BRIEF CONTENTS

Fourth Edition

ESSENTIALS OF
MARKETING

WITHDRAWN

Fourth Edition

ESSENTIALS OF
MARKETING

GEOFF LANCASTER
Professor of Marketing, University of North London and
Chairman, Durham Associates Group Ltd, Castle Eden, Co. Durham

LESTER MASSINGHAM
Chairman and Managing Director, CMC Pte Ltd
Singapore, Malaysia, Hong Kong and Indonesia
and Professor of Marketing, University of Tun Abdul Razak (UNITAR) in Malaysia

RUTH ASHFORD
Senior Lecturer in Marketing, Manchester Metropolitan University
CIM Senior Examiner

McGraw-Hill Publishing Company

London · Burr Ridge IL · New York · St Louis · San Francisco · Auckland · Bogotá
Caracas · Lisbon · Madrid · Mexico · Milan · Montreal · New Delhi · Panama · Paris
San Juan · São Paulo · Singapore · Sydney · Tokyo · Toronto

Published by
McGraw-Hill Education
Shoppenhangers Road, Maidenhead, Berkshire, SL6 2QL
Telephone: 44 (0) 1628 502 500
Fax: 44 (0) 1628 770 224
Website: www.mcgraw-hill.co.uk

Editorial Director:	Melissa Rosati
Development Editor:	Caroline Howell
Editorial Assistant:	Nicola Wimpory
Senior Marketing Manager:	Petra Skytte
Senior Production Manager:	Max Elvey
New Media Developer:	Doug Greenwood

British Library Cataloguing in Publication Data
A catalogue record for this book is available from the British Library

Library of Congress Cataloging in Publication Data
The Library of Congress data for this book has been applied for/is available from the
Library of Congress

McGraw-Hill
A Division of The **McGraw·Hill** Companies

Produced for McGraw-Hill by the independent production company
Steven Gardiner Ltd TEL +44 (0)1223 364868 FAX +44 (0)1223 364875
Cover design by Hybert Design
Printed and bound in Great Britain by The Bath Press
Text design by Design Deluxe, Bath

ISBN 0-07-70986-0

McGraw-Hill books are available at special quantity discounts.
Please contact the Corporate Sales Executive at the above address.

CONTENTS

PREFACE

This is the fourth edition of our textbook covering the Essentials of Marketing. This edition has been substantially updated and modified to meet the needs of those students preparing for the Marketing Fundamentals examination of the Chartered Institute of Marketing. In this process we have drawn in this edition upon the knowledge and experience of the current CIM Senior Examiner for this subject, Ruth Ashford. However, the original aims established right from the outset in the first edition remain unchanged.

The text still seeks to synthesize contemporary marketing knowledge and does not purport to break new ground. It is highly readable and does not assume previous knowledge of marketing.

We have continued to write this edition as the fundamental text that underpins any introductory marketing course. Throughout, other specialist texts are referenced and recommended for more advanced and specialist reading. However, where we have chosen to include more advanced and specialist material ourselves, as for example in the area of strategic marketing planning tools, this material has been included in Appendices. The text is now essential reading for the Chartered Institute of Marketing Fundamentals paper and as already indicated, has been specifically amended in both content and layout for this purpose. In addition, we feel the text is also suitable for other courses in marketing and indeed for further levels of the CIM qualification examinations. Although it is appropriate to purchase this textbook at certificate level, therefore, it will not become redundant as the diploma stage case study subject, Analysis and Decision, is still catered for in terms of advice on how to tackle extended marketing case studies. In this respect we have continued to include extended cases of the type used in the CIM Analysis and Decision paper. As the book is now essential reading for the certificate level Marketing Fundamentals paper, however, we have included a new chapter on how to deal with mini cases in marketing. In addition, at the end of each chapter we have included a mini case and questions in order to assist those needing to develop skills and expertise in tackling such material.

Marketing concepts and techniques continue to be applied across an increasing range of organizations. The text reflects this widening of the application of marketing by marketing-oriented organizations. Sections have been added to reflect recent developments in marketing including, for example, the use of technology across the full range of marketing applications. In addition, areas such as direct marketing, customer care and relationship marketing have been extended and reworked to reflect current thinking and developments in the marketing arena. The all-important area of marketing planning has been substantially reworked in this edition and includes an extensive new section on combining and extending the marketing mix. Areas such as buyer behaviour, the tools of marketing and how to achieve a marketing culture have all been reworked and updated.

Precisely how you use this textbook will depend on many factors including, perhaps most importantly, whether or not you have purchased it in pursuing a particular course of study including preparation for a particular examination, or perhaps whether you have purchased it for background reading, say, to help you in your organizational marketing role. You may therefore prefer to work systematically through the text beginning with Chapter 1, or you may simply dip into the various chapters as appropriate.

Given that many of you will have purchased this text as essential reading for the CIM Marketing Fundamentals paper, we would recommend that you not only work through the chapters systematically as indicated above, beginning with Chapter 1, but also that you attempt both the end of chapter questions and the mini case and questions which accompany each chapter. You will note from the contents page that Chapter 16 of the text covers the area of undertaking mini cases. In this chapter we provide a framework for how to tackle mini cases of the type used in the CIM examinations. We would suggest, therefore, that you read that chapter before tackling the first mini case at the end of Chapter 1. You can, of course, then return to Chapter 16 as you wish to remind yourself of how to approach the mini cases as you work through subsequent ones at the end of each chapter. Broadly, the chapters are organized to reflect the content and sequence of the CIM syllabus for the Marketing Fundamentals paper. You will note that some chapters cover areas which are not included as such in the Fundamentals syllabus, so, for example, the chapters on selling and sales forecasting are in much more detail than is required by the syllabus. Where this is the case the reason for including the material has been for the sake of completeness to meet the needs of students who are preparing for other courses of study and examinations. We believe it is useful to include these chapters and material as you progress through the text rather than to leave them out, even if they are in a little more detail than perhaps you might require if you are taking the Fundamentals examination.

For those who are preparing for examinations other than Marketing Fundamentals, including, for example, the Analysis and Decision examination of the CIM where you are required to deal with extended case studies, Chapter 15 covers how to undertake them and includes two full case studies on which to practise these skills. Because these extended case studies encompass several areas of marketing, including marketing planning and control, we would advise you to leave Chapter 15 until you have worked through the first fourteen chapters of the text.

Appendices 1 and 2 are included for those students who are preparing for examinations other than the Certificate level Fundamentals paper and may require more advanced knowledge.

Teaching and Learning Resources

For this new edition we have updated the website which contains the following additional material free of charge: Lecturer's Manual—including case study debriefs and lecture plans, PowerPoint slides, Multiple choice questions, Web links.

GUIDED TOUR

Learning objectives identify the abilities and skills the student should be able to demonstrate after reading the chapter.

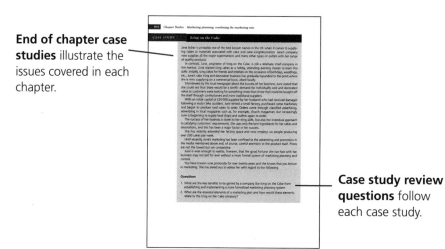

Chapter summary briefly reviews and reinforces the main topics covered in each chapter.

Chapter review questions check progress and encourage students to apply their knowledge of topics covered in the chapter.

References indicate sources used and encourage students to further explore the subject.

End of chapter case studies illustrate the issues covered in each chapter.

Case study review questions follow each case study.

Part One

MARKETING PERSPECTIVE AND CONTEXT

Chapter One

THE MARKETING CULTURE

LEARNING OBJECTIVES   *This chapter will help you to:*

- appreciate the scope and meaning of marketing in the contemporary organization;

- understand the distinction and links between marketing as a concept and marketing as a management function;

- understand the development of the marketing concept, the evolution of the marketing-oriented organization and the distinction of marketing from a sales or product-oriented approach;

- assess the implications of marketing orientation and the development of marketing activities within an organization;

- understand the basic tasks and responsibilities of the marketing manager;

- appreciate the changing nature of marketing in the contemporary organization and the factors which underpin these changes.

INTRODUCTION

The marketing way of management is not a particularly complex or original notion; indeed, the saying 'the customer is always right' is as old as business itself. Marketing is really a business orientation based on this principle, which has grown and developed into a management discipline over the years. Marketing is not narrowly confined to a particular office or department: it is an attitude of mind, an approach to business problems that should be adapted by the whole organization, from the chairman and chief executive down to the lowest levels. This company-wide view of marketing has led to the use of the term 'marketing culture' to describe the company-wide orientation which is needed to adopt the marketing philosophy effectively. Because a marketing culture is so important in contemporary marketing we shall examine this concept again later in the chapter, but briefly what is at the core of the marketing concept or culture?

Marketing is based on the concept that the customer is the most important person to the company. In order to prosper or even survive, every company must work hard to retain its existing markets and continually strive to secure new and profitable customers. The marketing concept puts the emphasis on *customers* and the identification and satisfaction of customer requirements. Such an orientation to business consequently results in the customer becoming the focus of the company's activities, and most successful companies in the world owe their prosperity to the adoption and application of this marketing concept.

In starting our discussion of marketing, it must be stated that, although the concept of marketing is relatively straightforward, the term 'marketing' often means different things to different people. This confusion is not restricted to the ordinary person in the street. There are still many business people who have not fully grasped the importance of the marketing concept. The objective of this first chapter is to explain clearly what the marketing concept is all about and to compare and contrast it with less sophisticated approaches to business which, even today, are still practised by many business firms. Of course, like most things to do with organizations, situations develop and change. This is as true for marketing as for any other area of business and indeed it might be argued that in fact the marketing function is subject to even more forces for change than other functional areas of the business. This chapter therefore is also concerned to look at recent trends in both the concept and application of marketing in the modern business. As we shall see, both thinking about what marketing is, and how it is being practised by organizations, is constantly evolving and changing. The successful practitioner of marketing must not only be aware of the key ways in which marketing is evolving and changing but indeed must increasingly be able to anticipate the way that marketing thinking and practice is moving.

A DEFINITION OF MARKETING

It was explained above that the marketing approach to business is really quite straightforward and that the basic principles of marketing have been used to a greater or lesser degree for as long as mankind has engaged in trading activity. In this sense, marketing is a rather old subject, although the name 'marketing' is relatively new.

As far back as 1775, Adam Smith,[1] the father of modern economics, wrote the following passage in his famous work, *The Wealth of Nations*:

> Consumption is the sole end and purpose of all production and the interests of the producer ought to be attended to, only so far as it may be necessary for promoting that of the consumer.

In the above statement Adam Smith has given the essence of what modern marketing is all about. The very word is *consumer*, as it is the identification and satisfaction of a *consumer's requirements* which forms the basis of modern marketing.

Although the essence of marketing is as old as trade itself, marketing emerged as a serious subject of study and has been accepted as a major management discipline only since the middle of the present century. In this sense, marketing is a very new subject concerned with the analysis of conditions and forces that make for successful commercial exchanges.

In certain commercial subjects, for example accountancy, it is possible to give a reasonably accurate definition of the scope of the subject in a few lines. Such a straightforward, simple definition, however, is more difficult to find in the case of such a wide-ranging subject to marketing. This is not because a definition of marketing does not exist. On the contrary, the problem is choosing the most appropriate one as there are so many definitions.

Because marketing is such a wide-ranging topic, different people often look on the subject from different viewpoints or give the subject a particular emphasis. To some extent such different viewpoints result from the academic background or the area of employment of the person giving the definition. For example, many people often go into marketing after studying economics, and tend to give the subject an economic slant. Others have worked for many years in a specialized area of marketing, e.g. market research or advertising, and hence tend to regard their particular area as the most important facet of marketing.

The following list is a sample of the wide range of definitions given for the subject:

Marketing is a social process by which individuals and groups obtain what they need and want through creating and exchanging products and value with others.[2]

Marketing consists of individual and organizational activities that facilitate and expedite satisfying exchange relationships in a dynamic environment through the creation, distribution, promotion and pricing of goods, services and ideas.[3]

Marketing is the process of planning and executing the conception, pricing, promotion and distribution of ideas, goods and services to create exchanges that satisfy individual and organizational objectives.[4]

Marketing is selling goods that don't come back to people who do.[5]

Marketing involves the integrated analysis, planning and control of the marketing mix variables (product, price, promotion and distribution) to create exchanges and satisfy both individual and organizational objectives.[6]

Marketing is the identification, establishment, maintenance and enhancement of relationships with customers and other stakeholders, at a profit, so that the objectives of the parties are met.[7]

The generally accepted UK definition is the one given by the *Chartered Institute of Marketing*, which reads as follows:

Marketing is the management process which identifies, anticipates, and supplies customer requirements efficiently and profitably.

The reader will appreciate that, although there are many generally accepted definitions of marketing, there is no one unified definition. All of the definitions given above are correct while at the same time all are slightly different. Because of the difficulty of incorporating all the facets of marketing into a simple definition, let us instead look at a number of key points which will help clarify the situation:

1. Marketing focuses the firm's or individual's attention towards the *needs* and *wants* of the marketplace.
2. Marketing is concerned with *satisfying* the genuine needs and wants of specifically defined target markets by creating products or services that satisfy customer requirements.
3. Marketing involves analysis, planning and control.
4. The principle of marketing states that all business decisions should be made with a careful and systematic consideration of the *user*.
5. The distinguishing feature of a marketing-oriented organization is the way in which it strives to provide *customer satisfaction* as a way of achieving its own business objectives.

6. Marketing is *dynamic* and operational, requiring action as well as planning.

7. Marketing requires an improved form of business organization in order for it to be able to lead and catalyse the application of the marketing approach.

8. Marketing is both an important functional area of management and an overall *business philosophy* which recognizes that the identification, satisfaction and retention of customers is the key to prosperity.

This last point is particularly important, as much of the problem of definition and misunderstanding over the term 'marketing' stems from the confusion between the *function* of marketing and its *philosophy*. The term 'marketing' is used to describe both the techniques used by the marketing department and the overall marketing orientation of the firm. Marketing is in fact both a functional area of management and a business philosophy or, as we termed it earlier, a company-wide culture

MARKETING AS AN OVERALL BUSINESS PHILOSOPHY: THE MARKETING CULTURE

Many successful companies see marketing as the keystone of their business. Such firms do not see marketing simply as yet another functional area of management but more as an overall business philosophy, a way of thinking about business, and a way of working which runs through *every aspect* of the firm's activities. Hence, marketing is viewed not as a separate function, but rather as a profit-oriented approach to business that permeates not just the marketing department but the *entire business*. Looked at from this point of view, marketing is seen as an attitude of mind or an approach to business rather than a specific discipline.

The holistic view of the role of marketing within the firm has been expressed by a leading authority on management thinking, Peter F. Drucker,[8] who stated:

> Marketing is not only much broader than selling, it is not a specialized activity at all. It encompasses the entire business. It is the whole business seen from the point of view of its final result, that is, from the customer's point of view. Concern and responsibility for marketing must therefore permeate all areas of the enterprise.

This marketing-oriented business philosophy is referred to as the *marketing concept* or *culture*. It is a philosophy that puts the customer at the very centre of the firm's corporate purpose. Marketing cannot exist in a vacuum. To be really effective it must permeate the whole company. What is needed is an integrated approach, not just the creation of a marketing department. It is the company's whole approach to business problems that is the key issue. It is the adoption of a business philosophy that puts customer satisfaction at the centre of management thinking throughout the organization that distinguishes a marketing-oriented firm from other less enlightened companies. Such an approach to business propels the marketing-oriented company into new activities and new opportunities and away from the narrow preoccupation with selling existing products to existing customers. Marketing cannot begin to be effective within a company unless it has the firm support of general management and penetrates every area of an organization. As we shall see later in the chapter, in fact perhaps one of the most significant developments in the concept of marketing and hence the application of marketing practices in organizations, is the increasing recognition of this need to adopt Drucker's holistic view of the role of marketing and for marketing therefore to become the guiding philosophy for the whole organization. Put simply, a marketing 'culture' must pervade every aspect of the organization's operations.

The question we must ask ourselves is why, if the marketing concept is so simple and straightforward, has it been only relatively recently that firms have adopted it as a serious business philosophy? To answer this question, and to see how the marketing concept has evolved over the years into the form accepted today, we need to take a historical perspective and look at the development of trade.

MARKETING IN A HISTORICAL CONTEXT

Marketing is principally concerned with exchange or trade. Trade in its most basic form has existed ever since mankind has been capable of producing a surplus.

In historical terms surplus was usually agricultural produce, which would then be traded for other goods such as pots or cloths. This early process of exchange brought about the existence of the local market and later the village fair to facilitate trading. The emergence of trade allowed people to specialize in producing particular goods and services and to exchange them in markets for other goods they needed.

THE ECONOMIC ROLE OF EXCHANGE

If individuals and organizations within our society were totally self-sufficient and could survive without the need for exchange, there would be no need for marketing. However, in a modern society, virtually everyone depends upon exchange for economic welfare. An organized system of exchange, based on formalized procedures and an explicit legal framework, is fundamental to the working of any modern industrial economy.

Exchange is the act of obtaining something of value, usually a product or service, from another party, an individual or organization, by offering something of value to the other party. The thing of value offered can be another product or service resulting in a simple barter agreement, although in modern exchange transactions money is usually used as a medium of exchange. The act of exchange is an important economic process because it actually *creates value*. The act of production creates wealth, but the value of this wealth is greatly enhanced through the exchange process, which allows an individual or organization a greater range of consumption possibilities, resulting in greater satisfaction and utility all round.

Hence the exchange process is central to the subject of marketing, which, broadly speaking, can be said to be concerned with how, why and when consumers choose to satisfy needs and wants through exchange.

THE INDUSTRIAL REVOLUTION

Before the Industrial Revolution the production and distribution of goods tended to be on a small scale. Producers generally sold their products to a very localized market. The period 1760–1830 saw the British economy transformed from its dependence on agriculture with a dramatic increase in industrial production. With industrialization and the development of machines, production became more geographically concentrated, carried out in purpose-built mills or factories. Enterprises were now on a much larger scale and manufacturers produced relatively large volumes of products, not only for a localized market but for a national and even an international market. Although this period brought many social problems, economic activity and production expanded dramatically, particularly from the end of the eighteenth century. The development of the heavy industries such as iron and coal, the availability of steam power to drive machinery, the greater use of machines in all industries, particularly textiles, and the equally dramatic developments in communications, transport, agriculture and commerce transformed the economy, resulted in the growth of the factory system and saw the migration of the population from the countryside to the new industrial towns.

During this period trade flourished, but because consumption had now become more dispersed over greater geographical distances, producers no longer had immediate contact with their markets. In order for producers to be able to manufacture goods and services that would sell in such markets, it became necessary for them to *analyse* carefully and *interpret* the needs and wants of customers and to manufacture products that would 'fit in' with those needs and wants.

This process of matching the resources of a firm to the needs and wants of customers was termed 'entrepreneurship'. Generally, the entrepreneur was the individual who 'carried' the firm; for example, Josiah Wedgwood epitomizes the traditional entrepreneur. In a sense, the entrepreneurs were practising an early form of marketing although they did not actually call it such.

This period also saw advancements in production techniques based on job specialization and the division of labour. Prior to industrialization, production was carried out by the craft industries. In the craft industries, work was based on specialization in the production of a particular product, with the producer engaged in all the processes of production. The craftsmen would then trade their specialist product in order to obtain goods and services produced by other craftsmen, who of course also specialized in the production of a particular product. A skilled craftsman, e.g. a blacksmith or a cobbler, develops a high degree of skill in carrying out a particular activity. The craft industries were based on an early form of division and specialization of labour, productivity and output.

Industrialization saw the process of specialization and division of labour taken even further. The process of producing a product was broken down into stages or activities. Individuals then specialized in a particular operation. This resulted in a higher level of skill and speed and a greater amount of output than was possible when individuals had to carry out all the operations in the production of a product. The increase in job specialization increased the need for *exchange*. Specialization resulted in greater productivity, which in turn reduced costs and hence the price of products. Larger scale production meant that channels of distribution had to be created to enable the effective demand from a much larger market to be met. The period of the first Industrial Revolution laid the foundations of the modern industrial economy, in which we now have a sophisticated system of institutions and economic organizations carrying out specialized activities in manufacturing, distribution, communication and finance to facilitate modern-day commercial activity, which of course is still based on the fundamental concept of trade or exchange.

THE MID-NINETEENTH CENTURY TO THE PRESENT DAY

From the middle of the nineteenth century to almost the beginning of the twentieth century, Britain was a dominant force in the world's economy. Throughout the nineteenth century both Britain's industrial output and the world's demand for that output had dramatically increased. The main factor underlying this industrial growth was the development of international trade. Britain was still seen as the 'workshop of the world' and held a virtual monopoly in the supply of manufactured goods to the relatively underdeveloped countries of the British Empire.

The latter half of the nineteenth century saw the emergence of other countries as competing industrial powers, most notably the United States of America and Germany. The rapid development of industry in these countries resulted in a significant increase in total output. Although Britain faced fierce competition in the areas of coal, steel and textiles, the period up to the First World War continued to be one of industrial expansion. Although Britain's share of world trade declined, the actual value of her trade increased as the incomes generated in other countries resulted in an increase in total demand.

During the First World War Britain's economy was concerned with the war effort. After the war Britain discovered that many of her previous overseas markets were now trading with her new industrial *competitors*. The financing of the Second World War resulted in Britain selling off many of her overseas investments. As a result, trade was even more important to the country's future. The period since 1945 has seen a decline in the importance of the traditional Empire and Commonwealth countries as overseas markets. Attention is now focused on the United States, Japan, and particularly countries in the European Union.

Despite an overall growth in world demand, the increase in world productivity has resulted in the excess supply of many products, e.g. steel and textiles. The international situation has changed from a sellers' market, where there was once a virtually insatiable demand for everything produced, to a buyers' market. Today we have a large number of producers competing to supply a finite market. Modern industry, as we have seen, is based on the process of mass production which necessitates *mass consumption*. Today, in order for a product to be commercially successful, it must be produced in sufficient volume. In order for producers to achieve a sufficient level of demand, they must produce products that the market *wants to buy*. Simply to produce is no longer enough. To be competitive, firms not only have to take the needs and wants of the market into consideration: they have to *start with them*.

Today's modern organizations have become larger and more complex to manage. Markets too have changed and consumers' tastes have become more sophisticated. In the modern firm the entrepreneurial function is rarely left to one individual, but has developed into a management function and overall business philosophy that we now term marketing.

It can be seen then that marketing has its historical roots in trade and entrepreneurship. Marketing to a greater or lesser degree has always been practised by successful firms, albeit in a rather unsophisticated manner. It is only in modern times that it has developed as a formalized business concept with a codified philosophy and set of techniques. The realization by producers that they needed to take the buyers' points of view into account has slowly developed since the onset of industrialization. However, it has only been over the last 30 years that this growing realization has matured into the ideological breakthrough we now call marketing. Manufacturers eventually realized that, not only must they take the buyers' needs and wants into account, but these were the starting-point in the production of goods and services. This 'marketing maturity' did not happen overnight, but was a gradual process. Even today there are many firms that really only pay 'lip service' to the marketing concept and have still some way to go before they can truly claim to be *marketing-oriented*.

THE PRODUCTION-, SALES- AND MARKETING-ORIENTED FIRM

Many organizations pass through several stages of business orientation before fully adopting the marketing concept. Broadly speaking, even today there are three types of company:

1. Production-oriented
2. Sales-oriented
3. Marketing-oriented

Most marketing-oriented companies have evolved over the years, passing through the first two stages before reaching the third. Let us look at these various stages in a little more detail.

Production orientation

We saw earlier that in the nineteenth century and early part of the twentieth century the fundamental role of business was seen as production. Manufacturers were in a suppliers' market and were faced with a virtually insatiable demand for goods and services. Firms concentrated on production and productive efficiency in order to bring down costs. Product decisions were taken first and foremost with production implications in mind. Firms tended to manufacture and offer products that they were *good at producing*, with customers' requirements and satisfactions of secondary importance. Firms tended to be 'production-oriented', and the production man was the most important person in the organization, as it was thought that he held the key to the firm's prosperity. This production mentality was a workable philosophy as long as a sellers' market existed. However, many firms had to change their attitude as the world economy drifted into recession in the 1920s and 1930s and to produce was no longer enough.

Manufacturers who focus their attention on existing products and pay little or no attention to the changing needs and wants of the marketplace are in danger of one day discovering that they have no customers. Such firms suffer from what is often termed 'marketing myopia'. This is a very shortsighted viewpoint where firms are so busy concentrating on their products that they fail to take customers' requirements into account.

It is strange that even today firms can be found who pay little regard to the needs and wants of their customers and still have the production concept as the guiding philosophy of their businesses. Such firms take the attitude that they produce excellent products and common sense dictates that people will want to buy them.

Naturally, consumers have to be informed and convinced of the superiority of the company's products, and this task is entrusted to the salesforce. If consumers are not buying the firm's products, then as far as the company is concerned there can only be two possible reasons:

1. The customer is ignorant and does not appreciate a good product.
2. The salesforce is inept.

Many firms have, in their own opinions, produced excellent products, but not necessarily of the type customers want to buy. The British motorcycle industry produced fine-quality machines, but consumers preferred the styling and range offered by Japanese manufacturers.

In a production-oriented company senior personnel such as the chairman and managing director are likely to have production backgrounds. Such companies are likely to have a small sales department which handles traditional marketing functions such as advertising. The greatest importance is placed on production. Under the production concept the salesperson's task is a relatively minor one; he or she has to sell what the firm has produced. Such a firm is typically organized as shown in Fig. 1.1. The sales area is viewed as a service function, and so the sales manager is not part of top-level management.

Sales orientation

The world economic recession of the early twentieth century concentrated the minds of business people. Many firms failed and fortunes were lost. Unemployment was high and effective demand slumped. Production capacity was underutilized and there were many unsold goods. Gradually business people began to realize that it was not enough simply to produce goods as efficiently as possible. For profits to materialize, such goods had to be sold.

The guiding business philosophy of many firms switched from production to sales orientation. The salespersons and the sales manager now became the most important people in the organization. The firm could manufacture the goods, but these goods still

FIGURE 1.1

The organization of a production-oriented firm

had to be *sold*. The sales concept stated that effective demand could be created by sales techniques, and it was thought that the sales department held the key to the firm's future prosperity and survival.

In a sense, sales orientation was a conceptual step forward because, although goods and services were still produced with little regard to customer requirements, at least it was realized that products did not sell themselves as a matter of course.

This period saw the development of a number of techniques that are still used today in modern marketing. In order to achieve a competitive advantage, greater importance was attached to product differentiation and branding. Advertising, sales promotions and other sales techniques were increasingly used to achieve a 'sales angle'. These techniques were still used to *sell* the product rather than to communicate and inform or to increase customer satisfaction. Although these methods are still used today, it was the ethos with which they were used that distinguishes the sales approach from modern marketing practices, with the emphasis on the *hard sell*.

Even today many people think of marketing as being synonymous with selling and promotion. In a wide-ranging study of the meaning and practice of marketing in UK business, Hooley *et al*[9] found that nearly 10 per cent of the organizations in their sample still viewed marketing's primary functions as being sales and promotional support. For perhaps obvious reasons they described these types of companies as being '*sales supporters*' with regard to their view of the nature and practice of marketing. Although personal selling forms an important part of a firm's marketing programme, especially in industrial markets where personal contact with customers is of particular importance, it is not necessarily the most important element of marketing. In fact, selling is only one of several functions for which the marketing department is responsible. Personal selling is but one of an array of marketing tools, each of which has a particular part to play in the overall scheme of things. Individually, such tools are only part of the firm's overall 'marketing mix' or set of marketing tools which must be finely tuned to achieve maximum impact in the marketplace.

This is not to say that selling is of no importance: rather that, if the firm has applied the concept and techniques of marketing, i.e. identified consumer needs, produced appropriate products, priced, packaged, promoted and distributed the product correctly, then consumers should *want to buy* the product rather than the firm having to rely on intense selling. At the extreme, Peter Drucker,[10] one of the world's most respected management theorists, has stated:

> There will always, one can assume, be need for some selling. But the aim of marketing is to *make selling superfluous*. The aim of marketing is to know and understand the customer so well that the product or service fits him and sells itself. Ideally, marketing should result in a customer who is ready to buy. All that should be needed then is to make the product or service available . . .

In a sales-oriented firm its whole business philosophy is centred around sales. Often these firms believe that with some young, highly motivated salesmen, hungry for success and with a well worked out incentive scheme, they can sell anything. Sales volume is the most important criterion, and planning horizons tend to be relatively short term. The actual customer, and how customers might perceive the value or utility of the goods being 'sold', is of secondary importance. Philip Kotler[11] defines this selling concept as one which holds that:

> Consumers, if left alone, will ordinarily not buy enough of the organization's products. The organization must therefore undertake an aggressive selling and promotion effort.

From the above definition, the implicit premises of the selling concept are as follows:

1. Consumers can always be induced to buy more through various 'sales techniques'.
2. Consumers tend to resist purchasing and it is the salesperson's job to overcome this.
3. The firm's key task is to organize an effective salesforce.

In a sales-oriented company the sales function is given equal seniority with finance and production. Such a firm is likely to be organized as shown in Fig. 1.2.

The basic assumption of firms practising the selling concept is that their goods and services are 'sold' not *bought*. The aim of these firms is to get the sale and not worry about post-purchase satisfaction; customer satisfaction is considered secondary to getting the sale.

Examples of such selling situations are:

1. Certain double-glazing, burglar alarm, loft conversion, cavity wall insulation and other home 'improvement' companies: once they have a 'lead' from an unsuspecting target, they send round a high-pressure salesman with a 'foot in the door' approach.
2. Many insurance companies, which search out potential customers and 'hard sell' them on the benefits of life insurance.
3. Encyclopedia companies, which often disguise their real intention through an 'educational survey' and other devious methods.

A sales approach to business is all very well to those companies that are 'here today and gone tomorrow', but not to firms that want to remain in business and build their business on the basis of trust, respect and genuine *customer satisfaction*. A good high-power salesperson can sell virtually anything to anyone—once! For repeat business over the long term, however, the typical selling mentality of many firms is not enough: a more 'customer-' or market-oriented approach is necessary for long-term success.

Marketing orientation

As discussed earlier, the modern marketing concept is a twentieth-century phenomenon. The concept has evolved from the rather myopic production and sales orientation of earlier times as a direct response to the obvious shortcomings of these less sophisticated business philosophies. The concept started to be seriously put into practice in the United States during the 1950s and has, since that time, been adopted as the central business philosophy by many firms throughout the world.

The marketing concept is sometimes referred to as a 'marketing' or 'customer' orientation. Simply stated, the marketing concept suggests that in order for a firm to survive in the *long term* and make a profit it must ascertain the genuine needs and wants of specifically defined target markets and then produce goods and services that satisfy customer requirements.

FIGURE 1.2

The organization of a sales-oriented firm

Under the marketing concept, it is the customer who takes the central place on the business stage. It is the satisfaction of customers that is seen as the key to prosperity, growth and survival. A marketing-oriented firm produces goods and services that customers *want to buy* rather than what the firm wants to make. The emphasis is put on the customer buying rather than on the firm selling the goods.

The management of a sales-oriented company tends to be short-run-oriented and preoccupied with achieving current sales. In such a company customer considerations are often limited to the sales department. To progress from this position to a marketing orientation, the firm must be able to cultivate a 'company-wide' approach to customer requirements. Marketing cannot begin to be effective within a company unless it has the full support of general management and penetrates every area of an organization, from the lowest to the highest levels.

Levitt[12] has drawn a sharp contrast between the selling and the marketing concept:

> Selling focuses on the needs of the seller; marketing on the needs of the buyer. Selling is preoccupied with the seller's need to convert his product into cash; marketing with the idea of satisfying the needs of the customer by means of the product and the whole cluster of things associated with creating, delivering and finally consuming it.

The contrast is illustrated diagrammatically by Kotler[13] and shown here in Fig. 1.3.

To change from a sales- to a marketing-oriented company, the firm will have to become long-run oriented and preoccupied with planning the right products, the right channels, level of service and marketing strategy to meet the customer's long-run needs. The marketing approach challenges every member of a company, whatever his or her specialist function, to relate his or her work to the needs of the marketplace and to balance it against the firm's own profit needs. Nowhere is this more important than in the area of product design, where customers' views, rather than the views of production, should be the starting-point.

It was shown in Fig. 1.2 that a sales-oriented company is likely to be organized in the form of specialized departments charged with carrying out different company tasks; each department directly or indirectly will have an impact on customer satisfaction through its own activities and decisions. Under the marketing concept, it is desirable to coordinate these activities because the ultimate satisfaction gained by the customer is a function of the *totality* of all company departments acting in *unison*.

Changing from a simple sales to a more sophisticated marketing orientation will mean that marketing will have much more influence and authority over other departments to bring about *integrated* coordinated marketing. The sales department and

FIGURE 1.3

The selling and marketing concepts contrasted

Source: P. Kotler, *Marketing Management: Analysis, Planning, Implementation and Control*, 8th edn, Prentice-Hall International, Englewood Cliffs, NJ, 1994, p. 19

other functional management departments may resent having to bend their efforts to the will of the marketing department. The major departmental differences or organizational conflicts between marketing and other departments are summarized in Table 1.1.

The Hooley study, referred to earlier, found that the most successful organizations in their study—as measured by return on investment—were those where marketing was seen not only as a function primarily responsible for identifying and meeting consumer needs, but also where marketing was viewed as the guiding philosophy for the whole organization. As you will recall, we have already come across this view regarding marketing in Drucker's holistic notion of the marketing concept. These types of organizations, where marketing represented a guiding philosophy for the whole organization, Hooley understandably referred to as *'marketing philosophers'*.[14] In a similar vein, Gummesson[15] has argued that in his view everybody in the organization must become what he refers to as a *'part-time marketer'*, each making their own respective contribution to ensuring customer satisfaction.

The main problem facing the sales-oriented firm in progressing to a marketing orientation is the management of organizational change. Marketing will set the strategies and plans in consultation with the departments concerned, but these departments will retain the authority to execute the agreed programme in the way they think best. The human implications of this organizational change should not be under-rated, bearing in mind that it will involve a reallocation of power within the company. Functions previously carried out by other departments will become the responsibility of marketing, and every part of the firm will have to conform to a plan drawn up by marketing in consultation with other departments.

Traditionally, perhaps nowhere in the organization has the potential for conflict from implementing a company-wide marketing orientation been greater than between the marketing and 'technological functions' of the business including, for example, design, research and development and manufacturing functions. But in addition, there is

TABLE 1.1 *Major differences/conflicts between marketing and other departments*

Department	Emphasis	Marketing's emphasis
Sales	Short-term sales Sales most important One department	Long-term profits Customer satisfaction most important Whole organization
Purchasing	Narrow product line Standard parts	Broad product line Non-standard parts
Finance	Hard-and-fast budgets Price to cover costs	Flexible budgets Market-oriented pricing
Accounting	Standard transactions	Special terms and discounts
Manufacturing	Long runs Few models Standard orders Long production lead times	Short runs Many models Custom orders Short production lead times

also potential for conflict between marketing and the sales department, marketing and purchasing, and marketing and the finance and accountancy functions. Most of these conflicts arise from differences in emphasis between the marketing department and these other functional areas of the business, examples of which are shown in Table 1.1. In a recent study of conflict between marketing personnel and engineers in organizations, Lancaster[16] has argued that in addition to these inherent differences in emphasis, conflict between marketers and engineers in organizations is often compounded by a lack of understanding on the part of many engineering personnel as to what marketing can do for a company. Lancaster argues, however, that developments in markets and competition allied to philosophies such as just-in-time (JIT), total quality, and quality function deployment increase the need for a more company-wide approach to customer orientation but particularly among design and production functions. This in turn requires more coordination and teamwork between marketing and the engineering functions of the business. Furthermore, marketing techniques continue to improve which means that marketers are now in a position to provide better information to the engineering and design functions of a business so that, for example, new product development programmes can be specifically designed around pre-determined customer needs at the outset, hence increasing the chances of successful new product development programmes. Needless to say, often engineers and design personnel can resent such 'interference' from marketers in what they see as their responsibilities in the business. It is therefore important to obtain their support by demonstrating how a customer-oriented approach, backed by the tools and techniques of modern marketing, can help increase their efficiency and effectiveness without detracting from their roles and responsibilities.

In a marketing-oriented firm, the chairman and managing director are likely to come from a marketing background. In addition, there is likely to be a marketing director with a position of equal status to that of the production and financial directors. Such a firm is likely to be organized as shown in Fig. 1.4.

Although the proper organizational structure is an important element in a firm becoming marketing-oriented, such an orientation is not achieved simply by adopting an organizational chart. Management must also adopt and use the marketing concept

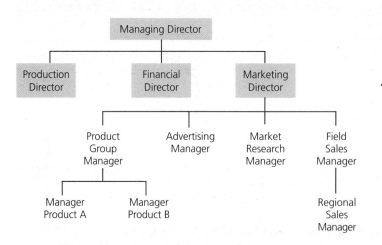

FIGURE 1.4

The organization of a marketing-oriented firm

as a business philosophy. Hence in a marketing-oriented firm marketing is not confined to the marketing director and the marketing department. As already suggested, to be really effective, it must permeate the whole company. A change of management labels and titles will not achieve the necessary fundamental change in company attitudes. It is the company's *whole approach* to business problems that is the key issue. It is the adoption of a business philosophy that puts customer satisfaction at the *centre* of management thinking throughout the organization. It is this that distinguishes a marketing-oriented firm from a production- or sales-oriented firm.

IMPLEMENTING THE MARKETING CONCEPT

As we have seen then an essential element of implementing the marketing concept is the need for the marketing function, or rather the managers in it, to develop effective working relationships and systems for ensuring coordination and cooperation between marketing and the different functional areas. In practice, implementing the marketing concept often gives rise to conflict between marketing and other functions. A company needs to understand the sources and issues of such conflict, and also needs to look for ways to convert potentially damaging conflict into more constructive forms of management behaviour. In other words, the marketing manager needs to consider the intra-firm environment in marketing plans.

Perhaps one of the best ways to appreciate the range and nature of the types of problems encountered when translating the marketing concept into practice is to reflect for a moment on the following problems:

1. Suppose that you wanted to gauge the extent to which a company had implemented the marketing concept: how would you assess this; what would you look for in the company; what would be the signs?

2. Alternatively, and now that you know what the marketing concept is, if you were made responsible for turning the production- or sales-oriented company into one that is marketing-oriented, what steps would you take?

How these problems are approached, and indeed the identification of the problems themselves, is not just one more academic exercise. These questions go right to the heart of the very practical issue of moving from what seems to be a statement of fundamental common sense—the marketing concept—to a position where a company can rightly be judged to be 'good' at marketing. After all, for many years now politicians, academics, industry pundits and so on have extolled the virtues, indeed the necessity, for British companies to improve in this respect. Further, and interestingly, not many practising managers, from whatever function, would deny the central importance of the customer and his or her needs. Fewer, but perhaps still not an insignificant number, of these same managers, including those directly involved in marketing management, would be willing to admit that there is still plenty of room for improvement.

It appears, therefore, that for some reason translating the concept into practice poses problems which some companies find insurmountable. To explore this further, let us return to the first of our hypothetical problems—that of gauging the extent of implementation.

A doctoral thesis completed at the University of Bradford as long ago as 1969 remains one of the most thought-provoking and, therefore, useful frameworks for judging the extent to which a company has moved from marketing concept to marketing practice.

In his thesis, Saddik[17] suggested that in order to make this judgement we should look to seven key areas or aspects of a company's operations:

- Company philosophy/managerial attitudes
- Organizational structure
- Planning procedures—particularly as they relate to marketing planning
- New product development activities and decisions
- Intelligence and information-fostering activities and decisions
- Promotional activities and decisions
- Distribution activities and decisions

Using these seven areas of measurement, Saddik investigated the extent to which companies in two of the important local industries in the area—engineering and textiles—had implemented the marketing concept. With so much time now having passed since Saddik completed his findings, there would be little point in detailing them other than to note that at the time he concluded that the marketing concept was far from being fully accepted and implemented in the industries studied. It is perhaps disappointing, therefore, that the Hooley study already referred to still reported a similar situation in many companies in the late 1980s in the UK, though thankfully they also found that marketing has increased in importance in the companies studied.

Nevertheless, even after all these years, Saddik's framework for measurements is still relevant, particularly if we reclassify some of his seven criteria. This reclassification is shown below:

- Company philosophy/business definition
- Managerial/workforce attitudes
- Organizational structure
- Planning and information gathering
- Processes and procedures for decision-making

We shall examine each of these in turn in order to clarify their significance to the implementation issue.

Company philosophy/business definition

We have already seen that the marketing concept is an idea or rather a philosophy of the essential purpose and conduct of a business. This philosophy is based on the notion of *consumer sovereignty*: that the purpose of a business is to create customers, and unless a business satisfies the needs of its customers it will not, in the long run, and under normal competitive conditions, survive and prosper. In order to begin the process of implementation, it could be argued that the first step is the acceptance of this philosophy. In the context of the measurement problem, which was posed earlier, we could perhaps gauge the extent to which a company had implemented the marketing concept by examining its philosophy. But where in a company would we look to for evidence of its having accepted this philosophy? How could we measure it? Although there is no doubt some difficulty in such measurement—after all, companies as such do not have philosophies: rather, it is the people in them who have—there are a variety of signs which would indicate the extent to which a company had passed this important first test. For example, an indication of company philosophy can often be gleaned from a company's annual report; alternatively, one might look to a company's Articles and Memorandum of Association. Perhaps the clearest, and certainly the most important, indication (and therefore the best measure) would be found in how the organization defined its business.

The importance of business definition in the context of implementing the marketing concept was perhaps most clearly highlighted by Levitt.[18] In his article 'Marketing myopia', Levitt illustrates that failure to define what business a company is currently in is a clear indication of a failure, or an unwillingness, to implement the marketing concept. An incorrect business definition, in Levitt's terms, is one which is too narrow and/or is based on a false premise. For example, how would you define the business of the following companies?

- General Motors
- Max Factor
- IBM

Even with no particular or detailed knowledge of any of these companies, no doubt you could at least guess what business they are in. Certainly you would think that the companies themselves would have little difficulty answering Levitt's question. But would you, or they, be correct? More specifically, would your or the companies' answers indicate that progress had been made towards implementing the marketing concept? Let us take one of the companies mentioned above to explore this further.

IBM represents the initial letters of a company called International Business Machines. Founded in America in the early 1920s, this now large and very successful multinational company currently produces a range of products primarily for use in the business office. IBM is probably best known for its computer products, both hardware and software. In fact this is a market which it has come to dominate. The answer to the question 'what business is it in?', therefore, would appear to be straightforward. After all, the company name itself gives us the answer. Surely this is a company that is in the business of making machines for business; or, alternatively, given the prime focus on computing, this company is in the business computing market.

Perhaps your thoughts were moving along the same lines in terms of defining IBM's business. If so, you may be accused of suffering from Levitt's marketing myopia. If IBM were to define its business in this way, it would be a strong indication that the company had not begun to implement the marketing concept.

The reason for this can be found in Levitt's original article. Here Levitt proposed that a company which defined its business in terms of the products it produces is invariably suffering from what was termed earlier as production or product orientation. In our terms, its company philosophy—as represented by business definition—would imply that it has not begun to implement the marketing concept. Such a company, Levitt argues, would have a shortsighted and blinkered view of its markets and customers and would, therefore, tend to miss both marketing opportunities and marketing threats. Because of this, a business definition based on products or production would in most cases eventually lead to the long-run decline of a business.

In contrast, Levitt suggested that market-/customer-based business definitions should be used to condition company philosophy. Using our earlier example, a customer-/market-based business definition for IBM might be represented by the following:

IBM is in the business of meeting the needs of businessmen for speedy and economic systems for data production, handling and interpretation.

Remember of course that the definition is only hypothetical; business definition is not easy. Some companies have spent considerable time and effort arriving at a meaningful definition. The purpose of this hypothetical definition for IBM is to demonstrate the difference between a marketing philosophy and a product or production philosophy. Our second IBM business definition is based on customer/market needs rather than being couched in terms of what IBM predominantly produces, i.e. computers. There are many advantages to be gained from such a market-/need-based definition; for example:

- It helps to identify competitors, present and potential.
- It acts as a guide for strategic decision-making.
- It forces the company to consider what the customer is actually purchasing and why. Customers buy benefits not products.

Because of these and other advantages of properly defining the business, we shall return to this aspect again in Chapter 2 when we consider marketing decisions. At this point it should be noted that the redefinition of a business from a product- to a customer-based one represents a fundamental shift in company philosophy and would represent a key signal to the effect that a company had begun to implement the marketing concept. A second key signal would be in managerial and workforce attitudes.

Managerial/workforce attitudes

It has been suggested that one of the difficulties of assessing company philosophy stems from the fact that companies do not have philosophies: rather it is the people in them, and in particular their senior management, who do. A customer-/market-based business definition is thus in itself a reflection of a certain attitude on the part of management. Perhaps, then, in gauging the extent to which a company has begun to implement the marketing concept, we should focus on the pre-disposition of the managers in a company, particularly as they relate to marketing in general and customer needs in particular. In fact, an essential second step in implementing the marketing concept is the recognition and acceptance throughout a company, in every function, and at every level from shopfloor to chairman, of the importance of satisfying customer needs. The point is that redefining the business alone is not sufficient to ensure that a company has become marketing-oriented. After all, such a redefinition may reflect an acceptance of the marketing concept by only the senior management of a company or even by only the marketing team itself. Neither of these is sufficient. Remember, implementing the marketing concept requires that the whole of a company and the people in it be oriented towards the needs of the customer. But what are the practical issues and problems to which this assertion gives rise, and in particular what steps can a company take to instil this attitude?

   As we have seen, a critical issue to which this need to change attitudes gives rise is the possibility of conflict between marketing and other functional areas. For example, the production or accountancy departments have their own jobs to do, their own set of specific problems to solve and activities to perform. Their task is not to take account of customer needs—this is the responsibility of the marketing function. Again, few of these other functional managers would deny the importance of customer needs, but they often find it difficult to relate this to their own activities. If not carefully managed, attempting to instil a customer-oriented attitude throughout a company can result in antagonism, and often open hostility, to the ideas of marketing in general and towards the marketing function in particular. A carefully planned, and above all diplomatic, programme of activities is essential in achieving this second step in implementing— instilling the right attitude.

To achieve this, some companies have taken the step of organizing seminars, teach-ins, familiarization programmes, etc., for company personnel designed to acquaint them with customer needs and their own role in meeting these. We have referred to this type of activity as internal marketing. The limited evidence available on the success of such schemes would appear to suggest that they can contribute significantly in turning a concept into a practice. After all, most of us respond well to being kept informed and to being able to see how we can contribute to the achievement of objectives. Some of the best examples of this sort of practice leading to positive attitudes and improved company performance have come from the Japanese companies, many of which hold regular meetings with representatives of the workforce to discuss consumer-related problems. We shall return to some of these ideas in this chapter when we consider the issue of conflict. You should realize by now, however, that in redefining the business— the first step in implementation—we should not expect, as if by some process of osmosis, for this to filter automatically through the different layers of the company. We need to take steps to ensure that it does. In particular, we need to ensure that the organizational structure is appropriate.

Organizational structure

Remember, the development of the marketing concept can be viewed as a series of evolutionary changes, from production to sales orientation, and so on. We saw also that accompanying these different steps of evolution may be changes in the organizational structure of a company. Reorganizing the structure of a company is often seen as being essential to the implementation of the concept. Stanton[19] encapsulates this notion in his two suggestions for translating the philosophy of marketing into action:

> . . . the marketing activities in a firm must be better co-ordinated and managed . . .
> [and]
> the chief marketing executive must be accorded a more important role in company planning . . .

In implementing the marketing concept, various activities that traditionally may have been the province of other management functions, for example sales, product planning and inventory control, should come within the remit and control of the marketing function.

Stanton's ideas about the organizational requirements for implementing marketing are not unique; indeed, they are broadly representative of most marketing authors on this topic. Not surprisingly, then, a frequently used indicator of the extent of marketing commitment in companies has been the organizational chart. After all, can a company be said to have implemented the marketing concept if the marketing function and the managers in it occupy a very lowly position in the company hierarchy? More extreme still, can the company that does not have a marketing department at all be said to have implemented the concept? It may surprise you to learn that the answer to both these questions can be yes! In other words, it is possible for a company to have implemented the concept fully without this being accompanied by changes in its organization chart. More importantly, and again reinforcing what was said earlier, you should understand that it matters little what we call it, or where it appears in the organization chart—if at all—so long as someone is responsible for representing the customer and his or her needs to the rest of the company, and for coordinating those activities necessary to meet those needs.

This should not be interpreted as meaning that organizing for marketing and assessing its overall role or position in company structure is unimportant. We have already acknowledged that implementing the concept will often necessitate changes in company structure. All that is being said is that the organizational chart alone is not sufficient to judge the extent to which a company has implemented the concept. Nor, therefore, are exercises in chartmanship, changing job titles, elevating the status of marketing in the hierarchy, etc., of themselves sufficient to bring about marketing orientation.

If anything, if we want to look to organizational factors in assessing the extent of implementation (and if we want to ensure that our company is taking the right steps in its programme of implementing), we would be better advised to look at *what activities are performed*—by whom; involving what relationships and authority; and to what purpose—than simply looking at the job titles in a box on the organization chart. It is to some of these 'activities' of marketing, in the context of implementing the marketing concept, that we now turn our attention.

Planning and information gathering

There is no doubt that implementing the marketing concept requires that planning, and the gathering of information on which such plans are based, assumes a greater importance in overall company activities. In addition, in the marketing-oriented company the focus for planning and information-gathering activities centres around the hub of company decision-making—customer needs and satisfaction.

These implications of implementing the marketing concept provide yet another basis for gauging the extent to which a company has in fact become marketing-oriented. To return to our earlier measurement problem, if we look at the extent to which a company plans for its future, and in particular the procedures and information on which such plans are based, this will enable us to assess the extent to which the marketing concept has been implemented. In order to appreciate this, consider the following example:

> . . . your company has just completed its annual marketing plan for the forthcoming year. The planning process commenced with the preparation of a sales forecast based on the pattern and trends of the previous five years' sales. On the basis of this forecast, a sales budget has been prepared and translated into production and operating budgets for the company as a whole. The plan includes a detailed schedule of activities and decision-making required to implement the plan including product, pricing, distribution and promotion decisions . . .

The question is, to what extent is your company marketing-oriented?

The answer is that we cannot tell without knowing on what basis the plan was prepared, and in particular with what knowledge of the facts about the market and the customers. To continue our example:

> . . . your company has recently acquired a new managing director who was previously employed in the capacity of marketing director by a fast-moving consumer goods company. Her experience in marketing is substantial. After considering your company's proposed marketing plan, she calls in the marketing manager responsible for preparing it. Specifically, she is worried that the plan contains no details of the information and market facts on which the plan is based . . .

The marketing manager explains again that the plan is based on his sales forecast. When asked what market research has been carried out in recent years, he replies that this expensive luxury has never been considered necessary. After all, both he and most of his staff have worked in the industry for some twenty years.

The newly appointed managing director then proceeds to ask the marketing manager the following questions:

- Who are our customers?
- What do they buy?
- How do they consider value?
- How do they buy?
- When do they buy?

To the marketing manager's consternation, he finds these questions difficult to answer. The simple fact is that he has never before considered them.

The evidence suggests that planning is not customer-based. No attempt has been made to gather the necessary information and facts on which to base effective marketing decisions. In short, the company has a long way to go in implementing the marketing concept.

The example illustrates that an essential step in implementing the marketing concept is the establishment of planning based on an accurate, factual understanding of customer needs. This, in turn, requires that a company has adequate sensing mechanisms for analysing and interpreting these needs. In most companies this sensing mechanism is provided by the marketing research function. However, you should be careful not to interpret this as meaning that implementing the marketing concept will always require the establishment of a marketing research function. The smaller company may not be in a position to afford this. What matters is not how much a company spends on it, nor who does it, and certainly not what we call it, as long as a company is basing its decision-making on an adequate and accurate mechanism for sensing market and customer needs. It is to these decision-making aspects of implementation that we now turn our attention.

Processes and procedures for decision-making

Perhaps the clearest indication of the extent to which a company has implemented the marketing concept is contained in its activities related to decision-making, and in particular how decisions are made with regard to the elements of the so-called 'marketing mix'. Again, an example will serve to illustrate this:

> . . . your company spends some 2 per cent of its annual turnover on developing new products in its research laboratories. On average, over the past ten years the company has launched four new products every year. Only three of the last 25 products launched have been successful, but these have earned good profits. The research and development team is given a free hand to develop any products which the company is technically and commercially able to produce and market. Once the technical and production problems have been overcome for a new product, it is passed over to marketing for commercial evaluation and possible launch. This year the company has only two products which it feels are worth launching; these products have reached the stage where a decision has to be made with respect to their market price. In fact, the pricing of the company's new products presents few

problems. All products, including new ones, are priced on a cost-plus basis. The procedure is that the accountancy department calculates the variable costs of producing the product (raw materials and labour costs) and adds to this a proportion of the fixed costs of factory overheads (rent, rates, etc.). To this 'total cost' is added a percentage profit margin according to the estimated life of the product and the investment required to develop and launch the product. This result is the final price of the product . . .

At first glance the company does not appear to be doing too much wrong—certainly, its success rate for new products is low, but this is not unusual as new product development is risky. But to what extent is the company a marketing-oriented company, and what clues are there in the example which would enable us to assess this?

In fact, on the basis of the relatively small amount of information given in the example, it is almost certain that the company has not implemented the marketing concept to any great extent. The evidence for this conclusion lies in the processes and procedures for decision-making. There appears to be little communication between research and development and marketing, at least in the early, and most crucial, stages of new product development. Similarly, the procedure for pricing of products is distinctly non-marketing-oriented. Demand considerations appear to play little part in this decision-making process.

What the example illustrates is the fact that perhaps the most fundamental change that is required to implement marketing in a company is often a subtle, but nevertheless vital, change in how decisions are taken. There are two related aspects to this.

The first change in decision-making required to implement the marketing concept is for every department or function—and not just marketing—in the company to place the customer and his or her needs at the very centre of its decision-making. This is a question not only of what was referred to earlier as education, but also of the establishment of a system of processes and procedures for functional decision-making which is customer-oriented in every department of the company and one which is based on adequate and accurate market facts.

The second aspect of changed decision-making in the company that implements the marketing concept is that the different areas of functional decision-making, however customer-oriented they may be individually, must be effectively *coordinated* to achieve a concerted and consistent, company-wide marketing effort. This is a key function of marketing management, but again, if misunderstood (by other functions) and/or badly

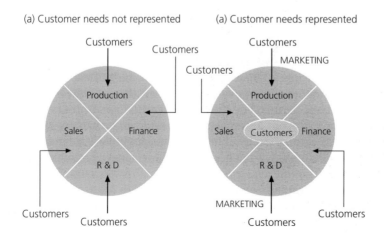

(a) Customer needs not represented

(a) Customer needs represented

FIGURE 1.5

The boundary-spanning role of marketing

Source: adapted from P. Kotler, *Marketing Management: Analysis, Planning, Implementation and Control*, 7th edn, Prentice-Hall, Englewood Cliffs, NJ, 1991

managed (by marketing or senior management), can give rise to problems and further hostility.

In effect, it is in its decision-making that a company evidences the extent to which it has been successful in all of the previously discussed facets of the implementation issue. But what of marketing's role in this process, and more specifically, what are the functional responsibilities of the marketing department in a company?

THE MARKETING FUNCTION: RESPONSIBILITIES AND ROLES

Our discussion of the requirements of implementing the marketing concept points to a number of key responsibilities and roles for the marketing function in a company. First, the marketing function must act as an intermediary between the company and its customers' needs. In fulfilling this boundary-spanning role, marketing acts as a sort of representative for the customer, interpreting his motives for purchase and ensuring that the company comes closest to satisfying the customer's requirements. This notion is shown in Fig. 1.5.

In addition to this boundary-spanning role for the marketing function, and because of the importance of planning referred to earlier, a further key role for marketing in a company is the formulation of company and marketing plans based on market facts and information. This notion is shown in Fig. 1.6.

Finally, the marketing function must attempt to ensure that decision-making throughout the company adequately reflects both company and marketing plans, and

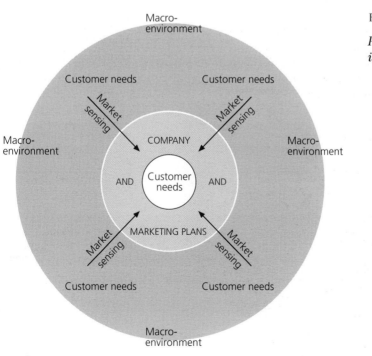

FIGURE 1.6

Planning and information gathering

the assessment of market and customer needs on which these are based. This is shown in Fig. 1.7.

These three broad areas of responsibility for the marketing function must be translated into a specific set of responsibilities and activities for marketing personnel—a job description, in other words. Some marketing textbooks go further than this and list what these are likely to be in the typical company. An example of this approach is that given by Buell.[20] Unfortunately, such 'lists' often do not take account of the fact that there is no such thing as the typical company. All companies are different and we should expect to find that, within the three broad areas of responsibilities for marketing described above, specific responsibilities and activities for marketing will differ between companies. We should also remember that, as in other functional areas of business, marketing may comprise of a hierarchy of management levels, each of which will have its own set of responsibilities and activities. The product or brand manager level of the marketing hierarchy, for example, faces a very different (if inter-related) set of issues from those facing the senior marketing manager in a company.

Marketing relations with other functions

We have seen that becoming more marketing-oriented may entail an enlarged role for marketing in overall company decision-making. Functions and responsibilities that had previously been the province of other functional areas in a company may, under the marketing concept, come within the remit of the marketing department. Although it is not inevitably the case, both enlarged responsibility and increased status are often the outcome of this process. Remember, this can give rise to conflict between marketing and other departments. Some of the possible issues of such conflict were discussed earlier; you will recall, for example, that marketing and production may have very different notions as to what constitutes effective management and decision-making

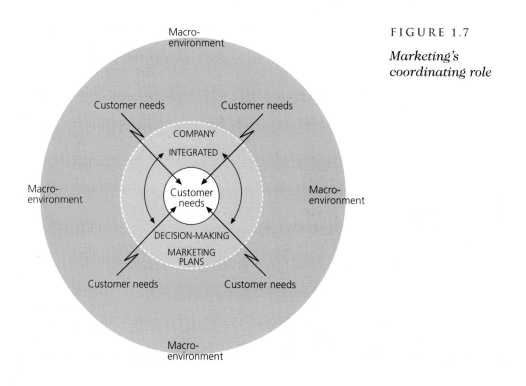

FIGURE 1.7

Marketing's coordinating role

within each of their respective functions. So too may marketing and research and development, and marketing and sales, and marketing and finance. In fact, it would not be an exaggeration to suggest that the potential for inter-functional conflict is at its greatest when we consider the relationship between marketing and virtually every other functional area of a business. Of course, conflict in itself is not always undesirable, as Shapiro points out;[21] not unlike market competition, conflict can ensure effectiveness and efficiency. However, conflict can reach such levels as to be dysfunctional; it can effectively disable the participants and reduce efficiency. Unfortunately, some companies have attempted to minimize the potential for conflict between marketing and others (or, rather, have provided a mechanism for reducing the outcome of such conflict situations) by increasing the power and authority of one of the protagonists—marketing. The usual result of enforcing 'agreement' in this way is more, not less, conflict. The reason for this is that simply increasing the authority of marketing over other functional areas does not remove the basic issues which probably gave rise to the conflict in the first place. On the contrary, the nature of marketing's authority and power relationships will often be at the heart of it.

What is required is a mechanism whereby there are no 'losers'. Handy[22] suggests a number of procedures which a company might use to achieve this, and which may bring about more effective coordination between the various functional groups. Some of these and their relevance to marketing's relationships in a company are as follows:

1. The agreement of common, overriding and realistic goals or objectives. 'Customer satisfaction' is not a meaningful goal if a department is not judged upon it. Nor is it likely to become an accepted goal if one or more of the parties does not contribute to it or is unsure of how precisely they might contribute.

2. The establishment of information and control systems such that the different departments or parties can appreciate and evaluate their contribution to the goal of customer satisfaction. For example, quality control and inspection might be kept informed of the role of their efforts in increasing sales and reducing customer complaints.

3. The stimulation of high interaction and frequent communication between functional groups. Trust, or the lack of it, often lies at the heart of conflict between departments. Regular contact and communication between marketing and other managers can help considerably in building a climate of trust.

4. The establishment of clear *and agreed* terms of reference for marketing and other departments with respect to duties, authority, etc.

5. The establishment of clear and explicit overall company policies within which each functional area will operate. For example, if it is company policy to produce a full product line, both marketing and production know precisely where they each stand and the potential for conflict between these departments is much reduced.

Even with these mechanisms, conflict can arise between marketing and other departments. Where the parties themselves cannot settle such conflict in a manner that is conducive to effective company management, procedures for arbitration and conciliation will be required. Above all, both effective implementation of the marketing concept and the establishment of effective working relationships between marketing and other functions require positive commitment and support from the most senior management in a company.

To summarize then, marketing is both a philosophy or, if you like, a particular approach to running a business and a management. As a philosophy marketing stresses the importance of the customer. Not only the marketing department and its personnel, but all the functions and members of the organization need to recognize the importance of the customer. In other words, we need a marketing culture. The extent to which a company has adopted and implemented such a culture can be assessed by looking at, for example, managerial attitudes, organizational structures and procedures for planning and decision-making.

As a management function the marketing department is responsible for representing the needs of the customer to the organization and developing plans to meet these needs while ensuring that all the other functions play their necessary role in this process.

Although these represent the key ideas about what marketing is as both a philosophy and a function, over time both the nature and practice of marketing are evolving. We can now turn our attentions to some of the more important developments in the concept and practice of marketing.

DEVELOPMENTS IN THE CONCEPT AND PRACTICE OF MARKETING

Like most areas of management and business, both the marketing concept itself and, as a result, the practice of marketing management have continued to evolve and develop and no doubt will continue to do so in the future. It is impossible to trace all of these developments and changes in this chapter, but among some of the more important are the following.

Internal marketing: Total customer care and total quality

Conventionally, of course, the role of marketing in the organization has been looked at as being one of focusing externally on the needs of the customer. A recognition of the need for a company-wide marketing orientation and for the development of aspects such as Gummesson's 'part-time marketers' (referred to earlier), has led to the recognition that marketers and the marketing function also need to look inwards to the staff in other functions of the organization and the need to 'market' a customer orientation to these other functions. This is now often referred to as 'internal marketing'. Although there are several perspectives as to the meaning and application of internal marketing, the following definition from Ballantyre et al.[23] reflects what many would consider to be the essence of internal marketing:

> Internal marketing is any form of marketing in an organisation which focuses staff attention on the internal activities that need to be changed in order to enhance external marketplace performance.

Overall, internal marketing is aimed at increasing customer awareness throughout the entire organization, together with the motivation of all employees to play their part in achieving customer satisfaction.

Needless to say, achieving effective internal marketing is often problematical and can require considerable commitment and patience on the part of a company trying to implement internal marketing. Successful internal marketing requires the development of systems, procedures and plans for improving customer consciousness throughout an organization together with the motivation to improve customer satisfaction. In turn, successful internal marketing requires, for example: good internal communication, suitable organizational structures and adequate training and resources. Above all, a total commitment on the part of senior management to improving customer service and satisfaction is required. Lancaster[24] argues that internal marketing is essential in improving company performance and competitiveness but requires the recognition that in addition to outside customers, employees too are in a sense customers of the managers who wish to carry out the company's objectives.

Internal marketing is closely linked to the philosophy and practice of total customer care and total quality. Increasingly, companies are having to give much more attention to the role of quality and customer care. Customer care has become the focus of a new approach for organizations and encompasses every facet of a company's activities which can impinge on customer satisfaction and service. It covers all activities at the pre-, during and post-transaction stages and thereby encompassing all aspects of customer/supplier relationships. The idea is to offer superior value to customers thereby enabling the company to develop a competitive edge and achieve customer retention and loyalty. Customer care is more than just simply customer service and should affect every aspect of corporate policy and strategy. It includes, for example, the way that customers are dealt with over the telephone, the application of the marketing mix elements and obviously customer after-sales and service. Total quality management (TQM) links with customer care with the aim of developing better services to meet customer requirements first time every time. Quality programmes and total quality management involve more than simply product quality. Indeed, TQM encompasses every element which impinges on the customer's perception of quality. Customer care and TQM then are very closely related. They are also related to the recognition of the long-term value of a customer and hence need to be considered with another important development in the concept and practice of marketing, described below, namely relationship marketing. Total customer care, total quality and relationship marketing are in fact so important in contemporary marketing that we have devoted a whole chapter to these areas. Chapter 13 then, considers these aspects in more detail. But let us now examine the concept of relationship marketing.

Relationship marketing

Perhaps one of the most significant developments in recent years has been the growth of the notion of *'relationship marketing'*. It is increasingly argued that the traditional concept of marketing as exemplified in some of the definitions given earlier in this chapter, do not adequately reflect the recognition of the *'long-term value'* of a customer. The argument is that many of the traditional definitions of marketing, although stressing the importance of customer needs and satisfaction, are essentially concerned with maximizing the profitability of each transaction. Buttle[25] argues that this philosophy is no longer appropriate for today's markets and customers, rather, he argues that marketing should instead seek to develop long-term relationships with customers which cannot easily be duplicated by competitors. Building successful long-term relationships with customers, he suggests, provides for a unique and sustained competitive advantage. Similarly, Kotler[26] suggests that relationship marketing attempts to build up long-term, trusting, relationships with valued customers to the benefit of both customer and organization. This trend towards a longer term non-transactional view of marketing is captured in the definitions of marketing as exemplified by Gronroos[27] referred to earlier. Kotler argues that the effective relationship marketer must supply good consistent quality backed up by good consistent service and fair prices. The aim is to develop and maintain strong economic, technical and social ties with valued customers.

In some ways these descriptions of relationship marketing at first glance appear to represent nothing particularly different or special about relationship marketing compared to more conventional marketing. However, in fact, relationship marketing requires a whole new approach to customers and marketing compared to traditional marketing approaches. All aspects of marketing from planning marketing strategy to developing and implementing the marketing mix need to be approached differently using a relationship marketing philosophy. In fact, the relationship marketing concept is so important to the contemporary marketer, and has so many far-reaching implications for marketing practice that we will consider relationship marketing and its implications at several points in later chapters. So, for example, we shall see some of the implications of relationship marketing when we consider areas such as product management, the management of distribution and logistics, planning customer service, and in particular, the management of personal selling. As already mentioned, however, relationship marketing is so important that we consider this area of marketing again in more detail in Chapter 13.

Communications and information technology (IT)

As in many other areas of our daily lives, marketing, too, has been not only affected but some would argue, fundamentally changed through developments in technology and particularly developments which are related to and/or stem from communications and information technology. In particular, the ubiquitous computer continues to change the face of marketing practice. It is impossible to go into detail here but examples of areas of marketing affected by developments in communication and IT range from techniques of marketing research and data collection which are increasingly computer-based, through to developments which stem from database marketing such as the growth in direct marketing techniques. Perhaps one of the most significant developments which has already affected marketing but which will grow in importance in the future is the growth of the use of the Internet. As with relationship marketing, so many facets of marketing technique and practice are affected by developments in communications and information technology, including the growth of the Internet, that we shall highlight the implications and effects of these changes and developments as appropriate throughout the text.

In the context of this chapter, however, it is worth emphasizing that developments in communications and information technology have in very practical ways helped marketers to implement the marketing concept. There are many ways in which this has happened, but overall technology offers the marketer a better ability to understand, anticipate and deliver the needs of customers. For example, information technology has facilitated more sophisticated and insightful marketing research. Both secondary and primary information can now be accessed, analysed and interpreted to increase the speed of response to customers' changing needs. Information and communication technology has also helped in the marketing planning process. For example, new technology is increasingly being used to analyse markets and identify market segments. Customer care, too, has benefited from advances in technology thereby helping the marketer to develop a marketing culture within the organization. Moreover, improved databases have facilitated easier tracking of customer satisfaction and the following up of complaints thereby improving customer service and increasing customer loyalty and retention rates. More effective internal communication, too, via the intranet has also facilitated the development of more marketing-oriented cultures in organizations by improving internal communication regarding customer needs and market developments. All the staff, and not just the marketing department, can be kept informed of, and therefore feel able to play a part in, developments in improved customer relationships.

Ecological/environmental and consumer welfare issues: social marketing

Recent years have witnessed an increased interest in protecting the environment, together with a recognition of the complex and potentially fragile nature of the ecological system of our planet. Coupled with these developments has been an increased emphasis on protecting consumers against marketing malpractice and dangerous or unhealthy products. Effective and aware marketers have responded to these developments by, for example, producing recyclable products and packaging, reducing the pollution that the use of their products causes, and even protecting consumers against their own worst excesses by stopping the selling of certain products. The consumer movement and so-called 'green' issues are considered further in Chapter 2, but there is no doubt that these developments have had far-reaching effects on marketing practice. There are some that argue that the marketing concept itself needs to change to reflect this increased concern for consumer and environmental welfare, calling for a societal-based marketing concept. A 'societal-based' view of marketing, or as it is often termed 'social marketing' involves a widening of both the concept and the application of marketing. The traditional viewpoint of marketing was that the principal responsibility of marketing was simply to provide products that satisfied consumers' needs efficiently and profitably.

Proponents of social marketing would greatly extend this responsibility. They see marketing as a social force which not only transmits a standard of living, but also serves as a force that reflects and influences cultural values and norms. Thus, the boundaries of social marketing extend far beyond purely economic criteria. The idea is that marketing concepts and techniques should be used to promote the welfare of society as a whole, encompassing such areas as the reduction of poverty, improved education, improved healthcare, etc. So, for example, marketing tools are used in promoting healthier lifestyles through, say, better diet or reduced alcohol or tobacco consumption. In addition, social marketing suggests that a more ethical/social orientation be incorporated into companies' marketing strategies so that, for example, marketers consider and take account of the wider social implications of their products and services. Obviously there is potential here for a conflict between the interests of society and those of business or even individual consumers. It is certainly not clear where the boundaries of social marketing should be erected and where the marketer's responsibility to society, other than in purely economic resource usage and profit terms, start and end. However, there is no doubt that more and more marketers are considering the social consequences and implications of their actions. Social marketing does not imply a replacement of the traditional marketing concept, but rather its extension so as to recognize and encompass the wider needs of society. As we shall see later in this chapter many of the criticisms of marketing focus on ethical issues and the extent to which marketing is responsible for various social and environmental problems. In Chapter 2, we shall also consider the growth of consumerism and legislation as responses to some of the more antisocial activities in marketing. Whatever the reasons, voluntarily or otherwise, marketers are having to consider ecological, environmental and consumer welfare issues together with their wider social role more frequently in their marketing plans and activities.

WIDENING THE APPLICATIONS OF MARKETING

In addition to the developments in the concept and practice of marketing, marketing is increasingly being used in new and ever-widening applications. Originally the concept of marketing together with the application of its tools and techniques was not only limited to the profit-making organization, but also primarily to the marketing of consumer products. Gradually, the application of marketing concepts and techniques has widened beyond this initial remit. Marketing is now extensively being used in the applications below:

- Business-to-business markets
- Not-for-profit/non-business marketing
- Services marketing
- Small- and medium-sized enterprises (SMEs)
- International and global markets.

Each of these application areas of marketing involve sometimes subtle but often major changes to the use and application of some of the marketing tools and techniques. In particular, these different applications for marketing have major implications for combining the marketing mix elements. These implications are considered in more depth in Chapter 12, so we shall at this stage simply introduce some of the key areas encompassing a widened use of marketing thinking and practices.

Business-to-business markets

Marketing first spread from consumer markets into business-to-business applications. Although there are different types of business-to-business markets, in the main they are characterized and distinguished from consumer markets by the fact that customers in these markets are purchasing in order to further the objectives of their organizations rather than personal motives and use. Some of the key differences between organizational buyers are considered in more detail in Chapter 3. It has long been recognized, however, that the importance of a marketing culture and the general principles of marketing apply to just the same extent as in consumer goods markets. However, because of the differences in business-to-business markets, primarily it has to be said, because of the different nature of the buyers and the buying process, there are some major implications for the marketer in managing and planning marketing activities. Primarily these differences are seen in the design and use of the elements of the marketing mix. We shall return to these differences in the mix in business-to-business markets in Chapter 12.

Not-for-profit/non-business marketing

Our first important development in marketing practice has been the increasing use of marketing tools and techniques in not-for-profit and non-business organizations. Traditionally, marketing was conceived as a means of generating and sustaining profits. However, many organizations have objectives other than profits, and many are not business organizations in the conventional sense. Examples of such organizations include churches, charities, political parties and 'public' organizations such as local authorities, police and fire services and government departments. Once spurned by such organizations, or at the very least thought of as not being relevant, marketing is increasingly being used as part of their plans. Remember, we shall consider the special issues of marketing approach and application in these types of organizations in more detail in Chapter 13.

Services marketing

Unlike not-for-profit and non-business marketing, many providers of services have long recognized the value and importance of marketing and of being marketing-oriented. As mentioned earlier, the marketing concept applies just as much to service products as to physical products; however, probably because of the growth in importance of services in the economies of many developed countries, more and more attention has focused on the special issues and problems of applying marketing in this area. As we shall see in Chapter 6, the characteristics of services compared with tangible physical products gives rise to additional considerations in their marketing. The marketing mix for services marketing is also considered further in Chapter 13.

Marketing in small- and medium-sized enterprises (SMEs)

Although never exclusively intended only for the larger organization, it is fair to say that many small- to medium-sized enterprises have been reluctant, or felt unable, to implement and use many of the marketing tools and techniques. There are many reasons for this, not the least of which is the attitude of many managers in such organizations who have, at least in the past, thought of marketing as an expensive luxury. Such organizations are increasingly recognizing, however, that effective marketing and a marketing culture are necessities rather than luxuries. Having said this, the small- to medium-sized enterprise does face different issues and problems in the application of marketing concepts and techniques, not the least because of limitations in access to resources and expertise. This therefore means that sometimes the marketing approach of the larger organization is inappropriate or at least has to be modified. Again, this often presents itself as differences or modifications to the elements of the marketing mix. We shall consider the applications of marketing in SMEs in more detail in Chapter 12.

Global marketing

Finally, in terms of widening applications of marketing, business and trade, and hence marketing, have become more and more global in nature in recent years. As with services, the application of marketing—in this case by companies trading across international frontiers—is not new, but again, the growth in activity in this area, and particularly the spread of the global marketing organization, has focused more and more attention on this aspect of marketing. International and global aspects of marketing are considered in more detail in Chapter 14. Of particular significance for European marketers, of course, are the developments concerning the activities of the members of the European Union (EU). These are discussed in more detail, therefore, in the next chapter when we consider the marketing environment.

CRITICISMS AND LIMITATIONS OF MARKETING

Lest we begin to believe that marketing offers a perfect solution to all the problems, not only of business, but potentially of society in general, it is important to balance this possible perspective with the fact that marketing is not without, and often quite rightly, its critics. There are also limitations as to what marketing can achieve for a company in pursuing its objectives. As consumer markets have become more complex, marketing more sophisticated and its applications wider, its practice has increasingly become the subject of increasing controversy and criticism. This is due, to some extent, to media and sometimes consumer misuse and misunderstanding of the word 'marketing' itself. Unfortunately, the term 'marketing' as used in some of the media and by some consumers often becomes the generic term which describes a multitude of malpractices ranging from actual dishonest trading to over-exaggerated advertising claims. A company that describes itself as 'marketing-oriented' can run the risk of being grouped with those firms that do not practise marketing at all in the real sense. This is one explanation for the poor image which marketing has in the minds of many consumers and media controllers.

However, it must be recognized that, even among those companies that adhere to the marketing concept, some criticism as to its functions is justified. Typical criticisms are outlined in the following list:

- Many products are at least wasteful of resources and in some cases dangerous to health.
- Much packaging and labelling is unnecessary or deceptive.
- Advertising is misleading.
- Advertising exploits children and makes people dissatisfied.
- Delivery is unreliable.
- After-sales service is inefficient.
- Market research invades privacy.

There are no excuses for such (valid) criticisms, and there is obviously much room for improvement. It must be remembered that in a competitive environment firms do not set out to antagonize customers if they wish to remain in business. Moreover, consumers usually have the sanction of spending their money where levels of service are more acceptable. The onus here is on marketing practitioners to recognize and remedy their areas of weakness and to promote themselves and their activities so as to be distinguished from the less savoury and often purely sales-oriented approaches that some companies employ.

There is a more intellectual and more fundamental basis from which marketing can be criticized. This concerns marketing's economic and ethical role in the way in which needs are satisfied and resources are allocated. The fundamental debate as to the validity of respective political systems and their approach to resource allocation is beyond the scope of this text; the intention is to consider the problem within the context of 'market' economies. Within such a framework, it is perhaps inevitable that the marketing manager has, in his or her professional role, typically viewed the problems of society from a different viewpoint from that of the external or public observer. The former has tended to emphasize the success and contribution which business in general has made to society, while the latter looks beyond the individual firm and highlights the negative aspects of marketing in society. This section deals with criticisms that call into question marketing's impact on society and are, therefore, 'macro' in nature.

Although it is difficult to classify such criticisms conveniently because of their wide variety, they can be roughly divided into 'economic' and 'ethical' sub-groups. Economic criticism centres around the theme that marketing is inefficient and chiefly concerns the following proposals.

Marketing creates monopoly and limits consumer choice

The possibility of a company becoming so powerful that it will decide what the consumer will buy and at what price, is a denial of the marketing concept and one of the chief fears of the consumer movement. In the private sectors of the developed world, although the development of even larger and more powerful companies is recognized, true monopolies rarely exist. As well as government regulation (in the form of the Monopolies and Mergers Commission in the UK and Anti-trust Legislation in the USA) the buying public is rarely sufficiently homogeneous to permit exclusive control by a monopolistic power.

Part of the opposition to monopoly is rooted in the economist's notion that perfect competition among sellers is the fairest way in which business can serve society and that a state of monopoly will allow the worst fears of marketing critics to materialize. It is true that monopoly is the antithesis of perfect competition, but these represent extremes of economic theory: the reality lies somewhat between the two. Marketing is in fact characterized by many economic business conditions. Some markets are supplied by numerous small- to medium-sized companies, while others are represented by the state of oligopoly.

We should remember that good marketing strategy should centre around a distinctive competence of the firm.[28] In this way the most successful companies become something like monopolists in their fields. For the consumer, the most important factor is that such a firm's competitors will continually strive to emulate this success. Thus, the current leader has little room for complacency. Such competition acknowledges the idea of consumer sovereignty and is the best safeguard that consumers have against exploitation by powerful companies.

The reality that increased market share leads to a disproportionate increase in market advantages, profits and thus power has led many markets to a state of oligopoly.[29] The existence of such power has caused marketing's critics to prophesy that such firms will eventually dictate what, where and when consumers will buy. Certainly there are instances of the abuse of power, and such activities must be deplored. In Western markets such power is tempered by competition as well as the ability of the consumer to remove his or her custom. In the UK in the early 1970s, genuine fears were expressed about the power of large bakeries and breweries to 'impose' white sliced bread and gas-filled beer upon the nation. Although these markets were in fact oligopolistic, it seemed that they were in possession of monopoly-like powers, supplying only what was profitable and convenient for them to produce. The resurgence of more traditional products was testimony to consumer power and a timely reminder to those firms that had neglected the marketing concept. Britain's largest bankers have had to shake off any complacency that they may have had in the 1970s. Not only has competition increased between them, but also they are realizing that they have no 'divine right' to exclusivity in the marketing of their services, as evidenced by the ending of their power through legislation which has opened up their traditional market to other financial institutions like building societies.

Similar examples are not difficult to find; they usually reveal that successful companies gain power so long as they efficiently satisfy demand, while at the same time, the standards of other companies are raised in their efforts to emulate the leader. Such a leader is constantly under threat from potential competition, differentiated and substitute products, and changes in the nature of consumer demand. Critics of marketing play a valuable social role—it would be naive to bestow complete altruism on all the business world, or indeed to overlook genuine mistakes. It is proposed that the nature of markets themselves will militate against monopoly, and that if situations approaching monopoly exist, these will remain only so long as they efficiently satisfy consumer needs and wants.

Marketing involves too much competitive promotion

The major criticisms of competitive promotion are directed at the advertising industry. Indeed, advertising is criticized by business itself because of the notorious difficulties involved in evaluating its effectiveness. Our main concern is with external critics who contend that purely competitive advertising is wasteful and that the consumers' real need is for advertising to be informative. If advertising were reduced or did not exist (so the argument runs) manufacturers' overheads would decrease and this would result in cheaper goods. The argument is extended to question the need for the multiplicity of apparently similar products which advertising is engaged in promoting.

The desire of consumers to have brand choice is well known, but marketers should not reject such criticism out of hand. When the US government banned cigarette advertising, it was interesting to note that sales did not fall significantly and that the relative market share of the cigarette manufacturers (all of whom were heavy advertising spenders) did not change. Cigarettes may, of course, present a special case, but the event certainly caused large spenders of advertising money to stop and think.

More usually, marketers are able to provide economic justification for their promotional expenditure. So as to maintain profitability, manufacturers place great reliance on their ability to achieve an optimum production–overhead ratio. Advertising can help to achieve and maintain such a position, but it must be remembered that, if sales that exceed the optimum are induced, such effort may become counter-productive.

Marketing is wasteful

The 'middleman' is often the butt of marketing criticism. A long and complicated channel system is seen as wasteful and unnecessary. Students of channel structure should be able to present cogent reasons justifying the need for middlemen—that is, from the manufacturer's point of view. There is no doubt that some channel systems are less than efficient. In the macro sense, critics bemoan the transportation around the country of apparently identical goods which are produced by different manufacturers. Frequently these goods are in fact highly differentiated with respect to style, design and brand name. There is, moreover, an important movement towards the simplification of channel systems which is discernible in the rise of discount stores and hypermarkets.

Despite the inefficiencies of marketing, it is logical to assume that companies will endeavour to reduce costs whenever possible. Efficiency is, of course, necessary for profit, and profit is essential for survival, but the implication for the consumer is that it allows the company to increase competitiveness and so reduce prices or improve service.

From the social perspective, critics question social values which it is claimed marketing is largely responsible for creating.

Marketing promotes materialism and creates artificial needs and values

The economist and social philosopher J. K. Galbraith described, as early as 1952, the creation of wants as the 'dependence effect'. He criticized the process of production and marketing for satisfying wants that were not 'original' within the consumer, but which were actually created by marketing in the first place.[30] Much of the blame for so-called stimulation of wants is laid at the door of advertising. Whether the source of our desire to acquire products and life styles which we could physically live without is inherent in ourselves, or is imposed upon us by phenomena such as advertising, is the subject of major philosophical debate. Some psychologists maintain that our wants are not really concerned with the acquisition of, say, an expensive hi-fi system, but rather that such an act realizes an inner psychological need. If this is the case, then marketing plays the valuable social role of want fulfilment, satisfying wants that otherwise, it could be argued, the consumer would search to fulfil in some other way. To this extent, if blame is to be attached, it must be shared by the buyer and the seller.

Questions as to the power of marketing and advertising to distort values and create artificial wants cannot be easily resolved. Is marketing to be blamed for the general rise in living standards which has facilitated the style of spending, which is itself the source of so much criticism? It may be that some critics underestimate the ability of consumers to discriminate and choose for themselves. The existence of social inequality has led to the comment that advertising dissatisfies the poor by portraying a world that is beyond their means. This is a socio-political comment as much as a direct criticism of marketing.

Advertising is offensive and deceptive

Fraudulent and deliberately deceptive advertising is infrequent as it is controlled by legislation. It is relatively rare because it is the advertiser's job to gain confidence among the target market and not to destroy it.

Much of the advertising deemed 'questionable' involves sins of omission as well as commission. The existence of advertising control is testimony to the fact that some advertising has presented half truths which, although not necessarily making blatantly false claims, have in reality set out to deceive. The socially responsible advertiser aims to communicate genuine product features to the public, and, while the need for regulatory bodies to control the less ethical is reprehensible, its existence appears to have raised the standards of advertising in general. In the United States, the Federal Trade Commission now reports that 97 per cent of advertisements checked each year satisfactorily adhere to its code of conduct.[31]

Marketing is unethical

Often the individual marketer's own personal standards may be compromised in the business situation. This problem of ethics is aggravated by the confusion that exists as to what the ethical obligations of marketing are. In recent years we have witnessed numerous examples of 'leaks' and revelations from individual employees of large organizations. If, for example, in detriment of his or her own career and financial security, an executive publicly discloses that the company has deceived or endangered its customers, the employee's corporate allegiance has then been overruled by his or her personal ethical code. For the average individual, the dilemma is unlikely to reach such critical proportions, but an ethical problem nevertheless remains.

Clearly, the solution lies with higher management, who could obviate the causes of ethical conflict. The power of the media and of consumerism has developed to such an extent that management is in any case under considerable pressure to adopt an increasingly responsible stance. Major initiatives have indeed been taken by enlightened companies that see valid marketing opportunities in such an approach. The question of social responsibility in marketing will be dealt with in a later section of this chapter. When we are discussing marketing ethics, though, we should be careful to note that the term 'ethics', and in particular what constitutes 'ethical' versus 'unethical' behaviour in the context of marketing, is very difficult to define. Dibb[32] suggests that ethics may be one of the most misunderstood and controversial concepts in marketing.

We can see then that marketing is not without its problems and certainly its critics, justified or not. In all honesty, there is little doubt that some marketing practices have been in the past, and will no doubt continue to be, offensive, deceptive, unethical and so on. Similarly, there will always be those who genuinely believe that marketing is wasteful and creates artificial needs and values. We shall see in Chapter 2 that such criticisms are responsible for the development of regulations and legislation to deter at least the worst potential excesses of the marketer. Another outcome of these criticisms of marketing has been the rise of the so-called consumer movement or as it is often called 'consumerism'.

Marketing proponents and practitioners must be careful not to claim too much for what marketing can achieve. Marketing on its own cannot make up for weak organizational structures or poor managerial expertise. Furthermore, marketing is not the answer to all the ills of society in general. Indeed, as we have seen, some believe that it is a major cause of these problems. Overall, however, with all its limitations, effective marketing probably offers one of the most powerful ways of generating corporate success and overall economic wellbeing.

CHAPTER SUMMARY

This chapter has traced the development of the modern marketing concept, and compared it with less sophisticated approaches to business. These approaches tended to put the product or product sales, rather than customer requirements, at the centre of business thinking. Even today the marketing concept is still often misunderstood by practising business people and, as a result, is often criticized as a management 'fad' or nothing more than rhetoric. If modern marketing principles are to gain acceptance by the senior managers who must put them into effect, the need is not for more elaborate marketing techniques, but for better communications between the marketing specialist and the general manager.

Unless the marketing way of thinking and caring about the business is practised at a level where effective action can be guaranteed, then the most up-to-date and sophisticated marketing techniques in the world will not succeed. Marketing can provide policies for profitable action, but top management must give the authority to form these policies into action.

Marketing is not narrowly confined to a particular office or department: it is an attitude of mind, an approach to business problems that should be adopted by the whole organization, from the chief executive downwards.

Every person working in an organization should realize that without customers there is no business and hence no jobs. If a company cannot attract and retain customers' business, it will eventually be forced into liquidation or merger. All departments within the organization should be *working together* as an integrated unit with a common purpose—the satisfaction of customers' needs and wants. They should strive to carry this out more effectively and efficiently than competitors and, in the case of profit-making organizations, to make a profit out of the whole operation.

The marketing concept acknowledges that a business geared to serve the needs and requirements of customers will achieve better results over a longer period of time than a company whose orientation is along different lines. When a company is said to be 'marketing-oriented' it puts the customer at the very centre of its corporate thinking. It sees its mission in life and its very purpose for existence as being the identification, satisfaction and retention of customers.

The marketing concept, together with the practice of marketing is itself evolving and changing. Marketers in particular are recognizing the importance of internal marketing and the link between this and total customer care and total quality. Relationship marketing is fundamentally altering many of the basic premises of marketing recognizing as it does the long-term value of a customer and the importance of building relationships. Like most areas of business, marketing is being strongly affected by developments in communications and information technology. In some cases this is revolutionizing marketing practices, but in the context of this chapter we have seen that developments in this area are helping the marketer develop a marketing culture. Ecological/environmental and consumer welfare issues, too, have increasingly affected marketing ideas and practice and in part have led to the development of the notion of social marketing.

In terms of the applications of marketing the philosophy and practice of marketing was once viewed as being most relevant to the profit-seeking organization selling consumer products. Increasingly, however, the marketing concept and tools of marketing are being used in an increasingly diverse range of situations and organizations. Spreading first into the business-to-business marketing arena, marketing is increasingly being used in not-for-profit organizations, services marketing, small- and medium-sized enterprises, and in the increasingly important arena of international and global marketing.

Finally, we have seen that there are many critics and criticisms of marketing. Marketers must not ignore these, and indeed have often responded positively to criticism. However, the growth of the consumer movement and the need for increased legislation to curb some of the worst potential excesses of marketing underline the fact that marketers do not always respond quickly or positively enough to such criticisms.

CHAPTER REVIEW QUESTIONS

1. How does marketing differ from selling?
2. Identify an organization which in your opinion has not adopted a marketing concept. What evidence have you found to support your view?
3. What are the key steps in introducing a marketing-oriented culture within an organization, and what might be the main problems in achieving this?
4. Outline and discuss what you feel are some of the key developments in the concept and practice of marketing in the contemporary organization.
5. How can communications and information technology help in the development of a marketing culture?
6. What are some of the major criticisms of marketing and how should marketers respond to these criticisms?

References

1. A. Smith, *The Wealth of Nations*, Random House, New York, [1775] 1937.
2. P. Kotler, G. Armstrong, J. Saunders, and V. Wong, *Principles of Marketing*, European 2nd edn, Prentice-Hall, London, 1998, p. 12.
3. S. Dibb, L. Simkin, W. M. Pride and O. C. Ferrell, *Marketing Concepts and Strategies*, European 3rd edn, Houghton Mifflin, Boston, MA, 1997, p. 5.
4. O. C. Ferrell and G. H. Lucas, 'An evaluation of progress in the development of a definition of marketing', *Journal of Marketing Management*, **3** (1), 1987, pp. 73–82.
5. M. J. Baker, *MacMillan Dictionary of Marketing and Advertising*, Macmillan Press, London, 1984.
6. 'AMA Board approves new marketing definition', *Marketing News*, 1 March 1985, p. 1.
7. C. Gronroos, 'The rebirth of modern marketing: six propositions about relationship marketing', Swedish School of Economics and Business Administration, Working Paper 307, Helsinki, 1995.
8. P. F. Drucker, *The Practice of Management*, Harper & Row, New York, 1954, p. 56.
9. G. J. Hooley, J. E. Lynch and J. Shepherd, 'The marketing concept: putting the theory into practice', *The European Journal of Marketing*, **24** (9), pp. 7–24.
10. P. F. Drucker, *Management: Tasks, Responsibilities, Practices*, Harper & Row, New York, 1973, pp. 64–5.
11. P. Kotler, *Marketing Management: Analysis, Planning, Implementation and Control*, 8th edn, Prentice-Hall, Englewood Cliffs, NJ, 1994, p. 17.
12. T. Levitt, 'Marketing myopia', *Harvard Business Review*, July–August 1960, pp. 45–6.
13. P. Kotler, op. cit., p. 19.
14. G. J. Hooley *et al.*, op. cit., p. 5.
15. E. Gummesson, 'Marketing orientation revisited: the crucial role of the part-time marketer', *European Journal of Marketing*, **25**, 1990, pp. 60–75.

16. G. A. Lancaster, 'Marketing and engineering: can there ever be synergy?', *Journal of Marketing Management*, **9**, 1993, pp. 141–53.

17. S. M. A. Saddik, 'Marketing in the wool textile, textile machinery, and clothing industries', Ph.D thesis, University of Bradford Management Centre, 1969.

18. T. Levitt, op. cit.

19. W. J. Stanton, *Fundamentals of Marketing*, 5th edn, McGraw-Hill, Tokyo, 1978, pp. 11–15.

20. V. P. Buell, *Marketing Management in Action*, McGraw-Hill, New York, 1966, pp. 22–7.

21. B. P. Shapiro, 'Can marketing and manufacturing co-exist', *Harvard Business Review*, September–October 1977, pp. 104–14.

22. C. B. Handy, *Understanding Organizations*, Penguin, Harmondsworth, 1976, p. 236.

23. D. Ballantyre, M. Christopher and A. Payne, 'Improving the quality of services marketing: service (re) design is the critical link', *Journal of Marketing Management*, **2**, 1995, pp. 7–24.

24. G. A. Lancaster, 'Marketing and engineering revisited', *Journal of Business and Industrial Marketing*, **10** (1), 1995, pp. 6–15.

25. F. Buttle (ed.), *Relationship Marketing: Theory and Practice*, Paul Chapman, London, 1996, pp. 1–16.

26. P. Kotler, op. cit., p. 11.

27. C. Gronroos, op. cit.

28. C. W. Hofer and D. Schendel, *Strategy Formulation, Analytical Concepts*, South West American Publishing, Edmond, OK, 1978, p. 151.

29. R. D. Buzzel *et al.*, 'Marketing share: a key to profitability', *Harvard Business Review*, January–February 1975, pp. 34–58.

30. J. K. Galbraith, *The Affluent Society*, Houghton Mifflin, Boston, MA, 1952, pp. 124–5.

31. S. W. Dunn and A. W. Barban, *Advertising: Its Role in Modern Marketing*, Dryden Press, Hindsdale, IL, 1978.

32. S. Dibb, L. Simkin, W. M. Pride and O. C. Ferrell, op. cit., p. 740.

Bruddersford Leisure Centre

Leisure, sports and recreation centres have, in recent years, been one of the fastest growing markets in the UK where there are now over 2000 such centres. Some of these are privately run but many of them are provided by local authorities.

With regard to the privately run centres, most of them are very sophisticated in their approach to their marketing and the degree of marketing orientation which they exhibit. They make sophisticated use of marketing research and understand the importance of identifying and satisfying customer needs. In short, they are very marketing-oriented.

In the case of centres run by local authorities, however, the opposite is the case. Many of these centres are run on product-oriented lines. Many of them are ill-equipped, have non-customer friendly opening times, and are often dirty and poorly maintained.

Bruddersford, a northern local authority, operates several sports and recreation centres. The largest of these was built only six years ago and is attached to the local football ground. Initially extremely successful, more recently this newest centre has faced intense competition from a recently opened private leisure centre. Despite much higher prices than the local authority centre the private one has taken an estimated 30 per cent of customers who were previously users of Bruddersford's council run facilities.

Partly as a result of this, Bruddersford Council advertised for, and have appointed, a marketing manager. The remit of this new manager is to recapture the customers lost to the private centre.

The new marketing manager believes that at the heart of the problem is the fact that traditionally local authority leisure, sports and recreation centres have not been sufficiently marketing-oriented. There are, however, perhaps good reasons for this. For example, the provision and use of such centres are not necessarily based upon profits, although obviously they have to contribute adequately towards their running costs. Furthermore, unlike privately owned centres, local authority centres have a responsibility towards the council tax payer and perhaps to the public in general. They therefore tend to provide, for example, minority sports facilities which can be grossly underutilized.

Having only been in the post for a month, the new marketing manager has already spoken to various staff at the centre to solicit their views about how lost customers could be recaptured. Below are some of the comments he has received.

'The facilities are for the local public and should be free': pool supervisor.

'The people who have gone to the new private centre aren't interested in sport and fitness at all—they are simply posers who want to be seen in the right places': assistant manager.

'I know we only open between 9.00 a.m. and 7 p.m. but surely if they wanted to people could get to use our facilities at some time during these hours': publicity assistant.

Questions

1. If you were the new marketing manager for Bruddersford's leisure centre explain why you might be concerned about the comments you have received back from some of the centre's staff.

2. Write a report for the members of Bruddersford Council outlining your recommendations for using the ideas and tools and techniques of marketing to recapture some of the centre's lost customers.

Chapter Two

THE MARKETING ENVIRONMENT

LEARNING OBJECTIVES   *This chapter will help you to:*

- appreciate the nature and importance of the marketing environment to the marketing manager;

- understand the range of environmental forces and factors which affect the marketing activities of an organization;

- be aware of how the marketer can respond to the marketing environment;

- understand how to conduct and use an environmental appraisal.

INTRODUCTION

We saw in Chapter 1 that the marketing-oriented firm places the customer, and the satisfaction of customers' needs and wants, at the very centre of all corporate thinking. Rather than establishing what the organization can produce and then going out and 'selling' it, the marketing-oriented firm first finds out the genuine needs and wants of consumers and then attempts to produce products and services that satisfy these requirements. It was also shown that, in a wider sense, the marketing concept is an attitude of mind or a customer-oriented business philosophy, as well as a functional area of management.

Although a clear understanding of consumers' requirements is of paramount importance in putting such a business philosophy into practice, there are also other factors to consider. The marketing firm operates within a complex, dynamic, environment. It is the task of the marketing-oriented firm to link the resources of the organization to the requirements of consumers within the framework of opportunities and threats presented by this environment. Hence, the marketing firm not only has to put consumers' requirements at the top of its list of priorities, but it also needs continually to adjust to environmental forces and factors.

The objective of this chapter is to develop an understanding of the factors making up the marketing environment. How these factors affect the marketing process and how to develop systems for identifying, scanning and forecasting key environmental forces and factors as an input to marketing-planning and decision-making. Firms cannot usually control their environment, but they can understand, and to a certain extent anticipate and react to, environmental forces.

In order to place the environment in its proper context, one should realize that the general term 'marketing environment' is often used to denote both *internal* organizational forces and forces *outside* the control of the firm. For example, Kotler[1] defines the general marketing environment as follows:

> A company's marketing environment consists of the actors and forces that affect the company's ability to develop and maintain successful transactions with its target customers.

Such a definition includes *all* environmental forces outside of the firm's marketing management function. This would also include inter-departmental influences.

Russ and Kirkpatrick[2] call the interaction between the marketing department and other functional areas of management the *intra-firm environment*. It is important, in order to understand the influences of external environment forces, to appreciate that, although the marketing function is the channel through which the firm adapts to changes in external conditions, marketing's ability to carry out this role is also influenced by internal factors. Marketing managers make decisions that have a bearing on other functional areas of the firm. Likewise, the decisions made by other departments have a direct effect on the marketing department's ability to carry out its job.

The *general* marketing environment, therefore, consists of *all* the factors and forces influencing the marketing function. This includes both internal and external forces. Internal forces, i.e. the intra-firm environment, are largely within the control of the firm, and, as we have already acknowledged, these internal factors are in their own way extremely important to the marketing function. However, there is no doubt that it is generally those forces and factors outside the organization which pose the greatest potential opportunities and threats to its continuing survival and hence it is these external environmental forces and factors that we shall concentrate on in this chapter. Nevertheless, as explained below, when considering the range of external environmental forces and factors it is useful to distinguish between two levels of the marketing environment. The first of these is the 'proximate' marketing environment and the second level encompasses the wider or 'macro'-environmental forces and factors. Our terms of reference for our discussion of the marketing environment then are as follows:

In the context of this chapter, the term 'marketing environment' denotes all these forces and agencies *external* to the marketing firm. Some of these outside factors and forces will be somewhat 'closer' to the firm than others, for example immediate suppliers and competitors. We will term this the *proximate marketing environment* (proximate meaning 'close', as in the word 'proximity'). This will serve to distinguish between the environmental influences close to the firm, and the wider macro-external forces such as economic or political forces, which of course also affect the people and organizations in the firm's proximate macro-environment as well as the firm itself.

THE IMPORTANCE OF THE MARKETING ENVIRONMENT: UNCONTROLLABLE AND CONTROLLABLE FACTORS

The only really certain thing in this world is change. Sometimes change occurs so slowly that it is virtually imperceptible. We are often unaware that change is occurring until it is too late to do anything about it. At other times change is so rapid that, even though it is obvious, we find it difficult to react quickly enough. The important point to remember about these changes is that, in the main, changes in the key marketing environmental forces and factors are largely uncontrollable. In other words, there is nothing the marketing manager can do to precipitate, accelerate, slow down or even affect them in any way. One might be tempted to argue then that the marketing manager may as well ignore them. After all, why should we bother if we cannot do anything about them? The answer, of course, is that the marketing manager can do something about these uncontrollable environmental forces and changes in them. Specifically the marketing manager can, and indeed should, ensure that the organization adapts to these changes. Moreover, the marketing manager should attempt to predict the changes which will occur in the future rather than having to adapt to them after the changes have taken place. Although none of us possess the power to foresee the future, we can be sure that it will be *different* from today, and that change is a fact of life. We have little power to stop it, and the sensible course of action is to welcome change and attempt to adapt to it. However, one can attempt to predict such changes through forecasting, a subject dealt with in more detail later.

Charles Darwin,[3] author of *On the Origin of the Species*, put forward the theory that many living organisms have been able to survive in a changing and hostile world because they were able to adapt successfully to changing conditions. Fossil records indicate that long ago there existed many forms of life that for some reason no longer exist today. Although many theories have been put forward to explain the demise of prehistoric animals, the main factor seems to have been their inability to adapt.

Firms also operate in a changing, and at times hostile, business environment. They too, in order to survive and prosper, need to take account of, and adapt to, changing environmental conditions. Firms that fail to do so are likely to end up as extinct as the prehistoric dinosaurs.

In order for a firm to be able to adapt successfully to changing circumstances, management needs to have an understanding and appreciation of the factors and forces influencing such changes. Ideally, a firm should be in a position to adapt to changes as they are occurring, or even in advance. Firms should attempt to capitalize upon change rather than merely reacting to it. By identifying environmental trends soon enough, management should be able, at least in part, to anticipate where such trends are leading and what future conditions are likely to result from such changes.

Unless firms are able to identify and react to changes quickly enough, they are likely to be dictated to by circumstances beyond their control. Instead of being part of the changes occurring, and *leading* the market, they will, of necessity, be forced into being market followers. Instead of adapting to change and even going some way towards *influencing* events, events will instead influence them, perhaps in an unfavourable way. The 'Mars' company not only makes Mars bars; it makes pet foods, convenience foods, computer software, etc. It makes no secret of the fact that its intention is to be market leader in all its operations.

In terms of its speed of response, and its ability to react to changing conditions, we can generally classify three types of firm:

1. Firms that identify and understand the forces and conditions bringing about change. Such firms adapt and move in line with such changes. To a certain extent, such a firm may itself play a part in influencing events.

2. Firms that fail to adapt to changes early enough to become part of that change. Such firms have little opportunity to influence events, but are usually forced to react to changes eventually, out of the necessity to survive.

3. Firms that fail to realize change has occurred, or refuse to adapt to changing circumstances. Such firms are unlikely to survive in the long term or, if they do, are unlikely to prosper.

In short then, organizations that ignore or fail to adapt to uncontrollable environmental forces will eventually go out of business. On the other hand, companies that identify, forecast, understand, and most importantly adapt to these forces will be among the most successful. But how can a company adapt, what does this mean, and in particular what actions can a company take to make such adaptations and, moreover, what role does the marketing function have to play in this process?

In a mixed economy, such as that to be found in the UK, firms enjoy a considerable amount of autonomy. Not only does the management of a firm have control over how it organizes and integrates its management functions, but generally it is free to decide what and how to manufacture as well as matters concerning, for example, pricing, packaging, advertising and distribution and so on. Generally speaking, the management of a firm is free to carry out its business affairs in any way it pleases, and so a number of marketing variables like price are directly under its control. Collectively, we call these controllable marketing variables the 'marketing mix', and this concept is discussed in detail in Chapter 4.

While marketing firms control much of their operations, they do not plan strategies in a vacuum. As we have seen, all organizations are influenced by a number of macro-environmental factors which are broadly outside their control. These environmental forces, and in particular changes in these forces, give rise to marketing opportunities and threats. Stanton *et al.*[4] suggest that the ability of a marketing decision-making executive may be measured by the skill with which he or she can carry out the following tasks:

1. Adjust to the external elements in the changing environment.

2. Forecast the direction and intensity of these changes.

3. Use the controllable variables at his or her command (the marketing mix) in adapting to this external environment.

The controllable variables to which Stanton *et al.* are referring here, are the decision areas pertaining to marketing strategies and plans and the tolls and techniques which the marketer has at his or her disposal to help make these decisions. For example, as already mentioned, the marketer has control over the selection and use of forecasting techniques to help predict changes in the marketing environment. Similarly, the marketer controls the tolls of market research to help in this process. Above all, as already mentioned, the marketer has control over the key decision areas in marketing strategies and plans. In simple terms, the key way in which the marketer ensures the organization's adaptation to the environment and the opportunities and threats it poses are through decisions in the marketing, planning and decision-making process. We shall examine marketing planning in some detail in Chapter 12, but examples of decisions which should reflect responses and adaptations to changes in the environment include decisions regarding the definition of the business; corporate decisions regarding corporate and marketing objectives; market targeting decisions; and decisions for marketing and overall competitive strategies. Above all, however, adaptations to the marketing environment are made through decisions about the controllable elements of the marketing mix. The tools of the marketing mix, then, are so central to the tasks of the marketing manager that well over half of most marketing textbooks of this kind, including this one, are usually devoted to discussing these controllable elements of marketing. Needless to say, we shall return to each of the elements of the marketing mix in several chapters of this text. At this stage, however, we need to identify and discuss the major factors in the marketing environment.

ELEMENTS OF THE MARKETING ENVIRONMENT

Remember we have suggested that it is useful to split the elements of the marketing environment into two layers or levels, namely those forces closest to the organization which we have termed the 'proximate' marketing environment and those forces and factors which constitute the wider external forces which, though less proximate, are as we shall see nonetheless equally if not more important. We shall now consider each of these levels and the most important elements within each of them. These are shown in Fig. 2.1 and are discussed below.

The proximate macro-environment

The proximate macro-environment consists of people, organizations and forces within the firm's immediate *external* environment. Of particular interest to marketing firms are the sub-environments in which we find:

1. Competitors
2. Suppliers
3. Intermediaries (e.g. distributors)

The people and organizations making up the above sub-environments all have a *direct*, and at times *immediate*, effect on the commercial well-being of the marketing firm.

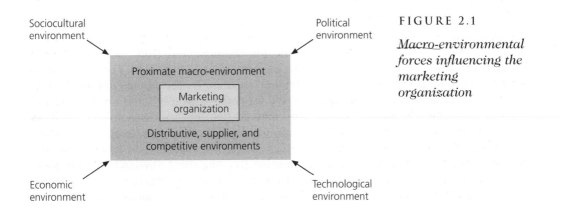

FIGURE 2.1

Macro-environmental forces influencing the marketing organization

The competitive environment

There are very few firms that are fortunate enough to have no competitors. Except in the case of the centrally planned economies, of which, of course, there are fewer and fewer as they increasingly turn towards free-market mechanisms. On the other hand, there are very few markets which possess all the characteristics of what the economist calls a 'perfectly competitive' market structure where no company has any differential advantage and where all products are homogeneous and companies therefore must accept the market price. Rather, most markets fall somewhere in between these two extremes but are characterized by intense competition. In some markets the market structure is dominated by three or four very large companies with a number of medium- and smaller-sized companies all vying for position. In such competitive market structures, in an attempt to reduce price competition and to secure a competitive advantage, companies will seek to make their products and services stand out in some way from their competitors. This attempt to '*differentiate*' products/services from those of competitors is a key feature therefore of modern marketing. Differentiation can be achieved in many ways, but essentially the extent to which differentiation is successful or otherwise is the responsibility of the marketing function. So, for example, the marketer will seek to gain a competitive edge through, say, branding, or perhaps packaging. Innovative distribution, or excellent customer service can also be used to differentiate the company's offerings from those of competitors. Clearly, marketing decisions therefore must reflect and indeed be based upon an analysis of the competitive environment. In fact, the competitive element of a company's environment is probably one of the most important elements in the development of marketing strategies and plans, and therefore in affecting the extent of a company's success, or otherwise, in the marketplace. Traditionally, economists have distinguished between market structures with different degrees of competition. As already mentioned, at one extreme we have the monopolistic market structure where there is only one supplier and hence little or no competition. We have also suggested that this type of market structure is increasingly rare apart from in centrally planned economies or where for some other reason an industry is state run or protected. Also, as already mentioned, at the other extreme is the perfectly competitive market structure where products are undifferentiated between competitors. In the 'real world' though the economists 'oligopolistic' (a market structure with a few relatively large companies) or 'monopolistic competition' (a market structure with many competitors and hence where product differentiation of some kind is crucial) are more realistic.

The marketer must understand who the key competitors are; their relative strengths and weaknesses; and their objectives and strategies in order to plan effective marketing programmes. Not only must the marketer understand existing competitors but must also assess likely new competitors in the form of new entrants or substitutes to the market. How competitors compete for business and their reactions to our planned strategies must also be taken into account. Some companies of course attempt to minimize the effects of the competitive environment by identifying and targeting a market niche which other competitors have for some reason ignored and/or avoided. Smaller companies in particular are able to avoid the disadvantages and problems of trying to compete against larger, much more powerful companies in this way. Some companies, however, deliberately attack their competitors particularly where they have some sort of cost or other advantage. Porter[5] has identified three alternative ways in which a company can attempt to build a competitive advantage. These three alternative routes are through 'cost leadership', 'differentiation', or 'focus' and he suggests that the company must select and pursue one of these alternative strategies which he suggests are mutually exclusive. Irrespective of which competitive strategies are pursued the point is that competitors, and hence the competitive environment, are a key element of a company's overall marketing environment. Furthermore, in virtually every market in the world, the degree of competitive rivalry is increasing. In particular, global competition continues to grow as throughout the world, countries continue to open their frontiers through the liberalization of world trade, while at the same time seeking their own marketing opportunities overseas. It is essential therefore that the marketer analyses and understands the competitive environment as one of the key inputs to marketing planning and decision-making. We shall return to competitor analysis and the range of competitive marketing strategies in Chapter 12.

Supplier environment

Suppliers are other business firms and individuals who provide the resources needed by the marketing firm to produce goods and/or services. Nearly every firm, whether engaged in manufacturing, wholesaling or retailing, is likely to have suppliers. Large firms such as IBM or the Ford Motor Company are likely to have numerous suppliers. For example, Ford must obtain glass windscreens, headlamp units, brakepads, tyres, steel sheet, fabric for interior upholstery and a number of other materials in order to produce cars. While some of these product constituents will come from major manufacturers such as Pilkington's Glass, Lucas and Firestone, other components, ranging from industrial fasteners to engine gaskets, will often be supplied by a large number of smaller, less well-known companies.

As you will appreciate, Ford depends on possibly hundreds of suppliers for its manufacturing capability and commercial prosperity. In the same way, hundreds of firms depend on Ford for orders. The firms that supply Ford with finished components are also likely to be supplied with raw materials or semi-processed goods by a host of other suppliers.

Purchasing is regarded as a very important management function in many organizations. The reason for this is that firms must be able to purchase products and services at an acceptable price and quality. The firm must also ensure that its suppliers are capable of offering an acceptable level of service on such matters as delivery, reliability, stock availability, servicing arrangements and credit facilities.

Manufacturing firms have to decide what proportion of their products actually to make themselves and what parts and components should be sub-contracted out to other manufacturers who are often specialists in their field. For those materials that have to be bought in, purchasing personnel will have to obtain detailed product specifications from engineers and designers, search for suppliers that are capable of producing or supplying materials to specification, rate them on potential suitability, obtain tenders and arrange contracts.

The buyer–supplier relationship is one of economic interdependence. Both parties rely on each other for their commercial well-being. Changes in the terms of the relationship are usually based on negotiation rather than on *ad hoc* unilateral decisions. Such relationships are usually long term, with each party realizing its dependence on the other. Both parties are seeking security and long-term stability from their commercial relationship. This is not to say that factors in the supplier environment do not change. Suppliers may be forced to raise their prices and may also be affected by industrial disputes which, in turn, will affect delivery of materials to the buying firm. Some suppliers may find themselves in financial difficulty and be forced into liquidation. In an attempt to limit the effect of such factors, many buying firms use a 'multiple sourcing' purchasing policy. This avoids over-dependency on any one supplier and reduces the vulnerability of the buying firm.

The trend is now for companies to hold as little stock of components as possible. This trend has been established by the Japanese, and it is not unusual to hold only four hours' stock of certain components. The aim is for 'zero defects' and is an extension of a school of thought called 'just-in-time management'. As Lancaster[6] points out just-in-time (JIT) is now used extensively in Japan and has made major inroads into organizations in the West. He also points out that a fully successful JIT system needs precise synchronization from suppliers, through manufacturing and production units, to retailers and finally, consumers. In turn, this synchronization requires very close cooperation between all suppliers and their customers. In particular there must be a full and frank exchange of information between the various parties in the supply chain, which in turn of course implies a relationship of trust. As we have already seen in Chapter 1 these changing relationships between the marketers and their customers away from a transaction-oriented approach to a relationship-based approach are giving rise to new perspectives on the nature and practice of marketing in organizations.

The advantages to the car company are that it saves on working capital in that stock-holding is minimal. However, the implication is that there must be absolute reliability on suppliers in terms of quality and delivery. The implication to companies marketing to large car firms is that quality and reliable delivery are as important (if not more important) than price.

Marketing firms are also buyers of specialist marketing services. For example, although the larger firms are likely to have their own 'in-house' marketing research department, they will often commission surveys, and test marketing programmes and product facilities, from outside specialist agencies.

Whatever the product or service being purchased by the marketing firm, developments in the supplier environment can have an immediate and possibly serious effect on the firm's commercial operations. Marketing management should be continually monitoring changes and trends in order to plan ahead.

The distributive environment

Many firms, particularly in industrial markets where products are often buyer-specified, market and deliver their products direct to the final customer. Other firms use some form of intermediate distribution system. The distribution system is then made up of one or more 'middlemen' who can be individuals or other organizations. They range from agents, distributors, factors and wholesalers to retailers.

Because of the seeming permanence of the distributive environment at any point in time, many firms make the mistake of thinking it is static. In fact, distribution channels change and evolve just like any other facet of business life. As Davidson[7] explains:

> Distribution channels resemble the hour hand of a watch. They are always moving, but each individual movement is so small as to be invisible in isolation. The cumulative movement over a number of years can, however, be massive.

In fact, although this is true of many of the other elements of the marketing environment, changes in distribution channels in particular are taking place at an ever faster pace. This once relatively stable element of the marketing environment for many organizations is now one of the most dynamic, and as such, a major source of opportunities and threats. Some of the major changes in channels and methods of distribution are considered further in Chapter 8.

These, then are some of the most important environment forces and factors in the proximate marketing environment of the firm. We shall now turn our attention to the most important factors that make up the wider marketing environment.

Wider macro-environmental factors

The macro-environment represents those factors and forces over which the organization has least control. They are, however, as already mentioned, the forces and factors which give rise to perhaps the greatest opportunities and threats facing organizations. The most important of the macro-environmental forces together with their relevance to the marketer, are discussed below.

Socio-cultural environment   Of all the elements in the wider marketing environment, the socio-cultural environment probably presents the greatest challenge. People's basic beliefs, attitudes and values are shaped by the society in which they grow up. Their general behaviour, including their purchasing behaviour, is influenced by social conditioning. A more detailed discussion of consumer behaviour is given in Chapter 3.

The main factor influencing a society's attitudes and behaviour is its culture. Core cultural values are firmly established within a society and are generally difficult to change. Such beliefs and values are passed on from generation to generation through the family and other social institutions such as the church, schools and government. Because core cultural values are difficult to change, they act as relatively fixed parameters within which marketing firms have to operate. Kotler[8] states that culture is the most fundamental determinant of a person's wants and behaviour. These values are less persistent than society's core values and tend to undergo changes over time. Social and cultural influences are so interrelated that it is extremely difficult to evaluate the effects of one factor without the other. Before we look at the role of culture in more detail, let us first summarize some of the major changes that have occurred in the socio-cultural environment that can have affected marketing.

Changes in social values   The 1960s saw the birth of the so-called 'permissive society'. Over a period of about 10 years, society's values went through a period of dramatic change. Society's attitude towards marriage, divorce, sex, religion, drugs, economic and social institutions and authority changed and the values of the previous generation were radically altered. People in general became more responsive to change; in fact they welcomed it. This was the period of 'individualism', 'do your own thing', and 'anything goes'. Today we have seen a reversal of many of the attitudes and beliefs of the permissive society. Today people value health, economic security and stable relationships and in many ways have returned to a lot of the social values and norms of the pre-1960s. We have already discussed the growth of social marketing partly as a result of a heightened interest in, and awareness of, ecological and environmental issues and the role which organizations and, in particular, marketing activities play with respect to these factors. Put simply, society is more and more aware now of the problems associated with some business and marketing practices. As a result, more and more consumers are concerned to protect the natural environment, or at least minimize the possible negative effects of business and marketing practices. As we have seen, as a result marketers, too, are having to pay careful attention to the implications of an increasingly socially responsible consumer society. A further implication of changes in social values in this area, as we shall see later in the chapter, is the growth of the consumer movement and consumerism. We shall also discuss the natural/ecological elements of the macro-marketing environment and the rise of the so-called green movement which this has given rise to.

Changes in attitudes towards credit   Over the past 20 years society's general attitude towards credit has dramatically altered. As recently as the 1960s, borrowing was generally frowned upon, except for major purchases such as cars and houses. Hire-purchase agreements were usually signed in the store manager's private office, and there was something of a social stigma attached to buying something on the 'never never'. Today, credit availability has become an intrinsic part in the marketing of many products. Credit has lost its social stigma, and many people carry Access, Visa, American Express or individual store credit cards. Credit transactions are now conducted openly, and it is the person who never buys using credit who is considered to be unusual.

Attitudes towards health   Twenty years ago people who went jogging or ate specific 'health' foods were regarded as being a little eccentric. Today people are more aware of the health implications of what they eat and drink, and regular exercise is an important part of many people's lives. Smoking, which was once considered the height of social sophistication, is now thought of as an anti-social habit. Changes in society's attitude to health have resulted in a multi-million-pound industry developing and supplying health foods, clothing, books and exercise equipment.

Change in attitudes towards working women   Not so very long ago, society's attitude towards working women tended to be chauvinistic. A woman's place was thought to be 'in the home' and the 'career woman' was viewed with a certain amount of suspicion. Today, such attitudes have changed and a high proportion of workers are women. This fact has doubtless contributed to the acceptance of convenience foods as a normal part of everyday life as well as to the widespread adoption of such products as home freezers and microwave ovens. The high proportion of working women has also contributed to the development of 'one-stop shopping'. With both spouses working, leisure time is at a premium. Many couples now do a major 'shop' once a month, buy in bulk, store in the freezer, and cook mainly in a microwave oven.

The changes in society mentioned here do not form an exhaustive list, but are illustrative of the sort of changes that have influenced, and will continue to influence, marketing firms. Although social change is not occurring at the speed that it was in the 1960s, it is nevertheless in evidence. Marketing firms need to monitor social trends and to be prepared to adapt to social changes if they intend to serve their customers effectively and remain competitive. As mentioned earlier, one of the major factors influencing changes within our society is changes in cultural beliefs and norms. It is to the subject of cultural influence, and in particular cultural change, to which the discussion now turns.

The role of culture

A society's culture is a completely learned way of life which is handed down from generation to generation. Cultural influences give each society its own peculiar attributes. Although the norms and values within a society are the result of many years of cultural conditioning, they are not static. It is cultural change, and the resulting revised norms and values within a society, that is of particular interest to the marketing firm. Nowhere is the aspect more poignant than when the company is marketing internationally, a point discussed in detail in Chapter 14.

The English anthropologist, E. B. Taylor,[9] defined culture as:

> that complex whole which includes knowledge, belief, art, morals, law, custom, and any other capabilities and habits acquired by man as a member of society.

Taylor's definition is an accepted classic in defining some of the major facets of culture, and in emphasizing that culture is very much a learned phenomenon. British culture has historically been largely materialistic, derived as it is from the Protestant work ethic of self-help, hard work, thrift and the accumulation of wealth. Arguably, other Western cultures such as the USA, Germany and Japan are even more materialistically oriented. This factor is often thought to be one of the reasons for these countries' superior economic performance. Cultural values do, however, change over time, and a number of Western core values are currently undergoing major changes. Some of the changing cultural values which are particularly prevalent among the young include:

- A questioning of materialism and its values.
- A decline in respect for authority and the law.
- A belief in the rightness of militancy and confrontation.
- A desire for innovation and change.
- A shift towards informality.

Sub-cultural influences

Within each culture are numerous sub-groups with their own distinguishing modes of behaviour. In the United States black Americans represent the largest racial/ethnic sub-culture. In the UK it is the Asian community. American marketing firms realize that it is impossible to treat such a large group of consumers as a homogeneous mass, a number of studies though indicate that their consumption habits are significantly different from those of the remainder of Americans. As a result, American firms are now designing products and advertising campaigns aimed specifically at this large minority market. This has now also happened in the UK.

Indeed, although the UK is more culturally homogeneous than the USA, firms can no longer ignore the cultural differences of the ethnic populations. Ethnic heterogeneity is slowly being recognized by more enlightened firms as potential source of marketing opportunities. Cannon[10] highlights a number of interesting examples of marketing opportunities and problems related to sub-cultures.

- Products may need to meet special religious needs (e.g. kosher foods).
- Marketing intermediaries may be different (e.g. the importance of small, Asian-run, shops).
- Consumer tastes may differ (e.g. Cadbury Typhoo's Poundo Yam, aimed mainly at consumers of Caribbean origin).
- Language can be a problem in marketing communications. For example sometimes words have different meanings between different sub-cultures in a society.

The culturally aware marketing firm will recognize that sub-cultures represent distinct market segments and will seek to increase their awareness of the needs, attitudes and motivations of sub-groups.

Culture and marketing awareness

An understanding of cultural values is of particular importance to a marketing firm involved with overseas markets. Many countries are geographically distant, but culturally close, while others that are geographically close are culturally distant. For example, France is geographically closer to the UK than, say, the USA or Australia, although both of these latter countries are 'closer' to the UK from a cultural point of view.

Often, because of cultural differences, a marketing programme that has been successful in the UK cannot be applied directly in international markets. Cultural differences exist between different countries, and the differences must be known and evaluated by the marketing firm. A number of factors contribute to a country's overall culture including religion, education and aesthetic appreciation. For a full understanding of a country's culture, management will have to have an understanding of the factors influencing that culture, a point that is taken up in Chapter 14.

Political environment

To an increasing extent, the operation of business firms is being influenced by the political framework and processes in our society. Marketing management must be alert to changes in the political attitudes or 'climate', which depend on the policies of the government of the day. The political environment cannot be examined in a vacuum. Political philosophies on their own are nothing without action. The outcome of political decisions can be seen in the legislation and economic policies of government. In this sense, you will appreciate that, although for clarity of exposition we are examining the various macro-environmental forces in isolation, in reality they are very much interrelated. Many of the legal, economic and social developments in our society and other countries are nothing more than the result of political decisions put into action. For example, in the 1980s the Conservative Party favoured a monetarist approach to the management of the UK economy. It attached great importance to the control of money supply and hence government public expenditure. The general philosophy of the Conservatives was one of 'self-help' and free enterprise, preferring to see business in the hands of private shareholders rather than being owned by the state. Its main concern was with the reduction of the level of inflation which is seen as being vital to long-term economic growth and stability. Business, entrepreneurship, private ownership and profit were seen as being a good thing, vital to the country's future prosperity.

The election of a Labour Government in the UK in May 1997 led to the start of the introduction of a whole set of new policies based on what the leaders of this newly elected government argued was a very different set of attitudes and philosophies to those which characterized the previous Conservative Government. So, for example, the newly elected Labour Government stressed the importance of, and therefore its commitment to, education, and health. Similarly, there have already been major changes in areas related to aspects such as welfare payments, training programmes to encourage the unemployed into work and the management of the economy, such as giving the Bank of England control over interest rates.

This discussion does not purport to make any normative statements about the running of the country or to proffer political ideologies. The important thing to realize is that the political climate is of great significance to the marketing firm and is likely to have a direct bearing on many aspects of the economy and society in general.

Although developments in the domestic political scene are likely to be of prime concern to the majority of companies, many will also be affected by international political developments. Many British firms import from, or export to, foreign countries and may even have subsidiary companies or divisions overseas. In the UK, political change is brought about through the democratic process. The UK enjoys a high degree of political stability which instils confidence in overseas buyers and suppliers, and this is good for business. In some overseas countries the political situation is more volatile. Change and political power are often obtained through force rather than the democratic process. Companies operating in such a climate have to monitor the local political situation very carefully.

The political environment is the starting point from which many other macro-environmental forces originate. Firms themselves can go some way in influencing the political climate through their trade associations or organizations like the Confederation of British Industry (CBI). Organizations such as these are often looked to by the government for advice, or may themselves act as 'pressure groups' in lobbying the government over political or economic issues. Whatever industry the marketing firm is involved in, factors in the political environment at both national and international levels should be carefully monitored and understood.

Economic environment

Marketing management must understand the effects of the many economic variables that are likely to affect their business operations. We see in the media that inflation is rising or falling, that exchange rates are affecting the value of the pound or influencing the level of interest rates. We hear discussions on the level of unemployment, industrial output, or the current state of the balance of payments. Such economic factors are of concern to marketing firms because they influence costs, prices and demand.

Some of the major economic trends and changes affecting UK marketers recently have included, for example, relatively stable interest rates which in turn have led to an extremely strong pound and hence problems for exporters; increases in real disposable incomes have also helped fuel consumer retail spending which in turn has given rise to fears of a return to high levels of inflation; a return of consumer confidence, particularly in some of the markets where long-term investment is involved, such as the housing market, has helped to boost the prospects of the UK building industry. These, of course, are simply examples of the ways in which economic factors affect markets. These examples, however, relate to the economic trends and changes within an economy. We should not forget that some of the most significant economic trends and changes are those which relate to the international and global operation of world markets. Increasingly, it is global aspects of competition and economic policies and decisions which must be taken into account by the marketer. In this respect perhaps some of the most significant economic and political developments in recent years in a European context have been those associated with the growth and development of the European Union or EU as it is now usually referred to. The UK's membership of the, then, European Economic Community goes back to 1 January 1973. The 'Common Market', as it was called, was initially essentially a customs union. A customs union implies two things: first, that all tariffs between members on industrial products be abolished; and, second, that a uniform tariff be adopted for other nations' products imported into the customs union area. Membership of the European Economic Community subjected British firms to new economic pressures to which companies needed to adjust. The pressure to adjust became even greater with the passage of the so-called

'Single European Act' in December 1992. Set into operation in 1987, the objective of this Act was to abolish all barriers to trade between the member countries of the Community by the deadline referred to above. Technically, after this date, goods, services, capital and labour were to enjoy freedom of movement between all member countries—the culmination of a process of moving towards a genuinely 'common' market.

The Single European Act has posed both opportunities and threats to business in each of the member countries. Companies that have adapted to the new competitive conditions have thrived; those that have not have floundered. Changes in economic policy and legislation are continuing developments and it is essential for marketing firms to monitor continually all business facets affected by the Community's actual or proposed economic policies.

The EU in particular has proved to be extremely dynamic. The number of member countries continues to expand and there are still several further European countries, particularly in the former Eastern European/Soviet bloc which are likely to join in the near future. Of particular significance for European marketers is the introduction of a Single European Currency—the so-called ECU. After years of discussion and planning, 11 EU countries—Germany, France, Italy, The Netherlands, Austria, Belgium, Finland, Ireland, Luxembourg, Portugal and Spain have joined the Single Currency. The UK and the other remaining EU countries did not, for a variety of reasons, join the Single Currency on that date. In the case of the UK, the Labour Government decided to defer the decision regarding whether or not to join until a later date. Nevertheless, irrespective of whether a country has elected to join the Single Currency, marketers in all of the member countries have been affected by, and therefore need to take account of, the Single Currency in their marketing planning and decision-making. So, for example, since July 1998 decisions on European interest rates are largely influenced by a European Central Bank. Economic policy in the Euro zone is largely coordinated through a European committee on which members of the Single Currency sit. Euro currency will gradually be introduced until national currencies in those countries that have elected to join will have been replaced. Marketers even in member countries, such as the UK, who have not made a decision about joining the Single Currency are planning their marketing strategies, including for example, pricing strategies in the context of the new Single Currency.

On a wider scale, recent years have witnessed dramatic changes in trading practices and patterns in other areas of the world. Perhaps some of the most notable of these changes are those brought about by political changes in the Eastern bloc countries. *Perestroika* and *glasnost*, the policies of Mikhail Gorbachev in what was previously the Soviet Union, resulted in what were once centrally planned economies becoming more market-driven.

Other important developments include the continuing efforts of Far Eastern competitors—not only Japan but also Singapore, Malaysia, Thailand and China—in world markets; the harmonization of East and West Germany; the near breakdown of the most recent round of the World Trade Organization talks. In short, the international economic environment is dynamic, and needs to be constantly monitored and adapted to in marketing plans.

Although world economic forces are of paramount importance to marketing firms, particularly those involved with either importing or exporting, domestic economic forces usually have the most immediate impact. The level of domestic unemployment affects the demand for many consumer products, especially those classed as 'luxury goods'. This in turn affects the demand for many industrial products, particularly manufacturing plant such as machine tools. The rate of inflation and the cost of borrowing capital affect the potential returns from new investment and inhibit the adoption of new technologies. Governments of every persuasion attempt to encourage economic growth through various policy measures. Tax concessions, government grants, employment subsidies and capital depreciation allowances are some of the measures that have been used.

The marketing firm needs to monitor continually the economic environment at both the domestic and international level. The 'ebb and flow' of economic forces and the policies that governments use to attempt to manage their economies could have a significant impact on a firm's business operations. As with all other environmental factors, economic factors can be viewed as a source of both opportunities and threats to the marketing firm. By carefully monitoring and understanding the economic environment, a firm's management should be in a better position to capitalize upon the opportunities and to do something about reducing the threats.

Technological environment

Technology is a major environmental influence upon the marketing firm. It affects not only the firm's operations and products, but also consumers' lifestyles and consumption patterns. Management must be aware of the impact of technological changes. As Wilson[11] explains in relation to electronics:

> The development of the microprocessor and its large scale production has revolutionised information collection, processing and dissemination which in turn is affecting the whole spectrum of marketing activity.

The impact of new information technology has been particularly marked in the marketing research area. For example, it is now possible to design and administer questionnaires via computer terminals. In the past this method has been used on a limited basis, but is being more and more frequently used. Computer assisted telephone interviewing (CATI) has revolutionized the speed with which surveys can be completed. Responses are fed immediately into a computer and a report 'hard copy' can be available immediately after the final interview is completed. As Thomas[12] explains:

> On-line interviewing is now in widespread use in the larger data gathering market research firms. Interviews, using telephones, work from a questionnaire which is displayed on a VDU and responses are keyed straight into the computer.

Sales forecasting has always been, and always will be, an important marketing activity. Until recently, the majority of firms tended to use subjective or judgemental sales forecasting methods. The development of computers and available software programs has brought the use of sophisticated forecasting techniques within the reach of all companies. The role of sales forecasting is discussed in greater detail in Chapter 11.

Technology also affects the way in which goods are distributed and promoted. Containerized freight and automated warehousing have increased the efficiency with which products can be distributed. Sales representatives can now use audio-visual equipment for presentations and demonstrations. Technology is also affecting marketing at the retail level. Electronic point-of-scale (EPOS) data capture is now used by the major retailers. The 'laser checkout' automatically records consumer purchases and is used to analyse sales and to control and re-order stock. Operation of the laser checkout system depends on the electronic reading of codes. Many fast-moving-consumer-goods (FMCG) manufacturers have responded to these developments by incorporating 'bar codes' on their product labels.

Technology has influenced the development of products themselves. Genetic engineering, aerosol cans, digital television, compact disc players, dvd players and digital cameras have all come into widespread use over the past few years. While older industries are in decline, whole new industries, sometimes referred to as the 'sunrise industries', have developed and grown to take their place. These new industries have capitalized on developments in the technological environment (e.g. information technology, biotechnology and aerospace).

As already mentioned, one of the most significant technological developments for the marketer in recent years has been the growth of the Internet. Innovation in IT technology has encouraged more and more businesses and households to link up to the Internet. Access and connection to the Internet throughout the world is likely to continue to grow substantially over the next few years. As a result, we have seen such developments as home shopping over the Internet. Similarly, more and more marketers are using the Internet to provide company and product information to potential customers and to promote their products and services. We have also seen the growth of home-working in many countries which in turn is giving rise to changes in demand for many products. So, for example, in future years the growth of home-working may see a decline in demand for, say, transport while at the same time increasing demand for products which are used to communicate with the office, such as faxes and, of course, e-mail, etc.

The rate of technological change would appear to be accelerating. Marketing firms themselves play a part in technological advancement and must make use of current technology. They must ask themselves what products or processes are likely to be demanded and technologically feasible to produce in, say, the next 10 or 20 years that are not available now. Management must anticipate the impact of technological change not only on the firm, but also on all other elements in the macro-environment.

The wide-ranging impact of technological advances on marketing and the importance of these is such that we shall return to this area throughout the remaining chapters of this text. So, for example, we shall look at the role of technological advances in the sales forecasting and marketing planning process in Chapters 11 and 12; in the marketing research process in Chapter 5; in the process of segmentation, targeting and positioning in Chapter 4; in areas pertaining to the management of the marketing mix in Chapters 6 to 10 and including the combining of these marketing mix elements in Chapter 12. Finally, our chapters on customer care and relationship marketing (Chapter 13) and international marketing (Chapter 14) also include specific reference to the impact of new technological advances. We have taken the trouble to spell this out in order to underline our point about the ubiquitous and far-reaching impact of technological advances on contemporary marketing. We would also point out that we felt it would be useful to discuss technological advances as they pertain to each area (and therefore in our case each chapter) of the essentials of marketing allowing us to show how and where such advances are impacting upon the practice of contemporary marketing.

Legal/regulatory environment

We have seen how criticisms of marketing allied to an increasing interest in and awareness of their rights by customers has provided an impetus to a growth in legal and regulatory aspects of marketing. The contemporary marketer now faces an abundance of regulatory and legal factors affecting virtually every aspect of marketing operations and decision-making. The contemporary marketer therefore must at least be broadly familiar with the key areas of legislation and regulation affecting marketing practices. As you will no doubt appreciate it is neither possible nor even desirable to cover every facet of the regulatory and legal environment. When it comes to assessing the implications in detail regarding legal and regulatory matters you are advised to consult a legal expert. However, we can perhaps gain some awareness of the importance of legal and regulatory factors by considering briefly some of the main areas of consumer law and protection as they pertain to the UK legal system. Again, in this case if you are not from the United Kingdom or you are considering marketing in other countries, you are advised to consult a legal expert. Some of the more important legal and regulatory factors pertaining to the UK marketing environment include the following.

Consumer law and protection

The rate of change in consumer marketing since the early 1960s has brought with it equivalent change in the law, which has been considerably modified to protect the consumer from unfair practices. The law relating to consumer protection is not a clearly defined code; it is made up of extensions and amendments to contract law. In Britain there is no such thing as a 'consumer law' as a single entity, nor is there a comprehensive code of consumer protection. There is, nevertheless, a wealth of statutory instruments which have been introduced during the last 20 years designed to effect specific control over potential injustices and to exploit actions of the consumer. There is also the existing contract law, which has a high degree of relevance to current situations in which the consumer may be at a disadvantage.

What follows is a brief discussion of some of the more important legislation pertaining to consumers and hence marketing. As already mentioned, clearly, this is a specialist area of marketing and one which is subject to constant change and interpretation as a result of both new legislation and case law. We can, therefore, only try to give just a flavour of this important area simply to demonstrate the range and variety of consumer protection under the law. You should note that our discussion applies principally to the UK, although increasingly of course, EU legislation and regulations pertain.

Further legal remedies for the consumer are to be found in contract law. Although it has already been stated that there is no such thing as 'consumer law', and although existing legislation is somewhat hybrid in nature, it is possible to place the law as it relates to the consumer into two broad categories. First, remedies exist under private law and second, remedies have been created by administrative and governmental action. These latter remedies are backed up by criminal law and come under the jurisdiction of the Director General of Fair Trading.

Before continuing, it is important that one should understand the nature of a 'contract'. To be binding in law, a contract need not necessarily be formally drawn up by solicitors and signed by both parties. All that is necessary is that an 'offer' be made which is 'accepted' and that the exchange take place for some 'consideration': in most cases this is financial. The implication for consumers is that such a contract takes place every time a purchase is made.

Remedies available under private law: the Sale of Goods Act

The original Sale of Goods Act was passed in 1893 and has been constantly amended since then. The Act defines the statutory rights of the buyer (and seller) with respect to the transfer of property and goods for a money consideration (the price). The 'inalienable' rights of the consumer are set out by the Act. These concern the transference of title from the seller to the buyer, and the description and quality of the goods.

An important component of the Act concerns the question of 'merchantable quality'. The definition of merchantable quality is the cause of some debate. The question is covered by the implied terms of the Act and should not be equated with mere 'description' of the goods. 'Merchantable' means 'as fit for the purpose or purposes for which goods of that kind are commonly bought as it is reasonable to expect having regard to any description applied to them, the price (if relevant) and all the other relevant circumstances'.

Linked to the idea of merchantable quality is the 'fitness for purpose' for which goods are bought and the 'availability' of those goods, which are also implied terms of the Act.

The supply of services

As marketing is concerned with the provision of both goods and services, we should also consider consumer rights when the product is a service rather than a tangible good. Separate, and perhaps less exhaustive, legislation covers this area, but there are well-established precedents which refer to contracts for services. The Unfair Contract Terms Act was particularly concerned with the application of exemption clauses by the supplier of services. The 'reasonableness test' afforded protection for both buyer and seller when such clauses were included in a contract.

The more recent Supply of Goods and Services Act furnished the consumer with further specific attention. Services must be carried out with 'reasonable care and skill', 'within a reasonable time' and at 'a reasonable charge'. Of course, what is 'reasonable' is dependent on the facts and circumstances of the case and how these are interpreted by the judge.

Misrepresentation and false trade descriptions of goods

Perhaps the most often quoted piece of consumer legislation is the Trade Descriptions Act (TDA). It is also likely that, while the seller should be aware of all consumer legislation, the TDA has the widest scope of application. The Act overlaps to some extent with other legal remedies, but it is specific in that it applies only where a trader has made a claim about the goods offered for sale. This is of particular relevance to the consumer nowadays when advertising, promotion and direct mail campaigns have reached an intensive level. Test cases in the courts have tended to concern malpractices in second-hand car trading, but the precedents that have been set have equal applications in all manner of consumer transactions.

The TDA is clearly of particular relevance to advertising practice. While the Act does not specifically deal with claims as to 'value' and 'worth', the creative jargon of the advertiser's copy may lead to the making of intentional or unintentional false claims about a good or service. This leads us to an important legal point on the subject of advertising—that of the traders' 'puff'. Claims made about a brand of perfume or beer, or the hackneyed 'desirable residence' of the estate agent's jargon, are not likely to be construed as being legally binding. If, however, the advertiser uses a phrase such as 'results guaranteed', such a promise *is* sufficiently definite as to be legally enforceable. If a company makes a claim about its product, it is up to the courts to decide whether the statement is legally enforceable or merely a 'puff' of creative imagination.

The subject of false trade descriptions is linked to that of misrepresentation, which is dealt with separately under the Misrepresentation Act. The easiest way to understand misrepresentation is to remember that it must relate to a question of fact and that any representation becomes legally significant only if it turns out to be false. The categories of misrepresentation should also be appreciated. These are: fraudulent, negligent or innocent. In the latter case, damages are not usually available to the consumer, although costs and expenses arising from the trader's action may be awarded.

Consumer credit

The Consumer Credit Act is an example of direct response to consumer protection as the purchase transaction becomes more complicated and open to abuse.

The Act controls the advertising of credit and canvassing where dishonesty is concerned, and it requires the company offering credit to disclose fully all information about the agreement, including the rights of cancellation. The consumer also has the 'right to a remedy' if a so-called 'credit bargain' is subsequently found to be extortionate. More recently, a 'cooling off' period has been introduced during which the consumer may reflect on a purchase, and decide whether or not to go ahead with the responsibilities of a credit agreement.

The proliferation of credit facilities that now exist has led to a whole series of legislation on the subject. The principal intention here is to bring attention to the significance of this legislation, rather than to expand upon the individual statutes.

Product liability

The consumer usually makes a contract of sale with a retailer. Under the terms of the Sale of Goods Act, the usual recourse to justice in the event of complaint is made to the retailer and not to the manufacturer. There are, however, occasions when the consumer has the right to bring a case against the manufacturer of defective goods. Such liability with respect to safety is set out in the Consumer Safety Act and the Consumer Protection Act. Similarly, where a guarantee is offered by the manufacturer, the offer for sale is deemed to have been made by that party and not the retailer.

In civil law, a consumer has the right to sue in the 'tort' of negligence, because a manufacturer has the legal duty of care to ensure that his goods are not dangerous (this being subject to a series of limitations). Although remedies in fact existed long before the consumer movement, such an action is nevertheless a powerful weapon in the modern consumer's armoury in cases of negligence.

Remedies available due to administrative and governmental action

The failure of traders and manufacturers to comply with government regulations may result in civil or criminal action being taken against them. The rationale behind the establishment of the various consumer bodies is not to facilitate a flood of legal actions. The principal idea is to create a system whereby the existence of such bodies performs a self-regulatory function on behalf of manufacturers, advertisers and similar business practitioners. Before 'going to law', the consumer has (in the event of complaint) various sources of advice, plus the opportunity to take advantage of official assistance which will bring pressure to bear upon the offending party. The regulatory bodies established to oversee some of the recently privatized industries, such as OFGAS in the gas industry, or OFWAT in the water industry, are good examples of this.

In addition to, and in conjunction with, legal remedies, the consumer is protected by the following bodies that 'supervise' the law.

Self-regulation by manufacturers   The setting up of voluntary codes of practice by various industries is valuable for consumer protection in that it is beneficial for companies to be seen to be adhering to the code. Moreover, a company will usually support the elements of the code because miscreants will damage the image of the industry as a whole. Voluntary codes will not, however, protect consumers from companies that are determined not to take part in such schemes. Such industry codes do, in many cases, obviate the need for legislative action. The Office of Fair Trading is a useful arbitrator in consumer/trade disputes. The duties of the office are also to approve, monitor and revise codes that are not functioning satisfactorily.

The advertising industry set up the British Code of Advertising Practice as early as 1962. Consumer complaints are brought before the Advertising Standards Authority, whose duty it is to see that advertisements are 'legal, decent, honest and truthful' and that they are prepared with 'a sense of responsibility to the consumer'.

Sources of advice and assistance for the consumer   Consumer activism has identified the fact that, for a large proportion of the population, legal remedies, however comprehensive, are beyond their financial reach. Similarly, many consumers are not able to articulate their complaints in the manner which the law often requires. To compensate for this, a conscious effort has been made by volunteers (often from within the legal profession) and by local authorities, to establish advice centres. These centres do not deal exclusively with consumer problems, but provide a wide range of legal advice and consumer information.

All local authorities have a Trading Standards Department which exists expressly for the protection of the consumer. This was originally established to ensure the proper execution of the Weights and Measures and Food and Drugs Acts. While this is still the case, the remit of the department now encompasses an advisory role in the event of consumer disputes. Since 1972, such assistance has been augmented by the creation of Consumer Advice Centres although these were abolished in 1980. These also publish a wide range of informative leaflets which help consumers to know what is available and what their rights are but their role has now been taken over by Citizens Advice Bureaux.

Finally, Citizens Advice Bureaux are run on a volunteer basis in most UK cities. As with law centres, the work of the bureaux is not exclusively concerned with 'consumer affairs'. They are particularly involved with social issues such as housing and payment of social security.

Although the range of legal remedies, and the scope of advice sources, may seem daunting to a prospective business person, it must be remembered that they are merely designed to uphold the law and ensure fair treatment of the consumer. A business that is seriously engaged in satisfying consumer 'wants' and 'needs' need not feel threatened or led to treat the protectors of consumers as adversaries.

These, then, are some of the more important areas of legislation and regulation in the UK at the present pertaining to marketing and in particular to consumer protection. However, once again we would stress that we have only scratched the surface here. Below are listed just some of the other areas where legislation and regulation of marketing activities, both voluntary and non-voluntary, exists.

● Advertising and promotion
● Direct mail
● Databases and marketing research

- Labelling
- Pricing
- Distribution arrangements
- Telephone selling
- Questionnaires
- Exporting

In fact, virtually every facet of marketing is covered by some sort of regulation. The move towards more socially oriented marketing described in Chapter 1 is in some cases no longer an option, but a question of legislative enforcement. It is probably preferable that marketing becomes more socially aware and oriented as a result of its own efforts and practices. In the absence of this governments and regulatory bodies will continue to impose their own regulations. This is not to say that governments have enacted bad legislation or that they do not have an important role to play in the development of more socially responsible marketing. Unfortunately, there exist many companies that would have ignored their social responsibilities had not governments forced them to recognize them. Another important environmental pressure forcing companies to be more socially responsible in their marketing has been the growth of the so-called 'consumer movement'. Although not strictly legal/regulatory in the sense that this movement is always backed by statutory legal and regulatory requirements, there is no doubt that consumerism has had an important effect on the marketing activities of many organizations and will no doubt continue to have an important effect in the future. We shall now examine the nature and impact of the consumer movement.

THE CONSUMER MOVEMENT

The origins of the consumer movement are firmly based in the USA. This is not to say that the need for consumerism did not exist in Europe and the UK. Rather, factors such as mass production and mass marketing were quicker to develop in the USA. Here, organized consumers successfully achieved their aims both at the turn of the century and in the 1930s. However, these were isolated movements which were directed at specific targets. Once successful, there appeared to be no need to continue with further organized action. It was not until the late 1950s and early 1960s that the consumer movement as we know it today began to materialize. Social commentators such as J. K. Galbraith, Vance Packard and Rachel Carson began to alert the American nation, not only to specific cases, but to the whole philosophy and social rationale on which society (as it related to the business world) was based. The Second World War probably developed the birth of such a movement, because the austerity of the immediate post-war environment made consumers more likely to be grateful for the luxury of being able to acquire goods that had previously been scarce than to complain about their quality or the marketing methods associated with them. Moreover, during the war period itself, organized groups of dissatisfied consumers were not conducive to the spirit of patriotism which prevailed. By the early 1960s, however, definite challenges to the *status quo* that business had enjoyed were emerging.

The Second World War notwithstanding, it is likely that consumerism was an inevitable development of our economic system, and it is equally likely that the movement will not only endure, but will continue to to grow.[13] In America the 'champion' of consumerism was Ralph Nader, whose book *Unsafe at Any Speed* was a challenge to, and a formidable indictment of, the American automobile industry—and in particular General Motors. Nader was an influential figure of the 1960s who was responsible for a number of federal laws such as the Meat Inspection Bill and the Fire Research and Safety Law, but his influence was far wider than in these specific spheres. His greatest impact was that he engendered in the public the idea that monolithic business institutions could in fact be challenged and that those who were at fault could no longer act with impunity. This notion spread through the USA via the mass media and was transferred (albeit more slowly) to the UK.

Within the UK itself, an important parallel to Ralph Nader (in terms of influence on the public attitude) was the development of the consumer magazine *Which?* From very humble beginnings in a garage in South London, circulation experienced a dramatic rise, such that within a very short time *Which?* became a household name. *Which?* selects a series of consumer goods for each publication, objectively tests them on a variety of counts and then publishes its conclusions. The result is that products and their companies are classified according to their relative performance. Such a concept was hitherto undreamed of. Like Nader, *Which?* has not only achieved a specific task, but has also contributed to the feeling, or notion, that consumers need no longer accept the offerings of big and small businesses alike without voicing their opinions.

The meaning of consumerism

Consumerism is well defined as 'a social movement seeking to augment the rights and power of buyers in relation to sellers'.

To understand the full implications of such a definition, it is worth while examining what these rights have traditionally been held to be.

Sellers have the following rights:

1. To introduce any product in any style or size, provided that it is not injurious to health and safety and provided that potentially hazardous products are supplied together with appropriate warnings.

2. To price products at any level, provided that there is no discrimination among similar classes of buyers.

3. To say what they like in promotion of their products, provided that any message is not dishonest or misleading in content or execution.

4. To spend any amount of money they wish, to promote their product and to introduce any buying incentive schemes, provided that these cannot be defined as unfair competition.

Buyers in their turn have their own rights and the right to expect certain things from sellers and their products:

1. Not to buy products offered to them.

2. To expect the product to be safe.

3. To expect that the product is in fact essentially the same as the seller has represented.

An appreciation and a knowledge of the respective rights of the buyer and seller help to put the consumer problem into perspective.

The biggest weapon of the consumer has traditionally been held to be that of the 'silent vote', that is, the right not to buy unsatisfactory goods; this is the concept of consumer sovereignty. Logically, therefore, companies who mis-serve the market will usually run out of customers. This is indeed a powerful sanction and has been cited earlier when discussing major criticisms of marketing. Consumerists argue that the onus is not on the consumer to veto unsatisfactory goods after having first been disappointed; rather, it is up to the sellers of goods to take all reasonable steps to ensure satisfaction before offering goods for sale. They further argue that such a step will be greatly facilitated if certain basic consumer 'rights' are recognized.

What should consumer rights be?

In 1962 President John F. Kennedy clearly delineated four basic consumer rights. His declaration was probably the most important single step in the advancement of consumerism. He proposed the following:

1. *The right to safety*   Consumers have the right to expect that products do not possess hidden dangers. This was the basis of Nader's campaign against the automobile industry. In the UK, the aftermath of the thalidomide affair forced attention to turn on food and drugs. Occasionally, such attention has led to allegations of alarmist activity by consumerists. In the USA, the use of cyclamates in artificial sweeteners was alleged to have a carcinogenic effect. Subsequent investigations held that such products were harmless in the quantities normally consumed by human beings.

2. *The right to be informed*   Consumers should be protected from inadequate and misleading product information and from deceptions in advertising, guarantees and product labelling. Possibly the most extreme example is that of cigarette advertising and the introduction of government health warnings. Other examples are less controversial, but the idea remains the same: consumers should be responsible for their purchase decisions only after having been in receipt of adequate product information.

3. *The right to choose*   Consumers have the right to real competition among sellers and should not be subjected to confusing promotion and product labelling. An experiment in California showed that such was the variety and complexity of labelling, that supermarket shoppers were incapable of relating quantity to cost when making purchases.[14]

4. *The right to be heard*   Consumers have the right to express their dissatisfactions in a manner that will attract attention and so achieve positive results. Consumerists argue that individual consumers, apart from having no 'voice', do not necessarily have the time or the skills to make complex choice decisions or to absorb product information when it is preferred. Organized bodies should, therefore, be established to speak for them. A further argument is that modern shopping methods have distanced the seller from the buyer so that dissatisfactions are difficult to voice with any degree of success.

These rights were cited in 1962, and since then further issues have been raised through the 'green' movement which we shall consider shortly and information that is kept on databases in relation to members of the public. Therefore, the following additional rights should now be added to those cited by Kennedy:

- The right to a clean, healthy environment
- The right to privacy.

A great deal of the demands which the consumer movement originally made have now been met. This is not to say that the need for consumer protection has diminished, or that it is likely to do so. There is also the danger that, after several years of success, those responsible for administering and improving consumer protection will become complacent, less dynamic and less responsive to change. Consumerists are also becoming involved with protection at the macro level. The progress already made must not be allowed to slide, but it is likely that future consumerist interest will focus more on macro-price levels (such as lobbying the EU on food prices) and on multinational business, than on the day-to-day problems of the high street.

Marketing's ethical issues are, of course, inextricably bound up with consumerism, and the implications for both reach beyond the boundaries of 'marketing management' in the commonly accepted sense of the term. The response of marketing to consumerism presents us with philosophical as well as practical questions. Kotler's call for a 'revised marketing concept'[15] would take into account the long-term moral and social issues with which marketing should now concern itself. Before examining further such a concept, we should recognize certain practicalities which complicate the issue.

The essence of marketing strategy is to think and plan for the long term. This strategic approach is also essential if a firm wishes to adopt an increased social orientation and to respond positively to consumerism. The economies of business life, on the other hand, tend to invoke short-term concern, and while the evidence of successful long-term strategy is all around us, this is never easily achieved. It is likely that such difficulties will be accentuated by the addition of a consumerist/social dimension to long-range planning.

The second important consideration is that of the social/economic environment itself. Consumerism, taken to its logical and ultimate conclusion, implies a major redistribution of wealth and power. By how much the business world is willing, or able, to subscribe to such a movement is an important subject of debate. This in turn is closely linked to the attitudes of government, which may vary according to the social and economic conditions that prevail. In theory, pro-consumer government action should benefit the government (in terms of popularity) plus business; if a positive response is made, then consumers themselves will react favourably. Major initiatives have already been taken by various governments, and such a sequence of benefits has already occurred. However, it is important that we do not underestimate the complexity of this process.

Having taken into account the above considerations, we can examine how marketing should react to consumerism. It is apparent that the consumer movement has graduated beyond the realms of 'micro' issues, although it has been suggested that the need for vigilance in this respect will continue. The future concerns of marketing should involve the long-term and broader issues of consumerism. The immediate realization must be that consumerism must be seen as an opportunity, and that the suspicion previously associated with it should be abandoned. Many firms have already proved this to be a viable and profitable approach. In many respects, consumerism has done the work of the marketer by identifying a whole range of previously unsatisfied needs and wants. These opportunities concern such items as unit pricing, honesty in labelling and credit agreements, and new green products. They extend into the satisfaction of psychological needs. The manufacturer who, for example, produces a product and includes and conceals a hazardous component in order to save costs, will suffer in the long term at the hands of a competitor who treats safety as a 'feature' and builds this into marketing strategy and tactics. Consumerism, properly viewed, does not challenge the marketing concept, but is a major reinforcement of it.

Natural/ecological environment

The final element of the wider macro-environment facing the marketer concerns the natural environment including aspects such as, for example, resource usage and depletion, environmental pollution and degrading, related to environmental pollution—climate changes such as, for example, global warming and the so-called greenhouse effect. Clearly this aspect of the marketing environment touches on, and is related to several of the areas already discussed, after all there is plenty of legislation and regulation encompassing the natural/ecological environment. Similarly, the consumer movement has taken to its heart the protection of the natural environment and the ecology of the planet. Of specific relevance to the marketer with regard to this element of the environment, however, has been the growth in importance of green issues in marketing and the emergence of the so-called 'green consumer'.

Green issues and marketing   In 1989 a Market Intelligence Report[16] published the results of a UK survey in which respondents were asked to list the issues they considered to be among the most serious problems facing the country. Pollution of the environment ranked second on the list only to the then much disliked poll tax. In the same report, the following is a sample of some of the views expressed:

- 90 per cent of respondents considered our sea and river pollution as fairly or very serious.
- 80 per cent were aware of the problems of acid rain, nuclear waste and leaded petrol.
- 65 per cent were concerned about the use of chemicals in farming.

These examples of consumer attitudes are indicative of the increased awareness, and in some cases alarm, about the state of the environment. Moreover, rightly or wrongly, marketers and marketing practices are seen as being at the heart of many of these and other environmental issues. The result has been the emergence of what is now often referred to as the 'green' consumer. Put simply, an increasing number of consumers are interested in, and in some cases will only buy, environmentally friendly products. Only a few short years ago such green consumers were considered an oddity, and the numbers involved meant that only a few, usually small and specialized, companies catered for their needs. With the increased awareness of environmental issues referred to earlier, however, green consumers are no longer a fringe group, and as a result marketers have had to respond to changing customer needs in this area. There is little doubt that the impact of this greening of the customer is significant and far-reaching. Moreover, the number of green customers continues to grow.

Although there are many ways in which the impact of the green consumer has made itself felt on marketing practice, perhaps the most obvious impact has been the recognition by marketers of the marketing opportunities for green products. Ozone-friendly aerosols, CFC-free fridges and freezers and lead-free petrol have perhaps been the subject of the best known marketing campaigns, but other products include batteries (e.g. Varta), disposable nappies (e.g. Peaudouce), cars (e.g. Volkswagen) and biodegradable washing powders (e.g. Unilever). Moreover, the impact is not restricted to the physical products themselves, but also affects their packaging and labelling, their development and testing (e.g. non-animal-based testing of cosmetics) and their promotion.

Only one thing is certain, and that is that green issues in marketing are here to stay. As with the broader issue of consumerism, of which green issues are a part, the greening of consumers represents both an opportunity and a threat.

Companies that are prepared to identify opportunities for more environmentally friendly products and practices, and which can produce genuinely green products and practices to meet these, will find a growing market. Companies that continue to ignore the green consumer and/or to address green issues only in a superficial way will increasingly find their sales threatened by a more environmentally aware consumer.

The undoubted success of the green movement cannot be wholly ascribed to a positive response on behalf of the business world. During the 1960s and 1970s in particular, mistrust, misunderstanding and complacency were typical corporate responses to the green phenomenon. Just as few motorists are likely to consider themselves as being bad drivers, few firms are able to appreciate or be willing to admit that the green movement has been aimed against them. It is not suggested that companies have decided to persevere with a policy of deception or poor service; the real answer is that, until consumer issues began to take on national importance, most companies genuinely believed that they were fulfilling their ecological responsibilities.

Despite the initial reluctance of firms to respond to the green movement, the 1980s witnessed definite progress in the attitudes and actions of business organizations. That this was due to enlightenment and altruism is the subject of debate. What is more certain is that governmental and legal action has not only obliged companies to initiate change, but has also permitted the realization that the green consumer has become a fixture of society which, if properly approached, can provide positive opportunities for marketing management. The creation of a whole set of green legislation testifies to the government's commitment to environmental protection. It is, therefore, perhaps lamentable that statutes and official bodies have had to be the instrument of change, but what is important for the consumer is the fact that change has taken place. It is significant that major companies in the retail sector have adopted green policies voluntarily. As we have seen, yet others have responded to green issues by producing more environmentally friendly products. Whether this is altruism or a response to legislation is not really relevant; the important thing is that these initiatives have been taken.

Scanning and adapting to the environment

Our discussion so far has concentrated upon reviewing the range of environmental factors and their potential importance to marketing management. Because of this importance, it is vital that the marketing function regularly scans the environment so that trends and changes can be spotted and adapted by the organization. This task of marketing management, however, is both difficult and complex. A full review of environmental scanning and appraisal systems is beyond the scope of this text, though interested readers may consult *Marketing Management*, by Lancaster and Massingham,[17] for a more detailed discussion. The essential stages in an environmental scanning and appraisal system, however, are outlined below.

- *Identifying key environmental factors*   First, the key environmental factors must be identified. Not all environmental factors are equally important to all organizations. Indeed, the effect of external environmental factors varies with the type and purpose of the organization; for example, a multinational organization is obviously affected more than a purely domestic firm by such factors as international regulators and trade. Senior management, therefore, just identify the key components of the environment which are critical to their particular organization and its plans.

- *Monitoring and forecasting trends and changes in key environmental factors*   Having identified key environmental factors, the next step is to monitor and forecast any trends and changes. For example, a manufacturer of luxury products may need to forecast trends in personal disposable income to which sales of the organization's products may be sensitive. Similarly, most firms will need to monitor trends in those regulations that affect their particular product markets. A systematic and continuous system of scanning and forecasting is essential. More sophisticated modern forecasting techniques now make it increasingly possible for managers to anticipate changes in technology, government regulations, social/cultural factors and so on.

- *Assessing the likely/potential impact of environmental trends and changes*   The third step in coping with the external environment is the assessment of the likely/potential impact of trends and changes in key environmental factors. Put simply, some trends and changes will have a potentially adverse effect on an organization, for example a predicted new technology from a competitor. These are normally and understandably referred to as threats. On the other hand, some trends and changes will have a potentially positive effect and hence can be referred to as opportunities. Both opportunities and threats must be identified and appraised for their likely impact on the organization.

- *Planning to adjust to the external environment*   The final step in coping with the external environment is adjusting to the trend and changes in the external environment and the opportunities and threats that are potentially posed. Sometimes the organization can influence the environment in order to reduce threats and maximize opportunities, for example by taking over a new competitor who is posing a threat. Often, however, the environment must be treated as a non-controllable variable and adaptations made within the organization. Controllable or uncontrollable, however, the most important way that organizations cope with the external environment is through the development and implementation of marketing plans. In other words, the environment needs to be managed through the marketing planning process; threats must be minimized and opportunities maximized.

CHAPTER SUMMARY

In this chapter we have looked at the marketing environment. We have seen that changes and trends in this environment give rise to major marketing opportunities and threats, therefore marketers have to be aware of these changes, anticipate them in advance and respond and adjust to them through their marketing decisions and in particular through their strategies and plans. The marketer, in turn, requires an understanding of what constitutes the major elements of the marketing environment plus an awareness and understanding of how these factors are changing and the implications for marketing planning.

We have seen that the marketing environment comprises of two layers or levels. The near or proximate marketing environment includes the key environmental factors of competitors, suppliers and intermediaries. In the second level of the environment, broader macro-environmental forces and factors include social/cultural factors, political factors, technological factors, economic factors, legal/regulatory factors and natural/ecological factors. Among some of the more recent developments in the marketing environment has been the growth of consumerism as part of the legal/regulatory environment and the green movement related to the natural/ecological environment. Together these two movements have forced marketers to rethink their marketing policies and practices. Effective marketers, however, have looked at these movements as representing opportunities rather than threats and have adapted their marketing policies and plans to meet the consumer and green movements' aspirations and hopes. The marketer must try to constantly plan ahead of changes and trends in the marketing environment. The tasks of scanning and forecasting, therefore, are crucial. Scanning and forecasting involve identifying those environmental forces and factors which are most important to the particular organization. These forces and factors can then be monitored and forecast looking for key trends and changes. The marketer must then proceed to assess the likely potential impact of any environmental trends and changes and in particular to assess the likelihood and impact of any opportunities and threats. Finally, the marketing environment must be adjusted to through the marketing plans and decisions of the organization. The marketing environment is essentially non-controllable so the marketer must adapt through the controllable elements of marketing activities and especially the combination of the elements of the marketing mix.

CHAPTER REVIEW QUESTIONS

1. Using examples, describe the importance of the marketing environment to the marketing manager.
2. For an organization of your choice explain the importance of the economic factors in the environment.
3. For an organization of your choice explain the importance of the political factors in the environment.
4. For an organization of your choice explain the importance of the social/cultural factors in the environment.
5. For an organization of your choice explain the importance of the technological factors in the environment.
6. For an organization of your choice explain the importance of the legal/regulatory factors in the environment.
7. For an organization of your choice explain the importance of the natural/ecological factors in the environment.
8. Discuss the essential stages in an environmental scanning and appraisal system.

References

1. P. Kotler, *Marketing Management: Analysis, Planning, Implementation and Control*, 7th edn, Prentice-Hall, Englewood Cliffs, NJ, 1991, p. 129.
2. F. A. Russ and C. A. Kirkpatrick, *Marketing*, Little, Brown & Co., Boston, MA, 1982, p. 24.
3. C. R. Darwin, *On the Origin of the Species*, 1859.
4. W. J. Stanton, M. S. Sommers and J. G. Barnes, *Fundamentals of Marketing*, McGraw-Hill, New York, 1977, p. 27.
5. M. E. Porter, *Competitive Strategy*, Free Press, New York, 1980.
6. G. A. Lancaster, 'Marketing and engineering, can there ever be synergy?', *Journal of Marketing Management*, **9**, 1993, pp. 141–53.
7. J. H. Davidson, *Offensive Marketing*, Pelican Books, Harmondsworth, 1979, p. 232.

8. P. Kotler, *Marketing Management: Analysis, Planning, Implementation and Control*, 8th edn, Prentice-Hall, Englewood Cliffs, NJ, 1994, p. 174.

9. E. B. Taylor, *Primitive Culture*, Murray, London, 1971, p. 1.

10. T. Cannon, *Basic Marketing, Principles and Practice*, Holt, Rinehart and Winston, New York, 1985, pp. 38–9.

11. M. Wilson, *The Management of Marketing*, Gower Press, New York, 1980, p. 5.

12. M. Thomas, 'World of research', *MRS Newsletter*, no. 174, September 1980.

13. P. Kotler, 'What consumerism means for marketers', *Harvard Business Review*, May–June 1972, pp. 48–57.

14. M. L. Bell, *Marketing Concepts and Strategy*, 2nd edn, Houghton Mifflin, Boston, MA, 1972.

15. Kotler, *Marketing Management*, p. 174.

16. *Market Intelligence*, MINTEL, July 1989.

17. G. A. Lancaster and L. C. Massingham, *Marketing Management*, 3rd edn, McGraw-Hill, London, 2001, pp. 22–42.

McShelley Distillery   CASE STUDY

Looking over the Scottish hills from his office of the McShelley Distillery, Jack Murray was pondering the future.

The McShelley Distillery had been in the Murray family for over a hundred and fifty years now. McShelley produced single malt whiskies marketed under the brand name McSporran.

Good single malt whiskies, usually maturing for over ten years before bottling, account for approximately 3 per cent of the total sales volume of whiskies produced and marketed by the Scottish whisky industry. In recent years, however, all the Scottish distilleries producing deluxe malt whiskies had seen their sales fall by over 15 per cent. No single factor accounted for this fall, but rather a combination of the following.

First of all, so-called 'brown spirits' of which whisky is a part, had become unfashionable among the drinking public of the UK. The white spirits, and particularly vodka and white rum, had become much more fashionable, particularly among younger drinkers. In addition, many of the traditional drinkers of first-class premium brand single malt whiskies were quite literally dying out. The price and the image associated with this type of whisky meant that it was generally older drinkers who formed the largest part of the market in the UK. As they grew older and died the market was literally disappearing.

Social/cultural factors, too, were causing the market for malt whisky to diminish. The better brands including that of the McShelley Distillery are 75 per cent proof and therefore contributed greatly to the now recommended upper limit of units of alcohol that drinkers were advised not to exceed. Quite simply, drinking strong malt whiskies on a regular basis was frowned on by many members of the medical profession.

The drinks market is highly competitive and innovative. The larger companies often have brands with turnovers of hundreds of millions of pounds and can afford extensive and expensive promotional campaigns. As a small independent manufacturer McShelleys simply could not compete with these types of spends on promotion. Moreover, many of these larger companies have been very active in developing and launching new alcoholic products in recent years. Many of these were mixers, again aimed at the younger end of the market.

The Scottish whisky industry, McShelley included, had, of course, always enjoyed strong export sales. Japan in particular had been a lucrative market and McShelley exported some 30 per cent of their product to that country. The strength of the pound, however, had also hit McShelley's export sales. To date the potential for exports to the EU had not been fulfilled, in part because the UK was at this juncture not intending to join the single currency.

In the recent budget the Chancellor of the Exchequer had not increased excise duty on whisky which was at least one thing working in the industry's favour.

Many of the companies in the industry had responded to a loss of sales by introducing new technology. This helped cut the costs of producing the product but the long storage costs before bottling in oak casks was still a major expense. The major breakthroughs in technology in this industry in recent years have been in bottling plants which are now totally automated and help in keeping costs down while maintaining quality.

Channels of distribution too have changed in recent years. The major multiple super-markets continue to grow in strength at the expense of the small independent off-licence type of outlet and even the specialist wine and spirit outlets such as Oddbins. As a small manufacturer McShelley had found its margins squeezed by the multiples. An interesting development with regard to distribution has been the growth of the Internet channel of distribution for wines and spirits. Slowly but surely customers were gradually turning to the Internet for ordering these products.

Jack Murray is wondering what the future holds for the McShelley company and what avenues might be open to recapture some of the company's lost sales.

Questions

1. What elements of the marketing environment are affecting the markets of the McShelley company?

2. How can the company ensure that it adequately scans and adapts to the marketing environment in the future?

Chapter Three

UNDERSTANDING THE BEHAVIOUR OF CUSTOMERS

LEARNING OBJECTIVES   *This chapter will help you to:*

- appreciate why it is important for marketers to understand consumer and industrial buyer behaviour;

- understand the key questions which marketers need to answer in understanding the behaviour of their customers;

- understand the key steps in the consumer and organizational buyer decision-making process;

- analyse the factors which affect consumer and organizational buyer behaviour;

- be aware of some of the most important and useful models of buyer behaviour;

- be aware of some of the recent developments with regard to our understanding of customer behaviour.

INTRODUCTION

It might seem obvious, but if the essence of marketing centres on identifying and satisfying customer needs, then it is vital that marketers understand these needs. Moreover, they need to understand what influences these needs and how consumers go about satisfying them. In short, marketers need to understand the buying behaviour of existing and potential customers. Unfortunately, however, this behaviour can be extremely complex and multifaceted. Partly for this reason, marketers have increasingly called upon the knowledge and techniques of the behavioural scientists in order to gain insights into buyer behaviour. In this chapter we shall examine some of these insights. Specifically, we shall be looking at the way in which customers purchase and the behavioural forces and factors that affect this choice process. We shall also be looking at some of the implications of this process for marketers.

Because it is felt that there are fundamental differences between the way individuals buy for their own purposes and the way they buy on behalf of an organization, we shall refer to the former as *consumer buyers*, and to the latter as *organizational buyers*. Each type of buyer will be considered separately below. Clearly, in a single chapter we are not able fully to discuss all the behavioural concepts relevant to understanding consumer and organizational buyer behaviour. For a more detailed treatment of the subject area, readers are advised to consult one of the specialist texts in this area such as Solomon,[1] Hoyer and MacInnis[2] or Schiffman and Kanuk.[3]

CONSUMER BUYER BEHAVIOUR

The distinguishing feature of consumer buyer behaviour as opposed to organizational buyer behaviour is the fact that consumer buying consists of the activities involved in the buying and using of products or services for personal and household use, whereas organizational buyers purchase primarily for organizational purposes. As we shall see, this seemingly obvious difference in fact gives rise to further major differences between the two types of buying.

As stated earlier in this chapter, consumer behaviour is complex. An illustration of this complexity can be seen if we examine some of the questions that relate to consumer buyer behaviour, the answers to which, therefore, the marketer must seek. Kotler[4] suggests that the following key questions need to be answered:

- Who constitutes the market?   Occupants
- What does the market buy?   Objects
- When does the market buy?   Occasions
- Who participates in the buying?   Organizations
- Why does the market buy?   Objectives
- How does the market buy?   Operations
- Where does the market buy?   Outlets

Answers to these questions will give a company an added advantage over less aware competitors. They will enable the company to fit its product offerings to the customer more closely and therefore to satisfy customer needs more fully than competitors. Marketers will also need to know whether their controllable variables, e.g. marketing mix variables, will affect buying behaviour.

However, as mentioned earlier, understanding consumer buyer behaviour in order to address these questions raises complex issues. In order to investigate these in detail, it is advantageous to break down the purchase process into a framework so as to simplify the process and factors influencing purchase behaviour. Figure 3.1 shows a simplified framework of consumer behaviour. As can be seen, environmental influences that are external to the consumer have an effect on purchase behaviour. The consumer also has influences that are individually determined. Both types of influence are carried, consciously or subconsciously, within the consumer's memory. The third box in the diagram shows the decision-making process an individual goes through when purchasing a product. The directional lines show that at any stage, information can be fed back and the purchase process can be stopped and resumed at an earlier stage. The framework will now be discussed in greater detail.

Environmental influences

Consumer buyer behaviour is influenced by a range of outside stimuli.

Cultural Culture is the broadest environmental factor and can be defined as:[5]

> Norms, beliefs and customs that are learned from society and lead to common patterns of behaviour.

So, as behaviour is learned, culture determines the broad values and attitudes an individual holds. Culture can be investigated by using an inventory of values. A child growing up in a certain culture learns its cultural values from the people with whom it socializes. So family, school and friends have a large impact on the cultural values with which the child grows up. Some aspects of culture—for instance, freedom in the UK—have not changed over time. Other aspects as we have seen, however, are dynamic; for example, we suggested that the role of women in society has changed over the years. So, even though culture is a basic foundation of society, in the strategic management process it has to be monitored for changes. In addition, culture is often assumed, and this has meant that many mistakes have been made when companies have tried to market their products abroad, where there are cultural barriers to entry. Other aspects of the socio-cultural environment include sub-culture, social class, and group and family influences.

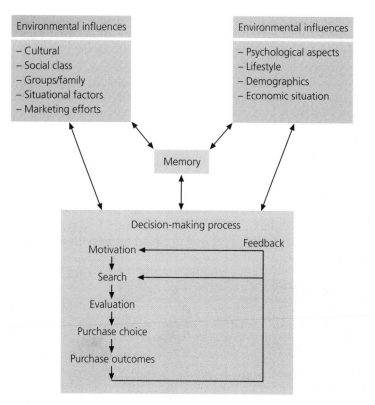

FIGURE 3.1

A framework of consumer buyer behaviour

'Sub-culture' refers to groups in society that have distinct cultural differences. This includes nationality groups such as Indian, West Indian, Italian or Irish, who may have individual lifestyles and values. Religious groups, such as Jews, Muslims, Christians and Hindus, are another sub-culture within the larger cultural group. Blacks, whites and Asians are examples of broad racial groupings, and geographical groups can include northerners, southerners or Scots as distinct groups. Sub-cultural groups can vary in the products they wish to buy, the outlets they buy from, the prices paid, the media they watch, etc.

Marketers ignore cultural factors, including sub-cultures, at their peril, especially, as we shall see in Chapter 14, when they operate in different cultures such as in international markets. Take, for example, the case of a UK company planning to launch a new consumer product in France for the first time. What questions pertaining to cultural factors would need to be considered by this company? For example:

- What needs does our product fulfil in the French culture? (relevant motivations)
- What broad French cultural values are relevant to this product? (e.g. attitudes to work, health)
- What are the characteristic forms of family (or household) decision-making in France?
- Are there any characteristic French behaviour patterns that are relevant to this product? (e.g. shopping habits)
- Through what type of marketing institutions would we be expected to market this product in France?

We could go on listing relevant questions, but we can see that cultural factors are very important to marketers. Indeed, in the widest sense cultural factors shape many of the elements of individual behaviour that we shall consider later. The marketer, too, must be aware of cultural trends and changes, for these give rise to new marketing opportunities and threats. True, cultural changes tend to be relatively slow (although the pace of cultural change is quickening), but again we would stress that cultures do change. We saw in Chapter 2 that in many societies cultural attitudes towards sex, religion, and family and marriage, health, youth and leisure have changed dramatically over the past 20 years. The successful marketer must keep abreast of these changes and anticipate them.

Social class   'Social class' refers to the grouping together of individuals or families who have certain common social or economic characteristics. Members of the same social class exhibit similar patterns of behaviour and have similar values and interests. Criteria used for this type of grouping can be occupation, education or income. Traditionally though, in the UK, marketing researchers and advertising agencies have used occupation to identify and group the different social classes. A simplified summary of these, together with the types of occupations associated in broad terms with each class group, is shown below:

Social class	Types of occupation
AB	Managerial and professional
C1	Supervisory and clerical
C2	Skilled manual
DE	Unskilled manual and unemployed

A more detailed breakdown of these groupings is given in Chapter 4 when we consider the use of social class as a basis for segmentation and targeting. People from the same social class are supposed to be more alike than people from differing classes. Social class is seen in terms of higher or lower classes (although individuals can move from one class to another), but this does depend upon the rigidity of the social system in the society in question. Social class is a major influence on buyer behaviour because classes show different product purchase behaviour in certain product categories. Examples include cars and holidays, where social class is a determining factor of the types of product purchased. The 'best' measures of social class have a number of factors included in them rather than just one, for example occupation. Social class may determine not only the products people choose to purchase but also the store type chosen. For example, department stores, market stalls, mail order or independent retailers may be favoured by certain social classes.

In recent years, however, it has increasingly become recognized that the once strong association between social class and purchasing patterns and behaviour has weakened. Put another way, social class is no longer felt to be such a strong predictor of behaviour and particularly buying behaviour. At the very least, some of the very distinctions between the social class groups are now very blurred, and because of this many feel that lifestyle and aspirations may be much more important than social class, particularly where, as in the UK social class is designated primarily on the basis of the occupation of the 'head of household'. Indeed, there is now substantial evidence that social class may in fact be misleading in terms of predicting consumer behaviour. There are still areas of consumption behaviour which appear to be strongly related to social class. For example, newspaper purchasing and reading habits still seem to be an area where social class distinctions predominate, but for many products and services social class is increasingly a poor predictor of behaviour, especially where used in isolation. We shall return to some of the implications of this in Chapter 4 again when we consider segmentation and targeting and the use of social class for this purpose.

Groups and family   Group and family influences can also affect purchase decisions. *Reference groups* are all the groups that an individual is exposed to that have a direct or an indirect influence on behaviour and attitudes. *Primary groups* are those with which the contact is continuous, and can include family, neighbours, friends and colleagues or peers. *Secondary groups* are groups that have less contact with individual members, for example a football team. People also have aspirations and may then be affected by group pressure from an *aspirational group*. For example, this is used quite often in the marketing of cosmetics, where advertisements show women from the aspirational group of beauty, wealth and desirability using the product. Reference groups affect individuals in three ways:

1. They influence self-image and attitudes.
2. They expose individuals to new behaviour.
3. They create pressure to conform.

Of course, reference group importance will depend greatly upon the product in question. If group influences are strong, it is worthwhile for the marketer to identify opinion leaders in the group. Opinion leaders have influence over members of their reference group. For instance, if a friend you know is interested in computers and you wish to purchase one, you may ask your friend for advice. Then the friend is an opinion leader. The family group also has an influence on purchase behaviour. Indeed, some purchases are made by the family as a group—for example houses, holidays, cars and furniture. In family decision-making, individual members may assume different roles. Depending on the purchase and individuals involved, they may perform one or many roles, such as:

1. Information gatherer
2. Influencer
3. Decision-maker
4. Purchaser
5. Consumer

So for the purchase of a holiday, say, a mother and daughter may go into a travel agent's and pick up brochures; all the family will influence the decision; the final decision may be made by the father; but the mother books the holiday and is then the purchaser; all the family are consumers. Some products within family decision-making are dominated by the husband or wife; others are made jointly.

Situational factors   These may also determine a purchase or consumption situation, and may be a major aspect in purchase behaviour. If you were asked about your favourite food, it would be quite acceptable to state that it depends upon the situation. At times you may prefer a snack, at others a meal with the family and at other times a special meal, perhaps in a restaurant. The consumption situation will directly influence consumer brand perceptions and purchase behaviour—that is, where precisely the product is going to be consumed. The purchase situation is also important. Product availability, change in price, the existence of queues and the amount of time available for buying may all have an effect on purchase behaviour.

Marketing efforts   The final environmental factor affecting consumer buyer behaviour is the marketing effort of organizations. Much of this text concentrates on the planning of decisions aimed at influencing buyer behaviour. For example, as we shall see, the marketer makes decisions concerning products, prices, distribution and promotional campaigns aimed at influencing consumers to purchase the marketer's brands. We shall look at the combination of the marketing mix elements in different marketing settings in Chapter 12. This will include some of the key differences in the marketing mix when considering consumer versus organizational markets. But at this stage it might be useful to consider an example of how marketing efforts, and in particular the application of one of the marketing mix elements is linked to buyer behaviour. A good example is in the area of marketing communications.

Marketing communications from companies are always around us. Some of these are retained in memory, and we then have an image of companies and the goods and services they provide. This may lead to a motivation to purchase the product or to be aware of the product and provide for future use. Recent television campaigns promoting personal pensions have stimulated a perceived need in this area.

Marketing efforts, therefore, are—at one and the same time—both a cause and a result of buyer behaviour.

Individual influences

The second major group of factors that influence a consumer's purchase decisions are those that are personal or individual to the consumer. The major ones are outlined below.

Psychological factors   A number of complex behavioural factors come under this heading. They include perception, motivations, attitudes and personality. Again, we must stress that the full complexity of each of these factors cannot be explored here; but as an indication of the relevance of some of these psychological factors to marketers, and the way they are interrelated, we can briefly consider perception and attitudes.

Perception is the way in which individuals select, organize and interpret stimuli. This includes how they see and interpret a company and its products. When a message is perceived, it is modified by the individual's interpretation. Each person selects (subconsciously) the exposure, attention, comprehension and retention of stimuli. This information is then organized so that it can be easily understood. This can be effected by placing information in categories or combining these into brand images. It is therefore important that marketers build up brand awareness so that a personality for the brand is developed in the minds of existing or potential buyers.

Attitudes are specific. An attitude is held about a certain good or supplier in the context of consumer behaviour. Attitudes are very difficult to change, so companies finding that certain products are associated with a poor attitude would, if at all possible, be better advised to change the product than to try to change consumer attitudes.

Lifestyle variables   These encompass an individual's activities, interests and opinions. (Indeed, as we shall see in Chapter 4, one approach to assessing and grouping lifestyle groups is called AIO research.) A person's lifestyle describes how a person interacts with his or her environment. This again will have consequences for purchase behaviour. Lifestyle variables are increasingly being used in segmentation and targeting.

Demographic variables   These describe individuals according to age, sex, income, education and occupation. Demographic factors will have a bearing on the types of product individuals want, where they shop and how they evaluate possible purchases. For instance, a teenage girl will want, in the main, different products from her mother. A concept similar to age is the life cycle stage. Throughout life, people go through stages—single, married, married with children, children left home, and retired. At each of these stages their product needs will be somewhat different. As we shall see in Chapter 4, there are now some very sophisticated approaches to using the notion of life cycle stages in identifying different target customers.

The economic situation   This factor encompasses not only how much income individuals have but whether they have borrowing power, and their attitude towards spending. Clearly, the economic situation of individual consumers is of prime concern to marketing managers when planning their marketing strategies.

The decision-making process

A further aspect of consumer behaviour is the decision-making process involved in a purchase. In Fig. 3.1 this is shown in the lower box and encompasses five stages. In the first an individual feels a need which a certain product will satisfy and is motivated to evaluate the goods on offer. People have many varying needs; if a need is intense, then they become motivated to purchase the good that will satisfy it. Maslow[6] described the different needs of human beings as being hierarchical. Figure 3.2 shows Maslow's hierarchy of needs. This shows, at the bottom of the pyramid, physiological needs.

These are the most basic and important of human needs. When needs lower in the pyramid are met, individuals move up the hierarchy to fulfil 'higher' needs. Motivation to satisfy such needs can be stimulated by marketing. For instance, when people see an advertisement for a burger they may then feel hungry and purchase one. Alternatively, they may search for alternatives to fulfil the need to satisfy hunger—they could, perhaps, go to a restaurant, or have a pizza or a sandwich in a café. This searching for alternatives may be *external*, that is a physical search for alternatives, or *internal*, i.e. searching the memory for what a person knows about products and suppliers. Marketers, then, need to research (a) how they can stimulate a need for their products and (b) the type of information consumers want on their products.

There are many sources of information on products. Friends and relatives can be used as information sources in addition to company information such as advertising. There may be some public media sources of information, for example press articles about product areas. Another source is the actual handling of the products. When information has been assimilated by the individual, he or she can then make judgements about the brands that are available. Marketers then, as well as building awareness, need to ensure that their products have *unique selling propositions* (USPs) so that they stand out from competing brands.

When consumers have enough information, they will evaluate the alternatives in the market place. The criteria on which products are evaluated vary depending on the products and on how many brands are available. The evaluative criteria used will depend on what need is being fulfilled by the product. Most often discussed are the role of price and the brand image. Again, it is imperative that marketers know on what basis their products are being judged. If there are common themes from consumers for the evaluation of alternative products and the ideal product offering, this has implications for marketing management. It means that products can be tailored to suit consumer needs and marketing communications can respond to the evaluating criteria they use. Evaluating products often coincides with the search for such products.

When products or brands have been evaluated, one product is selected for purchase. However, purchase intention can be affected by unforeseen factors; for example, the price may rise. Also, other people can have an effect on purchase choice even at this late stage. There may now be no purchase at all.

FIGURE 3.2

Maslow's hierarchy of needs

Purchase outcomes or *post-purchase behaviour* will be either satisfaction or dissatisfaction with the purchase choice. Again, the product will be judged against the needs that were to be fulfilled by the product and by the criteria on which alternative brands were judged. Satisfaction occurs when expectations of the product are either met or exceeded. This is remembered the next time the product is purchased. Also, the satisfied consumer may tell friends about the product. If expectations have not been met, the consumer experiences some *post-purchase dissonance*. There are many ways in which consumers try to reduce such dissonance. They can find information to support their product choice, or avoid information that will not confirm their purchase. If dissonance is strong, the consumer may take action either with the company directly, perhaps asking for a refund, or indirectly, for example by telling friends about the problems with the product.

Of course, whether all these stages are experienced and the amount of time spent at each stage depends on the individual and the product purchased. Some products require extensive problem-solving where a great deal of information is required in order to make a decision. This type of product is usually expensive, complex to understand, and/or has not been bought previously, for example a house, a personal computer or a car. Limited search and evaluation would be used when there is some knowledge of the products on offer, for example a small item of furniture for the house, or a car radio. When customers know quite a good deal about the products, then there is little search and evaluation. The purchase may be habitual, for example the repeat buying of the same brand of toothpaste or washing powder. This 'low-involvement' decision-making causes some problems for marketers. Should they try to make such decisions higher-involvement? Are consumers being brand-loyal to products in an active way, or are they displaying inertia? What is the best way of promoting the product in low-involvement market? Ways in which marketers try to increase involvement of consumers include:

1. Link the product with an issue; a recent example here is the marketing of relatively mundane products being described as environmentally friendly or 'green'.

2. Use advertising that involves consumers, e.g. 'Try the Pepsi challenge'.

3. Change product benefits; for example, Radion advertisements emphasize the 'new' benefit of clean-*smelling* clothes.

For a more detailed investigation of the marketing strategies that are successful for low, medium and high-involvement purchasing, see Assael.[7]

A framework such as Fig. 3.1 shows the marketer how to break down consumer behaviour into aspects that can be analysed for effective strategic marketing planning. However, as acknowledged earlier, this framework is very much simplified and therefore understates the full complexity of the range of factors affecting consumer buyer behaviour and the interrelationships between them. Because of this, marketers and behavioural scientists have turned to developing more comprehensive (and complex) models of consumer buyer behaviour.

Models of consumer buyer behaviour

The use of models has for some been one of the more significant developments in the study of consumer behaviour. They reflect an effort to order and integrate the various components of information that are known about consumer behaviour. Models are useful in aiding research design to give a deeper understanding of consumer behaviour.

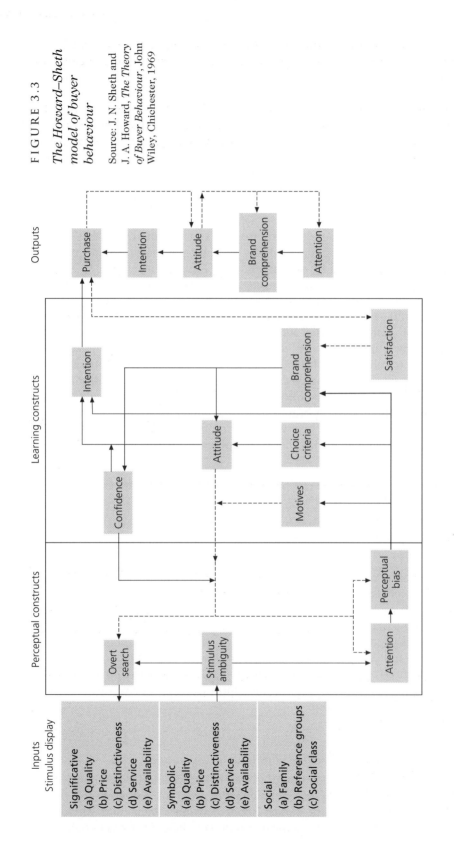

FIGURE 3.3

The Howard–Sheth model of buyer behaviour

Source: J. N. Sheth and J. A. Howard, *The Theory of Buyer Behaviour*, John Wiley, Chichester, 1969

Chisnall was one of the first UK authors to document and discuss such work in the mid-1970s, and his *Marketing: A Behavioural Analysis* still provides one of the best discussions of such models.[8]

The Howard–Sheth model[9] (Fig. 3.3) Howard and Sheth provided one of the earliest and most comprehensive models of consumer behaviour. Their model uses the concept of stimulus–response to explain brand choice behaviour over time, using four major components:

1. Input variables
2. Output variables
3. Hypothetical constructs
4. Exogenous variables

Input variables Input variables are those stimuli that come from the environment. There are three types:

1. *Significance stimuli* These are actual elements of a brand which the buyer confronts, for example price.
2. *Symbolic stimuli* These are generated by manufacturers representing their products in symbolic form, for example in advertisements.
3. *Social stimuli* These are generated by the social environment, for example in reference groups.

Output variables The five positions shown in the right-hand portion of Fig. 3.3 are the buyer's observable stimulus–response inputs. They consist of

● Attention
● Comprehension
● Attitude
● Intention
● Purchase behaviour

Hypothetical constructs These are intervening variables which can be categorized into two major groups: perceptual constructs and learning constructs.

1. There are three *perceptual constructs*; these deal with information processing:
   a. Sensitivity to information—the degree to which the buyer regulates the stimulus information flow.
   b. Perceptual bias—distorting or altering information.
   c. Search for information—active seeking of information about brands or their characteristics.
2. There are six *learning constructs*; these deal with the buyer's formation of concepts:
   a. Motive—general or specific goals impelling action.
   b. Brand potential of the evoked set—the buyer's perception of the ability of brands to satisfy goals.
   c. Decision mediators—the buyer's mental rules for matching and ranking purchase alternatives according to his or her motives.
   d. Predisposition—a preference towards brands in the evoked set expressed as an attitude towards them.

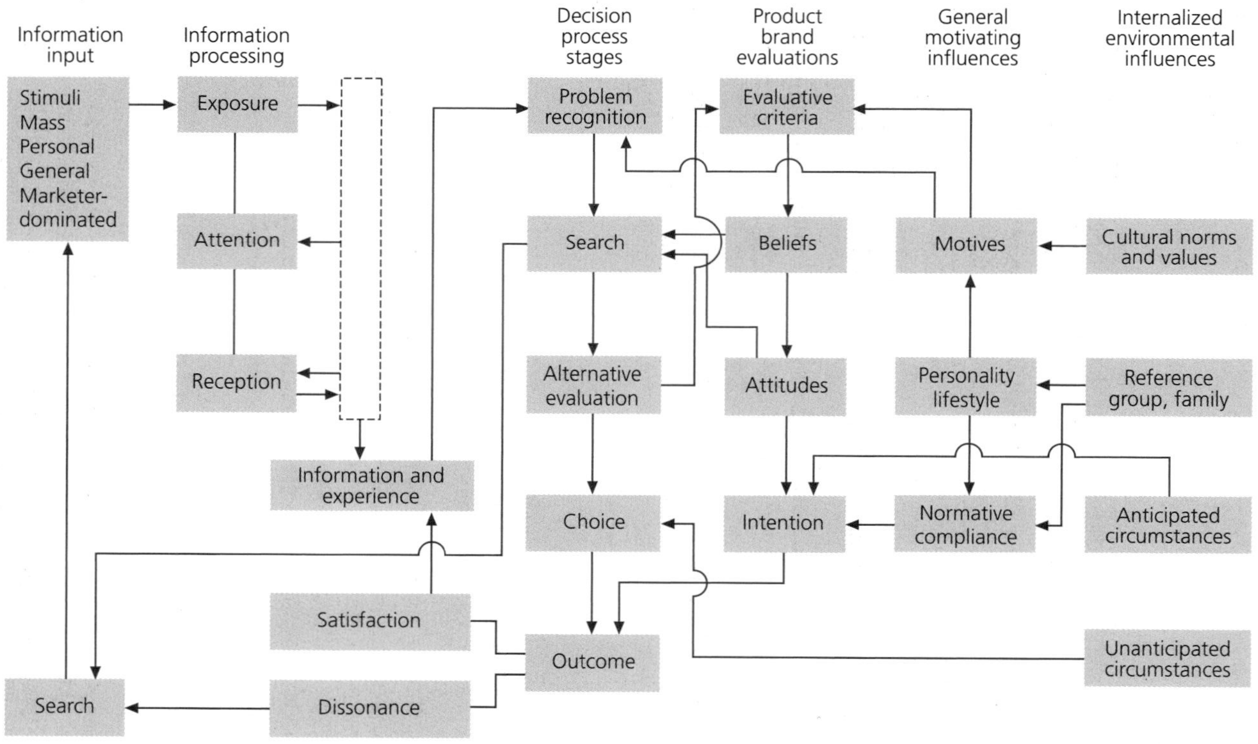

FIGURE 3.4
The Engel–Kollat–Blackwell model

Source: J. Engel, D. Kollat and R. Blackwell, *Consumer Behaviour*, Dryden Press, NY, 1978

e. Inhibitors—environmental forces such as price and time pressure which restrain purchase of a preferred brand.

f. Satisfaction—the degree to which the consequences of a purchase measure up to the buyer's expectations.

Exogenous variables   These external variables can significantly influence buyer decisions. Because such variables are external to the buyer, they are not as sharply defined as other aspects of the model.

The process of operating the model begins when the buyer confronts an input stimulus and it achieves attention. The stimulus is then subjected to perceptual bias as a result of the influence of the buyer's predisposition as affected by his or her motives, decision mediators and evoked set. The modified information will also influence these variables, which in turn will influence the buyer's predisposition to purchase. The purchase will be influenced by the buyer's intentions and inhibitions which are confronted. After the purchase, the buyer evaluates satisfaction, and satisfaction increases the buyer's predisposition towards the brand. More information means that the buyer engages in less of an external search for information and exhibits more routine purchasing behaviour.

The Howard–Sheth model made an important contribution towards the understanding of consumer behaviour. It identified many of the variables that influence consumers and how they interact with one another. The model also recognized that there are different types of consumer problem-solving and information search behaviour. There are, however, a number of limitations to the model: there is no distinction made between exogenous and other variables; some variables are difficult to measure because they are not well defined; and its greatest limitation is its complexity.

The Engel–Kollat–Blackwell model[10] (Fig. 3.4)   This model considered consumer behaviour as a decision process concerning five activities which occur over time:

1. Problem recognition
2. Information search
3. Alternative evaluation
4. Choice
5. Outcomes

These steps provide the basic core. The model also took into account a number of other variables that influence the decision process. These variables are grouped into five general categories:

● Information input
● Information processing
● Product brand evaluation
● General motivating influences
● Internalized environmental influences

The arrows in the model show the direction in which the influence is exerted.

Problem recognition   The consumer detects a difference between his or her actual and ideal state of affairs. This may occur through external stimuli, for example an

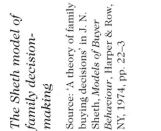

FIGURE 3.5
The Sheth model of family decision-making

Source: 'A theory of family buying decisions' in J. N. Sheth, *Models of Buyer Behaviour*, Harper & Row, NY, 1974, pp. 22–3

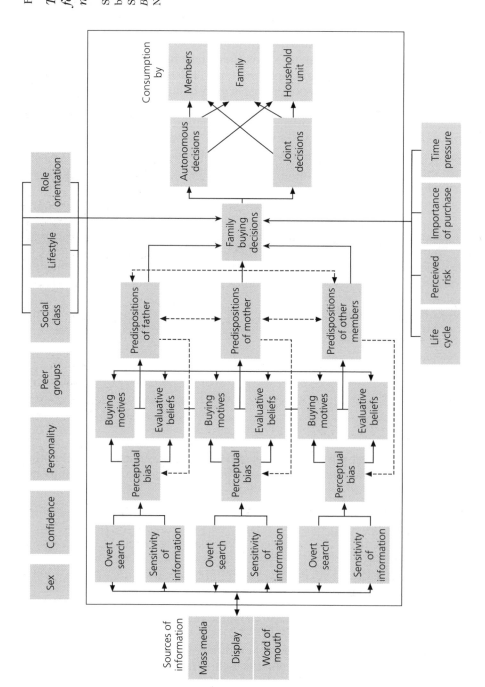

advertisement, or the activation of a motive, for example hunger. In order for action to occur, the consumer must perceive a sufficiently large discrepancy between actual and ideal states.

Information search   The initial information may consist of beliefs and attitudes the consumer already holds. If more information is needed, a consumer may look to friends, salespeople or the mass media. The processing of this information is carried out in a number of stages. The individual is first exposed to stimuli which may be attention-catching. The information is then received and stored in memory. Information processing is highly selective, and individuals may distort information depending on their predisposition to accept what they perceive.

Alternative evaluation   The standards by which products are judged are derived from the consumer's underlying goals or motives. The consumer also has beliefs about which brands possess which characteristics and hence will respond positively or negatively towards a particular brand.

Choice   The consumer's attitude will influence his or her choice. Other influences will comprise normative compliance and anticipated circumstances. *Normative compliance* is the extent to which the consumer is influenced by others, for example friends or family. It considers their attempts to influence, and the susceptibility of the individual to influence from anticipated circumstances—that is, factors a consumer expects (e.g. availability of funds for purchase). At this stage a purchase is likely to occur. However, a barrier to purchase would be *un*anticipated circumstances, such as a drop in income.

Outcomes   If the outcome is perceived as positive, the result is satisfaction. The alternative to this is dissonance—a feeling of discord brought about by doubt about the chosen alternative relative to another, or a range of, unchosen alternatives. The consumer may require more information to support his or her choice.

The Engel–Kollat–Blackwell model considered a number of variables that influence consumers, and its emphasis was on the conscious decision-making process that consumers adopt. The flow of the model is fairly easy and relatively flexible, recognizing that in some purchase decisions many of the detailed steps are passed through very quickly or are bypassed, for example in repeat purchases.

   One weakness in the model, however, is the inclusion of a number of variables whose effect on behaviour is not well specified, for example environmental variables and motives.

The Sheth model of family decision-making[11] (Fig. 3.5)   This model depicts separate psychological systems, which represent the distinct predispositions of father, mother and other family members. These lead into 'family buying decisions', which may be either individually or jointly determined.

   The right-hand side of the model depicted in Fig. 3.5 lists seven family and product factors that influence whether a specific purchase will be autonomous or joint:

1. Social class
2. Life style
3. Role orientation

4. Family life cycle stage
5. Perceived risk
6. Product importance
7. Time pressure

The model suggests that joint decision-making tends to prevail in families that are middle class, closely knit and with few prescribed family roles, and among the newly married. In more specific terms of product purchasing, it suggests that joint decision-making is more prevalent when there is a great deal of perceived risk, when the purchase decision is considered to be important, and when there is ample time to make the decision.

The models of consumer behaviour that have been outlined above are three of the most comprehensive models that describe the decision-making of choice processes of consumers. Even now, such models tend to be theoretical, and are not of direct practical use to marketing practitioners. The models will need to be developed and tested for them to become useful devices for synthesizing behaviour in further studies in consumer behaviour.

Theory versus practice in consumer behaviour   Research into the behaviour of consumers continues to evolve, and as it does it is likely to become more relevant. Consumer researchers are having to justify the relevance of their search, not only in terms of cost, but also in terms of how useful it is to marketing practice and theory.

Researchers are less willing to accept the conclusions of an investigation merely at face value. More frequently research strategies are being questioned, resulting in replications and critiques of prior research studies. Furthermore, research investigations tend to have a strong theoretical basis and are part of ongoing research programmes. These factors point towards a discipline that is becoming mature, with more valid results and realistic findings.

There has been an increase in awareness about what can and cannot be achieved through consumer research. Part of this increased awareness is the result of better training and tuition in the subject. An increasing number of universities now offer specific courses in consumer behaviour, and many institutions run professional seminars.

With increased awareness, consumer researchers have had to consider how they should approach investigations. For example, questions that have been asked of the consumer have mostly been determined by the marketer or researcher; yet many of the product characteristics determined in this way may not be the most relevant to consumers in their purchase decisions. A number of researchers have overcome this problem by using consumer-originated questions when investigating product attributes. This has been achieved through using group interviews and such techniques as the repertory grid test.[12]

Researchers are also recognizing that the wrong questions may have been asked of consumers because those questioned did not always know what they wanted in a product. Since consumers are generally not creative enough to be of direct assistance in designing new products, it is often more productive to find out what they do *not* want.

Future trends in understanding the behaviour of customers   There is likely to be a continuous re-evaluation of the concepts, data and techniques being employed in consumer behaviour investigations. Standard approaches to the study of consumer behaviour will continue to be evaluated and if necessary refined or eliminated. Consumer behaviour research is likely to come under more interactive examination concerning its managerial implications. Hence studies should become more relevant for decision-making purposes.

As consumer research expands, it is likely that expenditure on this subject will increase. While increased expenditure may be the rule, more attention also needs to be given to the cost/benefit of such projects. This will increase attempts to use the most cost-efficient research tools and techniques.

Schiffman and Kanuk[13] have suggested that there are two distinct perspectives concerning the study of consumer behaviour which each stem from different theoretical assumptions and which, in turn, have given rise to two different research approaches to studying consumers.

The first of these is what they refer to as the *'positivist'* approach. This approach to studying consumer behaviour looks for causes of behaviour and is largely empirical using large samples. The idea is to generate knowledge/results which can be generalized to larger populations. In contrast, Schiffman and Kanuk suggest that the second and more recent approach to studying consumer behaviour have tended to be more qualitative using relatively small samples. This theoretical perspective they term *'interpretivist'*. This perspective is based on the assumption that each consumption situation is essentially unique, and hence cannot be generalized. However, it is possible to identify common patterns of behaviour, the analysis of which will lead to a greater understanding of consumers. We need not concern ourselves here too much with the implications of the distinctions between these two approaches regarding the theory and study of consumer behaviour other than to note that as an area of study and research, consumer behaviour remains a very dynamic area of marketing theory, the study of which and our knowledge of which continues to expand and evolve. Irrespective of arguments and debates between academic researchers in this area the primary purpose for researching and studying consumer behaviour remains the same: namely to understand why and how consumers make their purchase decisions so that the marketer may in turn design more effective marketing strategies. Having said this, as the study of consumer behaviour has progressed and developed over the years, the focus of this consumer behaviour research has widened. Nowadays the tools and techniques of researching consumers has been applied to the study and understanding of such diverse elements of consumer behaviour as:

- *Addictive consumption*, e.g. gambling, drugs, alcohol, cigarettes, etc.
- *Illegal consumption activities*, e.g. drugs, prostitution, etc.
- *Compulsive consumption*, e.g. 'shopaholics'.

These and similar aspects of consumer behaviour are sometimes referred to as the 'dark side of consumer behaviour', Solomon,[14] but they constitute a legitimate area for the contemporary student of consumer behaviour. Understanding these types of consumer behaviour is not only of importance to marketers, however, but is also increasingly of interest to, for example, legislators who have the task of understanding the ethics and potential abuses of consumers by marketers, including the extent to which consumers may be manipulated. Increasingly, therefore, knowledge about consumer behaviour is being used to shape policies regarding, for example, consumer protection. It is not possible to go into detail here about some of these uses of consumer behaviour research and understanding but the interested reader should consult some of the more recent contributions in this area as, for example, reported in the article by Andreasen.[15]

In the future it is likely that more integrated research programmes will be initiated, tracking consumer behaviour over time and monitoring trends in behaviour and attitudes. Despite the fact that integrated research programmes require a high level of commitment in terms of effort, time and resources, the need for them seems to be critical for yielding more valid and reliable data than have previously been available.

Getting closer to customers: Relationship marketing and buyer behaviour

Obviously the closer we are to customers, the more likely we are to understand their behaviour. The growth of relationship marketing is helping to facilitate this understanding by allowing the marketer to get closer to customers, gaining useful insights into what makes them purchase or not purchase. The behavioural scientist studying consumers and their behaviour is now moving towards interactive models of buyer behaviour based on the relationships between buyers and sellers. Marketers themselves are developing a better understanding of customers as they communicate more with their customers.

Advances in technology

Once again, advances in technology are helping marketers to understand their customers better. As with relationship marketing, this is particularly true of those technologies which facilitate improved communication between marketers and customers. The Internet, then, is allowing much better feedback about customers' needs and wants and how they respond to particular marketing initiatives. Improved databases, too, are proving particularly useful in understanding the behaviour of customers.

ORGANIZATIONAL BUYING BEHAVIOUR

Consumer behaviour relates to the buying behaviour of individuals (or families) for products for their own use. Organizations buy to enable them to provide goods and services to the final customer. This has implications for marketing management, as we shall see later. Organizational buying behaviour has many similarities to consumer behaviour. Both encompass the behaviour of human beings, whether individually or in groups. Organizational buyers do not necessarily act in a more rational manner than individual consumers. One study in Canada[16] showed that only 30 per cent of buyers followed a rational buying style. Organizational buyers are also affected by environmental and individual factors, as outlined in the previous section.

One of the main differences from consumer buying is that organizational buying usually involves group decision-making. In such a group individuals may have different roles in the purchase process. These can be categorized as follows:

1. *Users*   These are the people in the organization who will be using the product. Sometimes they will also be involved in devising product specifications.

2. *Buyers*   Buyers have the formal authority to purchase the product.

3. *Deciders*   Deciders actually make the buying decision.

4. *Influencers* Influencers affect the buying decision in many different ways. For example, they might be technical personnel who have developed the product specifications.

5. *Gatekeepers* Gatekeepers control the flow of information to and from the buying group (or 'buying centre').

One person may play all the above roles in the purchase decision, or each role may be represented by a number of personnel. The salesperson trying to sell to an organization should be aware of the roles people assume in the buying centre. In the UK this notion is referred to as the 'decision-making unit' (DMU).

Another difference in organizational buying is that products tend to be more complex and require specialist knowledge to purchase. As many products are changed according to the specifications of the buyer, there has to be more communication and negotiation between buyers and sellers. After-sales service is also very important in organizational buying, and suppliers are often evaluated quite rigorously after purchase. In general, organizational markets have fewer, larger buyers who are geographically concentrated. Another aspect of organizational buying is the nature of *derived demand*; that is, demand for organizational (especially industrial) goods is derived from consumer markets. If demand for the end-product consumer good falls, then this has an effect along the production line to all the inputs. So in organizational marketing the end-consumers cannot be ignored, and trends should be monitored.

Organizational buying decisions can also be categorized as to how complex they are, similar to the low high-involvement decision-making in consumer markets:

1. *Straight re-buys* These occur often, are relatively cheap and are usually a matter of routine. If the supplier is an 'in-supplier', that is if it is on the company's approved list of suppliers, then it has to perform so as not to get taken off the list. If it is an 'out-supplier', it has to try to get on to the approved list.

2. *Modified re-buy* This situation requires some additional information or evaluation of suppliers. It is usually the case that specifications, etc., have been modified since the last purchase.

3. *New task* A new task or new 'buy' situation is the most complex purchase decision when the company has not bought this product before. Search and evaluation procedures are extensive here.

The process of organizational buying The process involved in organizational buying has many similarities to consumer buying. Both go through a form of need recognition, search, evaluation, choice and post-purchase evaluation. Figure 3.6 shows the specific stages that organizations go through when buying. Need recognition occurs when the company has a need that can be fulfilled by the purchase of a product. Need can be stimulated internally from within the organization or through external means (for example if a salesperson visits with a new product). The company will then draw up general specifications. This can be done in consultation with the prospective seller. Then more detailed specifications are assimilated. Value analysis can be used to reduce the costs of components in the production process. In the search stage, buyers can use numerous sources of information. They may advertise for tenders for certain products, investigate trade journals or directories, speak to salespeople, look at their own records or visit trade shows.

For suppliers, marketing considerations would lead them to aim for a good reputation in the marketplace, attend trade shows, maintain a certain level of advertising, and try to identify prospective customers. By so doing, the purchasing company can be considered early in the decision process and may even be involved in the formulation of specifications.

Evaluation may be systematic, involving some form of supplier evaluation technique. These can be very detailed, covering quality, price, delivery and after-sales service, for example. The buying centre will evaluate the proposals and alternative product offerings and decide upon the most suitable purchase choice. At this stage there may be further negotiations to alter the price on certain product specifications. The buying centre may choose to have a number of suppliers so as to protect it from being too dependent on one source. The selection stage may also incorporate some form of reordering system, and evaluation of the product after purchase is often formalized.

Again, the time spent, resources committed and, indeed, whether or not all the stages are passed through depends on the type of product bought. A 'new task' product will mean that all the stages will probably be passed through. A straight re-buy situation will be a relatively quick process, missing a number of stages; indeed, this type of purchasing is often accessed by computerized buying.

The people involved in the decision-making process can also change over time, although it is still very important for marketers to be aware of the process and the ways in which they can develop marketing strategy around this. Cardozo[17] stated that it is very important for the seller to be involved in the buying process at an early stage.

Members of the buying centre are influenced by both rational and emotional factors in their decision-making. Marketers should be aware of the different influences on the buying centre, although emotional factors are much more difficult to predict and interpret. Hutt and Speh[18] discuss the different types of motivation in the following buying process:

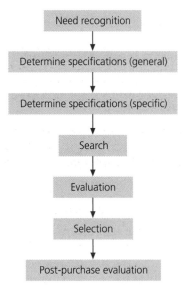

FIGURE 3.6

Organizational buying process

Rational motives	Emotional motives
Price	Status and rewards
Quality	Perceived risk
Service	Friendship
Continuity of supply	
Reciprocity	

These motivations for purchase are not the only influences on organizational buyers of which strategic marketers should be aware. We will now examine other factors that influence organizational buyer behaviour.

Influences on organizational buying   In consumer buying behaviour we discussed two main influences on purchase behaviour: environmental factors and individual factors. In organizational buying we have a more complex environment for buying decisions. Figure 3.7 shows the main influences in the purchase process.

Environmental forces on buyer behaviour include economic, legal, political, cultural, physical and technological factors, so the general economic trends of the area in which the buying organization is located are important, as are the economic trends of any areas in which it trades (owing to derived demand). Increasingly, as world trade expands, when evaluating economic trends the marketer should take a global perspective. The political and legal environment, which includes government spending, taxation and import and export controls, should also be evaluated for their influence upon buying decisions. In the developing global markets for goods and services, it is easy to disregard cultural differences; however, there are still many different cultural climates in the world, and they do not appear to be diminishing in importance. Physical influences involve the geographical location of the organization. The changing technological environment also influences buying decisions.

Marketers must take account of group force purchasing influences:

1. Who is involved in the buying decision?
2. What influence does each member have?
3. How does each member of the buying centre evaluate alternative products?

The type of information that is needed on group forces is the type that becomes available only when close contact is maintained with the buyer. This reinforces the role of the salesperson in the buying decision process. Members of the buying centre were outlined earlier in this chapter, when the roles that various individuals carried out were described.

Organizational forces, such as the organizational culture of the business, also have an effect on the buying decision. For instance, marketing to an organization that has a highly centralized structure, including the buying function, needs a different marketing approach from that of companies that have a decentralized structure.

It is easy to assume that organizational buying has little to do with individual factors. However, in any buying centre it is individuals who make the buying decisions, not the organization. Different members of the buying centre may evaluate products using different criteria, which complicates the issue for the organizational marketer. Some of

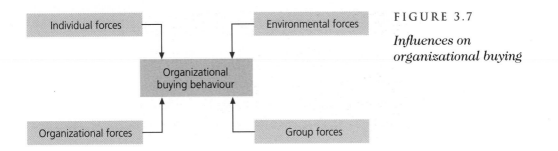

FIGURE 3.7

Influences on organizational buying

the motivations of individual buyers were outlined earlier in this chapter. Individuals will also try to reduce the level of risk they are exposed to in the purchase decision, for example by using multiple sources or making use of an extensive information search.

Models of organizational buyer behaviour

Just as in consumer buyer behaviour, attempts have been made to capture the full complexity of organizational buyer behaviour by developing comprehensive models of the process. Each model incorporates a number of variables and processes and attempts to show how these interrelate. Some of the concepts in organizational buying already discussed in this chapter directly derive from some of these models—for example, the concept of a buying centre, types of buying decisions, and the range of factors affecting these decisions. Two of the more influential of these models are outlined below.

The Webster–Wind model (Fig. 3.8)   This model is concerned with environmental, organizational, interpersonal and individual buying determinants.[19] The model implies that these determinants affect individual and group decision-making processes and final buying decisions. The environmental influences in this model are seen to act as constraints on the buying goals of the organization. Although the marketer cannot control any of these factors, an understanding of the parts they play may be critical to success.

An explanation of the organizational influence relies upon four elements of the buying organization: people, technology, structure and task. The concept of the buying centre is one example of how the model uses these elements. The buying centre concept discussed earlier recognizes that a number of people participate in the buying decision, including individuals and groups from various departments in the organization.

The model also suggests that within the decision-making unit there are a number of roles that people play. These roles were outlined earlier in our discussion and are a valuable contribution of this model.

Although this model is a valuable contribution to the theory of organizational buying behaviour, in that it indicates a whole range of factors that can directly or indirectly influence the outcome of a buying decision, it still provides only a static representation of a dynamic situation.

The Sheth model (Fig. 3.9)   This model was proposed by Sheth as early as 1973[20] and was developed from the Howard–Sheth model of consumer behaviour. The model concentrates on information sources and portrays a more dynamic situation. The buying centre consists of purchasing agents, engineers, users and others. The actions and expectations of the individuals are influenced by previous experience, and the information received by the individuals is subject to their own perceptual distortion.

The Sheth model is dynamic in that it considers time and acknowledges that any future decisions that are made will use continually updated information. It is successful in four ways:

1. It demonstrates the complexity of industrial buying behaviour.

2. It depicts the most important variables in a systematic way.

3. It is a generalized stimulus–response model of the behaviour of industrial buyers.

4. A number of theories and concepts are brought together and are supported by empirical research.

The two major weaknesses of the model are that it does not elaborate much on the process of industrial buying and on how the relationships of the variables might change during that process; in addition, it does not look closely at the various methods of conflict resolution that may be involved in decision-making.

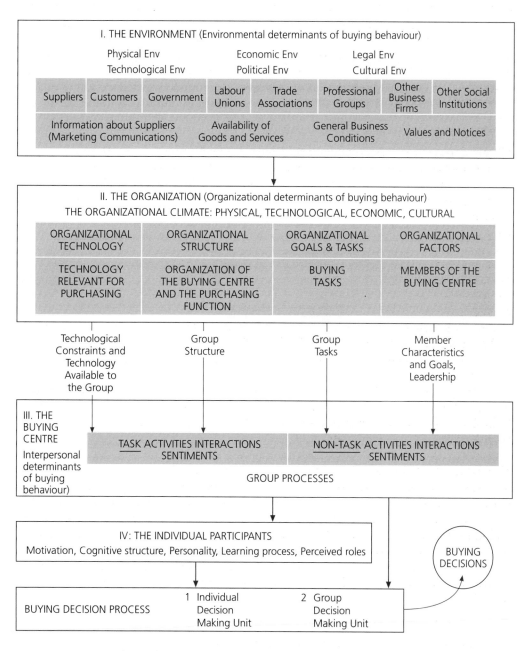

FIGURE 3.8 *The Webster–Wind model of organizational buying behaviour*

Source: W. Webster and Y. Wind, *Organizational Buying Behaviour*, Prentice-Hall, Englewood Cliffs, NJ, 1972

There is no doubt that these two early models of organizational buyer behaviour have helped enormously in our understanding of this potentially complex buying process. As with consumer buyer behaviour though, our knowledge and understanding regarding the organizational buyer has advanced considerably since these early models were first proposed. In addition, the very nature of organizational purchasing and hence organizational buyer behaviour has changed over the years. It is to some of these changes, together with the developments in our knowledge about organizational buyer behaviour to which we now turn our attention.

Theory versus practice in organizational buying behaviour

Over the past 20 years, substantial efforts have been made to advance knowledge on this subject. As a result there has been a considerable output of literature in this area, even if it still receives less attention in comparison with consumer buying. The majority of research, particularly in the United States, has centred on the industrial buying approach and has concentrated on three main areas. First, there have been studies of the process of industrial buying behaviour and the factors that affect the choice of supplier. Second, there have been studies of the effect of individual elements of the marketing mix on industrial markets. Again, remember that we shall be looking

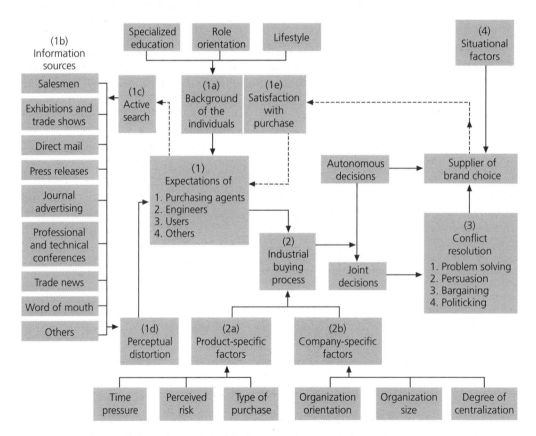

FIGURE 3.9 *The Sheth model of industrial buying behaviour*

Source: J. N. Sheth, 'A model of industrial buying behaviour', *Journal of Marketing*, **37** (4), October 1973

at the marketing mix elements in this case with regard to industrial or organizational markets in more detail in Chapter 12. Last but not least, recently considerable research has focused on the notion of *exchange processes* or *interactions* between organizational marketers and their customers. As we shall see, these notions of exchange and interaction have in turn led to the development of new models of organizational buyer behaviour.

To some extent, at least initially, industrial marketing practice did not keep pace with the conceptual development of organizational buying behaviour. Initially, models were developed from research carried out in the 1960s which focused on identifying variables that influence behaviour. The framework provided by the models supported the variables, and this represented the most advanced thinking in this area. However, the evidence presented by these theoretical models was not backed up by sufficient research to show that this was how organizations bought. In addition, even 10 years ago, the industrial marketer was not encouraged to implement these concepts. Sheth commented in the 1970s that the work carried out within the area of industrial buying seemed to have had little impact on marketing thought and practice. He also felt that marketers had been led to believe that little was known about industrial buying behaviour. Hence there was a reluctance among practitioners to move in the direction suggested by conceptual developments in organizational buying.

Another reason for the early gaps between theory and practice was that data on organizational buying was more problematical to obtain in industrial markets, and as a result the usefulness of such data in formulating marketing strategies was often not demonstrated. The difficulty of obtaining reliable data caused a number of problems. Consumer behaviour was researched in greater depth than industrial buying behaviour, because consumers were more accessible, more numerous, more identifiable and generally more cooperative than participants in industrial buying decisions. In addition, organizational buying decisions tended to be more complex, and hence more difficult to research.

All this has now changed. Certainly researching industrial buyer behaviour and hence developing our knowledge in this area still perhaps remains more complex and difficult than researching consumer behaviour for the reasons stated. But developments in research methodology, coupled with the increasing skills of contemporary research in this area has helped overcome many of these problems. Perhaps more importantly, however, the potential practical value of such research and knowledge is now increasingly recognized by today's marketing manager.

We should also note that organizational purchasing itself is changing. Indeed, this is one of the most dynamic areas of commercial practice. Some of the most important trends and developments within organizational purchasing include the following:

1. Purchasing is more specialized and professional.
2. There is more centralized purchasing.
3. Computerized purchasing has increased.
4. As we have already seen, there are new philosophies of purchasing and manufacturing, e.g. just-in-time, zero defects and materials management.
5. There is more, and improved, supplier capability and performance analysis.

These trends have meant that there have had to be closer links with buyers and sellers. If just-in-time purchasing is to work successfully, close contact has to be maintained between buyers and sellers. There has been an increased emphasis on product quality and delivery schedules. The emphasis is not now on single-product attributes but rather on the overall 'profile' of the good in question. The salesforce of organizational marketing has a great responsibility through the purchase decision, and there is much greater emphasis on its role and specific training requirements. Yet again this has meant an increased profile of what is termed 'relationship marketing'. Over time, a close relationship is actively built up between the seller and the buyer. This is often on a social level and has been called 'lunch', 'golf', or 'dinner marketing', but as we have seen relationship marketing requires extremely close co-operation and trust between suppliers and customers, which can often be established through such social contacts. It is only really worth while on high-value accounts, as a relationship marketing strategy can be very expensive.

As already mentioned several times in this text the growth of relationship marketing is perhaps one of the most significant developments in marketing in recent years. It is fair to say that the notion on which relationship marketing is based, namely the creation of loyal, long-term customers, has implications for virtually every element of a company's marketing activities, from selection of target markets through to product pricing and distribution strategies. Perhaps one of the greatest impacts of a relationship marketing approach when it comes to organizational customers, however, is felt in the area of marketing promotion, and in particular the organization and conduct of sales activities. Because of this we shall return to a more detailed discussion of the growth, meaning and application of relationship marketing in Chapter 10 when we look specifically at selling and sales management. However, although as already mentioned, the growth of relationship marketing has itself been a response to a changing industrial environment and particularly the growth of, for example, new systems of manufacturing and purchasing, many of the concepts and techniques of relationship marketing stem from models of organizational buyer behaviour based on the notions referred to earlier in this chapter of 'exchange' and 'interactions' between business-to-business marketers and their customers. It is to these theoretical antecedents of relationship marketing therefore to which we now turn our attention in the final part of this chapter.

Exchange processes and customer/supplier interactions in organizational buyer behaviour

In recent years a number of models of organizational buyer behaviour have been developed which suggest that organizational buying and selling can usefully be viewed as essentially an exchange process in which the two parties (buyer and seller) 'exchange items of value'. Typical of such exchange models of organizational buying and selling is that offered by Hutt and Speh[21] and shown in Fig. 3.10.

The model reflects the notion of an exchange perspective on business marketing, illustrating what each party to the transaction potentially exchanges and gains. This model also illustrates that there are potentially several participants in each party to the exchange. So, for example, in the selling firm, not only marketing is a participant in the exchange but also manufacturing, R&D, engineering and so on. In the buying firm, not only is purchasing involved but also manufacturing, engineering, R&D and marketing. However, the key representatives in the exchange process responsible for much of the negotiations and exchanges which take place are the salesperson, for the selling firm, and the purchasing agent for the buying firm. The model also illustrates that there are several possible areas of exchange, not only do the most obvious exchanges take place, i.e. products and services from the selling firm in exchange for payment from the buying firm, but also there are complex exchanges of, for example, information, problem-solving, negotiation, friendship and trust, and reciprocity. Such exchange models including this one proposed by Hutt and Speh are based on the premise that the marketer must effectively manage all the complex exchanges that take place in buyer/seller relationships.

Related to this concept of organizational buying and selling involving exchange processes are the models developed by Hakansson[22] who formed the International Marketing and Purchasing (IMP) project group. This research group is studying buying in several European countries and as a result have developed the so-called '*interaction models*' of organizational buying and selling. Hakansson's own contribution to this type of model is shown in Fig. 3.11.

The model describes four basic elements relating to the interaction process between buyers and sellers, namely:

1. The interaction process itself
2. The participants in the process
3. The interaction environment
4. The atmosphere created by the interaction

Using these elements Hakansson describes how they interact in potentially complex ways to determine the outcome of the interaction. We need not concern ourselves here with the detail of these complex relationships and possible outcomes other than to note that it is increasingly recognized that organizational buying and marketing is as complex as these interaction models imply and in turn that successful organizational marketing requires the marketer to appreciate the nature and significance of these complexities. The key importance however, of these more recent exchange and inter-action models of organizational buyer behaviour is that yet again they illustrate the importance of relationship management and marketing. Both exchange and interactive

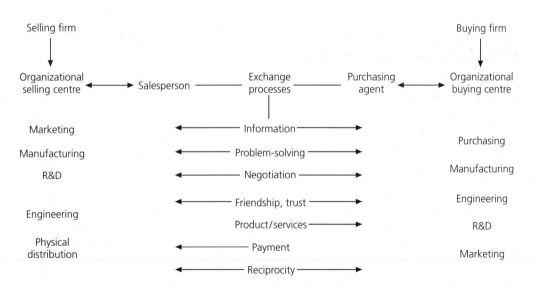

FIGURE 3.10   *Diagnosing exchange processes in business marketing*

Source: M. D. Hutt and T. W. Speh, *Business Marketing Management*, 6th edn, Dryden Press, London, 1999, p. 71

models emphasize that the marketer is responsible for planning and coordinating the range of complex exchange and interactive processes which take place between buyers and sellers. Again we shall return to the meaning and practice of relationship marketing in Chapter 13.

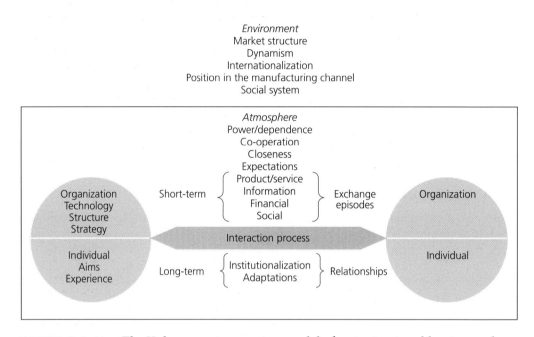

FIGURE 3.11   *The Hakansson interaction model of organizational buying and selling*

Source: H. Hakansson, *International Marketing and Purchasing of Industrial Goods: An Interaction Approach*, John Wiley, Chichester, 1983, p. 79

CHAPTER SUMMARY

This chapter has sought to provide an overview of buyer behaviour and a study of buyer behaviour from the point of view of the contemporary marketer. It has been shown that there are significant implications from a marketing point of view in the analysis of buyer behaviour. The concept of fulfilling consumer needs is central to successful marketing strategy. The study of buyer behaviour is a relatively new discipline and has become a specialist area of marketing, owing to its complexity. It covers questions concerning who is in the market, what they buy, when they buy, how they buy, and where. Marketing mix variables—price, product, place and promotion—have effects on buyer behaviour, so the marketer should be aware of the impact of these controllable variables.

Buying behaviour does not simply encompass the straightforward decision process, but also covers the underlying influences and motives for purchase. These are difficult to measure but are none the less very important in a thorough understanding of purchase behaviour. The principles of buyer behaviour theory can be applied to the commercial sector (both consumer and organizational), to non-profit-making institutions and to service providers. A simple framework has been used in this chapter to describe the factors that might influence purchase behaviour, but more complex models of both consumer and organizational buyer behaviour have also been introduced. They are useful in providing a framework for study.

In organizational decision-making, additional influences were included. These included group influences and organizational factors. The actual decision-making process will depend on whether the purchase is a new task, a modified re-buy or a straight re-buy for the organization. The process involved is similar to the consumer decision-making process. Within organizational buying, motivation is not simply rational: *emotional* motives for purchase also play a part in the decision to purchase. Recent trends in organizational purchasing have implications for marketing management. For example, just-in-time purchasing, computerized purchasing and centralized purchasing have meant that salespersons' roles and responsibilities have changed. In particular, we now know that organizational purchasing can usefully be viewed as a set of exchanges between two parties. This interactive view of marketing underpins the notion of relationship marketing.

The growth of relationship marketing and developments in new technology are allowing the marketer to gain new insights into the behaviour of customers. Relationship marketing because it facilitates an increased closeness to customers and new technology because it facilitates better communication and information exchange.

CHAPTER REVIEW QUESTIONS

1. What are some of the major differences between organizational and consumer buying decisions?
2. Using examples, show how a knowledge of buyer behaviour can help the marketer.
3. What are the main influences on consumer buyer behaviour?
4. What are the main stages in the decision-making process in consumer buyer behaviour?
5. What are the main influences on organizational buyer behaviour?
6. What are the main stages in organizational buyer behaviour?

References

1. M. R. Solomon, *Consumer Behaviour*, 4th edn, Prentice-Hall, Englewood Cliffs, NJ, 2000.
2. W. D. Hoyer and D. J. MacInnis, *Consumer Behaviour*, Houghton-Mifflin Company, Boston, MA, 1997.
3. L. G. Schiffman and L. L. Kanuk, *Consumer Behaviour*, 6th edn, Prentice-Hall, Englewood Cliffs, NJ, 1999.
4. P. Kotler, *Marketing Management: Analysis, Planning, Implementation and Control*, 8th edn, Prentice-Hall, Englewood Cliffs, NJ, 1994, p. 173.
5. H. Assael, *Consumer Behaviour and Marketing Action*, 4th edn, Kent Publishing Co., Boston, MA, 1992.
6. A. Maslow, *Motivation and Personality*, Harper & Row, New York, 1954.
7. Assael, op. cit., Chapter 12.
8. P. M. Chisnall, *Marketing: A Behavioural Analysis*, 4th edn, McGraw-Hill, London, 1998.
9. J. N. Sheth and J. A. Howard, *The Theory of Buyer Behaviour*, John Wiley, Chichester, 1969.
10. J. Engel, D. Kollat and R. Blackwell, *Consumer Behaviour*, Dryden Press, New York, 1978.
11. J. N. Sheth, 'A theory of family buying decisions', in *Models of Buyer Behaviour*, Harper & Row, New York, 1974, pp. 22–3.
12. G. A. Churchill, *Marketing Research: Methodological Foundations*. Dryden Press, Hinsdale, IL, 1976, pp. 17–21.
13. L. J. Schiffman and L. L. Kanuk, op. cit., p. 13.
14. M. R. Soloman, op. cit., p. 624.
15. A. R. Andreasen, 'Consumer behaviour research and social policy', in T. S. Robertson, and H. H. Kassarjian (eds), *Handbook of Consumer Behaviour*, Prentice-Hall, Englewood Cliffs, NJ, 1991.
16. D. T. Wilson, 'Industrial buyers' decision making styles', *Journal of Marketing Research*, November 1971, pp. 433–6.
17. R. N. Cardozo, 'Modelling organisational buying as a sequence of decisions', *Industrial Marketing Management*, **12**, February 1983.
18. M. D. Hutt and T. W. Speh, *Business Marketing Management*, 6th edn, Dryden Press, London, 1998.
19. W. Webster and Y. Wind, *Organizational Buying Behaviour*, Prentice-Hall, Englewood Cliffs, NJ, 1972.
20. J. N. Sheth, 'A model of industrial buyer behaviour', *Journal of Marketing*, **37** (4), October 1973, pp. 50–6.
21. M. Hutt and D. Speh, op. cit., p. 71.
22. H. Hakansson, *International Marketing and Purchasing of Industrial Goods: An Interaction Approach*, John Wiley, Chichester, 1983.

Dalton Dynamics

Dalton Dynamics is a small company set up by its owner/manager, Ian Quayle. The company produces electronic monitoring systems for production machinery principally in the canning industry.

Ian Quayle had for most of his life worked as a design and electronics engineer for a large multinational company. Recent compulsory redundancy had forced him at the ripe old age of 51 to have to look elsewhere to use his talents and earn a living.

Using his redundancy payment, Quayle had spent twelve months designing a new electronic device for monitoring contamination during the canning process for food products. In recent years there had been several major scares for food-processing companies involving both accidental, and sometimes deliberate contamination of their foodstuffs during the canning process. Although systems did exist for detecting this, Quayle's system is innovatory and increases the reliability of detection while at the same time decreasing costs.

Quayle is now considering how to market his new product through Dalton Dynamics. He is unsure what is the best way of encouraging potential customers to even consider his product. In particular he is unsure about the buying behaviour of his potential customers and in particular the following:

First of all how to identify the right people in the purchase process for a product of this type.

Second, he is not sure what sort of procedures and processes customers are likely to use in considering a new supplier.

Finally, he is unsure what will be the key influences on this buying process.

Quayle knows that you, a close friend of his son, have been studying marketing in order to qualify for the Chartered Institute of Marketing qualifications.

Questions

1. Write a brief report to Ian Quayle outlining what he ideally needs to know about the buying behaviour of his potential customers.

2. How might he proceed to make use of this information in marketing his new product?

Chapter Four

MARKET SEGMENTATION, TARGETING AND POSITIONING

LEARNING OBJECTIVES *This chapter will help you to:*

- appreciate the meaning and importance of target marketing;

- understand the steps in effective target marketing

- distinguish the major alternative bases for segmenting consumer and industrial markets;

- understand the range of marketing strategies available to the marketer;

- understand the product positioning and repositioning processes.

INTRODUCTION

The central message of the marketing concept is the need for firms to identify and attempt to satisfy the genuine needs and wants of customers more effectively and efficiently than competitors. As a result of attempting to put this philosophy into practice, many firms have realized that, in order to relate their product and service offerings to the needs of customers, it is not always possible, except in a few special circumstances, to treat the entire market as a homogeneous mass of potential purchasers. Doing this would be 'product-oriented' rather than 'market-oriented'. Market orientation means looking at the marketplace through the medium of marketing research and sales forecasting which have been considered in the previous two chapters.

One of the most important developments in the history of marketing has been the realization that many overall markets are made up of significantly different groups or sub-markets. The people or organizations comprising each of these groups are often sufficiently similar as to be treated as a separate 'market' in terms of product offering, communication strategy, pricing policy, distribution and other marketing mix elements.

Hence, in the selection of 'markets', many firms are not so much concerned with the entire population of potential purchasers for a given product category (e.g. a motor car). They are more concerned with the most commercially attractive sectors in segments of the market for a given product form (e.g. the family saloon market or the sports car market).

This process of 'homing in' to particular segments of a given overall market is known as *target marketing*. This chapter discusses how much target markets can be identified, evaluated and selected, and includes the three related steps of segmentation, targeting and positioning.

THE CONCEPT OF A MARKET

The term 'market' often means different things to different people. There are many usages of the term in economics and in business in general. A market may be defined as a *place* where buyers and sellers meet, where goods are offered for sale and where transfer of ownership takes place. A market may also be defined as the total *demand* for a given product or service, for example the television market or the market for contract cleaning. Markets are also defined in *money* terms; for example, we may say the UK market for Axminster carpets is currently at around £120 million per year. Economists talk of a market as a set of conditions and forces that determine price levels.

We can see from the above examples that modern usage has given several meanings to the word 'market'. Whatever the context in which the term is used, it generally implies a demand for a product or service. Stanton *et al.*[1] state that, in the market demand for any given product or service, there are three factors to consider:

- People with needs
- Their purchasing power
- Their buying behaviour

A market, therefore, can be defined as people with needs to satisfy, the money to spend and the willingness to spend it. From a marketing point of view, a market consists of not only existing customers but also potential customers. As Foster explains,[2]

> for marketing executives the market is not only present customers but all those persons and organisations who may be persuaded to buy the products or services they offer.

THE DEVELOPMENT OF TARGET MARKETING

The development of mass production and the mass markets of today has been discussed in Chapter 1. We saw that, as both domestic and international competition increased from the latter part of the nineteenth century, companies found themselves in a 'buyers' market' rather than a 'sellers' market'. This change required greater sophistication on the part of firms in the marketing of their products and services. This eventually led to the wide-scale adoption of the marketing concept as a central business philosophy from around the middle of the present century.

The concept of target marketing is a refinement of the basic philosophy of marketing. It is an attempt by companies to relate the characteristics or attributes of the goods and services they provide more closely to customer requirements. When mass production techniques were first introduced, out of necessity they imposed a large degree of uniformity upon consumers. However, such techniques also brought an improvement in most people's standards of living. Mass production reduced unit costs and resulted in cheaper goods. Many products that were once considered luxuries of the rich became available to the ordinary people at affordable prices, and they did not really mind that their cars or sewing machines were of the same design or colour. To be even able to purchase such goods was a new experience for most people. Hence, in the early stages of mass production consumers did not really mind being treated as a homogeneous mass.

As consumers became more affluent, their aspirations also increased. They were no longer satisfied with 'a car' or 'a sewing machine', but wanted a particular type of product with *specific characteristics* that suited their requirements more accurately. Advances in production technology made a degree of product differentiation possible with little reduction in the economies of scale of the former mass production techniques. It was now possible to mass-produce a basic product such as a car, which in the later stages of production would take different routes in the assembly process. The result was different variants of the same basic model. The process was applied to many products other than motor cars.

Advancements in production techniques allowed firms to cater for disparities in consumer demand. Today, products are no longer regarded as commodities like 'coffee', or generic products such as 'cars', but are differentiated to suit the requirements of specific groups of consumers. For example, we now have a plethora of brands of coffee catering to different tastes, e.g. strong coffee, weak coffee, decaffeinated coffee, etc. Likewise with cars, we no longer have just one Ford model as we did, say, with the Model 'T' Ford. Today, there is such a wide choice of Ford vehicles and models that it virtually amounts to buying a custom-built vehicle.

The situation today is that, while certain firms attempt to service an entire market for a particular product or service, this tends to be the exception rather than the rule. In such cases, either the market in question is very specialized and relatively small, or the firm enjoys some form of monopoly power. Many organizations operate in very large markets. Such firms recognize that the overall market is so large that it may not be possible to serve the entire population of that market effectively.

The overall market may be geographically dispersed and the firm may lack the resources to service it properly. For example, the computer 'market' is international. Very often the overall market for a particular product or service is too heterogeneous, in terms of the purchasing requirements of individuals or organizations making up the market, for any one firm to service adequately.

By targeting onto specific groups of consumers or 'market segments', instead of attempting to service the demand requirements of an entire population for a particular product category, the firm is able to develop more effective marketing programmes. To speak of the market for shampoo, audio equipment or even industrial valves is to ignore the fact that, within the total market for each of these products, there exist sub-markets which differ from one another in some commercially significant manner. This lack of homogeneity may be due to differences in the amount of money consumers are willing to pay, the way in which the product is used, motives for buying or other factors.

STAGES IN TARGET MARKETING

The process of target marketing needs to be carried out systematically and scientifically to be effective. Kotler[3] states that the process of target marketing has three distinct stages:

- *Stage One: Market segmentation*   The overall market is divided into distinct groups of buyers who are likely to respond favourably to different product/service offerings and marketing mixes. The firm determines the most appropriate basis for segmentation, identifies the important characteristics of each market segment, and develops criteria for evaluating their commercial attractiveness and viability.

- *Stage Two: Market targeting*   This is not to be confused with the overall process of target marketing. Market targeting is the process whereby one or more of the market segments previously identified are evaluated and selected.

- *Stage Three: Product positioning*   Even within a given market segment, competitors' products are likely to be positioned in a particular 'niche' or position. Product positioning is the process whereby the product or service and all the other marketing mix elements are designed to fit a given place within a particular segment. Such a position may be more implied than real. It is how the consumer perceives the product's position relative to competitors' products that is important.

We shall now look at each of the three stages shown in Fig. 4.1 in more detail.

Market segmentation

The growth of specialized market segments has resulted in firms producing goods and services that are more closely related to the requirements of particular kinds

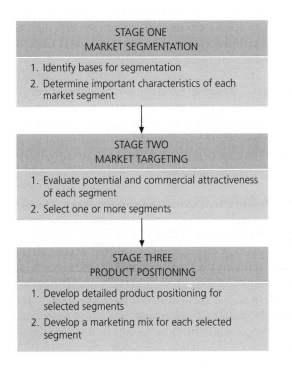

FIGURE 4.1

The three stages of target marketing

of customers. Instead of treating all customers as a homogeneous mass, firms have identified sub-groups of customers whose precise needs can be more effectively met.

As Levitt explains,[4] the marketer should:

> stop thinking of his customers as part of some massively homogeneous market. He must start thinking of them as numerous small islands of distinctiveness, each of which requires its own unique strategies in product policy, in promotional strategy, in pricing, in distribution methods, and in direct selling techniques.

The whole process of target marketing can be illustrated schematically as shown in Fig. 4.1.

Manufacturers have always been aware that certain products were purchased by certain types of people. Rich people tended to buy fine wines and fashionable clothes, whereas poorer people tended to buy ale and more basic items of clothing. Much of this early 'segmentation' was accidental. It just so happened that products were purchased by certain types of people. Producers rarely had any particular target groups in mind, or if they did it was largely based on common sense rather than being a conscious segmentation policy.

As business people began to pay greater attention to the needs and wants of the marketplace, they began to realize that, since the people or organizations that make up a particular market are likely to be heterogeneous, they are unlikely to have identical preferences. Consequently, it was highly unlikely that one product would satisfy everyone. The outcome of this realization can be seen today in the many everyday products we see on our supermarket shelves. For example, most brands of toothpaste were originally marketed with one simple flavour. However, the fact that people do not have identical preferences suggested the possibility of a number of market segments. In order to serve their customers more effectively, companies like Procter and Gamble now market toothpastes in different flavours, different formulations (e.g. paste and gel), and with different ingredients (e.g. regular or 'tartar control' formula). Hence the total market is broken down into smaller groups or segments made up of people who may be prepared to pay a little more to obtain a toothpaste that suits their personal taste or preferences more closely than the 'standard' flavour or formulation.

Bases for segmenting consumer markets   There is no 'golden rule' when it comes to segmenting consumer markets. The marketing firm may have to investigate using many different segmentation variables in order to gain an insight into the structure of the overall market. Very often it may be necessary to use a combination of variables in order to define a precise market segment. The sections that follow describe the main discriminating variables used to segment consumer markets.

Demographic variables   Demographic factors are perhaps one of the more straightforward bases for segmenting consumer markets; they are also one of the most meaningful. The main demographic variables are given below.

Age   For many products purchase behaviour is strongly related to age. For example, the 18–24-year age group tends to buy the latest style of clothing and a large proportion of 'pop' recordings, to eat a lot of 'take-away' food and to read certain magazines and newspapers aimed mainly at the 'youth market', e.g. *New Musical Express*. The 'youth market' is a specific market segment, as is the 25–35-year and 60+ year segments. Although age is one of the more straightforward segmentation variables, it is also one of the most important.

Gender   Many product purchases are also related to gender. Some of these products will be obvious to the reader, e.g. dresses, lingerie, cosmetics (including men's cosmetics) and 'women's' magazines such as *Woman's Weekly*. Some products are not so obvious; for example, certain motor cars tend to be regarded as 'female' cars; this is also true of certain brands of cigarettes.

Family size   This is usually categorized as 1–2, 3–4, 5+. Obviously, the size of family will have some effect on the types of product purchased and this is especially so of pack size, e.g. family size pack.

Family life cycle   In the UK the family remains the basic social unit. The demand for many products, for example consumer durables such as washing machines, refrigerators, etc., is related to stage reached in the family life cycle. These stages are often defined as:

Young	Young single, no children	Young couple, youngest child under 6	Young couple, youngest child 6+	Older couple with children 18+ at home	Older couple, no children at home	Older single

A development in the use of family life cycle segmentation is the approach developed by Research Services[5] and branded as SAGACITY. In fact, this segmentation approach combines life cycle with income and occupation to delineate different consumer groups. The approach is as follows.

First, consumers are divided into one of four possible life cycle groups:

1. *Dependent*   Adults 15–34 who are not heads of household or housewives unless they are childless students in full-time education.
2. *Pre-family*   Adults 15–34 who are heads of household or housewives but childless.
3. *Family*   Adults under 65 who are heads of household or housewives in households with one or more children under 21 years of age.
4. *Late*   All other adults whose children have already left home or who are 35 or over and childless.

These four major life cycle groups are then broken down further by a combination of occupation and/or income to produce 12 major SAGACITY groupings. These, together with a description of each group and the approximate size of each group as a percentage of the total UK adult population, are shown in Fig. 4.2. The evidence suggests that SAGACITY is a powerful discriminator between customer groups for a wide variety of products and services, ranging from package holidays to cars, use of financial services and so on.

Social class/income   The current convention in the UK is to use a mixture of social class and income. Classifications are based on the occupation of the head of the household.

The socio-economic groupings used in the UK are those established by the National Readership Survey, and fall into the following categories:

A   Higher managerial, administrative or professional

B   Intermediate managerial, administrative or professional

C1 Supervisory, clerical, junior administrative or professional

C2 Skilled manual workers

D   Semi-skilled and unskilled manual workers

E   State pensioners, widows, casual and lowest grade earners

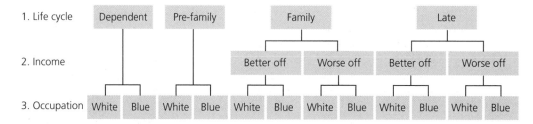

4. Sex

—*Dependent, white (DW) 6%* Mainly under 24s, living at home or full-time students, where head of household is in an ABC1 occupation group.

—*Dependent, blue (DB) 9%* Mainly under 24s, living at home or full-time students, where head of household is in a C2DE occupation group.

—*Pre-family, white (PFW) 4%* Under 35s, who have established their own households but have no children and where the head of household is in an ABC1 occupation group.

—*Pre-family, blue (PFB) 4%* Under 35s, who have established their own households but have no children and where the head of household is in a C2DE occupation group.

—*Family, better off, white (FW+) 6%* Housewives and heads of household, under 65, with one or more children in the household, in the 'better off' income group and where the head of household is in an ABC1 occupation group (65% are AB).

—*Family, better off, blue (FB+) 9%* Housewives and heads of household, under 65, with one or more children in the household, in the 'better off' income group and where the head of household is in a C2DE occupation group (72% are C2).

—*Family, worse off, white (FW−) 8%* Housewives and heads of household, under 65, with one or more children in the household, in the 'worse off' income group and where the head of household is in an ABC1 occupation group (72% are C1).

—*Family, worse off, blue (FW−) 14%* Housewives and heads of household, under 65, with one or more children in the household, in the 'worse off' income group and where the head of household is in a C2DE occupation group (47% are DE).

—*Late, better off, white (LW+) 5%* Includes all adults whose children have left home or who are over 35 and childless, who are in the 'better off' income group and where the head of household is in an ABC1 occupation group (60% are AB).

—*Late, better off, blue (LB+) 7%* Includes all adults whose children have left home or who are over 35 and childless, who are in the 'better off' income group and where the head of household is in a C2DE occupation group (69% are C2).

—*Late, worse off, white (LW−) 9%* Includes all adults whose children have left home or who are over 35 and childless, who are in the 'worse off' income group and where the head of household is in an ABC1 occupation group (71% are C1).

—*Late, worse off, blue (LB−) 19%* Includes all adults whose children have left home or who are over 35 and childless, who are in the 'worse off' income group and where the head of household is in a C2DE occupation group (70% are DE).

FIGURE 4.2   *SAGACITY system and group descriptions*

In more recent years the use of socio-economic groups as a segmentation variable has been criticized. As occupation is the only factor used to ascribe social class in the United Kingdom, it is obviously important that the occupations used to designate it are relevant and valid. In particular, it is important that the different occupations used to designate social class actually discriminate and distinguish between different customer groups and their purchasing habits. It is this aspect of the social class grading system which has been causing marketers most concern in recent years. There is now increasing doubt as to the extent to which the traditional social class groupings and the occupations on which they are based truly reflects differences in buyer behaviour in any meaningful and predictive way. In part, this problem arises from the fact that the traditional occupations used in this social class grouping method are no longer so strongly related to income. For example, it is often the case that the skilled manual group (C2) earn higher incomes than their lower or even intermediate management counterparts (C1) or (B) in industry. Such groups therefore are often in a position to purchase products and services which were once thought of as being the prerogative of the upper social grades. There is now increasing evidence to suggest that the social class groupings shown above, or at least again, the occupations on which they are based, are possibly misleading and therefore ineffective in segmenting today's markets.

Because of this efforts are now being made to develop an updated social class system which more nearly reflects the social groupings of today. One such system is currently being developed for the UK Office of National Statistics. This system, although still based on occupation, proposes eight new categories of socio-economic groups, as opposed to the existing six. In this system the familiar alphabet of As, Bs, C1s, C2s, and D/Es is replaced with a numerical system ranged from 1–8. Although this system of classification is still being researched it is interesting to see how some of the occupations of the former system of social grading have been reassigned; for example, social workers, previously at maximum social grade B according to their precise managerial level in the old system are now classified in Group 1 under the proposed system. Cooks and chefs have moved from a previous Group C2 or C1 to Group 1 or 2—an indication of the increase in status of the 'celebrity chef' in the UK. Whatever the merits of the new system it is an indication that marketers and social scientists are aware of the problems of the long-used A, B, C1, etc. system. It remains to be seen how meaningful and predictive the new system of social class grading in the UK will be for the marketer.

The use of socio-economic grade in market segmentation is discussed in more technical detail by Buttle.[6]

Geodemographic techniques   Partly because of some limitations of either geographic or social class segmentation, considerable effort and research has focused on finding newer and more powerful bases of segmenting and targeting markets. Aided and abetted by the power of the modern computer, a number of approaches have been developed which are based on a combination of where the customer lives and a variety of socio-demographic variables, e.g. occupation, home ownership, size of family, etc. Not surprisingly, these approaches have come to be termed 'geodemographic', and they represent one of the most significant and potentially far-reaching developments in target marketing to date. Although a full explanation of all the geodemographic techniques is beyond the scope of this text, some of the more widely used ones are outlined below.

1. A significant recent development in segmentation studies, related to geographic, cultural, socio-economic and other factors, is 'A Classification of Residential Neighbourhoods' (*ACORN*). The ACORN system is a method of 'mapping' geographically the

concentrations of particular types of people. The assumption is that the demographic/ socio-economic characteristics of people can be correlated to the housing characteristics of a particular area. The original ACORN classifications were derived using a multi-variable statistical treatment of Census of Population data and were divided into major ACORN categories, each category in turn being made up of several subcategories. A summary of these for the UK is shown in Table 4.1.

The ACORN system has proved useful in many areas of marketing, such as retail store location and poster site location. It is of particular importance when a firm is considering using direct mail. Instead of wasting a lot of mail shots on people who are unlikely to be interested in the product, ACORN allows the firm to 'target in' accurately on the market segment of interest.

Although developed at the Centre for Environmental Studies by Richard Webber, the principal uses of ACORN are now in marketing applications. Consolidated Analysis Centres Ltd (CACI), offers a variety of research services based on ACORN data.

For example, 'sample plan' is a service that can be used by marketing research organizations. A computer program is used to select ACORN areas and then individual addresses which will provide the most representative sampling frame for the survey in question. Interviewers can then be provided with clear instructions as to which householders to interview and how to sample them.

Similarly, SITE is a CACI service for determining store location. Potential sites can be assessed by comparing the potential buying power and purchasing patterns of the

TABLE 4.1   *ACORN groups in the UK*

Major ACORN categories	Sub-groups within each category
A Thriving	1. Wealth achievers, suburban areas 2. Affluent greys, rural communities 3. Prosperous pensioners, retirement areas
B Expanding	4. Affluent executives, family areas 5. Well-off workers, family areas
C Rising	6. Affluent urbanites, town and city areas 7. Prosperous professionals, metropolitan areas 8. Better-off executives, inner city areas
D Settling	9. Comfortable middle ages, mature home-owning areas 10. Skilled workers, home-owning areas
E Aspiring	11. New home-owners, mature communities 12. White-collar workers, better-off multi-ethnic areas
F Striving	13. Older people, less prosperous areas 14. Council estate residents, better-off homes 15. Council estate residents, high unemployment 16. Council estate residents, greatest hardship 17. People in multi-ethnic, low income areas

Source: © CACI Ltd (1993). ACORN is a registered trademark of CACI Ltd. Reproduced with permission

various ACORN groups in the vicinity of a proposed location in order to find sites with maximum potential.

These are just some examples of the applications of ACORN in segmentation and targeting. The power of ACORN is evidenced by the fact that British Market Research Bureau (BMRB) analysed the 24 000 panel data respondents in its Target Group Index (TGI) survey on the basis of ACORN groups. For a wide variety of products and services, the TGI data indicated that ACORN segmentation was very effective.

This effectiveness of segmentation based on census data and neighbourhoods has spawned a number of similar approaches.

2. *Pinpoint (PIN) analysis* was also based on analysing census enumeration districts, but with a larger sample. A system of Ordnance Survey grid referencing provided very accurate targeting. A total of some 104 census variables were used to delineate a possible 60 neighbourhood types which were further clustered into 12 main types.

3. *MOSAIC* is, again, based essentially on census enumeration districts. This system used added data on the financial circumstances of potential target customers living within each enumeration district, together with techniques for eliminating errors in relating postcodes to enumeration districts.

Geodemographic segmentation systems are now widely available throughout Europe and may potentially become much more important to marketers in the future, particularly when considering marketing in the different countries of Europe. As with any basis for segmentation the ACORN and other systems of geographic segmentation are not perfect. We know, for example, that in some census enumeration districts the types of neighbourhood and property can differ considerably even though they are grouped into one ACORN category. We must be very careful therefore to establish that the geodemographic system being used is appropriate to our particular market and products. Systems such as ACORN are usually linked with market research survey systems such as the Target Group Index survey conducted in the UK by the British Market Research Bureau which can be used to assess the potential and effectiveness of any proposed geographic segmentation basis for a particular product market.

Education Many products are related, in a general way, to the purchaser's level of formal education. Classical music recordings, certain types of books, items of clothing and the purchase of more exotic kinds of food and wine are examples of this. This is very much a generalization, as there are many people with little formal education who appreciate such products.

Perhaps of greater importance is the fact that consumers' media habits are related to education. Taken as an aggregate, it would be true to say that the better educated tend to read the better quality broadsheet newspapers such as *The Times* or the *Guardian*. Such people are also more likely to watch the more 'highbrow' commercial television programmes, such as *Newsnight*.

Education is also related to social class group because, as a rule, the better educated tend to obtain better jobs. Clearly, a firm wishing to advertise a product aimed at the higher socio-economic/better educated segments of the market would be wise to use the appropriate types of media.

As a segmentation variable, education is usually expressed as terminal education age (TEA). A person's TEA is based on age on finishing full-time education. This particular classification is open to criticism, especially today, where cut-backs in full-time education provision have increased the emphasis on part-time studies. Many people today go back to education in later life to study for degrees and professional qualifications. Therefore, the standard question, 'How old were you when you finished your *full-time* education?' may not really give an indication of a person's true level of educational attainment.

Benefit segmentation   Benefit segmentation uses *causal* rather than *descriptive* variables to group consumers. Different people buy the same or similar products for different reasons. For example, some people buy a car purely as a means of transport, others because the shape and design of the car give them pleasure, others as a status symbol or as an extension of their personality, and others for patriotic reasons; e.g. they might always buy British.

Haley[7] first introduced this approach, based on the idea that consumers could be grouped according to the *principal benefit* sought. The now classic example given by Haley concerned the benefit segmentation of the US toothpaste market. Although this is now somewhat 'historical', the example showed that the use of a combination of different types of segmentation variables could lead to the conclusion that the main criterion for segmentation is the 'principal benefit sought'. Hence, although this approach acknowledges the fact that no single variable is likely to be of sufficient discriminatory power adequately to segment a market on its own, it regards the benefit sought as the *main variable*. As Haley himself states:

> the benefits which people are seeking in consuming a given product are the basic reasons for the existence of true market segments.

A further illustration of the principle of benefit segmentation is given by Bass *et al.*[8] An investigation into the principal benefits sought by consumers from a milk substitute allowed Cadbury Schweppes to develop the brand 'Marvel' to offer the following benefits:

1. As an emergency standby in case a household ran out of milk.
2. As a fat-free healthy substitute for conventional milk.
3. As an aid to slimming.
4. As a convenient way of using 'milk' for people who only use very little, i.e. less than a whole pint per week.

In using benefit segmentation, the marketing firm needs to determine the major benefits people are seeking from a particular product class, to identify the profiles of the people seeking each benefit, and to recognize the existing competitors' products that are close to delivering each of the benefits. Some of the benefits sought may not be serviced by existing products. This will give the firm the opportunity of capitalizing on an unsatisfied market segment.

Segmentation by usage   Consumption rates for many consumer products are not evenly distributed across all households. Hence, meaningful segments could be defined in terms of usage of the product itself. As Frain[9] explains:

> Research does indeed indicate that a 'skewed' purchasing pattern often does apply—even to products intended for a mass market: 50 percent to 80 percent of the purchases of some commonly-bought products are made by 20 percent to 30 percent of all UK housewives.

If the firm can identify such heavy users, it may be able to develop a special marketing strategy aimed at winning more of them to the brand. For example, Bass *et al.* showed that heavy users of beer in the United States tended to be working-class, between 25 and 50 years of age, watched television more than 3½ hours per day and preferred to watch sports programmes. Consumer profiles such as this are obviously helpful to the marketing firm in developing pricing and communication strategies.

Loyalty status   A market can also be segmented according to the degree of consumers' brand loyalty. Kotler[10] divided consumers into four groups according to their loyalty status. To illustrate the principle, let us assume we are analysing purchasing behaviour relating to five brands of toilet soap which we will call simply A, B, C, D and E.

- *Hard-core loyals*   These are consumers with undivided loyalty to one brand. Their purchasing pattern over six periods would be say, A,A,A,A,A,A.
- *Soft-core loyals*   These consumers have divided loyalty between two or more brands. The purchasing pattern of such people may look something like A,B,B,A,A,B.
- *Shifting loyals*   These consumers 'brand-switch' their loyalty between two or more brands. Their purchasing pattern may look something like B,B,B,A,A,A.
- *Switchers*   This class of consumer shows no brand loyalty at all, but instead 'switches' from one brand to another. Their purchasing pattern may look something like B,E,C,A,E.

A company can usually attract switchers, at least in the short term, by price reductions or other forms of sales promotions. A careful analysis of brand loyalty categories can tell the firm a lot about its present marketing strategy and can point the way to improvements. For example, from an analysis of 'shifting loyals', the firm may learn about possible inadequacies in its marketing programme that are causing people to switch brands.

Geographical and cultural segmentation   In Britain the indigenous population tends to be very similar culturally, although some people would argue that there are distinct regional differences (e.g. North and South of England, for beer and certain types of food). There are certainly areas of the country that are suffering more than others from declining industries and unemployment. These factors clearly act as a constraint on purchasing behaviour.

In certain parts of the UK, such as the Scottish Highlands and certain parts of Wales, the cultural differences are more marked. This is also true of areas of high immigrant concentration, which are often culturally distinct, and hence may be treated as a separate market segment for certain products and services.

Needless to say, geographic and cultural differences are even more marked when we cross national boundaries and hence this basis of segmentation is extremely important in export and international markets.

Lifestyle and psychographics   As we have seen, many of the more traditional bases for segmenting consumer markets, at the very least, lack a certain richness in describing consumer segments and at worst are misleading predictors of buyer behaviour. Lifestyle and psychographic segmentation is an attempt to remedy these problems. But what is meant by 'lifestyle' and 'psychographics'?

Lifestyle is a term used to describe how individuals spend both their time and money, reflecting in turn their underpinning attitudes, personality, and social, educational and cultural backgrounds. One of the clearest definitions is given by Chisnall:[11]

> The concept of lifestyle refers to the distinctive or characteristic ways of living adopted by certain communities or segments of communities. It relates to the general attitudes and behaviour towards the allocation of time, money and effort in pursuit of objectives considered desirable by particular types of individuals.

Psychographics is more difficult to define—indeed, there is a lack of general agreement as to its precise meaning. However, broadly, psychographics is the process, and collection of related techniques, for measuring the lifestyles of individual consumers. A number of approaches and techniques have been developed for measuring and classifying lifestyle groups.

The meaning and uses of lifestyle and psychographics in market segmentation are perhaps easiest understood if we examine one of the earliest and best known approaches to identifying lifestyle segments. In the early 1970s, J. T. Plummer[12] reported a lifestyle study based on the following measures:

- How individuals spent their time on *activities*.
- Their major *interests*.
- Their *opinions* about themselves and the world in general.

Perhaps not surprisingly, this approach was referred to as the AIO framework. Respondents were asked to respond to a series of questions designed to measure their *activities*, *interests* and *opinions*. Information was also collected on background demographic characteristics. Table 4.2 illustrates the major elements that formed the focus of the AIO questions, together with information on demographics. Approximately 300 AIO statements were included, and respondents were asked to indicate their agreement or disagreement on a six-point scale, from 'Definitely agree' to 'Definitely disagree'. Examples of 'typical' AIO statements are:

'I like active sports.'

'I enjoy classical music.'

'I go out most evenings.'

'Sex is more important to men than to women.'

'Buying on credit is immoral.'

Using a statistical analysis of responses to such AIO statements, respondents were clustered together into distinct lifestyle groups with descriptive labels being issued to capture the essential characteristics of each group.

TABLE 4.2   *Lifestyle dimensions*

Activities	Interests	Opinions	Demographics
Work	Family	Themselves	Age
Hobbies	Home	Social issues	Education
Social events	Job	Politics	Income
Vacation	Community	Business	Occupation
Entertainment	Recreation	Economics	Family size
Club membership	Fashion	Education	Dwelling
Community	Food	Products	Geography
Shopping	Media	Future	City size
Sports	Achievements	Culture	Stage in life cycle

Source: J. T. Plummer, 'The concept and application of lifestyle segmentation', *Journal of Marketing*, **38**, January 1974, p. 34.

Over the past few years, interest in the application of lifestyle research in marketing has grown substantially, with many studies of lifestyle groups being conducted in both Europe and the USA.

An example of early lifestyle research in the UK is that conducted by Research Bureau Ltd. Using AIO statements with a sample of 3500 housewives under the age of 45, the following lifestyle groups were identified.[13] Here we can see the use of the descriptor labels referred to above.

- *'The young sophisticates' (15%)*   Generally: extravagant, experimental, non-traditional, young, well educated, owner-occupiers, full-time employed, interested in new products, sociable.
- *'Cabbages' (12%)*   Generally: conservative, demographically average, middle-class, average income, home-centred, little entertaining.
- *'Traditional working class' (12%)*   Generally: traditional, quality-conscious, enjoy cooking but do not experiment, middle-aged, lower socio-economic group, lower incomes, sociable, husband and wife share activities.
- *'Middle-aged sophisticates' (14%)*   Generally: not traditional, experimental, middle-aged, ABC1 social class, well educated and affluent, interested in new products, sociable, cultural interests.
- *'Coronation Street housewives' (14%)*   Generally: conservative, traditional, quality-conscious, obsessive, DE social class, less educated, lower incomes, part-time employment, not interested in new products, not sociable.
- *'The self-confident' (13%)*   Generally: self-confident, quality-conscious, young, well educated, owner-occupiers, average incomes.
- *'The homely' (10%)*   Generally: bargain seekers, not self-confident, house-proud, social class C1, C2, part-time employed, some entertaining.
- *'The penny-pinchers' (10%)*   Generally: self-confident, traditional, not quality-conscious, 25–35 years, social class C2DE, less education, average income, husband and wife share activities, sociable.

Similarly, in the United States, the advertising agency Needham, Harper & Stears used AIO measures to identify the following male and female lifestyle groups:

- *Male lifestyle groups*

    1. The self-made businessman   (17%)
    2. The devoted family man   (17%)
    3. The frustrated factory worker (19%)
    4. The successful professional   (21%)
    5. The retired homebody   (26%)

- *Female lifestyle groups*

    1. The socialite   (17%)
    2. The contented housewife   (18%)
    3. The militant mother   (20%)
    4. The suburbanite   (20%)
    5. The traditionalist   (25%)

We can see from these examples how lifestyle segmentation attempts to categorize consumers into distinct groups (segments) with a clear picture of the dominant motives, habits, aspirations and so on of each group. This information can then be used to develop clear targeting and positioning strategies, with the marketing mix being formulated to the specific lifestyle requirements of each group.

The examples shown so far of lifestyle research fall into the category of general lifestyle segmentation; i.e. the AIO statements, and hence the lifestyle categories, are general and not product-specific. Product-specific lifestyle research measures product-related activities, interests and opinions. Some believe that product-specific lifestyle research is a much better predictor of product and brand choice. As we might expect, product-specific lifestyle research uses AIO statements relating to the product category in question. For example, respondents might be given AIO statements relating to, say, the motor car and driving, or alcohol consumption. A number of product-related lifestyle studies have resulted in the targeting of certain types of cigarette smokers, beer drinkers, drivers, users of financial services, coffee drinkers and so on.

It is not difficult to see the appeal of lifestyle segmentation to marketers. Not only does it provide a means of identifying different potential target groups, but it also provides a rich tapestry of insights into the different customer types and their needs and wants, and hence provides valuable clues for planning the marketing mix. Advertising in particular can be more effectively planned with lifestyle information. Examples of advertising campaigns based on some form of lifestyle research include: the advertising for Guinness stout; Colgate Palmolive's 'Irish Spring' soaps; Schlitz beer; many of the utility privatization campaigns; and Legal & General's insurance policies.

One of the problems with lifestyle research and segmentation is that it can potentially involve the marketer in extensive data collection and analysis in order to identify and classify lifestyle groups. In turn, lifestyle research requires quite specialized skills in questionnaire design and the techniques of statistical analysis, including, for example, factor analysis. Because of this, increasingly market research and advertising agencies are offering marketers their own lifestyle groupings based on their own in-house research and analysis. Two examples of such 'off the peg' lifestyle studies are the so-called *'four Cs system'* developed by the advertising agency Young and Rubicam, and the *'VALS system'* originally developed by the Stamford Research Institute.

Using these two examples of lifestyle/psychographic segmentation techniques will serve to illustrate this approach to segmenting consumer markets, and the potential power and hence increasing use of these bases for segmentation into today's consumer markets.

Young and Rubicams 'four Cs'   The advertising agency Young and Rubicam have developed a lifestyle segmentation system which analyses how consumers perceive themselves and in turn how these perceptions are reflected in their interests, values, and activities, and subsequently give rise to different purchasing preferences, brand choices, etc. Using extensive marketing research involving in-depth interviews, focus groups, and questionnaires, Young and Rubicam have identified three main lifestyle groups which are based on a cross-cultural consumer characterization (the 'four Cs'). Each of these three main lifestyle groups contains a number of sub-groups as follows:

Lifestyle group	Sub-groups
The constrained	Resigned poor Struggling poor
The middle majority	Mainstreamers Aspirers Succeeders
The innovators	Transitionals Reformers

As already mentioned, and indeed in all segmentation bases, this classification is based on the notion that each group and sub-group, in this case because of their lifestyles/personalities, has differing needs and will exhibit different purchasing patterns, brand choices, etc. So, for example, in the 'four Cs' system, in the middle majority group, mainstreamers are consumers who are conventional in their lifestyle patterns, values etc. Young and Rubicam have found that the mainstreamers will tend to prefer and purchase well-known brands. They tend not to purchase own-label brands. Similarly, the mainstreamer will tend to buy from domestic rather than overseas producers wherever possible. In contrast, the aspirers, who are motivated to improve themselves in life, will tend to purchase the latest products and brands which in their view will bestow higher status on them. They tend to indulge in the latest activities and pastimes and purchase conspicuously. Young and Rubicam therefore suggest that knowing which lifestyle group an individual belongs to can be used in market segmentation and targeting, and in particular in the development of promotional campaigns to appeal to the various target groups.

The VALS system   Originally developed by the Stamford Research Institute this approach to lifestyle/psychographic segmentation is based principally on information collected from self-administered questionnaires embracing respondents' *activities, interests, and opinions* (AIO measures) together with motives, attitudes, and various other aspects such as values. The updated system of VALS (VALS 2) uses two key dimensions to classify customers into eight lifestyle types. These two dimensions are 'self-orientation', and 'resources available to sustain the self-orientation'. For our purposes we need not concern ourselves with the details of precisely what is encompassed by these two dimensions, but they are used to classify a customer into one of the following lifestyle categories:

- 'fulfilled'
- 'believer'
- 'actualizer'
- 'achiever'
- 'striver'
- 'struggler'
- 'experiencer'
- 'maker'

So, for example, 'experiences' are action-oriented with regard to the self-orientation dimension and therefore have a lifestyle characterized by a high degree of physical and social activity coupled with variety seeking and risk-taking behaviour. With regard to the resources available dimension, they have the most resources of any of the eight lifestyle groups to sustain their self-orientation. Stamford Research Institute claim that this lifestyle group seek wealth, power and fame, and are substantial consumers of exercise and sports products, and tend to be non-conformist in their purchasing. Like the 'four Cs' system, VALS 2 is used predominantly to develop promotional appeals and has been used extensively for this purpose in the United States.

It is important to remember that these are just two of a large and increasing number of lifestyle systems for classifying consumers. In recent years, marketers have become increasingly interested in the potential of lifestyle segmentation for developing more effective marketing strategies. Although not without their problems, both with regard to underpinning concepts and, as already mentioned, in particular problems of data collection and analysis often associated with many of the lifestyle segmentation techniques, lifestyle segmentation has proved powerful for developing marketing and particularly promotional strategies. This usefulness of lifestyle segmentation bases for developing advertising and promotional strategies in part explains the fact that many of the approaches and techniques of lifestyle segmentation have been developed as packages by some of the leading advertising and market research agencies.

Lifestyle and psychographics is not without its critics and problems. The research required can be expensive and difficult to interpret. Some doubt the validity of some of the underpinning concepts. Finally, lifestyles change, and hence the lifestyle categories being used, can become outmoded. However, the distinct advantages of lifestyle segmentation stemming from the richness of the insights it gives into consumer behaviour mean that lifestyle segmentation is here to stay.

This section has covered the main variables used to segment consumer markets. The list is not exhaustive; there are other variables which can be used depending on the situation. Many of the variables discussed here, and other less frequently used methods of segmentation, are discussed further by Frank *et al.*[14]

Industrial market segmentation

The concept of segmentation can also be applied to industrial markets, although the bases used are likely to be different. A more detailed discussion is given by Hutt and Speh, in their book on business marketing.[15] The following is an example of the most frequently used industrial segmentation variables:

1. *Size of firms*   The criteria used could be turnover, capital employed or number of employees. Large firms tend to have different criteria for evaluating a supplier and its products than smaller firms. This is due partly to the fact that larger firms are able to employ professional buyers.

2. *Type of industry*   The criteria used may be manufacturing or service industry, nationalized/private industry, or actual type of activity, e.g. electronics or glass industry. Different industries may have different requirements in terms of product specifications, price, or after-sales service. A firm selling, say, industrial valves may need a different marketing strategy and marketing mix for each industrial segment it deals with.

3. *Geographical region*   Some areas of the UK are designated 'Enterprise Zones' or 'Assisted Areas'. The firms operating in such areas often qualify for government grants or other financial assistance. Again, a firm marketing to organizations in such areas is likely to have a different marketing strategy, especially in relation to pricing and communication policy, from that used in other parts of the country. Other geographical criteria may be urban, rural, European Union, developing country, etc.

4. *Type of buying organization*   This segmentation variable is also related to size of firm. How an organization purchases its products affects the way a marketing firm negotiates and communicates with it. Larger firms tend to have a very formal purchasing procedure. Smaller firms tend to be more informal.

Many organizations have factories or divisions located in different parts of the country or in different countries. Some of these firms will have a centralized purchasing system, where the whole company's requirements are purchased from Head Office. Other firms may have a decentralized purchasing system which allows each factory or division a certain amount of purchasing autonomy. How an organization's purchasing system is organized will have an effect on the policies of marketing to that firm.

Industrial buying situations   In organizational purchasing, the following situations can be observed:

1. *New buy*   As far as the buying firm is concerned, a 'new buy' situation would be:
   a. The marketing firm was offering a totally new product.
   b. It had never purchased from this supplier before so it was a 'new' situation.
   c. The product had been around for some time, but this was the first time the firm had actually bought it.

2. *Modified re-buy*   The buying organization had purchased a similar product before, but this one is slightly different, e.g. a new, more advanced machine tool.

3. *Routine re-buy*   The buying organization had been purchasing the same product from the same firm for a number of years.

In a 'new buy' situation, the buying firm experiences a high degree of perceived risk. Marketing strategies should be aimed at reducing this risk, e.g. through a free trial, after-sales service or a guarantee. A modified re-buy is perceived as being less risky although not risk-free, and a straight re-buy is perceived as a minimal-risk situation.

Service elasticity   Very often a firm attempts to market the same product to different industries. Service requirements, and the perceived importance of the level of service offered by the marketing firm, is likely to differ between industries. For example, a firm may be marketing industrial valves to both oil and sugar processing industries. In the oil industry price is of relatively little importance; delivery, reliability, stock availability and maintenance are very important. In the sugar industry price is likely to be one of the major purchasing criteria. The marketing firm will have to take a completely different approach in marketing these products to each industrial segment.

Price elasticity   Some firms or industries are more concerned about price than others. For large successful firms, price differentials between suppliers would have to be relatively large before they would consider switching from an established supplier. Smaller firms tend to look for the cheapest source of supply they can get, although extended credit is often of more importance. A computer firm marketing hardware to public authorities would have to use a different pricing strategy than if it was dealing with, say, IBM or Ford (UK). It can be said that some firms or industries are more price-elastic or 'price-sensitive' than others.

Market structure   When a firm is dealing with a number of different industries, it may be possible to segment by market structure. Some industries may be dominated by a few large, powerful firms (e.g. the motor car industry or the defence industry). Other industries may be made up of hundreds of smaller firms. The marketing firm's approach is likely to be different between industries; i.e. it would treat large firms that virtually dominate the market differently from smaller, less powerful firms.

Decision-making unit   In industrial firms, purchasing decisions are rarely taken by one individual, except perhaps in routine re-buy situations. Very often a number of individuals are involved in the overall purchasing process. The group of people involved are known as the decision-making unit (DMU).

Again, the composition of a firm's DMU is likely to differ by type of industry, size of firm, whether the firm is a public or private-sector firm, whether the purchasing function is organized on an informal/formal basis or on a centralized/decentralized basis. The composition of the DMU is therefore related to some of the other factors mentioned earlier. However, when used as a basis for segmentation, it is the actual structure of the DMU that is used as the *main* discriminatory segmentation variable.

Until relatively recently, certainly compared with consumer markets, industrial market segmentation has been a neglected area by academics and researchers. However, recognition of the value of effective segmentation in business markets has led to the development of more powerful industrial segmentation models based on step-by-step, hierarchical approach. An early example of this type of approach is that developed by Wind and Cardozo[16] and illustrated in Fig. 4.3. Basically, the approach is to segment industrial markets into two successive stages. The first stage involves forming what are referred to as 'macro segments', based on characteristics of the organization. The second stage involves dividing these macro segments into *'micro* segments', based on the characteristics of the decision-making units (DMUs).

This hierarchical approach enables an initial screening of organizations and a selection of those macro segments that, on the basis of organizational characteristics,

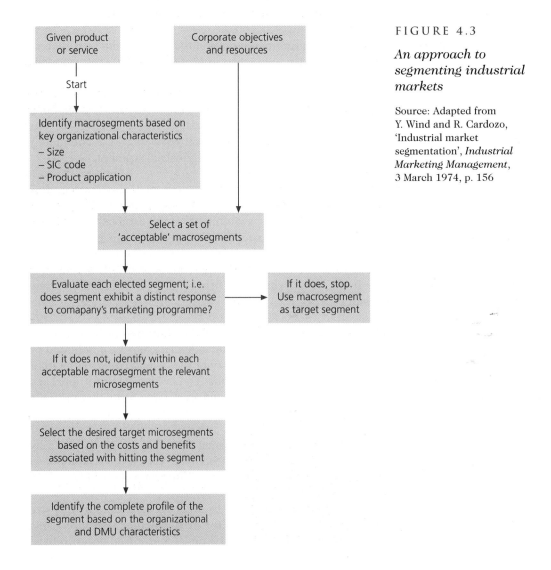

FIGURE 4.3

An approach to segmenting industrial markets

Source: Adapted from Y. Wind and R. Cardozo, 'Industrial market segmentation', *Industrial Marketing Management*, 3 March 1974, p. 156

provide potentially attractive market opportunities. Organizations that may have no use for the given product or service can be eliminated. Starting with the grouping of organizations into homogeneous macro segments also provides a reduction in total research effort and cost. Instead of examining detailed buying patterns and attempting to identify the characteristics of the DMU in each organization individually, such analysis is limited to those macro segments that have passed the initial screening.

Once a set of acceptable macro segments has been formed, and the marketer may divide each of them into micro segments, or small groups of firms, on the basis of similarities and differences among DMUs within each macro segment. Information for this second stage will come primarily from the salesforce, based on sales people's analysis of situations in particular firms, or from specially designed market segmentation studies.

It is argued that the outcome from this segmentation model should include a *key dependent variable*, on which firms can be assigned to segments, i.e. the basis for segmentation; and a set of *independent variables*, which allow a marketer to predict where along the key dependent variable a particular group of customers may lie, as well as providing a greater insight into the key characteristics of the segment.

This concept of successively combining industrial market segmentation bases, giving (it is hoped) more and more precise and hence meaningful segments, is taken even further in the model developed by Shapiro and Bonoma.[17] Their 'nested' approach is shown in Fig. 4.4.

This approach identifies five general segmentation bases which are arranged in the nested hierarchy shown. Moving from the outer nests towards the inner, these bases are: demographics, operating variables, purchasing approach, situational factors, and personal characteristics (of the buyer). We shall examine each of these in turn.

Demographics   This category represents the outermost nest, which contains the most general segmentation criteria. These variables give a broad description of the segments in the market and relate to general customer needs and usage patterns. They can be determined without visiting the customer, and include industry and company size and customer location.

Operating variables   The second segmentation nest contains a variety of segmentation criteria called 'operating variables'. Most of these enable more precise identification of existing and potential customers within demographic categories. Operating variables are generally stable and include technology, user/non-user status (by product and brand), and customer capabilities (operating, technical and financial).

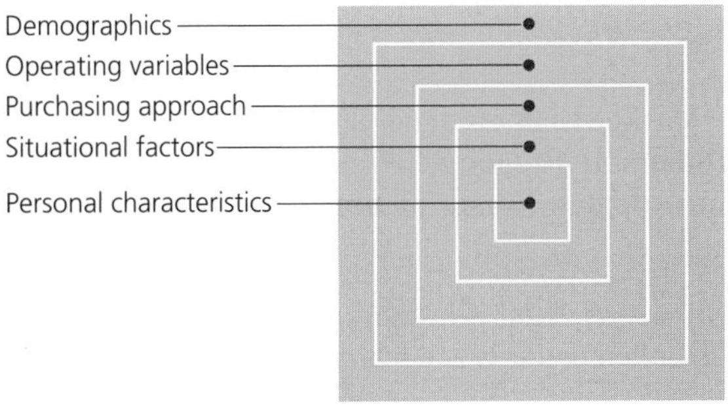

FIGURE 4.4

A 'nested' approach to industrial market segmentation

Source: Adapted from B. P. Shapiro and T. V. Bonoma, 'How to segment industrial markets', *Harvard Business Review*, May–June 1984, pp. 104–10

Purchasing approaches One of the most neglected but valuable methods of segmenting an industrial market involves customers' purchasing approaches and company philosophy. The factors in this middle segmentation nest include the formal organization of the purchasing function, the power structure, the nature of the buyer–seller relationship, purchasing policies and purchasing criteria.

Situational factors Up to this point the model has focused on the grouping of customer firms. Now it moves to consider the tactical role of the purchasing situation. Situational factors resemble operating variables, but are temporary and require a more detailed knowledge of the customer. They include the urgency of order fulfilment, product application and the size of order.

Buyers' personal characteristics People, not companies, make purchase decisions, although the organizational framework in which they work and company policies and needs may constrain their choices. Marketers for industrial goods, like those for consumer products, can segment markets according to the individuals involved in a purchase in terms of buyer/seller similarity, buyer motivation, individual perceptions and risk management strategies.

These then are some of the major approaches to identifying market segments in both consumer and industrial markets. Having identified potential segments, however, the marketer must determine the extent to which these are likely to be suitable as potential target markets.

Criteria for effective segmentation The marketing firm not only has to identify potential market segments, but also has to establish whether segments are commercially viable and cost-effective. The test is whether the individuals in firms making up the segment can be serviced with a marketing mix probably specific to them. As a rule of thumb, to be commercially meaningful, the individuals or firms making up a segment must be more homogeneous in relation to some exploitable characteristic than the overall market from which they have been chosen. For this to be so, the variation of difference within each segment must be less than the variation between each of the segments. The following factors are useful in evaluating the suitability of a potential market segment:

1. *Measurability* The marketing firm should be able to identify and quantify the potential of each segment.
2. *Accessibility* To have any commercial meaning, the marketing firm must be able to reach each segment with a specific marketing programme. It must, therefore, be possible to communicate with individuals or firms making up the segment in a cost-effective way.
3. *Viability* To be viable, each segment must be large enough or commercially lucrative enough to warrant treating as a separate sub-market.

Benefits of market segmentation Market segmentation should result in benefits for both the marketing firm and its customers. If no such benefits accrue to either party, then the segmentation exercise is a meaningless waste of time. The following is an example of possible benefits:

1. Effective segmentation should result in greater sales and profitability.
2. Segmentation should allow the producer to design products and market appeals that are more 'finely tuned' to the needs of the market.

3. Segmentation should result in greater consumer satisfaction.

4. Segmentation allows the marketing firm to focus on those sub-markets with the greatest potential.

5. It allows for greater product differentiation and variety as firms seek further market opportunities by developing new segments.

6. It may result in a better competitive position for existing brands.

Market targeting

Market segmentation is only the first, albeit essential, step in the overall process of target marketing. The firm also has to evaluate each segment and decide how many of the segments to serve. It was discussed earlier that the criteria of measurability, accessibility and viability form the basis of segmentation evaluation. To establish viability, we need not only an indication of the size of the segment, but also estimates of likely turnover and profit, and an indication of where the segment is going; i.e. forecasts of future trends in demand are also necessary, which was the subject of Chapter 11.

Very often the trend in the overall market is different from that in the individual sub-markets. For example, the overall demand for cigarettes in the UK is declining, whereas the demand for 'low-tar' cigarettes is on the increase as consumers switch to less harmful forms of smoking. Many tobacco companies are now exploiting the low-tar segment of the market in reaction to consumers' changes in tastes and in order to retain their share of the cigarette market.

For a proper evaluation, each market segment must be expressed in terms of its cost and revenue implications. Buzby and Heitger[18] recommend the use of individual segmentation budgets. These can then be aggregated to form the firm's overall marketing budget.

Market coverage strategies   Once market segments have been identified and evaluated, the marketing firm has to decide on its level of market involvement. It may determine that no meaningful segments exist and decide to cover the whole market with one basic product or service offering. It may establish a number of meaningful segments and decide to service all or a number of them with a differential product and/or marketing mix. It may identify a number of segments, but decide to service only one or very few of them. Hence the firm can adopt one of three market coverage strategies:

1. *Undifferentiated marketing*   With this strategy, the firm focuses on what is common to all potential consumers rather than attempting to exploit differences. One product and one marketing mix are offered to all consumers without any form of differentiation. Its product features and marketing programmes are designed to appeal to as many potential buyers as possible within the overall market. The overall market is treated as a homogeneous mass, and the firm uses mass production, mass communication and mass distribution.

2. *Differentiated marketing*   With this strategy the firm decides to operate in a number of market segments. The firm offers a slightly 'different' product and related marketing mix to each segment. Washing powder, toothpaste and motor car markets are good examples of this approach used by marketing firms.

3. *Concentrated marketing*   Here the firm decides to attempt to cater for one, or possibly a few, market segments. It concentrates on a limited group of customers and aims to service them more effectively and efficiently than competitors. This strategy is used by the Savoy Hotel, Rolls-Royce cars and Rolex watches, which tend to cater solely for high-income groups.

Product positioning

After segments have been identified and a segmentation strategy developed, a firm needs to develop and communicate a product positioning strategy. Product positioning is the act of designing the company's product and marketing mix to fit a given place in the consumer's mind. Using marketing research, the firm should establish the position of competitors' products in any given market segment and then decide whether to compete on a 'me-too' basis (to offer a product very close to a competitor's offering) or to attempt to fill a gap in the market.

A technique that has gained popularity, especially in the 'positioning' of products, is multidimensional scaling (MDS). MDS is a term that is applied to a variety of techniques for representing brands, stores or products as points in multidimensional space. The dimensions used in the analysis are the attributes which research indicates that consumers use to differentiate products.

Tull and Hawkins[19] show how a two-dimensional scale can be used to plot the market position of soft drinks. The two primary dimensions used in the evaluation are 'cola-ness' and 'diet-ness'. This example is shown in Fig. 4.5.

Tull and Hawkins show that with the aid of a computer an 'ideal' brand position can be developed. Existing brands are ranked in terms of preference by each respondent in the test. This provides the coordinates or scores of the individual's 'ideal' brand on each dimension. The example shows a relatively simple two-dimensional map (called 'brand mapping'). The use of computers allows similar analysis on more than two dimensions, thus increasing the usefulness of the technique.

Product positioning is the final stage in the overall process of target marketing. Once the firm has established its product positioning strategy, it is then in a position to go on to plan the details of its marketing mix.

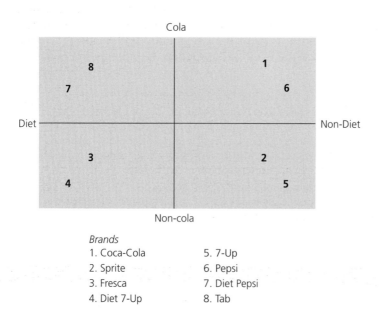

FIGURE 4.5

Multidimensional space for soft drinks

Brands
1. Coca-Cola   5. 7-Up
2. Sprite   6. Pepsi
3. Fresca   7. Diet Pepsi
4. Diet 7-Up   8. Tab

Repositioning

Although positioning is particularly crucial when developing and launching a new product for a market, it is also relevant to the management of existing products and brands. Because markets evolve and change over time, including, for example, changes in customer tastes, competition, etc., the marketer must continuously assess the effectiveness of existing positioning strategies for products and brands. Often, existing brands will need to be repositioned to reflect changing market dynamics. Some of the most common repositioning strategies are as follows.

Repositioning with existing segments   This approach to repositioning is often done in order to revitalize a brand which is losing sales/market share and/or has approached the end of its product life cycle. This type of repositioning does not target new customers but seeks rather to update the image and/or features of a brand. A good example of a brand which has been updated consistently over its life is the Oxo Stock cubes brand which has changed its image, particularly through its advertising, to reflect changing social and family attitudes.

Repositioning to attract new customers   Sometimes a company may deliberately reposition a brand in order to attract new customers. This may often involve significant changes to one or more of the marketing mix elements. Again, this may be done to take account of market dynamics and/or to revitalize flagging sales. A good example of repositioning is the Lucozade drink brand which over time has been repositioned from its original positioning as a product for the sick to a brand which is essentially for the fit and healthy, particularly where they participate in exercise and/or sports activities. A consideration in repositioning brands in this way is the effect it has on existing customers and sales.

Innovative repositioning   Sometimes a marketer can create a new position in a market for a brand by introducing new criteria for brand choice based on attributes in which the marketer is strong. So, for example, Volvo have kept ahead of their competition by deliberately positioning their products on the basis of the 'safety' attribute. Sometimes, the innovative marketer can come up with entirely new attributes to use in such a repositioning exercise. So, for example, Daewoo have successfully introduced the notion of 'no hassle' showroom staff in order to sell their cars.

Competitor depositioning   In this approach the strategy is essentially based on repositioning competitor brands rather than actually changing the position of one's own brand. Essentially, this means altering the perceived position of competitive brands from the perspective of the customer. Understandably, competitor depositioning normally means repositioning competitor brands in a less favourable light. Competitor depositioning should be approached with caution as it can involve legal implications where, for example, a competitor brand is publicly denigrated through, say, media advertising. It is normally safer to deposition competitors by more subtle and sometimes veiled comparisons involving competitor brands.

CHAPTER SUMMARY

Today, companies are finding it increasingly difficult to practise mass marketing. As a result, many firms are embracing the concept of target marketing. Target marketing enables firms to focus on marketing opportunities more effectively. Instead of spreading their marketing effort too thinly, target marketing enables firms to produce product offerings, pricing, advertising and distribution strategies that can 'home in' on specific groups of buyers more efficiently.

To be effective, the overall process of target marketing needs to be carried out in a logical and systematic manner. The first, and perhaps the most important, stage after suitably researching the market is the process of market segmentation. The identification of commercially meaningful market segments forms the bedrock of the rest of the target marketing programme. The remaining two stages are market targeting and, finally, product positioning.

If the process of target marketing is carried out thoroughly and scientifically, the firm should then be in a position to formulate a more meaningful strategy. Target marketing results in benefits for both the marketing firm and its customers. The firm should benefit in terms of a better competitive position for its products, resulting in greater sales and profitability. The customer should derive greater satisfaction from the goods and services purchased. This is a particularly important point as the whole rationale of the marketing concept is increased business effectiveness through the provision of consumer satisfaction.

CHAPTER REVIEW QUESTIONS

1. A microwave oven manufacturer wants to develop a benefit segmentation of the microwave oven market. Suggest some possible benefit segments.

2. In what circumstances might a marketing firm use a concentrated marketing strategy? Illustrate your answer with examples.

3. Marketing firms use certain criteria in evaluating the commercial attractiveness of market segments. Discuss the usefulness of such criteria for evaluating potential segments in the shampoo market.

4. Using the two primary dimensions of expensive/not expensive and serious/not serious, plot the product positioning of existing titles of national daily newspapers on a two-dimensional scale similar to that shown in Fig. 4.5. Discuss a possible product positioning for a new daily newspaper.

5. Show how the segmentation variables
   a. service elasticity and
   b. market structure

   might be useful in determining a marketing strategy for a firm producing industrial valves.

6. Explain lifestyle segmentation and discuss its use in market segmentation.

References

1. W. J. Stanton, M. S. Sommers and J. G. Barnes, *Fundamentals of Marketing*, McGraw-Hill, New York, 1977, p. 49.
2. D. Foster, *Mastering Marketing*, Macmillan, London, 1982, p. 151.
3. P. Kotler, *Marketing Management: Analysis, Planning Implementation and Control*, Millennium edn, Prentice-Hall, Englewood Cliffs, NJ, 2000, p. 192.
4. T. Levitt, *Marketing for Business Growth*, McGraw-Hill, New York, 1974, p. 69.
5. Research Services Ltd, *SAGACITY: a special analysis of JICNARS NRS 1980 Data*, London, 1981.
6. F. Buttle and S. Pettitt, *Principles of Marketing*, 2nd edn, Prentice-Hall, London, 2000, pp. 177–203.
7. R. I. Haley, 'Benefit segmentation: a decision-oriented tool', *Journal of Marketing*, July 1968, pp. 30–5.
8. F. M. Bass, D. J. Tigert and D. T. Lonsdale, 'Market segmentation: group versus individual behaviour', *Journal of Marketing Research*, **5**, August 1978, p. 276.
9. J. Frain, *Introduction to Marketing*, Macdonald and Evans, London, 1981, p. 103.
10. Kotler, op. cit., p. 275.
11. P. M. Chisnall, *Marketing: A Behavioural Analysis*, 2nd edn, McGraw-Hill, London, 1985, p. 92.
12. J. T. Plummer, 'The concept and application of lifestyle segmentation', *Journal of Marketing*, **38**, January 1974.
13. T. Lunn, S. Baldwin and J. Dickens, 'Monitoring consumer lifestyles', *Admap*, November 1982.
14. R. E. Frank, W. F. Massy and Y. Wind, *Market Segmentation*, Prentice-Hall, Englewood Cliffs, NJ, 1972.
15. M. D. Hutt and T. W. Speh, *Business Marketing Management*, 6th edn, Dryden Press, New York, 1999, Chapter 6.
16. Y. Wind and R. Cardozo, 'Industrial market segmentation', *Industrial Marketing Management*, **3**, March 1974, pp. 142–64.
17. B. P. Shapiro and T. V. Bonoma, 'How to segment industrial markets', *Harvard Business Review*, May–June 1984, pp. 104–10.
18. S. L. Buzby and L. E. Heitger, 'Profit oriented reporting for marketing decision makers', *MSU Business Topics*, **24** (3), 1976.
19. D. A. Tull and D. I. Hawkins, *Marketing Research, Measurement and Methods*, 3rd edn, Macmillan, New York, 1984, p. 316.

Starting from an office in his spare bedroom some fifteen years ago, Brian Benson had started selling holidays in French *gîtes*. Brian had long been a lover of France and had spent most of his own holidays there usually in a rented *gîte*. One year the owner of the *gîte* he was staying in asked him if he could find people to stay there, for example his friends, colleagues and so on. The deal was that if he could 'rent out' the *gîte* for 10 weeks during the summer, he would receive his own week free of charge. On return to the UK Brian found it surprisingly easy to sell the holidays to his friends. As a result, two or three other *gîte* owners, friends of the owners of the original one which Brian had rented out, also contacted him and asked him to find visitors for their properties. From these humble beginnings Brian had built a very successful *gîte* holiday business. He still worked from home, but now his home was a substantial Victorian mansion, half of which was given over to running the business. Brian's turnover is now nearly £5 million and he employs 20 staff with some employed in France.

Brian is now considering moving into other geographical markets. In particular he is considering adding holidays in farmhouses and cottages in Italy to his portfolio. The problem here is that he knows nothing about the Italian market for such holidays, and in particular is not sure about what sort of customer groups he should target his marketing at.

In France, his target market is principally socio-economic groups B/C1, younger married couples with children under the age of 18. The properties he mainly deals with in France are quite large, often sleeping up to 12 and this, too, affects his choice of target markets and how he markets the products.

Initial research and visits to Italy suggest that many of the properties for holiday rentals and smaller, often bed and breakfast, establishments run under the auspices of the agrotourismo operation. Here, small farmhouses rent out part of the property or even one room with the facilities being monitored by the Italian Tourist Board.

Visitors to Italy taking this sort of holiday tend to be interested in cultural activities and many of the most popular regions for these properties are in Tuscany and in particular around the major towns of Sienna, Pisa and so on. Prices are not likely to be cheap and are some 50 per cent more expensive than their French counterparts.

Brian has not yet decided how to proceed, but at this stage he feels he needs to address the following issues:

a. Which market segments in the UK he should principally target and why.

b. How to establish the commercial viability of any potential market segment.

c. How to position the product in the market compared to competitor products.

Question

Prepare a report for Brian outlining how he might address the issues in a, b and c above.

Part Two

THE MARKETING TOOLS

Chapter Five

MARKETING INFORMATION SYSTEMS AND RESEARCH

LEARNING OBJECTIVES   *This chapter will help you to:*

- understand the importance of marketing information for marketing decision-making and planning;

- appreciate the different types of marketing research;

- understand the key steps in the marketing research process;

- understand the different types of data collection methods;

- define the differences between primary and secondary data;

- understand the uses of market research information;

- understand the role of marketing information systems;

- be aware of the uses of new technology in contemporary marketing research.

INTRODUCTION

We have examined the place of marketing in business and society, its relationship with customers and how the company can better serve the marketplace through adopting a customer-oriented culture. Achieving such a culture involves examining the marketplace through techniques of marketing research, which is the focus of this chapter. This chapter specifically gives an overview of marketing research—its nature, its role and its limitations—followed by some practical discussion of specific techniques. For a more comprehensive and professional treatment of marketing research, the reader is directed to the work of Chisnall.[1] In this chapter we shall also consider the uses of marketing information systems in contemporary marketing. Again, no discussion of marketing information systems and research would be complete these days without considering at least some of the new techniques that are used and particularly developments in information technology in this area.

Information is required to identify marketing problems and opportunities; it is also required to assist with the formation of an organization's response to problems and opportunities that have been identified. The function of marketing research, therefore, is to generate information that will assist marketers in making decisions. There are two sources of marketing research data: primary (collection of new data) and secondary (data previously collected, or data that are already there), which is the focus of a later part of this chapter.

TYPES OF MARKETING RESEARCH

Marketing research can contribute to the decision-making process in all aspects of marketing activity. Some of the major types of marketing research that are conducted include:

1. Market research and sales research cover:

    a. Estimates of market size of both developed and new markets
    b. Identification of market characteristics and segments
    c. Identification of market trends
    d. Sales forecasting (although this is sometimes considered to be a separate activity)
    e. Obtaining information on customers and potential customers
    f. Obtaining information on competitors

2. Product research covers:

    a. The generation of new product ideas
    b. Product concept testing
    c. Product testing
    d. Test marketing of products
    e. Investigations into different types of packaging (sometimes called packaging research or package testing)

3. Pricing research is concerned with:

    The identification of the relationship between a product or service's price and demand

4. Marketing communications research covers:

    a. Research into the effectiveness of marketing communications (sometimes called advertising research, but it is felt that that term is a rather restrictive definition)
    b. Media selection research
    c. Copy testing
    d. Sales territory planning

5. Distribution research covers:

    a. Warehouse location research
    b. Retail outlet location research

This listing demonstrates that the term 'marketing research' implies a broader sphere of activity than 'market research'. The term 'market research' could be interpreted not to include key marketing research activities such as the generation of new product ideas and pricing investigations and tends to be restricted to research that merely looks into the marketplace itself.

THE MARKET RESEARCH SOCIETY (MRS)

The Market Research Society is the major professional body for marketing researchers in the United Kingdom. It was founded in 1947 and now has in excess of 4500 members. Its name is perhaps peculiar in view of the fact that it has already been established that market research is part of marketing research. This is probably because in 1947 it was set up simply as a body of market researchers, and it is since then that its remit has widened to embrace the broader aspects of marketing research. Among its many activities, the society publishes, in association with the Industrial Marketing Research Association (IMRA), a code of conduct to which its members undertake to adhere.

The following extract from the code is particularly relevant to modern marketing:

No activity should be deliberately, or inadvertently, misrepresented as being market research.
Specifically, the following activities shall in no way be associated, directly or by implication, with market or social research intervening:
(a) Sales approaches for profit.
(b) The compilation of lists for canvassing.
(c) Attempts to influence opinions *per se*.
(d) Industrial espionage.
(e) Enquiries about private individuals *per se*.

It has already been explained that the marketing concept uses the customer as the starting-point for planning activities, and this essentially means asking customers questions through the medium of marketing research. Thus, as companies adopt the marketing concept, so more marketing research will be undertaken. At the same time, companies will explore other means of obtaining business in an increasingly competitive environment. Many less scrupulous companies have taken to conducting selling activities under the guise of marketing research with a questionnaire aimed at obtaining the respondent's name and address for future selling approaches. This unscrupulous activity is often referred to as 'sugging', namely—selling—under the guise of market research. Examples of such companies are double glazing/patio door manufacturers and insurance companies (not, we would hasten to add, from the well-known national names, but from lesser known smaller companies whose salespeople are often working only for commission, whose products and services usually cost more than better known companies and who often cease to trade after a short period of time). Such activity gives marketing research a bad name (not to mention reputable double glazing and insurance companies) and serves to make respondents wary when they are approached to take part in a consumer survey.

Perhaps with the above-mentioned fears in mind, the Market Research Society has a scheme whereby marketing researchers have an identification issued with the authority of the MRS. The problem is that members of the public do not generally know what the MRS is, and unscrupulous companies can still issue a letter of introduction or other form of identification pertaining to claim that the 'researcher' is conducting a bona fide survey—and then use the addresses obtained for subsequent sales canvassing.

IN-HOUSE RESEARCH VERSUS OUTSIDE AGENCY RESEARCH

Sometimes a company may choose to conduct a research study by using internal company personnel. On other occasions it may employ an outside marketing research agency. In this 'make or buy' decision, the following criteria should be considered:

1. *Cost*   Many companies believe that it is cheaper to use internal personnel. It is, however, important to consider that, while these personnel are conducting research, other aspects of their company employment may be neglected. This is particularly true in the case of salespeople being used for interviewing purposes.

2. *Research expertise*   Here one must consider whether or not there is the necessary expertise available internally, particularly when sophisticated research techniques are to be employed in the research project. Similarly, the analysis may call for complicated statistical analysis which might well be outside the scope of internal company personnel. The problem here is that internal personnel, who are not specialist marketing researchers, may not be aware of the existence of such sophisticated techniques in the first place.

3. *Product or service knowledge*   Research requiring an in-depth technical knowledge might be more suited to an 'in-house' team, because it would be time-consuming (and expensive) to impart such information to a team of outside researchers.

4. *Objectivity*   Here, outside agencies are more likely to be objective because an 'in-house' team will perhaps be too familiar with the subject under discussion, and may come to conclusions largely based upon their own prejudices and preconceptions.

5. *Special equipment*   Depending upon the nature of the inquiry, it may be that the research calls for specialist computer programs or specialist test equipment, which may not warrant the expenditure by an 'in-house' team for, say, an *ad hoc* (one-off) study.

6. *Confidentiality*   Although it has already been mentioned that the code of the MRS places importance upon the confidentiality of completed results, it is, nevertheless, a risk to impart confidential information about, say, new products and processes to individuals from outside the company unless it can be ensured that security can be assured. For this reason, some companies are reluctant to use outside marketing research agencies.

In order that a company can obtain the benefits of the optimum use of resources, it is often the case that some parts of a marketing research project are handled internally and other parts are contracted out to external agencies.

Responsibility for marketing research

Sound organization is as essential to effective marketing research as to any other area of business activity.

Companies vary a great deal, not only in size but in their own internal organization, and it is difficult to lay down a general rule as to who should be responsible for the market research operation. In practice, it varies from company to company, depending on size and resources. Here we can simply give an idea of the various alternatives available and the circumstances in which each is likely to be used. There are four generally accepted sources:

- The company's own research department
- Outside research organizations

- Advertising agencies with marketing research departments
- The sales manager and the salespeople

Each is now looked at in more detail.

Company's own research department   There is no doubt that this is the ideal solution if it can be afforded, but a well organized marketing research department with a qualified manager and a trained staff is costly. It is, therefore, found only among large companies, and particularly those that are selling consumer products. Most organizations commission their market research from a market research agency.

The difficulty in laying down general principles regarding the size of a marketing research department is that each firm has different ideas about the division of responsibilities between sales, marketing and market research. In practice, the marketing department is different in each company, and so is its marketing research activity. Nevertheless, if we imagine a sizeable company of importance in the consumer products field, its marketing research department would probably be organized something like that shown in Fig. 5.1.

Generally, the marketing research manager will be responsible to the marketing director of the company, and he or she must work closely, not only with the rest of the marketing department, but also with the sales department, which, because of its specialized knowledge of the company's products, of competitors, and above all of customers, can give a great deal of invaluable information to the marketing research department.

The success or failure of the marketing research department will depend mostly on its manager. In a company, many people view with distrust a newly established marketing research department because they believe it will destroy many of the myths and prejudices that exist; but if the department has a good manager, who is tactful and shows the benefits that can be reaped from marketing research, its acceptance will be much quicker.

A good market research manager should:

- Be a good organizer
- Be a good administrator, able to control staff
- Have a critical mind
- Know all aspects of marketing thoroughly
- Be able to get on with other managers in the company
- Have a sound knowledge of the company's products and their manufacture, and of the industry as a whole
- Above all, be honest, in that he or she reports what has been found and does not tell the management what it wants to hear

FIGURE 5.1

Typical organization of a marketing research department

The advantages of an in-house research department are that it is more convenient, more speedy and more specialized than an outside agency; the work of the department can be organized according to the firm's requirements, while that done by an outside body has to be fitted in with work for other clients. Furthermore, a firm's own department is bound to have a deeper knowledge of its own products than an outside agency, and research can be more confidential if handled within the firm. Agencies should treat their clients' work as confidential, but 'leaks' can occur more easily.

Disadvantages are that there is always the danger of bias in favour of one's own products. A marketing research agency which handles a wide range of clients and products is bound to have a broader knowledge of techniques than the staff of a company's own research department, whose experience is probably more limited.

Outside research organizations   Some firms are too small to justify a research department of their own, so they naturally turn to a specialist research firm if they require some specific research to be carried out. A team of specially trained people, using modern methods, with a great deal of practical experience and a completely impartial view, will produce a report for them.

The drawback is that, however well briefed it may be, such an organization will lack a depth of knowledge of the product unless it works closely and regularly with the client. Furthermore, while continuous research over a long period can be carried out with one's own staff, it is too costly to use an outside organization, which is mainly used for 'one-off' investigations.

There are often cases where a firm that has its own research department uses an outside organization as well—for instance, when a particularly large investigation is needed which requires more staff than the company has at its disposal, or when the information is needed quickly and the staff is not large enough to cope with it.

Very often, outside research organizations are used for overseas research, perhaps because of language difficulties, but also because a local agency will have a much better knowledge of the market and of its problems and can do the survey much more quickly.

Advertising agencies with market research departments   Most of the large advertising agencies have their own marketing research facilities, in the form of either a separate department or an associate or subsidiary company. Therefore, much of what has just been said about specialist organizations applies here.

Agencies generally have a very sound all-round marketing background, but there is a danger that the staff doing the actual research work may be drawn from people who originated in the advertising or publicity world, and whose tendency may be more to influence people than to study their reactions impartially. This is a difficult point, and it can be overcome by enquiring first as to how closely the marketing research section works together with the advertising one. Each case will have to be judged on its merits.

Sales manager and salespeople   In many smaller companies, marketing research is carried out by the sales manager and staff. This is relatively expensive and easily organized. The salesforce is in constant touch with customers, so what could be easier than to ask a few questions about sales policy, packaging, and the product itself? Indeed, there is a lot to be said for this method if resources are scarce—and provided one realizes the inherent limitations.

The weakness of this method lies in the fact that sales staff cannot be impartial. If they are good salespeople, they must be enthusiastic about the product they sell, and convinced that it is the best value for money. They will therefore lack the critical approach that is needed for research. So the use of salespeople for this type of work will depend on the type of research that is being carried out. If one is trying to assess the respective values of one's products against competitors', it is unlikely that sales staff will produce the really impartial information that is needed, but what they do come up with will be better than no information at all.

If such research attempts to find neutral information, such as whether dealers handle one or several brands, and if so which ones; whether they put their products on shelves or hang them on pegboards; what types of customer they supply; and what the response has been to the latest coupon offer, then this can perfectly well be obtained by the salesforce working in conjunction with marketing research staff, who will have prepared the questions in the first place.

THE RESEARCH PROCESS

Research should be conducted only when it is expected that the value of information to be obtained will be greater than the cost of obtaining it. Calculating the cost of a research project is a relatively simple matter and merely involves a calculation of interviewer time, equipment used, data processing, etc. The difficulty arises in determining the value of the information that will be obtained as a result of the research, and this involves the following considerations:

- The relative profitability of the alternative decisions
- The likely contribution the information will make to effective decision-making

When it is decided that research value will be likely to exceed the cost of research, the research process can begin. This process usually consists of a series of nine steps, the first five of which are research design phases:

1. Definition of the marketing problem to be solved, together with a specification of the research objectives.
2. Selection of data collection method(s) to be used. In marketing research there are two basic data collection methods: secondary research and primary research. Secondary data are collected mainly for background purposes and not necessarily to solve the specific problem under consideration; primary data are collected to solve the specific problem at hand. Primary data collection techniques cover: survey research, depth interviews, observational research and experimentation.
3. Selection of sampling method to be used. In some circumstances this may not be appropriate; for instance, when the universe is small, it may be decided to conduct a census.
4. Development of an analysis plan. This step specifically involves specifying the data that will be reported together with the selection of the statistical procedures that will be employed in analysing the results.
5. Estimation of the time and resources required to complete the research.
6. Obtaining approval of the research design outlined in steps 1–5 from the individual(s) requesting the research.
7. Data collection.
8. Data analysis.
9. Research reporting.

LIMITATIONS OF MARKETING RESEARCH

While it is virtually impossible to remove all sources of error in such a behaviourally based field as marketing research, it is the aim of research design to minimize the probable occurrence of the following types of error:

1. *Sampling errors*   These are errors in the specification of the target population and errors caused by the selection of a non-representative sample.

2. *Non-response errors*   These include a failure to contact all members of a sample and failure by such members to respond to the survey.

3. *Data collection errors*   These include occasions where respondents provide answers to please, impress or irritate the interviewer. For instance, in responding to a question (especially open-ended questions where the respondent is encouraged to give a response that is not a pre-determined one from a list of alternatives) a respondent may be unable to articulate a response accurately. Data collection errors may also be caused by leading questions, and here it is the fault of the questionnaire designer, in that the way the question is worded may lead the respondent to give a certain answer (e.g. the question 'Do you believe that children should have a good breakfast?' is almost bound to produce a positive response). Similarly, interviewers may also produce such biases by the way they read out such questions to respondents with, say, a positive or negative bias in the tone of the voice. Simple clerical errors can also be included under this category, where interviewers may record incorrect response information due to misinterpretation or carelessness in recording answers. There will, of course, be a minority of anarchical individuals among respondents who will deliberately set out to give incorrect responses. Such problems, together with the possible problem of interviewer dishonesty, can sometimes be detected statistically, wherein such answers will deviate from the 'norm' of answers, or through the use of 'check' questions, wherein a question is asked to check upon the validity of a question asked earlier, and where there is a disparity then the questionnaire may be regarded as being 'suspect'.

4. *Analytical and reporting errors.*

5. *Experimental errors*   Experiments are designed to measure the impact of one variable (e.g. advertising) on another (e.g. sales). Experimental error may arise if uncontrollable events occur during the experiment (e.g. if a competitor launches a new product during a test period—which is quite often done deliberately, to confuse the results!).

Before a company embarks upon an expensive primary data collection exercise, it makes sense to use information already in existence. Such data are termed secondary data and are the subject of the next section.

SECONDARY RESEARCH

The major sources of secondary data are as follows:

1. *Internal sources*   These data are generated by the organization itself and include: accounting records, salesforce reports, reports from previous marketing research studies, and customer complaints records.

2. *External sources*   These data are generated by sources outside the organization including data produced by the government and publishers of directories, newspapers, periodicals and research reports.

Published data of particular interest to marketers may be grouped into social and industrial statistics, company information, media information (including miscellaneous information from newspapers and periodicals) and market reports. The following listing is a sample selection of major publications relating to the UK market, and they cover what are commonly termed 'social and industrial statistics'. A fuller listing is given in Chisnall's text.[2]

- *Business monitors*   The object of individual business monitors is to bring together the most up-to-date official statistical information covering production, imports and exports relating to a particular industry.

  a. The *Production Series* covers items such as: food, drink and tobacco; coal and petroleum products; chemical and allied industries; metal manufacture; engineering; textiles; clothing and footwear; printing and publishing; timber; furniture; pottery; glass; cement.
  b. The *Service and Distribution Series* covers: food shops; clothing and footwear shops; durable goods shops; catering trades; finance houses.
  c. The *Miscellaneous Series* covers motor vehicle registrations; cinema; insurance companies; overseas travel and tourism; acquisitions and mergers; company finance.

- *Census of Population*   This is taken every ten years during the year that ends with the digit 1, with a 10 per cent sample being taken during every year that ends with a 6. It collects information on numbers in the population, including age, sex, marital status, socio-economic class, country of birth and economic activity.

  The Economic Activity Tables contain statistics of the working population based on their personal occupations and the employed population classified into branches of industry. Key statistics, covering age, distribution, socio-economic status, housing conditions, housing tenure, car ownership and many others, are available for each of the 106 000 enumeration districts (i.e. precisely mapped areas containing approximately 150 households each and based on wards and parishes).

  These statistics have been extensively used in the past by marketing organizations in order to evaluate potential markets and now form the basis of several of the so-called '*geo-demographic*' approaches to identifying and targeting market segments which we considered in Chapter 4.

- *Family Expenditure Survey*   This annual publication provides an analysis of total household income and expenditure. The analysis is based upon a postal survey of 10 500 households.

- *Overseas Trade Statistics of the UK*   This provides monthly and annual import and export statistics by commodity and by country, by both volume and value.

- *Census of Distribution*   Although it is called a census, this series samples various retail outlets, e.g. grocers, confectioners, tobacconists, newsagents, clothing and footwear shops, furniture and electrical goods shops. It provides information on numbers, sizes, type and turnover of shops.

- *Census of Production*   This series samples establishments engaged in: manufacturing; mining and quarrying; electricity; gas and water supply. It provides information on employment, wages and salaries, stocks, capital expenditure, purchases of materials and fuel, sales and work done.

- *Economic Trends*   This is published monthly and contains information on the value of: imports and exports, volume of retail sales, index of production, new car registrations, retail prices, gross domestic product, personal disposable income, saving and borrowing, consumer expenditure, investment, relationship of stocks and output, changes in stocks.

- *Monthly Digest of Statistics* and *Annual Abstract of Statistics*   These publications are very popular and are quite often a good starting-point for a marketing researcher, before going on to the more specialist statistical publications. Statistics are provided on such matters as population trends, employment statistics, manufactured goods, external trade and shipping. As the titles suggest, these are general publications, and as such they are more useful for background information.

- *Family Expenditure Survey*   This is an annual publication based upon a continuous sample survey of approximately 7000 private households on a personal interview basis. It includes data on housing, employment, education and health.

In addition to government statistics, statistics are also produced by trade associations which reflect their members' interests. It is not the purpose of this text to produce a list of such publications, because the best course of action for any researcher here is to contact the individual trade association and enquire whether or not the information sought is available. There may, however, be difficulty in obtaining such information if the sponsoring company is not a member of that trade association. There are also a number of independent research report publishers (for example *MINTEL*, published by Market Intelligence).

There are a number of statistical publications that provide information relating to individual companies and groups of companies, examples of which are as follows:

- *Guide to Key British Enterprises*   This is produced by Dun and Bradstreet on an annual basis. It is arranged alphabetically by company name and has a product index. The addresses, telephone numbers and names of directors are given, together with brief details of company activities, ownership of the company and its approximate turnover and its number of employees. Approximately 20 000 companies are included in this publication.

- *Kompass (UK)* is published annually by Kompass Directories. It is arranged in two volumes, the first of which is arranged geographically, alphabetically and by county, town and name of company. An alphabetical index by company name is also provided. The second volume is arranged by Standard Industrial Classification coding and by company, and this volume is probably of more use to purchasers wishing to obtain details of companies manufacturing certain types of products. The guide also gives brief details of company turnover, number of employees and names of directors.

There are also a large number of trade directories for specific industries, e.g. *The Food Trades Directory*, which lists producers, retailers and all other potential outlets for food products. A full list of specialist trade directories is provided in *Current British Directories*. There are a number of other general directories, which, although not as ambitious as those mentioned, are useful and easy to use.

- *The Times 1000* is published annually by Times Books Ltd and it contains listings of the top 1000 UK companies by turnover plus 500 European top companies, 100 top American companies and 50 top Japanese companies.

- *Who Owns Whom (UK)* is published annually by Dun and Bradstreet and gives details of parent companies, associate companies and subsidiary companies.

- *Extel cards* provide details of company financial results and chairmen's statements.

- *Datastream*, produced by Datastream International, is a computerized database of company financial results available 'on line'. There are now many such on-line databases the use of which has been facilitated by the growth of the World Wide Web and developments in IT. We shall consider some of these in more detail later.

Information can also be obtained directly from companies themselves. Such information can include the annual report and product literature. Information of interest to marketers is not limited to information on industrial and social statistics and company performance. Newspapers and periodicals contain a vast amount of potentially useful marketing information. For example, stories about mergers, announcements of new products, new personnel appointments and the opening of new premises can be useful for general background market intelligence.

To assist in the location of relevant news items, there are several indexes of news-paper and periodical articles:

- *McCarthy Information Services* This publication is useful, for example, when the researcher has identified something of interest from other information sources. This information service will then provide fuller details which the client requires. Such data are reprinted on cards and indexed by company and market.

- *Chambers of commerce* Although this is not a publication, these establishments can sometimes be fruitful sources of information. Many large towns and conurbations have their own chambers of commerce. Some have useful libraries which contain reports on countries and areas of the world, to which export missions may have been sponsored by that particular chamber of commerce. They mainly contain useful local commercial information relating to the area which they serve.

- *Market reports* From the number of secondary sources already mentioned (and this is by no means the full listing) the reader will begin to appreciate the volume of work that secondary research can cover. Various research agencies have recognized that companies often require similar collections of published data. Such agencies undertake to collect, analyse and then sell published reports to interested companies. In essence, they perform desk research and distil whatever information is available into a concise report. Commercial libraries usually contain indexes of the range of reports available.

In fact, most of the publications mentioned are available at major commercial reference libraries; it should be emphasized that there are often surprisingly good commercial sections in modestly sized town libraries. It is always better to investigate these local sources first before visiting one of the major commercial libraries. This is because the larger libraries tend to be more for the professional user, whereas local libraries will contain staff who are more 'in tune' with the needs of 'learners', and will personally show them how to use certain facilities and how to reference the information they require.

Secondary data collection and new technology

In Chapter 1 we touched on what is felt by many to be one of the most significant technological developments affecting marketers now and in the future, namely the growth of the Internet. The Internet of course is now beginning to affect every facet of our lives but it is certainly already having a major effect on marketing activities. Needless to say, one of the areas of marketing most crucially affected by the growth of the Internet is access to, and the exchange of, information. The Internet already offers significant potential to explore and utilize secondary information sources, so, for example, most major international companies, and many smaller ones too, supply information about themselves and their activities to the Internet. Clearly, this is primarily intended to promote their products and services but we can also use this information as a source of cheap and easy secondary information regarding their products, prices, etc. Potentially at least, the Internet offers a way of reducing one of the biggest disadvantages regarding secondary information and its use in marketing research. Namely that secondary information is often out of date. On the Internet however, such information can be, and often is, regularly updated. Not only can we access company information on the Internet, but also increasingly on-line information is available regarding, for example developments in the business world, new legislation that may affect the marketer in a particular product sector, government statistics and information, etc. The growth of the World Wide Web together with related developments in information technology including, in particular, access to both internal and external databases is helping to facilitate the marketers' access to, and interpretation of, secondary data.

Many of the secondary data sources listed here are now available on-line via the Internet. Furthermore, the global reach of the World Wide Web means that marketers can now readily access sources of secondary data and information from virtually anywhere in the world. Clearly this is of particular interest to the marketer considering international markets. Below are listed just some examples of web-based information sources for international marketing:

http://www.europages.com	(European business directory)
http:www.eiv.com	(Survey of country reports and news)
http:www.dti.gov.uk	(UK government international trade and market information)
http://www.lexis-nexis.com	(International database with over 28 000 sources of international information)

These are just some examples of what is a wealth of on-line secondary information available to today's marketer. Admittedly, in some ways this is simply an extension of existing secondary information sources, but on-line information is obviously much easier and quicker to tap into. It also can be regularly updated so as to provide more accurate information for the marketer. A particularly good element of on-line secondary data information is the availability of databases on the net.

Databases and secondary marketing research

Developments in information technology have given an impetus to the growth and importance and use of databases. Simply stated, a database is a pool of extant data which the marketer can access, analyse and manipulate in order to produce information for marketing decision-making. The database may comprise of either internal—inhouse—data, external data or both. Marketers have, of course, used both internal and external databases for years. After all, a salesperson's filed reports on customer visits is effectively a database. Similarly, many of the secondary information sources available to marketers listed earlier are essentially external databases. What is different about the contemporary database and its usage is the sheer volume of data which can be accessed, analysed and utilized, together with the speed and level of detail which can now be achieved.

In the past, often access to large amounts of data, even if it were available, posed the marketer more problems than it solved in as much as the marketer could easily be over-whelmed by large amounts of data. Needless to say, it is access to cheap and powerful computers which have enabled the marketer to overcome this problem. So much so that coupled with powerful programs for analysing and manipulating data, modern information technology has served to put databases right at the centre of much of contemporary marketing research and marketing decision-making. Databases are now being used in every area of marketing including the following:

- Marketing planning and strategy
- Market segmentation and targeting
- Customer care and customer relationship management programs
- Direct market and marketing communications
- Pricing strategies

- Appraisal and selection of international markets
- Competitor analysis

Clearly as this list indicates there is now a wide range of uses for databases. It is perhaps not going too far to suggest that effective database management and use is now one of the most effective competitive weapons which a company can have. Databases can help the marketer to sense new needs and trends early thereby spotting problems and opportunities before competitors and developing pre-emptive marketing plans and strategies to stay ahead of them. Needless to say, these potential advantages of databases can only be achieved if the database systems are effectively designed and managed. It is not possible to describe all the facets of database design and management here, but we can outline some of the key considerations.

Starting with sources of information for databases. As already mentioned, database information can come from internal and external sources. Information can come from, for example, customer orders, subscription lists, loyalty cards, company salespersons, customer complaints and enquiries, traditional market research and databased companies that specialize in providing market and customer information. Again, we can see how it is possible to be overwhelmed by data. Successful database design requires that the following areas be addressed.

First of all, the marketer must set specific objectives for the database specifying the types of information required and more importantly why this is required. Systems for data capture can then be designed to provide this information including the identification of internal and external data sources. In the main, perhaps for obvious reasons, where possible, internal data should be used before considering external data sources. The database system should include appropriate systems for data storage including effective database maintenance. Finally, and most importantly, the database planner should provide adequate systems of analysis and interpretation designed to provide information for marketing decision-making.

Many companies are now realizing that much of the internal data which could be useful for marketing decision-making is often distributed in an *ad hoc* way around the organization in different departments. Sometimes, in fact, different departments each have their own databases which are never accessed or even known about by other parts of the organization. Recognition of this has led to some companies using what is referred to as 'data-warehousing' which means that all data on customers throughout the organization are collected and analysed in a central database within the company.

In managing a marketing database it is important to ensure that the database is regularly maintained. This is sometimes referred to by database practitioners as 'database cleaning'. Obviously if a database contains out-of-date or inaccurate information it not only becomes meaningless, but potentially disastrous. For example, unfortunately there have been many cases where mailshots have been sent to customers who are no longer living. Similarly, it can be upsetting for the 38-year-old to receive a Saga mailshot. Companies should regularly check the information held on databases to ensure that the database is as up to date and accurate as is possible.

PRIMARY RESEARCH

If secondary data do not provide sufficient information to satisfy research objections, primary data must then be collected. In this section primary data collection methods are considered under the following headings:

- Survey research
- Depth interviews and group discussion
- Observation
- Experimentation

Survey research

This is concerned with the administration of questionnaires, and is the most common method of collecting primary data for marketing decisions. When planning a survey, there are four major issues to be considered:

1. Selection of communication method (i.e. mail, telephone or personal survey)
2. Maximizing response to a survey
3. Questionnaire design
4. Phrasing of questions

Mail, telephone or personal survey   The general strengths and weaknesses of these three methods are summarized in Table 5.1. An important criterion not featured in this table is 'probable response rate', which is discussed later.

Postal questionnaires   The main attraction of postal questionnaires is their low cost. The cost will vary with the numbers involved—the more questionnaires, the less the cost per unit. When you take the cost of each item, i.e. paper, printing, pre-paid cards or envelopes, testing, recalls, etc., the cost per copy is much higher than might be first thought. Nevertheless, it is still possibly the cheapest method of all. Where an industrial population is geographically dispersed, the postal questionnaire has obvious attractions in time and money. If the sample to be taken is large, the postal questionnaire yields results more quickly than personal interviewing and is almost as quick as telephone interviewing, without the need for such a large staff. There can be no bias because there is no interviewer, and the respondent has the choice of remaining unknown.

TABLE 5.1   *Relative effectiveness of different research techniques*

Criterion	Mail	Telephone	Personal
1. Ability to handle complex questionnaires	Poor	Fair	Excellent
2. Ability to collect large amounts of data	Fair	Fair	Excellent
3. Accuracy on 'sensitive' questions	Good	Good	Fair
4. Control of interviewer effects (e.g. interviewer interaction; unintentional cues from interviewer)	Excellent	Fair	Poor
5. Speed	Poor	Excellent	Fair
6. Cost	Good (but now low response rate is a problem)	Good	Poor

There are, however, a number of disadvantages, the chief one of which is that there is no control over the person actually filling in the questionnaire. (An advantage of personal interviewing is that it can be highly structured.) Also, the respondent can read the complete questionnaire before filling it in, thus perhaps prejudicing his or her answers to early questions.

There are not many people who are prepared to sit down and complete a long questionnaire. The more questions one asks, the less response one is likely to obtain. Questions should be kept simple. Complex questions which cannot be explained should not be included. (Contrast this situation with personal interviewing.) Moreover, despite pre-testing and piloting of questions, misinterpretation on the part of the respondent does arise. A further disadvantage is that, whereas the whole essence of personal and telephone interviews is the chance to follow up leads, this is obviously impossible in the case of a postal questionnaire. Finally, non-response is a problem. You may never know why those who did not reply did not. One must also ask whether a high non-response will affect the sample.

There is some evidence to show that questionnaires mailed on Mondays and Tuesdays have a better chance of being completed and returned. When mailing interviews, certain rules should be adhered to:

1. *Personalize*   Use the respondent's name. Do not address to 'The Sales Manager' or 'The Marketing Director', etc.
2. *Sponsorship*   Use of the sponsor's name helps to promote confidence in the respondent's mind by allaying suspicion.
3. *Reason*   State the reason for the request and explain any use that will be made of information supplied.
4. *Anonymity*   If people are given the impression that they can remain anonymous, they will be more inclined to reply. This is the case when the respondent does not have to state a name or address.
5. *Confidentiality*   The letter and questionnaire often display the word 'confidential' when it comes from a named respondent. However, there is evidence that confidentiality is not strictly necessary as this guarantee seems to have little effect on response.
6. *Premiums*   If any premium is enclosed in order to stimulate interest and response, then its inclusion should be explained in the letter.
7. *Additional questionnaires*   If you are dealing with business firms, it is often desirable to enclose a second copy so that the firm can file it for its own purpose.
8. *Stamped addressed envelope*   This is an absolute necessity.

Telephone interviews   When time is short, the telephone is frequently the only medium. The number of calls that can be made in a day will depend upon your luck in finding the respondent in, his or her garrulousness, and on the number of questions you intend to ask.

The cost of a call will obviously vary with the length of time and distance involved. However, research organizations have found that the telephone method costs roughly 25 per cent of the personal method for similar types of survey. Almost all industrial firms are connected to the telephone. Even in the consumer market, the majority of households in the UK now have a telephone. If certain industries are widely scattered, the telephone is the best method of contacting an adequate sample.

The interview can be run on organized, structured lines without upsetting interviewees by showing them a long questionnaire. If a person selected does not turn out to be suitable, you can ask to be transferred to someone who *can* help.

There are, however, a number of disadvantages, including the fact that you cannot readily ask questions over the telephone the answers to which require a search of company records. The questions must be limited to those that can readily be answered without resort to company records or other research. Bias can arise on the part of the interviewer in similar fashion to personal interviewing. It can also be introduced in a quite different way; for example, if the telephone directory is used as a sampling frame, bias can be introduced in selection because a certain percentage of firms will be listed more than once.

Maximizing response   Error caused by a difference between those who respond to a survey and those who do not is termed non-response error. Non-response can involve the refusal to answer an entire questionnaire or just a particular question. It is one of the most significant problems faced by a survey researcher. In general, the lower the response rate to a survey, the higher is the probability of non-response error. However, a low response rate does not automatically mean that there have been non-response errors. Non-response error occurs only when a difference between the respondents and the non-respondents leads the researcher to an incorrect conclusion or decision.

In telephone and personal surveys, reply refusal and respondent non-availability are the major factors that reduce response rates. The number of 'not-availables' may usually be reduced by a series of callbacks at varying times. Refusal rates (the percentage of contacted respondents who refuse to participate) for telephone surveys can vary considerably. Interest in the survey topic is a primary factor in the cooperate–refuse decision. Prior communication with the interviewee by letter also helps to reduce the refusal rate. Attempts to increase the response rate to mail surveys focus on increasing the potential respondents' motivation to reply. As with telephone and personal surveys, the respondent's interest in the subject matter is a key factor. Response rates may usually be increased by offering token incentives to reply and sending reminder letters, which include another copy of the original questionnaire.

Questionnaire design   A questionnaire can be used to collect data on the respondent's behaviour (past, present or intended), demographic characteristics (age, sex, income, occupation), level of knowledge, attitudes and opinions. Before a questionnaire can be designed and used, answers are required to the following questions:

- What information is required?
- From whom is it required?
- Which method of communication will be used, i.e. mail, telephone or personal interview?
- Are all the questions really needed?
- Is each question sufficient to generate the required information? (Does the respondent have the information? Can the respondent find or remember the information? Is the respondent able to express his or her answer?)
- Will the respondent answer the question correctly? (Is the answer confidential or potentially embarrassing? Do the words used have the same meaning for all respondents? Are any of the words or phrases put in a leading way?)
- Are the questions in a logical sequence?

When designing a questionnaire the following guidelines should be applied:

- The overall questionnaire should move from topic to topic in a logical manner, with all questions on one topic completed before moving to the next.

- Sensitive questions, such as the respondent's income, should be at the end.
- The first few questions should be simple, objective and interesting.
- The questionnaire should be designed so as to minimize recording errors and assist analysis.
- The questionnaire should be pre-tested with respondents similar to those who will be included in the final survey.

Question phrasing   There are three types of question format: direct questions, attitude questions and indirect questions.

Direct questions   The direct question format may be subdivided into open and closed questions. Open questions allow the respondent to answer in his own words. Closed questions include all possible answers, and the respondent makes a choice from among them. Closed questions may be dichotomous or multiple-choice. Dichotomous questions allow only two responses; such as 'yes–no', 'agree–disagree' and 'male–female'. The two responses of dichotomous questions are often supplemented by a third neutral category such as 'don't know'. Multiple-choice questions allow three or more responses. To clarify the various types of direct questions, here are some examples:

Open	'Why did you stop travelling by train?'
Closed—dichotomous	'Do you like travelling by train?'
	Yes ☐
	No ☐
Closed—multiple-choice	'What is your favourite method of travelling to work?'
	Car ☐
	Bus ☐
	Train ☐
	Walking ☐
	Bicycle ☐
	Other ☐

Open questions have the advantage that the respondent is not influenced by stated response categories. The major disadvantages of open questions are respondents' difficulties in articulating answers; interviewers' difficulties are in recording answers, introduction of bias through probing, and the complexity of categorizing answers.

Closed questions have two main advantages: they are easier for the respondent and interviewer, and they aid questionnaire analysis. Closed questions have two disadvantages: research is required to ensure that a comprehensive range of alternative responses is presented, and considerable skill is required to ensure that the presentation of alternative responses does not sometimes stimulate response bias.

To benefit from the advantages of both open and closed questions, researchers will often use open questions in preliminary research situations. Feedback from this preliminary research is then used to formulate closed questions for a final and more extensive survey.

Attitude questions   Consumer attitudes and opinions help to predict their function behaviour, and for this reason collection of this type of data is of vital importance to marketers. Attitude data may be collected using direct or indirect questions. We shall discuss some of the direct questioning scales used, of which there are four types, for the direct questioning of attitudes. These scales are the non-comparative rating scale, the comparative rating scale, the semantic differential scale and the Likert scale, which can be most easily explained using examples.

Non-comparative rating scale   How would you rate the taste of
Furgekin Lager?

5	4	3	2	1
Probably the best	Very good, I like it	All right, neither good nor bad	Not at all good, I do not like it	Probably the worst

This scale is non-comparative, as the respondent has not been asked to compare one product with another.

Comparative rating scale   How do you like the taste of
Bonzo compared to Gonzo?

5	4	3	2	1
Vastly superior	Superior	Neither superior nor inferior	Inferior	Vastly inferior

Semantic differential scale   What are your opinions of the Vega Estate car?
Please tick the box that best describes your opinions.

	Extremely	Very	Some- what	Neither nor	Some- what	Very	Extremely	
Fast	☐	☐	☐	☐	☐	☐	☐	Slow
Good	☐	☐	☐	☐	☐	☐	☐	Bad
Large	☐	☐	☐	☐	☐	☐	☐	Small
Inexpensive	☐	☐	☐	☐	☐	☐	☐	Expensive

Likert scale   The Vega Anglian is the best small car on the market.
Do you . . .

Strongly agree	Agree	Neither agree nor disagree	Disagree	Strongly disagree
☐	☐	☐	☐	☐

Research has shown that when the various scaling techniques have been compared the results have been similar across all techniques.[3] Therefore, the selection of a scaling technique will depend largely upon the information that is to be collected.

Piloting the questionnaire   Before a questionnaire is ready for final use in the field, it needs to be pre-tested under field conditions. The questionnaire is piloted to discover if there are any problems in the areas we have been discussing. A small number of respondents, representative of the types of respondent to be interviewed in the actual survey, are selected and the questionnaire tried out on them.

The findings of a pilot survey regarding the product will not be included in the final report. These interviews are conducted not to test the product, but to test the efficiency of the questionnaire. The researchers are examining the ease with which the question-naire elicits the required information:

- Are some of the questions superfluous?
- Should others be added to get a fuller picture?
- Are the questions clear enough to be understood by the public at large?

In the nature of things, it is not practicable to try out the draft questionnaire on a large and elaborately selected sample. Nevertheless, the pilot survey must be undertaken under actual conditions with people representative of those who will finally be inter-viewed. To try out the questionnaire on members of the Market Research Department, for instance, would give a distorted answer, as the reactions of specialists in this field are likely to be quite different from those of the public at large. Instead, interviewers will go out and put the questions to passers-by in the street, or will call on various households taken at random, with the aim of getting a cross-section of informants approximately similar to that selected for the actual survey.

Panel research   A panel refers to a group of respondents who have agreed to provide information over a period of time. In effect, panel research is continuous survey research. Panels are normally operated by research agencies rather than by individual organizations. Two of the most common types of panel operated are retail audits and consumer panels.

Retail audits   A retail audit (such as that produced by A. C. Neilsen Company) records sales to consumers through a panel of retail outlets. The estimate of consumer sales is based on observations. It is arrived at as follows:

$$\begin{array}{c}\text{Opening stock}\\ \text{for period}\\ \text{(checked at}\\ \text{last audit)}\end{array} + \begin{array}{c}\text{Net}\\ \text{deliveries}\\ \text{since}\\ \text{last audit}\end{array} - \begin{array}{c}\text{Stock}\\ \text{held at}\\ \text{present}\\ \text{audit}\end{array} = \begin{array}{c}\text{Sales to}\\ \text{consumers}\\ \text{during}\\ \text{period}\end{array}$$

The information obtained from such an audit is sold to manufacturers, who can see how their brands are performing alongside others. The reports issued to such subscribers include information such as the following:

- Retail purchases by brand and by product.
- Retail stocks by brand and by product.
- Consumer sales by brand and by product.
- Percentage of shops handling the product.
- Percentage of shops out of stock of various brands.
- Retail and wholesale prices of various products.
- Average size of retail order from average retailer.
- Proportion of retailers buying direct from manufacturers and from wholesalers.
- Display material, promotions and advertising carried out for individual brands.

The advantages of an audit of retail sales are as follows:

1. It is factual research, based on the actual stock levels and examination of sales. It is therefore not distorted by likes, dislikes, prejudices or the wish to please, which is so often the pitfall of interview research.

2. It provides the manufacturer with a continuous picture of a constantly changing market.

3. It shows the manufacturer its position in relation to competitors and to the trade in general.

4. Seasonal variations and other fluctuations in consumer behaviour can be observed, and the effect of such things as price changes, special offers and advertising campaigns can be assessed.

5. The manufacturer can base its selling tactics on a knowledge of the effects of various factors, not only on its own products but also on those of its competitors.

Disadvantages are:

1. A retail audit shows the picture only at those retail outlets that are taking part in the scheme, and their selection is not random. Only some shops wish to cooperate, so important types of outlet can be left out if they are among those unwilling to participate. Retail outlets that generally refuse to cooperate usually sell a high proportion of 'own-label' merchandise, and do not want their success (or otherwise) to become public knowledge.

2. Retail audits can be expensive and time-consuming.

3. They tell only part of the story. An audit of retail sales will not reveal the reasons for sales patterns, and there is still a great deal of research to be carried out to ascertain such underlying factors.

Developments in retail technology and audit data   It has already been mentioned that retail audits are carried out by people from the research agency conducting a regular physical audit in a selection of retail outlets. However, new developments in retail technology are starting to have an effect on the way sales data are collected at the retail level. The development of computerized checkout points combined with the bar-coding of products, particularly in the area of packaged grocery, has meant that retail audit companies are able to assess accurate sales figures from retail outlets via on-line computer terminals from head office, without the necessity of actually visiting the store and carrying out a physical stock-take.

These developments do not remove entirely the need for researchers to visit stores, as some of the information can only be recorded through human observation, but they have made the whole retail audit task more efficient and less inconvenient to the stores taking part. Such developments have also reduced the cost of such research to the end-users.

Consumer panels   Consumer panels are typically used to study media exposure and purchasing behaviour. Data are gathered using diaries (data entered by respondents), regular telephone surveys, or increasingly, direct links via a computer.

A consumer panel consists of a reasonably permanent set of consumers, usually a sample of housewives, selected on a purposive basis to represent accurately a cross-section of housewives in the country.

In the UK, the Attwood Consumer Panel consists of 5000 housewives in Great Britain and 500 housewives in Northern Ireland. Members of the panel are defined by age, ACORN class (dealt with in detail in Chapter 4), social class and district. Each member of the panel is given a diary in which she records information.

The housewife reports the information concerning the product in her 'diary'. For example:

● Brand name and description

● Number of items bought

● Size and weight of each item and price

- Day of purchase
- Type of outlet
- Full description of any 'special offer'
- Information on flavour of product, type and colour of container, if applicable

The housewife returns the diary to the market research organization weekly. The market research organization sells reports of this activity to individual manufacturers. The diaries are intended to reveal:

- The performance of brands
- The total number of people buying specific products
- Sales volume by type of shop and geographic area
- The effect of promotions, price changes or competition
- Consumer purchasing patterns concerning brand switching

Probably the most important single advantage of the panel design is that it is analytical. The panel involves collecting data from the same individual over time, and from this one can note the specific individuals who change or do not change, e.g. those who switch to different brands and those who are loyal to a specific brand. From this, one can determine the kind of person who changes brands and the kind who does not change. This can suggest the segment of the population on which promotion effort can most successfully be concentrated. The timing of such changes may help in the formulation of hypotheses as to the reasons for the change.

As panels are maintained over a period of time, it enables one to introduce new products, change advertising strategy, alter the price, etc., and observe any change in behaviour and purchasing patterns on the part of the panel members. In other words, what alterations in the marketing mix can one make in order to increase sales?

Much more detailed data can be gathered about panel members than would be the case for a one-off sample of respondents. Panel members often submit to long interviews, at the end of which the research organization will have collected a large volume of classification data. Furthermore, as the same individuals are involved in the 'before' and 'after' measurements, small changes can be identified more easily than if separate studies were made using two independent but comparable samples.

In addition, if panel members record their purchases or viewing habits during or immediately after the event, the information gained will tend to be more accurate than if an interviewer inquired about the purchase or programmes a day, a week, or a month later.

Well-run consumer panels using continuous reporting diaries can yield reasonably accurate projections of total retail sales of a variety of consumer products.

With regard to the cost factor, there can be advantages and disadvantages. If data are required at frequent intervals, it is cheaper to maintain a continuous panel than to select a new sample at each interval. If the data are required less frequently, this advantage may turn into a disadvantage.

As panel members have agreed to cooperate on projects as they come along, data can frequently be obtained from them by mail with close to 100 per cent response—and, of course, it is much cheaper than collecting information by personal interview.

Panel members may be divided into control and experimental groups, e.g. those who have satellite television and those who do not. This can aid the interpretation of the effect of introducing experiment variables.

Panels are without doubt invaluable for the study of trends over time periods and for the accumulation of data over time. Casual relationships can be better studied. More information can be obtained through cooperative effort.

There are, however, disadvantages with consumer panels, the principal one of which is that membership involves cooperating with a research organization continuously or at regular intervals. As this no doubt involves some effort, many individuals will decline to serve on panels. This raises the question of whether the sample can be truly representative of the population being studied, irrespective of whether the sample corresponds with the population on certain selected characteristics. In order to offset this, panels do pay members in money or merchandise; but this raises the further question of whether or not premiums attract a special type of panel member.

It is often assumed that both the highest and lowest social classes are under-represented on panels. Furthermore, the kind of people attracted to panels, even when selected by the quota sampling method, tend to be the more intelligent, literate and expressive section of the population.

Unfortunately, panel members die, move away, or just quit. They are replaced by new members with similar characteristics as far as these are known, but the probability is always present that the replacements differ from the original group in some significant, but unknown, way. There is evidence that those who have the least interest in the subject under study are most apt to drop out.

Response errors by panel members are usually thought to result from change of habits, self-consciousness, development of 'expertise', attempts by the panel members to 'look good', the bias of boredom or annoyance from repeated interviews or continuous reporting, failure to keep diaries on a current basis, and fatigue from completing long questionnaires or diaries.

The actions of new members to the panel are often atypical in that there is a tendency to increase the activity that is being recorded, e.g. television viewing or food purchasing. To eliminate the effects of this bias, data from new members are excluded from final results for four to six weeks.

After some time as a member of a panel, the individual may begin to think of him- or herself as an 'expert' and act accordingly, at the expense of acting normally. Other panel members may try to 'look good' by buying higher priced goods or shopping at high-class stores. However, these actions are found not to be of crucial significance, as often the first report of the panel member is discounted.

Once the novelty of panel membership wears off, interest can decline and cooperation tends to become mechanical. Diaries may be filled out just before they are sent in. Regular submission of diaries and forms is often lacking.

There must be constant vigilance of the tendency to develop a 'panel sophistication'; i.e. constant interviewing may lead to specially conditioned responses. Furthermore, control must be exercised over what is known as 'socially acceptable' responses.

There is a variety of panel types available. Some of the most frequently used are the continuous consumer purchasing panels, short-term consumer purchasing panels, television viewing panels, consumer product consumption panels, shopping panels and product testing panels.

Brand barometers   This is a service offered by market research firms to subscribers on a quarterly basis. Brand barometers each cover a particular market; for example, the private motorist brand barometer and grocer brands barometer, etc. While the subject covered by the inquiry remains the same, the informants are chosen at random for each quarterly survey.

In each type barometer, a range of products is chosen. For instance, one barometer covers pet foods, bread, cleaning materials, butter, cooking fats, etc. The questions basically ask informants whether they buy each commodity, and if so when, what brand, and at what type of shop. The data are analysed into regions, age groups, ACORN and social class.

Omnibus surveys   Omnibus surveys are organized by a research agency on behalf of several clients rather than a single client. As clients participate in a single survey, interviewers ask different questions, but to the same sample of people. The costs of the survey are divided between them. Each client receives only the answers and analysis relating to his or her own questions, and there is exactly the same degree of confidentiality as with an *ad hoc* study.

This type of survey is particularly suitable where a client needs original research, but only needs to ask a limited number of questions, as costs are usually based on the number of questions asked. Other factors which usually govern the cost per client are the proportion of the total sample available that the client wants to access. If the whole sample is not required, and the types of questions required are open-ended, then questions are likely to be more expressive.

There are several large, general omnibus surveys available, plus quite a wide variety of specialized ones. Specialist ones concentrate on particular types of product or customer. Anyone considering using an omnibus survey is advised to look at recent issues of the Market Research Society's newsletter, as this carries advertisements to recruit clients for omnibus surveys.

Personal interviews

If it is decided to conduct a series of interviews, one should do everything possible at the desk research stage before going out into the field. There are two basic reasons for this:

1. It is desirable to have some knowledge of the background to the discussions that will take place in the field.
2. Many executives do not have time to examine trends and ascertain the state of the market in five or ten years' time, but a market researcher, with a knowledge of market forecasting, can indicate to the respondent the way he or she thinks the market is going to move.

Before embarking on the main programme of visits, it is advisable to undertake some pilot visits to test out the questionnaire, the area of investigation, which respondents in a company to interview, etc.

Interviewers' characteristics   The characteristics of a prospective interviewer warrant analysis. In the industrial market, the interviewer will have to be somebody who is going to be acceptable at all levels, from foreman to managing director. In general terms (and this includes interviewing in the consumer market), he or she needs to be a good mixer and have a pleasant personality, because interviewers are likely to confront people who may be uncommunicative, hostile or suspicious.

General approach   In the industrial market, it is advisable *not* to produce a tightly written questionnaire, filling it in point by point when talking to senior officials in companies. This approach can cause antagonism. One should really begin with a general discussion. The use of an *aide-mémoire*, with ten or so key areas for discussion, is advisable.

Whereas industrial interviewing has necessarily to be much more in the nature of a discussion, in consumer interviewing a structured questionnaire is often used.

There are several advantages to be gained by employing the personal interview method:

- It permits a longer questionnaire with more comprehensive questions, and the interviewer can clear up any misunderstandings as they arise.

- Complex questions can therefore be used.

- The interviewer can probe the respondent, thereby eliciting further useful information.

- It is possible to assess the validity of some answers by observation, e.g. answers on personal details—age, education, income. The researcher can check whether answers are in line with obvious visual facts.

- The rate of response to a personal interview is higher; in effect, it reduces non-response.

There are also some disadvantages:

- It can be expensive.

- It requires a great deal of technical and administrative planning and supervision.

- Bias on the part of the interviewer can arise in the interview.

Depth interviews and group discussions—qualitative data

Much survey research is concerned with the collection of quantitative data. That is data that, for the most part, can be objectively and quantitatively measured, evaluated and manipulated. It is concerned with issues such as, for example, 'how many' or 'how large' or with 'what rate of growth', etc. Marketers though are also interested in more subjective elements such as, for example, how customers feel, what their underpinning attitudes are, or even the innermost fears and hopes of customers. Information of this more subjective, non-quantified type is not surprisingly usually referred to as 'qualitative data' and it is the collection of this type of data which the primary data collection methods of depth interviews and group discussions are particularly well suited. Another group of research techniques which have also been developed specifically for the collection of qualitative data are those techniques which have come to be known under the heading of 'motivation research'. This group of techniques is considered later in the chapter.

Depth interviews normally involve either one face-to-face respondent (individual depth interview) or a group of 5–25 respondents (group discussions).

In the individual depth interview, the interviewer has a list of subjects of interest as opposed to a structured questionnaire. He or she is free to create questions and probe responses in greater depth.

Individual depth interviews are particularly useful in the following situations:

- Where the subject matter is of a confidential or potentially embarrassing nature.

- Where a highly detailed understanding of complicated behaviour on decision-making patterns (e.g. planning the family holiday) is required. This is usually the case in industrial/organizational research problems where executives are interviewed on a one-to-one basis.

Group discussions (or focus groups) are often used for

- Generating ideas for new product concepts and new products.

- Exploring consumer response to promotional and packaging ideas.

● Conducting preliminary research prior to carrying out a more structured survey, e.g. to establish consumer knowledge and vocabulary.

Group discussions are normally recorded (on audio or video tape) or viewed 'live' by the client (possibly behind a one-way mirror). The researcher is responsible for leading the discussion, probing interesting comments and preparing a summary of the group's major comments. The major advantage of group discussions over individual interviews is that the interaction process tends to generate more information than could be derived from individuals separately.

It is probably fair to say that the use of focus groups on marketing research has been one of the fastest growing types of marketing research technique in recent years. Although developed as far back as the 1950s, it was during the 1980s that they began to be used extensively by marketers. In the 1990s, and for the foreseeable future, focus group interviews look set to remain one of the most widely used types of marketing research. Focus groups are now used in situations and product markets as diverse as consumer packaged goods, through to financial services, and industrial products. In the UK, focus groups were used extensively by the Labour Party in the run up to their success in the 1997 General Election and were used to monitor voter attitudes and perceptions on a regular basis, the information being used to develop policies and also to react quickly to any changes in, for example, voter perception, 'hot issues', etc. Focus groups are now used by all the major political parties in the UK on an ongoing basis.

Traditionally focus group interviews were used to determine and structure quantitative studies, and in particular the design of questionnaires. Increasingly, however, focus group interviews are now used to investigate further, issues highlighted through initial quantitative studies. Focus group interviewing and the analysis of focus group information is now much more sophisticated than it was even five years ago as market researchers have learned how to utilize the technique better. Focus group interviews are now often designed involving respondents in the design process itself and also post-focus group debriefing will often now include participants to check their reactions, hence improving validity and reliability. An interesting development in focus group techniques is the use of information technology and specifically of course the computer to facilitate three-party (or more) discussions. So, for example, the focus group might involve, say, existing customers, distributors, and past customers, in interactive group discussions using electronic information interchange.

Certainly, focus groups are not cheap to conduct, an average today would be approximately between £1000 and £1600 per group. However, marketers have found that focus groups offer potentially 'very rich' information for improving marketing decision-making.

There are, however, two problems with both individual and group interviews. First, they can be biased, as respondents are normally given an incentive to participate. Second, sample sizes are small and often non-representative. As with projective techniques and open questions, depth interviews are an excellent tool for preliminary research, but results from them normally require validation by more extensive and structured research.

Observational research

An ice-cream manufacturer was concerned that sales of some of its products were not achieving the levels that had been expected (based on survey research). A direct observation study in a sample of shops revealed why. The ice-cream was kept in top-loading refrigerators with sides that were so high that many of the children could not see in to pick out the products they wanted. A picture display was devised for the side of the cabinet to enable the children to recognize each product and to indicate their choice by pointing to it. Sales increased.[4]

Observational research includes viewing and listening to situations. It also encompasses recording human behaviour with monitoring instruments.

Personal observation is used when it would be impossible or expensive to obtain data through a survey. Examples include:

- Monitoring traffic flow both inside and outside a shop.
- Studying a retail outlet (e.g. display methods, prices and customer flows).
- Viewing competitors' products at an exhibition.
- Viewing product usage by, say, children.

Monitoring instruments are sometimes preferable to personal observations for reasons of accuracy, cost or for functional reasons. Examples of their use include:

- Monitoring traffic flow through a district.
- Monitoring television viewing habits.
- Monitoring physiological reactions to promotional and packaging ideas. Physiological measures are measurements of physical responses (including eye movement, brain-wave analysis, perspiration rate, eye pupil size) to a stimulus such as an advertisement.

Computer-assisted interviewing   This technique once used to be regarded as a gimmick with which to impress clients. However, it is increasingly now part of the contemporary market researcher's toolbox for collecting interview data. The advantage, of course, is that results can be analysed almost instantly. Today researchers can now use 'computer clipboards' wherein responses to questions can actually be punched into the computer clipboard. An instant read-out can then be achieved and, of course, the results downloaded for central computing. There is little doubt, as with all other aspects of the computer, that computer-aided personal interviewing (or 'CAPI' as it is often referred to in the trade) together with computer-aided telephone interviewing (CATI) will continue to grow. Other facets of new technology in primary data collection, analysis and application are considered in more detail later in the chapter.

Experimentation

Experimentation involves the manipulation of one or more variables by the experimenter in such a way that its effect on another variable can be determined, e.g. manipulating price in order that its effect on sales can be determined.

Marketing experiments may be conducted in the field or in a 'laboratory' situation.

Field experimentation is also known as 'test marketing'. This involves the replication of the planned national marketing programme for a product in one or more limited market sectors. Marketing mix variables are manipulated in an attempt to identify the optimal marketing mix for the national launch. Test marketing is not limited to new products. It can be used to evaluate price changes, new packages, variations in distribution strategy or alternative advertising strategies.

In laboratory experimentation, an environment is simulated (e.g. home or shopping environment) and the environment is used to test consumer reactions to new products, packaging, displays or advertising themes.

Types of errors affecting experimental results In order for an experiment to be useful, care must be taken to ensure that all sources of error are minimized. Such possible sources of error include:

- *Motivation* Respondents may alter their responses to a specific stimulant over a period of time, irrespective of external events. For example, in a prolonged 'taste testing' experiment, respondents may develop more sophisticated palates as the experiment progresses and this may affect their response to a particular flavour.

- *Exogenous occurrences* These are events not controlled by the experimenter, e.g. competitive actions and macro-environmental changes.

- *Selection* Selection error occurs when the groups formed for the purposes of the experiment are unequal.

- *Instrument variability* This refers to changes in the measuring instrument over time. These changes are most likely to occur when the measurement process involves people, either as observers or interviewers; their interest and professionalism may cease or become better as time passes.

- *Lost respondents* After a period of time, respondents in an experiment may refuse to continue their participation. The experimental results at a later stage in the experiment may not be representative of what might have emerged had all the original respondents been present.

- *Experiment effect* The fact that an experiment is being conducted often has an important effect on the respondents. Even pre-measurement can, by alerting the subjects to the topic of study, cause them to change behaviour.

Rodger[5] provides a more detailed discussion on experimental design and shows how this can measure the impact of a single variable or several variables.

Once the optimum research method has been selected, the researcher must decide who and where to study. This decision process normally involves a sampling procedure. After data have been collected, the researcher must analyse and report research findings. Sampling, data analysis and research reporting are discussed in the next section.

SAMPLING, DATA ANALYSIS AND RESEARCH APPLICATIONS

Sampling

Sampling is a necessary and inescapable part of human affairs. Each of us samples and is regularly sampled. We sample the performance of a new car by a test drive, a wine by a few sips and a new acquaintance by an initial meeting.

It is sometimes possible and practical to take a *census*; that is, to study each member of the population of interest. This is sometimes the situation in industrial market research situations where the number of companies to be investigated is small. More often than not, however, a *sample* is taken because of cost, time, accuracy and research considerations. Cost and time benefits are obvious, but the last two reasons require explanation:

- *Research effect* The purpose of marketing research is to collect data about markets: not to influence markets. Yet responding to survey questions forces the respondent to examine his or her attitudes towards the survey topic. This examination may lead to a change in behaviour.

To minimize the occurrence of behavioural changes, a sample is sometimes preferable to a census.

- *Accuracy*   As sample size increases, the occurrence of non-sampling errors may also increase. Non-sampling errors include errors in data collection and analysis.

Five criteria are important when evaluating *sample frames*, or target populations:

1. *Adequacy*.
2. *Completeness*   All the units of population under survey should be represented, and proportionately so.
3. *Accuracy*   Totally up-to-date sampling frames are rarely available. The frame may contain units that no longer exist, e.g. the Electoral Register will contain people who have moved house.
4. *Duplication*   Bias will occur where names of sampling units occur more than once, e.g. some firms may have multiple listings in telephone directories.
5. *Convenience*   Sampling lists should be accessible and suitable for sampling purposes.

The sampling process consists of three steps:

1. Specify the target population.
2. Select the sampling method.
3. Determine the sample size.

Specifying the target population   The target population, or frame, is that part of the total population (universe) to which the study is directed. For example, for a company selling cars in the UK, the universe could be the entire UK population plus foreign visitors, and the frame might be people aged 18 or over. Elements (e.g. prospective respondents) from the target population are selected using reference material (including directories and maps) or after preliminary questioning or observation.

Selecting the sampling method   Five basic choices must be made when deciding on a sampling method:

1. *Random v. non-random sampling*   In random samples, each member of the target population has a fixed (often equal) probability of being a member of the target sample. Random samples have to be sufficiently large to ensure that all sections of the population are surveyed. In non-random (also known as *purposive* or *quota*) samples, on the other hand, respondents are selected to fit a quota designed to mirror relevant characteristics of the population, and in this way fewer respondents are required.

A random sample design has two advantages. First, a statistical relationship exists between the sample estimates and population. Second, the composition of the sample is not affected by interviewer likes and dislikes. These two benefits have made random sample designs particularly useful for surveys that are politically sensitive.

A non-random sample may be as reliable as a random sample if the following requirements are met:

- Up-to-date statistics relating to the structure of the population are available.
- Classification questions are carefully designed.
- The interviewer's selection of respondents is carefully controlled.

In a *simple random sample*, every individual in the target population has an equal chance of being drawn. Each individual is allocated a number and the sample can be drawn using random number tables. This method is equivalent to the classic lottery where names are placed in a hat and drawn out randomly.

In a *systematic random sample*, a random starting-point is selected and every Nth unit in the frame is drawn where:

$$N = \frac{\text{Population size}}{\text{Sample size}}.$$

This method is quicker and cheaper than simple random sampling as the procedure involving random number tables is avoided.

2. *Single-stage v. multi-stage sampling*   If a survey population is large and widely dispersed, a probability sample will often be drawn in more than one stage. For example, a survey of voters could be sampled first by constituencies, then polling districts, then the register of electors. Multi-stage sample ensures that interview calls are not too widely dispersed.

3. *Single-unit v. cluster sampling*   In single-unit sampling, each sampling unit is selected separately; in cluster sampling the units are selected in groups; e.g. a household might be a single unit but a street would be a cluster. Cluster sampling has the advantage of reducing interviewing costs, but within-cluster variability may be low.

4. *Unstratified v. stratified sampling*   A stratum in a population is a segment of that population having one or more common characteristics, e.g. companies with a turnover of £5 million–£10 million annually. Stratified random sampling involves treating each stratum as a separate sub-population for sampling purposes. The reasons for stratifying a population for sampling purposes are:

- It may help to ensure representativeness (and thus reduce sampling error).
- The required sample size for the same level of sampling error will usually be smaller than for a non-stratified sample.

Stratification is commonly used in industrial marketing research. In consumer research, details of strata are not normally readily available, e.g. individuals' incomes. The ACORN[6] method (a classification of residential neighbourhoods) does enable some stratified random sampling in consumer research. It provides 11 classifications of residential neighbourhoods according to type of housing.

5. *Proportionate v. disproportionate sampling*   In proportionate sampling an equal percentage of respondents is sampled for each stratum. In disproportionate sampling a small (but important) stratum is over-sampled but restored to its due weight when considering total results. Disproportionate samples are, therefore, most cost-effective.

Determining sample size   In determining sample size, there are two major considerations:

- Research budget available.
- Degree of precision required.

Research budget   Based purely on resources available, sample size may be calculated using the following formula:

$$\text{Sample size} = \frac{\text{Total budget} - \text{research planning, analysis and reporting costs}}{\text{Variable cost per interview (or observation)}}.$$

Precision required For random samples, there is a statistical relationship between sample estimates and population values. Using probability theory, we are able to relate precision required to sample size. The larger the sample size, the more confident the researcher can be that the results are representative of the population. If the level of precision required can be specified in advance, it is possible to determine the minimum required sample size. This sample size refers to the number of usable responses, and allowance should be made for the likely non-response level. A more detailed discussion of sampling accuracy is given by Rodger,[7] who explains the statistical methodology behind sample size determination.

Editing and coding responses After data collection the next step is to edit illegible, incomplete and inconsistent responses. There are three ways to deal with imperfect responses:

1. *Ask the respondent to clarify response* This is usually avoided except in the case of surveys with a small sample size and a high level of imperfect responses.

2. *Use responses* This approach is often used by research agencies as they are often committed to obtaining a certain number of responses. Tabulation can keep track of non-responses as a separate category. Inconsistent responses might be assumed to average out over the sample.

3. *Discard responses* The researcher may judge that the end results will be more useful if incomplete responses are discarded.

For small studies (less than 25 respondents), it is possible to conduct analysis manually, provided only basic analysis is required. Data from large studies are coded prior to computer input.

The process of coding involves converting responses to code values on coding sheets. Coding sheets are normally 80 columns wide and one or more column is allocated to each survey question. Each line (horizontal) of the sheet is devoted to one respondent. Closed questions may be *pre-coded*; that is, a code is allocated to each possible response before the survey. Responses to open questions are normally grouped into convenient categories and a code is allocated to each category after the survey.

Figure 5.2 illustrates a typical coding procedure. Two commonly employed conversions are used in this example:

- Possible responses are coded from left to right beginning with 1.
- Non-responses are normally coded 9.

It can thus be seen how the system works from the questionnaire to the coding sheet, and thereafter for computer punching. In this particular example, the partial toothpaste questionnaire has been hypothetically filled in, and the partial coding sheet has been filled in from the response on this questionnaire.

Data analysis

After input to the computer, it is often desirable to create new variables. Two types of new variable may be created:

- *Combination of variables* For example, data on a respondent's age, marital status and children may be combined to generate a new variable called 'stage in the family life cycle'.
- *Introduction of secondary data*

Basic analysis Marketing research analysis usually involves simple tabulation, calculation of summarizing and cross-tabulation.

Sampling tabulation involves calculating the number and percentage of respondents who choose each of the available answers. Table 5.2 provides an example of simple tabulation. In this example an adjusted frequency discards data that are missing as a result of non-responsive or incorrect coding.

There are two kinds of *summarizing statistics*. The first provides measures of the mid-point of the distribution and is known as *measures of central tendency*. The second gives an indication of the amount of variation in the data comprising the distribution and is known as *measures of dispersion*.

Mean, mode and median are the major measures of central tendency, and the reader is again directed to Rodger[8] for a detailed discussion of their computation.

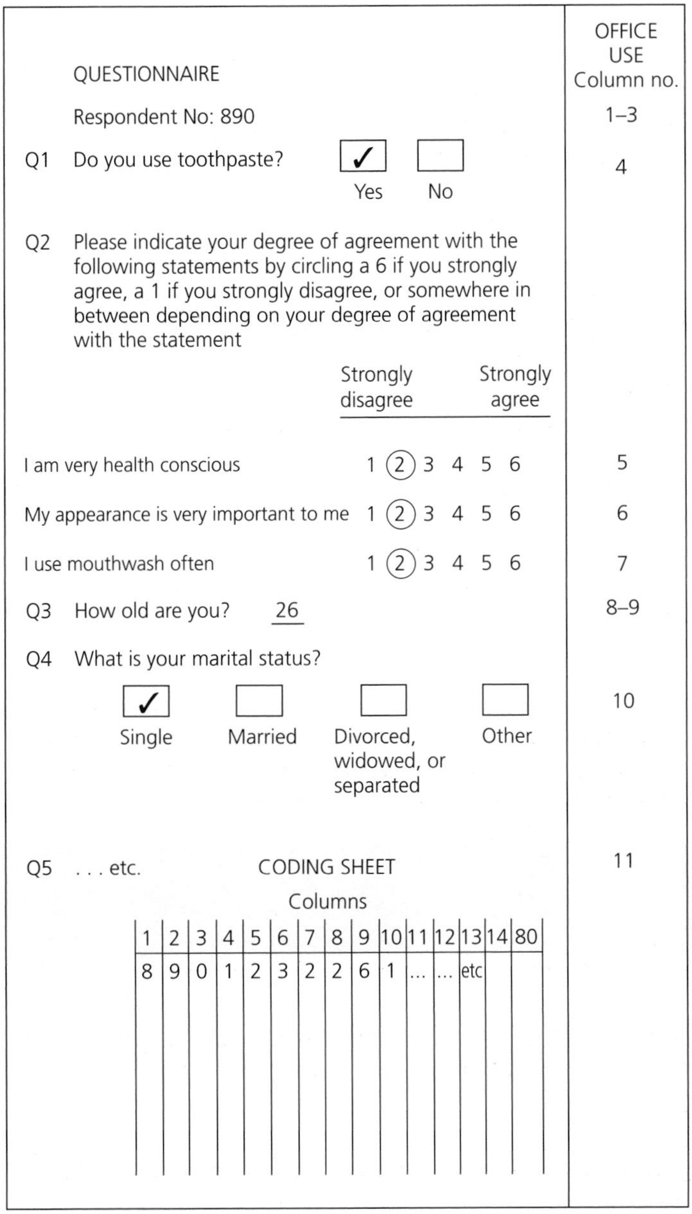

FIGURE 5.2

Coding procedure

QUESTIONNAIRE	OFFICE USE Column no.
Respondent No: 890	1–3
Q1 Do you use toothpaste? ✓ Yes ☐ No	4
Q2 Please indicate your degree of agreement with the following statements by circling a 6 if you strongly agree, a 1 if you strongly disagree, or somewhere in between depending on your degree of agreement with the statement	
	Strongly disagree — Strongly agree	
I am very health conscious 1 ②3 4 5 6	5
My appearance is very important to me 1 ②3 4 5 6	6
I use mouthwash often 1 ②3 4 5 6	7
Q3 How old are you? 26	8–9
Q4 What is your marital status? ✓ Single ☐ Married ☐ Divorced, widowed, or separated ☐ Other	10
Q5 ... etc.	11

CODING SHEET

Columns

1	2	3	4	5	6	7	8	9	10	11	12	13	14	80
8	9	0	1	2	3	2	2	6	1	...	...	etc		

Cross-tabulation involves constructing a table so that responses to two or more questions may be compared. Table 5.3 provides a cross-tabulation example produced using the SPSS(X)[9] software package. Here the response to a question on income groups is compared to the response to a question on weekly food expenditure.

Measurement scales   The various ways of phrasing questions have been outlined earlier. From an analysis viewpoint, it is useful to categorize questioning/measurement scales into four groups.

Nominal scales   Nominal scales are used to categorize responses. For example, the number 1 is assigned to female respondents and number 0 to male respondents. Nominal scales may be used to calculate the number (or percentage or frequency) of items falling within each category. The calculation of median for nominal data is meaningless, but the mode may be calculated.

Ordinal scales   Ordinal scales are used to rank items. For example, a consumer is asked to rank his or her performance for brands A, B and C. In this example, if the consumer ranks B as his or her preferred brand, an ordinal scale will not reveal how much more the consumer prefers brand B to brands A and C. An ordinal scale may be used to calculate frequency, mode and median, but not mean.

Interval scales   An interval scale where intervals on the scale are equal distances. For example, respondents are asked to state their degree of agreement or disagreement with a statement by selecting a response from a list such as:

1. Agree very strongly
2. Agree fairly strongly
3. Agree
4. Undecided
5. Disagree
6. Disagree fairly strongly
7. Disagree very strongly

Virtually the entire range of statistical analysis can be applied to interval scales, including frequency, mean, median, mode, range and standard deviation.

TABLE 5.2   *Simple tabulation*

Age of respondent	Absolute frequency	Relative frequency (%)	Adjusted frequency (%)	Cumulative frequency (%)
0–17	1	1.9	1.9	1.9
18–40	20	37.7	38.5	40.4
41–64	21	39.6	40.4	80.8
65+	10	18.9	19.2	100.0
Not ascertained	1	1.9	(missing)	100.0
	53	100.0	100.0	100.0

Ratio scales A ratio scale is an interval scale with a zero point. Simple counting of any set of objects produces a ratio scale. Thus, sales, costs and number of purchasers are all ratio scales. Ratio scales allow, in addition to the analysis permitted by interval scales, some specialized calculations.

Interval and ratio scales can thus be subjected to more analytical procedures, and hence they are easier to analyse.

More complete analyses Most marketing research analysis is limited to the basic analytical procedures described. However, IT now enables more complex analytical procedures to be used by marketers. Many of these procedures are concerned with analysing the degree of association (or relationship) between two or more variables. Pearson's correlation coefficient is the most common formula employed.[10]

Research reporting The results of a research project may be reported in written or oral format, or both. The importance of effective reporting cannot be overemphasized. Regardless of the quality of the research process and the accuracy and usefulness of the

TABLE 5.3 *Cross-tabulation of income versus food expenditure*

COUNT Row % Col. % Tot. %	Food expenditure					
	Less than £15	£15–29	£30–44	£45–59	£60+	ROW
Less than £15 000	33 7.1 84.6 3.5	226 48.7 70.2 24.2	149 32.1 7.8 16.0	45 9.7 23.1 4.8	11 2.4 16.5 1.2	464 49.7
£15 000 to £25 000	5 1.5 12.8 0.5	73 22.0 22.7 7.8	121 36.4 38.8 13.0	102 30.7 52.3 10.8	31 5.3 47.7 3.3	332 35.6
£25 000+	1 0.7 2.6 6.1	23 16.8 7.1 2.5	42 30.7 13.5 4.5	48 35.0 24.6 5.1	23 16.8 35.4 2.5	137 14.7
Column Total	39 4.2	322 34.5	312 33.4	195 20.9	65 7.0	933 100.0

Each cell contains four numbers:

Count The number of people in the cell (i.e. 33 respondents had incomes under £10 000 and spent less than £15 per week on food).

Row % The percentage of people in the row who are in the column (i.e. 33/464 = 7.1 per cent of the people with incomes under £10 000 spent less than £15 per week on food).

Col. % The percentage of people in the column who were in the row (i.e. 33/39 = 84.6 per cent of people who spent less than £15 per week on food had incomes under £10 000).

Total % The percentage of the total sample in the particular cell (i.e. 33/933 = 3.5 per cent).

resulting data, the data will not be used if they are not effectively communicated to the appropriate decision-makers.

For written reports, the following guidelines normally apply:

1. The report sequence is usually title page, table of contents, summary, introduction/research objectives, research methodology, findings, conclusions, recommendations (if appropriate), appendices.

2. Most report readers will not be particularly concerned with the technical aspects of the report, such as sampling procedure and questionnaire design. For this reason, technical details should be placed in the appendix section rather than in the methodology section.

3. Use terminology that matches the vocabulary of the reader.

4. Use diagrams (such as graphs, bar charts and pie charts) whenever possible.

For oral presentations, the report sequence is normally research objectives, research methodology, major findings, conclusions and recommendations; to maintain audience attention, full use should be made of visual aids.

Application of research techniques

Marketing research techniques may be applied to assist decision-making in all the functions of the marketing mix. It should also be borne in mind that 'mixed' research tactics can be used (e.g. personal interviews combined with group discussions). The application of research techniques in product, pricing, marketing communications and distribution research is now briefly outlined; sales forecasting research is discussed in detail in Chapter 11. For a fuller discussion of the techniques, the reader is again directed to the work of Chisnall.[11]

Product research   This encompasses the following aspects:

- *Generating new product ideas*   Sources of new product ideas include monitoring secondary sources (particularly trade journals, the competition's literature), group discussions with consumers and/or industry 'experts', studies of product use and surveys of consumer requirements.

- *Product concept testing*   A product concept is a product idea that has been defined in terms of its applications and benefits. Before embarking on the costly process of developing a prototype, it is usually advisable to research demand for the product concept. Product concept testing often involves describing the concept to consumers and asking the following question:

  'If this product were available, would you be likely to buy it? Would you say that you:

  ☐ would definitely buy it
  ☐ would probably buy it
  ☐ might or might not buy it
  ☐ would probably not buy it
  ☐ would definitely not buy it?'

- *Product testing*   In product testing, consumers are asked to use or examine product prototypes. The consumers are then asked if they would buy such a product and to state their opinions of the test product.

- *Test marketing* of products in a limited geographical area.

- *Packaging research*, including laboratory and field experimentation.

A fuller discussion of product research, especially in relation to fast moving consumer goods, is given in a text by Watkins.[12]

Pricing research   This includes the setting of prices for both new and current products and involves forecasting sales and estimating costs. Methods for forecasting sales are described in Chapter 11, but the estimation of costs is more the subject of accountancy. Pricing also forms part of marketing tactics, whereby prices can be manipulated in the short term to fight a tactical battle (e.g. short-term petrol price reductions) or in longer term for product positional tactics. A fuller discussion is provided by Greenley within the context of marketing plans.[13]

Marketing communications research   This includes the following.

Marketing communications effectiveness research   Under this heading, the effectiveness of advertising, personal selling, sales promotion and public relations activity is measured. This involves measuring its communication and/or sales effect. An assessment of communications effectiveness is concerned with measuring awareness, attitudes or 'intention to buy' before and after a campaign. A sales effectiveness measurement may be conducted by statistical analysis of past sales versus promotion expenditure. For new products, field experiments with 'control' markets are used.

Media selection research   In order to select a suitable publication or medium, a marketer should aim to collect the following data:

- Media distribution (the number of copies or sets carrying the advertisement).
- Audience size (the number of people actually exposed to an advertisement, also known as 'reach').
- Audience exposure (the number of people exposed times the number of times they are exposed, i.e. reach × frequency, also known as 'gross rating points').
- Cost per exposure.

Media distribution details are normally available from the media and these statistics are normally audited by an independent organization, e.g. Audit Bureau of Circulation for the UK. Audience 'reach' and 'exposure' data are collected and published by research organizations such as Research Services Ltd. Media effectiveness can vary greatly for different products and may be measured using the techniques mentioned in the previous sub-section.

Copy testing   This is concerned with determining the effectiveness of the creative aspects (headline, pictures, etc.) of advertising or promotional material. Creative ideas may be tested using physiological measures, surveys of advertising recall, field and 'laboratory' experiments.

Researching the number and location of sales representations required   Two main types of research are used for sales territory planning:

1. *Statistical analysis of sales data*   For current products, an analysis of actual sales versus market potential for each territory will indicate if the optimum number of representatives is being employed.
2. *Sales effort approach*   This approach is particularly appropriate for new products; it involves four stages:
   a. Compiling lists of prospective customers from secondary sources.
   b. Estimating the number of sales calls per year required to sell to selected prospective customers.

c. Estimating the average number of sales calls per representative that can be made in that territory in a year.

d. Dividing b by c to obtain the number of representatives required.

Distribution research   This includes the following:

- *Warehouse location research*   Here, the marketing research function is normally required to provide data on customer location (from secondary sources).

- *Retail outlet location research*   To assist with the process of planning the location of retail outlets, marketing research can provide a great deal of useful data. Useful data on a prospective site would include volume of pedestrians, number of nearby competitors, and the socio-economic profile of the neighbourhood.

Test marketing   Test marketing is a research technique in which the product under study is placed on sale in one or more selected localities or areas, and its reception by consumer and trade is observed, recorded and analysed.

Performance in these test markets is supposed to give some indication of the performance to be expected when the product goes into general distribution. 'Performance' includes two aspects:

1. The likely sales and profitability of the product when marketed on a national scale.

2. 'Feasibility' of the marketing operation, by which we mean the soundness and integration of all the elements that enter into the marketing operation.

Today, it has become an economic necessity to reduce new product risk by using one or more small and relatively self-contained marketing areas, wherein the market can apply a full-plan marketing strategy in order to gain at least a reasonably reliable indication that the product can be sold profitably in the (eventual) total marketplace.

Test marketing can be expensive, time-consuming, and can give competitors a window on your activities. At best, it provides only gross measures when one would like precision. This leads us on to the question, 'Why is it used?'

Other market research methods may indicate the *likelihood* that a new product or marketing approach will be successful. These methods have their place and should be used; but something more is ultimately needed—greater assurance than an indication or more 'likelihood'. All signs may be encouraging, but one nagging question usually remains: Will it sell? This is the question to which the answer is sought. In a market test, the product is actually placed on sale in a number of stores, and this provides a decisive acid test.

Test marketing is the final and most complex of a series of marketing research techniques used to reduce the tremendous risks inherent in new product development. It tends to be largely related to consumer products (particularly products such as groceries, confectionery, alcohol and cigarettes). Industrial products, particularly large items of capital equipment, do not permit concentrated area testing as envisaged in a test marketing programme. Industrial companies obtain their new product feedback in more informal ways. With an industrial product, e.g. computers, sales representatives and technical specialists arrange for a demonstration with potential users. Reaction on the part of potential customers to this 'trial run' may require the company to alter the product in some way.

Test marketing in the industrial situation really amounts to a 'market probe' and the emphasis is very often on the product itself. Contrast this with the consumer field and the products mentioned above, where one is testing not only the product but the price, advertising, selling effort, distribution, the package, etc. Products such as office equipment are often tested at trade shows where selected clients are permitted to use them. There are many successful industrial products on the market which have, unlike most consumer goods, started life as a special order for a particular client. That is a form of test marketing.

However, as Lancaster and Jobber[14] have pointed out, test marketing proper, needs to be much more carefully designed and controlled than this if it is to serve as a basis for sales and market forecasting. With consumer durables, e.g. TV sets, refrigerators, washing machines, furniture, etc., it is unlikely that a company would go into a full-scale regional test market, with, say, a half-million pound advertising spend or more on TV coverage, commando salesforces, discounts to the trade and everything else, unless it had every intention of marketing the product nationally. For such products, test marketing is essentially a preliminary skirmish into the marketing battlefield, designed to iron out the problems before the final product 'roll-out'.

We shall now look at the various stages involved in establishing a test market and the important factors that must be considered.

Defining objectives   The market research process, whatever set of techniques is employed, starts with a clear set of objectives. The same applies to test marketing.

Some of the more frequently encountered objectives for a product test market are:

- To provide the basis for total market production, i.e. giving you an idea of potential product sales after the launch.
- To check the entire operation, including production, distribution and marketing plan.
- To check the advertising campaign.
- To check the presentation/packaging of the product.
- To check the selling method.
- To check the distribution plan.

Setting criteria for success   Performance should be assessed against pre-determined and agreed standards of success. There is no sense in conducting an expensive test marketing operation only to find more disagreement after the test than before it as to whether the product is successful.

Standards can be set in such areas as sales volume, level of distribution, market share, etc. If you are studying advertising, then it is necessary to determine the degree of increase in sales that would be regarded as successful and therefore indicative of the wisdom of extending the advertising campaign, say, from one or two selected regions to national level.

Integrating marketing operations   The test marketing campaign must fit into the overall marketing plan, e.g. top salesmen should not be used in test areas if this is not to be repeated on a national scale because it will produce abnormal and misleading results. Furthermore, you should not indulge in excessive advertising if this is not to be repeated in the national launch.

Establishing controls   This involves three aspects:

1. What is the market situation before the test campaign starts?
   - What is the level of competition?
   - How successful are competitors' brands?

- What are the buying habits of the consumer?
- What are the attitudes to the product type?
- Is there brand loyalty?
- Is there price sensitivity?
- How do shopping habits affect the types of outlet through which a product can be sold?
- Has there been sufficient trade research—for example, attitudes to product type, customary discount structure, quantity discount terms, merchandising practices by companies, degree of cooperation expected from the trade?

2. During the test campaign, marketing movement should be monitored so that trends may be identified quickly, and also to assess the likely outcome of the campaign. Use of consumer panels and retail audits in test areas can be of immense help in this respect.

3. Post-test survey research should be extended to dealers so that an overall appreciation of market influences is gathered. The frank assessment of the test operation by dealers is very important.

Selecting areas   The ultimate aim should be to select test areas that reflect in miniature the national market. The reasoning behind this is that management wants to project results from test markets to entire target markets. One could take the view that there are a few large 'favourite' cities/test areas that are believed to be representative of the nation, based on analysis of demographic and socio-economic characteristics. However, this selection procedure may suffer from a number of drawbacks, including:

1. Possible reduction of market representativeness owing to continual use of test market cities/areas and to multiple tests being conducted at the same time.

2. The ease with which competition can discover that a new product introduction is being evaluated.

3. The questionable ability of a few cities/test areas to be representative of the entire country.

Selection of a greater number of smaller, more widely dispersed, cities could overcome these difficulties.

It can be seen that the choice of a test marketing area is not an easy one. Nevertheless, consider the following factors, which stand out as being the most important influence on the choice:

- *Size*   The area must provide an adequate base from which to project your findings on to a national scale, e.g. 100 000–200 000 inhabitants, yet at the same time be small enough to offer coverage at a reasonable cost. The ultimate market potential will, of course, influence the size of the test market area. A new pet food aimed at the huge pet food market would require a larger test market area than a product aimed at a small specialist market.

- *Population characteristics*   Clearly, the people a product is aimed at may be defined in terms of age, sex and socio-economic grouping. It is important to try to match a test area population with the national market.

- *Research services and marketing techniques that a media owner can offer the advertiser*

- *Range of different media available*

- *Isolation*   The ability to isolate and observe without interference from outside variables is, of course, a precondition of much scientific research. It applies to some extent to test marketing and is certainly a point the media owners themselves like to stress. The marketing manager at Westminster Press has stated that: 'Our test towns and their newspapers have the special advantages of being isolated. You know where you are when you are researching them and have greater control. Wholesalers, for example, have much less chance to blur distribution of the product than in any other towns.'

The main point is that it is essential to have a deep and full understanding of the test area you use so that results can be adjusted to allow for known variations from national behaviour patterns, media availability, media costs, etc.

Determining the number of test markets   Results may be more representative as the number of test market areas used increases, but in so doing you increase the cost. You should use a larger number of test market areas under the following circumstances:

1. If the risk of loss is great in a national launch.
2. If a number of alternative marketing plans are being tested.
3. If the opportunity of interference by competitors is likely.

In practice, it is unwise to use fewer than two test market areas.

Establishing the length of tests   There is no one answer to this question. Naturally, the ideal test period is the shortest time it takes to find out what you want to know. However, *three factors* do exert an influence on the length of the test period:

1. *Average repurchase period*   This can be defined as the time period that normally elapses before the consumer restocks the product. You need to observe a few repurchase periods to obtain a fair picture of attitude towards and usage of your product. This is not a problem with a product consumed as regularly as shampoo, but it may be a problem with a consumer durable such as a washing machine.
2. *The competitor situation*   No business likes to tell the competition what it is doing or give the opponent the opportunity to go national first. There is plenty of justification for this fear because the first manufacturer into a market can be overtaken by another only with great difficulty or luck. The dilemma is one of testing long enough useful information, but not so long that competitors are given a chance to catch up.
3. *Cost*   As the duration of the test increases, so does the cost. Thus, everyone is anxious to make test marketing short and sweet—but not too short, because the chances of correctly forecasting the national results increase dramatically with each extra week of a test.

Deciding the cost and information required   As was stressed earlier, perhaps the most important rule of all in test marketing is that objective yardsticks for assessing satisfactory performance should be established in advance of the test itself. Obviously, criteria relating to sales performance and market penetration must form the basis for the ultimate 'go'/'no go' decision. However, of equal importance are the costs involved. Is it a proper decision to say that we must go ahead because it would cost too much to pull out? I think not!

In line with this, therefore, it is important to establish what information is to be collected during the test market and from what sources. Examples of different types of information that might be collected include:

- *Data on goods delivered to the trade*   This is perhaps the least informative and costly.
- *Store audits*   This will inform you of actual retail sales. One can utilize the services of the Neilsen Company in this respect However, you must remember that store audits only provide you with retail sales figures; they do not tell you anything about the characteristics of buyers, such as the proportion of new buyers to repeat buyers.
- *Consumer panels*   A consumer panel can provide you with information on buyer characteristics.

● *Buyer surveys*   A company may wish to obtain direct data on buyer attitudes and reactions to the new product. This would involve obtaining a sample of new buyers and proceeding to interview them with a view to determining the characteristics of the buyers and reactions to using the product.

It goes without saying that test results should be evaluated properly, because on that rest important business decisions, e.g. heavy capital investment, and the setting up of volume production lines. You may have achieved a certain percentage market success in the test market, but you cannot simply deduce from that a similar performance if you were to go national. You must examine other significant factors, namely:

● Demographic structure of the population.

● Types of outlet available.

● Strength of competing brands.

● Variations among regions in competitors' activities, which may result in variations between the test area and the national market.

After this, you should attempt to make a forecast of future likely demand for the new product on a national basis.

Criticisms of test marketing   There are, of course, problems with test marketing. For example, it is difficult to 'isolate' test areas in order to ensure that the experiment is controlled. Similarly, it is almost impossible to hold constant all the factors that might affect the results of competitor activity. For these and other reasons, many researchers have cautioned against the use of this technique for certain purposes. Nevertheless, used wisely and properly planned and exercised, test marketing is a very powerful and useful aid to marketing decision-making.

Motivation research   Remember that we suggested earlier that much of marketing research, and especially survey research, is concerned with the collection of measurable quantitative data. We also suggested that the marketer is concerned as well to collect qualitative data about customers. We have already discussed the use of depth interviews and group discussions for collecting qualitative data, but a third group of primary research techniques for collecting and analysing qualitative data on customers are the techniques of motivational research. Again, remember that much of marketing research is concerned with the collection of statistical data and market facts including market size and numbers of competitors. It may also involve direct questioning of potential and actual consumers about their behaviour and attitudes.

However, a buyer's real motives and other behavioural influences are often unknown, hidden, or too complex to be determined by direct questioning. Marketing has thus borrowed some indirect research techniques from the behavioural science fields, especially psychology and psychiatry, to help gain a better understanding of why people respond as they do to various products, advertisements and other marketing variables. The term 'motivation research' is used to describe these indirect techniques.

In order to appreciate the need for motivation research, consider the complexity of purchase decisions that are influenced by attitudes, beliefs, motivations and environmental factors. The consumer's perception of him/herself (self-image) and the product (product image) should be appreciated by marketers. Products are bought not only for physical benefits and functional performance, but also for psychological satisfactions.

Bradley[15] has said that motivation research helps in designing the product, its package, pricing and advertising.

Certain mechanical aids also help motivational researchers, including speeded up and slowed down video recordings, traffic counters, psycho-galvanometers, scanners, eye cameras (pupilometers), tachistoscopes, people meters (for measuring TV viewing patterns), electro-encephalograms, one-way mirrors and voice pitch analysis. Some of their uses border on clinical research, and criticism has been voiced about some of the results obtained, largely owing to the fact that skill in interpreting the results is often extremely specialist. Some results have been drawn by marketers that are scientifically suspect.

We shall now examine the main techniques used in motivation research.

Projective techniques A person who is relieved of direct responsibility for his or her expressions will tend to answer more freely and truthfully. Projective tests are designed to achieve this end. They are called 'projective tests' because respondents are required to project themselves into someone else's place or into some ambiguous situation. Consider the following examples:

1. *Word association test* This type of test, also known as 'free association', involves firing a series of words at respondents, who must state immediately any other words that come into their minds. Association tests can be used to determine consumer attitudes towards products, stores, advertising themes, product features, selection of brand names, etc. Let us look at some examples:

   ● The interviewer says 'soap', to which the respondent might reply 'hygiene', 'lather', 'beauty', and so on.
   ● The interviewer says 'margarine', to which the respondent might reply 'health', 'cholesterol', 'convenient', 'butter', 'cost', and so on.

2. *Sentence completion test* Here the respondent is asked to complete a number of sentences. The following are some examples:

   ● In comparing margarine with butter, one might state:
   'A housewife using margarine instead of butter is _____.'
   or
   'The healthfulness of margarine is _____.'
   ● Considering a certain brand of cigars, one might state:
   'A man who smokes Hamlet cigars is _____.'
   This test can provide more information than word association.

3. *Story completion test* This is an extension of the sentence completion technique. Consider the following example:

   ● A man bought petrol at his regular petrol station which sold a nationally advertised brand. The petrol attendant, who knew the man, said: 'Mr Smith, your battery is now nearly two years old. We have just got in a new product which, when added to the water in your battery, will prolong its life by about a year. It's a bargain at £2.50.' What is the customer's response? Why?

   This technique can provide the seller with data on the images and feelings that people have about a particular product.
   Another example might be where a group of housewives is asked to complete a story in which the opening sentence is related to supermarket shopping.

4. *Psychodrama* Here the respondent is asked to play a role, and to do so he is given a complete description of the circumstances. This test is similar to the 'third-person' test. A famous example is the study by Mason-Haire of instant coffee usage in America in 1949. The study involved giving housewives two identical shopping lists, the only differences being that one list contained instant coffee while the other list contained coffee beans. The findings revealed that the buyer of instant coffee was seen as lazier, less well organized, more spendthrift and not as good a wife as

the woman who bought the traditional type of coffee. This study uncovered the true motivations. The original reason given for disliking the instant coffee was the flavour.

5. *Thematic apperception test (TAT)* In this test, a series of pictures is shown to respondents, who are then asked to describe what conditions give rise to the situation, what is happening, and what the outcome will be. The assumption is that, in explaining the picture, the subject will tell something about him- or herself. For example:

   ● The picture might show a young housewife looking at a display of 'bargain offer' tights, or the same woman casting her eyes over a merchandising unit offering expensive 'branded' tights. The respondent would be asked to comment on the person in the cartoon and the quality of the tights.

6. *Cartoon test* This is a variation of the TAT method and is commonly referred to as a 'balloon test'. Informants are presented with a rough sketch showing two people talking. One of them has just said something represented by words written into a 'speech balloon' as in a comic strip. The other person's balloon is empty and the informant is asked what he or she is replying. Consider the following example:

   ● Two women are pictured outside Smith's department store and one woman is saying: 'What do you think of Smith's department store?' The respondent is asked to give the reply of the other woman.

Many marketing situations could be usefully tested by this technique. Consider the following examples:

   ● A chemist is pictured saying: 'This bottle of Disprin gives you 100 tablets for £2; and this bottle gives you 100 soluble Aspirin for £1.50.' What is the customer's reply?
   ● You could show a situation between a shopper returning faulty merchandise and a store assistant.
   ● You could picture a husband and wife considering the purchase of an expensive product.
   ● Another particular example might be to use a cartoon showing a conference in progress. One of the delegates says: 'Now this is our present supplier list. We have been with them for quite some time and they have been doing a good job. There is no reason for making any changes. The next subject is . . . .' Another delegate interrupts to say: 'Wait a minute . . . Loyalty is fine, but there are a lot of other considerations which I think are due for a change.'

The respondent is then asked with which delegate he or she is in most agreement, and why.

Issues and problems involved You should note that motivation research, like test marketing, is not without its own special problems and issues.

A major problem is the fact that all the above mentioned techniques require the use of highly skilled interviewers and analysts trained in psychology and/or sociology. This, of course, is a problem that can be overcome, albeit at a cost.

Potentially more serious issues/problems relate to the extent to which these techniques are (a) scientific and (b) ethical. With regard to *scientific status*, the controversy continues. Critics argue that the techniques are shaky to say the least, with little comparability between various research studies. On the other hand, confirmed advocates of motivation research such as Dichter[16] suggest that the techniques are powerful marketing tools. With regard to *ethical status*, critics such as Packard[17] have long argued that the use of such techniques is tantamount to an invasion of the privacy of the consumer's mind and lays the customer open to manipulation.

No doubt the debate will continue, although it must be said that in recent years the use of these techniques in marketing has probably declined somewhat.

The professional marketer would perhaps be best advised to keep an open mind, picking and choosing from the techniques available, as and where appropriate.

Primary data collection and new technology

Again, the use of information and computing technology in general are becoming increasingly important in the collection and analysis of primary research data. Some examples of the uses of the new technology in this respect will illustrate this. Increasingly, companies are administering questionnaires on the Internet. An interesting related development in this respect is the use of e-mails to reach potential respondents. Chat rooms and even focus groups run through websites are increasingly being used by market researchers. Chat rooms are proving to be particularly useful in this respect as there is an element of self-selection by respondents with regard to interest in a particular product category. Technology, too, is also allowing information to be collected at, for example, point of purchase via on-line scanners linked to powerful computer analyses. Digital television is increasingly being used to gather quantitative information directly from respondents. Information technology developments are also facilitating the analysis and interpretation stages of marketing research. In consumer interviews, for example, the responses are now often entered directly into lap-top computers which then can be fed through a modem for immediate analysis and feedback. Increasingly powerful computer packages are enabling the marketer to use much more sophisticated techniques of analysis such as, for example, multi-dimensional scaling and cluster and factor analysis.

MARKETING INFORMATION SYSTEMS

A marketing information system (MkIS) can be defined as a system designed to generate and disseminate an orderly flow of pertinent information to marketing managers. Thus, marketing research is concerned with the task of generating information, whereas the marketing information system is focused on managing the flow of information decision-makers. This distinction is important because information is worthless unless it is relevant and effectively communicated. This section comes at the end of this chapter because you will appreciate that it is possible to have marketing research without a marketing information system, but not vice versa.

The marketing information system of a company is a sub-system of its management information system. A marketing information system, in turn, consists of a number of sub-systems or elements. These are shown in Fig. 5.3 and discussed below.

FIGURE 5.3

Elements of the marketing information system

The first three elements shown at the left-hand side of Fig. 5.3 represent the information inputs of the marketing information system. These three elements as shown comprise of marketing research encompassing one-off problem-based research programmes; marketing intelligence which comprises all those activities aimed at generating information on markets, customers and competitors which are collected through less formal channels than for marketing research projects such as feedback from the salesforce; and finally internal company information which should include information not just from sales and marketing, but also from other functional areas of the business which can be used in marketing decision-making such as production, financial, and quality control information. These three sources of information feed into the marketing database which was discussed earlier in the chapter. The marketing database can then be analysed and information manipulated so as to provide the necessary information for improved marketing decision-making. This element of the marketing information system includes systems of data analysis and manipulation including, for example, statistical analysis.

Finally, the system must include effective channels and procedures for feeding information in a way which is appropriate and useful to the marketing decision maker. Although this is shown as the output of the system, it is also in fact the start point for the design of the marketing information system. In as much as the design of the marketing information system should centre around management's decision-making needs.

Perhaps not surprisingly, once again the ubiquitous computer, and developments in data storage, handling and retrieval in particular, have facilitated the growth and use of marketing information systems. Indeed the main focus of the marketing information system is on data storage and retrieval designed around management's information requirements. Unlike marketing research, which is information-gathering in relation to specific marketing problems, the idea of the marketing information system is to provide continuous information for decision-making. Of particular importance in the modern marketing information system is the *marketing database*. As we have seen earlier in the chapter many companies now have substantial databases based on information collected both through internal and external information-gathering systems including traditional marketing research studies. Some companies have such extensive information in their databanks about, say, customers and their purchasing habits and characteristics that the database itself containing this information becomes a 'product' that can be sold to other marketing organizations. Needless to say there is some controversy regarding the use of databases on customers in this way. Nevertheless, we can expect companies to want to continue to widen and deepen their databases on their customers and potential customers. In the UK the introduction of store loyalty cards by some of the leading grocery multiples has enabled these marketers to obtain very detailed information about their customers' shopping habits, the brands they buy, the offers they are susceptible to, etc. There is little doubt that marketing databases as part of the overall marketing information system in organizations are now very sophisticated indeed.

CHAPTER SUMMARY

This chapter has covered the subject of marketing research. It has been acknowledged that this subject is an involved and detailed study in its own right. The areas covered have included an introductory description of the development of marketing research followed by secondary research methods. Primary research was then examined under the headings of: survey research, depth research, observation and experimentation. Sampling was discussed followed by data analysis. This was followed by a detailed explanation of test marketing and motivation research. The chapter concluded with an indication of how marketing research techniques could be applied to the marketing function including the adoption of a marketing information system. Lancaster and Massingham[18] provide a more strategic view of marketing research when they consider the marketing research as an element of the marketing information system.

Throughout the chapter we have seen that not surprisingly marketing research has been affected by new technology and particularly developments in IT and communications technology including databases, web-based research, the use of the Internet and computer-based packages for analysis and data manipulation.

CHAPTER REVISION QUESTIONS

1. What problems are to be encountered in assessing the cost effectiveness of marketing research?
2. In which research circumstances are observation techniques more suitable than other fieldwork techniques?
3. Distinguish between the universe and the sample frame.
4. What are the essential elements of a marketing information system?
5. Explain what is meant by the following in the context of questionnaire design:
   a. Open-ended questions.
   b. Closed dichotomous questions.
   c. Closed multiple-choice questions.
   d. Semantic differential scales.
6. Explain how information technology can help in the marketing research process.
7. Outline and discuss the main elements of a marketing information system.

References

1. P. M. Chisnall, *Marketing Research*, 3rd edn, McGraw-Hill, London, 1986.
2. Chisnall, op. cit., p. 38.
3. H. H. Kassarjion and M. Nakanishi, 'A study of selected opinion measurement techniques', *Journal of Marketing Research*, May 1969.
4. J. Kitchen, 'Observation, ethology and marketing research', *European Research*, January 1981, p. 22.
5. L. W. Rodger, *Statistics for Marketing*, McGraw-Hill, London, 1984, pp. 179–86.
6. ACORN is supplied by CACI London. It is discussed in detail in Chapter 7 'Selection of Markets'.
7. Rodger, op. cit., pp. 103–22.
8. Rodger, op. cit., Chapter 2, pp. 22–39.
9. N. H. Nie, *et al.*, *SPSS–X*, SPSS–X, Chicago, IL, 1985.
10. See Rodger, op. cit., for a fuller discussion, pp. 122–32.
11. Chisnall, op. cit.
12. T. Watkins, *The Economics of the Brand*, McGraw-Hill, London, 1986.
13. G. E. Greenley, *The Strategic and Operational Planning of Marketing*, McGraw-Hill, London, 1986, pp. 124–39.
14. G. A. Lancaster and D. Jobber, *Selling and Sales Management*, Pitman, London 2000.
15. V. Bradley, *Applied Marketing and Social Research*, Van Nostrand Rineholt, New York, 1982.
16. E. Dichter, *Handbook of Consumer Motivations*, McGraw-Hill, New York, 1964.
17. V. Packard, *The Hidden Persuaders*, Longman, London, 1957.
18. G. A. Lancaster and L. C. Massingham, *Marketing Management*, 3rd edn, McGraw-Hill, London, 2001, p. 299.

Mettricks Auctions

Mettricks Auctions is an internationally famous auction house based in Station Road, London. Although Mettricks auction any type of antique and fine paintings in recent years it has tended to specialize in the auctioning of Middle Eastern artefacts. Partly as a result of increased controls regarding the removal and sale of such artefacts particularly from archaeological sites, prices of such objects have trebled over the last 10 years. In addition, and as usual, the limited supply allied to an already rare product has led to even greater demand by collectors and international museums alike. Mettricks has an international reputation for quality and for establishing the provenance of items which pass through its auction rooms in London. Its expertise is frequently sought after and is reflected in the number of clients wishing to sell their antiques and artefacts through the firm.

Although marketing has only recently been introduced into the auction house business, Mettricks now feel that it could well make use of more marketing and particularly more marketing information and research.

Although Mettricks has impeccable information about the products that pass through its hands and can, for example, help date, identify and provide guide prices for clients, it has surprisingly little information about the people who buy or might buy at their auctions. All that Mettricks currently holds is a list of clients who have purchased from it before, detailing what they have bought, when and prices paid. Clients who have purchased in a particular category of auction before, e.g. have purchased, say, Middle Eastern antiques, are usually sent a catalogue advising them of any forthcoming sale. It knows nothing, however, about why these customers buy, what they are particularly interested in and the extent to which they purchase from other auction houses. It also has no information other than in general terms about competitors both in London and in other major art centres of the world.

Mettricks has recently established a website which enables prospective buyers to view products for forthcoming auctions.

It is not even sure what the total market for products sold through auction houses like itself in the United Kingdom, and certainly not for any other part of the world.

By far the majority of customers usually visit the auction house in person during a viewing period of normally two to three days before a sale. No information about these customers is collected at this point so it is not known how many, for example, of these pre-sale customers actually turn up for the sale itself let alone bid.

Questions

1. What sorts of marketing information might Mettricks find it useful to collect and analyse? Explain your reasons.
2. Suggest practical and cost-effective ways in which Mettricks might collect and analyse such information.

Chapter Six

THE PRODUCT (OR SERVICE)

LEARNING OBJECTIVES   *This chapter will help you to:*

- understand the nature and importance of product decisions in the marketing mix;

- appreciate the range and types of products marketed;

- identify the benefits related to the functional, physical and symbolic aspects of the product;

- appreciate the importance of new product development and the key steps in the new product development process;

- understand the product life cycle concept and its uses and limitations in developing marketing programmes;

- describe the importance and role of packaging;

- understand the role and responsibilities of the product manager;

- appreciate the key elements of product strategies;

- understand the special characteristics of service products and their marketing.

INTRODUCTION

People who are unfamiliar with marketing often hold the erroneous view that a 'product' is always a physical object with readily identifiable and tangible attributes. They would not, for example, consider an insurance policy or a package holiday to be a 'product'. Marketing practitioners must, however, adopt a very much wider view of the product. In a more abstract sense, products should be distinguished not only by their actual utilities, but also by the perceptions that consumers have of them. These can be real, or imagined by the customer, or the specific creations of the marketer. Thus, in the case of a frozen ready meal, the 'product' is not the physical food ingredients, but a convenience—a labour- and time-saving device. This is the basis for 'benefit segmentation', as explained in Chapter 4.

For the marketer, the product becomes any want-satisfying good or service that is considered together with its perceived tangible and intangible attributes. From the consumer's point of view, a product is a series or a bundle of satisfactions. It is important to realize that, whatever we as marketers 'would like' our products to be, the real nature of the product lies in the consumer's perception of it. This emphasizes the essence of marketing—a policy of customer orientation.

PRODUCT CLASSIFICATION

It should by now be clear that the product is much more than simply the physical product or 'object'. We can now consider the product in its widest possible context so as to obtain a complete understanding of its nature. This final consideration has been described as the 'Total Product Concept' and its understanding lies at the heart of successful marketing. In his text, *Differentiation of Anything*,[1] Levitt proposes four concepts of the product which go to make up the 'total product'.

First, as we already know, we must consider the physical product or service. This is the generic bar of chocolate, the machine tool or the two-week package holiday. Without this there can be no sale—no offer or acceptance. The customer, however, expects more than this. The expected product is, of course, wider in scope than the generic product, but it still represents the consumer's minimum expectations. Such expectations would include price, delivery or availability, after-sales service or packaging. A third dimension is the 'augmented product'; this is closely linked with the development of a policy of product differentiation, as opposed to customer-originated 'expectations'. 'Augmentations' are the creations of the marketer. Many consumers now select between different competing products and brands on the basis of what is being offered at the augmented product level. Examples of ways in which consumer product marketers augment their product offerings include, for example, delivery systems and services, free technical help and back-up service, extended warranties and after-sales service. A further and in some ways more subtle aspect of the augmented product relates to the symbolic aspects of a product. In addition to the physical and functional attributes and qualities of a product such as its design, its features, the materials it is made from or what it does in purely functional terms, you must not forget that an important attribute of many products, and often a major facet in customer choice, are aspects such as the brand image of the product or service. Customers often choose between products on the basis of the brand reputation of the product. Clearly prestige manufacturers such as Mercedes Benz, Bang & Olufson, Lexus, Gucci, Prada and so on recognize and trade on the symbolic aspects of the product or rather brand. In the industrial context, such things as a special 'tailor-made' delivery or storage service would 'augment' the product from its original basic parameters. Over time, there may be a tendency for customers to regard attributes of the augmented product as standard items, thus necessitating a further reassessment of the product's nature. This leads us finally to the 'potential' product, which encompasses all those things that 'could' be added to a product but which, as yet, have not been realized.

The product is, therefore, a complex idea, central to marketing and central to the consumer. It should never be viewed in the narrow terms of a physical object or service, but rather in the context of what satisfactions it brings to the consumer. In addition to this, it cannot be considered in isolation. From both the buyer's and the seller's viewpoint, the product is inextricable from the total approach that a firm adopts towards its market and customers.

We now have an insight into the scope and nature of a product. In order to aid market planning, products can be classified in a formal way. Such a classification system helps us to identify the way in which people view products, and thus why and how they subsequently purchase them.

A PRODUCT AND SERVICE CLASSIFICATION SYSTEM

Products can be divided into two main groups. 'Consumer goods' are purchased by the ultimate buyer, while 'industrial goods' are used by all the firms in the manufacturing chain. Many industrial goods, therefore, can go to make up one retail or consumer product. In other words, industrial goods are purchased in order to make other products.

Consumer goods

Figure 6.1 sets out a formal classification for consumer goods.

Convenience goods   The purchase of these goods requires very little effort and more often than not they are relatively inexpensive. Most of the contents of the average weekly shopping basket fall into this category, and any planning is usually restricted to the preparation of a simple shopping list. The presence of brands may cause the shopper to prevaricate over purchases, but this does not detract from the fact that, in general, little effort is required from the shopper in order for the store to make a profit, because the store's profit is assured no matter which brand is bought.

Convenience goods can be subdivided into emergency, staple and impulse items. If sudden necessity is the motivator for a purchase, even less effort than usual will be required. Many small neighbourhood grocery shops owe their survival (faced with price competition from supermarkets) to our need for *emergency convenience goods. Staple convenience goods* form the bulk of everyday shopping. Items such as milk, bread, sugar or potatoes fall into this category, although it is true to say that nowadays many of these goods possess some sort of branding or other differentiation. *Impulse items* are self-explanatory—pre-planning is obviously nil; these are goods that simply 'catch the eye', and price and price comparison plays a minimum role.

Shopping goods   This is the category of major, durable or semi-durable appliances. Owing to the fact that they are usually more expensive than convenience goods, their purchase is characterized by a fair degree of pre-planning, information search and price comparison. This is due not only to their relative expense, but also because these purchases are made less frequently and the consumer is less knowledgeable about the respective merits of the products that are available. As well as price comparison, place of purchase, purchase terms, service and guarantees will all form part of the purchase decision equation.

Homogeneous shopping goods would include such products as 'white goods', prams and pushchairs or DIY equipment. Although these purchases can, in many ways, be 'special' to the consumer because of their relative infrequence of purchase, they are not classed as 'speciality' in marketing terms because the products themselves are not rare or exclusive, but are in fact almost necessities and form a part of everyday life.

Heterogeneous shopping goods are by definition 'non-standard', stylized and possess a degree of exclusivity. Price is usually of secondary importance—behavioural factors playing a more important role than for homogeneous goods. In the car market, the Porsche can be compared with the family saloon to illustrate this difference. Similarly, certain clothing labels can be classed as heterogeneous goods when compared with the more standardized ranges available from the high street multiples.

Speciality goods   These are characterized by extensive search and an extreme reluctance to accept substitutes for the chosen product. Exclusivity is a prime purchase criterion. Certain 'long-haul' holidays, designer clothing and jewellery, gourmet foods and Rolls Royce cars would fit into this category. While behavioural and lifestyle factors are important for all consumer purchases, it is likely that this category of goods provides the consumer with the greatest opportunity for self-actualization, ego-satisfaction and the satisfaction of esteem-orientated physical and psychological needs. The marketer also has the best opportunity for targeting and segmenting consumers with a 'tailor-made' marketing effort. Although prices will usually be extremely high for such goods, we must remember that the number of consumers in a given population who will be able to afford speciality goods will always be relatively small.

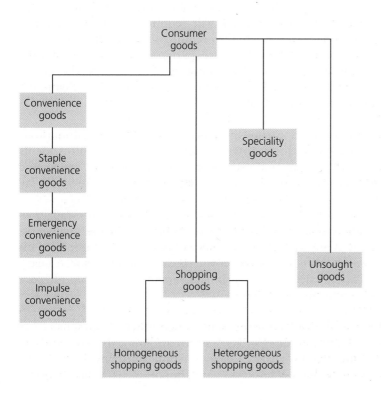

FIGURE 6.1

A formal classification system for consumer goods

Unsought goods   By definition, these goods are those that the consumer does not actively seek out. Indeed the consumer may not even have been aware of them immediately prior to any purchase. New products are 'unsought' initially, but this category is also characterized by aggressive personal selling, direct mail and telephone campaigns. In this respect, unsought goods represent that aspect of marketing which is most open to criticism. Typically, insurance policies that are sold by the above means are classed as unsought. This is not to say that sales generated in this way do not uncover a genuine need within a previously unaware consumer.

Finally, we must be aware of the fact that, while such a classification system has relevance for most consumers, there are, as always, 'grey areas' where a degree of overlap can take place. A television set may be a speciality good for some consumers, whereas Beluga caviar may, for some, represent a mere convenience item! The important implication for marketers is that for large groups of the population such a classification accurately reflects consumer behaviour and allows a firm to develop an optimum utilization of the marketing mix.

Industrial goods

Industrial goods tend to be characterized on a functional rather than a behavioural basis. This is because the primary use of industrial goods is in the manufacture, directly or indirectly, of other goods. As with consumer goods, the purpose of a formal classification system is to enable a better understanding of the market by gaining knowledge of the use to which the goods are put and by gaining an insight into the reasons for their purchase.

A simple way to imagine the complex range of industrial goods is to imagine any company and think of all the things that that company will require in order to function efficiently. Obviously, a manufacturing company will require machinery and raw materials to make the basic product, but it will also require all of the ancillary items that any company needs—cleaning materials, spare parts, stationery, typewriters, office furniture and so on. All of these items, while not being integral to the manufacturing process, are nevertheless essential to the running of the company. Figure 6.2 classifies these requirements into formal groups.

Installations   These can be regarded as the 'speciality' goods of industrial markets. They are the major items of plant and machinery which a company requires for its production. Their purchase is critical and can determine the nature, scope and efficiency of the company. For a haulage company, the heavy goods vehicle would fall into this category.

Not surprisingly, final purchase is the culmination of extensive search and comparison, because that decision is essentially long term and is likely to be the single most important capital investment at any given time. Because of the long-term implications of purchase, price, while important, is almost never the single deciding factor. A heavy reliance is also placed on expert sales advice, technical support, availability of spare parts and the general level of after-sales service.

Accessories   These comprise of ancillary plant maintenance, office equipment and so on. Although still considered as capital items, accessories are less expensive and are depreciated over a fewer number of years. Fewer personnel are involved in the purchase decision, and this decision itself has less overall importance for the company.

One only has to compare the often misguided purchase of office furniture with the implications of a similar decision involving a major piece of production machinery.

Raw materials   Unlike all the other goods in industrial product classification, these go to make up the final product. How close any particular manufacturer's output is to the final product will obviously depend on the position held in the manufacturing chain. It is also worth remembering that much industrial output is not necessarily destined for the consumer market, but goes to provide products for other industries so as to facilitate their manufacturing process.

The purchase of raw materials typically makes the largest share of the expenditure of the traditional 'buying department' of a company. Efficient purchasing is of the utmost importance, because the quality of the raw materials will have a direct bearing on the quality of the product to be produced. It is probably fair to say that the importance of price diminishes, the more the raw material forms part of a commodity market. Price is, however, by no means the only deciding factor of purchase, even in the most homogeneous of commodity markets: delivery, continuity of supply, quality and the general level of service all play a vital part in the decision to deal or not to deal with a particular raw material supplier.

Component parts and materials   These are similar in nature to 'raw materials' in that they go to make up the end products. A vehicle manufacturer may purchase steel as a 'raw material' while engine parts would be classed as components. Similarly, a textile manufacturer might purchase natural or synthetic fibre as a raw material, but would also require chemical finishes, dyestuffs and so on as 'materials'. Machinery would also require replacement items: these too would be classified here, and should not be compared with 'accessories'. As with raw material supply, non-price considerations figure highly in reaching the purchase decision.

Supplies   If we draw another parallel with the consumer market, supplies can be thought of as the 'convenience goods' of industrial supply. Supplies represent the multiplicity of items that most companies probably take for granted. These are

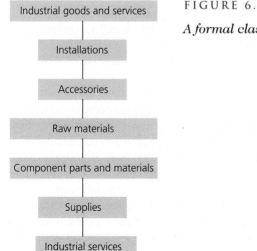

FIGURE 6.2

A formal classification system for industrial goods

cleaning items—soap, brooms, cloths, etc.; office stationery; as well as items for general maintenance (other than those required for plant) such as light bulbs, fuel oil and numerous 'repairs and renewals'. Purchase procedure is often routine and conducted through the medium of wholesalers. Owing to the relatively homogeneous nature of supplies, and their wide availability, price is a major influencing factor of supply.

Industrial services   The supply of industrial services has greatly increased in recent years. One only needs to think of the field of marketing itself, where the opportunity to purchase the services of management consultants and market research agencies has increased many-fold during the past decade. There has been a similar increase in the use of contract cleaners and services such as 'express delivery' for urgent or fragile correspondence. The principal factor in deciding to use outside services rather than the firm's own personnel is cost effectiveness. Frequently, when such services are not required on a continuous basis, or when the long-term cost of employing expert personnel would exceed the cost of the required service, the use of outside agencies offers a convenient solution to the problem. The special issues of marketing both industrial and consumer service products are considered later in this chapter.

A classification of industrial products is an ideal aid and companion to the study of industrial buyer behaviour. Each category of products performs a different role for the firm, and this knowledge can be used by suppliers in the design of their marketing and sales strategy. It should be uppermost in the minds of both buyer and seller that the finished products can be only as good as the machinery that makes them. The product classification system also permits emphasis of the fact that, just as consumers 'perceive' benefits other than the physical form of a given product, industrial buyers are equally concerned with factors other than the immediate product and its price.

NEW PRODUCT DEVELOPMENT

The development of a new product is a component of overall marketing strategy. For most firms new products involve the effort and cooperation of the total management structure as well as a wide cross-section of the total workforce. New products involve large sums of money and higher than normal levels of risk when compared with many other major marketing decisions. It is for these reasons that it is thought worthwhile to highlight this subject as a separate element of product strategy.

What is a new product?

Most of us must be familiar with the bewildering selection of goods displayed in any supermarket. In industry, the professional buyer is consistently confronted with 'variations on themes' and occasionally with a product designed to 'revolutionize' a particular manufacturing process. Both in consumer markets and in industry, the purchaser has a tendency to adopt a blasé attitude towards the latest offering from any given firm. From the manufacturer's point of view, the picture is very different—a new chocolate bar or machine part is the culmination of a vast commitment of resources, time and research. Before going on to examine in detail how this process is carried out, we should be aware of the variety of definitions that can be applied to a new product.

1. *Innovative products*   These are products that are truly 'new' to the consumer: they provide totally different alternatives to existing products which serve existing markets. Among such goods can be included television, or the motor car, which was made possible by the invention of the internal combustion engine. These new products provided an alternative to radio and cinema entertainment and to horse-drawn methods of transport. In more recent times, genetically engineered food products, lasers and solar power would fall into this category.

2. *Replacement products*   These are replacements for existing products which, while not being wholly 'innovative', do provide significant differentiations from those that are currently on offer. Using a previous example, one could say that a radically new design of car offers a 'replacement' product. Similarly, the Polaroid camera 'replaced' those cameras that required films to be developed independently from the taking of the picture. The compact disc, however technically innovative, was a replacement for the conventional hi-fi system, as was the hi-fi system a replacement for the original and truly 'innovative' (in the marketing sense) gramophone.

3. *Imitative products*   This final category involves all those products that are new to a company, but are already well established in the marketplace. These follow on from the replacement and innovative products which have been developed initially by individual firms. Occasionally, imitative products are perhaps disparagingly described as 'me-too' products because they imply a certain lack of imagination on behalf of the firm launching them. It is also fair to say that all firms cannot be pioneers of product inventiveness, and thus the bulk of new products are imitative. Certainly, if a firm's financial resources and marketing expertise are strong, then it is advantageous to be an innovator rather than a follower, but in practice many firms appear content to let another take the risks of an innovative product launch, and then join the market when 'the dust has settled'. It also happens that a firm launches an innovative product and then quickly loses market share to a more powerful imitation.

    Imitative products are most often found when the technical development costs are low and are obviously launched before the initiator has had the opportunity to set up too many barriers to market entry. It is also with imitative products where the highest rate of product failures is likely to occur.

A final criterion for new product definition, irrespective of the above categories, lies in the consumer's perception. This is, of course, determined by the manner in which the product is presented to the marketplace. Thus, a relaunched product can appear 'new' if different benefits are promoted, whether or not these are tangible or intangible. Appearance or performance need not be radically altered. Provided the consumer perceives a product as being significantly different from that which already exists, then it is effectively a new product.

The importance of new product development

In his famous article 'Marketing myopia',[2] Levitt emphasizes the absolute necessity of a 'total' commitment to new product development. This is the sole medium for adaptation to change and is, therefore, critical to the continued survival of the firm. This importance is mirrored and intensified by the fact that new products are the 'rocks on which many companies founder'.

The product (and its successors) is, therefore, central to the whole being of the firm. Any efficient sales manager will maintain that without customers there is no need for production. This perfectly valid standpoint can, however, be considered in a different way by stating that without a product one has no need for a salesforce! Thus we move to the inevitable conclusion that the product is essential to the firm's physical existence, not only because a product is necessary for profit generation to take place, but also because the product is the medium through which a company fulfils the marketing concept. Taking the strictest interpretation of the marketing concept, the total ethos of the firm should be to produce goods that provide consumer satisfaction, profit being the reward of this if effectively carried out. Such a view, which may appear overly altruistic (and which is certainly complicated), is not, however, far removed from reality. Whatever company policies may be, competitive forces tend, over time, to militate against the firm whose products are not specifically aimed at fulfilling the marketing concept.

The marketing mix too is a meaningless tool without the product. It should be evident that all elements of the marketing mix are totally dependent on each other, but quite logically the core of the marketing mix is the product and new product developments. All marketing planning is based on, and must start from, the product. If that product is intrinsically weak, it will not ultimately survive, however skilfully the other elements of the mix are employed. This last factor underlines the importance of the product as the basic profit determinant of the firm. New products, moreover, should ensure that profit is sustained in the long term as well as providing the opportunity for growth and diversification.

From the strategic viewpoint, the firm must utilize new products as a means towards market leadership, rather than market imitation. The underlying trends towards a more affluent society in Western post-war history imply that the more basic of consumer needs are now, to a great extent, fulfilled. The implications of this are that firms must be increasingly aware of the need to satisfy consumers on a higher plane than was previously necessary. Consistently, research studies have shown that successful new products can give a company a significant competitive advantage: often helping a company to become market leader. Wheelwright and Sasser[3] demonstrate how a successful new product can become the industry standard. Examples would include the Sony Walkman, and the Dyson vacuum cleaner. Booz, Allen and Hamilton[4] have conducted research which suggests that new products are increasingly making a greater contribution to overall company profits.

Finally, the increase in global marketing and competition has meant that companies must innovate or run the risk of going out of business. No longer can domestic companies expect 'loyal' customers to purchase from the indigenous producer. Rather, the overseas competitor with the more innovative products will now tend to be chosen instead.

Technological change and new product development

Obviously technological change, but more specifically the pace of this change, is having a major impact on the process of new product development. Understandably many new products stem directly from technological changes and breakthroughs. Technological change, of course, is not new but what is, is the pace of this change. There are several aspects regarding the impact of the pace of technological change on new product development. The first, and perhaps most obvious, is that in many industries product life cycles are shortening. This then creates a vicious circle in as much as the marketer must increasingly be looking for new products to replace the outdated and outmoded ones. A second consequence of the increased pace of technological change is that there is now a premium on being able to develop and launch new products quickly. Many companies are now looking at ways in which they can speed their process of NPD through approaches such as concurrent engineering where the different stages of new product development are worked on at the same time by different functional areas of the business instead of sequentially passing the new product idea through the different development stages starting with research and development until it eventually reaches sales and marketing. This aspect of new product development is so important that we shall consider it further when we look at recent developments and thinking in new product development and innovation.

Risks in new product development

Contrasted with the factors underlying the importance of and hence need for new product development are the risks associated with this marketing activity. It is fair to say that new product development represents perhaps one of the most risky activities that a company can undertake. Estimates of rates of new product failures range, for example, from that of Crawford,[5] at 35 per cent on average, to the frighteningly high average suggested by Cooper[6] of 90 per cent. Even the lower of these estimates illustrates the risk involved in new product development. Because of this, coupled with the fact that companies must innovate or go out of business, it is essential to try and reduce the risks and increase the chances of success of new product development. In order to do so, the marketer must understand and manage effectively the steps in the new product development process. It is to these steps and their management then that we now turn our attention.

STEPS IN THE DEVELOPMENT PROCESS

In view of the importance of new products, and of the high rate of product failure, it is axiomatic that any development programme should be embarked upon only with the utmost care. The ramifications of a new product are numerous, but the criteria for any developments and ultimate launch can be reduced to three basic questions; no undertakings should even be considered unless satisfactory answers to the following can be supplied:

1. Is there a real consumer need?
2. Does the company have the resources and technical ability to market and manufacture the product?
3. Is the potential market large enough to generate profit?

These are the key questions, but because new products do not just 'materialize', there must be a formal method for the generation of ideas, idea evaluation and establishing practical feasibility. The following steps should provide answers to the three fundamental questions and establish a clearly defined cut-off point after which the company should feel confident in launching a new product.

Idea generation

These emanate from a variety of sources, but the source itself is less important than the system and attitude which the company has towards idea evaluation. The groundwork that leads to ideas can be described as 'opportunity exploration'. This process can be carried on by formal *research and development* departments. Here, care should be taken to avoid the syndrome of developing a product and then saying 'let's see if anyone wants it!' The *production department* can, in the course of manufacture, provide ideas for modifying and improving the existing product. The *sales team* is another source of valuable ideas: they are the people who receive direct customer feedback and who are often able to say what competitors are providing which their firm is not. *Senior management*, if product-oriented, should be responsible for creating the correct attitude towards development within the firm and for organizing formal programmes which might include techniques such as brainstorming sessions and the organization of venture teams and planning committees. Finally, and irrespective of the firm's level of sophistication in the field of market intelligence, it is possible to draw heavily on *external sources* for inspiration and ideas. These would include: trade associations, published reports, governmental bodies, middlemen and foreign competitors.

Screening new ideas

Once equipped with a set of potentially viable ideas, it is necessary to devise a method of screening these ideas so as to reduce them to a manageable number which have real market prospects. Screening should also ensure that a good product is not eliminated at an early stage, which can be equally as damaging as having to bear the development cost of a product failure.

In order to develop a screening technique, it is essential that the firm isolates a series of factors which research has shown are desirable to the consumer, and which are desirable to the firm in that they make the best use of existing strengths. The product ideas can then be compared so as to establish a short list of those that fit most closely to these criteria. Typical factors under consideration might include: raw material availability, production, distribution and product line compatibility, and the effect on sales of other products. Market research techniques such as brand mapping might provide a series of features that are thought desirable from the consumer's point of view.

The technique of screening can be carried out by a numerical weighting of the factors involved. A minimum rating score must, of course, be established and those ideas whose score is superior to this can then proceed to the next development stage. The use of 'Likert'-type scales to construct client profiles rather than numerical values is probably less effective because of the semantic difficulties in establishing what is, say GOOD, POOR or FAIR.

Business analysis

This third step concerns the financial, rather than the practical, viability of the product idea. Research and forecasting techniques are used to establish demand. Cost analysis examines not only the basic cost of production, but also such factors as capital investment, marketing costs (perhaps advertising and new distribution channels) and in some cases the engagement of new personnel. Profitability can be established in terms of 'break-even' and 'rate-of-return' analysis.

Product development

Once it has been established by analytical methods that a product idea has market potential, it is necessary to develop some form of prototype in an effort to confirm this feasibility in physical terms. This confirmation must be related both to production and marketing. Marketing activities would include motivational research and concept testing. Physical testing of the prototype by the consumer would encompass performance, packaging and comparison with products where level of acceptance is already known.

It is also necessary at this stage to ensure that production and marketing departments are working in close harmony. The marketing responsibility is to communicate immediately any reaction that would suggest that the nature of the prototype should be altered, or that the whole project should be seriously called into question. The production department must be as sure as possible that the prototype corresponds precisely with any production model that would subsequently be launched. If this was not the case, all marketing research would be a fruitless exercise.

At the end of the product development stage, the firm faces a critical decision: whether to go ahead and market the new product or to 'cut its losses' by abandoning a project which appears to have an unlikely chance of success. Either decision requires considerable business competence, not to mention sheer courage! The 'go' decision involves the risk of product failure, while on the other hand the decision to abort requires that the firm must write off large expenditure and perhaps years of time spent in development. The decision must, however, be made, because this is the whole reason for having a 'planned' development programme.

Test marketing

Just as the prototype must correspond exactly to the final product, so it is vital that the 'test market' chosen for partial launch of the final product is highly representative of the total market.

Although, in practice, the test market and test marketing provide the firm with a final opportunity to withdraw the product before a full-scale launch, this is not the real purpose of the exercise. Test markets are not 'final screens'. At this stage the firm should have already made up its mind to commercialize the product. Test marketing objectives are: to predict the efficacy of the proposed marketing strategy (and refine this if needed) and to predict the effect of strategy in terms of market penetration.

As we have seen, the usual procedure for test marketing is to select an easily identifiable sector of the market which represents the total market in miniature and then to launch a product in the same way as a total market launch would be expected to take place, thus testing the feasibility of the full marketing programme. In the UK it is common to use ITV television areas as test marketing areas for consumer goods. As well as providing distinct geographical areas, television advertising can also be monitored area by area when experimenting with different campaigns, advertising frequency and so on. It is not uncommon to run more than one test market concurrently. In this way, different applications of the marketing mix can be experimented with, as can the attribution of marketing budgets. Market research agencies are increasingly active in test marketing, especially in the field of predictive analysis. As such predictive models increase in their level of sophistication, there is a tendency to reduce the scope of test markets in the physical sense by placing an increasing reliance on statistical hypotheses. This is less true in the industrial sense, but in consumer goods markets, 'mini' and 'micro' test markets are common.[7] For actual examples of UK test marketing procedure see Chapter 5.

Mini test markets provide one way of exercising greater control over the test itself. One danger of test marketing is that one is never completely sure that the test marketing accurately simulates the full-scale reality. This can be exacerbated by competitors who, aware that a test market is under way, can devise ways of creating artificial market conditions. An intense 'burst' of competitive advertising or a series of special offers would completely disrupt the effect of test marketing in a given area. A second danger is that, while company A is engaged in test marketing, company B can 'leapfrog' the whole process by bringing a product to market without pre-testing it. For these reasons, as well as for good statistical practice, it is always advisable to operate a 'control' test market so as to estimate the impact of a number of control variables—including competitive action.

Commercialization

The stages of product development have 'filtered' commercially viable product ideas from a wide selection of original propositions. Furthermore, a product has been chosen *and* prepared for acceptability in the marketplace. Test marketing has fine-tuned the appropriate marketing strategy, and the firm is now sufficiently confident and knowledgeable to launch and commercialize the product on a full-scale basis. New product strategy to 'skim' or go for 'market penetration' is dealt with later in this chapter and in Chapter 7 when we consider pricing.

Figure 6.3 shows a schematic relationship between product development and expenditure. The relationship is inverse in that early stages cost relatively little. At the stages of product development and test marketing, potential products have been reduced to a few, yet these are the stages where cost is highest. This underlines the importance of effective screening and business analysis. Ruthless decisions must be made to eliminate those products thought unsuitable at each stage of the process. It is also worth while re-emphasizing that, while development costs to the stage of a test market are high, the financial loss of launching a product 'full-scale' which is a subsequent failure are always considerably higher. Typically, the development cost of a new model in the car industry is between £500 and £1000 million over a time span of around five years. Imagine the cost of full production and market launch in addition to this, and the period of time required for break-even!

Despite the care and attention which goes into new product development, as we have already seen there exists an apparently endless list of product failures. In industrial markets, most go unnoticed by all but those who are directly involved. Consumers are, however, witness to a constant series of new products which are here today and gone tomorrow. No guarantees are attached to a careful development plan, and despite the best predictions, markets have a habit of being unpredictable. On the positive side,

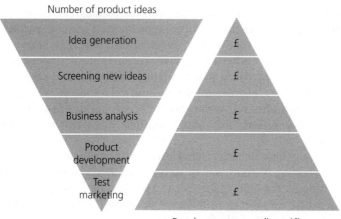

Number of product ideas

Idea generation

Screening new ideas

Business analysis

Product development

Test marketing

Development expenditure (£)

FIGURE 6.3

The relationship between cost and product development

what we can be sure of is that, like good marketing as a whole, the more thorough and professional is the development programme, the more this is likely to minimize the risk of product failure.

RECENT DEVELOPMENTS AND THINKING IN NEW PRODUCT DEVELOPMENT AND INNOVATION

Perhaps as we should expect, in an area of marketing which by its very nature is characterized by change, in recent years a number of key developments have been taking place regarding the management of new product development and innovation. In part, these developments reflect improvements in our knowledge regarding the key factors in managing this process more successfully, and in part, they reflect changes in the competitive and market environment. Of particular importance in the management of new product development has been the growing recognition of the role of the design function, and in particular the importance of relating design to all the elements of new product development from manufacturing through to the final marketing of the product. Another development has been the attention that has been focused on how to reduce product development times, in particular through more effective teamwork and better sequencing of the new product development process. Finally, the high costs and risks of new product development have led many companies to look at the possibilities of collaborative ventures with other members of the supply chain to develop new and improved products. We shall now consider each of these developments in turn.

Design and new product development

The design of a product is now a major source of product differentiation in an increasingly competitive marketplace. The importance of design in new product success has, of course, long been recognized by some; however, perhaps not since the 1930s has design been more strategically used to gain advantage in the marketplace. Block[8] has suggested that a distinctive design can render older competitors obsolete and make later competitors appear shallow copies. He also suggests that more durable product designs can have an impact on both users and non-users for many years. To be durable a product design does not have to be complicated, a good product design is one which satisfies the needs of the customer and makes a product eye-catching in the marketplace.

In addition to being one of the principal means of differentiating a company's products from those of its competitors, the product design process also determines product attributes such as functional capabilities and product lifespan. Similarly, the life cycle cost of a product is significantly influenced by how it is designed. Product design affects ease of manufacture and product serviceability. Simplifying product design results in many benefits and not only reduced costs but the marketing benefits of improved quality and potentially shorter product development lead time. Lee and Sasser[9] have suggested that the total cost of producing and delivering a product is largely determined by the design of the product itself. At the time of design completion only 5 per cent of the budget for new product development may have been spent but 80 per cent of the remaining budget has been committed through the design.

How products are designed has changed significantly in recent years. Customer-focused designs are replacing the expensive, slow, and above all, product-oriented, engineer-dominated design processes of the past. Neff[10] has proposed that *quality function deployment* be introduced to ensure that customers' ideas are incorporated into the product design process from the outset. Marketing, of course, has the responsibility of relating customer requirements to technical departments including design, so well-run organization marketing research should be used to evaluate the marketability of new designs at an early stage. Customer requirements in fact should be translated into technical requirements at each stage of product development but it is at the early design stages that they are most important. Competitive benchmarking is also an approach which can be used to ensure that proposed new product designs improve on those of competitors in aspects which have greatest importance and value to customers. The effect of quality function deployment in an organization requires potentially far-reaching changes in how a company operates with respect to design and new product development. In essence it requires different functional groups to interact simultaneously to identify and solve problems, and hence much greater teamwork and communication, particularly between marketing and design functions is required. An example of how quality function deployment can be used in the new product design and development process is outlined by Lockomy and Khurana.[11] In particular, they stress the significance of the role of quality function deployment in integrating functions horizontally through the process of design and new product development. This notion is illustrated in Fig. 6.4.

Lockomy suggests that one of the key advantages of implementing a system of quality function deployment is that 'a pioneer' in a market can charge premium prices in the early years of a product's life cycle, then use process improvement initiatives to generate savings in later years.

Overall then, effective management of the design process is essential if products are to compete successfully in the marketplace. More and more companies have come to realize this and have elevated their design function to a more important role in the overall process of innovation than that afforded it in past years.

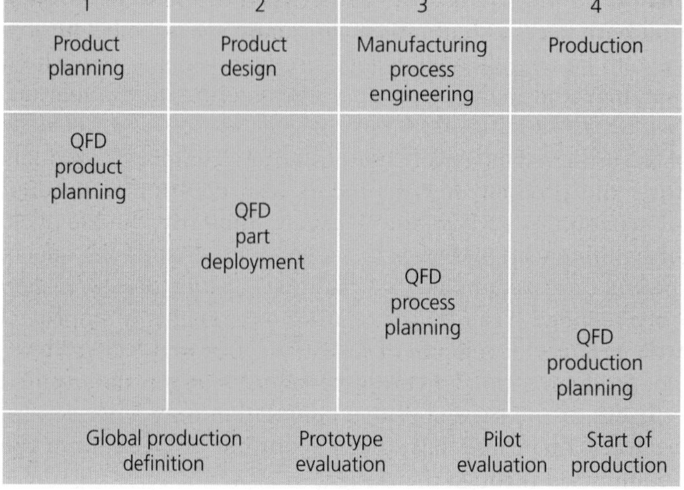

1	2	3	4
Product planning	Product design	Manufacturing process engineering	Production
QFD product planning			
	QFD part deployment		
		QFD process planning	
			QFD production planning
Global production definition	Prototype evaluation	Pilot evaluation	Start of production

FIGURE 6.4

Product development cycle and quality function deployment (QFD) key events

Source: A. Lockomy and A. Khurana, 'Quality function deployment in new product design', *International Journal of Quality and Reliability Management*, **12** (6), 1995, p. 75

Speed and flexibility in the new product development process

With competitive environments changing so rapidly, and in particular with changes in markets, technologies, and user needs, as we have already seen, causing product life cycles to become even shorter, there is an increased premium on speed and flexibility in managing new product development. Because of this, companies have sought to find ways of improving their performance with respect to both these attributes. The most important way in which companies have sought to increase their performance in the speed and flexibility of new product development has been to move from the traditional sequential approach to product design and development to one which is characterized by shorter overlapping phases between the different stages of new product development, and with interaction and feedback from cross-functional and multi-functional areas. Takeuchi and Nonaka[12] have suggested an holistic approach to new product development where several phases of development overlap. This idea is shown in Fig. 6.5.

With the sequential approach to product development the new product goes through each phase in a step-by-step manner, moving from phase to phase only after all the requirements of each phase have been completed. The 'type B approach' shown in Fig. 6.5 has moved from the traditional sequential approach to a process where development overlaps at the borders of each phase. The final truly holistic approach shown in type C of Fig. 6.5 is where the different phases of product development run together. This inevitably means an end to functions being specialized where marketing examines the customer needs, engineers select the design, and production are asked to build the product. Instead of this process, which is akin to running a relay race with each function passing the baton from one to another, the new product development process is organized around multi-functional teams who take charge of the product development process, developing products, manufacturing processes, and marketing plans simultaneously to collapse time. The increased speed of product development which this can give rise to can represent a major source of competitive advantage. For example, Ray[13] cites the case of Canon. In the early 1980s Canon's top management set an objective of reducing product development cost and time by 50 per cent. Ultimately, Canon reduced its development costs by 30 per cent and achieved its objective of reducing time-to-market by the 50 per cent figure. This enabled Canon to increase its market share by 10 per cent over a 10-year period. Similarly, when Yamaha threatened Honda's leadership in the motorcycle market, Honda unleashed 30 new motorcycle models within a six-month period, effectively thwarting the Yamaha threat.

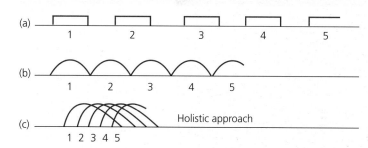

FIGURE 6.5

Sequential (a) versus overlapping (b) and (c) phases of new product development

Source: Adapted from H. Takeuchi and I. Nonaka, 'The new product development game', *Harvard Business Review*, January 1986, **64** (1), p. 139

The effect of these newer approaches to developing new products is illustrated in Table 6.1 below which shows some examples of how well-known companies have reduced their product development time for particular products over a 10-year period.

Inter-company collaboration in new product development

As many products become more complex and their design and manufacturing demand more and more resources, some companies are increasingly turning towards collaboration for the development of new products. Each of the collaborating companies concentrates on those activities which reflect their competencies and the product development process therefore is shared between the different members of the supply chain. Collaboration is increasingly being promoted as an effective strategy in dealing with some of the more problematic aspects of the product development process. Littler and Leverick[14] suggest that collaboration offers the means to secure access to technologies, skills or information, to share the costs and risks of product development and once again reduce the time taken to develop products. Styles[15] contends that the pooling of resources and capabilities can generate synergistic growth between organizations, either in terms of developing a current product or service offering, or through the creation of an entirely new venture.

THE PRODUCT LIFE CYCLE

The concept of the product life cycle (PLC) constitutes an important component of product and marketing strategy. The concept proposes that, once the product or service reaches the market, it enters a 'life cycle' and will eventually fade from the market. We must remember that the PLC is meant to serve as a conceptual base for examining product growth and development, and that not every product necessarily fits neatly into all the elements of the theoretical curve (see Fig. 6.6). A study of business

TABLE 6.1   *Reduced development times for new products*

Company	Product	Development time (years) 1980	1990
Rank Xerox	Copiers	5	3
Brother	Printers	4	2
Hewlett-Packard	Printers	4.5	2
Apple	Computers	3.5	1
Volvo	Trucks	7	5.5
Honda	Cars	8	3
AT&T	Telephone systems	2	1
Sony	Television sets	2	0.75

Source: M. B. Ray, 'Cost management for product development'. *Journal of Cost Management*, Spring 1995, **9** (1), p. 54

and economic history reveals that some predictable course of product development occurs sufficiently often for marketing planners to attach considerable credence to the concept. Thus, as well as providing a theoretical framework, the PLC can be used as a real managerial tool which is helpful in forecasting and, therefore, in strategic planning.

Figure 6.6 identifies four stages in the pattern of demand during the product's life. The life cycles of two hypothetical products are shown to illustrate that the life cycle concept is only a guide. The life cycles of different products will differ because they are a function of their intrinsic nature, their markets and their competitive environments.

Similarly, just as the shape of the curve is likely to differ according to the type of product, the time span of the cycle may vary from as little as a few days to as much as several decades.

Whatever the shape of time span of the life cycle curve, the implications for the marketer are of equal importance and are as follows:

1. The appropriate strategy for each stage.
2. The identification of movement from one stage to another.
3. The likely shape of the total curve.

The definition of the points where different stages in the life cycle begin is somewhat arbitrary, but each stage has characteristic phenomena which suggests a specific reaction and mode of strategy formulation.

Introduction

Characteristics   This stage is, of course, typified by conditions that relate to those of a new product launch.

1. A high product failure rate.
2. Relatively little competition.
3. Limited distribution.
4. Frequent product modification.
5. Company losses at least on that product because development costs have not yet been recouped, mass production economies are not possible and promotional expenditure is usually greater than profit return on sales.

Money spent at the 'introduction' phase should be regarded as an investment in the future.

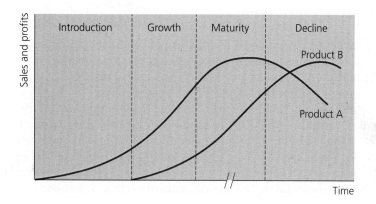

FIGURE 6.6

Product life cycle (PLC)

Introduction strategy   Promotion is directed at creating product awareness. This may require extra effort in personal selling. For consumer goods, advertising is the most common method of promotion. In extreme cases, advertising expenditure can exceed not only profits, but also sales revenue. In any case, introduction strategy requires that a firm's resources are deployed in larger than usual levels of marketing expenditure.

Pricing strategy will depend largely on the degree of distinctiveness of the product and on the length of time that this distinctiveness is likely to last. Two basic strategic options are open: either a 'skimming' or 'penetration' strategy may be adopted. 'Skimming' involves the application of a high price to a small section of consumers (the early adopters). It is appropriate when the product is unusually distinctive and demand is inelastic. Depending upon the circumstances (a critical factor being the degree of competitive activity), potential new groups of adopters are encouraged to buy the product by a planned series of progressive price reductions.

'Penetration' is likely to be appropriate where demand is elastic and the level of competitive activity is high. This is a relatively low price strategy which aims to attract the largest number of new buyers early in the product's life.

Neither strategy has an immediate profit-maximizing objective in the economic sense; rather, these are 'marketing' strategies which are designed to ensure long-term profitability, that is, profitability during the subsequent stages of the life cycle. These pricing strategy notions are explored more fully in the next chapter.

The decision to pursue a policy of market share acquisition is a matter of corporate strategy and is a highly complicated subject. Suffice it to say here that, if market share is considered as being strategically advantageous, then it is most easily accomplished during introduction while the distinctiveness of the product remains intact.

In the sense of 'market evolution' or a life cycle for markets, Hofer and Schendel[16] have identified a 'shake-out' stage between those of introduction and growth. This can be applied to individual products as well as to companies in a market, because in both cases the numbers falling 'by the wayside' can have significant implications for those that survive into the growth stage.

Growth

Characteristics

1. More competitors—less product distinctiveness.
2. Rising sales.
3. Profitable returns.
4. Company or product acquisition by larger companies.

Growth strategy   Although heavy promotion is a feature of the introduction stage, advertising and promotion also feature highly in the marketing budget during growth. However, there are two important differences: one is the promotional task itself, which in growth centres its emphasis on promotion of the 'brand' or trade name, rather than on creating product awareness, as this should already have been achieved. Second, the promotional budget, relative to sales, should allow room for a profit return, whereas in introduction it is not unusual for promotional expenditure to be grossly dispro-portionate to sales and profit. There are, however, exceptions to these guidelines. If, for example, a large company with an extensive product portfolio is determined to ensure market dominance for one of these products during maturity, then a promotional expenditure which continues to sap profits throughout the growth stage would not be unusual.

Distribution is also a major consideration during growth, and manufacturers will fight strongly to acquire dealership and distribution outlets. Trends in the UK retail sector during the last 10–15 years emphasize this phenomenon. In many instances the key to whole markets lies within a small nucleus of retail groups. Similarly, owing to the pressure for profitable shelf space, retail groups, especially supermarkets, will rationalize the number of brands carried as soon as a hierarchy of leaders has established itself. For fast-moving consumer goods, if a product fails to be stocked by even one of the major UK supermarket chains, a large section of that market will have been lost.

You will doubtless already be aware of the strongly 'interdependent' nature of the elements of the marketing mix: growth strategy ably demonstrates this. In growth, as indeed in the other stages of the PLC, the chosen strategy will fail if either one of the key elements (in the case of growth, promotion and place) is not efficiently effected.

The opportunity to achieve maximum profits usually peaks towards the end of the growth period. This is often because brand shares have stabilized to some extent and many companies are obliged to follow the leader. This last factor, coupled with the possible opportunity for economies of scale, sometimes leads to price decreases towards the end of this stage.

Finally, for the pessimistic as well as the cautious strategist, the end of growth also heralds the beginning of decline!

Maturity

The majority of products are in this stage of the life cycle. Much marketing activity is, therefore, directed at appropriate maturity strategies. This is also usually the longest stage of the life cycle.

Characteristics

1. Sales continue to increase, but at a greatly reduced rate.
2. Attempts are made to differentiate or re-differentiate the product, and the product line may be widened.
3. Prices begin to fall as manufacturers fight to regain market share.
4. Profits fall in line with falling prices and the continued need to promote the product.
5. Inventory and brand rationalization become common among retailers and dealers.
6. Marginal producers, faced with dwindling margins and severe competition, may drop out at this stage, although it is not impossible for new entrants to appear.

Maturity strategy   Promotional strategy is directed at reinforcement of the 'message' so as to encourage re-buys. Subtle differences in brands are emphasized to attract new customers as well as to reinforce the loyalty of existing users. It must be remembered at this stage actual market growth has ceased, and companies can increase their own market share only at the expense of their competitors. Such a situation implies that promotional activity must be sustained merely to hold on to the existing market share.

Price reductions (as a means of achieving the above) are often a feature of the maturity stage, but care must be taken to avoid a 'pyrrhic' victory, because very often the net result of initiating price cuts is to decrease the revenue for all firms in the industry unless sufficient increased purchases can be induced so as to offset revenue losses.

Distribution strategy must be designed to retain existing dealerships and retail outlets, because once lost, they are unlikely to be retained at this stage. To achieve this, the emphasis of promotional effort may move from consumer to distributor.

Decline

Whether because of innovation or changes in consumer preferences, a continued fall in industry sales signifies the 'decline' of the product.

Characteristics

1. Falling sales for the total industry.
2. Price cutting may intensify.
3. Producers decide to abandon the market.

Decline strategy The major strategic decision here is whether to leave the market or not, and, if the former decision is taken, when? Many firms have successfully 'hung on' in a declining market by outliving their competitors and finding 'niches' or speciality areas to serve. Cost control, although always important, becomes critical in retaining profitability when the decision to remain in a declining market is made.

On the other hand, the decision to abandon a previously profitable product is a crucial one and is the source of much 'soul searching' on management's behalf. Many firms find it difficult to accept that a product (on which the very company may have made its name) must sooner or later be abandoned. Such decisions are, however, the essence of marketing management.

Extending the product life cycle

It is important to note that at the maturity or even decline stage of the PLC many products have their lives extended and can sometimes experience a whole new growth process. The extent to which this is possible depends on many factors. For example, the nature of the replacement products, the amount of investment required and the factors overall which have caused maturity and decline. Extending the life of products and brands is not easy and in fact may not always be advisable, but there are plenty of examples of seemingly 'death-defying' products and brands. British Leyland's Mini, for example, started life over 50 years ago with the latest variant of this model having been recently launched by its now owner BMW. Product life cycles can be extended in a variety of ways, for example, by finding new users, i.e. different market segments, or new uses as in the case of, for example, Johnson's baby lotions. More frequent usage, too, is a way of rejuvenating products and brands through encouraging heavier usage among existing customers. Finally, of course, products and brands can have their lives extended through effective rejuvenations, brand remarketing and repositioning strategies.

Using the PLC concept

The key to successful use of the PLC concept lies in the accurate identification of where each stage starts and ends. This calls for a high degree of marketing orientation by management and thus for extensive use of marketing research and intelligence.

If we assume the above to be possible, management then has the basic medium for long-term strategic planning. As well as providing a predictable pattern of product development (during which the appropriate strategies can be planned and budgeted for), the PLC is particularly useful for planning 'beyond the life' of the existing product.

Figure 6.7 shows the likely course of profits for product A during its life cycle. Of particular importance, however, is the launch and overlap of product B.

It is essential that planning is such that companies are already beginning to receive revenue from a new product before or while the previous product is in decline. Similarly, the funding of product B must be derived from the profits of product A—and so the cycle continues.

As we have seen, though, one of the key uses of the PLC concept is in helping guide the marketer with respect to the use and combination of the marketing mix elements. We shall return to the relationship between the PLC and the combination of the marketing mix elements in Chapter 12.

Criticisms and variations of the concept

Despite criticisms, to many the value of the PLC as a strategic tool is undoubted, but, as the student of marketing should now be aware, management should not be constrained by dogmatic adherence to a theoretical course of events. Success is determined by the ability to react and adapt to 'market conditions'. The PLC provides a 'framework' for planning rather than a rigid curve that must be followed. As has already been stated, the time span of the curve can vary enormously according to the product type, but the 'actual' life of the product can in practice be modified by management. Thus, faced with difficult trading conditions or with the opportunity for a better allocation of resources, management can prematurely end the life of a product, say, in early maturity. By the same token, the product's life can be extended and re-extended by finding new end-users for it, or by applying it to totally new markets. There is the possibility of some confusion in considering the extension of a product's

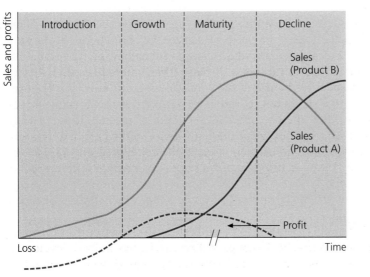

FIGURE 6.7

Sales/profit comparisons

life, because in some cases, if the product has changed significantly, then it could be said that this is in reality a 'new product'. One must also distinguish here between the company product and the generic product. Using Levitt's[17] example of nylon, we can see that the generic life of nylon has been constantly extended by finding new end-uses for it. We must be aware that some brands may themselves experience decline while the generic product lives on. The personal computer (PC) is a good example of a new product with which to study the PLC. Although a multitude of new brand personal computers may enter or leave the market at various stages, this will not affect the course of the PC's cycle as a generic product. Provided that it remains popular with consumers, the PC will not begin to decline until a radically new technology begins to supplant its use.

We must also consider the views of those who criticize the use of the PLC as a basic concept. It is not the intention here to engage in full-scale debate, but it is worth noting that critics of the PLC raise issues to which attention should be paid.

We have already pointed to some of the problems and limitations of the basic PLC concept. Some of the critics of this concept have gone further in their assessment of the limitations of the conventional life cycle in strategic market planning. Essentially, these criticisms are based on the extent to which the concept is, at best, irrelevant and, at worst, misleading and dangerous.

The most fundamental, and hence most important, of the criticisms of the PLC concept is that there is little or no consistent empirical evidence to support the notion of products following a natural and preordained life cycle with the distinct stages that we have outlined here. In short, some critics claim that the product life cycle simply does not exist.

Among the most cogent of these critics have been Dhalla and Yuspeh,[18] who have challenged the whole concept of the product life cycle. Indeed, in their influential article we are counselled to forget the concept, the use of which, they suggest, can lead to costly and potentially irrevocable mistakes in strategy.

Of course, any doubt about the existence or otherwise of both the S-shaped life cycle and the distinct stages of which it is suggested to comprise can be resolved only by an appeal to the facts. Needless to say, with such a long-standing piece of marketing theory, numerous empirical studies have been undertaken over the years designed to confirm or refute the PLC concept, including those of Cox,[19] Polli and Cook,[20] Cunningham[21] and Day.[22]

Overall, the evidence from these and other studies suggests that the classic S-shaped life cycle does indeed exist, but not for all products or for similar products on all occasions. In other words, we cannot (indeed, should not) consider the traditional PLC concept as a universal law or fact. But if this is the case, then where does this leave the marketing planner with respect to the use of the concept, and particularly with regard to the suggested application of the concepts that were outlined earlier? You will recall that we have already counselled the use of judgement and experience in interpreting the concept for marketing strategy; but does not the evidence of the lack of universality of the concept tend to undermine the wisdom of using the concept at all? Clearly, this is the Dhalla–Yuspeh view. However, the view taken here is that critics and researchers of the concept, and particularly those who have not supported the classic S-shaped PLC, have added to, rather than detracted from, the usefulness of the concept to strategic marketing planning.

The reason for this seemingly contradictory statement derives from our assertion that much of this criticism, coupled with empirical research, has helped develop and refine our knowledge of the basic concept. In particular, partly as a result of the criticisms of the basic concept and the research it has generated, it is now acknowl-edged that there are several possible variations on the traditional, S-shaped PLC curve. Some of these are shown in Fig. 6.8.

A number of factors give rise to these different possible shapes for the product life cycle, but there is some evidence to suggest that the shape of the PLC may be associated with the type of product/market under consideration.

For example, life cycle (a) of the figure is suggested by Kotler[23] as being frequently found in the small kitchen appliance market. Initial sales growth after a new product launch is rapid, followed by a quite severe drop in sales as the novelty wears off. Eventually, however, the decline in sales will stop and the product will enter a relatively long period of stability in sales as late adopters purchase the product and early buyers purchase again to become replacement purchasers.

The pattern shown in Fig. 6.8 (b) represents a 'truncated' pattern. The shape of this pattern illustrates that there is no introductory period. Sales grow rapidly right from product launch. This type of PLC curve may be associated with new products where there is a substantial market appeal and where little learning is required or risk perceived. Such products include new models of cars from the large manufacturers supported by appropriate high profile launch publicity.

Pattern (c) illustrates a rapid growth in sales, again with no introductory stage, followed by an equally rapid decline with no maturity stage. Products that exhibit this shape of life cycle are typical novelty products or fads, such as Rubik's Cube, or Teletubby products.

Finally, pattern (d) illustrates a success of PLC curves with a relatively short introductory period, rapid sales growth, a short maturity, followed by rapid decline. After this, the process is repeated. This pattern is frequently associated with fashion type products, such as clothing.

Another criticism is that, if used without imagination, the PLC can become a self-fulfilling prophecy. In other words, management may misinterpret market activity and

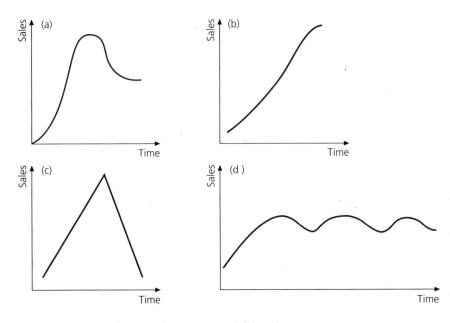

FIGURE 6.8   *Alternative product life cycle patterns*

think themselves into product decline and accept this as inevitable. One method of avoiding this is to extend or 'exploit' the PLC by imaginative application of the product to new markets. Thus, although the product may decline in its existing form and market, this is not to say that it cannot be profitably employed elsewhere. Such a strategy does not imply that the life cycle concept is being ignored—rather, it is the recognition of the concept that permits such a strategy.

A further danger and cause for criticism is linked to that described in the preceding paragraph. This concerns the capacity of management to identify accurately the beginning and end of progressive life cycle stages. This is, of course, no easy task, because each stage merges with another over a time span which may vary according to the product and its markets. In the case of a truly 'new' product, no empirical data will be available to aid decision-making: such situations will, therefore, be 'unique'. Successful use of the PLC concept is not, however, an unattainable goal. It should be the result of a coherent and long-term marketing strategy. This in turn is supported and made possible by 'continuous' marketing and market research and the employment of a comprehensive marketing intelligence system.

Modified models of the PLC

In addition to proposing alternative shapes for the PLC some researchers have sought to develop more radical developments to the original PLC concept.

One example is that proposed by Tellis and Crawford.[24] They have suggested the idea of the *'product evolutionary cycle' (PEC)* concept. The PEC concept is in fact similar to the conventional PLC concept inasmuch as it uses analogies from biological/ evolutionary life cycles of living organisms to explore the life cycle stages and patterns of products. However, the PEC model of the evolutionary cycle allows for much more diverse and complex possible patterns of the evolutionary cycle. The following types of evolutionary cycle and patterns of change are included in the PEC model.

Cumulative change   Cumulative change is the notion of each change stage in a product's life building on the previous one. From a biological perspective new species are no longer seen as isolated entities but as part of a continuous evolving pattern connected by vital links to the previous species that existed. From a marketing point of view, products therefore can be considered not as individual isolated entities but part of an evolving pattern. So, for example, the modern washing machine is simply the present result of cumulative change from the original hand- and foot-driven models.

Directed change   Cumulative change implies a change proceeding with greater complexity, efficiency and diversity. Directed change is where new products throughout their life cycle are characterized by ever greater sophistication in their efficiency and performance and greater diversity in the total offering to consumers. Tellis suggests that the car, ballpoint pen and shaving blades are all outstanding examples of directed change.

Motivated change   There are three forces working together in motivated changes: generative, selective and mediative. Continuing the biological analogy, the genetic system is the generative force and the environment, the selective force favouring those evolutions better suited for survival. Man serves as the mediative force altering both genetic and natural selection processes to eliminate unwanted species and develop only selected ones. Applying this notion to marketing, managerial creativity serves as the generative factor, consumers and competitors act as the selective factor and the government and other agencies play the role of mediators.

Patterned change   This type of change comprises a variety of possible change patterns which do not fit the three types of change already outlined. Five possible types of patterned change in biological evolution can be identified, namely:

1. *Cladogenesis*   This is where the pattern is one of divergence of a new species from the evolutionary line triggered by some sort of stimulus from the environment. In marketing terms this is the commencement of a whole new product type or category.

2. *Anagenesis*   This is where we see a pattern of adaptation by a species to a changing environment. In product terms this is where a new product is increasingly adapted to suit market needs over its life cycle.

3. *Adaptive radiation*   This is where, in biological terms, a species shows increasing variation over time leading to the formation of sub-species. In marketing terms this is equivalent to the process of differentiation where products are increasingly differentiated to suit different consumer interests.

4. *Stasigenesis*   In biological terms this is used to describe a period of stability where there is not much change in the species. In marketing terms this is where there are few major changes in the basic product but perhaps numerous minor changes in, say, packaging, service deals, etc.

5. *Extinction*   Needless to say, this is the dying out of a species that can no longer cope with environmental changes. In marketing terms it is equivalent to the decline stage of the conventional PLC where a product no longer meets customer needs.

The PEC concept attempts to capture more of the complexity of what we know about biological and evolutionary patterns in species. It is an attempt to move away from what many have argued is the oversimplistic notion of the conventional PLC patterns.

Another relatively recent attempt to modify the PLC concept is that suggested by David Mercer.[25] On the basis of empirical research of the product life cycle theory Mercer has suggested what he calls the 'competitive saw' model. This model is an attempt to deal with what Mercer sees as a limitation of the conventional PLC in that it specifically focuses on patterns of sales of products in relatively stable markets. In other words it is designed to deal with the less dramatic changes in markets which Mercer

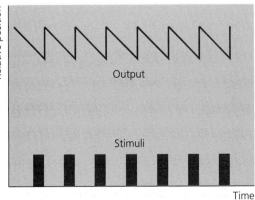

FIGURE 6.9

The competitive saw

Source: D. Mercer, 'Decline of the product lifecycle', *ADMAP*, September 1993

suggests represents the staple diet of most marketers. The principles of Mercer's competitive saw are shown in Fig. 6.9.

The stimuli referred to in Fig. 6.9 represent 'investments' in a product or service. These investments are bursts of marketing activity designed to boost the competitive position of the product or service and hence increase its sales. Such investments could be, for example, a new advertising or promotional campaign, a new feature added to the product, a new service deal, etc. If effective, these investments raise the product's or service's position in the market. Over time, however, this position is eroded as competitors respond and make their own investments in their products and services so that the initial advantage is slowly diluted and the competitive advantage or sales slowly drop until the next stimulus is made in the form of further investment. Mercer argues that this very simple model in fact mirrors what actually happens in practice in many markets.

The PLC and the product adoption process

It is important to consider product strategy and the PLC in conjunction with the reactions of consumers who are exposed to new products. The section on consumer behaviour in Chapter 3 deals in detail with this subject, but it is worth while here to consider briefly the relationship that the PLC concept has with product adoption. By doing this, marketing management can appreciate the nature of the target market and its needs as the product moves through its life cycle.

Consumers can be grouped into five 'adopter categories', each of which has distinct characteristics; therefore specific strategies need to be formulated which suit the individual needs of each group at a given time. The relationship between adoption theory and the PLC concept is shown in Fig. 6.10.

This figure does, of course, present an extremely simple and logical relationship, which is based on separate research studies. However, the implication is an essential ingredient of marketing strategy. This is that the marketing of a product should be seen in as many dimensions as possible. Marketing might say that the 'early majority' will require a specific approach to advertising, pricing and distribution. The fact that competitors will be employing the marketing mix in a similar way will in turn create market conditions that require decisions and action of a strategic nature, which in this case should be relevant to the 'growth' stage of the life cycle.

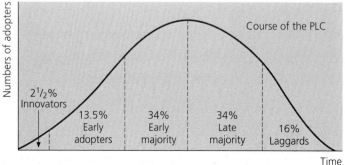

FIGURE 6.10

Adoption theory and the PLC

Source: E. M. Roger, *Diffusion of Innovation,* Free Press, NY, 1962, p. 162

PRODUCT MANAGEMENT AND ORGANIZATIONAL STRUCTURE

This section is concerned not with the total study of marketing organizational structure, but rather with the subject as it relates to the product. As usual with marketing, the interdependent theme is strong as no one aspect of the firm can be considered in isolation. A striking aspect of product organization *vis-à-vis* the complete organizational picture is the indispensable, motivational involvement of top management.

It is the responsibility of senior executives to create the correct environment for innovation and forward thinking and thus to initiate and motivate the development of new products. The extent of their involvement is very often the only determinant of eventual product success. Vital though attitude is, this must be translated into some concrete form of organizational structure and procedure so that the communication of ideas 'top down' and 'bottom up' can flourish. One of the following formal sections is commonly found in those companies that enjoy consistent success in product innovation.

The 'new product' section

The existence of such a section or department quite obviously implies a permanent commitment to product development. Typically, the section is small, perhaps four to six members, and it is their responsibility to set up a 'new product' programme and to steer this through the stages of development that have already been described.

The new product function has the authority and credence of being a section or department in its own right and should have the ability to 'streamline' ideas, whereas a committee, for example, has a tendency to operate in a manner rather abstracted from the running of the rest of the firm. It is vital that the members of the team are drawn from a wide cross-section of other departments, thus ensuring that they have the necessary experience and expertise to cover *all* aspects of the product; moreover, this experience should facilitate constructive communication with their peers throughout the firm. A real danger for 'new product' sections is that this communication breaks down and it becomes a remote 'boffin-like' institution in the eyes of other employees.

Often the head of the section will report directly to the chief executive of the firm and will possess substantial authority. When the development stage is complete, the product will be turned over to the respective functional areas for test marketing and commercialization.

'New product' committees

In common with 'new product' departments or sections, committee members are selected from key functional areas of the firm and in this case are usually senior managers in their respective fields. Their role is not as much in the actual conception of a product, but rather more in the approval and review of existing programmes. The strengths of committees are due to the authority of their members. Thus, if a particular plan is approved by, say, the production director, it is less likely that this will meet opposition later. On the other hand, there is a danger of the committee becoming remote from its purpose because members are often more anxious to concentrate on their own existing responsibilities. Moreover, decision-making can be slow, compromising in nature, and have a tendency to impede rather than accelerate the progress of promising developments.

In some companies, committees exist side by side with 'new product' sections or departments and are the final arbiters of crucial stages of development.

The venture team

This is the newest organizational concept for product development. Its role is to manage the development of a specific product from conception to full-scale marketing. Again, members are multi-disciplinary, but, unlike the two previous examples, the venture team operates outside the mainstream of the firm—almost like a 'mini-business' in itself. Its sole objective is to bring a new product to the market profitably. Most usually, team members are relieved of their existing responsibilities so as to concentrate fully on a given project. The life span of the team can run from a few months to several years—just as long as it takes to do the job.

The essence of the venture team is entrepreneurial spirit, and companies should endeavour to choose team members on this basis. How successful venture teams really are is uncertain. The 'entrepreneur' is often difficult to identify, and it is extremely difficult to segregate a small team away from the firm and retain its effectiveness, and to free such a team from 'bureaucratic' constraints and impediments, although this is the rationale on which the team is based.

Once a product reaches market launch, the team is usually disbanded and product management is then passed back to the mainstream of the firm and its functional departments.

Product managers

A product manager is an organizational unit in one person who has responsibility for the development of a new product and for the entire management of existing products. Functional marketing areas such as sales, marketing research and advertising exist on a 'company-wide' basis, and it is up to the product manager to utilize these services as he or she thinks fit.

A major criticism of the use of product managers for new product development is that, like committees, there is a tendency for them to become preoccupied with existing products and problems rather than new ideas. This is understandable, as their performance is usually assessed on the basis of established product success rather than idea generation, although the latter forms part of their remit in many firms. Similarly, it does not necessarily follow that the skills required for established product management coincide with those required for new product development. On balance, such role duality is likely to be neither fair nor efficient, and much current thinking places the product manager's responsibility with the management of established products. For this reason, the product manager's role will be re-examined below.

There is no single 'best' method to organize for new product development. Like many other aspects of marketing, this organization is a function of the company's make-up—its managerial skills, financial resources and existing organizational structure. There are, however, distinct guidelines which, if followed, considerably increase the opportunity for success.

Whatever method is employed, development should not be harmed by bureaucratic constraints. This is the surest way to stifle progress and enthusiasm. Development should take place in an entrepreneurial atmosphere fostered by top management and permeated throughout the firm. Representatives from all functional areas should be involved in development. Finally, the importance and involvement of top management cannot be overemphasized. As long as 25 years ago, E. J. McCarthy went so far as to say that 'new product development cannot be systemized'. Organizational plans can only 'facilitate' development whose key criterion for success is a 'dynamic, innovating attitude, instilled into and felt by the whole company'.[26]

THE PRODUCT MANAGER

The product manager as an organizational unit is not really a new or revolutionary breakthrough in marketing management. What is new is its rapid acceptance and adoption by most major companies during the past two decades. The principal reason for this can be ascribed to the emergence of multi-product organizations.

Where does the product manager 'fit in'?

The particular type of marketing organization a company chooses is of course dependent on the products it markets and the markets within which it operates. The arrangements and solutions that a company decides upon are almost as numerous as the companies themselves. One major theme is common whatever the circumstances of the firm. They all must accommodate three basic dimensions of marketing activity:

1. Functions
2. Products
3. Markets

The most common and least complicated approach to addressing the organizational problem is to organize the company around the marketing functions that must be performed. A marketing manager or marketing director is at the head of a function that coordinates and synchronizes the marketing operation in totality. This most simple structure is illustrated in Fig. 6.11. Advertising, sales and marketing research possess their own functional specialists, but work together under the unifying supervision of the marketing director. While the system is advantageous because of its simplicity, its appeal is considerably lessened as the number of products produced by a company begins to grow. When this happens, not only does management become physically complicated, but more importantly, there is a risk that some products will become neglected at the expense of others.

The product manager type structure offers the solution of providing each product (or sometimes brand) with someone who is directly responsible for its success, allocation of functional support and general well-being. Figure 6.12 locates the product manager in relation to the rest of the firm's marketing activities. Each product manager draws on

FIGURE 6.11

A functional marketing organization

the functional areas for appropriate support, and, because his or her activity is focused on one product only, the marketing of that product is uncluttered by dual roles and conflicting or confused product loyalties. Additionally, such a structure is highly flexible, as new managers who have very clearly defined objectives can be added as product expansion takes place.

If the product range is sufficiently large and diverse, the responsibilities can be broken down still further. A chemical company may have a manager for 'agricultural products'. Separate product managers may control 'insecticides', 'fertilizers', etc. These too can be broken down into individual 'brand managers', say, for brands within insecticides as in Fig. 6.13.

The role and responsibilities of the product manager

The product manager type company structure allows senior management to 'home in' on the progress and performance of any given product with relative ease and precision. As such, the system lends itself to marketing control and to marketing planning. Strategic planning and marketing 'audits' are, therefore, greatly improved by product manager feedback. Planning at the business level is also improved, because the product manager's primary role is to plan product objectives and strategy, ensure they are implemented, monitor their progress, take action if necessary, and coordinate budget development and control.

The responsibilities are, therefore, erroneous—in reality, the product manager runs a business within a business with direct responsibility for success or failure. Not only is the product manager a planner as well as an implementer, but a further burden is one of ensuring that the resources required to carry out a plan are readily available. In theory, as can be seen from Fig. 6.13, functional resources are shared and are at the disposal of each product. Problems arise, however, if a functional area becomes over-stretched and cannot share its resources equally. Here the product manager faces the task of negotiating, perhaps even fighting, for resources that are essential to carry out the job that senior management expects. In less difficult conditions, the least that is expected from a product manager (in addition to planning and implementation) is the ability to coordinate the functional resources at his or her disposal to the best advantage of the product plan.

The 'fundamental' tasks of the product manager have just been described. The remit is so wide that it is worth detailing the various involvements. The scope of product management is as follows:

1. Planning product strategy
2. Sales forecasting

FIGURE 6.12

A product manager marketing organization

3. Monitoring performance and gathering field intelligence

4. Advertising

5. Sales promotion

6. Marketing research

7. Merchandising

8. Packaging, branding, labelling

9. New product development—product improvements

10. Product line planning

11. Pricing

12. Inventories and warehousing

13. Production planning

14. Distribution

15. Sales—stimulating interest and support among the salesforce

Problems with product management

In view of the extent of the product manager's role, it is not surprising that certain problems are associated with this form of organization.

First, as has already been mentioned, the product manager, whose primary concern is the product, often extends much effort in vying for the functional resources which are shared with his or her peers. Time spent thus dilutes the amount of effort spent on planning. Such 'in-house competition' also has a psychological effect, in that the product manager is expected to be responsible for the results of, say, advertising decisions, but does not gain either personal expertise or the opportunity to be instrumental in the decision-making process. This syndrome can also be extended to profit accountability; the product manager is highly 'profit accountable', but rarely has the authority to make big profit decisions.

The product manager is therefore allocated great responsibility without the satisfaction of real control over the product's destiny. From the senior executives' viewpoints, the product manager's decision-making abilities are restricted because of his exclusive involvement in one product. For the product manager, this is a good reason to be afforded more executive control!

FIGURE 6.13

Expanded product manager organization

A final problem concerns organizational policy itself. At one extreme, a strictly functional structure (Fig. 6.11) is not sufficiently flexible for the demands of multi-product companies. However, there is a real danger of carrying the product manager concept too far. The structure of Fig. 6.13 shows product managers and brand managers, and here the difficulty for some companies is to know where to stop! If, for example, a product manager's time is being spent more and more on one aspect of management, an assistant may be appointed. So, in turn, a brand manager may request assistance. This process will in turn place increasing pressure on functional specialists. The end result may be an expensive and unwieldly 'superstructure' of personnel whose presence will defeat entirely the main object of product management—that of simplicity, direct responsibility and easy access to information.

Advantages of the product management structure

Much of the value of the product manager concept can be attributed to the direct responsibility and answerability that the system itself engenders. The product manager is a centre of information for planning. No single product is likely to be neglected because each manager has an obvious vested interest in obtaining the best possible level of resource support. With reference to overall product strategy, the product manager is uniquely placed as the firm's 'early warning system', giving information as to changes in the market which may require product adaptation, marketing mix modification or even the consideration of product deletion. Last, but not least, the job of the product or brand manager provides valuable experience and training to young men and women who aspire to higher managerial positions.

Despite these drawbacks, the product management structure is popular and workable in companies whose product range is too diverse to be adequately serviced by a 'functional' type of marketing organization. Any risk can be further reduced if the company clearly delineates the product manager's responsibilities, is aware of potential areas of conflict and takes steps to reduce their number, and, finally, ensures that the methods used for assessment are consistent with the product manager's responsibilities and authority.

PRODUCT STRATEGY

Many companies, while not necessarily requiring brand and product managers, do market more than one product. This is especially true of firms operating in consumer goods markets. The fact that a company has more than one product necessitates that some method be devised for monitoring and comparing their respective performances, and for enabling decisions to be made about the future. The PLC concept illustrates that, whatever the time span, the life of a product is finite. With this in mind, the essence of product strategy is simple: the firm must manage the marketing of existing products, decide when products are of no further use, and plan the development of new profit sources by providing new products to replace those that have been deleted.

In order that firms can organize for product planning, and that their products can be easily related to each other and to respective market areas, it is useful to consider products as a series of readily identifiable groups.

The first consideration is the *individual product*. This is any product considered as a separate entity irrespective of its relationship to other products and the type of market in which it is to be found. Provided that any product differs in some way from another, through either modification or market application, the firm can regard this as an individual product.

The sum total of the products offered for sale by a firm is referred to as the *product mix*.

Finally, those products that are related in some way to one another are classed as the *product line*. The relationship could be because they are simply different models of the same basic product, or because they have marketing similarities in that they are sold in similar outlets or serve the same customer groups.

It is common to attribute the product mix with 'width' and 'depth'. This enables an analysis of the consistency of the product mix to be made. The following example illustrates the idea of the product mix and product line, and forms the basic structure of analysis and selection of appropriate line strategies. A hypothetical example best illustrates this (Fig. 6.14).

A firm manufactures fountain pens, cigarette lighters and wrist watches. Each item is related in that they are marketed through similar channels and are targeted at approximately the same consumer segments.

The product mix represents the sum of the firm's products—in this case 30 products. The number of product lines is obviously three. 'Depth' refers to the number of products in each line—9, 13 and 8 with the average depth being 10. 'Width' refers to the number of product lines which a company has to offer.

By looking at its products in this way, a company is able to begin to see where existing strengths and weaknesses lie. Is there scope for adding to the product line by adding, say, digital watches to line 3? Do some products in the same line compete with each other? With respect to new products, will an addition to the line be consistent with its neighbours in terms of image, production, distribution and market segment? Conversely, is any one product so valuable in terms of image and reputation that its deletion will damage the product line or indeed the total mix? Finally, should the firm consider an addition to the width of the mix, and will these be consistent with the existing product mix and compatible with the current long-term marketing strategy?

Mix analysis is also vital to a review of marketing strategy itself. The firm is merely a representation of its products and its marketing strategy. In the case of Personal Products Ltd, the following are a few of the possible strategic options.

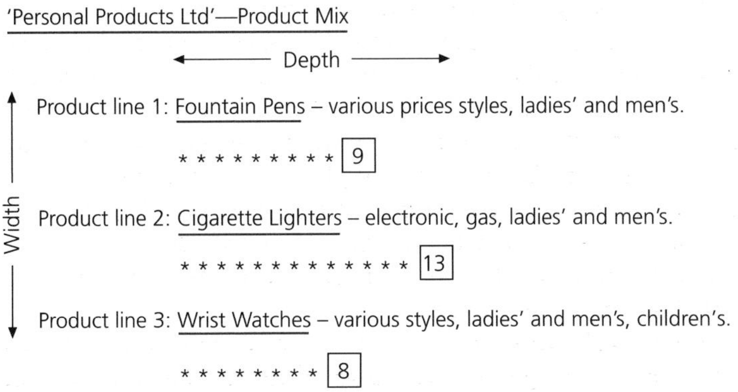

'Personal Products Ltd'—Product Mix

←———— Depth ————→

Product line 1: Fountain Pens – various prices styles, ladies' and men's.

★ ★ ★ ★ ★ ★ ★ ★ ★ 9

Width

Product line 2: Cigarette Lighters – electronic, gas, ladies' and men's.

★ ★ ★ ★ ★ ★ ★ ★ ★ ★ ★ ★ ★ 13

Product line 3: Wrist Watches – various styles, ladies' and men's, children's.

★ ★ ★ ★ ★ ★ ★ 8

FIGURE 6.14

The consistency of the product mix

1. Augment product line 1 by adding ball point pens. This would remove some measure of exclusivity and represent a strategy of being 'all things to all people'—a bid to serve the whole market for ink-based writing implements.

2. Delete all but the most expensive men's lighters from line 2. This would have the effect of making the company a market specialist in men's lighters—aiming at an exclusive market segment.

3. Delete lines 1 and 2 and become a specialist in a single product line—wrist watches. In such a situation, options 1 and 2 would still be available to the company.

4. Delete all but one product and become expert in its marketing and production.

5. Add another product line. In the case of 'Personal Products Ltd' it could be a new line of pens aimed at the designer or graphics market.

Some industrial companies become expert in supplying products for special situations, such as deep sea diving equipment. This represents a decision to reduce the product mix to its absolute minimum.

Given the existing product mix and the options available, the company must begin to take product decisions that are in line with long-term strategy, and are consistent with that mix. The introduction of ball point pens by Personal Products Ltd could influence the perception the consumer has of the company as a whole. Cheaper disposable pens might not be consistent with the firm's reputation for high-quality lighters. Similarly, the firm may be technically capable of producing an industrial line, but lacking in the marketing expertise required to serve this new market efficiently.

Analysis of the product mix thus questions every aspect of the company. Any decision has financial, technical, marketing and market connotations. The critical nature of product strategy becomes more apparent when one considers the consequences of failure and the necessity for success.

We must now consider ways in which the decision to choose any of the above options is made. First, we should remind ourselves of the absolute necessity of new products. If, at any time, the rate of new product development and launch is not equal or superior to the rate of product deletion or obsolescence, the company will lose profits rapidly and ultimately will be unable to survive. A long-term view of strategy must, therefore, be taken. Still keeping the product mix very much in mind, it is possible to look at the company's future from a more abstract viewpoint, which will stimulate and aid the long-term decision-making process.

The matrix shown in Fig. 6.15 presents possible alternatives for product strategy. Of course, any decisions must be evaluated in relation to the company itself and to the market conditions that are prevalent and likely in the future. In the first case, a marketing audit is designed to establish whether the firm is currently making the best use of opportunities available in existing markets and for existing products. Market share and sales analysis should establish whether last year's objectives are being achieved, and a study of profitability by product, geographical area and market segment should be made. When an internal analysis has been completed, marketing research and intelligence systems should be brought to bear to examine whether or not any prepared action is feasible.

Armed with knowledge of itself, and present and future markets, the company can address itself to the alternatives and go on to produce a plan for strategy realignment, new product development and possibly expansion. You may recognize that Fig. 6.15 is in fact a variation on the so-called 'Ansoff Matrix'. The Ansoff Matrix was in fact primarily developed for analysing and assessing overall marketing strategies but it can, in addition, be used as here to illustrate the various product strategies. We shall consider the Ansoff Matrix in the context of its marketing planning role again in Chapter 12.

We now know that product strategy requires a thorough examination of the firm's own strengths and shortcomings, thorough market knowledge and an unequivocal commitment to new product development and thus long-term strategy. Product strategy must, logically, also involve methods for phasing out certain products to make way for new ones. Very often it is judicious to withdraw products from the mix long before the PLC has run its course, and such a decision is usually due to one or more of three reasons:

- A decrease in market share due to competitive pressure.
- A reduction in profitability which is deemed irreversible.
- A slowing down of sales growth which suggests that marketing resources might be better employed elsewhere.

Given available marketing information, both internal and external, and the existence of products in varying market conditions and stages of development, it is possible to classify the total product mix according to each product's potential usefulness to the company. Again, as we shall see in Chapter 12, many of the strategic planning tools are also useful in the process of strategic product management. For example, we shall see that the BCG product portfolio technique can be used to analyse the elements of the product mix according to their position in the matrix. This analysis can then be used to classify products and to develop strategies according to where the products are located in the matrix.

In using portfolio techniques such as the BCG matrix to formulate product strategies, it should be remembered that the emphasis should be on managing the total product mix (the portfolio aspect). Understandably, product managers plan what they see as the best strategies for their own products or strategic business units. As Day[27] points out, this ignores the interdependency among products and the possibility that what is optimum for each product manager is not necessarily best for optimizing the product mix for the company as a whole. In addition, as with planning other elements of the marketing mix, strategic product decisions need to be considered in the interest of the organization's business mission, company objectives, environmental forces, and corporate strengths and weaknesses. Finally, strategic product decisions must also take into account competitors and their products and related strategies. An outline of these factors and the relationship between product planning and the strategic planning process is shown in Fig. 6.16.

	Existing markets	New markets
Existing products	Improved performance / Product performance / Realignments of the marketing mix	New market segments / Geographical expansion
New products	Same distribution channels, sales outlets and sales strategy	Diversification through innovation

FIGURE 6.15

A simple product strategy mix

SERVICE PRODUCTS

At the start of this chapter it was suggested that a product is a series or a bundle of satisfactions. It was also suggested that physical products such as a car or a machine tool include an 'intangible' service element when considered from the perspective of what the customer buys. Finally, we have seen that, when we discuss products and the planning of product decisions, a wide range of different types of products, from machine tools to office cleaning services and from baked beans to holidays, can be encompassed. All of what has been discussed throughout this chapter relating to the nature and importance of product planning decisions, plus the planning tools and frameworks, applies equally well to any category of product. We end this chapter by examining the special issues of marketing services.

The importance and nature of service products

In many developed economies of the world, and particularly the USA and the UK, service industries have outstripped manufacturing industry in terms of their contribution to gross national product. Put simply, the UK and the USA are now service economies. There are a variety of reasons for the growth of the service sectors, and many argue that the balance has tipped too far in favour of services for a 'healthy' economy. Both the reasons for the growth of services and the arguments for and against

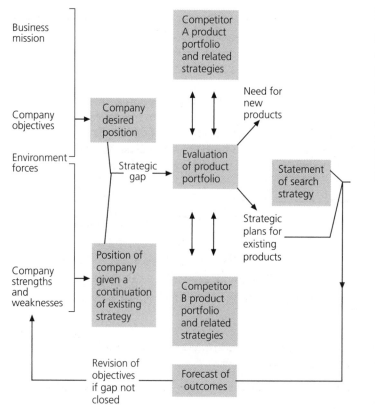

FIGURE 6.16

Product planning activities in the strategic planning process

Source: Adapted from G. S. Day, 'A strategic perspective on product planning', *Journal of Contemporary Business*, Spring 1975

this growth are outside the scope of this text. However, the importance of service products and the special issues that surround their marketing mean that it is worth while considering them further. But what is meant by the term 'service products', and what are the distinguishing characteristics of those products that give rise to special issues in their marketing?

'A service is an intangible product involving a deed, a performance, or an effort that cannot be physically possessed.'[28] This definition by Berry attempts to capture some of the key distinguishing characteristics of service products, in particular their intangibility and lack of physical ownership. For example, if we consider air travel as a service product, there is little doubt that this is a product that is largely intangible and of which the customer does not take physical possession as such. On the other hand, there is a tangible element to the product. The aeroplane itself, the seat we occupy, the meals and drinks we are served are all very much tangible aspects of the flight we purchase. In addition, we do take 'physical possession' of certain elements of the product—again, for example, the seat and the meals and drinks. In the same way as we argued that physical products usually contain an important non-physical, or largely intangible, element, so too are service products often accompanied by physical, tangible elements.

What all this means is that very few service products strictly meet the definition given earlier; rather, most products have a mixture of both tangible and intangible components. If we think of tangibility as a continuum, therefore, service products are those where the intangible element is dominant. This notion of a continuum of intangibility is frequently encountered in texts on services marketing and is a useful way of evaluating whether the customer is buying what is essentially a product or a service. An example for business product/services from Shostack[29] is shown in Fig. 6.17.

A brief list of examples of where the intangible element is dominant, and hence examples of what we would define as service products, includes:

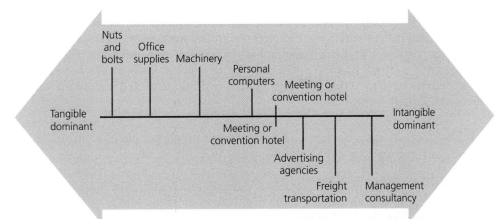

FIGURE 6.17   *A continuum of tangibility and intangibility: business product–service classifications*

Source: Adapted from G. L. Shostack, 'Breaking free from product marketing', *Journal of Marketing*, **41**, April 1977, p. 177

- Education
- Health care
- Legal/financial advice
- Hairdressing and beauty parlours
- Insurance
- Hotels/catering
- Public transport

Clearly, there are plenty of other examples of service products/industries, but note that it is the customer who decides whether or not a product or service is being purchased (and hence marketed) according to the relative importance he or she attaches to the tangible versus the intangible elements.

Intangibility, then, is the key dimension that distinguishes service products; but what about the notion of 'non-possession' referred to in our earlier definition, and do services have any other distinguishing characteristics that set them apart from physical products? Briefly, the other suggested special characteristics or service products, including the aspects of non-possession (or, as we have called it, non-ownership), are outlined below. As with the degree of tangibility, you should remember that these so-called 'special' characteristics are more a matter of degree than of distinguishing between physical and service products, and are also best thought of as a continuum.

Non-ownership   Many services are used rather than owned. For example, we use the services of a hairdresser rather than take physical possession of a product.

Inseparability   Services are generally consumed as they are produced. For example, when we pay a visit to the dentist, normally the dentist 'produces' his services while we are there in the dentist's chair. Production and consumption are simultaneous. Because of this, the person providing the service—in this case the dentist—is very much part of the service product.

Perishability   Generally, service products cannot be stored. For example, if a hotel room is not filled for the night, or if an aeroplane flies with empty seats, the room or seats for that particular night or flight cannot be 'stored' and sold later. The revenue that would have accrued had the room been let or the seat booked has been lost for ever. This characteristic makes effective matching of demand and supply for service products particularly important.

Variability   Largely because service products have a high 'people content', i.e. there is a significant human element in the provision of many services, the quality of the service product may vary each time the service is provided. As consumers, we are all probably familiar with this variability of services. For example, how many of us have gone to a hotel or restaurant which in the past has provided us with good service, only to be disappointed by the level of service we get from, say, a waiter who is new or who simply cannot be bothered to give good service on that particular day?

In addition to intangibility, then, these are some of the special characteristics of service products. These characteristics in themselves would be of little impact if they did not give rise to significant implications for marketing service products; but in fact they do.

Implications for marketing service products: The marketing mix for services

The characteristics of service products mean that they must be marketed in a somewhat different way from other products. Kotler[30] has argued that service businesses are more difficult to manage if using only a 'traditional marketing' approach.

For a detailed discussion of the issues and techniques of services marketing, readers are advised to consult one of the excellent texts that are now available in this once neglected area of marketing, such as Baron[31] or Lovelock.[32] Some of the more important implications of the special characteristics of service products for their marketing are summarized in Table 6.2. Perhaps one of the most significant implications of the special characteristics of service products, however, is the suggestion that it is necessary to add three additional elements to the conventional marketing mix when considering service products. It is now generally accepted that the traditional marketing mix of the original four Ps needs to be extended with three additional mix elements to give seven Ps for service. These additional three Ps for services comprise of 'People', 'Physical Evidence', and 'Process'. These are introduced briefly below but we shall be considering them together with the application of the other four Ps of the conventional marketing

TABLE 6.2   *Service characteristics: some implications for marketing*

Characteristic	Major effects/issues	Marketing implications
Intangibility	Difficult for consumers to evaluate service offerings, e.g. quality, etc. Positioning difficult to achieve/signal	'Tangibilize' the service offering by managing the 'physical evidence' that accompanies the service, e.g. staff appearance, buildings/ facilities, promotional material
Inseparability	Direct contact with service provider. Both provider and client affect 'quality' of relationship. Market may be limited by time constraints on provider	Selection and training of service provider's personnel is essential. Franchise/train other service providers. Develop systems/ procedures for increasing customer throughput
Variability	Difficult to ensure that service quality levels are maintained. Customer may have 'bad' experiences	Ensure strict quality control. Staff training essential. Develop customer care programmes and systems
Perishability	Periods of excess demand: period of excess supply	Manage demand and supply, e.g.: • Differential pricing • Develop complementary services • Effective pre-booking systems • Use part-time personnel
Non-ownership	Customer finds it difficult to assess advantages of purchasing service	Stress benefits of non-ownership in promotional programmes

mix to services marketing in more detail again in Chapter 12 when we consider the issues in combining the marketing mix in different marketing settings and segments.

People   The characteristics of services mean that an important element of marketing services are the service marketer's employees, and particularly those involved in direct contact with customers. The employees of the service marketer, therefore, must be considered in developing the marketing mix.

Physical evidence   Largely because of the intangibility characteristic of services, the marketer must carefully plan and communicate the nature of the service offering, including its quality level, by managing the more tangible elements of the service mix such as physical facilities, equipment and so on.

Process   How the service is provided is important to its marketing. Procedures for dealing with customers at the point of contact, and for supplying the service itself, to ensure consistency and quality of service supply must be carefully pre-planned and managed.

Again we should stress that these and the other marketing mix elements for services are discussed in greater detail in Chapter 12.

We shall now consider our last area related to the product or service, namely the important area of product packaging.

PACKAGING

It is a debatable point whether packaging is part of the product element of the mix or the promotional element. In fact, it is both. Perhaps in terms of the functional role of packaging such as protection and storage, the package is part of the physical product. However, packaging is a powerful tool of promotion and can be used, for example, to catch the eye of the customer or even in some markets, such as expensive gifts, be one of the major factors in brand choice. What is not in doubt is that packaging is a very expensive commodity both to marketer and ultimately to the customer. In fact, more is spent on packaging than on promotion. Packaging has also become more important as the result of changes in distribution channels and particularly the growth of self-selection in shopping in, for example, supermarkets. In terms of the specific roles which packaging plays are those of:

● Protection

● Ease of handling and storage

● Convenience for distributors and customers

● Information in terms of instructions for use and contents

● And, finally, as already mentioned, promotion in the sense of implying benefits, building image and brand recognition, etc.

Package design is in fact now a specialist area involving engineering, logistics and obviously design skills. From the perspective of the marketer packaging decisions involve considerations such as packaging materials, sizes, colours, information, convenience and handling. As with all marketing decisions the packaging for a product must be based around a careful identification of customer and market needs.

It is important for the marketer to consider the needs of distributors as well as final customers in packaging design.

An important development in the area of packaging is the increasing need for packaging to be tamper resistant. There have been several scares over recent years with the tampering of packages. Even where these have turned out to be hoaxes or false alarms they can have a major effect on the image of the manufacturer/marketer, and cause the almost certain need to recall all the products from the distributor's shelves, which is an expensive process. Many innovations have been made in recent years with respect to developing new safer, tamper-proof packaging.

The promotional role of packaging is a vital concern for the marketer. The package sends information to buyers about content, features, uses, competitive advantages, and so on. The marketer must carefully consider size, materials, colour and graphics when it comes to the packaging. We know that different colours on packaging are associated with certain feelings and moods. This is often culturally specific. In the Western world, for example, red is the signal for danger and suggests masculinity, green on the other hand is viewed as a soothing colour implying a certain degree of coldness or freshness. Most of the menthol cigarettes on the market, for example, use green- or blue-coloured packaging. Men and women like different colours in packaging. Pastel packaging colours are often used for products aimed at the female segment of the market.

Packaging can be used to make a product or brand distinctive on the shelves. Sometimes it is the most recognizable thing about a product or brand. This can be due to shape, colour, materials, graphics or a combination of these. Very few, for example, would not recognize the very distinctive style of the Cadbury's milk chocolate bar range. Similarly, the Heinz 57 logo is almost instantly recognizable. Perhaps one of the best examples of distinctive packaging in terms of brand identification, however, is the Coca-Cola bottle. The shape of this bottle is so distinctive that in fact it is protected worldwide.

Packaging attracts considerable criticism from some parties. Often it is viewed as being expensive and wasteful, particularly when it is not recyclable. As we have seen earlier, consumerism and the growth of the green movement have given impetus to this view of packaging. Many marketers, however, have responded positively to such criticisms by introducing recyclable and more environmentally friendly packaging such as CFC-free aerosols.

Perhaps surprisingly, at least for the non-packaging expert, packaging is one of the most innovative areas in marketing. New technologies and new materials continue to improve what is possible. Innovations such as shrink-wrap, bubble packaging, plastic squeeze toothpaste tubes, squeezy sauce bottles (which enable the last drop to be extracted), reusable/resealable packaging technologies, are all examples of innovations in packaging. Perhaps one of the most significant of recent developments that might affect packaging in the future is the growth of the ubiquitous Internet marketing. To some extent this may reverse the seemingly inexorable growth in importance of the promotional aspects of packaging with a return to a greater emphasis on the more functional areas of protection and ease of handling. This is primarily because purchasing via the Internet does not put such a premium role on the use of the package to sell itself from the supermarket shelf.

CHAPTER SUMMARY

This chapter has examined the product or service initially with a view to establishing what exactly the idea of a product or service is. The traditional, narrowly held, belief of a tangible item has been dispelled.

Product categorization has been investigated from the viewpoints of consumer and industrial goods and services.

New product development and its tactical and strategic implications have been viewed, followed by the product life cycle concept and its practical use to marketing strategists. The adoption process was then explained as an idea to complement the PLC concept.

The management of products was posed through the 'product manager' organizational concept, as opposed to the traditional view of the organization of a marketing department.

We have also examined product strategy matrices as vehicles through which product strategies could be formulated.

As we all know, many of us now live and work in service economies. Service products have a number of special characteristics which, in turn, give rise to additional issues and considerations when marketing such products. These special characteristics give rise to an additional three marketing mix elements for services, namely people, physical evidence and process.

Finally, we have looked at the importance and role of packaging in contemporary marketing. Although packaging plays a functional role with regard to, for example, protection and ease of handling, it is in its promotional role that the marketer can and should make use of effective packaging concepts and design.

CHAPTER REVIEW QUESTIONS

1. Define 'the product' in modern marketing terms. Give an example of a 'traditional' and 'modern' held view of a product (or service).

2. Explain and discuss the various product categorizations. What marketing approaches are normally associated with each?

3. Why is new product development so important to companies? Explain this with reference to the process of new product development.

4. How can the PLC concept be used as a tool for strategic marketing?

5. Explain the nature and role of product/brand management. Illustrate your answer with organizational structures most suited to different types of products and services.

6. What are the so-called 'special characteristics' of service products, and to what additional issues do these give rise when marketing this type of product?

7. Outline and discuss the role of packaging in the marketing process.

References

1. T. Levitt, *Differentiation of Anything: The Marketing Imagination*, Collier Macmillan, London, 1983, pp. 72–93.
2. T. Levitt, 'Marketing myopia', *Harvard Business Review*, **18** (1), July 1960.
3. S. C. Wheelwright and W. E. Sasser (Jnr), 'The new product development map', *Harvard Business Review*, May–June 1989, pp. 112–25.
4. Booz, Allen and Hamilton, *New Products Management for the 1980s*, Booz, Allen and Hamilton, New York, 1982.
5. C. M. Crawford, *New Products Management*, 5th edn, R. D. Irwin Inc., Homewood, IL, 1996.
6. W. Cooper, 'Failure rates in new product development', *Journal of Marketing*, Fall 1981, **45**, pp. 133–42.
7. M. Crimp, *The Marketing Research Process*, Prentice-Hall, London, 1981.
8. P. H. Block, 'Seeking the ideal form: product design and consumer response', *Journal of Marketing*, July 1995, **59** (3), pp. 16–29.
9. H. L. Lee and M. M. Sasser, 'Product universality and design for supply chain management' *Production Planning and Control*, **6** (3), May–June 1995, pp. 270–7.
10. R. Neff, 'Number one and trying harder', *International Business Week*, 2 December 1992, pp. 26–9.
11. A. Lockomy and A. Khurana, 'Quality function deployment in new product design', *International Journal of Quality and Reliability Management*, **12** (6), 1995, pp. 73–84.
12. H. Takeuchi and I. Nonaka, 'The new product development game', *Harvard Business Review*, January 1986, **64** (1), pp. 137–46.
13. M. B. Ray, 'Cost management for product development', *Journal of Cost Management*, Spring 1995, **9** (1), pp. 52–9.
14. D. Littler and F. Leverick, 'Joint ventures for product development: learning from experience', *International Journal of Strategic Management and Long Term Planning*, **28** (3), 1995, pp. 58–68.
15. J. Styles, 'Collaboration for competitive advantage: the changing world of alliances and partnerships', *International Journal of Strategic Management and Long Term Planning*, **28** (5), 1995, pp. 109–12.
16. C. W. Hofer and D. Schendel, *Strategy Formulation: Analytical Concepts*, West Publishing Company, St Paul, MN, 1978, p. 107.
17. T. Levitt, 'Exploit the product lifecycle', *Harvard Business Review*, November–December, 1965.
18. N. K. Dhalla and S. Yuspeh, 'Forget the product lifecycle concept', *Harvard Business Review*, January–February 1976, pp. 102–12.
19. W. E. Cox, 'Product lifecycles as marketing models', *Journal of Business*, October 1967, **40** (4), pp. 375–84.
20. R. Polli and V. Cook, 'Validity of the product lifecycle', *Journal of Business*, October 1969, **42**, pp. 385–400.
21. M. T. Cunningham, 'The application of product lifecycles to corporate strategy: some research findings', *British Journal of Marketing*, 1969, **3** (Spring), pp. 32–4.
22. G. S. Day, 'The product lifecycle: analysis and application issues', *Journal of Marketing,* Fall 1981, pp. 60–7.
23. P. Kotler, *Marketing Management: Analysis, Planning, Implementation and Control*, 7th edn, Prentice-Hall, Englewood Cliffs, NJ, 1991, pp. 551–2.

24. G. J. Tellis and C. M. Crawford, 'An evolutionary approach to product growth theory', *Journal of Marketing*, **45**, Fall 1981, pp. 125–32.

25. D. Mercer, 'Decline of the product lifecycle' *ADMAP*, September 1993.

26. E. J. McCarthy, 'Organisation for new product development', in *Product Strategy and Management*, T. Libery and A. Stuchman (eds), Holt, Rhinehart and Winston, New York, 1963, pp. 384–9.

27. G. S. Day 'A strategic perspective on product planning', *Journal of Contemporary Business*, Spring 1975, pp. 1–34.

28. L. L. Berry 'Services marketing is different', *Business Horizons*, May–June 1980, pp. 24–9.

29. G. L. Shostack, 'Breaking free from product marketing', *Journal of Marketing*, **41**, April 1977.

30. P. Kotler, op. cit., p. 459.

31. S. Baron, *Services Marketing: Text and Cases*, The Macmillan Press Ltd, Basingstoke, 1995.

32. H. Lovelock, *Services Marketing*, 3rd edn, Prentice-Hall, Englewood Cliffs, NJ, 1996.

Exley International

Exley International produce and market consumer electrical and electronic products. They are one of the world's largest manufacturers of televisions, video recorders and DVD equipment. They also produce computers and related hardware and small electrical and electronic appliances such as kitchen appliances.

The company is reckoned to be one of the most inventive in the industry. Many of the breakthroughs in electronics, in particular in recent years were originally developed and patented by Exley International. The company prides itself on this record which is due, they feel, mainly to the fact that they employ some of the most able technical people in the world. They spend over 10 per cent of their annual turnover on research and development and reckon to come up with at least 100 new ideas for products every year.

Despite all this, Exley International has an extremely poor record of launching commercially successful new products. Of the average 100 new ideas over the past five years, only five have made any reasonable return on their investment and only one is still being marketed. One of the most disappointing aspects of new product development for Exley International, however, is that many of their patented technologies have been successfully developed by other companies albeit under licence. Put simply, Exley International seem to have a problem proceeding from invention to successful introduction. In particular, they seem to be unable to exploit even technologies which their competitors subsequently prove to have commercial potential.

Perhaps surprisingly it is only relatively recently that they have considered that there might be something amiss with how they manage the new product development process. In particular they are wondering if they have been systematic enough about this process in the past.

Questions

1. What advice could you give this company about how to approach their new product development process more systematically?

2. What advice could you also proffer the company with regard to recent developments and thinking in new product development and innovation, and the implications of these for a company like Exley International?

Chapter Seven

PRICING

LEARNING OBJECTIVES   *This chapter will help you to:*

- understand the nature and role of pricing in the marketing mix;

- distinguish between the different perspectives on, and approaches to, pricing decisions;

- be aware of the inputs to, and considerations in, making pricing decisions;

- understand pricing methods, pricing policies and procedures

INTRODUCTION

Following the discussion in Chapter 1 on the marketing concept, it is true to say that, in general, until the 1950s price was considered to be one of the most important influences on buyer behaviour and choice. As a result of increasing competition, during the 1950s and 1960s non-price factors grew in importance, with companies attempting to differentiate their products from competitors on the bases of branding, advertising and packaging. A period of depressed demand, particularly during the early 1980s and early 1990s, combined with decreased levels of real disposable income, meant that competitive pricing began to re-emerge as an extremely potent marketing tool. Even now, many marketing managers are of the opinion that price is, after the product, the most important element in the marketing mix.

This chapter covers the variety of approaches to making pricing decisions, with an emphasis on the marketing approach to pricing. In order to understand and appreciate what represents this marketing approach to pricing, it is necessary to consider first the approach and contribution to pricing decisions of the economist and the accountant.

In fact, in many companies the final responsibility for making pricing decisions may, ultimately, rest outside of the marketing function. Of all the marketing mix decisions, pricing has the most obvious and clear-cut effect on company profit. Because of this, pricing is of central concern to all the managers in a company—not just marketing managers.

Given that it is logical to look first at the role that pricing plays in a company and in particular at the link between company and pricing objectives, against this background we can then consider the considerations or inputs to pricing decisions, including cost, demand and competitive considerations. Finally, we can consider pricing policies and procedures, including the important aspects of quoting and changing prices.

THE ROLE OF PRICING

It is through pricing that a company covers the costs of separate elements of its various activities: research and development, raw materials, labour and administrative costs must all, ultimately, be recovered through the price charged to the customer. Marketing costs, too, must be covered by the final price of the product, including those costs incurred in promoting, selling and distributing the product. Last, but not least, the price charged for a product is required to generate additional funds in excess of those costs to meet company profit objectives. Thus, pricing plays the following important roles:

1. Pricing fuses together the various elements of company activity necessary to fulfil customer requirements.
2. Pricing pays for their respective contributions to the final package offered to the customer.
3. To the extent that this package makes commercial sense in the marketplace, pricing generates residual profits in order to fulfil company objectives.

PRICING AS A STRATEGIC DECISION

It is sometimes asserted that, compared with decisions about the other elements of the marketing mix—product, place and promotion—pricing decisions are relatively simple. For example, if we know the costs of producing and marketing a product, and in addition have specified a percentage amount which is to be added to these costs for profit, we can 'easily' calculate the required selling price. Viewed in this way, pricing decisions become a matter of following simple rules or formulae. In addition, price is often viewed as being one of the most flexible elements of the marketing mix; that is, it can be readily changed to meet market conditions as and when required.

These notions about pricing are in fact based on a major misconception about pricing, namely that pricing decisions are tactical decisions. This is not to deny that short-term, tactical, price manoeuvres cannot—under certain conditions—be most effective; but as we shall see, in fact, pricing decisions are a strategic issue. This gives rise to the following implications:

1. Pricing decisions should be made in the context of overall marketing objectives and strategy.
2. To this end, pricing decisions should be related to, and be consistent with, the other elements of the marketing mix.

3. Care should be taken not to make price the overriding competitive factor. Alternatively, often more appropriate strategies for competing should not be neglected or ignored.

4. Pricing decisions should not become a matter of routine to be administered by the accounting department.

5. Pricing decisions should not place too much emphasis on cost inputs to the decision.

Some of these strategic implications of pricing are discussed in the excellent text on pricing by Hanna and Dodge,[1] however, we shall return to the need to think of pricing decisions from a strategic perspective towards the end of the chapter when we consider some of the more recent developments in approaches to pricing. First, though, it is necessary to consider some of the basic concepts and approaches to pricing together with some of the contributions made to our understanding of pricing from the areas of economics and accountancy. We shall turn first to the contribution of the economist to pricing decisions.

The economist and pricing decisions

The classical economists have put forward a well-developed conceptual framework for the establishment of price levels. In fact, for 150 years economists have regarded the price variable as the most important factor in determining the level of demand. This strong, almost exclusive, emphasis on price has led to the economist neglecting the other elements of marketing effort such as advertising, product differentiation and selling efforts.

The classical economist suggests that prices should be set at that level which *maximizes short-term profits*. To maximize profit, the notion of marginal cost and marginal revenue must be introduced.

- *Marginal cost* is the addition to total costs of producing one more unit of output.

- *Marginal revenue* is the addition to total revenue of selling one more unit of output.

Using these concepts, the following pricing rule can be derived from economists' models:

- Profits will be maximized when marginal revenue equals marginal cost.

This rule means that output should be set at a level that would imply a price at which the marginal revenue from selling one more unit equals the addition to total cost of producing that unit. This position is illustrated in Fig. 7.1. At output q, marginal cost equals marginal revenue, and the price required to sell this level of output is p.

The marginal revenue curve is a function of the demand curve facing a company, which in turn is a function of the nature and extent of competition in the market. The revenue curve shown in Fig. 7.1 is that faced by a firm in a 'perfectly competitive' market structure and is a particular, and somewhat unrealistic, type of market structure where the nature of competition condemns the individual company to being a *price-taker*. From this earliest model of market structure, economists have extended their analyses to take account of different, and more realistic, forms of market structure, including markets that are characterized by product differentiation. Regardless of the type of market structure, however, the same decision rule for pricing decisions applies; i.e. prices or output are set so as to equate marginal cost with marginal revenue. For a fuller description of the economists' model, readers are advised to consult a good basic textbook on economics, for example J. Harvey's *Modern Economics: An Introduction for Business and Professional Students*.[2]

This model of price-setting is appealing in that it suggests such a clear-cut decision rule for the price-setter. Nevertheless, the economists' price-maximizing theory has substantial shortcomings. In particular:

1. The assumption of the objective of profit-maximizing: undoubtedly, profits do figure very prominently in company objectives. Only by being profitable is the firm able to pay dividends to shareholders, generate the cash flow necessary to provide working capital and be attractive enough to potential investors when further capital is required. In practice, few, if any, companies set objectives in terms of profit maximization—much less do they even achieve it. Indeed, for most companies, profit objectives are couched in terms of a certain level of profitability, or return on investment (ROI). More specifically, the providers of the investment capital in a company are less interested in the absolute level of profit earned than in the percentage rate of return which they receive on their investment.

2. The assumption that price is the only factor determining the level of demand for a company's product: one only has to compare this assumption with what is known about the tools of marketing to see how restrictive this statement is.

3. The assumption that cost, and more particularly demand functions, can be measured with sufficient accuracy to be sure that the point of profit-maximizing has been reached.

4. The implicit assumption that in making pricing decisions one can ignore the trade, i.e. channels of distribution.

5. The assumption that price is set independently of the other variables in the marketing mix.

6. The assumption that the customer attempts to maximize satisfaction with respect to price alone.

These shortcomings in the economist's model are sufficient to render it of little value to the marketing decision-maker. Despite this, the model does point to one important consideration in practical price-setting; namely, *the importance of demand*. We shall return to this important contribution of the economist later in this chapter.

The accountant and pricing decisions

In contrast to the economist's focus on demand, the accountant's approach to pricing is often based essentially on costs. Such an emphasis on costs is perhaps not surprising, coming from a function that often has responsibility for their determination and control. A variety of approaches to cost-based pricing have been developed by companies. For example, a simple, and therefore, popular method of setting prices is to calculate the total costs of producing a product or service and to add to this total cost

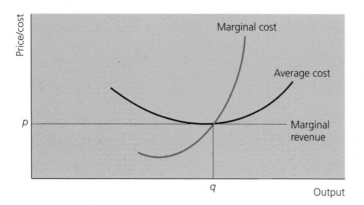

FIGURE 7.1

The economist's model of pricing in a competitive market

a set percentage for profit. This *cost-plus*, or *full-cost* pricing, as it is variously termed, is justified on a number of bases. First, as previously suggested, it is relatively simple. Second, it is argued that pricing in this way ensures that a known and pre-specified level of profit is attained, with all costs being covered. Finally, it is argued that cost-plus pricing is 'fair' to both trade and final customers. In fact, like the economist's profit-maximizing model, this deceptively simple approach to pricing also has significant shortcomings. In particular:

1. Total costs are usually arrived at by calculating the variable cost per unit and adding to this an allocation of a proportion of the total fixed costs. Total fixed costs are calculated on an assumption of either a standard volume or a forecast level of output. Both the calculation of total fixed costs and the methods of allocating this total between products give rise to serious problems when using this method of pricing. For example, the amount of fixed costs that will be added to each product, and consequently the price, clearly depend upon the number of products produced. In turn, the number of products that a firm will produce will, ignoring stockholding, be a function of how many it can sell. How many will be sold, in turn, depends upon the price charged. Pricing in this way then is nonsensical; it means that, for a given production capacity, if a company finds that it is selling less, and thus cuts its production, its market prices will need to increase. This, in turn, will probably lead to fewer sales, a further cut-back in production and even higher prices. To say the least, this is an unsatisfactory state of affairs.

2. A second major disadvantage with full-cost pricing is that strict adherence to a full-cost pricing policy can permit certain marketing opportunities to be passed by because the price the customer is willing or able to pay does not cover the full cost.

Clearly, then, there are problems if we base pricing decisions on total costs plus a margin for profit. In fact, we can go further and say that costs generally should not be used to determine prices. This being the case, what role do costs play in pricing decisions, and what contribution can cost information from the accountancy function play? Among the key roles that information on costs plays in pricing decisions are those that are concerned with the *evaluative* rather than the decision-making role of such information; in particular, it enables a company to:

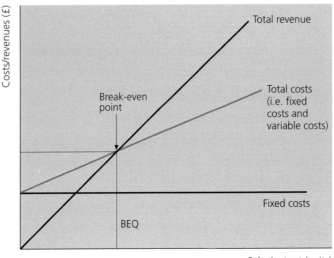

FIGURE 7.2

A simple break-even chart

- Measure the profit contribution of individual selling transactions.
- Determine the most profitable products, customers, or market segments.
- Evaluate the effect on profits of changes in volume.
- Determine whether a product can be made and sold profitably at any price.

In order to fulfil these evaluative functions, it is important that the marketing manager has access to *accurate* and *relevant* information on costs.

Accurate cost information allows a company to identify costs on a very specific basis directly related to each product, activity, customer, etc. In this way, management is able to make *informal* decisions about volume mix and pricing to target market segments.

Relevant cost information is information that is presented and analysed in such a way as to be pertinent and useful in decision-making. In particular, the cost analysis should enable the marketer to distinguish between *fixed* and *variable* costs and the relationship between those and volume. Such a cost analysis and its usefulness is perhaps best illustrated in the use of *break-even analysis*. A simple break-even chart is shown in Fig. 7.2.

Fixed costs are those that do not vary with the level of output and are, therefore, represented by the horizontal fixed cost curve in Fig. 7.2. Variable costs, on the other hand, are those that are more or less directly related to production or sales. Increases in output or sales will lead to a proportional increase in those costs with any decrease leading to an overall reduction of variable costs. Taken together, of course, fixed and variable costs combine to give total costs as shown in Fig. 7.2. The remaining information contained in a break-even chart is the revenue curve. This shows the total revenue that will accrue to the company at a given price–quantity combination.

The break-even point is normally represented as that level of output where the total revenue from sales of a product or service matches exactly the total costs of its production and marketing (break-even quantity, or BEQ in Fig. 7.2). Such an analysis of cost–revenue relationships can be very useful to the pricing decision-maker.

One use of break-even analysis is to compare the break-even points associated with different prices for a product. Again, a simplified example of this is shown in Fig. 7.3.

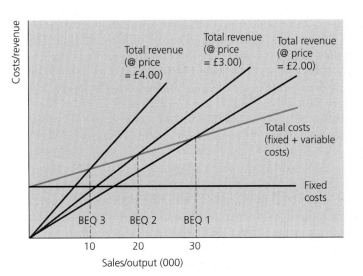

FIGURE 7.3

Break-even versus price (not to scale)

The effect of charging a higher price is to steepen the total revenue curve and as a consequence lower the break-even quantity (BEQ). The pricing decision-maker can then assess the effect of charging different prices in terms of what these different prices and break-even points mean to the company. Specifically, the information given by a break-even chart is:

- Profit or losses at varying levels of output
- Break-even points at varying levels of price
- Effect on break-even point and profits or losses if costs change

Break-even points can also be calculated using the following simple procedure:

$$\text{Selling price} - \text{Variable cost} = \text{Contribution}$$

$$\text{BEQ} = \frac{\text{Fixed costs}}{\text{Contribution}}$$

$$\begin{aligned}
\text{e.g.} \quad \text{Selling price} &= £10 \\
\text{Variable cost} &= £5 \\
\text{Fixed costs} &= £100\,000
\end{aligned}$$

$$\text{Contribution} = £10 - £5 = £5$$

$$\therefore \text{BEQ} = \frac{100\,000}{5\,\text{mm}} = 20\,000 \text{ units}$$

The notion of *contribution* is also a valuable addition to the price-maker's armoury. It illustrates that, in the short run at least, it may pay a company to sell a product at a price that is *less than the full cost* of producing it. Remember that fixed costs are those that do not vary with the level of output. If a company produces and sells nothing, it will still incur these costs. At any price over and above the variable cost of producing each product, then, the company is receiving a contribution towards those fixed costs. In the long run, of course, a company must cover all its costs through the price it sets on its products.

There is no doubt that break-even analysis, and the distinction between fixed and variable costs (and therefore contribution) on which it is based, is of much greater relevance to the price-setter than is the simple provision of total costs implied by the cost-plus approach. Nevertheless, one should note that, once again, its relevance is still more of an evaluative rather than a prescriptive one in terms of price-setting. This is because it is still cost- rather than demand-based. The total revenue curve in the break-even chart illustrates only the total revenue that would be received if we sell any given price–quantity combination. It is not, however, a demand curve. That is to say, it does not indicate the actual quantity that will be sold at any given price.

Another important and useful concept from the costing area is the relationship between costs and the cumulative volume of production, normally referred to as the *experience curve effect*.

In 1925, the commander of the Wright Patterson Air Force Base in the USA observed that the number of direct labour hours required to build an aeroplane decreased as the number of aircraft previously assembled increased. Eventually this phenomenon was explored across a wide range of industries and was found to be present in most of them. The phenomenon eventually came to be termed the *experience curve effect* (or, as it is sometimes called, the *learning curve*). Information on this effect is a vital input to pricing decisions and other elements of marketing strategy.

The basis and meaning of the experience curve effect are relatively easy to understand, and are encapsulated in the name of the phenomenon itself. Put simply, experience curve effects are derived from the fact that the more times we repeat an activity, the more proficient we become: in other words, 'practice makes perfect'. In the case of the Wright Patterson Air Force Base, the commander noticed that this led to a reduction in the time it took to assemble an aircraft as cumulative production increased. The assembly workers simply became more adept at assembling an aircraft because over time they had assembled increasing numbers. Further investigation into this effect established that, not only was the experience curve a phenomenon in most industries, but the relationship between costs and experience was predictable. The specific sources of experience curve effects are as follows:

1. Increased labour efficiency, e.g. the learning of short cuts, improved dexterity, greater familiarity with systems/procedures.

2. Greater specialization/redesign of working methods.

3. Process and production improvements, e.g. design of more effective plant, increased automation.

4. Changes in the resources mix, e.g. substitution of initially highly qualified labour for less qualified personnel.

5. Product standardization and product redesign.

The important point to note about these sources of experience curve effects is that many of them are not 'automatic'; i.e. in order to achieve experience curve effects, management must undertake the necessary steps and exercise initiative.

Experience effects provide the opportunities to lower costs, but appropriate strategies are required to grasp them.

Understandably, experience curve effects differ between industries and between companies. The basic formula for the experience curve is:

$$C_q = C_n \left(\frac{q}{n}\right)^{-b}$$

where:

q = the experience (cumulative production) to date
n = the experience (cumulative production) at an earlier date
C_q = the cost of a unit q (adjusted for inflation)
C_n = the cost of a unit n (adjusted for inflation)
b = a constant depending on the learning rate

Experience curves are normally expressed in percentage terms, e.g. an '85 per cent' experience curve or a '70 per cent' experience curve. Expressing the experience curve in this way tells us the expected reduction in costs for each doubling of cumulative production. An '85 per cent' curve means that the unit cost of producing, say, 2000 cumulative units of production will be only 85 per cent of the unit cost when cumulative production had reached only 1000 units.

It is important to note that the evidence shows that this percentage impact in costs is the same across the whole range of cumulative experience; i.e. doubling experience from 4 million to 8 million units results in exactly the same percentage cost reduction as doubling experience from 100 to 200 units in the company. This, too, has important strategic implications.

A typical experience curve is shown in Fig. 7.4. Note how the curve shows that, at higher levels of cumulative production (experience), larger and larger amounts of cumulative production are required to achieve any given percentage reduction in unit costs.

Information on the experience curve effect can be used to plan pricing strategies, especially for new products. Lancaster and Massingham[3] explore these strategic uses of the relationship between costs and cumulative production in greater detail; but it must be remembered that, like break-even analysis, the experience curve is merely a useful *tool* in the marketer's armoury for pricing decisions.

It is clear that neither the economist's model of price-setting nor the accountant's contribution of cost information is in itself a sufficient basis on which to determine prices. Nevertheless, taken together, they do point to a clear-cut and universal presumption for delineating pricing decisions which can be incorporated into a more realistic and marketing-oriented approach to pricing.

The marketer and pricing decisions

Notwithstanding the shortcomings of their approach to pricing, both the economist and the accountant have provided useful, if partial, insights into this area of the marketing mix. Specifically, we can take the economist's notion of demand and the accountant's emphasis on costs, and incorporate them into the following prescription:

- The upper limit to the price of a product (or service) is determined by *demand*. Therefore, this price should not exceed what the market will bear. Put another way, the price of a product (or service) should not exceed the value of its benefit to the buyer.

- In the long run, the price should not fall below the costs of making and distributing the product (or service).

Demand and costs, then, can be likened to the two blades of a pair of scissors as shown in Fig. 7.5.

This notion of demand and costs as determinants of upper and lower limits is important in a wider context than that of simply pricing decisions. You will note that

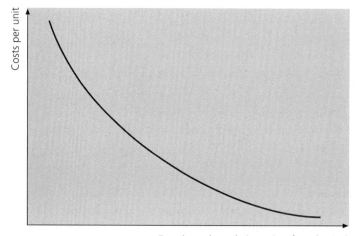

FIGURE 7.4

A typical experience curve

Costs per unit

Experience (cumulative units of production)

the gap between the blades in Fig. 7.5 gives the marketing decision-maker some discretion on pricing decisions. If there is no gap, then there is no profit and hence no discretion. A company can widen the gap between the blades in two ways:

1. It can reduce its costs, through improved manufacturing, greater efficiency, etc.

2. It can increase the perceived value of the benefits of its market offerings to the buyer.

The greater part of a company's marketing efforts is, or should be, aimed at the second of these. As far as is possible, effective marketing should 'desensitize' the customer to price. Unless the company is able and prepared to weather losses, price competition is the lowest form of competition. In order to be effective, competing primarily on price requires that rather stringent conditions be met:

- Sales volume must be much more sensitive to price changes than to changes in other elements of the marketing mix, e.g. advertising, salesforce, products, etc.

- Price advantages should be based on definite cost advantages that will not be easily lost over a period of time—for example when based on new and superior (patented) technology, or where barriers to entry are high.

In addition to cost and demand considerations, the marketing manager must consider the other elements of the marketing mix and the company's generic marketing strategy when considering pricing decisions. Similarly, the marketer's approach to pricing is characterized by a recognition of the need to consider a wide range of factors that will affect the pricing discretion and the eventual choice of a price level. Some of the more important of these factors are summarized below.

Input to, and considerations in, marketing pricing decisions

- Costs
- Demand
- Company and marketing objectives/resources
- Competition/market structure
- Social/legal aspects
- Distribution/trade
- Other factors

Each of these is considered in turn.

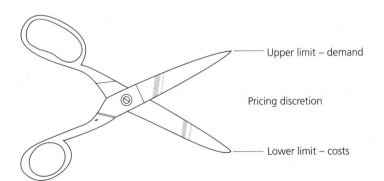

FIGURE 7.5

Upper and lower limits to price: pricing discretion

Upper limit – demand

Pricing discretion

Lower limit – costs

Costs   We have already seen how costs play an important role in pricing decisions. In addition, we have counselled against using costs alone to set prices. Nevertheless, costs do constitute the lower blade of the pricing decision, and the cost structure of the firm must be considered when setting prices. With respect to pricing generally, it is useful to consider three measures of the cost structure of the firm: the ratio of fixed to variable costs; the relationship between costs and volume, including, of course, cumulative volume of experience curves; and the costs of a firm relative to its competitors. Techniques such as break-even analysis, outlined earlier, and accurate and relevant cost information are extremely useful in the delineation and evaluation of price decisions.

Demand   We have stressed that demand constitutes the upper blade of the scissors of pricing decisions. We cannot charge prices higher than the market will bear. Ideally, the price-maker would like information bearing in mind the following two interrelated questions:

● What will be the quantity demanded at any given price?

● What will be the effect on sales volume of changes in price?

What we are discussing here can perhaps best be explained with the help of a simple diagram. Figure 7.6 shows a simple demand curve. Even this simple curve contains a substantial amount of information which is extremely useful for pricing decisions. In particular, it allows the company to ascertain the relation between the price charged and the resulting level of demand. As Kotler suggests,[4] normally demand and price are inversely related, i.e. the lower the price, the greater the demand.

The slope of the curve in Fig. 7.6 also indicates how sensitive demand is to price changes, i.e. it indicates what the effect on quantity demanded will be for any given change in price. We normally refer to this as *price elasticity* of demand. It is important to distinguish between the demand curve for the industry as a whole and that faced by the individual company. Ideally, we would like information on both.

Formally, price elasticity of demand can be calculated as follows:

$$\text{Price elasticity of demand} = \frac{\text{Percentage change in quantity demanded}}{\text{Percentage change in price}}$$

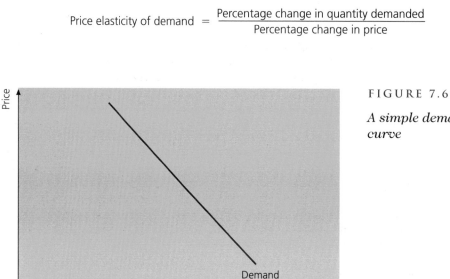

FIGURE 7.6

A simple demand curve

Measures of price elasticity commonly range through:

$e<1$: *Relatively price-inelastic*—a change in price results in a less than proportionate change in quantity demanded.

$e=1$: *Unit price elasticity*—a given change in price results in an equal proportionate change in quantity demanded.

$e>1$: *Relatively price-elastic*—a change in price results in a more than proportionate change in quantity demanded.

Useful though this information may be, in practice the relationship between demand and price, and therefore estimates of price elasticity, are difficult to ascertain and interpret. In particular, you should note the following considerations.

In markets where suppliers are able to *differentiate* their products from those of competitors, sales volume for the individual company is a function of:

- The total marketing effort of that company, i.e. marketing mix
- The marketing efforts of competitors

It is difficult to appraise the impact of our price policy upon sales without analysing the entire marketing mix relative to the marketing mix of our competitors.

Price sensitivity may be expected to differ between individual customers and/or groups of customers.

Taken together, differentiated 'products' and differences in price sensitivity mean that the price sensitivity of demand confronting a company is influenced by the choice of market segment and the extent to which prices are congruent with the *total marketing effort* to these segments.

In analysing demand, it is necessary to examine the *buyer's perception of value* as the key to pricing decisions. Essentially, that involves appraising the benefits sought by customers, these benefits being reflected in their buying criteria.

This enables a company to select the most appropriate market targets and then to develop a marketing mix for those targets with a particular marketing positioning in mind with respect to price, quality, service, etc.

Company and marketing objectives/resources   We have already stressed that all marketing decisions, including pricing decisions, need to reflect and be consistent with overall company and marketing objectives. A company with an objective of a minimum of 20 per cent return on investment based on rapid market penetration may well require a different pricing strategy from one that is seeking only a 10 per cent ROI and a relatively small rate of market growth. Effectively, therefore, the selection of company objectives, market targets and the formulation of a marketing mix serve to constrain or delimit the range of appropriate pricing strategies and specific price levels. A particularly good illustration of this delineating of price decisions is contained in Oxenfeldt's 'multi-stage' approach to pricing.[5] The essence of Oxenfeldt's approach is as follows:

1. *The selection of market targets*   The company's size, location, existing distributional arrangements, contracts with suppliers, customers and creditors, its reputation and past history will influence to a large extent the type of product the company can make, the service it can offer and its probable costs, and will determine the market that the company can command, and the segments of that market that it should attempt to cultivate. It must identify where its strengths and weaknesses lie.

2. *The selection of a brand image*   The image of a company or brand can have considerable bearing on the price that the company can charge, and will influence the type of customer that

the company can attract. Most companies will be constrained by the image they have already built up. Thus, to a large extent, steps 1 and 2 are totally interdependent.

3. *The formulation of a marketing mix*   The marketing mix (of advertising, promotion, selling, distribution, product, etc.) must be selected so as to help reinforce the desired brand image. The direction or emphasis of this marketing mix will be limited by the target market and the brand image.

4. *The selection of a pricing policy*   Oxenfeldt uses the term 'policy' to refer to overall pricing strategy, and suggests that the company should establish in advance a policy for dealing with general pricing conditions, answering such questions as:

   a. Do we price above or below the market average?
   b. Who are our competitors on price?
   c. Should we change price to meet competitors' price changes, and how quickly?
   d. Do we vary prices or aim for stability?
   e. Do we run price promotions?

   Thus, pricing policy deals with recurring pricing problems, and tries to anticipate answers in advance.

5. *Establish a pricing strategy*   Oxenfeldt uses the term 'strategy' to refer to the tactics that would be used to cope with unusual or irregular market conditions, such as:

   a. A change in legislation.
   b. A massive price reduction by a competitor.
   c. A radical fall-off in demand.
   d. A new entrant to the market.

   All of these might call for some pricing action as a counter-measure.

6. *The selection of a specific price*   The previous five steps will have narrowed down the choice of a final price to a fairly small price zone. The cost and revenue implications of various prices within this restricted range can be compared, elasticity within the range studied, etc. If the five steps leave no freedom of choice, then break-even analysis can be used to determine whether or not the demand that could be generated by that price would be profitable.

   Company resources, too, and particularly cash resources, must be considered in setting prices. For example, a decision to undercut competitors' prices often leads to a substantial drain on cash resources and should only be considered if a company can afford to sustain such a pricing approach.

Competition/market structure   Companies in differing product markets find themselves faced with varying degrees of competition. Some markets are characterized by large numbers of competitors, whereas others may comprise relatively few companies competing for the same customers. The number of competitors affects pricing decisions in the following ways:

● Where there are many competitors selling similar or identical products, competition on price will be severe.

● When there is only one supplier, that supplier can establish his own price, within the constraints of government legislation.

Between these two extremes are those market structures that more often characterize the market economy. The first of these is a market structure where there are relatively few competitors and where often one or two dominant firms emerge which set the lead in determining prices in the industry. In turn, smaller less dominant firms in the industry determine their price levels in relation to those determined by these price leaders. The second type of market structure frequently encountered is one in which, although there is a large number of competitors, firms in the industry attempt to escape from severe competition on price by differentiating their market offerings through advertising, quality and product features.

In addition to current competitors, the company must also consider the relative ease with which new competitors are able to enter the market.

Social/legal aspects   Legal and social considerations are also inputs to the pricing decision. Much of the legislation that pertains to trading practices and consumer protection relates to price-setting and pricing practices. Very few marketing managers are legal experts in this area, nor indeed can they be expected to be. Nevertheless, the variety of legal and social issues confronting the marketing manager today means that they must be treated as an additional input in the pricing decision.

Distribution/trade   We must not forget that most companies market their products via middlemen in the channels of distribution. For this reason marketing management must consider how this will affect pricing decisions. For example, do we set prices with the final consumer in mind, or do we set them with distributors in mind? What control, if any, do we have over the final price that our distributor, perhaps a retailer, will eventually put on our products? What quantity discounts and what credit terms are we willing to extend to our distributors? etc. Such considerations may serve to complicate what is already a difficult decision area, but they are considerations with which the price-setter must contend whenever he is dealing with distributors or the trade.

Other factors   The above are some of the main considerations in pricing decisions. In addition, the decision-maker may have to consider many other factors in setting prices. Some of these factors might be company-specific. For example, a supplier of products to the National Health Service may be involved in a system of tendering prices and may need to consider the policies and procedures of local authorities. Other factors may become important to the pricing decision as a result of unexpected changes in the company's market environment. For example, a major supplier might suddenly increase the prices of his raw materials; political events may cause commodity or energy prices to change as currency exchange rates fluctuate.

Psychology can also play a part in pricing, particularly at retail levels. This accounts for prices like 99 pence, £1.99, £9.99 and so on, because one penny more represents a psychological barrier. There are also psychological price brackets at work in which consumers are 'conditioned' to realize that goods falling within such brackets represent 'value for money'. Prices outside such brackets may infer that the goods are inferior or over-priced. It is well known that pricing goods or services cheaply, perhaps through mechanistic cost-plus procedures, can often be as bad as pricing too expensively.

PRICING METHODS, PRICING POLICIES AND PROCEDURES

Because of the wide range of possible factors that need to be taken into account in pricing, and because of the fact that their relative importance will vary from company to company, the marketing manager needs to be wary of adopting admittedly much simpler but possibly less effective heuristic pricing methods. Full-cost, or cost-plus, pricing is one example of such a pricing method, but there are many others, for example 'going-rate' pricing or 'target pricing'. Whatever the specific method used to set prices, it helps reduce the complexity of pricing decisions considerably if a company establishes a framework of pricing policy and procedures after due consideration of some of the factors outlined above.

A policy framework for pricing decisions should include processes and procedures covering the following areas:

1. *Pricing and company objectives*   This should cover the role of pricing in relation to company objectives viewed as a set of targets with respect to, e.g. return on investment, market share, etc.

2. *The role of price in marketing strategy*   This should delineate the major policy objectives for pricing in terms of its role in marketing. The policy should cover the extent to which price will be used to compete in the marketplace *vis-à-vis* the other element of the mix and market targets.

3. *Procedures and methods for determining specific pricing levels*   This should specify how specific prices shall be set on products and services and the considerations in such decisions, e.g. costs, demand, competition, etc. This part of pricing policy should also allocate responsibilities, i.e. who is to be involved in pricing decisions and on what basis.

4. *The administration of price changes*   In addition to setting prices, a company must also consider its procedures and policies with respect to administering and implementing price changes. The need to change prices may, of course, result from a number of factors, including increased costs, changed demand, etc. It is important that a system be established such that price changes are implemented effectively and efficiently. Also, care needs to be taken that frequent, short-term, price changes do not detract from the long-run overall pricing objectives determined earlier.

5. *Policies and procedures on credit, discounts, etc.*   In addition to pricing levels and price changes, we should not forget that credit policies and procedures for offering discounts for quantity and/or early payments are important facets of pricing policy.

SPECIAL ISSUES IN PRICING DECISIONS

So far in this chapter we have outlined and discussed the factors that need to be considered in making any pricing decision. Having said this, some categories of pricing decisions do give rise to certain problems and issues which deserve special attention. Two of the more important of these categories are: 'product-line pricing', and pricing to account for stages in the product life cycle.

Product-line pricing

The majority of companies produce and market not one but a variety of products and services. Provided that neither the costs nor the demand for a range of products is interrelated, decisions on the price of each product may be made independently. Where, as is usual, this is not the case, we must, at the very least, consider the possible effect of these interrelationships on our pricing decisions. In particular, we must consider establishing product-line pricing strategies. The meaning of interrelated demand and costs plus an outline of possible alternative product-line pricing strategies are detailed below.

Interrelated demand   Products are interrelated in demand when the price (or some other element of the marketing mix) of one affects the demand for the other, in either a positive or negative way.

Interrelated costs Two products are interrelated in cost when a change in the production of one affects the cost of the other.

Alternative product-line pricing strategies

1. Prices proportional to full cost, i.e. same net profit margin for all products.
2. Prices proportional to marginal cost, i.e. same percentage profit margin over marginal cost (contribution).
3. Prices proportional to conversion cost or 'value added'. Conversion cost is found by subtracting purchased material costs from the allocated full costs.
4. Prices that produce the same degree of contribution margins dependent upon conditions of demand in differing segments.
5. Prices related to target market requirements such as to yield an overall required rate of return from the product mix.

Strategies 1, 2 and 3 are dependent upon cost and ignore demand; 4 and 5 are more adequate. These are based on the criterion that prices should reflect the demand relationships existing between products in the line to yield the required return on average assets employed.

Pricing and the product life cycle

As we have seen, pricing decisions are not once-and-for-all decisions; they need to reflect changing competitive and market factors.

One of the factors that is suggested to affect the pricing decision is the stage of a product in its life cycle. In Chapter 6 we classified these stages as:

- Introduction
- Growth
- Maturity
- Decline

The suggestion is that each stage may require, or be best fitted to, a particular set of marketing strategies and marketing mix combinations, including, of course, price. For example, as we saw in Chapter 6, in the case of pricing *new products* at the introduction stage of the life cycle, we may distinguish between, for example:

- *Selective penetration strategy* High price/low promotion, often referred to as market skimming, with the price being lowered at successive stages in time as the product achieves larger sales.
- *Pre-emptive penetration strategy* Low price/heavy promotion.

The strategy selected at this stage then has clear implications for pricing.

Similarly, research indicates that market response to the different elements of the marketing mix may change over the life cycle of a product.[6]

Clearly, then, we must reflect these considerations in a dynamic pricing policy.

DEVELOPMENTS IN APPROACHES TO PRICING

You will recall that at the start of the chapter it was suggested that all too often pricing decisions have been treated as being essentially non-strategic. Indeed, in some organizations pricing is viewed as being more in the province of the accountancy rather than the marketing function. It was also suggested, however, that both treating pricing as being essentially tactical and relinquishing the responsibility for pricing decisions to the accountant are mistakes. Pricing is in fact very much a strategic issue and should be treated as such; similarly, as we implied, in the concept of the marketing mix, pricing is very much a marketing decision albeit that we may need the expertise of the accountant regarding aspects such as costs, break-even points and so on. In fact, it is now increasingly recognized that pricing is a core part of marketing strategy. Moreover, marketers are beginning to realize that pricing can be used much more creatively and proactively in strategy than perhaps it sometimes has been in the past. An excellent analysis of the value of approaching pricing decisions in this more strategic, creative and proactive manner, is provided in a recent article by Pitt *et al.*[7]

Arguing the need for what they term a more *'entrepreneurial'* approach to pricing, Pitt suggests that a more turbulent environment with rapid rates of change, increased competition, and more discerning customers has led to the need for all companies, large or small, established or new, to adopt new approaches to pricing. Specifically, their suggested approach to pricing entails pricing decisions having the following characteristics:

1. *Market based*   They suggest that above all pricing decisions need to be based primarily on customer and competitor considerations rather than, say, cost considerations.

2. *Reflect a willingness to take calculated risks*   They suggest that all too often in the past pricing decisions have tended to be on the conservative side. Trying to ensure, for example, that at least a satisfactory return is made rather than perhaps a willingness to take risks to earn higher rates of profit.

3. *Proactive*   Price should play a proactive role in marketing strategy rather than the more passive price-taking role it often does.

4. *Flexible*   Pricing strategies and decisions should be flexible in order to reflect changing market and demand conditions according to circumstances, albeit within a pre-planned strategic framework.

Pitt argues that together these characteristics reflect a company's *'orientation'* to pricing indicating the extent to which pricing is being used in a strategic and entre-preneurial manner as opposed to a tactical and mechanistic one. They further suggest that a company's orientation to pricing will potentially affect every aspect of a company's pricing decisions including:

1. *The formulation of pricing objectives*   A strategic orientation towards pricing decisions will tend to lead to the formation of pricing objectives which reflect market, and particularly competitive position objectives, rather than purely financial objectives. So, for example, pricing objectives will be set to, say, discourage new market entrants rather than, say, simply to reflect a desired rate of return on capital.

2. *Selection of pricing strategies*   A strategic/entrepreneurial orientation to pricing allows for the use of different pricing strategies for the same company in different markets and for different products.

3. *Determination of price structures*   This includes, for example, decisions on price bundling, differential pricing for various market segments, and price discounts. A strategic/entrepreneurial approach will be characterized by substantial creativity in the different aspects of price structure decisions rather than having a uniform/mechanistic approach.

4. *Pricing levels and tactics*   These elements of pricing decisions include the actual amounts charged for each product and include decisions such as the setting of odd or even prices,

product line pricing and price tactics such as rebates and promotional pricing. Again, a strategic/entrepreneurial orientation to pricing decisions in a company will result in these aspects of pricing decisions being much more flexible than in the non-strategic/entrepreneurial counterpart.

In fact, Pitt *et al.* suggest the use of an entrepreneurial pricing checklist which the marketer can use to assess the nature of the pricing orientation in his or her organization. Using a set of simple questions the marketing manager completes a Likert-type scale and then computes an overall score to assess the degree to which pricing decisions are being made in a strategic/entrepreneurial manner. The highest scores represent a company which is making pricing decisions in a proactive and creative way. These companies approach pricing strategically and understand the importance of not leaving pricing decisions to the accountant. Price is used very much as an element in competitive strategy. Such companies sometimes take risks in their pricing but more often than not these risks will pay off.

At the other extreme a firm with a low score from the entrepreneurial pricing checklist is not really using pricing as a creative or strategic part of its marketing. Such companies will tend to make pricing decisions in a mechanical way and will not be using price flexibly. Such companies also tend to be price followers rather than price leaders.

Overall, the approach of Pitt *et al.* is indicative of the way in which thinking on pricing as a marketing variable has changed. Price is now very much a means for strategically coping with complex changes in the external market and competitive environment.

Pricing and technological advances

Apart from in one important respect, in many ways pricing has remained relatively untouched by advances in technology compared to other elements of the marketing mix. However, the facet of pricing which has been affected by technological advances is potentially extremely significant for the marketer and the customer alike.

The Internet and the worldwide web are increasingly providing opportunities for customers to be able to compare and contrast different prices much more readily than they have been able to do so in the past. Using the Internet the customer can shop around for the cheapest prices and the best buys. Because of this, as use of the Internet grows as a channel for purchasing products we can expect consumers to become more price aware and potentially more price sensitive. This applies as much to conventional channels of distribution such as retailing as it does to Internet shopping. This does not, of course, mean that companies can only compete at the lowest price. It may, for example, encourage marketers to try to desensitize customers to prices by offering additional services, better products, etc. Companies that cannot do this, however, and who in addition cannot compete on price, will find themselves in trouble when trying to market via the Internet. It should be added that of course not only customers can surf the web to check out prices. This is a very useful way for companies themselves to find out information on competitors' prices and offers.

CHAPTER SUMMARY

In this chapter we have considered the role of pricing decisions in overall company and marketing strategies. We started by exploring a number of popular misconceptions about pricing: misconceptions that mitigate against effective strategic pricing.

Before considering how the marketing manager might approach pricing decisions, we looked at the approaches of the economist and the accountant. Despite limitations in each of their approaches, we saw that both contribute a number of useful concepts and techniques. In particular, the economist helps by stressing the importance of demand—the upper limit to pricing discretion, and the accountant contributes to our knowledge and recognition of the importance of cost—the lower limit. With these upper and lower limits in mind, we then examined a variety of other important inputs to the pricing decision, inputs which marketers must include if they are to arrive at sensible pricing strategies. In addition to demand and cost inputs, marketers must also consider, in particular, company and marketing objectives, company resources, competition and market structure, social and legal aspects, and middlemen, plus a number of other factors according to the circumstances.

The need to consider this number of factors makes it important that a company should establish a framework of pricing policies and procedures to include, for example, pricing and company objectives, pricing and marketing strategy, procedures and methods for setting specific prices, price changes, credit and discount policy.

We looked at special issues in pricing decisions, and in particular at the additional problems posed when pricing in a multi-product company and when considering setting prices for products in the different stages of their life cycle.

Finally, we considered some of the developments in approaches to pricing as the environment becomes more competitive and turbulent. In particular we looked at the notion and advantages of an entrepreneurial approach to pricing decisions.

CHAPTER REVIEW QUESTIONS

1. Why are pricing decisions strategic, and what misconceptions detract from this strategic role for pricing?

2. a. What does the economist contribute to the pricing decision?
   b. What does the accountant contribute to the pricing decision?

3. How does the marketer's approach to pricing differ from both that of the economist and the accountant?

4. What factors should be encompassed in a system of pricing policies and procedures?

5. What special pricing problems are posed
   a. In product-line pricing?
   b. In pricing to take account of the stage a product is at in its life cycle?

6. What do you understand by the term 'entrepreneurial' in the context of pricing?

References

1. N. Hanna and R. Dodge, *Pricing*, The Macmillan Press Ltd, Basingstoke, 1995.
2. J. Harvey, *Modern Economics: An Introduction for Business and Professional Students*, 7th edn, The Macmillan Press Ltd, Basingstoke, 1998.
3. G. Lancaster and L. Massingham, *Marketing Management*, 2nd edn, McGraw-Hill, London, 1998, Chapter 8.
4. P. Kotler, *Marketing Management: Analysis, Planning, Implementation and Control*, 7th edn, Prentice-Hall, Englewood Cliffs, NJ, 1991, pp. 478–9.
5. A. R. Oxenfeldt, 'A decision making structure for price decisions', *Journal of Marketing*, **37**, January 1973.
6. Kotler, op. cit., pp. 362–72.
7. L. F. Pitt, P. R. Berthon and M. H. Morris, 'Entrepreneurial pricing: The Cinderella of Marketing', *Management Decision*, **35** (5) & (6), 1997, pp. 344–50.

CASE STUDY   *Mini Prices for Maximum Profit*

One of the products which BMW held onto despite its recent split with a previous Rover Group was the Mini. Developed and launched in the 1950s, the Mini car is almost a legend in the automobile industry. An immediate success when it was launched, and despite not ever having made much profit for its succession of makers, the Mini is now one of the longest-running models of any car ever made. Only the original Volkswagen Beetle had a longer history.

For better or worse, rightly or wrongly, BMW decided that the Mini still had marketing life left in it. At the time of the split a new and almost completely redesigned model was in the pipeline at the then BMW/Rover Group. The new planned model was to be larger than its previous counterparts and was to include the latest engineering and design technology, as you would expect from a company like BMW.

BMW must have felt that the Mini had a part to play in its overall product portfolio. As with any new product, however, one of the major decisions which faces the company is what price to set on the product? As already mentioned, although enjoying a long life cycle, the Mini has never been very profitable. In some ways it was more of a flagship for the British companies which marketed it over the years. Again, as you would expect from BMW, however, this company is more interested in profits than simply flagships. Like any product in a profit-seeking organization, then, the new Mini would be required to generate sufficient sales, with sufficient margins, to recoup the undoubtedly large investment and marketing costs for the new product.

We now know that the new Mini is positioned as a fashionable car which is fun to drive and yet cheap to run. It is also positioned as being a second car in the family and is aimed at both male and female drivers.

A particular issue for pricing the new product is the overall image of the BMW company and the position of the new Mini in that prestigious, towards the top of the market range. Another factor particularly affecting the price of cars in Europe is also the fact that prices differ greatly between different parts of the European Union. There has, for example, been considerable controversy with regard to the fact that UK customers usually have to pay much higher prices than their counterparts in other countries in Europe. As a result, particularly of these differential prices, a whole new market, or rather distribution channel, for cars in Europe has developed, encouraging customers to buy from the cheapest parts of the European Union outside of the normal distributor channels established and effectively owned by the major car manufacturers.

Finally, again, as you would expect, BMW paid careful attention to competitor prices when launching the new Mini.

Questions

1. What factors do you feel BMW would have taken into account in pricing the newly launched Mini?

2. What special issues might have arisen with regard to pricing the new Mini?

Chapter Eight

CHANNELS OF DISTRIBUTION AND LOGISTICS

LEARNING OBJECTIVES   *This chapter will help you to:*

- understand the nature and role of distribution and logistics in the marketing mix;

- appreciate the structure and working of the alternative channel arrangements through which products and services flow from producer to consumer;

- identify the different types of channels and intermediaries, and the role they play in distributing products and services;

- be aware of some of the changes and trends affecting channels of distribution;

- understand the major strategic elements of channel design and management;

- be aware of the scope, nature and importance of logistics management in contemporary marketing.

INTRODUCTION

In this chapter we shall be examining the routes by which marketers of products and services can ensure that these reach their intended market. We normally refer to these routes as *marketing channels*, which include those intermediaries through which products and services pass from the point of production to the point of intermediate and final use.

In the first part of the chapter we shall concentrate on the development and structure of marketing channels; we shall find that this area of marketing is in fact among the most dynamic, being characterized by increasingly rapid technological and market change. Within marketing channels in the UK this change is particularly marked in the area of retailing. Not only has the structure of retailing in the UK undergone a period of rapid evolution, but increasingly this has been accompanied by innovations in technology which have changed the face of shopping as we know it. The modern marketer must adapt to and plan for future changes. Increasingly, the company that fails to take account of the dynamic nature of marketing channels will find itself at a disadvantage in the marketplace.

This first part of the chapter explains the place of marketing channels in the marketing mix. The marketing manager needs to appreciate the various types of channel intermediaries, their role and function. Here, again, we shall find that these roles and functions are themselves changing. Against this background of evolving and changing channels of distribution, we shall examine the use of limitations of the once much vaunted 'wheel of retailing' hypothesis in order to assess the extent to which the hypothesis is relevant to marketing decision-making in this important area of the mix. With this as a background, the second part of the chapter looks at the management of channels from the point of view of the marketing decision-maker. Here we shall find that channel decisions are among the most important of the marketing decisions made by a company and are therefore strategic rather than tactical.

If channel design and choice are strategic considerations, the manager must also devote sufficient attention to the implementation and control of these strategies. Individual middlemen must be encouraged to act for the company, and their activities must be monitored and assessed. Thought needs to be given to the minimizing of possible channel conflict and the achievement of maximum cooperation both within and between the variety of channel members.

Finally, in this chapter we shall look at how the concept of what constitutes the 'place' element of marketing has widened in recent years to include the management of physical distribution and logistics and why this element of managing the 'place' part of marketing mix is increasingly important in the development of a competitive advantage.

THE DEVELOPMENT OF CHANNELS OF DISTRIBUTION

It is a fact that today most producers do not sell directly to the final users. Instead, the majority of goods and services move from producer to user through a series of intermediaries or 'middlemen' who perform a variety of functions. Collectively, these intermediaries and the institution of which they form a part are variously referred to as trade, marketing or, as we shall term them here, *distribution channels*. Bucklin[1] offers the following definition of a channel of distribution:

> A channel of distribution comprises a set of institutions which performs all of the activities utilized to move a product and its title from production to consumption.

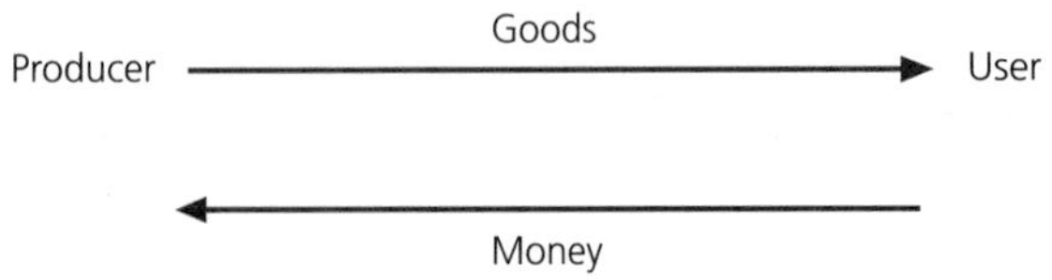

FIGURE 8.1

A simple system of exchange

Producer ——— Goods ———→ User

←——— Money ———

In discussing the development of channels, a basic question must be, why are they used at all? Or, put another way, why don't all producers themselves sell directly to the consumer? Some, of course, do, and indeed, as we shall see in this chapter and in Chapter 9, a growth area recently has been direct marketing, but the majority of marketers still use intermediaries. There are a variety of reasons for this.

One reason is simply that many producers lack the necessary skills and resources to perform all the activities referred to in Bucklin's definition. Figures 8.1 and 8.2, together, illustrate this.

Figure 8.1 would seem to indicate that the exchange relationship between producer and user is essentially very simple. Goods and services are provided to the final user, who in return for them passes back money to the provider. In fact, as shown in Fig. 8.2, today's business transactions are often characterized by a diverse range of complex and interacting activities which are required in order to facilitate the process of exchange. As McGarry[2] points out, a number of functions are necessary to bridge the time, place and possession gaps that separate producer and user. For example, a consumer may require to see the product before making a commitment to purchase. This may require that adequate display facilities are made available for the potential end-user. An individual producer may lack the necessary financial and skill resources to make such a facility available on a national basis.

Similarly, the end-user may require that a variety of products be made available to him at one geographical location. Imagine, for a moment, how much more complex, time-consuming and frustrating it would be if the shopper had to purchase sugar at one retail outlet, jam at another, soap at another and so on. It has long been a key function of middlemen to transform what Alderson[3] has referred to as 'heterogeneous mixtures' of products into 'meaningful assortments'.

A further, if connected, reason for the function of channels of distribution has been the increasing separation of the producer from his end-users. The households that purchase goods and services are not only separated geographically from producers, but are themselves often geographically dispersed. This dispersion, at both a national and

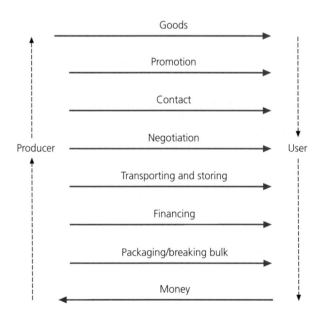

FIGURE 8.2

Today's system of exchange

an international level, has led to the growth of intermediaries who can bridge this spatial gap between producer and user.

Finally, the growth of channels of distribution is linked to the growth in complexity in industry itself, and in particular the increase in specialization. For example, the mining company extracts bauxite and from it produces aluminium. This aluminium is sold to a can manufacturer. The can manufacturer sells his product to the food processing company. The food processing company sells its canned products to the wholesaler, who in turn sells to the retailer. Finally, the retailer sells the food in aluminium cans made from the bauxite to the housewife. Industry today is comprised of a vertical chain of extractive, manufacturing and service companies, often each specializing in one part of the conversion process. This specialization gives rise to what might be referred to as 'breaks' in the industrial conversion process, and it is these break-points that the institutions and individuals that comprise channels of distribution have stepped in to bridge.

We can see from these reasons for the growth of channels of distribution that they play a very important role, not only in the marketing mix of the individual company, but in an economy as a whole. In fact at this second, macro level, channels of distribution can be said to form part of the marketing system of a country and, therefore, of the individual firm. As Howard points out,[4] a marketing system is for a total economy, it being the *means* by which all of the goods and services flow to the end-user from the different stages of manufacture and all of the funds flow in the reverse direction. An effective and efficient system of distribution, therefore, is essential to the well-being of an economy and the individual units that comprise it. Having said this, and notwithstanding the reason discussed for the development of distribution channels, there is no *a priori* reason why the functions performed by channels of distribution should not be performed by individual companies. In fact, the only economic justification for a company or a society entrusting these functions, or at least some of them, to middlemen is if they perform them more effectively and efficiently than would otherwise be achieved.

Figure 8.3 illustrates more specifically how using intermediaries can contribute in this respect. Without a middleman, each producer must contact all four customers. Therefore, 12 contacts are required for every producer's product to reach every customer. By including a retailer this cuts the number of contacts down to only seven, and in fact each producer need only make one contact to the retailer in order to reach all the prospective customers. Even this much simplified example illustrates how channel intermediaries can bring economic benefits both to the individual company and to the economic system as a whole. The example should also serve to dispel a widely held, but frequently misplaced, view that middlemen are economic 'parasites'. This view stems from the misconception that middlemen add nothing to benefit, but serve only to increase costs. Not only can middlemen substantially reduce the final cost to the consumer, but, in addition, they add to the utility the customer derives from products by means of, for example, variety, convenience, after-sales service, information, etc.

ELEMENTS OF CHANNELS OF DISTRIBUTION

It has already been shown in Chapter 4 that channel decisions constitute the 'place' element of the marketing mix. In ensuring that his or her products and services are available at the right time, in the right place and in the right quantities, the marketing manager is making decisions about distribution. Specifically, a company must decide the type of channel it will use to reach its target markets; it must select, recruit and organize channel intermediaries, and it must decide on stock levels, delivery modes and times. These aspects of decision-making—channel strategies, channel choice and logistics—are considered in more detail later in this chapter. In order to make these decisions, the marketing manager must understand the elements of channels of distribution. For example, the marketing manager must understand the various *dimensions* of channel structure, and, in particular, the *variety of channel types* to which these dimensions give rise. He or she should also be familiar with the *different sorts of channel intermediaries* or *middlemen*; their roles and relative advantages and disadvantages. Finally, the marketing manager must understand and appreciate the implication of the *dynamic and changing nature* of marketing channels.

(a) No middleman

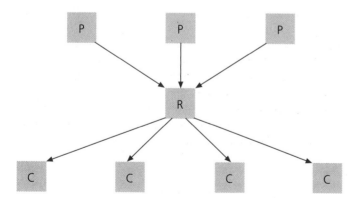

FIGURE 8.3

How the middleman can contribute to efficiency

P = Producer
C = Customer
Number of contacts = 3 × 4 = 12

(b) With a middleman

P = Producer
C = Customer
R = Retailer
Number of contacts = 3 + 4 = 7

Dimensions of channel structure

Channels of distribution are extremely complex marketing structures, and we can examine their components in a variety of ways and from a variety of angles. Nevertheless, one or two key characteristics of channel structure are associated with the 'personality' of a particular channel and are therefore associated with differences between various channels. One of these key characteristics is *channel length*.

Figure 8.4 illustrates several alternative channels of distribution distinguished primarily by channel length. Clearly channel length is determined by the number of different intermediaries through which a product passes *en route* from producer to consumer. The shortest channels are those where no intermediaries are involved, i.e. where the producer deals directly with the final consumer. One might be tempted to suppose that the most effective channels are those that involve fewer intermediaries and preferably none at all, i.e. direct marketing. Certainly, as already indicated, direct marketing has grown in importance, and there are distinct advantages to both producer and consumer of keeping channels as short as possible. Nevertheless, our discussion of why intermediaries are used should alert one to the fact that shorter channels are not invariably more effective and efficient. Remember that the justification for using intermediaries is that they can perform certain functions more efficiently than can the producer. In the long run, and certainly in a free market economy, competitive forces and the profit incentive will tend to lead towards that length of channel which is most efficient under the circumstances. Circumstances here would include, for example, factors such as type of product, number of customers, geographical dispersion of customers, variety required by customer, type and range of services required, etc. Of course, this is not to say that the length of marketing channels for established product markets has arrived at the optimum: the optimum length is likely to change, and as we shall see, the role of some intermediaries has diminished considerably in marketing certain products. Nor should we assume that what is the appropriate length of channel for one company is identical for another company in the same industry. As with all other marketing decisions, decisions about channel length are company-specific.

A second key aspect of channel structure concerns the *relationship between channel members* and, in particular, the relationships that pertain to the locus of power and decision-making in the channel structure. This, again, is an area of channel structure that has seen significant changes over the past few years. Today, three broad types of channel structure can be identified on the basis of different relationships: free flow or conventional marketing channels; single transaction channels; and vertical marketing systems.

The first of these, *free flow or conventional marketing channels*, is what many people have come to think of when they consider the relationship between different channel members. In this type of channel essentially each member in the channel—producer, wholesaler, retailer, etc.—operates as an autonomous business unit. Each level operates with its own aims and objectives in mind, and no one level of the channel has any degree of substantial control over the remaining levels. The primary force keeping the channel intact is a mutually beneficial trading arrangement which

1. Producer ⟶ Consumer

2. Producer ⟶ Wholesaler ⟶ Customer

3. Producer ⟶ Wholesaler ⟶ Retailer ⟶ Consumer

FIGURE 8.4

Channel length

can be ended by either party should the arrangement become less beneficial. Although no formalized or contractual arrangement exists between the different levels in the channel (other, that is, than those pertaining to each business transaction), such channels do tend to establish trading practices with respect to the expected behaviour of each channel member. Such behaviour would include, for example, services or functions to be performed, consumers to be served, mark-ups and prices, etc.

The second type of channel based on this aspect of structure is what Bowersox *et al.* refer to as *single transaction channels*.[5] In fact, this type of channel is not really a channel at all in the sense of its duration, although a substantial amount of transactions are executed in this way. A single transaction channel is a channel that is brought into being or use specifically for each transaction. After the transaction is completed, the channel has fulfilled its role and the business arrangement in the channel ceases to exist. Examples of transactions that require and use this form of channel relationship would include financial stock and bond purchases, sales and purchases of houses, etc.

The third type of channel structure, based on different relationships between channel members, is what has come to be termed the *vertical marketing system* (VMS).[6] In a vertical marketing system each level in the distribution channel acts in a planned and unified way so as to achieve maximum efficiency for the channel as a whole. Unlike the conventional marketing channel, therefore, each level in the channel acknowledges and functions on the basis of interdependence.

The concept of vertical marketing may be split into three distinct approaches according to how and on what basis coordination and cooperation are achieved in the system. These three approaches to VMSs are: the corporate VMS; the administered VMS; and the contractual VMS.[7]

In a *corporate vertical marketing system*, one of the channel members *owns* preceding and/or subsequent levels in the channel. So, for example, a manufacturer who moves forward into retailing or a retailer acquiring production facilities would constitute a corporate VMS.

An *administered vertical marketing system* is one in which channel cooperation and coordination at the various levels are achieved through the dominance and power of one of the channel members. This has been perhaps one of the most significant developments in channel structure in the UK. Increasingly, power in channels has shifted to the retail end of the distribution network. As we shall see shortly, the trend in UK retailing has been towards larger and much more powerful retailing organizations. This concentration of power has meant that the larger retailing organizations are able to secure strong cooperation and support from suppliers. Retailers now play a very prominent role in determining, for example, pricing levels, product specifications and features, displays and promotional and branding policies on the part of their suppliers.

A *contractual vertical marketing system* is one in which coordination and cooperation in the channel are achieved through a formal contractual arrangement. There are many forms of such contractual channel arrangements including, for example, exclusive dealerships, cooperative and voluntary groups and the rapidly growing area of franchising. Again, some of these developments in contractual VMSs, and particularly franchising, are considered later in this chapter. At this stage, however, one should note that the key difference between contractual and corporate VMSs is the absence of ownership.

There are many reasons for the growth of vertical marketing systems, but the prime reason has been to improve overall effectiveness in the channel through increased cooperation and control. As we shall see, one of the important factors in channel design is the minimization of conflicting interests in the channel. Vertical marketing systems may not eliminate potential sources of conflict in channels; indeed, they can give rise to such conflict. Nevertheless, VMSs do bring with them a variety of tools and arrangements for dealing with conflicting interests.

Together, channel length and channel relationships constitute the most important elements of channel structure. A related aspect to structure, however, are the channel intermediaries themselves and, in particular, their role and functions in the channel. It is to these considerations that we now turn our attention.

Channel intermediaries

We have seen that the reason for using intermediaries to move products and services from producer to consumer rests on their superior efficiency in the performance of basic tasks. We have also seen that the range and nature of these tasks that an intermediary is required to perform would include, for example, providing an assortment, breaking down bulk, promoting and merchandising products, etc. As in other areas of industry and business, over time, specialization has arisen in the intermediaries' industry. Because of this, the range of functions that a particular type of intermediary is customarily expected to perform can be broadly delineated for each of the major categories or types of marketing channel members. Some examples of these major types are briefly outlined and discussed below, although one should note that the tasks and responsibilities of a particular type of intermediary can vary considerably from company to company. It should also be noted that, within each broad category of intermediary, a variety of specific or specialized formats can operate. For example, in wholesale trading we can distinguish between wholesalers who deliver to their customers and often extend credit terms, and cash and carry wholesalers, where the purchaser selects and collects the goods from the wholesaler's warehouse with no credit being given.

Wholesalers   The primary function of the wholesaler was, and still is, the breaking down of bulk. The wholesale trader buys in bulk from one or more producers and sells in smaller quantities to the *retailer*. In addition to performing this key function, however, the wholesaler often provides the following services:

- Provides storage facilities, thereby reducing the need for the retailer and producer to carry extensive stocks.
- Reduces the contact costs between manufacturers and retailers.
- Reduces marketing risks for the producer—the wholesaler shoulders some of the risks involved in interpreting and forecasting consumer demand.

Recent trends and patterns in the distribution system of the UK have led to a significant reduction in this type of channel intermediary. In particular, the growth of the powerful multiple retailers which, as we shall see, has been such a feature of the changing structure of retailing in the UK, has put the wholesaling part of the channel under extreme pressure. Many of the conventional functions of the wholesaler have been increasingly taken over by the retailers themselves. However, wholesaling and wholesalers still remain important elements of many channels. Most wholesalers are so-called 'merchant wholesalers', who take title to goods and usually operate as independently owned businesses. There are several types of merchant wholesalers though. So, for example, *full service* merchant wholesalers, as the term implies, offer the full range of wholesaling functions. On the other hand, *limited service* merchant wholesalers, specialize in only a few of the wholesaler functions and hence can offer competitive rates, albeit with fewer services. A particularly successful type of limited service wholesaler in the UK has been the 'cash-and-carry' wholesaler.

Cash-and-carry wholesalers, as you would expect, stock goods which the customer (usually a small retailer or industrial customer) can pay for and take away immediately. There is no delivery and little or no additional services. The more effective cash-and-carry wholesalers have not only survived but have actually prospered in recent years. Dibb *et al.*[8] described the growth of the extremely successful Dutch cash-and-carry wholesaler Makro. They show that by the application of modern marketing techniques such as effective merchandising, the development of its own brands, and careful research and monitoring of customer needs, wholesalers such as Makro can respond successfully to the threat from the major retailers.

Agents   In many markets, particularly export markets, the agent is a widely used type of intermediary. Agents are of two basic types:

1. A *commission agent*, who secures orders from customers but does not, under normal circumstances, take title to the goods, and is not responsible for obtaining payment.

2. A *stockist agent*, who carries a stock of the manufacturer's products. They may either have purchased these stocks or may hold them on consignment. Often such agents will determine the mark-up on products and the discount that will be offered to dealers.

Retailers   As Pitfield points out,[9] the traditional functions of the retailer in the channel of distribution stem from the personal relationship with the customer. Among the traditional functions of the retailer in the channel can be included:

- The provision of variety (reducing shopping times and costs)
- Where appropriate, individual packing
- Customer and credit facilities
- Delivery and credit facilities
- Promotion and merchandising
- Final product pricing

As we shall shortly see, however, the modern retailer now performs other functions as well.

This relatively brief discussion of types of channel members and their functions illustrates that in channel decisions the marketer must not only consider the length and relationships of channel design, but must also be aware of the variety of channel intermediaries and the function they are best able to perform. In addition, the producer must take account of the trends and changes in channels and reflect these in channel decisions. It is to this dynamic aspect of channel management that we now turn our attention, with particular emphasis on one of the most rapidly evolving elements of channel structure in the UK—retailing.

Changing channels of distribution: the structure of retailing in the UK

Channels of distribution represent possibly one of the most rapidly evolving and dynamic areas of marketing. Nowhere is this more the case than in the area of retailing in the United Kingdom. Not only have these changes led to the growth of new types of intermediaries and the subsequent decline of more traditional ones; in addition, they have led to the growth of completely new channels for distributing products and services. Accompanying, and often under-pinning, these changes in overall structure have been equally important changes in the relationship between retailers and manufacturers and, in particular, in the locus of power channels.

Some of the more important of these changes and trends in the structure of UK retailing are as follows:

● Retailing has become, and is continuing to become, progressively more concentrated; i.e. a few very large retailers now account for a significant proportion of the retail market. Nowhere is this trend towards increased concentration in retailing more pronounced than in the area of grocery retailing, where the large multiples have grown to dominate this sector of the market. This growth has been achieved largely at the expense of the smaller independents and the co-operative societies. Initially this growth in dominance by the multiples was particularly prevalent in grocery retailing, with retail giants such as Tesco, J. Sainsbury, Asda and others. However, now virtually every product sector of UK retailing is accounted for by relatively few but extremely large multiples. So, for example, in the DIY sector multiples such as Kingfisher's B&Q, Homebase, Do-It-All, and Wickes dominate. In footwear it is multiples such as Sears—the British Shoe Corporation, Stylo-Barratts, and the C. J. Clark Group. Finally, as an example, electrical products and household appliance retailing is dominated by companies such as Dixons, Kingfisher-Comet and Currys.

The success of the large multiples is due to a number of factors. In particular:

● Their very marketing-oriented approach, based on responding to changes in consumer shopping and spending habits.

● Their willingness and ability to introduce new innovations in retailing.

● As they have grown in size, their ability and power to bulk-buy from manufacturers, coupled with centralized control has made them very cost competitive. They are in a position to specify exactly what they want in the products supplied to them by manufacturers and will often have products produced for them by a manufacturer and will market those products using their (the multiple's) own brand name.

These broad structural changes in retailing are the result of a number of factors. For example, as car ownership has increased, more and more consumers have begun to require stores with adequate car parking facilities and with a range of merchandise which allows the customer to purchase all or most of the household needs from the one store. Overall, the changes have occurred as a result of retailers, in search of higher profits, having adapted themselves to changing circumstances.

This description of broad changes, too, tends to mask some quite significant and more specific developments in retailing which will continue to affect the producer's marketing policies. Some of the more important of these are:

● A continuing growth in the tradeshare held by large multiples.

● A continuing shift of power from the producer to the retailing end of the distribution channel.

● Linked to the above factors, an increase in administered vertical marketing systems, with implications in particular for own-branding and specification buying.

● A continuing decline in both the numbers of independents and cooperatives, and the proportion of retail sales for which these types of outlets account.

● The continued growth of contractual vertical marketing systems, e.g. franchising.

● An increased internationalization of retailing within Europe.

● A continuing growth of one-stop and edge/out-of-town shopping.

- A growth of discount retailing.

- A continued growth of catalogue stores.

- The survival of convenience stores.

- The growth of non-store retailing and home retailing, including direct marketing, television and Internet shopping.

- A continued growth in the application of new technology to retailing and channels of distribution.

These factors represent changes that have taken place in UK retailing over the past 10–15 years, and they are trends that are likely to continue. They are also changes that are of considerable marketing significance to the various levels of the marketing channel, from producers to the retailers themselves. Some of these are discussed in more detail below.

The growth of one-stop and edge/out-of-town shopping and superstores

The trend towards larger, one-stop, retail outlets in the UK began in the early 1960s with the supermarket. Supermarkets began the trend for one-stop shopping. Previously this had involved visiting a small number of small specialist shops often located in different areas. This trend towards larger, one-shop outlets has continued with hypermarkets and superstores.

Both hypermarkets and superstores are likely to continue to take an increased proportion of retail business in the UK based on the competitive advantages of economy and convenience.

A study by Sanghari and Treadgold[10] on European retailing underlines the fact that the growth of hypermarkets and superstores is not exclusively a UK phenomenon. France, Germany, The Netherlands and Belgium have all experienced a growth in this type of retail outlet, facilitated by increased ownership of cars, refrigerators and freezers. The exception to this trend appears to be Italy, where, because the population remains concentrated in city centres, the growth of both supermarkets and hypermarkets has been restricted.

A further factor which has encouraged the growth of one-stop and edge/out-of-town shopping in the UK has been the trend towards retail parks and shopping malls. The UK has some of the largest shopping malls in Europe including, for example, the Gateshead Metro Centre and Meadowhall near Sheffield. These shopping malls offer the consumer the convenience of easy, usually free parking and all the major types of retailers and retail brands can be purchased under one roof. Not only can consumers do all their shopping in one location but they can do it in relative comfort, protected from the vagaries of the weather. In fact, visits to such shopping malls are now more than just 'shopping', but as with much of UK retailing, the whole experience of shopping has become more of a leisure experience. Customers often see visits to such shopping malls as a day out with the family and will often travel long distances on coach trips, etc. Similar to shopping malls, at least from the perspective of one-stop shopping, has been the growth of out-of-town retail parks. Although these parks may not contain shops under one roof as in the case of the shopping mall, they represent a collection of different retailers on one single site. So, for example, a customer can shop for furniture on one part of the retail park, and toys on another part. Again, parking is convenient and time is saved not having to drive from one retail outlet to another.

Recently the UK government and town planners have become worried that the continued growth of edge/out-of-town shopping is destroying trade in town centres. Many town centre retailers now find that they are struggling to survive against the competition from their non-centrally located counterparts. It seems that in the future planners are likely to be much more stringent in considering applications for new edge/out-of-town retail planning applications. Having said this, it is likely that edge/out-of-town retailing will continue to grow if customer demand has anything to do with it.

The decline of the independents and cooperatives   Accompanying the trends towards multiples and superstores, and in fact as a direct result of these, the independent and cooperative sectors of UK retailing have declined. Again, this trend is likely to continue. A knock-on effect of this decline has been the reduced importance of the trade wholesaler, whose principal customers are the independents. Independents, cooperatives and wholesalers have each fought against this decline by, for example, forming voluntary groups (sometimes called 'symbol' shops), improving marketing and merchandising and switching to cash-and-carry.

The survival of convenience stores   Although the independent and cooperative sectors of UK retailing have declined overall, the convenience store has managed to survive and to some extent has made a comeback in recent years. Convenience stores are usually local grocery stores selling a wide range of products from traditional grocery products to alcoholic drinks and newspapers. As the term implies, these stores survive because they are both conveniently located and offer convenient opening hours, in some cases even all night. Many of the so-called voluntary groups such as Spar, Mace, VG, etc. practise a convenience opening hours policy. Recently however, many of the major supermarket groups have begun to extend their opening hours, again sometimes with overnight shopping, and more recently Sunday opening. It remains to be seen what effect this will have on the convenience stores.

The growth of discount retailing   Although the general trend in much of retail shopping had been towards higher quality products and increased customer service, perhaps partly because of this we have also seen a growth of the discount section of the market. The discount segment is obviously designed to appeal to those customers who want, or perhaps can only afford, no-frills products and services that are at low prices. At one end of the market of discount retailers we have the discount sheds which are usually large superstores, situated again out of town with few or no window displays and customer amenities. In essence, these retail outlets are more like warehouses where customers can buy direct from stock and take their products home immediately. In fact, recently we have seen the growth of so-called '*warehouse clubs*' where customers must become members and having done so, effectively buy at cheaper rates on a cash-and-carry basis (e.g. Costco). Such warehouse clubs purchase in bulk but offer limited ranges. Merchandising and display are cut to a minimum and usually require customers to buy in minimum quantities. Finally, another form of discount retailing has been the increasing frequency of town centre shops and stores being taken on short-term leases in order to clear bankrupt stock or 'seconds' products at a cheap rate. Sometimes these types of retailers only occupy a store for a week or so until the stock is sold out.

The growth of discount retailing is, as already intimated, in part a response to the move upmarket by many of the more traditional retailing groups and the multiples in particular. As we shall see shortly, in some ways the growth of discount retailing then is perhaps due to the *wheel of retailing* hypothesis which we shall consider shortly.

Catalogue stores   Catalogue stores, in the context of the history of UK retailing are a relatively new development. Catalogue stores are where the customer uses a

catalogue that has either been mailed to their home or which they can look at in the store itself in order to fill in an order form which is then processed immediately in the store and the customer can take the product home. In effect, it operates like mail order, but without having to mail. The advantage to the retailer is that products do not need to be displayed and stocked on shelves, although sometimes a selection of the products in the catalogue will be on display. This means that the premises can be smaller than would otherwise be needed, and also there are fewer problems of, for example, shop-lifting and damage, etc. Little customer service or advice is usually available. So far as the customer is concerned, the advantage is normally a lower price than they would otherwise pay in a more conventional retail outlet and (on paper at least) more convenient shopping. In the UK two of the most successful catalogue retailers are Argos and Index.

Non-store retailing and home retailing: direct marketing, television and Internet shopping   The term retailing tends to imply a specific establishment (or chain of establishments) located in a particular area which the customer visits in order to purchase products and services. Although this description of retailing still accounts for the majority of sales, in fact an increasing proportion of purchases are made through non-store retailing and home retailing. In fact non-store retailing and home retailing represent part of what is probably one of the fastest growing areas of marketing activity, namely the growth of *direct marketing*. There are many different types of direct marketing including non-store and home retailing. Some of the more important ones are outlined below:

- *Automatic vending*   Although not accounting for a large proportion of retail sales, automatic vending, which of course is not new, is for some products particularly important. As you probably know, automatic vending involves the use of self-service machines, sometimes requiring payment, usually through a coin, and sometimes provided 'free' by, say, an employer. Types of products which are sold through this type of system include, for example, cigarettes, soft drinks and coffee, and snack/confectionery items such as biscuits, chocolate, etc. By far the largest proportion of vending machines are found in plants and factories, public locations such as airports and stores, and offices.

- *Mail order retailing*   Again, mail order retailing is not new. This type of retailing, too, uses a catalogue from which the customer selects products for purchase. Unlike catalogue retailing however, delivery of the catalogue itself, ordering, delivery and return of goods are done by post. In the UK large mail order companies include Littlewoods and Freemans who have been selling through mail order for many years. However, recently a large number of more traditional retailers have begun to establish mail order services for their products, including, for example, Next, Laura Ashley and Habitat. In addition, mail order is particularly suited to smaller, more specialist retailers. Essentially, the convenience of mail order has meant that this type of retailing is now growing again. Changes in technology and a decrease in the amount of time available for shopping will probably mean that this growth will continue.

- *Telephone selling (telemarketing)*   An increasing number of marketers are now contacting customers directly by telephone in order to try to gain an order, or at least an agreement to see a sales representative. Telephone selling, or as it is now more frequently referred to, 'telemarketing' has, of course, always been a feature of business-to-business marketing but it is increasingly being used in consumer marketing. The reason is the low costs involved for the selling company, coupled with the now almost universal connection to a telephone service among UK households. One of the problems with telephone selling, however, particularly when contacting householders, is that many customers see this as being an invasion of privacy and will refuse to purchase, or even speak, to companies using this method. Fortunately, marketers are now becoming aware of some of the worries of consumers in this respect and increasingly there is an industry code of practice which mitigates against the worst potential abuses of telephone selling. Sometimes telemarketing is based on a cold-canvass, for example using the telephone directory, of prospective customers but more effectively some sort of pre-screening of potential purchasers is used to draw up a telephone list. Often telemarketing uses more conventional advertising methods such as television, magazine or newspaper advertising to encourage the customer to make the telephone contact, often using 0800 Freephone numbers.

- *Direct mail*   Perhaps the fastest growing area of direct marketing, direct mail, involves selling by contacting customers through the postal service in an attempt to encourage them to make a purchase through the same system. Direct mail is such an important and fast growing area of marketing that in many ways it can be considered as a promotional tool in its own right. We shall therefore consider direct mail in this context in more detail in Chapter 9 when we consider marketing communications. Briefly, though, direct mail normally involves sending out a 'mailshot' of say promotional material for a company's products or services to a pre-selected target mailing list. The effectiveness of direct mail is very much dependent on the accuracy with which potential target customers can be identified and located as represented in the mailing list. The growth of direct mail then is almost entirely due to improved information and databases pertaining to the identification of potential purchasers. As we shall see in Chapter 9 one of the problems with using direct mail is that of response rates, that is, customers often 'junk' direct mail straight into the wastebasket. Another related problem is that the majority of direct mail is 'unsolicited', that is, the customer receives it without requesting it, and therefore does not value it. There is no doubt that direct mail is a major source of annoyance to many customers.

  A variation on the conventional use of direct mail is the sending of promotional information to prospective customers via the fax network. An increasing number of companies are using this method to try and sell their products, particularly to business and/or organizational customers. As with other forms of direct mail, however, this use of unsolicited promotional material transferred via customers' fax machines can be very annoying to customers. In particular of course it 'ties up' the fax facilities of an organization which are essentially intended for other purposes.

- *New technology and distribution: television and Internet home shopping*   Recent developments in technology have led to the growth of entirely new types of shopping. One area has been the growth of television shopping, itself prompted of course by the growth of cable and satellite television. Most of the cable and satellite companies offer a shopping channel which customers can tune into and watch presenters demonstrating products for sale. These products can then be ordered immediately over the telephone using, for example, a credit card number. A second area, however, represents what many pundits believe will be the biggest growth area in shopping in the future, namely shopping using the Internet. You will recall that we have mentioned the Internet several times throughout this text in different contexts but there is no doubt that shopping via the Internet is here to stay and will grow. More and more companies are now listed on the Internet and one can not only call up details of their products and services, including of course photographs, demonstrations and so on, but one can also order these products directly. Many retailers have introduced websites so that customers can 'visit the store' on the Internet, and then place their orders and have these orders delivered direct to their homes. Obviously, the convenience of such home shopping, together with the increase in the ownership of home computers connected to the Internet, means that the pundits who predicted growth were right. Certainly today's marketing manager needs to be fully familiar with current and future developments in Internet marketing and particularly Internet shopping.

The growth of franchising   One of the fastest-growing types of retailing in the UK in recent years has been franchising. Introduced into the UK in the early 1950s, the original image of the typical franchise operation was one of high risk and dubious trading practices. However, since those early days franchising has become respectable and often very profitable with, as a result, an explosion in the number and range of franchises being operated. Today, franchising encompasses products from pipes to

pastries and includes such well-known names as the Body Shop, Prontaprint, Kentucky Fried Chicken and Spud-U-Like.

This surge in franchising has been underpinned by the efforts of the British Franchising Association, which has developed codes of practice for franchising[11] and in doing so has greatly helped to reduce the risks to both franchisor and franchisee alike.

Irrespective of the different patterns of franchising systems, they all share a set of common features and operating procedures as follows:

1. A franchise essentially sells a nationally, or often internationally recognized trade name, process, or business format to the franchisee.
2. The franchisor normally offers expert advice on, for example, location selection, capitalization, operation, and marketing.
3. Most franchise systems operate a central purchasing system at the national or international level to enable cost savings to be made at the individual franchise level.
4. The franchise is subject to a contract binding both parties.
5. This contract normally requires the franchisee to pay a franchise fee and royalty fees, but the franchisee owns the business as opposed to being employed.
6. The franchisor normally provides initial and continuous training to the franchisee.

As already mentioned, contractual vertical marketing systems, and particularly franchising, have been one of the fastest growing areas of marketing activity and distribution arrangements. Clearly this would not have occurred if there were not substantial advantages which derive from the franchising system. As we would expect from a system which essentially involves two independent parties voluntarily agreeing to contract with each other, these advantages accrue to both the franchisee and franchisor. The main advantages are as follows, beginning with the franchisees, and continuing with those for the franchisor.

Some key advantages for the franchisees

- The franchisee gains the benefit of being able to sell a well known product or service that has been market tested and known to work.
- The franchisee enjoys access to the knowledge, experience, reputation and image of the franchisor. Because of this the franchisee is able to enter a business much more easily than setting up from scratch. The learning curve is shortened, expensive mistakes can be avoided, and overall there is less chance of business failure.
- Although the franchisee has the backing of what is often the large organization of the franchisor, the franchisee is still essentially an independent business with all this implies for enjoyment and motivation.
- The franchisee is helped by often national or international advertising and promotion by the franchisor which would be beyond the means of a small independent business.
- The franchisee enjoys the use of the franchisor's trademark, continuous research and development, and market information.
- The franchisor will normally provide a system of management controls such as accountancy, sales and stock control procedures, etc.

Some key advantages for the franchisor

- Recruiting a network of franchisees enables rapid growth as wider distribution can be achieved with less capital.
- The individual franchisee is, as already mentioned, more interested and motivated than the hired manager might be.

- The franchisor secures captive outlets for his products or services, especially in the case of trade name franchising and private labels.

- Franchise fees and royalty fees provide a regular stream of income for the franchisor.

- The terms of the franchise contract normally give the franchisor substantial control over how the franchise is operated. Normally, the franchisor can terminate a franchisee's contract should he or she find the relationship unsatisfactory. The costs of such terminations are likely to be much less than if the franchisor were operating corporate-owned facilities and where the staff involved were on the payroll. Normally the terms and restrictions on location and sale of the business by the franchisee ensure that the franchisor is able to maintain territorial exclusivity for its franchisees.

These advantages therefore explain the rapid growth of franchising as a system of distribution. Of course there are also potential disadvantages and pitfalls to franchising both for franchisee and franchisor, however, the franchise relationship is such that it combines the strengths of both small- and large-scale businesses. The franchisee is the small businessperson who is able to respond to local market conditions and offer personal service to customers. The franchisor passes on economies of scale in national advertising and bulk purchasing.

The internationalization of retailing   A further important development in retailing has been the way in which European retailers, including those of the UK, have sought to expand their retailing operations abroad. There are many reasons for this, not the least of course being the growth of the European Union and the continued moves towards free trade between member countries. These developments in trade are discussed more fully in Chapter 14, but at this stage it is sufficient to note that European retailers have been in the forefront of expansion across international boundaries. In the UK we have seen the establishment of retailers such as IKEA, originally a flat-pack furniture manufacturer of Swedish origin, Aldi, the largest German food retailer, and Benetton, the Italian clothing group. Successful international forays from the UK include retailers such as Body Shop, Safeway, Laura Ashley and John Menzies' Early Learning Centre. This trend towards the internationalization of retailing across the globe is one that is likely to continue as retailers seek out new profit opportunities.

Technology and retailing/channels of distribution   There is little doubt that the broad structural changes that have occurred in retailing, and the more specific events on which these are based, have resulted in changes in the marketing and distribution policies of channel members. Technology, too, is now beginning to change the face of UK retailing and, in particular, the application of the ubiquitous microchip. Computerized stock control and order processing, often linked through computerized, laser-aided checkouts, have become commonplace in retailing. As we have already seen, the 'shopper' is now able to order products directly from the home via a computer terminal/ television link. Such schemes will become more widespread in the future as the technology continues to improve. These and other developments pose questions as to the future shape of retailing in the UK.

THE WHEEL OF RETAILING

In the 1960s McNair and May[12] suggested a hypothesis to explain and help predict changes in retailing structure—the so-called '*wheel of retailing*' hypothesis. Essentially, this hypothesis suggests that new forms of retailing operation begin as low-price, utility operations, established to challenge the higher margin and, by comparison, luxurious established outlets. These low-cost, low-margin operations attract price-conscious customers. Their success leads to expansion, with an upgrading of facilities, services and eventually prices. They, in turn, become susceptible to newer low-cost/low-price operations. The 'wheel' has turned full circle.

There is no doubt that at least some of the structural changes that have taken place in UK retailing do in fact accord with this hypothesis. For example, the growth of the warehouse clubs discussed earlier. More recently, however, McNair himself has concluded that the term is too narrow and limited to explain adequately the changes that have taken place. Nevertheless, what McNair's hypothesis does point to is the fact that retailing institutions, much like products, have life cycles. Moreover, a marked trend in retailing is the shortening of the life cycle for a particular type of institution and for each successive retailing innovation. It took, say, 50 years for department stores to achieve maturity, only 25 years for supermarkets, and hypermarkets will probably reach it in 10. Only one thing is certain about the shape of UK retailing in 10 years' time, and that is that it will be different from that which exists today.

These, then, are some of the major facets of channels and intermediaries, together with some of the major structural changes that are taking place in this important area of marketing. In the next part of this chapter we turn our attention to the design of channels and the important aspects of channel strategy.

CHANNEL STRATEGY

It is now recognized that channel decisions are strategic decisions in a company. There are two major reasons for this:

1. Channel decisions generally involve a company in long-term commitments—often to other organizations. Once established, a company's channels of distribution can be difficult to change, at least in the short run. Of course, as we have seen, the dynamic nature of marketing channels inevitably means that at some stage a company will need to re-assess the extent to which its channel strategy is optimum, and perhaps to make changes. Few companies, however, change channels at the same frequency, or with the same relative degree of ease, with which they might and can change their advertising or their prices.

2. Channel decisions intimately affect, and are affected by, virtually all of a company's marketing and operating activities. For example, the selection of target markets is affected by, and in turn affects, channel design and choice. Similarly, decisions about the individual marketing mix elements—for example, pricing, product and promotion—must reflect a company's channel choice.

The four major strategic elements of channel choice and design are as follows:

1. *The delineation and selection of basic channel structure*   Included under this element would be considerations as to channel length, types of intermediaries and functions of intermediaries.

2. *The determination of required market exposure*   Included under this element would be the decisions concerning the number of intermediaries to be used and their geographical dispersion.

3. *Systems and procedures for ensuring maximum cooperation in the channel and the minimum of channel conflict*   This would include, for example, the specification of territorial rights, franchising conditions, etc.

4. *Marketing and channel support strategies* In particular, under this heading would be the relative emphasis and focus for marketing efforts in the channel.

These key elements are considered in more detail below.

Basic channel structure

We saw earlier that one of the principal differences between channel types is in the number and types of intermediaries used. At one extreme, the manufacturer may opt for the shortest channel available, i.e. direct distribution with no intermediaries being used. On the other hand, some channel structures incorporate several distinct levels, with a variety of intermediaries being involved in many products from producer to final user. Because of the variety of basic channel alternatives in this respect, we should be careful not to suggest what Stanton[13] refers to as an 'orthodoxy which does not exist'. Nevertheless, some of the basic channel structures, ranging from the most direct and shortest channel to one involving several levels, are illustrated in Fig. 8.5.

It should also be noted that channels with the same degree of directness (or indirectness), i.e. number of intermediaries, may differ in terms of the types of intermediaries used. An example of this is shown in Fig. 8.6.

To reiterate, the choice of basic channel structure involves both the choice of number and types of intermediaries that will be used. Very many factors will influence the basic range of channel alternatives and the choice between them by the marketer. At this stage, one should recall why channel intermediaries are used at all—i.e. that their use is justified when they perform functions more effectively and efficiently than would be the case if they were not used. Both the number and types of intermediaries that will be used depend upon the range and nature of the tasks involved in moving products and services from producer to final consumer, and upon the extent to which one particular channel alternative is superior to another. Against this general consideration, and again at the risk of oversimplifying this aspect of strategic channel choice, some of the factors influencing the choice between direct and more indirect channels of distribution are as follows:

More direct (shorter)		*Less direct* (larger)
Indirect products	→	Consumer products
Services	→	Tangible products

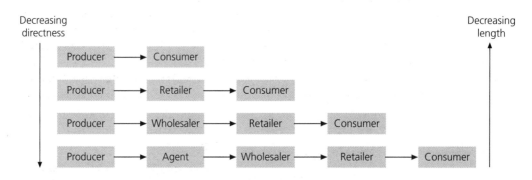

FIGURE 8.5 *Some basic channel alternatives*

Few, more-concentrated customer groupings	→	Larger numbers of customers; geographically dispersed
More control required, e.g. quality, aftersales service, etc.	→	Control less important
Customer purchase in large amounts at infrequent intervals	→	Customers purchase frequently but in small amounts
Products that are bulky/expensive to handle, custom-built, have a high unit value, or are perishable	→	Less bulky, cheaper, standardized, non-perishable products

One is counselled to treat these facts affecting choice of channel length and types of intermediaries with caution. For example, many tangible consumer products of a non-perishable, low-value, standardized nature are distributed very effectively direct from producer to final consumer through mail order.

Required market exposure

A second key element of strategic channel decision-making is the decision concerning the required degree of market exposure. This is underpinned by decisions about the number of intermediaries that will be used at each level and their degree of geographical dispersion.

If a company wishes to have its product available through as many intermediaries as possible, then it must design an *intensive* system of distribution. For example, it will seek to recruit or encourage as many different types of retailers as possible to stock and sell its products. Further, it may seek as wide a geographical dispersion of these stockists as it can. Again, many factors would affect choice of channel strategy, including the marketing objectives and particularly the target markets envisaged by the company. One of the most influential factors in determining this element of distribution strategy is the extent to which the customer is likely to require a place and/or convenience utility from the distributor. For example, few buyers of razor blades would welcome having to travel long distances to purchase this relatively simple, inexpensive and frequently purchased product from one of a relatively few specialist retailers of this product.

In contrast to this form of intensive distribution, the marketer may instead opt for a system of *selective* or *exclusive* distribution. Whereas intensive distribution involves the sale of company products or services through as many outlets as possible, selective and exclusive distribution refer to the distribution of those products and services through a deliberately restricted number of intermediaries.

In fact, there are two dimensions to the 'selective'/'exclusive' decision. The first relates to the earlier decision as to the type of intermediaries to be used. For example, the marketer may determine that its products will be made available only through multiple retail outlets and not, say, through mail order. The second dimension relates to the possible choice of certain intermediaries within a particular type. For example, the marketer may determine that only a few selected multiples, or dealers or agents,

FIGURE 8.6

Channel valuations based on different intermediaries

will be encouraged to handle its products. The extreme form of this aspect of channel strategy is exclusive distribution, where only a few, or possibly only one, intermediary is given exclusive rights to distribute the company's products.

Since, by implication, a selective or exclusive system of distribution provides less 'convenience' and 'place utility' than an intensive distribution system, there must be other reasons for selecting those systems. Some of the factors that would incline a company towards selecting a more exclusive system of distribution would include:

● Where the product and/or service is such that the customer expects and/or requires specialist advice, service facilities, etc.

● Where the marketer and distribution would benefit from the possibly enhanced image associated with more selective distribution.

● Where the potential volume of market/territorial sales would not warrant more intensive distribution.

● Where the marketer wishes to retain more control of the intermediaries' marketing of the product, including, for example, pricing, promotion, credit, etc.

● Where more intensive distribution may give rise to problems associated with channel conflict between intermediaries at the same level in the channel, e.g. between different agents, different retailers, etc.

This last aspect of this element of channel strategy illustrates an important consideration in our discussion so far on this topic: namely, that the elements themselves overlap. Decisions between intensive and selective or exclusive distribution have implications for the third element of channel strategy, i.e. channel cooperation and conflict.

Channel cooperation and conflict

Earlier in this chapter vertical marketing systems were outlined and discussed. We saw that channel relationships constitute an important dimension of channel structure. We also saw that the growth of various types of VMSs is explained in part by the need to achieve coordination throughout the full length of the channel. An important strategic element of channel decisions, therefore, are those decisions that relate to channel cooperation and conflict.

Essentially, it is in the interests of all the members of a channel for there to be a substantial degree of cooperation. After all, a marketing channel is, or should be, a set of interlocking and mutually dependent elements which combine with a complete system for achieving a given set of tasks. Having said this, an almost inevitable feature of marketing channels is the potential for conflict between channel members. This should be considered by the marketer in the strategic design of his channels.

Stern and El-Ansary[14] point to two distinct types of conflict in channels based on the level in a channel at which such conflict may arise. The first of these is *horizontal channel conflict*. This is conflict that occurs between intermediaries at the same level in the channel. This type of conflict is primarily competitive and may occur between similar intermediaries (e.g. multiple versus multiple) or between dissimilar intermediaries (e.g. discount store versus multiple). Horizontal conflict may also arise between the members of a company's own channel. An example would be where conflict arises, say, between two of a company's own distributors, possibly concerning trading rights and practices.

The second, and much more prevalent, type of conflict is *vertical channel conflict*.

This is conflict that occurs between different levels of the same channel, e.g. between producer, wholesaler and retailer. This type of conflict is primarily power conflict between channel members.

Clearly, some types of channel conflict are natural and healthy. For example, it is to be expected that, in a competitive market environment, channel intermediaries at the same level will lock in competitive conflict. As we have seen, at the retailing level in the UK, the multiples appear to have emerged victorious from this competitive struggle. Nevertheless, we can expect both more traditional and newer forms of retailing institutions to continue to challenge this supremacy.

If this type of conflict is healthy and even functional, then, potentially at least, conflict between channel members may be very damaging indeed to one side and/or the other. For example, the producer may come into conflict with his retailers about the way they are merchandising and promoting his product. Retailers, on the other hand, may come into conflict with their suppliers about, say, the issue of own-label brands. The issue is not so much of totally eliminating such conflict, but rather of designing channel structures and relationships in such a way that the potential for conflict is reduced; and, where some conflict is inevitable, it should be better managed. Examples of mechanisms for achieving this, and thereby increasing cooperation in the channel, would include clear and enforceable dealer and franchising policies, arbitration procedures, producer/distributor councils and, as we have seen, the use of vertical marketing systems. Regardless of the mechanisms, or administrative and contractual procedures, for improving cooperation in the channel, one issue will be as to which level or type of organization should act as channel leader and exercise control over the channel. In practice, the resolution of this issue comes down to where the power lies in the channel. Various views have been put forward as to where this power is, or should be, concentrated in the channel. For example, some argue that the power, and therefore the leadership, in a channel should rest with the manufacturer who is best suited to translate consumer needs and wants, and scarce economic resources, into marketable products and services.

Others argue that this type of argument is 'vague' and 'subjective',[15] or that today the retailer is uniquely placed in the channel system to interpret end-user or consumer needs.[16] Again, as we have seen, there is no doubt that the developments in UK retailing have, in fact, led to channel power increasingly being vested at this end of the distribution system, and this fact must be taken into account in strategic channel decision-making. But why should any one channel level or intermediary exercise channel power? The hypothesis appears to be that without channel leadership there is a substantial possibility of conflicting dynamics destroying the channel; if leadership exists, on whatever basis and however it is exercised, there is less chance of this occurring. An alternative hypothesis is that the exercise of channel leadership in fact creates increased instability in the channel, since controlled cooperation is in effect only subdued conflict.

These contrary arguments illustrate that the study of the cooperation and conflict aspects of distribution decisions, and the concepts of leadership and power on which they are based, is still very much in its infancy. The decision-maker will need to exercise his knowledge, experience and simple common sense. Simply to suggest or argue for a particular arrangement of channel leadership and power ignores the complexity of markets, products and channel relationships. In general terms, in order to fulfil the primary objective of the marketing channel, channel leadership and power should devolve, or preferably should be arranged to devolve, to the channel members who are best able to fulfil this objective.

Marketing and channel support strategies

The fourth major element of strategic channel decisions concerns the relative emphasis and focus for marketing efforts in the channel. Of particular importance in this respect would be the choice between 'push' and 'pull' marketing strategies.

In some companies, marketing efforts and tactics are aimed primarily at 'the trade', i.e. at wholesalers, distributors, retailers, etc. For example, advertising and sales promotion, selling effort and pricing strategies are aimed at generating trade interest and demand for the company's products. This focus of company marketing effort is designed to 'push' a product or service into the distribution pipeline by increasing sales-force and/or dealer interest and motivation to stock and sell the products.

A 'pull' marketing strategy, on the other hand, is one where the primary focus of company marketing efforts is concentrated on the final consumer. The objective with this strategy is to generate sufficient consumer interest and demand for the company's products to be 'pulled' through the distribution pipeline. The distinction between 'push' and 'pull' strategies in relation to channels of distribution is shown in Fig. 8.7.

Examples of marketing efforts within each category of channel strategy include:

1. 'Push' strategies

    a. Cash discounts and increased margins for dealers.
    b. Direct mail shots to dealers.
    c. Dealers competitions, free gifts or premiums.
    d. Merchandising and dealer points of sale display material.
    e. Salespeople's incentive schemes: competitions, bonuses, sales rallies, etc.
    f. Trade advertising.
    g. Trade exhibitions.

2. 'Pull' strategies

    a. Consumer advertising.
    b. Reduced price offers to consumers.
    c. Consumer sales promotion.

In fact, as we shall see in Chapter 9, there are many more tools available to a company to implement 'push' or 'pull' activities. However, it is usually not a case of deciding between one or other of these strategies, but more one of determining where the balance should lie—towards push or towards pull.

Again, many factors will influence the choice of an appropriate balance, for example types of product, target market, marketing objectives, etc. What is important, in terms of strategic channel decisions, is that this relative balance should be determined in advance of, or at least in conjunction with, the strategic channel decisions that it so intimately affects.

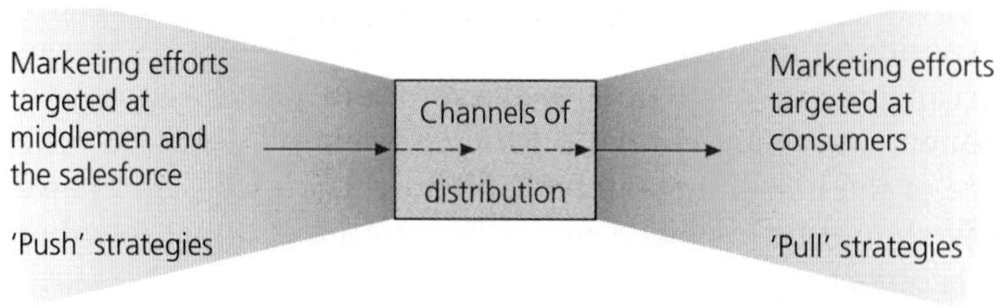

FIGURE 8.7

'Push' versus 'pull' strategies

In summary, we have looked at some of the key elements of strategic channel decision-making. In doing so we have also touched on some of the factors that will affect what would be an appropriate choice of channels for a company and their design. In the next section we will consider further some of the major factors that will serve to constrain and affect the channel decision. We shall also examine some of the specific criteria against which the variety of channel alternatives may be evaluated.

IDENTIFYING AND EVALUATING CHANNEL ALTERNATIVES

Bearing in mind the four key elements of channel strategy outlined earlier, the marketing decision-maker will need to delineate the major alternatives available to him or her in channel choice and design. In delineating these alternatives, he or she needs to consider a number of factors which effectively serve to constrain the channel choice. Some of the more important of these considerations are as follows.

Company and marketing objectives and resources

A key factor in delineating options for channel decisions is the company itself and, in particular, overall company and marketing objectives and company resources. For example, a company with long-run growth objectives based on increasing market share may have to look towards extending the breadth and depth of its distribution channels. Similarly, companies wishing to become market leaders in the grocery market have little option but to consider distributing through the multiples. The smaller company with fewer financial and staff resources may be forced into using more indirect channels for its products and will certainly have little power in the administration of the channel as a whole. Remember, as with other marketing mix decisions, distribution decisions should be consistent with and reflect overall company objectives and marketing strategy.

Target markets/customers

The design of channels of distribution is greatly influenced by the choice of target markets and the nature of customer characteristics within this market.

Before a company begins to consider the alternatives for channel choice and design, it should, ideally, have determined its target markets. In particular, the choice of target markets and channel alternatives may be interdependent. A company may discover that it cannot reach its preferred target market with the channel alternatives available, or it may find that this target market can be served profitably only with a particular system of distribution. In either case, target market selection and channel decisions must be made together. In addition, the company must take account of customer characteristics, in the target market(s). Examples of possibly important customer characteristics would include:

1. *The number of customers*   As we saw earlier, large numbers of customers for a product tend to favour a more indirect channel of distribution, particularly where this is associated with a second key customer characteristic (see point 2 below).

2. *Their geographical dispersion*

3. *Customer needs, habits and preferences*   Together, these probably represent one of the most important considerations in channel design. It is pointless selecting a particular channel design which satisfies the company but does not satisfy the needs of the customer. For example, customers in the target market may have a preference for a particular type of channel intermediary, or they may have particular needs in purchasing the product which certain channel arrangements cannot provide. Sometimes consumer preferences may be based on custom and habit. Although it does not pay to ignore such preferences, where they are based only on habit a company should consider the possibility of developing other and possibly innovative channels of distribution for its products.

Product

The influence of product characteristics on channel decisions was outlined earlier in this chapter. For example, it was suggested that, generally, bulkier perishable, non-standard products will tend towards a more direct system of distribution. It must also be remembered that there are no rules here. We often find that essentially the same types of product are distributed in very different ways by different companies.

Competition

Channel decisions must, like other aspects of marketing, reflect competitive consider-ations. Again, one should be careful to note that we are not suggesting that a company should utilize the same or even similar channels to those used by its competitors. Indeed, a company may seek to examine the practices of its competitors in order to devise alternative methods.

Together, these considerations will constrain the range of appropriate channels and systems available to a company. It is likely that the decision-maker will still be faced with a range of channel alternatives including a range of possible intermediaries for which he or she must make the final choice. At this point, each of the remaining alternatives needs to be assessed against a set of additional and more specific criteria. Kotler[17] suggests that among the more important of these criteria are those that relate to *control*, *adaptive* and *economic* factors; to these we would add an additional element—that of *coverage*.

In terms of control criteria and channel choice, a company must consider carefully the extent to which its channel design will allow the company to exercise control over the marketing effort. As a general rule, a company has more control where it uses more direct channels for its products. Of course, it is often the case that the producer determines to relinquish some degree of control over how its products are marketed. After all, it may not have the necessary resources to, say, promote the product extensively. There is no 'recipe' as to what constitutes an appropriate degree of control, but it is important that this aspect be considered in the channel decision.

Adaptability in channel choice relates to the extent to which a company is able to change its distribution policy to accord with changed conditions. We know that today's marketer operates in a dynamic environment. Further, we have seen that channels themselves represent one of the most turbulent components of this environment. In this context, adaptability in channels relates to two important factors. First, the marketer must consider how easily he or she can change to an entirely new system of distribution, although it must be remembered that often channel decisions commit the marketer to long-term contractual relationships with channel intermediaries. A company can find itself at a serious disadvantage in the market if a long-term channel arrangement becomes inappropriate. A second aspect of channel adaptability relates to the relative ease with which a company can adapt its marketing effort *within* existing channels. This aspect is related to the control issue discussed earlier. For example, selling through multiples may afford the producer little option as to how his products are marketed to the final customer so as to take account of changed market and competitive conditions.

In terms of coverage criteria, again there are two related aspects. The first relates to the extent to which a particular channel arrangement affords the marketer access to sufficient numbers of customers and/or market segments. The second relates to the extent to which the channel alternatives will lead to the required degree of coverage for the entire product range. For example, it is often the case that intermediaries will stock only the more profitable (for them) product lines and will refuse to have, or will neglect, other, less profitable products in the product range.

The final criterion for assessing specific channel alternatives is possibly the most important. After all, controllability, adaptability and coverage are important only in that they affect long-term profits. Economic criteria, then, are predominant in the assessment procedure. Selection of channel structures and individual middlemen should be based on a careful assessment of the costs and revenues associated with each. On the basis of this assessment, the marketer should choose those channel arrangements that meet both the company's requirements—including that of profit—and customer requirements at the lowest possible cost.

FURTHER CONSIDERATIONS IN CHANNEL DECISIONS

So far we have outlined the key elements of strategic channel decisions and some of the considerations and constraints that will affect these. Having arrived at a strategic channel choice, a company must act to implement, evaluate and control this strategy. Individual intermediaries must be encouraged and/or recruited to suggest the channel choice. Marketing efforts and resources must be swung into operation—sales teams organized, merchandising and promotional material developed, delivery and warehousing systems developed, etc. Further, channels, and the intermediaries that comprise them, should be subjected to continuous and rigorous evaluation and control procedures with regard to both effectiveness and efficiency. These additional considerations point to the fact that the management of distribution in a company involves wider issues than those associated only with overall channel design. Increasingly, this is being recognized and has given rise to the growth of a total systems approach to distribution. We shall conclude this chapter by examining this systems approach. Before we do so, two further considerations about channel decisions should be noted.

Throughout this chapter we have discussed channel design and choice from the point of view of the producer. Remember, intermediaries themselves, from wholesalers to agents, distributors and retailers, are marketers too, and have their own marketing decisions to make including distribution. Finally, you should note that increasingly the question for the producer in channel decisions is not so much: 'What channels should we choose?' as 'Which channels will choose us?'

THE TOTAL SYSTEMS APPROACH TO DISTRIBUTION: LOGISTICS

In recent years, views on what constitute the elements of distribution management have increasingly taken into account additional elements over and above those associated only with the channel itself. It is now recognized that the effective management of the total system of distribution can contribute significantly to overall company success and profits. This total systems approach is variously referred to as *physical distribution* or *logistics* management. The more encompassing nature of the total systems approach to distribution is illustrated in the following definition of physical distribution offered by Arbury[18] as long ago as 1967:

> By 'physical distribution' we mean the interrelationship of all the factors which affect the flow of both goods and orders necessary to fill orders. This flow starts when the customer decides to place an order and ends when the order is delivered to the customer. Physical distribution involves not only the action required to fill a particular order, but also the action necessary to prepare oneself to meet customer needs.

The term 'logistics' is essentially a military one and was applied originally to the science and practice of moving, lodging and supplying troops. Some authors in fact make a distinction between marketing logistics and physical distribution, suggesting for example that the management of physical distribution is more concerned with the planning and control of distribution activities in order to minimize costs, whereas logistics broadens this to include the notion of customer and market needs. For our purpose, the terms 'physical distribution', 'logistics' and 'total distribution' systems are used interchangeably. Two vital considerations, however, will guide our discussion of this aspect of distribution:

1. The design of the total distribution should begin with customer needs and wants.

2. The total system should be designed so as to provide the required level of customer service or utility at the minimum system cost.

Before we discuss these considerations further, it is useful to explain the reasons for the growth in importance of this area of company operations and also some of the more important elements in the system. We shall start by examining the background to marketing logistics.

Two related factors explain the growth of marketing logistics. The first of these is the increasing awareness of the potential cost savings to be derived from the more effective management of physical distribution. In some companies the total cost of all the activities implied in Arbury's definition can represent the most significant simple element of cost on the organization. Important though this may be, it does not ask itself why companies have only comparatively recently turned their attention to these costs. A clue to this recent interest is given by Drucker,[19] when in an article in *Fortune* magazine he referred to physical distribution as 'The economy's dark continent'. What he was highlighting in the use of this colourful phrase was the fact that, unlike so many other areas of company activity with well-developed systems of monitoring effectiveness and well-established costs, physical distribution activities represent a broadly uncharted area in this respect. Together, high costs and relatively underdeveloped cost control mean that in many companies physical distribution represents one of the last remaining areas for potentially substantial cost savings.

The second factor that has given rise to growth in the application of marketing logistics is the recognition that properly managed, effective marketing logistics represents a powerful competitive tool in the marketplace. We shall now give further consideration to this potential for competitive advantage.

Logistics and competitive advantage

Perhaps the most important reason for the growth in importance and interest in physical distribution and logistics is the fact that the logistics system offers substantial potential for achieving a competitive edge and hence for winning and keeping customers. Particularly in industrial markets, where products may be relatively undifferentiated and prices and margins cut to the bone, companies may find that they can gain a competitive edge by using their logistics system to improve customer service levels. This in turn may allow a company to increase the volume of sales and/or to increase prices. Because of this, identifying appropriate levels of and types of customer service to be achieved by the logistics management system is a key aspect of planning in this area.

In the same vein, a number of the developments and trends in industrial purchasing and materials management discussed earlier have heightened the importance attached by many customers to the service elements of the logistics systems of their suppliers and potential suppliers. Some of these were touched on in Chapter 3, when we looked at organizational buyer behaviour. But, for example, with modern continuous flow and large-batch manufacturing systems, a stock-out situation of even a relatively minor and inexpensive component may incur substantial costs in down-time. This potential problem is heightened where, as is increasingly the case, a firm's customers are using just-in-time (JIT) inventory principles. Clearly, where a manufacturer is using a JIT system, delivery, and hence the logistics performance of the supplier, is crucial and its importance heightened. A company that can achieve well on its delivery performance, therefore, has a strong competitive edge over those suppliers who cannot. In fact, for many companies these days, an inability to supply JIT deliveries means that a supplier would simply not be considered.

Similarly, the trend in industrial purchasing towards materials management systems has put an increased emphasis on the logistics performance of a firm's potential suppliers.

These trends towards JIT and materials management are themselves, of course, indicative of the recognition on the part of the customers of the substantial costs, and hence potential cost savings, associated with elements of their own logistics systems, including stocks of raw materials, work-in-progress, the consequences of stock-outs, and defective raw materials and components from suppliers.

As a result, logistics service is now a key factor in supplier choice in industrial markets. Suppliers with poor logistics service, evidenced in late deliveries or stock-outs, are quickly dropped by industrial purchasers in today's competitive conditions. By improving the design and execution of marketing logistics, a marketer can develop a substantial competitive edge over other suppliers. Product availability, prompt delivery and efficient and accurate order processing are just a few of the services that can help capture and keep customers. Hence determination of the nature and level of logistics service elements is crucial to the effective planning of this area of marketing if it is to be used as a demand-generating marketing tool. In this way, physical distribution and logistics can be considered in just the same way as the product, price and promotional elements of the mix.[20] This concept is shown in Fig. 8.8. Some of the elements that comprise logistics can be used, through service levels, to influence demand, as shown.

The components and related activities of a company's total system of distribution will vary from company to company, but will broadly encompass some of the following factors:

- Materials procurement
- Raw material inventories
- Sales forecasting and production planning
- Packaging
- Warehousing and delivery
- Order processing
- Customer service

You will note from this list that marketing logistics involves the total system of inputting, transferring and outputting materials, goods and services in a company. The idea is that the system as a whole be designed to provide the required level of customer service at minimum total cost. In planning the logistics system, therefore, the starting-point is customer needs and service requirements. We shall now briefly outline the steps in planning marketing logistics.

Planning marketing logistics

Planning marketing logistics is a complex process, requiring many elements to be coordinated and controlled. A fuller description is given in one of the many excellent specialist texts available on this area of marketing,[21] but the following represents an outline of the key steps offered by Lancaster and Massingham.[22]

FIGURE 8.8

The demand-creating role of physical distribution efforts

Source: Adapted from E. H. Ballou, *Basic Business Logistics*, 2nd edn, Prentice-Hall, Englewood Cliffs, NJ, 1987

Step 1: Establishing customer service needs   We have already stated that the design of the logistics system should start with customer needs with respect to the service elements provided by the system. Because of this, therefore, it is important to establish what these are. For example, do customers require speedy delivery, or is reliability of delivery more important? Do customers require flexibility in dealing with, say, special orders, or do they require only standard products? And so on. It is essential to establish not only the customer's service needs, but also the relative importance attached to each need. Both needs and relative importance, of course, may vary between different industries, different customers, and even for different products supplied to the same customer. For example, on this last point we may find that certain components are more critical to a customer's production process than others, with a consequent increased importance attached by the customer to the reliability of delivery of these particular components. Similarly, if we take order cycle or lead times, in some industries—the motor car industry for example—order lead times must be kept to a minimum. In fact, this is an industry where most suppliers must increasingly supply on a just-in-time basis. These differences in the degree of importance attached to logistics service elements by different customers or industries have the potential to be used to segment and target markets by a supplier, where the basis of segmentation is differences in sensitivity to different service levels. What is important throughout this process is the need to establish the importance of the various elements from the customer's perspective.

Elements of customer service that are a direct result of the marketer's logistics system are:

- Order cycle time (time from order placement to delivery)
- Consistency of order cycle time (reliability)
- Information on order status
- Flexibility in dealing with special requests
- Returns—damaged and surplus goods
- Response to emergencies
- Freedom from errors in delivery, paperwork, etc.
- Quality of delivered products

Step 2: Establishing current company and competitor performance with regard to service elements   The second step of designing the business logistics system is to establish how well (or badly) the company and its competitors are performing in areas of logistics services seen as important by customers. In general terms, we need to be performing as well in these areas as our competitors. Any significant underperformance is likely to result in lost sales and market share. However, even if we are performing as well as our competitors, this is not to say that customers will be happy with current levels. Indeed, they may be distinctly unhappy about the service they are receiving from current suppliers. In other words, there may be significant marketing opportunities available to the company that is able and willing to improve its service performance. On the other hand, in assessing competitor performance we also need to look carefully at areas where we are significantly outperforming our competitors in order to assess whether or not our extra performance is justifying the additional cost of providing it. This brings us to the third and most difficult step in designing the business logistics system.

Step 3: Determining cost and benefits of making changes to current company performance in levels of logistics service: profit maximization Before we can make decisions about specific objectives for service elements and the design of the logistics system to achieve them, we need to assess carefully the likely costs and benefits, and hence profit potential, associated with different service levels. This brings us to a very important point about the overall design of the logistics system. You will recall that earlier we stressed the fact that logistics services can be important demand-generators. However, improvements in these services are also likely to be costly to the firm providing them. Therefore, in determining the appropriateness, or otherwise, of current company logistics services and any proposed changes in these, we need to assess the likely impact on company profits. In other words, the optimal logistics system is not likely to be one that operates at lowest cost, as we may be losing too many sales. On the other hand, nor is the optimal system likely to be one that generates the greatest demand, as these sales will probably be generated at too great a cost. Put simply, the optimal business logistics system is one that generates the maximum profit. In turn, this requires that the company understands the relationships between service levels and demand, and between service levels and costs. We can then determine whether to increase or decrease service levels to generate maximum contribution. This notion of optimizing the profit contribution of the logistics system is shown in Fig. 8.9. We can see from the figure that maximum contribution is obtained at neither the lowest cost nor the highest service levels. Too low a level of service and we are losing revenue; too high, and we incur too high costs for the extra revenue generated. In theory, maximum contribution is obtained where the marginal cost of additional service levels is equal to the marginal revenue generated by these additional service levels. Needless to say, in practice, actually deriving the demand response functional (revenue) curve with respect to different levels of service can be difficult. Nevertheless, our earlier steps of identifying customer service requirements and current company and competitor performance in this area should at least give some indication of the likely response to increases or decreases in service levels.

As mentioned earlier, having established what types and levels of customer service the logistics system is to provide in order to support our competitive market strategy,

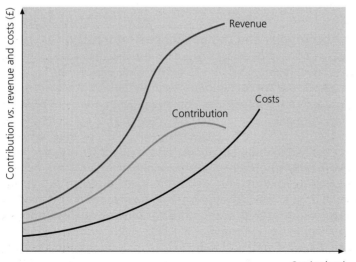

FIGURE 8.9

Costs, revenues and contribution versus service levels

the task of the logistics manager is to provide this service at minimum cost. It is not our intention to discuss the details of operating the logistics system, but it is important for the marketer to understand and recognize the existence of 'trade-offs' between costs and revenue.

In practice, therefore, as we stressed earlier, the system should be designed from a demand perspective. Essentially, based on our earlier analysis of customer needs, we should define our service level objectives based on the role we have determined for logistics services in our overall competitive strategy. The design of the total logistics systems should then be aimed at delivering this predetermined level of logistics services at minimum cost.

Step 4: Establishing specific objectives for areas and levels of logistics services

Overall objectives for logistics service levels will need to be translated to specific objectives for the various areas of such service. The variety of possible customer service elements were outlined earlier, but, for example, we will need to set quantified objectives for order cycle times, response to emergencies, consistency of order cycle time and so on.

Step 5: Planning, implementing and controlling the logistics system   From a

marketer's perspective, at this stage we can now pass the responsibility for the detailed planning, implementation and control of the logistics system over to the logistics experts. Their task is to design the system to give the desired level of service support in each of the elements of our prescribed customer service strategy. This will involve the planning, implementation and control of factors such as purchasing, inbound transport, production planning, inventory control, warehousing, order processing, outbound transport and so on.

We should be careful not to seem to be suggesting that it is only at this stage that the logistics experts should be involved. Even though customer and market needs must be paramount throughout the design of the logistics system, this can be achieved only through the cooperation and expertise of functions such as materials management, production planning and control and so on. In addition, we will need the help and cooperation of the channel members and suppliers, who must therefore be consulted. We should also note that the continued operation of an effective logistics system requires on-going information from sales and marketing, including sales forecasting, customer feedback and competitor information. Of all the elements of the marketing mix, perhaps the 'place' element requires more inter- and intra-firm communication and coordination than any other.

We have already come across the notion of a trade-off, but in this case we are applying it to the system as a whole, where the costs of the total system are traded off against revenue. In planning and operating the system, however, the logistics manager must also make trade-offs between the individual elements of the system in order to achieve the desired levels of customer service at minimum cost. This in turn, will require what logistics planners refer to as a *total cost approach* to distribution, and it recognizes the interdependence between the demands of logistics activities. So, for example, minimizing costs in one area, say inventory, may lead to more than proportional increases in another, say transport. To achieve this, a total systems approach to logistics is required.

Effective planning, implementation and control of the business logistics system is greatly enhanced by the introduction of a service policy and quantified service standards. Again, these need to be determined on the basis of customer and market needs.

The service policy should include written statements concerning the level of customer service in the form of promises to customers which the company will fulfil. These can represent a powerful promotional tool in helping to secure and keep customers, and can also inform staff as to the role and value of a logistics service in overall company and marketing strategy. Policy statements may be relatively simple, such as 'all orders received by noon will be shipped the same day', or more elaborate, covering in detail factors such as time, condition of goods, order communication, service contingencies and so on. The policy statement may then be translated into detailed operating standards for the logistics system. In turn, these standards form the basis of the logistics control system, against which logistics inefficiencies and out-of-line service situations can be quickly addressed.

CHAPTER SUMMARY

In this chapter we have looked at the means by which products and services are channelled from producer to final customer. A channel of distribution is made up of institutions and middlemen where activities centre on the activities required to achieve this. The question is not, should we perform these activities? It is more, who should perform them? The reason for utilizing the services of intermediaries is that often they perform these activities much more effectively and efficiently than can the producer alone.

In order to make decisions about channels, the marketing manager must understand the elements of these channels. In particular, he or she must understand the key dimensions of channel structure: length, and relationships; the role, function, and types of intermediaries; and finally, the dynamic and changing nature of marketing channels.

Against this background, we looked briefly at the changing nature of retailing in the United Kingdom. We have seen that the face of retailing is changing, with recent trends being towards larger, more concentrated retail institutions. The multiples, in particular, have dominated UK retailing over the past 10 years. We have also considered some of the more recent and innovative developments in retail and channels of distribution such as the growth of franchising, one-stop and edge/out-of-town shopping, and discount and catalogue retailing. Of particular significance in this respect are the fast growing areas of direct marketing and home shopping via the television and the Internet. Finally, we have looked at the wheel of retailing hypothesis in order to gauge the extent to which this explains the changes we have seen; it does not. What we have noted, however, is that the pace of retail change is increasing, a factor which the marketing manager will undoubtedly need to take account of in planning for the future.

In addition, we have seen that channel decisions and management are among the most important decisions a company faces. In fact, channel design and selection is a strategic consideration. Among the key elements of this strategic decision are the delineation and selection of the basic channel structure, the determination of required market exposure, systems and procedures for ensuring maximum cooperation and minimum conflict, and marketing and channel support efforts.

Channel design and operating decisions are company and situation-specific—in short, there is no one superior method for distributing products and services. Important considerations in identifying channel alternatives in a company would include: company and marketing objectives and resources, target markets and customers, products and competitive factors. The final choice of specific channel(s) needs to be assessed against control, adaptive, economic and coverage criteria.

Finally, we have seen that, increasingly, companies are assessing their distribution activities from a marketing logistics or total systems viewpoint. Not only does this approach offer potentially large cost savings in the often high-cost area of distribution, but in addition, it can help a company become more marketing-oriented in the design of its system of physical distribution, and hence increase its competitiveness.

CHAPTER REVIEW QUESTIONS

1. What reasons account for the development of channels of distribution?
2. Explain the importance of 'channel length' and 'channel relationships' in channel structure.
3. Outline some of the more significant changes in UK retailing over the past 10 years. To what extent are these changes indicative of a life cycle for retailing institutions?
4. a. Outline the major strategic elements of channel choice indicating the significance of each to channel design.
   b. Outline and discuss the criteria you would use in selecting a particular channel structure.
5. What are the key concepts in marketing logistics, and what do these mean in terms of designing the total distribution system in a company?

References

1. L. P. Bucklin, *A Theory of Distribution Channel Structure*, Institute of Business and Economic Research, University of California, Berkeley, 1966, p. 5.
2. E. D. McGarry, 'Some functions of marketing reconsidered', in *Theory in Marketing*, R. Cox and W. Alderson (eds), R. D. Irwin, Homewood, IL, 1950.
3. W. Alderson, *Marketing Behaviour and Executive Action: A Functionalist Approach to Marketing Theory*, R. D. Irwin, Homewood, IL, 1957.
4. J. A. Howard, *Marketing Management: Operating, Strategic, and Administrative*, 3rd edn, R. D. Irwin, Homewood, IL, 1973, pp. 4–5.
5. D. J. Bowersox, *et al.*, *Management in Marketing Channels*, Macmillan, London, 1968, p. 69.
6. L. P. Bucklin (ed.), *Vertical Marketing Systems*, Scott, Foresman, Glenview, IL, 1970.
7. P. Kotler, *Marketing Management, Analysis, Planning, Implementation and Control*, 8th edn, Prentice-Hall, Englewood Cliffs, NJ, 1994, pp. 543–6.
8. S. Dibb, L. Simkin, W. M. Pride and O. C. Ferrell, *Marketing: Concepts and Strategies*, 3rd edn, Houghton-Mifflin, Boston, MA, 1997, p. 376.
9. R. Pitfield, *Business Organization*, Macdonald and Evans, London, 1982.
10. N. Sanghari and A. Treadgold, *Developments in European Retailing*. Dower House Publications, Taunton, 1990.
11. British Franchising Association and National Westminster Bank, 'Franchising in the United Kingdom', London, November 1991.
12. M. P. McNair and E. G. May, 'The evolution of retail institutions in the United States', Report 76–100, Marketing Science Institute, Cambridge, MA, April 1976.
13. W. J. Stanton, *Fundamentals of Marketing*, 5th edn, McGraw-Hill, London, 1978, pp. 364–5.
14. L. W. Stern and A. I. El-Ansary, *Marketing Channels*, 2nd edn, Prentice-Hall, Englewood Cliffs, NJ, 1982, Chapter 7.
15. I. F. Wilkinson, 'Power and influence structures in distribution channels', *European Journal of Marketing*, **7** (2), 1973.
16. B. Mallen, 'Conflict and co-operation in marketing channels', in *Reflections on Progress in Marketing*, L. G. Smith (ed.), American Marketing Association, Chicago, IL, 1965, pp. 74–7.
17. Kotler, op. cit., pp. 516–18.
18. J. N. Arbury, *A New Approach to Physical Distribution*, Dryden Press, Hinsdale, IL, 1967.
19. P. Drucker, 'The economy's dark continent', *Fortune*, April 1962, p. 103.
20. E. H. Ballou, *Basic Business Logistics*, 2nd edn, Prentice-Hall, Englewood Cliffs, NJ, 1987.
21. M. Christopher, *Total Distribution: A Framework for Analysis, Costing and Control*, Gower Press, London, 1971.
22. G. Lancaster and L. Massingham, *Marketing Management*, 3rd edn, McGraw-Hill, London, 2001, Chapter 11.

Andrea's Rissoles

Andrea had started experimenting in her kitchen much to the surprise of her husband who knew that she wasn't really interested in cooking. One evening three years ago, however, Andrea had been trying out a new recipe for rissoles. Almost by chance she came up with a recipe which involved a particular and novel combination of herbs and spices in her rissoles which essentially was based on what was available in her spice cupboard at the time. Notwithstanding this, the resulting rissoles were delicious.

For some time she cooked the said rissoles mainly for family and friends, but everyone who tried them loved them and often asked her for the recipe, which partly through embarrassment (knowing what the ingredients were) she always refused to give. Some two years after inventing the recipe one of her friends mentioned how delicious the rissoles were to a local takeaway outlet. Knowing Andrea, the proprietor of the outlet approached her for a sample. As a result, the owner of the takeaway asked Andrea for her recipe which again Andrea refused to divulge. He therefore came to an agreement whereby Andrea would undertake to supply the local takeaway with her rissoles.

Andrea then began to supply other outlets and then proceeded to supply small independent local shopkeepers with packaged rissoles for people to cook at home.

From these humble beginnings, Andrea now produces her rissoles in a small factory initially funded by the local enterprise council. She has a staff of six full-time workers on production, but all sales and marketing are handled by herself.

She now wants to expand the business considerably and plans to introduce new products including a range of chutneys, a recipe for which has been passed down through the family for years. She feels, however, that one of the major obstacles to continued expansion is securing adequate distribution.

She is ambitious and is therefore thinking ultimately of national distribution for her pre-packaged rissole products through the multiple supermarkets. She recognizes, however, that she has very little marketing muscle in this respect and that it will be difficult to gain listings. She is prepared to consider any channel of distribution which will enable her to keep control over the quality of her products and the brand while enabling her to achieve the growth that she would like for her company.

She is also aware that if she can expand the business she will need to pay much more attention to the logistics aspects of distribution, especially as this is a perishable product to be sold, hopefully, on a national scale.

Questions

1. What are the major channel alternatives and decisions that Andrea would be faced with in seeking to expand her business?

2. What aspects of logistics will she need to pay attention to if her business expands as planned?

Chapter Nine

MARKETING COMMUNICATIONS

LEARNING OBJECTIVES *This chapter will help you to:*

- understand the nature and role of marketing communications in the marketing mix;

- appreciate how communication works and the key elements of the communications process;

- distinguish between the key elements of the promotional mix including their characteristics and uses;

- identify the steps in planning, implementing and evaluating marketing communications programmes;

- appreciate how technology is affecting contemporary marketing communications.

INTRODUCTION

Marketing communications is one of the most rapidly changing elements within the marketing mix, although many companies continue to ignore its importance. Despite the fact that above-the-line (direct) advertising currently accounts for expenditure running into billions of pounds per annum in the UK, with below-the-line (indirect promotional) expenditure at equally high levels, the application of management in these areas is subject to much criticism.

The purpose of this chapter and Chapter 10 is to examine the scope of the conventional marketing communications mix in some detail—advertising, sales promotion, public relations and personal selling—and to discuss the nature, role and principles of these communication tools. In addition to these four conventional and accepted tools of the communications mix, though, we shall also return to the area of direct marketing introduced in Chapter 8, or more specifically to the area of direct mail. Direct mail is, of course, a promotional tool and used to be considered primarily as a sub-element of sales promotion. Today though direct mail is so widely used by marketers that it is now considered by many to constitute the fifth element of the marketing communications mix. The basic purpose of such tools is to communicate with consumers in order to persuade them to buy the company's products. As we shall see, this is by no means the only objective of this type of communication method open to marketing practitioners. To view it as being only sales-oriented is to underestimate the complexity of modern marketing communications.

COMMUNICATIONS EXPLAINED

H. Lasswell[1] puts forward the proposition that five basic questions form the basis of analysis in communications:

1. Who is the communicator? In this, *the control analysis*, the main task is to discover the purpose of the sender so that his or her message can be correctly interpreted.

2. What is the content of the message? *Content analysis* very often revolves around the question of informative and persuasive messages—while D. Ogilvy[2] claims that informative advertising is the most profitable, quoting the example of how effective it would be at emptying a building simply to tell people that there was a fire; to try to *persuade* them to leave could lead to arguments and delays.

3. Who is the audience for which the message is intended? *Audience analysis* is concerned with the identifying of prospects, the target audiences and the segmentation of markets.

4. What information media or means of transmitting the message are employed? *Media analysis* can be viewed as discovering where audiences are located and selecting the media and media vehicles that will reach them most effectively.

5. What behaviour follows the receipt of the message? *Effect analysis* is concerned with the relationship between message content and the subsequent behaviour of the audience.

These five basic analyses will be a recurring theme in this chapter and in Chapter 10.

A communication process can thus be summarized as who says what, in what channel, to whom, and with what effect. The four basic components of the process are:

1. The communicator (the encoder)
2. The message (the symbols)
3. The channel (method of communication)
4. The audience (the decoder)

Figure 9.1 is a very simplistic analysis, and the process of marketing communications calls for countless problems to be considered. For the communications to be effective, these problems must be researched and then overcome.

One of the major problem areas is *channel noise*. This is a term used to describe anything that interferes with the message during its time in the selected channel. We may view it as a variety of distractions between the communicator and his or her audience. With reference to marketing communications, the advertisement might be subjected to poor reproduction in the mass media in some way, or the salesperson might have to put up with a variety of interruptions while in the middle of his or her presentation. Not all of these can be planned for in advance, but some ways in which channel noise might be overcome are:

- *The use of attention-getting devices*—highlighting the need for good, effective creative ideas, and using methods of communication that secure the attention of the audience. This applies in all areas of marketing communications, whether it is the memorable jingle used in the advertising campaign or the tactics employed in below-the-line and personal selling efforts.

- *Repetition of the key part of the message*—in an effort to try to ensure that this is received and remembered by the audience, even if other parts of the message are lost.

Another interference which presents problems for the communicator is that of *semantic noise*; even though the message is received exactly as it was transmitted by the encoder, for some reason it is misunderstood. Each person in the decoder group aimed at by the marketing communicator will have his or her own frame of reference. Any words, for example, that are unknown to the audience, or that mean different things to the audience from what the communicator intended, may very well result in misinterpretation. A need for the perceptions of the encoder and decoder to be common is thus highlighted, since any disparity between what the communicator perceives and what the audience perceives can result in severe problems, and ineffective communications. Advertisers are often criticized for being out of touch with their audiences' tastes and attitudes, while salespeople may not possess the technical know-how and expertise to be able to relate to prospects.

Frye[3] argues that this problem, while being a key one for marketing management to contend with, may be less harmful in the early stages of the product life cycle, when the target audience (the innovators) may tend to be on a similar social and economic scale as the marketing communicator. This may be true in some instances, but it is equally untrue in many others. For example, in industrial markets there may be little difference between the various decision-making units in potential buying companies; or at least the differences may exist among groups of buyers at all stages.

The need for commonality of perceptions between communicator and audience is illustrated by Frye as a Venn diagram (see Fig. 9.2).

The marketing communications management team must therefore identify the possible problem areas. Where perceptions are not shared, they must try to reduce the problem areas by careful definition of terms used and by adjustment of the vocabulary used.

It must also be realized that the context in which words appear may affect interpretation, and also that material that is deemed to be too complex or too simplistic by the audience may then be dismissed. Audiences might then turn to competitors' communications in their search for more rewarding material.

A further problem area that the marketing communicator may face is a result of the *beliefs* and *attitudes* held by the various people in his audience. As already stated,

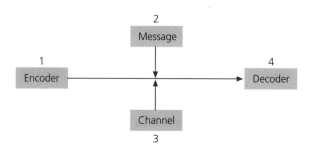

FIGURE 9.1

Components of communication

interpretation of the message may depend upon the terms of the frame of reference. Each person has certain beliefs and attitudes, which may be individual (ego-related) or may stem from reference groups that affect him or her (family, friends, etc.). A message that challenges these may lead the audience to distort, misinterpret or reject the communication. Many authors believe that it is easier to try to redirect attitudes in some way, rather than meet them in a head-on clash.

Related to this is the concept of *cognitive dissonance*, put forward by Festinger.[4] When a person takes an action which is inconsistent with what he or she believes, then the cognitive elements are in conflict. This provides the marketing communicator with a most useful analysis framework, in both the pre- and post-purchase situations. The underlying principle is that new information must be in harmony with existing knowledge if dissonance is to be avoided. This also has implications for personal selling, which is discussed in Chapter 10. Suffice it to say here that marketing communicators must realize that audiences will attempt to reduce dissonance by exposing themselves to further messages in order to reduce the conflict. They will turn again to the advertisements, the sales literature and the salespeople in their attempts to seek reassurance.

The final problem area facing the marketing communicator is that of *feedback*. These are the reactions that take place along the communication process, but which are transmitted backwards—from audience to communicator. This flow might, of course, not be a direct one, but rather could pass through a number of intermediary stages before it is received by the communicator. The obtaining of feedback is vital to communications management, if campaigns are to be correctly evaluated and controlled and the question, 'Why were we successful or otherwise?' answered. Within the area of marketing communications, feedback is one of the principal differences between the various activities. For example, in personal selling it can be instantaneous, whereas in advertising it is often slow, difficult and expensive to obtain.

COMMUNICATIONS STRATEGIES

All of these problems mean that the tasks facing marketing communications management are not as simple as the process initially outlined in Fig. 9.1. There are many

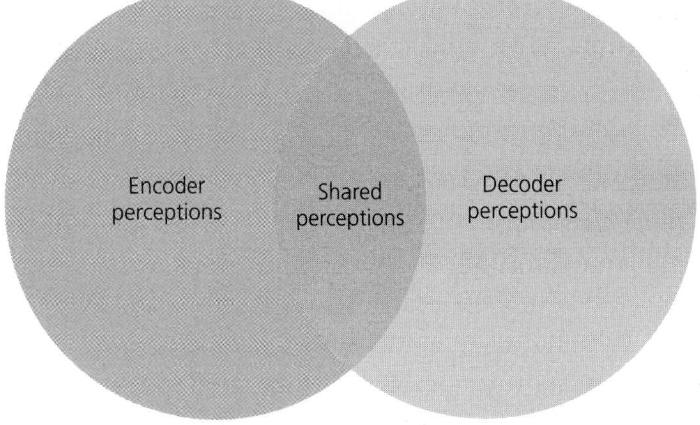

FIGURE 9.2

Encoder/decoder perceptions

Encoder perceptions

Shared perceptions

Decoder perceptions

potential problems that may have to be surmounted, but at least the recognition of these problems provides a useful starting-point in the formulation of communication strategies. Marketers must recognize that even the most effective communication strategy is unlikely to lead to effective communication with all the consumers at which it is aimed.

Once the scope and limitations of various communication strategies have been recognized, a strategy adapted to particular needs may be formulated.

Questions that should now be asked are as follows:

1. To which consumer group should the communications be directed?
2. What information will these consumer groups seek from our communications when deciding whether or not to buy?
3. What objectives should be set in order to communicate effectively with these groups?
4. How much will it cost to achieve these objectives? What size should the total budget be?
5. How should this total budget be apportioned among the various marketing communications activities available?
6. How much responsibility is to be assumed by the manufacturers and by the channel intermediaries?
7. How might the effectiveness of the campaign be evaluated and controlled?

CAMPAIGN PLANNING

This campaign planning process highlights the major decision areas faced by management. In order to provide insights into these, the rest of this chapter and Chapter 10 are devoted to close examination of many of the more important aspects of promotional planning. A marketing communications campaign planning process is put forward in Fig. 9.3.

By planning and implementing their communications campaigns in this structured way, it is suggested that a more professional approach can be adopted by communications management teams. Many authors have criticized the lack of management application in the area of marketing communications. Wills[5] asserts that it is not surprising that not many companies can truthfully answer the question of how good

FIGURE 9.3   *A marketing communications campaign planning framework*

or bad their marketing communication efforts are. Wills puts forward the following reasons for this being the case:

- The inertia of existing organizational structures.
- The lack of realization about the potential benefits of adopting a more professional approach to marketing communications.

There appears to be far more attention paid to other areas of the marketing mix, most notably product and pricing policies, while marketing communications tend to be ignored.

The organizational solution proposed is, as Wills points out, relatively simple. In Fig. 9.4, we see the need to raise marketing communications in the hierarchy of management thinking. Referring back to Fig. 9.3, we find that the prime need in the planning and implementation of marketing communication campaigns is for management to be objective-oriented.

Product strategy, as has been pointed out in Chapter 6, is seen as providing the initial sense of direction for the campaign. It acts as the key between the consumer, the product and market analysis, which form the basis of strategy formulation and the determination of the marketing communication programmes. The purpose of product strategy is to provide a single, unified direction for *all* of an organization's marketing programmes—including marketing communications. In this way, all the efforts are coordinated, and the product is moved towards the same goal by all of the organization's marketing efforts.

Product strategy receives inputs, and in turn provides guidance not just for marketing efforts. All of the organization's functional areas—production, financial, legal, personnel, etc.—are likewise coordinated by means of the overall product strategy, so that all of these efforts are directed towards a single, unified goal. There should only be one direction for a product, and the marketing communication activities should be coordinated with all of the other efforts in this way.

The strategy decision is long term, first decided upon before the product is even produced or marketed; it will be adjusted only when major events happen—such as changes in the product itself or a change in consumer tastes.

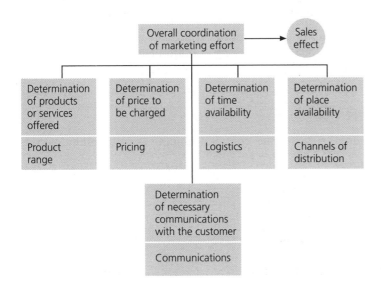

FIGURE 9.4

Marketing communications coordination

Marketing communications objectives have now to be determined. These are, of course, more specific and short term, and must be in line with the overall product strategy. The determination of these objectives is a key area in the planning of campaigns, and forms the cornerstone of the analysis. If good objectives are developed and clearly stated at the beginning of the process, then all the planners involved in the marketing communications process can attack their particular problem areas with good purpose and with their tasks having been eased. Copy specialists can prepare messages which are directed at achieving a specific purpose; personal selling, advertising and below-the-line promotional activities can all be coordinated; and the experts in media planning can use their expertise more effectively.

As Majaro[6] points out, the setting of clear, precise and measurable objectives can help in the following ways:

1. To integrate the marketing communications campaign with other marketing activities.
2. To improve the liaison with external agencies.
3. To determine communications budgets and appropriations.
4. To secure appraisal of the plans by top management.
5. To measure the results of communications efforts.

Too often, communications objectives are set which are too general, are confused with overall marketing objectives, or are non-existent. In a major survey of campaigns planned and implemented by advertising agencies in the USA, Britt[7] examined two major aspects of each campaign:

1. Were specific objectives set well enough for subsequent measurement to be made?
2. Did the agency attempt to measure effectiveness by clearly stating how the campaign fulfilled any previously stated objectives?

Only two of the campaigns met Britt's criteria for adequate objective setting, and most failed to specify what criteria were to be used for evaluation.

Under the circumstances discovered by Majaro and Britt, everyone concerned with the campaign building process lacks direction, with the inevitable reduction in the utilization of skills. Unless valid objectives are set, then the tendency will be for each manager in sales, advertising, sales promotions and public relations to set his or her own targets. These might be good objectives viewed individually, but because they are not coordinated they must be sub-optimal. Optimization can only be sought when there is a common goal, with all of the marketing communications activities being coordinated in the pursuit of this.

Communications objectives

It may prove useful to list here some of the common objectives of communications campaigns:

1. Consumer communications
   a. To inform about a new product.
   b. To correct misconceptions about a product.
   c. To increase frequency of use.
   d. To remind.
   e. To present special offers.
   f. To educate consumers in how to use a product.

g. To build an image for the product/company.
h. To build up consumer loyalty.

2. Trade communications

a. To provide information.
b. To inform about promotional programmes.
c. To present special trade offers.
d. To avoid stockpiling.
e. To educate the trade on product usage.
f. To build patronage motives.

These are not, however, all-inclusive, and when used as the basis of a specific campaign they must be expressed in precise, measurable terms. The fact, however, that consumers and trade will receive not only commercial information via the organization's communication campaigns, but also information from non-commercial sources, presents major problems to the communications manager. Editorial comments from the various media, and word of mouth, are both examples of communications that are not under the control of the marketer, and may contradict the messages he or she is conveying. Marketers must, therefore, recognize that even the most effective communications strategy is unlikely to lead to effective communications with all of the prospects all of the time. The recognition of these limitations puts marketers in a position to formulate a strategy adapted to their own needs. The identification of problems to be surmounted is the first vital step in the formulation of any strategy.

Having specified the objectives of the campaign, the next step facing the marketer is the selection of tools to disseminate the necessary information to the target audience. The nature of the programme objectives will obviously play a large part in establishing some guidelines for the overall communications budget. For example, the task of creating awareness for a product may require a smaller budget than, say, the task of instilling consumer loyalty for the product. Here communications management must try to achieve the following:

1. Identify and satisfy the target audience's interests in information.

2. Optimize the expenditure, so that the marginal cost of disseminating the information does not exceed the marginal revenue that is brought about.

3. Identify the extent to which the informational needs of the prospects can be resolved by promotional elements of the marketing mix, or by non-promotional elements.

There are many considerations to be taken into account:

● Overall marketing objectives and strategy.

● The level of competitive promotional spending in the target markets. Here, smaller producers tend to take their cue from larger manufacturers and adjust their budgets in line with the market leader.

● The level of sales generated by promotional activities.

● The objectives sought (called the 'objective and task' method). This calls for an ascertainment of advertising expenditure needed to reach marketing objectives that have been laid down in the marketing plan.

● The affordability of the proposals. Here the philosophy is that, after other cost centres have received their budgets, what is left over goes to advertising.

Each of these may be used as the basis for determining the budget. On an individual level, they may provide only limited insights. For example, if competitive spending is the only variable that is taken into account, then one major problem may be that the budget fails to consider the fact that the problems/opportunities faced by the company may be very different from those of its competitors.

Equally, if sales is the sole determinant of the budget total (whether this is a last year's, per unit or an adjusted sales figure), then a major criticism of this approach is that it regards the sales as the stimulus with communications as the response. It is obvious that this is wrong, and that the stimulus should be communications—leading to the response of sales. Taken further, the notion of sales determining the promotional budget implies that falling sales means a decreased budget and, conversely, increasing sales generates a larger budget. Logic must dictate that the opposite should be the case!

The whole area of budget determination within the field of marketing communication is full of controversy and criticism. A paper presented by Roberts[8] warns management of what he calls planning blight, and points out that advertising budgets are some of the last budgets to be set and the first to be slashed! The danger is one of the spiral decay.

An asset-based method of budget allocation is one of the most logical ones. It assumes that advertising is a tangible item that extends beyond the budget period, looks at it as a long-term investment and attempts to ascertain the return on such expenditures. The 'incremental method' is its corollary, and this assumes that the least unit of money spent on advertising should bring in an equal amount of revenue.

Much support from many academic sources comes for the 'task approach'. This involves the marketer, once an objective has been specified, in costing out the various promotional tasks that are necessary to achieve this objective. Once again, we see the need for valid objective-setting within the area of marketing communications. The best guideline to management must be to realize the importance of all these factors—sales, competitors, objectives and affordability, etc.—and to take account of them all when determining the budget. Adequate returns on investment will enable the marketer to command the resources necessary to continue satisfying consumers' interests.

Communications practice

The marketer, when deciding which promotional tools to use, is faced with a wide range of alternatives. Sometimes it is mistakenly assumed that advertising and personal selling are the only marketing tools through which to disseminate information. This view is far too narrow, since, through publicity and public relations activities, short- and long-term promotions and by means such as packaging, and increasingly, direct mail, information can be conveyed most effectively by the marketer.

Determining which combination of these tools to use in particular situations is a very complex operation involving many considerations. One of the most important of these is determining how many and which decisions are made at the possible locations. For example, is the decision made chiefly in the home, at the office or in the store? When decision-making occurs mainly in the store, for example, the emphasis should be placed on point-of-sale and personal selling activities.

The nature of the product is also important in this respect. Although there are many dangers in putting forward rigid guidelines here, it would appear that advertising may be most effective when the information needs are not overly complex, as may be the case with convenience goods. Personal selling, on the other hand, with its obvious advantages of face-to-face exchanges, may be most suitable in disseminating information about more technical, specialist goods where the individual needs of particular customers have to be taken into account. The kinds of information to be disseminated must have a bearing on the selection of the marketing communication tools. It is the function of the creative programme to specify what message is to be communicated to the audience. The creative programme provides direction for the creative people, who will implement the campaign when the plan is completed and approved.

The basic direction for creative ideas is provided by the product strategy, since the market position that is to be aimed for must be the starting-point. The more specific communications objectives specify the steps to be taken to solve immediate problems facing the product, and the consumer, product and market analyses will have provided information upon which the creative programme should be based. In particular, the nature of the target audience and the problems that consumers are trying to solve will form the basis of the creative programme.

The three essential steps in building this programme for a product are:

1. The determination of the content of the message, aiming for consistency of information from various sources.

2. The presentation of the message; identifying a central idea and the way in which it is to be expressed and creating the advertisements and sales approaches.

3. Determining how the communications effort will be produced—for example, estimates of the production costs and production time schedules of advertisements, point-of-sale material and sales literature.

Communications management delegates much of the work involved in this process, since it involves very specialized skills. In most instances there is clearly a need to employ the services of the creative specialists to be found in the agencies. Responsibilities remain for providing information and directions to the creative team and for evaluating the output in terms of specific, predetermined criteria.

Advertising agencies are examined in more detail later in the chapter, together with other detailed examinations of various aspects of advertising. Personal selling is considered in Chapter 10. The next sections are devoted to the remaining aspects of the communications campaign plan—below-the-line promotions and public relations—in order to assess their applications in campaign planning and implementation.

Below-the-line promotions

Below-the-line promotions have been defined by Christopher[9] as 'all non-media promotion'. Engel *et al.*[10] define it as 'the supplementary selling activity which coordinates personal selling and advertising into an effective persuasive force'. There are, however, many problems of definition, since the 'line' is an artificial concept, used originally by advertising agencies to distinguish between promotional expenditures that were commissionable and those that were not. 'The implication of the line is that there is some radical difference between the purpose and effect of expenditures above and below the line.'[11] To some extent, any definition of below the line assumed a false dichotomy, since many promotions are dependent on media advertising—for example when reduced offers are backed by national press advertising.

Within the context of communications planning, the marketer should be more concerned with adopting a total approach, whereby above the line and below the line are integrated to complement and support each other in the total communications process. A useful distinction has been drawn between those promotions that aim to move products from the marketing channel intermediary, and those aimed at moving the product from the manufacturers into the channels of distribution. These have been referred to as 'pull' and 'push' promotional techniques, which have already been detailed in Chapter 8.

The methods employed in promotional efforts must depend upon the objectives sought, the nature of the product, the type of distribution channel employed and the target audience.

The range of 'pull' (consumer incentives) includes the following:

- Price reductions—by the manufacturer, or by the retailer in the form of store price cuts
- Coupons—a form of price reduction
- Self-liquidators—where profits made on the merchandise offered (in return for money and 'box tops') cover the cost of the promotional effort
- Premiums given free in/on/off the pack
- Personality promotions
- Consumer competitions
- Free samples—offered either by post or through in-store demonstrations
- Merchandising and point-of-sale displays, and advertising in the stores
- Packaging
- Sponsorship
- Purchase privilege plans (buy one, get one free)
- Container premiums—where the container can be used after the contents have been consumed
- Trade-in facilities
- Credit facilities
- Training schemes
- Guarantees
- Direct mail 'shots'
- Saving schemes
- Banded (i.e. banded together) and twin packs

Over the past 20 years there has been tremendous growth in expenditure on these consumer incentives, to such an extent that it is estimated that the level of expenditure in the UK today exceeds that of above the line. Indeed, as already mentioned, some of these such as direct mail have become so important as areas of spend within the promotional mix that they have become important promotional tools in their own right, as opposed to simply being just part of a general assortment of below-the-line-promotions. Several factors have contributed to this growth in the use of sales promotion in consumer markets. The main ones are as follows.

Internal factors

1. Promotion is now more accepted by senior management as an effective sales tool.
2. More brand/marketing managers are qualified and have experience of using sales promotions.
3. The store managers are under increasing pressure to increase (or at least maintain) their sales in what has been a difficult economic and marketing environment.

External factors

1. The number of brands has increased.
2. Competitors have become more promotion-minded.

3. Inflation and recession have made consumers more 'deal'-oriented.

4. The changing trade structure in many markets has meant greater competition between retailers.

5. The threat from retailers' own brands has increased.

The range of 'push' (trade and salesforce incentives) includes the following:

- Cash discounts
- Increased margins
- Competitions—trade and salesforce
- Dealer premiums
- Salesforce cash incentives
- Exhibitions
- Demonstrations
- Direct mail 'shots'
- Training schemes
- Credit facilities

The marketer may be faced with a number of problems, which offer him the opportunity to utilize some of these 'push' and 'pull' techniques. Spillard[12] states that the main advantages of these below-the-line techniques stem from their being:

- Very flexible and adaptable
- Capable of specific action
- Wide-ranging in applicability
- Economical and cost-saving
- Swift in action

The marketing situations in which sales promotion may make a valuable contribution can range from payment problems to the need for advertising to have more 'punch', from consumer purchase to dealers not stocking the product, from the need to motivate the salesforce to blockages in the distribution channel, from the need for expert advice to the need for additional market information.

The decision whether or not to use sales promotion, and which particular techniques, is summed up by Ann Morgan,[13] who suggests the following:

1. Determine, in order of priority, the problems faced by the product/brand.

2. Determine the money available to solve these problems.

3. List and cost all the possible alternative solutions to the problems, e.g. theme advertising, pricing or product strategy, consumer promotions, etc.

4. Estimate the effectiveness of each solution.

5. If the answers to 3 and 4 suggest that a promotion is the most efficient answer to the problem, and if there is enough money available in 2, then a promotion is indicated. The marketer then needs to plan, implement and control the promotional campaign.

Managing sales promotion   For effective sales promotion, the marketer must establish the objectives, select the appropriate promotional tool, develop and implement the programme, and evaluate the results.

Establishing the sales promotion objective   As you would expect, the starting-point in planning sales promotion is the identification of the target audience and the specific objectives that the sales promotion is intended to achieve. Sales promotion can be aimed at one or more of the following:

- Consumers
- The 'trade' (retailers, wholesalers, distributors, etc.)
- The salesforce

Basically, sales promotion objectives derive from the basic marketing communication objectives for the brand. The specific objectives will vary depending on the type of market and the position of the product. For consumers, objectives might include:

- Announce a new product
- Encourage product trial
- Encourage greater use
- Stimulate purchase of larger sizes
- Attract non-users
- Encourage brand-switching

For retailers:

- Encourage stocking
- Increase inventory levels
- Encourage off-peak buying
- Promote related products
- Offset competitive marketing
- Open up new outlets
- Build retailer loyalty

For the salesforce, the aim would be essentially to support retailer objectives, e.g.:

- Build display
- Increase order size
- Increase shelf space utilization

Obviously, it is important to set realistic objectives for any sales promotion; and, although objectives should be simple and clear, it is possible to include both consumer trade and salesforce objectives; e.g.:

> To increase sales by *X* per cent during a sweepstake promotion period by obtaining special promotion related off-shelf displays of the brand in *Y* per cent of large retail stores and *Z* per cent in medium retail stores.

This type of objective has the advantage of stating how the goal is to be achieved and of identifying the outside support that will be needed.

Choosing the promotional tools   Having established what the sales promotion is intended to achieve and with whom, the next step is to select the most appropriate and cost-effective sales promotion tools. Again, with such a variety of tools available, this is not easy. Each of the tools tends to have its relative advantages and disadvantages, and there is little consistent empirical evidence to suggest which tools work best in which situation and why. In most circumstances, it is advisable to make use of a specialist sales promotion agency when devising sales promotion programmes.

As an indication of the types of sales promotion tools available for each target audience, we now briefly outline some of the major tools used for consumers, for trade and for the salesforce.

Bargain packages   There are two main forms of this promotional technique. One is where the product is advertised at a particular price but the pack is marked '5p off', which means that the purchase price will be reduced by that amount, but only on the products so marked, which is another way of saying 'while stocks last'. Many people take advantage of this type of offer, but they include all the regular purchasers of the product, many of whom just stock up with the product at the bargain price but then do not purchase the product again until their own stocks have been run down, by which time there might be another 'offer' on the same product. Packs marked for such a discount are often known as 'flash' packs.

The second form of this technique is where the offer is advertised as 'two for the price of one', or where, attached to the large size—of toothpaste, for example—is a smaller-sized pack. This method does not help the retailer so much as the manufacturer, who is able to increase the turnover of the large packs, sales of which may have been sluggish, and at the same time maintain his turnover of the smaller pack. At the same time, it means that less of the competitors' toothpaste will be purchased by the same customer during the following few weeks. This technique, whereby one pack is attached to another (often larger) pack, is known as the 'limpet' method. The title is self-explanatory.

Give-aways   This is aimed at the younger end of the various market segments, and has been used extensively by the breakfast cereal companies. Into every packet of cereal is put a small toy or gift in an attempt to use the influencing power of children in this market.

Trade promotions   Some of the more frequently used trade promotions include *discounts/cash allowances*, whereby a percentage discount or cash allowance is given for each case purchased.

Consumer sales promotions   The following paragraphs cite some examples of techniques used in the promotion of consumer products.

Coupons   The consumer must be in possession of a coupon or voucher of a particular value, which can then be 'redeemed' at the local store in exchange for the product or products named on the voucher at the usual price less the value of the voucher. There is usually a deadline, and the offer often applies to a particular size in the range of products, which usually means that the consumer, in order to take advantage of the offer, must purchase the product within a shorter space of time than he or she would normally have done. The effect of this is to increase the rate of stock-turn for both the retailer and the manufacturer.

One problem is, of course, that the majority of redemptions are made by people who would have bought the product anyway, and so to that extent the value of the scheme is doubtful. But where the voucher constitutes an introductory offer on a relatively new product, the 'bargain' element often persuades consumers to switch brand loyalties, perhaps (it is hoped) more than temporarily.

Self-liquidating offers   An example of this would be where a manufacturer of tinned food purchases a quantity of kitchen knives from a supplier at a price of £3 per knife. The food manufacturer then 'offers' to sell the knives to the consuming public at the cost price of £3 or thereabouts, plus five labels from a particular size of the tinned food.

Again, the advantage to the retailer and the manufacturer is that the rate of stock-turn is increased, and the consumer also benefits by being able to purchase the knives at trade price. This type of operation is termed 'self-liquidating' because all the capital used by the manufacturer in purchasing the knives is returned by the consumer.

Sampling   Many manufacturers—again, particularly in the areas of fast-moving consumer goods—give away free samples of their products. The sample is very often of a smaller size than the normal pack size, and it is hoped that customers will try the product, like it, and purchase the product in future. Once again, this operation is usually reserved for new entrants to a market. It has the added advantage that, if consumers are given a tablet of soap, for example, they are less likely to buy their usual brand that week, or until they have used up the free gift.

Additional products with order   Extra products are sometimes given with each unit ordered; e.g. if a case of 12 is purchased, two extra products are given free.

Merchandising allowances   A merchandising allowance compensates the retailer for featuring the manufacturer's products.

Advertising allowance/cooperative advertising   An advertising allowance compensates the retailer for featuring the manufacturer's products in newspaper advertisements; alternatively, the supplier may organize collaborative advertising with the trade.

Exhibitions   Exhibitions are, in some trades, almost obligatory. A well-known example in the UK is the Ideal Home Exhibition, which is held annually. It features all possible goods that can be used in a home and exhibits 'model homes' which are fully furnished and can be visited and inspected.

The bulk of exhibitions are industrial, however, and they include examples such as the Motor Show, the Office Equipment Exhibition, the Hardware Trades Fair and a number of others appropriate to various industries. Many of the exhibitions are mounted solely for the trade and the public are not allowed admittance.

Sales force promotion   This is a growing area for the application of sales promotional techniques. Some of the more frequently used techniques are:

- Sales contests
- Bonus prizes
- Sales incentives and gifts

With such a wide variety of sales promotion tools to choose from, it is important that the most cost-effective ones are selected. The most appropriate tools in this respect will vary according to a number of factors, including type of product market, specific sales promotion objectives, target audience and the emphasis of the marketing strategy, e.g. 'push' versus 'pull' strategies. It is also important to recall that very often all three areas, i.e. consumers, trade and salesforce, will be targeted; such multifaceted campaigns must therefore be coordinated.

Developing the sales promotion programme   The marketer, in addition to selecting the promotion type, needs to consider some additional decisions:

- *The size of the incentive*   For example, how much should be offered—5p off or 20p off? A certain minimum incentive is necessary, but too high an incentive may be counter-productive.

- *Conditions for participation*   Is everyone invited to be involved? What do consumers need to do in return, e.g. collect a number of packet tops?

- *Distribution vehicle*   On-pack, in-pack, door-to-door, in-store (etc.)? The decisions here might be crucial.

- *Duration of promotion*   How long should it run? Too short may mean missing many consumers; too long loses 'immediacy/impact'.

- *Quantity of promotion*   How many packs, prizes (etc.) are there?

- *Timing and coordination*   Here, seasonality in market, other retailer activities, production (etc.) must be considered.

- *Budget*   Promotions should be properly thought out and costed in the light of their objectives (see against the background of the complete and coordinated marketing effort). It is easy to make mistakes.

- *Pre-testing*   Whenever possible, the promotion should be pre-tested so that objectives and budgets can be properly tuned.

- *Legality*   It is important to ensure that the proposed promotion is legal.

- *Responding to unforeseen events*   Examples would be the launch of competitors, or a major crisis in the marketplace. Here the marketer must respond quickly and tactically.

The importance of the right theme   It is now almost universally accepted that a brand is a complex assimilation of ideas, attitudes, values and beliefs on the part of its consumers. It is not just a physical, tangible and functional entity, but a reflection of aspirations and self-actualizations. It stands to reason, therefore, that promotions can and should encourage favourable attitudes to the brand. They must not demote the brand in consumers' estimations. This poses problems for a money-off deal, banded pack (etc.) which might be construed as devaluing the brand. Conversely, a 'value' or budget brand might be harmed by some up-market offer or appeal.

We know from research that the relationship between the functional, evaluative and psychological components of a brand are subtle.

Functional   = What does the product do?

Evaluative   = How well does it do it?

Psychological = Which of the consumers' basic motivational needs or roles does the brand
                 imagery deliver?

In sales promotional terms, it is very important not to disturb the psychological beliefs built up via brand advertising. Here are some examples:

Domestos   = 'Impregnable security'

Comfort   = 'Loving softness'

Fairy Liquid = 'Gentle relationships'

Persil   = 'Caring whiteness'

Sales promotional themes for these brands should therefore aim to reinforce the beliefs.

Implementation and evaluation   As each promotion needs to be planned at the outset as an integral part of the overall marketing communications plan, proper lead times should be established. Production, the salesforce, the advertising agency and the trade will all be actively involved in the successful implementation (with the one concern of trade security *vis-à-vis* competition).

A further major consideration is whether the promotion should be backed by advertising. There is evidence that sales promotions are most effective when used together with advertising.

In terms of evaluation, a checklist should be produced and the promotion evaluated under the following headings:

1. Salesforce

2. Trade

3. Consumer

4. Achievement of objectives

5. Budget

6. Handling

7. Supplier service

8. Outside influences

Before the full-scale sales promotion is launched, it is advisable to pre-test the promotional vehicles selected. This can be done relatively quickly by using, for example, focus groups, selected in-store tests, or full-scale test marketing. If the testing is successful—indicating that the sales promotion will achieve the required objectives—the full-scale campaign can then be implemented.

The final stage, of course, is evaluation and control. Often the formal evaluation of sales promotion campaigns is overlooked by marketers. The chief factor in assessing the success of a sales promotion campaign is usually the effect on sales. However, this should also be compared with both the costs of the campaign and alternative ways of spending these monies, e.g. on other elements of the promotional mix.

In measuring the sales effectiveness of sales promotion, it is important to monitor sales over a longer period than the duration of the campaign itself. The explanation for this is given by P. Spillard and is shown in Fig. 9.5. The area $A + B$ in the diagram represents the additional sales volume generated by the sales promotion. Area A represents extra sales during the time the promotion is in effect, and B is the carry-over effect. Area C, however, represents future lost sales as a result of such sales being brought forward to take advantage of the promotion. For example, customers may stock up on the product concerned, causing a lagged effect. In addition, Doyle and Saunders[14] have pointed to a possible 'lead' effect; this is where, in anticipation of the sales promotion, customers delay the purchases they would otherwise have made. Similarly, salespersons may hold back on selling effort if they expect a sales contest with prizes to be introduced in the future.

These complications do not detract from the need to evaluate and control sales promotion; indeed, they add to it.

Planned and managed effectively, there is little doubt that sales promotion is one of the most effective of the promotional tools.

Among the most effective, and therefore fastest growing promotional tools in recent years, however, has been the use of direct mail. Indeed, as already indicated, many now feel that this promotional tool is so important that it should be considered as the fifth promotional element of the promotional mix, alongside the other four conventional elements of advertising, sales promotion, public relations, and personal selling. We shall therefore now consider direct mail in more detail.

Direct mail

In Chapter 8 we discussed some of the changes taking place in channels of distribution. You will recall that we suggested that one of the growth areas of channels in recent years has been direct marketing, including home shopping. Direct mail, as we also saw, is a key part of direct marketing, and indeed accounts for much of the growth in this area. Besides being a key element of channel management though, it is also a promotional tool. Understandably this growth of direct marketing, and direct mail in particular, is because it is potentially so cost-effective in marketing. However, we have also indicated that direct mail is not without its problems. Like any area of marketing activity it is only cost-effective if it is planned, implemented and evaluated properly. We shall therefore examine the key steps in undertaking a direct mail campaign, but first of all let us remind ourselves about the nature, purpose and scope of direct mail.

The nature, purpose and scope of direct mail   Direct mail may involve sending out technical information, notice of special offers, general information about a company and its products; it can include free samples, questionnaires, promotional gifts, order forms, and so on; it may be sent to householders or organizational buyers; it may be directed at existing or prospective customers; it may be aimed at eliciting an immediate response, or simply at increasing awareness or interest; and finally, it is used by profit-making organizations, not-for-profit organizations, for example, charities, and even by political parties. In other words, the nature, purpose and scope of direct mail are all very wide-ranging. In essence, though, direct mail represents an impersonal promotional activity sent directly to prospective customers in their own homes or offices.

Planning direct mail   The following represent the key steps in conducting a direct mail campaign.

Identifying target recipients/compiling the mailing list   We know that by far the greatest proportion of direct mail is thrown away unopened. That which is opened is

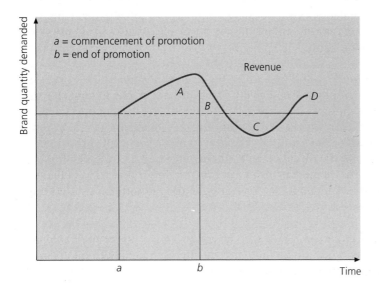

FIGURE 9.5

Sales promotion in its marketing strategy

Source: P. Spillard, *Sales Promotion—Its Place in Marketing Strategy*, Business Publications, Plano, TX, 1966, p. 112

often only partly read, and even less is acted upon. Indeed, much to the concern of the direct mail industry, direct mail is often referred to as 'junk mail' by many consumers, and worse still, even by many marketers. One of the reasons for this, of course, is that most direct mail is unsolicited by the recipient. One of the most important factors determining the effectiveness of direct mail is the identification on the part of the direct mail campaign planner of the target recipients of the mail campaign. Specifically, it is vital to identify those recipients who are most likely to be interested in the subject of the direct mail campaign and are therefore most likely to respond positively. Identifying and understanding the target audience is, of course, essential in planning any marketing communications. In the case of direct mail, this identification is normally done using a mailing list. A mailing list obviously contains the names and addresses of targets for the mail campaign, but, in turn, the mailing list itself must be based on customer details and information which allows only the most appropriate recipients for the mailshot to be identified. Because of this, in addition to straight-forward names and addresses, a mailing list is built using information and data about the potential recipients. This information and data may include details of, for example, life styles, incomes, qualifications, family details, past purchases, etc.

As mentioned in Chapter 5, the growth of ever more detailed and accurate databases about consumers has facilitated this process. Put another way, a major reason for the growth of direct mail is the growth in consumer information and databases. The mailing list therefore is the driving force of direct mail planning and clearly any data and information on which the mailing list is based must be relevant and up to date. Some companies produce their own mailing lists using their own internally and externally generated information. Increasingly though, commercial market research companies, advertising agencies, and specialist direct mail and mailing list agencies will supply appropriate mailing lists for a campaign. So, for example, CACI, the developer of the ACORN system also supply mailing lists, in this case linked to ACORN groups. Similarly, the Royal Mail is a major supplier of mailing lists and direct mail expertise.

As we have already seen, developments in information technology and computer power are allowing the marketer to develop extremely powerful databases on customers using a mixture of both internal and external information sources. A major use of data-bases in contemporary marketing is in direct mail campaigns. Databases allow much more accurate identification of target recipients for direct mail campaigns. Moreover, the content of the direct mailshot can be designed much more effectively using data-base information. Finally, databases enable much more effective co-ordination and evaluation of direct mail campaigns.

Setting objectives   As with all marketing activities it is important to determine the objectives of a direct mail campaign. Specifically, the marketer needs to consider what response from the target recipients the direct mail campaign is designed to elicit. So, for example, we need to determine if the mailing shot is designed to elicit, say, a telephone enquiry from a customer, or if, on the other hand, it is designed to 'break the ice' with a potential customer, the direct mail shot being followed up by a telephone call from the company, etc. At this stage it is also important to determine what constitutes an appropriate target for the campaign. So, for example, the marketer must determine what percentage rates of return, say, are being sought.

Producing the direct mail package   This step in conducting a direct mail campaign includes decisions such as what to include in the direct mail shot, for example, samples, the covering letter, any free gifts to be used, etc. In addition to what is inside the direct mail package, decisions must also be made about the outside of the package, that is, the envelope or parcel which the recipient will receive. Finally, decisions must also be made about, for example, what to say in the direct mail campaign. Needless to say, designing effective direct mail packages is a specialized and skilled task. Thanks to considerable research in this area, backed up by substantial experience over the years, we now know a considerable amount about how to produce an effective direct mail package. Again we would reiterate, though, that for most marketing managers, design of the direct mail package is best left to a specialist in this area. Above all, the direct mail package must be designed to ensure that at the very least the customer is interested enough to open the package in the first place. As mentioned earlier, this is obviously a crucial step determining the effectiveness or otherwise of the campaign. Again, both the inside and the outside of the direct mail package must be carefully designed to meet the interests and needs of a predefined target audience, hence the importance of an effective mailing list built upon information about target customers.

Evaluation, control and follow-up   All marketing communication spends should be evaluated and controlled. Direct mail is no exception. The marketer must consider if pre-determined objectives have been met or not, and if not, why not. Direct mail will often require a planned follow-up, say, for example, contacting mailed customers by telephone, etc. Obviously the campaign will only be as good as the quality of the follow-up initiated in this respect. As already mentioned, databases enable much more effective evaluation, control and follow-up of direct mail campaigns.

In conclusion then, direct mail is likely to continue to increase as a marketing tool in the future. Direct mail can never be perfect, and response rates in percentage terms are unlikely ever to be high. But it can, if well planned, be an extremely cost-effective way of communicating with customers and prospective customers.

Public relations

Defined by the Institute of Public Relations[15] as 'the deliberate, planned and sustained effort to establish and maintain mutual understanding between an organisation and its public', this is a key element in the discussion of communication tools. Public relations is concerned with the behaviour of the organization, its products, services and individuals which give rise to publicity. Unlike publicity, which is a result of information being made known, the results of public relations are controllable.

Control will result from public relations activities only if, as Jenkins[16] states, 'the communications with various publics are planned with the purpose of achieving specific objectives'. Here again, we see the need for providing our marketing communications activities with a clear meaning and purpose.

The 'publics' that should provide the direction for an organization's public relations activities are as follows:

1. *The community*   This is where the clear need is for the organization to act as if it were a member—just like a private citizen. Involvement in community activities and the development of a community relations programme are ways to achieve this goal.

2. *Employees*   This internal aspect of public relations is often a neglected area in many organizations, but there are obvious benefits in involving the workforce in organizational goals and establishing mutual understanding.

3. *Government*   Both local and national politicians are important sources of information for an organization, for example concerning proposed legislative changes affecting the business. The

lobbying of politicians is not without criticism, but it should be recognized as an acceptable procedure in industrial/government relations.

4. *The financial community*   Commercial and merchant banks, investors and share analysts, and city journalists provide a 'public' with whom an organization should communicate if it is to be seen as financially credible. The recent spate of mergers in the UK has highlighted the need to establish consistent relations over a period of time.

5. *Distributors*   All types of middlemen in a company's channel of distribution—wholesalers, retailers, brokers, agents and dealerships, etc.—need information about products and services if they are to have the knowledge and confidence necessary to become effective re-sellers.

6. *Consumers*   Often thought to be the only 'public' that concerns public relations. Here, as with distributors, there is a need for a company's public relations activities to be coordinated with other areas of marketing communications: advertising, sales promotion and personal selling. Educating consumers and creating and maintaining interest among target audiences can lead to favourable attitudes being generated towards a company's products and services.

7. *Opinion leaders*   These include trade associations and pressure groups. Public relations must attempt to understand the position of all important external groups—even if the group is opposed to them—if effective communications with them are to take place. It is far better for factual information to be the basis of discussion, not hearsay and exaggeration.

8. *Media*   Public relations has a role to play in the development of relationships with the press. By aiming to achieve maximum publication and broadcasting of information, a company may create understanding in many target markets. Press relations is therefore seen as part of a well-organized public relations campaign.

There is a variety of techniques available to secure effective communications with the above 'publics'. These are discussed in detail by Haywood,[17] who also discusses the specific tactics to be employed. Such techniques include:

- Visits to the workplace
- Open days
- Sponsorship
- Community projects
- In-house publications
- Annual reports
- Video films
- Training courses
- Press releases

Public relations has come a long way from its origins. No longer should it be viewed as merely 'free advertising', 'propaganda' or 'publicity'. It has a key role to play in the planning and implementation of marketing communications campaigns. A 'personality' must be developed by an organization with a clear need for true and full information.

ADVERTISING

A dictionary definition of 'advertise' would be 'to make known: to inform'. All advertisements can be seen to offer information, and can be regarded as communications about products, services and organizations. Viewed in this way, advertising's purpose can be seen as communication, but since all advertisements contain persuasive elements directed at the ultimate purpose of a sale, advertising must also provide motives. Consumers must be moved towards purchase; ideas must be communicated. These ideas might be generated by the creative people; at other times the ideas might be in the product, the service or the organization itself. A business definition of advertising would include this origination of ideas and the subsequent communication of such ideas with the purpose of motivating consumers along the path to purchase.

Advertising is concerned with the identification and presentation of desirable and believable benefits to the target audience in the most cost-effective manner. Most advertising expenditure is devoted to the promotion of brands by manufacturers. Currently, in the UK this area of advertising accounts for approximately 40 per cent of the total advertising 'spend'.

Advertising thrives on product differentiation, and an essential element here is the strategy of *branding*. Brand names are the vehicles through which manufacturers can establish an identity for their product; consumers relate to brands and form images of them. Whether the company aims for the same brand name for all its products or brands each of its products separately is a question of policy, and there are many promotional advantages available for each alternative. 'Family' brands might make the introduction of new products into the marketplace a comparatively easy task. Of course, there is always the danger that if the new product fails then damage might have been done to the whole of the product range; consumers might begin to perceive all of the company's products as being inferior. Individual branding of various products produced by a company, where different brand names are used for each, might offer more segmentation possibilities. Different varieties of a fast-moving consumer good might be individually branded and aimed at different segments of the market.

The defensive role of advertising should not be ignored, and it is often the case in situations of heavy branding that manufacturers advertise merely to preserve the *status quo*, knowing that their advertising efforts will be cancelled out by competitors.

It is not only with consumers that we find advantages of branding. Promotional effectiveness might also be increased in the case of trade advertising. Channel intermediaries might want to take on new brands from a manufacturer whose previous successes indicate that the new brand will also succeed. Indeed, in many cases where the middlemen find that they cannot refuse a new brand, the power within the distribution channel is often in the hands of manufacturers—strong, effective branding having put them in this powerful position.

In the case of private branding by retailers, not only does a manufacturer stand to increase output with possible resultant economies of scale, but also the promotional onus is on the retailer. These possible advantages must be carefully weighted against any possible disadvantages that may accrue from distributional power having been sacrificed.

Imagery is concerned with personality. Brand image is what consumers will see and feel when the brand name is called to their attention by means of advertising. The task of the advertiser is to ensure that consumer reactions are favourable when the brand name is mentioned. Advertising is seen as being an important determinant of brand image, along with the physical characteristics of the brand, the price charged, the satisfaction it provides and the retailers who stock it.

Consumer knowledge about a brand is often quite high, particularly when the decision-making process has involved a lot of fact-finding and comparisons between alternatives—often the case when purchasing a speciality good. But such consumers do not always know so much about the company itself.

Corporate image

To establish, maintain and improve a corporate image, institutional advertising can be utilized. Corporate advertising, as practised today, is a relatively new phenomenon, but is very often misunderstood. Critics accuse it of being:

- Self-indulgent
- A waste of money
- Too general, since it has no specific targets

Companies should, however, regard it as being a valuable public relations tool which may be directed at consumers, middlemen, financiers, employees, pressure groups, etc., in order to build up goodwill and confidence in the firm, create identity and publicize the firm's strengths. It is a long-term activity, requiring careful planning in order that the company is not faced with sudden crises which threaten its perceived standing. Not all events can be catered for, but corporate advertising—although it does involve the costs of buying the media time and space—is more controllable than public relations. The timing and content of the messages are no longer subject to the whims of editors, sub-editors and journalists.

Generic advertising

Advertising may be used to stimulate primary demand for a type of product or service, for example, the promotion of wool by the International Wool Secretariat and the promotion of milk deliveries by the Milk Marketing Board. The aims of generic advertising are to increase primary demand by promoting new uses, securing new users and persuading current users to buy more. A *group* of sellers often sponsor these programmes, these sellers being an association of manufacturers, service firms, agricultural producers, etc., all with a similar product to sell.

Seldom does a single producer use generic appeals in advertising, but an interesting example was the 'Put Mustard On It' campaign run by Colman's. A dominant market position and research findings indicated that the problem was one of frequency of usage, and this led Colman's to put forward this generic appeal rather than use a specific brand message. Primary demand determines the total market, with the commodity being pitched against a competing commodity (e.g. tea versus coffee) compared with brand competition, which is the basis of selective demand.

Sales effects

The ultimate purpose of all advertising is to generate sales. Direct, immediate responses are sometimes the objectives of advertising campaigns, as in the case of mail-order firms which aim for consumers to buy at once through the post. For instance, producers of records use television to generate as many sales as possible in the minimum amount of time. The objectives here are usually short-term in nature, and consumers are urged to act upon needs of which they are already aware.

To view sales as being the only valid objective of advertising is, however, too narrow a viewpoint. Modern advertising is far more complex than this. Indirect actions are also aimed for, although the ultimate purpose remains that of sales. In order that sales might eventually be brought about, the advertiser might direct the advertising campaign at other objectives, for example:

- Influencing attitudes
- Creating awareness about products and services
- Increasing knowledge of brands and companies
- Acting as a reminder
- Motivating enquiries
- Providing leads for the salesforce

Here, advertising is often used to make buyers aware of needs they feel.

Sequential models

In order to determine *what* to say in advertisements, the advertiser must understand the advertising process in his target markets. Advertising works in a myriad of different ways: it varies according to many factors, including:

- The product of service being advertised
- The organization doing the advertising
- The target markets aimed at
- The competitive environment
- The time period in which the advertising is done
- The media being used
- The message content of the advertisement
- The level of advertising being employed

In order that specific, measurable objectives may be set for the advertising campaign, marketing must familiarize itself with current knowledge about how advertising works. Theories can only put forward general perspectives; the task for marketing is to analyse how these may be applied in the specific task under consideration.

The behavioural scientists have formulated a number of sequential models, attempting to shed light on the process consumers pass through on their way to action (purchase). In the 1920s, the AIDA approach was put forward, stating that consumers pass through the successive stages of: Attention–Interest–Desire–Action. Criticism of this approach mainly centres around the fact that there is no allowance for 'build-up' and that the emphasis is far too much on the message, with little consideration of the role of the prospect.[18]

Daniel Starch[19] wrote in 1925:

An advertisement, to be successful:
(a) must be seen;
(b) must be read;
(c) must be believed;
(d) must be remembered;
(e) must be acted upon.

Again, the assumptions are focused on the advertisement itself, rather than the consumer, and there is far too much emphasis on the stimulus. There is too little analysis of the responses of the potential customer. There is also no allowance for 'build-up' in the model, with the implication being that successive exposures to the same advertisement will not interact. In practice, it is far more likely that there will be increasing (or diminishing) returns from additional advertising efforts.

In 1961 Colley[20] put forward the DAGMAR treatise—Defining Advertising Goals for Measured Advertising Results.

This is an attempt to identify the steps in the consumer decision-making process in order to allow for more precise definitions of advertising objectives and their measurement. Goals should be set in order to move prospects through the various levels; progression through the sequence increasing the likelihood of purchase (see Fig. 9.6). Colley drew attention to the fact that often the people concerned with implementing the advertising decisions may not have a common understanding of the purpose of the advertising effort: a point also commented on by Bernstein.[21]

In 1961, Lavidge and Steiner[22] proposed that consumers pass through the sequence shown in Fig. 9.7. As consumers perceive advertisements, they move along the hierarchical sequence of effects towards purchase.

Evaluation of the sequential models   These sequential models have been used extensively by advertising researchers, but they are put forward not on the basis of empirical evidence but on the basis of common sense. In fact, Colley, when putting forward the DAGMAR model, stated: 'The concept of the Marketing Communications Spectrum is applied common sense.' The implications of these models are that the objectives of advertising are to get the consumer to learn something; to present persuasive messages which appeal to rational decision-making; and to turn non-buyers into buyers.

Palda,[23] in a critique of the models, draws attention to the following:

- Consumers may not always have favourable attitudes before purchasing a product.
- The models may be operationally weak because of the lack of dependable measurement devices.
- Consumers may not move through the sequence in a forward manner: they may also move backwards (from, say, 'conviction' back to 'liking' a product).

Sequential models are thus more theoretical than practical, and clearly work needs to be done in this area before actionable models can be put forward as active advertising tools.

Practical theories

Reeves[24] states: 'the consumer tends to remember just one thing from an advertisement—one strong claim, or one strong concept'. This theory of the unique selling proposition (USP) proposes that, because of the problems of memory and credibility, if an advertisement tries to tell consumers too much it may fail. Effective advertising is secured by making a single, strong and motivating proposition to 'pull over new customers to your product'.

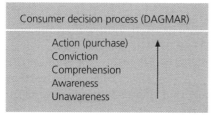

FIGURE 9.6

Consumer decision process (DAGMAR)

An alternative approach to the USP theory is that of 'brand image', often associated with David Ogilvy.[25] The claim here is that the purpose of advertising is 'to give a brand a first-class ticket through life'. This approach seems to be concerned with non-verbal methods of communication. By the evocation of moods, it is proposed that emotions will be generated which will lead to effective advertising. If consumers purchase on an emotional basis, then this approach may well prove to be effective, and rationality may not be necessary. Consider for a moment how the Martini advertisements successfully put forward the 'jet set image' and how the consumers would react if the 'voice over' finished by saying 'and only £1.25 a bottle'!

Emotion is also proposed by Martineau.[26] His opinion is that all human behaviour is a form of self-expression and that 'user images' are important. However, since people need to think of themselves as being rational, a rationalization is required by the consumer to justify his or her decision. The ideal advertisement proposed here is a combination of emotion and rationality, in line with the needs, perceptions and attitudes of the target audiences.

Joyce[27] states that the advertising/purchasing system is a rather complex system of interacting variables. The question of *what* to say is a key question for all advertisers, and it is proposed that the discussion of the various theories has shed some light on the question of how advertising works. The general perspectives provide insights. Joyce states 'the model itself is tentative' but this general conclusion seems unlikely to be overthrown.

MANAGING ADVERTISING

Planning, implementing and controlling advertising is a complex and difficult process which often requires specialist skills. For example, media selection and scheduling is often conducted by trained specialists whose sole task is to ensure that this part of the advertising process is carried out effectively. We cannot look at all of the facets of managing advertising in great detail, but it is important to understand and appreciate the basic elements of managing the advertising effort before considering some of them in more detail.

The six basic elements of managing the advertising effort are:

1. Identification of the target audience.

2. Determination of clear, realistic and measurable objectives for advertising.

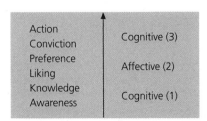

FIGURE 9.7

Hierarchy of effects

Stage (1) is concerned with knowledge and the process of thinking.
Stage (2) is concerned with attitudes, feeling or emotion.
Stage (2) is concerned with motives and the desire for action.

3. Determination of the advertising budget.

4. Message selection/creative platform.

5. Media selection and media scheduling.

6. Control and evaluation of advertising effectiveness.

Before considering each of these separately, it is important to stress once again that the planning and implementation of advertising, as with all the promotional elements, need to be set against the rest of the marketing mix and to be consistent with overall marketing objectives and strategy. In addition, external factors will also need to be taken into account including, for example, social and legal constraints, the choice of advertising agencies, competitors, and, of course, customers, and particularly their needs and motives. Finally, the overall role and emphasis given to advertising, together with some indication of the preliminary budget for advertising, should be set in the overall context of the promotional mix. This wider framework for advertising decisions is shown in Fig. 9.8.[28]

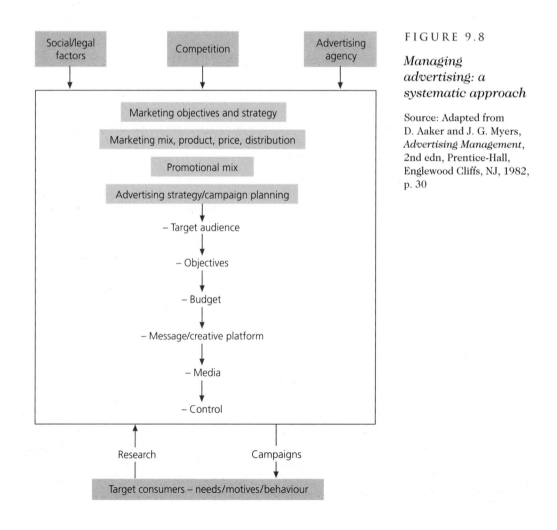

FIGURE 9.8

Managing advertising: a systematic approach

Source: Adapted from D. Aaker and J. G. Myers, *Advertising Management*, 2nd edn, Prentice-Hall, Englewood Cliffs, NJ, 1982, p. 30

Identifying and analysing the target audience

> Generally, the more advertisers know about the advertising target, the more likely they are to develop an effective advertising campaign.

This quote from Dibb *et al.*[29] captures the importance of starting the management of an advertising campaign by understanding the target audience. The target audience will stem from broader marketing objectives and strategies—particularly, of course, segmentation strategies. Details of the target audience should include not only demographic data, e.g. age, sex, etc., but also location, ACORN group and so on.

It is not sufficient simply to *delineate* target audiences; the marketing communicator must also *understand* the target audience. There are many pertinent factors here, but, to take an example, in planning effective marketing communications the marketer needs to understand the buying decision process, i.e. how customers buy. The importance, in more general terms, of understanding this process was discussed in Chapter 3. In the context of communications decisions, the stage at which the target audience is in the buying decision process begins to provide important information for planning communications. For example, in the case of a new product, communications will have to stimulate the start of the buying process by encouraging problem or need recognition. Alternatively, if the target audience includes mainly those who are already regular purchasers of the product in question, our marketing communications might be aimed at minimizing post-purchase dissonance.

In addition to understanding how the target market buys and the stage of the buying process it has reached, it is also important to understand who is involved in the purchase process. For example, in Chapter 3 we saw that we can usefully distinguish between different roles in the buying process. So if, for example, we are launching a new brand of breakfast cereal, it is important to distinguish between 'influencers', 'deciders', 'purchasers' and 'users'. Of course, all of these roles might be embodied in the one target group, but, as we have seen in both consumer and industrial markets, these roles may also be filled by a range of individuals.

Sometimes it is also important to establish existing preferences, attitudes and so on of our target audience. For example, given that with marketing communications we are very often concerned with image, it might be important to establish our target audience's current image of the company and/or its products.

The analysis of the target audience should help the marketing communicator to assess the information needs of customers. For example, analysis of the search, and alternative stages of the buying process, will help to establish where our target market looks for information, the degree of reliance on word-of-mouth versus marketer-dominated sources of information, and the type of information sought.

Setting advertising objectives

Once we have determined the target audience for our advertising, we need to determine what we intend our advertising to achieve with that audience. In broad terms, it might be intended to inform, persuade or remind. While this might be useful in beginning to delineate the reasons and role of advertising in the overall marketing and communications mix, these broad classifications are not a sufficient guide to the next steps in the advertising management and campaign planning process. Ideally, we need to prescribe specific communications goals for advertising. Needless to say, this is where our earlier models of the sequences in buyer behaviour related to communications are useful. For example, Colley's earlier described DAGMAR model translates into some 52 possible communication goals for advertising. Notwithstanding the controversy over these models, they are helpful in setting specific objectives for advertising couched in terms of objectives for communications designed to move customers through the buying stages. These objectives should, whenever possible, be defined in quantitative terms and specify a time scale.

Determining advertising budgets

Earlier we briefly discussed some of the approaches to determining the overall budget for marketing communications. Having gone through the process of broadly determining the thrust or emphasis of promotional strategy between the different promotional tools, we should have at least a preliminary idea as to how much of the total budget will be allocated to advertising. However, at this stage, and taking into account our first two steps of advertising management, we now need to refine this process to arrive at a precise budget for advertising. In fact, the advertising budget can be arrived at on the same variety of bases as the overall budget for communications, i.e. it can be based on percentages of sales and/or profits, on competitors' spend, or on the objective and task method. Once again, the only justifiable method is the objective and task approach. Indeed, this is a distinct advantage if setting clear and quantified communications objectives for advertising in the preceding stage.

Deciding on the message/creative platform

The creative element of advertising is an area that can have the greatest impact on the success or failure of an advertising campaign. Unfortunately, it is also an area that, despite much research, generates considerable controversy as to what makes a successful creative advertisement.

The creative plan is normally based upon research that provides answers about:

1. The key unique features of the brand.
2. The criteria used by consumers in evaluating brands.
3. The brand image in relation to competition.

This platform for the creative plan should feature the basic promise to consumers and should provide substantiation first.

There are three essential steps in developing a creative programme. The first is to determine the content of the message. The advertising content serves the advertiser by carrying out the strategy and objectives set for the product. It serves the consumer by providing useful information about solving problems. Second, in addition to deciding what is to be said, the programme must consider how it is to be said. Finally, the creative programme must determine how the advertising will be produced (i.e. the creative execution).

The advertiser also faces numerous difficult choices in weighing up the promise or appeal. It has been suggested that advertisers should use rational appeals when their prospects face utilitarian problems and emotional appeals when problems are social or psychological! Research evidence indicates that 'fear appeals' raise consumer defences if the problem is a vital or unavoidable one, but they may be effective with less important problems.

Determining media selection and scheduling

This element of advertising management should be prepared concurrently with the budget decision. A wide variety of media vehicles are available to the advertiser, especially in the developed economies. Media planning, however, is made easier by adherence to the preceding steps in our advertising management programme. Overall marketing strategy, advertising objectives, budgets and creative strategy all serve to delineate and point to the required media strategy. Above all, media strategy is determined by the target audience.

This extremely important element of managing advertising is considered in more detail later in this chapter.

Evaluating and controlling advertising

Given the importance and expense of advertising, it is vital to assess how effective it is. Again, this is where the importance of the previous stage of setting clear and quantified objectives comes in. You will recall that when we discussed objectives for communication it was suggested that, although sales and profits may be the ultimate reasons for advertising (at least in the profit-making organization), there are distinct difficulties in relating these to advertising. Furthermore, because of this, it was suggested that advertising objectives be set in communications terms, e.g. increasing recognition and brand awareness. It is also important to recognize that advertising, and particularly the creative/copy content of advertising, must be evaluated before actually implementing the campaign as well as after the campaign. In the next part of this chapter we give an overview of the range of research techniques available for both pre-testing and post-testing advertisements. Briefly, though, the overall approach to evaluating and controlling advertising is set out below.

The evaluation programme begins by defining the elements and decisions to be evaluated, including elements from the budget programme, the media programme and the creative programme. Next, an *effectiveness evaluation procedure* is designed for each element. This must include specification of a standard as a base for comparison; when actual performance is measured it will be compared with the standard to determine whether or not performance is satisfactory.

For each programme element to be evaluated, the evaluation programme should specify the measurement technique to be used. For example, the *media audience measurement* evaluates the effectiveness of media programmes, the *recognition and recall tests* measure the effectiveness of individual advertisements, and techniques such as *consumer and retail audits* measure the effectiveness of overall campaigns.

Clearly, evaluating advertising requires research. We now turn our attention to some of the techniques of advertising research.

ADVERTISING RESEARCH

Claims that advertising efforts have been successful must often be viewed with a good deal of uncertainty. There are many variables over which the advertiser cannot hope to have complete control (e.g. competitors' actions, economic factors and prices), all of which may affect the advertising–sales relationship. The sequential models of the advertising process are used extensively in practice as a means to establish objectives for the measurement of advertising success or failure.

The amount of marketing communications research carried out is a frequent source of criticism—including the level of advertising research (see Table 9.1). It appears that research into advertising and other marketing communication efforts is far less extensive than research into other areas of marketing. Hodgson[30] surveyed the types of marketing research undertaken in the UK, and discovered that research into marketing communications was only a minor part of the total.

One reason often given to explain the lack of advertising research activity is the amount of confidence that marketing managers have in the available techniques.

Advertising research techniques

Although marketing research has already been covered in Chapter 5, this discussion centres more specifically upon research into advertising. A fuller discussion of this subject is also provided by Chisnall.[31] Generally, the tools of advertising research are referred to as 'pre-measurement' or 'pre-testing' and 'post-measurement' or 'post-testing'. In other words, the probable effectiveness of advertising may be assessed before the campaign is implemented, and evaluation of an advertising effort, once it has been run, may also take place. The measurements provided by both types of advertising research are potentially of immense value to advertising management. Indications of the ability of advertising to communicate messages effectively to target audiences will enable operational principles and guidelines to be developed.

Pre-testing advertisements

Advertising management may feel that an advertisement appears to be promising, but it is vital that the likely reactions of the potential buyers are first assessed. Advertisers must decide what responses will constitute effectiveness in line with pre-stated objectives, and then set out to see how likely it is that consumers will react accordingly to proposed advertisements. The effectiveness of the creative elements of individual advertisements—headlines, body copy, illustrations, slogans, etc.—may be tested, or the entire advertisement may be tested.

TABLE 9.1   *Marketing communications research*

Turnover of research agency	Advertising research (%)	Sales promotion research (%)	Other marketing research (%)
£500 000+	9½	1½	89
£150 000–499 000	16½	1½	82
Under £150 000	23	3	74
Total average	13	2	85

Based on 28 UK agencies, including 18 of the 23 major UK research companies represented in the Association of Market Survey Organizations (AMSO)

The major techniques employed in pre-testing are as follows.

1. *Checklists* This is a form of internal assessment by the advertiser, who picks the elements that he or she considers should be in an advertisement, to enable the systematic review of proposed advertisements to take place, point by point, against this list. The weakness of this approach is that a company is dependent upon the validity of the points that are contained in the list, and some important ones may also be omitted or overlooked when the checklist is compiled.

2. *Consumer juries* A sample of prospects independently visited or contacted by mail, or interviewed on a group basis, is used to test advertisements. Simple or complex responses from jury members are sought in order to gain insights into how well an audience has understood an advertisement just seen or heard by them. The major weakness of this technique is that assessment is on the basis of what people say, and this may not always reflect their behaviour in the market.

3. *Enquiry tests* Alternative advertisements, published independently or together on a split-run basis (where different advertisements appear in the same issue of a magazine), are coded and the levels of enquiries generated are measured. In order to elicit enquiries, the advertiser must offer some reason for the audience to reply (e.g. a free sample of the product or an information brochure). The major weakness of this technique is that the advertiser has to assess the quality of the enquiry (some people write in just to receive mail!) and to assess further how effective the advertisement would be in communicating messages of a less direct nature (when offers are not made).

4. *Laboratory measurement devices* Sample consumers are placed in a controlled setting and shown proposed advertisements, and their physical responses are then measured. Sweat gland activity is measured by means of the psycho-galvanometer; pupil dilation can be recorded by a perceptoscope; images are flashed on a screen for a fraction of a second by the tachistoscope; the movement of an individual's eyes across the printed page is traced by an eye movement camera. These devices have the advantage of being apparently objective and conceptually simple, and distortion is limited since involuntary responses are measured (except in the case of the tachistoscope). Major shortcomings are that the laboratory setting may affect responses, and the relative sales effectiveness is not being measured.

5. *Focus groups* Focus groups, as discussed in Chapter 5, are an excellent way of gauging reactions to proposed advertising campaigns.

6. *Experimentation* This is where representative areas are chosen to test advertising ideas. Different advertisements may be evaluated in this way, by publishing them in different parts of the market, and sales data obtained to enable measurement to take place.

There are many managerial problems in conducting these experiments. These are summarized under three main headings:

- The setting of valid objectives.
- The control aspects when designing and running the test.
- The interpretation of the data.

Post-testing advertisements

1. *Enquiry tests* These may be used to post-evaluate advertising efforts, when offers are made to which the potential buyer can be expected to reply. In the case of mail-order selling, the yardstick used to measure the level of effectiveness may consist of sales generated as well as enquiries for further information.

    By varying the advertisements used over time, and by maintaining detailed records, the advertiser is able to discover significant variations which can then be attributed to the differences in the advertisements.

2. *Recall/recognition tests*   These are attempts to measure the number of people who have actually read a particular advertisement. The readership levels of various magazines are measured on a regular basis by the Starch Message Report Service, whereby readers 'recognize' advertisements or parts of them. A more rigorous version of recall testing does not involve showing advertisements to respondents, and advertisements must be recalled from memory (e.g. Gallup and Robinson's Impact Service).

   Recall testing may also involve 'dummy' magazines, where the respondent has advertisements in a scrapbook left for a few days. He or she is then tested by being asked questions about the various advertisements contained in the portfolio.

   Recognition studies may be subject to biased or distorted responses by consumers, in that sample members may tend to exaggerate their actual readership. Recall tests attempt to control this by more vigorous screening of sample members and by counting only recall. A major criticism is that simple ideas and facts are favoured. The communication of complex ideas—which may be necessary for technical or novel products—may score low in recall tests.

3. *Consumer audits*   A random group of consumers are asked if they have bought a product, how often they have bought it and what they have on hand—prior to the advertising being launched. Re-interviewing of these consumers then takes place after the advertising has been conducted in order to assess the percentage increase or decrease in the sales of the advertiser's product.

4. *Retail audits*   These are similar to consumer audits except that the retailer's stocks are measured before and after the advertising. The major problems with measuring the sales effects of advertising in these ways is that it is difficult to conclude that advertising has been responsible for the sales.

5. *Focus groups*   Again, our now familiar friend focus groups are increasingly being used to post-test advertising campaigns.

The pre-testing and post-testing of individual advertisements in the above ways can provide some insight into the overall effectiveness of advertising, but one is seldom able to measure all of its effects. At times, because the results of advertising may not happen immediately, it is difficult to relate the response to a particular stimulus. A lot depends on what other selling efforts are employed by the company and its competitors, how fast the turnover of the product is and how important advertising is to the sale of the product. Specific, measurable goals must be clearly defined in line with the DAGMAR treatise.

MEDIA SELECTION

In using media, the objective of management is to plan a media schedule which consists of the combination of media, and media vehicles, which most efficiently reach the target audience while still meeting various constraints (e.g. creative and budget). The first task for marketing is to identify and define the prospects (i.e. buyers and potential buyers of the product or service). In this way, various media alternatives will be seen to have more potential than others and the range of choice will become narrower. For example, if the campaign is to be directed to a group of potential female buyers, then magazines that are read predominantly by males are clearly ruled out.

More specific requirements of the media programme may be obtained by analysing the following:

1. *Budget constraints*   The aim should be for audience requirements to be fulfilled in the most cost-effective manner. The usual measure used here is 'cost per thousand', provided by the formula:

$$\frac{\text{Cost of the insertion of the advertisement}}{\text{Number of prospects}} \times 1000$$

← could do this for mags

$$\text{e.g.} \quad \frac{\text{£60 000 for TV spot}}{\text{15 million audience}} \times 1000 = \text{£4 to reach every 1000 viewers}$$

The major weaknesses of this approach are:

- It assumes that all of the audience are prospects.
- It makes no allowances for effectiveness; i.e. to evaluate on a purely cost basis overlooks the fact that an alternative medium that has a more expensive 'cost per 1000' could be far more effective in getting the message across.

2. *Creative constraints*   The media must also comply with creative requirements, and various messages may lend themselves to words/pictures, colour/black-and-white, prestigious/dominating medium, etc. The media planner must analyse these features of the various media alternative closely.

   Each of the various mass media has its attributes and shortcomings, as shown in Table 9.2.

3. *'Reach' vs. 'frequency'*   It must be decided whether the message should be distributed very widely among the prospects (termed 'reach') or concentrated on a smaller number of prospects ('frequency'). Where all potential buyers are estimated to be of equal value, it may be better for the advertiser to reach as many of them as possible; in cases where there are better prospects (heavier users of the product, for example) it may be better to build up frequency by providing them with many opportunities to see (OTS).

4. *Other constraints*   These may be important depending upon the product, its strategy and objectives. For example, there may be a need for the quick production and insertion of advertisements in dynamic markets.

Matching prospects with media

A profile of the prospects should already have been obtained. The remaining alternatives still under consideration should now be profiled in more detail. The audience characteristics (the total size of audiences; the demographic, geographical and psychographic details of the audience); the production requirements of the medium/vehicle; the size of insertions and potential effects on salesforce and trade must now be analysed.

A decision must also be taken on the number of media to be used. Many larger advertisers do use a single medium, and television is used particularly because it is so dominating. In cases where the advertiser dominates a medium relative to competitors, it may be expected that the audience is more familiar with the advertiser's brand and preference may result. There are, however, many advertisers who spread their budgets among the media. The potential advantages of this strategy are:

- Synergism—the '2 + 2 = 5' idea of media working in combination to produce a greater output than the sum of the individual parts. Primary media may be chosen by the advertiser, with supportive media being used to back these up.

- Coverage may be extended beyond what could be achieved via a single medium.

- Greater segmentation capabilities—different messages attracting different market segments through different media.

Timing of campaigns

The two decisions to be taken now are:

1. The duration of the media schedule (i.e. when the campaign is to start and when it is to stop). Concentration should be placed when prospects feel most need for the product, or when they feel the particular need that is the key part of the message.

2. The spread of activity over this time period.

Advertisers may choose between spreading the messages fairly evenly over the time period, and alternating between heavy and light periods of activity within the time period (see Fig. 9.9).

TABLE 9.2   *Media comparisons for advertisers*

Media	Advantages/disadvantages
Television	Large audiences; demonstration of product in use (sound and vision); compulsiveness; viewed at home in a relaxed manner. Commercial breaks may be seen as irritating; a transient medium.
Cinema	Has many of the above advantages, but problem is the size of the audiences, which do, however, still retain segmentation possibilities.
Newspapers	Great flexibility in terms of timing—booked at short notice; illustrations can be used; regularly purchased by large numbers of people. Do have short life spans; may be difficult to get people to notice the advertising content.
Magazines	Have 'editorial' facilities with which to integrate advertising content; advertisements are expected by readers; magazines have long life spans; read at leisure; high readership compared with circulation. May have 'desert' areas which are seldom noted by readers, e.g. front and back pages.
Commercial radio	May be perceived as an 'intimate companion'; use of sound; segmentation possibilities. Has disadvantages of small audience size; transient medium—how well are the messages perceived or retained?
Outdoor and transportation	Many people have an OTS (opportunity to see)—most of the population spend some time outdoors; relatively low costs; short- and long-term possibilities; national campaigns are possible; segmentation possibilities. May be subject to effects of the weather; how eye-catching and noticeable are they? Sites are subject to environmental criticism.
Newspaper supplements	Offer vast circulations at relatively low cost; opportunity to expose message at concentrated times; Sundays are a day of rest and family gatherings. Not passed around as much as magazines; have 'desert' areas.

The media schedule

The media requirements, and the reasoning that leads to the selection of final media choices, should now be stated in full. This has meant that the advertiser has reached this stage by a gradual process of elimination, and the listing of the purchases to be made. Such purchases include: the size/length of insertion; insertion dates and times; the anticipated costs; and the projected reach. Frequency and cost efficiency of the insertions provide the benchmark against which actual performance may be compared.

ADVERTISING AGENCIES

Most advertisers use the services of an advertising agency for major parts of their advertising programmes. The selection of the agency is a key decision area, since the success of the advertising depends to a large extent upon the contribution of these specialists. The 'full service' agency offers a wide range of services—creative, media planning, marketing research; sales promotions and public relations; account planning and customer contact. It should be noted that a client may use such an agency over some or all of this wide range. Perhaps because of a feeling that the temptation exists to use more services than originally anticipated, or because of a feeling that the 'specialists' are better, there has been a growth of specialist 'hot shops'. These media and creative specialists offer their specialism and nothing more.

Using an agency

The first question to be asked is: 'Do we need to use an agency at all?' A major consideration here is the likely costs of the deal—in financial terms, agencies derive most of their incomes from the *commission system*. This tripartite arrangement is the subject of much criticism (i.e. who is the agency working for?) but it continues, despite various threats that it should be modified.

Under this system, agencies pay the media owner for mass media time/space purchases, minus a commission, usually in the 10–15 per cent range, and then collect the full amount from the client. In the UK income from commission currently accounts for 70 per cent of all advertising agency incomes. In addition, 'service fees' are charged by advertising agencies and account for the remaining 30 per cent of income.

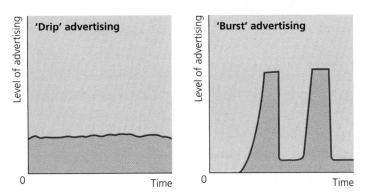

FIGURE 9.9

Advertising expenditure strategies

Advantages for the advertiser in using an agency

1. Administrative economies—high salaries of full-time staff may be avoided.
2. Provision of monthly invoices—no 'hidden' costs; better recording of the costs and monitoring of budgets.
3. Commission system may 'subsidize' specialized services provided by the agency.
4. Agencies have more power in cases of disputes with the media owners.
5. Specialist services provided by the agency—particularly creative and media expertise—may make advertising more effective.

Disadvantages in using an agency

1. Service fees may make the work expensive—particularly if a lot of creative work is undertaken.
2. If the client is a relatively small customer, its work may be delayed or handled by agency juniors.
3. Possible security leaks—agency personnel, particularly account executives (the agency contact men) must work very closely with and within the client's organization.

Advantages to the media owner

1. Contact with fewer people—costs reduced and operations simplified.
2. Agency acts as a 'salesforce', getting orders for the media owner.
3. Agencies act as a 'principal' in law; i.e. the media owner collects from the agencies, who in turn stand any bad debts from clients.
4. Agencies possess specialist knowledge which may be of use to the media owner in improving the quality of reproduction of the advertisement and other content of the media.
5. The specialist skills provided by agencies may improve the effectiveness of advertising, and indirectly help to bring in more clients and advertising revenue.

Client/agency relations

Corkindale and Kennedy[32] put forward the following recommendations:

- Client and agency should agree a written advertising brief specifically on advertising objectives.
- Someone in the company must be responsible for coordinating the activities undertaken in the agency.
- Someone in the company must be able to justify the work being done in the agency.

The client must develop selection criteria once it has decided to use an advertising agency. The initial screening process will narrow down the range of alternatives, and hopefully lead to a more effective relationship. Factors to be taken account of here are:

- Size of proposed agency.
- Specialist skills offered by the agency.
- Range of services to be used.
- Skills of existing marketing/advertising personnel in the company.
- Agencies used by competitors.
- 'Track record' of agencies.
- Location of agencies.
- The need for establishing rapport, and the likelihood of a long-term working relationship.

DEVELOPMENTS IN TECHNOLOGY AND MARKETING COMMUNICATIONS

In contrast to particularly the pricing element of the marketing mix, new technology is having a major effect on the marketing communications area of the mix. Some of the more important ones include the following:

1. *Direct response television advertising (DRTV)*   A growth area in marketing communications is a move towards direct response television advertising. This in itself has been prompted by the availability of additional television channels to facilitate this. Needless to say then DRTV is underpinned by the growth of satellite, cable and more recently digital television. DRTV advertising is aimed at invoking an immediate response from the customer through his or her telephone or increasingly now, directly through interactive facilities on the television to generate an order. Increasingly, digital developments in television will enable more and more customers to access the Web and associated activities such as e-mail services. Many believe that it is the television rather than the personal computer which will be the major interactive channel of the future.

2. *Wireless communications/mobile technologies*   Again underpinned by developments in digital communications is the growth of wireless technologies and the mobile communications which are associated with this. Already consumers can learn about products and services, check prices and availability and place orders using a mobile phone. Future developments in mobile phone technology will increase this usage. More and more companies therefore will have to think about placing at least part of their budget for marketing communications into this area, especially where the target market is the younger end of the market.

3. *The Internet*   The Internet yet again is one of the most significant developments for marketing communications planning and practice. In a matter of only three or four years at the most, advertising via the Internet and the use of company websites have become major strategic tools in the marketing communications mix of most organizations. Despite recent setbacks in the growth of some of the Internet marketers, there is no doubt that the Internet and associated activities will continue to increase in importance for marketing communications. Understandably perhaps many marketers are only just beginning to realize the potential of the Internet as a promotional tool, and many are relatively inexperienced in areas such as, for example, the design and operation of websites in marketing communications. Equally understandable though today's marketers are having to learn quickly about these matters. We know now, for example, that some of the basic principles of effective website design and use in marketing communications include the following:

    a. As with other areas of marketing communications websites must be designed with specific communications objectives in mind.
    b. Websites should enable the customer to readily access information and should offer the visitor more than just a listing of the company and its products.
    c. Websites should be operated and planned to be consistent with the overall communications strategy and with the other elements of the marketing communications mix.
    d. Websites should offer access to secure ordering systems.
    e. Websites should be continually evaluated, controlled, and where appropriate, updated.

    These then are some of the basic principles for using the Internet as a promotional tool. We should also note that the Internet can also be used for marketing communications with target audiences other than customers. So, for example, a company can use it to develop effective publicity and public relations with, for example, the media, investors, local communities and so on. Until recently one of the problems with websites as a marketing communications tool has been the lack of agreement on how to assess the effectiveness of website communication. Initially such effectiveness was limited to recording the number of people visiting the site via a server. This is known as the 'hit record'. However, such hit records in fact give very little indication of the communications effectiveness of a website. Realizing this, a number of improved web-tracking control and evaluation methods are now available. Using these, a company can establish, for example, background information on the website visitor, what pages have been visited, and which products assessed, what the website visitor did on each page and so on.

4. *The Extranet*   The Extranet is a system of electronic communication which connects members of a value/supply chain together. So, for example, suppliers, producers, distributors, intermediaries and even customers are now increasingly being linked together through electronic data interchange (EDI) systems. The EDI networks allow much closer working relationships to be developed between the members of the value chain. An increasing number of companies now insist that their suppliers be linked through EDI systems. The EDI also helps to encourage trust and commitment between members of a value chain thereby accelerating the move towards relationship marketing. The Extranet helps cut down stock-holding costs and minimizes the possibility of disruptions in the supply chain process. Not only do the members of the Extranet system benefit from this, but it also adds to customer satisfaction and competitiveness.

5. *The Intranet*   We should not forget that marketing communication is not only concerned with external communication, but that it is also concerned with internal customers with regard to the development of internal marketing. The Intranet is a system of electronic internal communication that operates within an organizational system. The Intranet connects functions and activities within an organization thereby allowing employees to access information from other parts of the company. It can be used to convey information on important external activities affecting the organization thereby fostering group communications, or in the same way, informing colleagues of marketing initiatives including, for example, new product launches. It may also be used to advantage for internal promotional material such as company newsletters.

CHAPTER SUMMARY

This chapter has shown the place of communications in the marketing mix. Communication strategies have been examined. Sales promotion (below-the-line) was discussed, as was the role of public relations. We also looked at the increasingly important area of direct mail. This was followed by an explanation of the purpose of advertising from the viewpoint of a company marketing its products or services. It further explored brand image and corporate image. Generic advertising was then discussed and the potential effect of advertising was summarized in terms of its effect on sales.

Theoretical models of advertising were considered and their usefulness assessed, followed by a practical assessment of advertising effectiveness through the medium of advertising research.

The selection of agencies and media is an important consideration in communication strategy, and criteria surrounding such selection were considered.

Chapter 10 considers the more personal elements of promotion in the form of selling and sales management.

CHAPTER REVIEW QUESTIONS

1. With examples of your choice, show the usefulness of the following:

   a. Brand advertising.
   b. Corporate advertising.
   c. Generic advertising.

2. Outline some of the major sales promotion tools available to the marketer.

3. Which 'publics' might a public relations campaign be aimed at?

4. Why are the sequential models of the advertising process so called? What insights may be gained by studying these?

5. Give three examples of each of the following:

   a. Advertisements using the USP.
   b. Advertisements based on 'imagery'.
   c. Advertisements using rationality as the main motivator.

6. To what extent do you believe that below-the-line promotions are particularly useful in encouraging impulse purchases?

7. What do you understand by the terms 'internal' and 'external publics' in the context of public relations?

8. Using examples, outline how new technology is being used in contemporary marketing communications.

References

1. H. Lasswell, in *Communication of Ideas*, L. Bryson (ed.), Institute for Religious and Social Studies, 1975.
2. D. Ogilvy, *Confessions of an Advertising Man*, Atheneum, New York, 1963.
3. J. Frye, *Introduction to the Marketing Systems*, Stanford University Press, Stanford, CA, 1973.
4. L. Festinger, *A Theory of Cognitive Dissonance*, Row, Peterson & Co., Evanston, IL, 1957.
5. G. Wills, 'How Good or Bad are Your Marketing Communications?' MEG Conference, 1976.
6. S. Majaro, 'Advertising by objectives', *Management Today*, January 1970.
7. S. H. Britt, *Marketing Management and Administrative Action*, McGraw-Hill, London, 1973.
8. A. Roberts, *Selling Advertising Budgets*, Advertising Association, London, 1986.
9. M. Christopher, *Marketing Below-the-Line*, George Allen & Unwin, London, 1969.
10. J. F. Engel, H. G. Wales and M. R. Warshaw, *Promotional Strategy*, R. D. Irwin, Homewood, IL, 1975.
11. W. Schlackman, *Some Psychological Aspects of Dealing*, MRS Papers, 1964.
12. P. Spillard, *Sales Promotion—Its Place in Marketing Strategy*, Business Publications, Plano, TX, 1966.
13. A. Morgan, *A Guide to Consumer Promotions*, Ogilvy and Mather, 1980.
14. P. Doyle and J. Saunders, 'The lead effect of marketing decisions', *Journal of Marketing*, February 1985, pp. 54–65.

15. Institute of Public Relations London, Public Relations Definition, 1986.

16. F. Jenkins, *Public Relations*, 2nd edn, International Ideas, Philadelphia, PA, 1983, pp. 1–11.

17. R. Haywood, *All about PR*, McGraw-Hill, London, 1984, pp. 141–244.

18. D. Corkindale and S. H. Kennedy, *Process of Advertising*, MCB Publications, Bradford, 1978.

19. D. Starch, *Principles of Advertising*, McGraw-Hill, New York, 1925.

20. R. H. Colley, *Defining Advertising Goals for Measured Advertising Results*, Association of National Advertisers, New York, 1961 and 1983.

21. D. Bernstein, 'Advertising: inexact science–bastard art', *Business Graduate*, Summer 1975.

22. R. T. Lavidge and G. A. Steiner, 'A model for predictive measurement of advertising effectiveness', *Journal of Marketing*, October 1962.

23. K. S. Palda, 'The hypothesis of a hierarchy of effects—a partial evaluation', *Journal of Marketing Research*, **3** (1), February 1966.

24. R. Reeves, *Reality of Advertising*, A. A. Knopf, New York, 1961.

25. Ogilvy, op. cit.

26. P. Martineau, *Reality in Advertising*, McGraw-Hill, London, 1961.

27. T. Joyce, 'What do we know about how advertising works', *Advertising Age*, 1967.

28. D. Aaker and J. G. Myers, *Advertising Management*, 2nd edn, Prentice-Hall, Englewood Cliffs, NJ, 1982, p. 30.

29. S. Dibb, L. Simkin, W. M. Pride and O. C. Ferrell, *Marketing Concepts and Strategies*, 3rd European edn, Houghton-Mifflin, Boston, MA, 1997, p. 491.

30. P. Hodgson, 'What happened to sales promotion research?' *Marketing*, April 1977, pp. 71–4.

31. P. Chisnall, *Marketing Research*, McGraw-Hill, London, 1986, pp. 204–40.

32. Corkindale and Kennedy, op. cit.

CASE STUDY   *A different division*

Manchester United is one of the largest and most successful football clubs in the world. Essentially, the success of any football club stems from its activities and results on the field of play. In the last few years, for example, Manchester United have won the league championship five times, the European Cup and the FA Cup. However, its commercial success is also due in large measure to the success of its marketing activities as well.

Manchester United is probably one of the most effectively marketed and promoted clubs in the world and certainly in the UK. It has made especially good use of merchandising and areas of marketing promotion such as sponsorship. As a result, it has built a strong brand image and an awareness of its activities and success even among those who do not support Manchester United. Although Manchester United understandably does not divulge full details of its promotional spends, it is almost certainly one of the largest spenders in the football league on promotion. It can, of course, afford to do so with the return from its consistently large attendances, its previously mentioned merchandising, football league and television revenues, and, of course, its sponsorship. These returns complete the cycle of success by enabling the club to buy the best players in the world and offer the best deals to its management and ground staff.

At the other extreme are the clubs who struggle to survive in the lower divisions of the Football League. Many of these clubs have barely sufficient revenue to keep their grounds open and many are constantly in debt. Because they are in lower divisions they often struggle to attract sufficient fans through the turnstiles, but also, of course, they are paid less from the FA league levy and from the satellite and digital TV networks. The vicious circle is completed by the fact that they are unable to spend large amounts on promoting their clubs or even their clubs' products, and so again they receive less revenue than their more famous, or at least successful, counterparts in the highest division.

Promotion in general and advertising in particular is often thought of as being the prerogative of the larger organization. Admittedly, many smaller companies, like the lower division football clubs, do struggle and cannot match their larger competitors in terms of spends on promotion.

Bruddersfield Football Club has recently been relegated to the second division of the football league and is currently running at a loss. The management of the club feel that they must attract more fans for the coming season, and, in particular, the all-important season ticket holders who purchase their tickets for a year in advance. They also want to seek more sponsorship money although they already have a major sponsor whose name appears on the club's football shirts. They have a large, recently built stadium with seating for 30 000 and there are facilities at the ground for hospitality boxes and for dinners and conferences with seating for 200 in the club's restaurants together with all facilities. Like most clubs, including Manchester United, Bruddersfield Town have a supporters club and shop and sell club merchandise through this and other outlets in the town. Again they are seeking to expand the merchandising part of their operation.

They cannot afford large budgets for marketing communications, but their newly arrived commercial and marketing manager, Bob Townend, feels that the club has not made good use of the money it has spent on marketing communications in the past. The club has allocated him £150 000 for promotion purposes in the coming year.

Questions

1. How can relatively small organizations make effective use of the tools of marketing communications.
2. Propose an outline plan for spending Bruddersfield Town's £150 000 budget next year. Justify your proposals.

Chapter Ten

SELLING AND
SALES MANAGEMENT

LEARNING OBJECTIVES   *This chapter will help you to:*

- understand the nature and role of personal selling in the marketing mix;

- be aware of the key elements in the selling process;

- appreciate the scope and nature of sales management;

- be aware of the changes in the role of personal selling and sales management in contemporary marketing.

INTRODUCTION

Personal selling is one element in a company's marketing efforts. It is in fact usually classed within the 'promotion' (or communications) element of the four Ps, but it warrants a separate treatment in its own right. In industrial marketing, personal selling is likely to be the main communications tool, with expenditure in this area very much higher than for non-personal communications such as advertising or public relations. Highly technical products require a talk to prospective customers to put across their merits and to answer questions about their use. Consumer goods' companies also use salespersons, primarily to sell into the trade, but in this area expenditure is likely to be higher for advertising than personal selling.

   Personal selling must, therefore, be integrated with the whole marketing programme and should not be seen as a distinct activity divorced from the other elements of the communications and marketing mixes. Selling and sales management within a marketing-oriented firm are concerned with the analysis of customers' needs and wants and, through the company's total marketing efforts, with the provision of benefits to satisfy these needs and wants. Although the selling process might seem to be simple at first sight, a body of theory surrounds the subject; this has been documented by Saunders *et al.*[1]

Clearly, we feel that it is important for any student and/or practitioner of marketing —even if he or she never has any intention of working in sales—to appreciate and understand the nature and role of personal selling and in particular the relationship between the sales and marketing functions in a business. It is important to note that this chapter is intended to provide this appreciation and understanding. The intention is certainly not to cover sales and sales management in great detail nor, indeed, is it appropriate to do so. We have therefore tried to keep this chapter relatively brief so as to concentrate on those key areas that are needed to set selling and sales management in their marketing context.

SELLING AND MARKETING

Marketing encompasses many functions and has a number of key activities, of which selling is one. Each has its part to play, but it is important that the various activities be coordinated so that the marketing policy can be carried through effectively. There is often controversy over which of the activities is the most important. Such a controversy is generally meaningless, because the relative importance will vary between industries and between companies within a single industry. Selling generally, but not always, entails a personal meeting between seller and buyer. For a sale to be made successfully, it is usually necessary for the product to be of a satisfactory quality (i.e. value for money), to be available when required, to be packaged adequately, and to be competitive. It is the salesperson's task to present this information persuasively to the customers. When there is no salesforce, the information may have to be presented by means of a catalogue or brochure.

Relationship with marketing research

The function of marketing research is that of fact-finding. From the facts obtained, policies may be changed and products amended. Much of the information obtained from marketing research is fed to the sales department and can be used by the salesforce to counter competition. On other occasions, the salesforce can be used to provide information for the marketing research department. In this case, however, the kind of information that is obtained is usually of a limited nature. Salespeople do not make good researchers. It is common practice in most companies that use marketing research for the findings to be passed to the sales department for comment and sometimes for verification.

The marketing research department should never be thought of as *reporting on* the salesforce, but rather should be considered as a source of information that can be put to good use.

Relationship with other elements of the promotional programme

The relationship between the salesforce and other aspects of promotion should be a cooperative one. The sales department can be helped by *and* can help the advertising manager. Typical examples are where the salesforce obtains the agreement of customers either to donate window space for displays or to distribute display material themselves. Similarly, the promotional department helps the salesforce by 'softening up' customers through the pressure of advertising, sales promotion, direct mail, and so on. Everyone is to some extent susceptible to marketing promotions.

Both personal selling and various kinds of publicity activity such as advertising are forms of marketing communications. All forms of marketing communications are inter-related, and all elements in the organization's marketing communications mix have a specific part to play in the overall scheme of things. Non-personal communications, in the form of advertising, public relations and sales promotion, and direct mail, should 'push' the customer, previously ignorant of the firm's products, towards them. It is then the role of personal selling to capitalize on the preceding communications and to actually close the sale. Hence, personal selling and other forms of publicity should all contribute to an overall marketing communications strategy.

THE NATURE AND ROLE OF PERSONAL SELLING

Personal selling is an element of an organization's marketing activities. Specifically it is part of the marketing mix and, even more specifically, it is usually considered to be part of the overall promotional or communication element of the mix alongside activities such as advertising, sales promotion, public relations and so on. Probably nothing that we have stated here in this description of personal selling will strike you as controversial. However, unfortunately, in many organizations selling and the sales function from which this process is managed are still often treated as if they were entirely separate functions to the marketing one. Where sales and marketing do overlap it is in terms of perhaps the marketing department providing background information on customers, designing sales promotion material and so on. Often there is substantial animosity and conflict between the sales director and the marketing director. It is important to reiterate therefore that selling is part of overall marketing activity. This is not to say that the selling function is in any way inferior to the marketing one or is only of relatively minor importance. As we shall see, in some organizations and for some markets personal selling is the most important of the marketing mix and certainly the communication mix activities. It is also true to say that personal selling is one of the promotional tools available to a company. Certainly it is the case that personal selling is closest to the promotional tools and for sure effective selling requires effective communication. However, this view of selling as just another tool of the marketing communications mix perhaps tends to understate the importance of selling in the overall marketing activities of many organizations. Perhaps the emphasis now given to the need to be marketing- rather than sales-oriented, as we discussed in Chapter 1, has had the unintended result of perhaps suggesting that the selling function is unimportant. As already suggested this is without doubt not the case. Certainly, selling is part of marketing. Furthermore, it is also the case that to succeed, organizations must be marketing- rather than sales-oriented. This does not mean that selling and sales management are unimportant or even minor in the context of marketing efforts, and it does not mean that these activities should always be subservient to marketing. Admittedly, the adoption of the marketing concept does alter the role of the selling function. Instead of, as in the past, the adoption of an aggressive 'hard sell' approach to customers, we now know that selling and marketing must work hand in hand to identify and satisfy customer needs. Indeed, in some organizations, the sales function may play a major—and sometimes the most important—role in this process.

Clearly, the importance of personal selling in the overall marketing effort of a company will vary from one organization and one situation to another. The type of customer; the nature of the product; the stage of the buyer's decision-making process; custom and practice in the industry are all examples of factors that will affect the nature of the selling process and its role in the marketing mix. In broad terms, personal selling is likely to be more important in the following situations and circumstances:

- With business-to-business as opposed to consumer product markets.
- Related to the above—with institutional/organizational customers.
- When marketing complex and/or expensive products.
- In later stages of the buyer's decision-making process.

The term selling itself encompasses an enormous range of different types of selling activities and sales processes. To some extent this is reflected in the range of titles used to describe the salesperson's position. Just some examples of these titles include: salespersons, sales representatives, sales agents, field representatives, sales consultants, account executives, area and district managers and sales engineers.

A useful way of classifying the different types of selling is from the perspective of the extent to which the salesperson is required to simply take orders from customers rather than actively create them. A second factor distinguishing the different types of selling is the extent to which the emphasis is on selling to existing customers and markets as opposed to attempting to open new accounts and develop new markets. Two further factors giving rise to different types of selling activities are the different types of settings within which the selling takes place, and the types of customers and/or markets to which sales are being made.

Using these factors we can distinguish between the following types of selling:

1. *Delivery salespersons*   As the term implies, here the primary role of the salesperson is to simply make deliveries. In reality this is not a selling activity at all, although the customer might sometimes come into contact with the salesperson and hence the ambassadorial and intelligence-gathering roles of the salesperson may come into play. Because of this, our subsequent discussion of the selling process will only touch on this type of selling activity.

2. *Inside order takers*   In this type of selling the salesperson simply responds to orders placed by customers. Often this ordering input takes place via the telephone or increasingly via a direct interface system with customers, as for example the customer's stocks are depleted. Sometimes the order taker may be dealing with orders generated through other promotional tools and marketing efforts, such as say direct mail or classified advertising, although there may be some degree of active selling such as dealing with customer enquiries. Still the selling process is relatively passive.

3. *Order creators*   Here the role of the salesperson in generating orders is much more proactive. Although the salesperson might be dealing with existing customers sales still have to be generated and completed by the salesperson and many of the elements of the selling process which we shall be looking at shortly are closely involved. Order creating salespersons may work from within the organization such as in say telephone selling or retail selling, or outside of the organization visiting customers at their own premises.

4. *Missionary selling*   Acknowledged as being the most challenging type of selling. Here the salesperson is required to seek out and sell to new customers and markets. It is understandable, then, that this type of selling involves the most difficult and challenging sales situations. To some extent special skills and characteristics are required of the missionary salesperson. However, the

basic process of selling is essentially that required for successful order-creating and as such will be encompassed by our discussion of this process.

5. *Sales support activities*   In the same way as delivery salespersons, sales support activities are not really selling as such at all. Sales support may take the form of, for example, technical support and advice to customers or, in the case of retailing, merchandising support. The fact that this cannot really be classified as selling proper is not to denigrate the importance of these support activities and the people who provide them in an organization. Indeed, effective sales support may be the very thing that helps clinch a new order or perhaps keeps an existing customer loyal.

To summarize, personal selling is part of the organization's overall marketing effort, but can most appropriately be viewed as being an element of the promotional mix. Sales should not be seen as in any way subservient to marketing and, indeed, in some markets and sales situations such as business-to-business marketing, may well remain the most important element of the marketing mix. Sales and marketing should work together to produce the most effective marketing plans to achieve competitive success. The selling process itself covers a myriad of different situations and types of selling. On the one hand, we have situations where selling consists almost entirely of simply delivering products to existing customers, possibly taking a regular order back for processing for the next delivery. Other situations do involve selling activities, but are still largely passive and consist of taking orders over the telephone or by direct mail. Yet other sales situations involve primarily a customer support role, such as technical or merchandising support, rather than 'pure' selling. Finally, we have the types of selling situation that involves a much more proactive role for selling skills and techniques to be utilized. These types of selling situations encompass 'order creating' and 'missionary' selling.

Compared to elements of the marketing communication mix such as advertising or sales promotion, selling has a number of advantages. It is a flexible medium that can be adapted to suit individual purchasing situations and respond and react as the sales interview proceeds. Each presentation can be different and parts of the sales routine can be cut or adapted to suit the circumstances. Its best asset is that it is more likely to achieve a sale, because other elements of the marketing communications mix simply move the prospect towards the sale.

In recent years, the importance of selling in the overall marketing process has begun to increase once again. There are a number of reasons for this, but among the most significant has been the growth of relationship marketing, which we have encountered several times throughout the text so far and which we shall explore further both in this chapter, but in more detail in Chapter 13.

Clearly the primary role of the sales function is to help generate and make a sale. However, in so doing through the salesperson, the selling function performs the following range of activities and functions in the overall marketing effort:

- Salespersons perform an 'ambassadorial' role for the organization—they represent the image of the organization to its customers.

- Salespersons often play a key role in collecting information and opinions directly from customers and feeding this information back to the marketing department.

- Salespersons can help increase customer satisfaction by representing the customer's interests to the salesperson's company.

Personal selling often involves more than simply securing the customer's order, but obviously most selling is aimed at achieving this. Research has shown that the difference between the effective and ineffective salesperson can translate into as much as a tenfold difference in sales revenue and profits for the company. Despite all the important other roles for the salesperson and sales function in the organization then ultimately making a sale should be their overriding contribution to the success of the organization.

THE SELLING PROCESS

Although no sales interview follows a rigid pattern, it is useful to distinguish seven elements in the sales process:

1. The opening
2. Need identification and stimulation
3. The presentation
4. Dealing with objections
5. Negotiation
6. Closing the sale
7. The follow-up

The fragmentation of the selling process into these phases is helpful when training salespeople, since development of skills within each area can be worked upon until proficiency is achieved.

The opening

Experienced salespeople know the importance of initial impressions. Consequently, they pay great attention to their appearance, manner and opening remarks. Buyers expect salespeople to be businesslike in their personal appearance and behaviour. Untidy hair and unbuttoned shirts with loose ties can create a lack of confidence in a salesman. Further, the salesperson who does not respect the fact that the buyer is likely to be a busy person, with many demands on his or her time, may cause irritation on the part of the prospective buyer.

Opening remarks are important since they set the tone for the rest of the sales interview. Normally they should be business-related since this is the purpose of the visit; they should show the buyer that the salesperson is not about to waste time. Where the buyer is well known to the salesperson and where, by his or her own remarks, the buyer indicates a willingness to talk about a more social matter, the salesperson will obviously follow. This can generate close *rapport* with the buyers; but the salesperson must be aware of the reason for being there, and not be excessively diverted from talking business.

Need identification and stimulation

Customers buy products to meet needs and solve problems. Consequently, key factors in sales success are the identification of customer needs and problems, and in certain circumstances the recognition of a need or problem on the part of the buyer.

This 'needs analysis' approach suggests that early in the sales process the sales-person should adopt a question-and-listen posture. In order to encourage the buyer to discuss his or her problems and needs, salespeople tend to use 'open' rather than 'closed' questions. An open question is one that requires more than a one-word or one-phrase answer.

- 'Why do you believe that a computer system is inappropriate for your business?'
- 'What were the main reasons for buying the XYZ photocopier?'

A closed question, on the other hand, invites a one-word or one-phrase answer. These can be used to obtain purely factual information, but excessive use can hinder *rapport* and lead to an abrupt type of conversation which lacks flow. Examples of closed questions are:

- 'Would you tell me the name of the equipment you currently use?'
- 'Does your company manufacture 1000 cc marine engines?'

Salespeople should avoid the temptation of making a sales presentation without finding out the needs of their customers. It is all too easy to start a presentation in the same rigid way, perhaps by highlighting the current bargain of the week, without first enquiring about the customer's needs.

Need and problem stimulation are necessary when a prospect is happy with the *status quo* and does not recognize that the purchase of the salesperson's product or service could, for example, improve productivity, lower costs, or give greater financial security. In these cases, the sales task may involve the process of 'disturbing', whereby the salesperson *disturbs* the buyer's perception of life by showing, for example, how present methods are inefficient, or costly, or how present insurance cover is inadequate.

The presentation

The advantages conferred by carrying out a 'needs analysis' are realized during the presentation. The salesperson knows which product or brand, from the range of products or brands he or she is selling, best fits the customer's requirements, and is also aware of which benefits to stress.

The key to this task is to recognize that buyers purchase benefits and are only interested in product features inasmuch as they provide the benefits that the customer is looking for. Training programmes and personal preparation of salespeople should pay particular attention to deriving the customer benefits their products bestow.

Benefits should be analysed at two levels: those benefits that can be obtained by purchase of a particular type of product, and those that can be obtained by purchasing that product from a particular supplier. For example, automatic washing machine salespeople need to consider the benefits of an automatic washing machine compared with a twin-tub, as well as the benefits that their company's automatic washing machines have over competitors' models. This proffers maximum flexibility for the salesperson in meeting various sales situations.

Dealing with objections

Objections should not always be viewed with dismay by salespeople. Many objections are simply expressions of interest by the buyer. What the buyer is asking for is further information because he or she is interested in what the salesperson is saying. The problem is that he or she is not, as yet, convinced. Objections highlight the issues that are important to the buyer.

An example will illustrate these points. Suppose an industrial salesperson working for an adhesives' manufacturer is faced with the following objection: 'Why should I buy your new adhesive gun when my present method of applying adhesive—direct from the tube—is perfectly satisfactory?' This type of objection is clearly an expression of a desire for additional information. The salesperson's task is to provide it in a manner that does not antagonize the buyer and, yet, is convincing. It is a fact of human personality that the argument which is supported by the greater weight of evidence does not always win the day; people do not like to be proved wrong. The very act of changing a supplier may be resisted because it may imply criticism of a past decision on the part of the buyer. For a salesperson to disregard the emotional aspects of dealing with objections is to court disaster. The situation to be avoided is where the buyer 'digs his heels in' on principle, because of the attitude of the salesperson.

The effective approach for dealing with objections involves two courses of action: the preparation of convincing answers, and the development of a range of techniques for answering objections in a manner which permits the acceptance of these answers without loss of face on the part of the buyer. Two commonly used methods for dealing with objections are the 'agree and counter' and the 'forestalling' techniques.

Agree and counter   This approach maintains the respect the salesperson shows to the buyer. The salesperson first agrees that what the buyer is saying is sensible and reasonable, before putting forward an alternative point of view. It takes the edge off the objection and creates a climate of agreement rather than conflict. For example:

Buyer: The problem with your tractor is that it costs more than your competition.
Salesperson: Yes, the initial cost of the tractor is a little higher than competitors' models, but I should like to show you how, over the lifetime of the machine, ours works out to be far more economical.

Forestall the objection   Perhaps buyers are continually raising the objection that the salesperson is working for one of the smallest companies in the industry. One way of dealing with this objection is to forestall, by raising the objection as part of the sales presentation. This allows it to be dealt with effectively by changing the objection into a benefit. Thus, the salesperson may say, 'My company is smaller than most in the industry which means that we respond more quickly to our customers' needs and try that bit harder to make sure our customers are happy.'

Negotiation

Many salespeople are given some discretion regarding the terms of the sale. They may negotiate price, credit terms, trade-in values and delivery times. It is a fact of much commercial life that the profit realized from a transaction will be dependent upon the outcome of negotiations. Success in negotiating derives from two factors: preparation, and the application of negotiating skills.

Preparation   Before the parties to the negotiation meet, each should make careful preparations. This involves four factors: (1) assessment of the balance of power; (2) determination of objectives; (3) concession analysis; and (4) proposal analysis.

A seller's position will be strengthened if the buyer has very few options available to him or her, if the salesperson's products offer better solutions to the buyer's problems than the competition, and if the problem is of high importance and visibility to the buying organization. The salesperson should assess his or her position so that objectives can be set and the level of concessions to be given can be planned.

When setting objectives it is useful to consider two types: 'must have' and 'would like'. 'Must have' objectives are the minimum requirements of the deal, e.g. the lowest price at which a seller is willing to trade. 'Would like' objectives are the maximum a negotiator can realistically achieve. They define the opening positions of buyers and sellers.

Concessions analysis is vital to negotiating success as it allows calm consideration at what can be traded. A skilful negotiator will attempt to trade concession for concession so that ultimately an agreement which satisfies both parties is reached.

Proposal analysis involves determining the likely demands of the buyer, and the reactions to them. By this kind of anticipation, the seller can plan the kinds of counter-proposals he or she wishes to make, and thus avoid making mistakes in the heat of the negotiating battle.

Application at negotiating skills   Two basic principles of negotiation are: to start high but be realistic, and to trade concession for concession. Making the opening stance high has two benefits. First, the buyer might agree to it. Second, it provides room for negotiation if he or she does not agree. Indeed, a buyer may have become accustomed to concessions from the seller in return for purchasing. Trading concession for concession can be achieved by means of the 'if . . . then' technique.[2] For example, the seller might say, 'If you are willing to collect these goods at our premises, then I am prepared to reduce the price by £10.' This is a valuable tool at the disposal of the negotiator since it promotes movement towards agreement and yet ensures that proposals to give the buyer something are matched by proposals for a concession in return.

Closing the sale

Some salespeople are reluctant to close the sale because they fear rejection. Yet in many sales situations failure to close will mean the order being placed with a competitor. In other situations, often industrial, it is inappropriate to attempt to close the sale since the buying process is lengthy. However, when the time has come for the close to be made there are a number of techniques available. Two methods are: the summary close, and the concession close.

Summarize and then ask for order   This technique allows the salesperson to remind the buyer of the main points in the sales argument in a manner which implies that the moment for decision has come and that buying is the natural extension of the proceedings.

> Well, Mr Smith, we have agreed that the ZDXL4 model meets your requirements of low noise, high productivity and driver comfort at a cost that you can afford. May I go ahead and place an order for this model?

The concession close   This involves keeping one concession in reserve to use as the final push towards agreement: 'If you are willing to place an order now, I'm willing to offer an extra 2½ per cent discount.'

The follow-up

Immediately after closing the sale, the salesperson should 'tie up' any loose ends (e.g. delivery times). In addition, the salesperson should make an appointment for a follow-up call after the initial order has been received to make sure that everything is going according to plan and to deal with any unexpected problems.

Many products also require the provision of after-sales service. Some manufacturers rely on their dealers to provide after-sales service (e.g. the motor trade); the manufacturer in such cases should be satisfied that dealers are capable of providing the required level of service. For many products, after-sales service is an important element in the marketing mix and needs to be costed into the final selling price of the product.

SALES MANAGEMENT

The sales manager's job is particularly difficult because subordinates are usually geographically separated from him or her. This can produce problems of communication and control not experienced by a purchasing or financial manager whose staff are located within the same building. However, the key responsibilities of sales management are similar to other managerial positions:

1. Setting of sales objectives and strategies
2. Recruitment and selection of salespeople
3. Motivation
4. Organization
5. Training
6. Evaluation and control

Setting sales objectives and strategies

The sales manager is unlikely to be the only person involved in setting corporate sales objectives. Top management, marketing personnel and statisticians as well as sales managers may influence the level of the sales target for the forthcoming year. Once agreed, the performance targets for individual salespeople are likely to be set by sales management after consultation with the salespeople themselves. Performance targets may be set in terms of sales volume, call rates, profit margin achieved, numbers of new customers, etc. Sales strategy is the method by which objectives are achieved. For example, an increase in target sales may be achieved by the strategy of increasing calls to new customers, spending more time with existing customers or setting up a telesales team to give increased service to small customers. Sales management plays a key role in determining the most effective strategy to achieve corporate sales objectives.

Recruitment and selection of salespeople

The selection of salespeople, while of obvious importance to the long-term future of the business, is a task that does not always receive the attention it should from sales managers. All too often, the 'man profile' is ill-defined and the selection procedure designed for maximum convenience rather than optimal choice. The assumption is that the right person should emerge whatever procedure is used. Consequently, the interview is poorly handled, the smooth talker gets the job, and another mediocre salesperson emerges.

Two key aspects of recruitment and selection are the preparation of the job description, and personal specification and interviewing. A job description usually covers the following factors:

- The title of the job.

  Duties and responsibilities—the tasks that will be expected of the new recruit, e.g. selling, after-sales service, information feedback, and the range of products/markets/type of consumer with which he or she will be associated.

- The person to whom he or she will report.

  Technical requirements, e.g. the degree to which the salesperson needs to understand the technical aspects of the products to be sold.

- Location and geographical area to be covered.

- Degree of autonomy—the degree to which the salesperson will be able to control his or her own work programme.

Once generated, the job description will act as the blueprint for the personnel specification which outlines the type of applicant the company is seeking. The technical requirements of the job, for example, and the nature of the customers the salespeople will meet, will be factors that will influence the level of education and, possibly, the age of the required salesperson. A personnel specification may contain all or some of the following factors:

- Physical requirements, e.g. speech, appearance.
- Attainments, e.g. standard of education and qualifications; experience and successes.
- Aptitudes and qualities, e.g. ability to communicate; self-motivation.
- Disposition, e.g. maturity, sense of responsibility.
- Interests, e.g. degree to which interests are social; active or inactive.
- Personal circumstances, e.g. married, single, etc.

The factors chosen to define the personnel specification will be used as criteria of selection in the interview itself.

The objective of the interview is to enable interviewers to form a clear impression of the strengths and weaknesses of the candidates with respect to the selection criteria. Candidates should be encouraged to talk openly about themselves, but interviewers should take care to control the interview so that all relevant areas are covered. Otherwise a candidate may be allowed to talk about his strengths without due consideration of his weaknesses.

What happens at the beginning of the interview is crucial to subsequent events. The objective at this stage is to set the candidate at ease. Most interviewees are naturally anxious before the interview and when they first enter the interview setting. They may feel embarrassed or be worried about exposing weaknesses; they may feel inadequate and lack confidence; and above all, they may feel worried about rejection. This anxiety is compounded by the fact that the candidate may never have met the interviewers before and may thus be uncertain about how aggressive they will be, the degree of pressure that will be applied and the type of questions likely to be asked. Some sales managers may argue that the salesperson is likely to meet this situation out in the field and therefore needs to be able to deal with it without the use of anxiety-reducing techniques on the part of the interviewers. A valid response to this viewpoint is that the objective of the interview is to get to know the candidate in terms of the criteria laid down in the personnel specification, or 'man profile' as it is sometimes called. In order to do this, the interviewee must be encouraged to talk about him- or herself. If sales ability under stress is to be tested, role playing can be employed as part of the selection procedure.

Motivation

Motivation in theory Although motivation is dependent on each salesperson's individual needs and desires, a sales manager can influence motivation both positively and negatively by his or her actions and policies. Some people have the opinion that salespeople are motivated solely by money; and indeed, the type of compensation plan a firm adopts can be a factor in achieving enhanced performance. However, there are other job-related factors which can influence motivation. A major contribution in this area was made by Herzberg et al.[3]

Herzberg distinguished between factors that can cause dissatisfaction but cannot motivate (hygiene factors) and factors that can cause positive motivation. Hygiene factors included physical working conditions, security and interpersonal relationships. Directing managerial attention to these factors, postulated Herzberg, would bring motivation up to a 'theoretical zero' but would not result in positive motivation. If this was to be achieved, attention would have to be given to true motivators. These included the nature of the work itself, which allows the person to make some concrete achievement; the recognition of achievement; the responsibility exercised by the person; and the interest value of the work itself.

The inclusion of salary as a hygiene factor rather than as a motivator was subject to criticisms from sales managers whose experience led them to believe that commission paid to their salespeople was a powerful motivator in practice. Herzberg accommodated their view to some extent by arguing that increased salary through higher commission was a motivator through the automatic recognition it gave to sales achievement.

The salesperson is fortunate in that achievement is directly observable in terms of higher sales (except in 'missionary' selling, where orders are not taken—e.g. pharmaceuticals, beer and selling to specifiers). However, the degree of responsibility afforded to salespeople varies a great deal. Opportunities for giving a greater degree of responsibility to (and hence motivating) salespersons include giving authority to grant credit (up to a certain value), discretion to offer discounts, and handing over responsibility for calling frequencies to the salespeople.

Herzberg's theory has been well received, in general, by practitioners, although academics, especially Dessler,[4] have criticized it in terms of methodology and oversimplification. The theory has undoubtedly made a substantial contribution to the understanding of motivation at work, particularly in highlighting the importance of job content factors which had hitherto been badly neglected.

Other theorists, such as Maslow,[5] Vroom[6] and Likert,[7] have worked within the area of motivation. For an evaluation of their contribution, see Lancaster and Jobber,[8] who have given a detailed review.

Motivation in practice Three key elements in motivating salespeople in practice are the type of compensation plan adopted, the setting of sales targets, and manager–salesperson relationships.

Type of compensation plan   There are, basically, three types of compensation plan:

- Fixed salary
- Commission only
- Salary plus commission

Each will now be evaluated in terms of benefits and drawbacks to management and salespeople, with particular reference to motivation.

Fixed salary   This method of payment encourages sales personnel to consider all aspects of the selling function rather than just those that lead to a quick sales return. Salespeople who are paid on fixed salary are likely to be more willing to provide technical service and complete information feedback reports and to carry out prospecting than if they were paid solely by commission. The system provides security to the salesperson, who knows how much income he or she will receive each month, and it is relatively cheap to administer, since calculation of commissions and bonuses is not required.

The system also overcomes the problem of deciding how much commission to give to each salesperson when a complex buying decision is made by a number of DMU members who have been influenced by different salespeople, perhaps in different parts of the country. Wilson[9] cites the case of a sale of building materials to a local authority in Lancashire being the result of one salesman influencing an architect in London, another calling on the contractor in Norwich, and a third persuading the local authority itself.

However, the method does have a number of drawbacks. First, no direct financial incentive is provided for increasing sales (no profits). Second, high-performing salespeople may not be attracted, and holding on to them may be different using fixed salary since they may perceive the system as being unfair and may be tempted to apply for jobs where financial rewards are high for outstanding performers. Third, selling costs remain static in the short term when sales decrease; thus, the system does not provide the in-built flexibility provided by the other compensation systems.

Because of its inherent characteristics, this system is used primarily in industrial selling, where technical service is an important element in the selling task and the time necessary to conclude a sale may be long. It is particularly appropriate when the salesperson sells very high-value products at very low volumes. Under these conditions, a commission-based compensation scheme would lead to widely varying monthly income levels depending on when orders were placed.

Commission-only   The commission-only system of payment provides an obvious incentive to sell. However, since income is dependent on sales results, salespeople will be reluctant to spend time on tasks which they do not perceive as being directly related to sales. The result is that salespeople may pursue short-term goals, to the detriment of activities that may have an effect in the longer term; salespeople may be reluctant to write reports providing market information to management and to spend time out of the field attending sales training courses, for example.

The system provides little security for salespeople whose earnings may suffer through no fault of their own, and the pressure to sell may damage customer–salesperson relationships. This is particularly relevant to industrial selling, where the decision-making process may be long and where pressure applied by the salesperson to close the sale prematurely may be detrimental.

From management's perspective, the system not only has the advantage of directly financing costs automatically, but also allows some control over salespeople's activities through the use of higher commission rates on products and accounts in which management is particularly interested.

It is most often used in situations where there are a large number of potential customers, the buying process is relatively short, and technical assistance and service are not required. Insurance selling is an example where commission-only payments are often used.

Salary-plus-commission   This system attempts to combine the benefits of both the previous methods in order to provide financial incentives with a level of security. Since income is not solely dependent upon commission, management gains a greater degree of control over the salesperson's time than under the commission only system, and sales costs are, to some extent, related to revenue generated. The method is attractive to ambitious salespeople who wish to combine security with the capability of earning more by greater effort and ability. According to Donaldson,[10] 65 per cent of salesforces are remunerated on such a combination plan basis.

Clearly, managers who wish to use the incentive of extra money for good performance are going to choose commission-only or salary-plus-commission as their method of compensation. However, fixed salary schemes may be used where it is difficult to tie performance to individual salespeople's achievements, and where to do so may cause resentment and feelings of unfairness which may lead to demotivation.

Setting sales targets   A key feature of the commission-only or salary-plus-commission payment plan may be the determination of each salesperson's sales target or quota. If a sales target or quota is to be effective in motivating a salesperson, it must be regarded as fair and attainable and yet offer a challenge. Because the salesperson should regard the quota as fair, it is usually sensible to allow him or her to participate in the setting of the quota. However, the establishment of the quotas is ultimately the sales manager's responsibility, and he or she will inevitably be constrained by overall company objectives. If sales are planned to increase by 10 per cent, then salespeople's quotas must be consistent with this. Variations around this average figure will arise through the sales manager's knowledge of individual salespeople and changes in commercial activity within each territory; for example, the liquidation of a key customer in a territory may be reflected in a reduced quota. The attainment of a sales target usually results in some form of extra payment to the salesperson.

Sales manager–salesperson meetings   There are a number of ways in which meetings between the sales manager and his salespeople can lead to better motivation. First, they allow the sales manager to understand the personality, needs and problems of each salesperson. The manager can then better understand the causes of demotivation in individual salespeople and respond in a manner that takes into account the needs, problems and personality of the salesperson. Second, meetings in the field, which may form part of an evaluation and training programme, can also provide an opportunity to motivate. Sales technique can be improved and confidence boosted, both of which may motivate by restoring in the salesperson the belief that performance will improve through extra effort. Third, group meetings can motivate, according to Likert, when the sales manager encourages an 'open' style of meeting. Salespeople are encouraged to discuss their sales problems and opportunities so that the entire sales team benefits from the experience of each salesperson. This leads to a greater sense of group loyalty and improved performance. Finally, meetings between manager and salespeople provide the opportunity for performance feedback where weaknesses are identified and recognition for good work is given.

Organization

A major aspect of organizing a sales team is the decision regarding organizational structure. There are three basic alternatives: geographical, product-based and customer-based structures.

Geographical structure   An advantage of this form of organization is its simplicity. Each salesperson is assigned a territory over which he or she has sole responsibility for sales achievement. Their close geographical proximity to customers encourages the development of personal friendships which aids sales effectiveness. Also, compared with other organization forms, for example product or market specialization, travelling expenses are likely to be lower.

A potential weakness of the geographical structure is that the salesperson is required to sell the full range of the company's products. These may be very different technically and may sell into a number of diverse markets. In such a situation it may be unreasonable to expect the salesperson to have the required depth of technical knowledge for each product and to be conversant with the full range of potential applications within each market. This expertise can be developed only if the salesperson is given a more specialized role.

Product-based structure   One method of specialization is along product lines. Conditions that are conducive to this form of organization are where the company sells a wide range of technically complex and diverse products, and where key members of the decision-making unit of the buying organizations are different for each product group. However, if the company's products sell essentially to the same customers, problems of route duplication (and hence higher travel costs) and customer annoyance can arise. Inappropriate use of this method can lead to a customer being called upon by different salespersons representing the same company on the same day. When a company contemplates a move from the geographically based to a product-based structure, some customer overlap is inevitable; but, if only of a limited extent, the problem should be manageable.

Customer-based structures   Three customer-based methods of organization are the market-centred, the account size and the new/existing account structures.

Market-centred structure   Another method of specialization is by the type of market served. Often, in industrial selling, the market is defined by industry type. Thus, although the range of products sold is essentially the same, it might be sensible for a computer firm to allocate its salespeople on the basis of the industry served, e.g. banking, manufacturing companies, retailers, given that different industry groups have widely varying needs, problems and potential applications. Specialization by market served allows a salesperson to gain greater insights into these factors for his or her particular industry, as well as to monitor changes and trends within the industry which might affect demand for his or her products. The cost of increased customer knowledge is increased travel expenses compared with geographically determined territories.

Account size structure   Some companies structure their salesforce by account size. The importance of a few large customers in many trade and industrial markets has given rise to the establishment of a 'key account' salesforce. The team comprises senior salespeople who specialize in dealing with large customers who may have different buying habits and may demand more sophisticated sales arguments than smaller companies. The team will be conversant with negotiation skills since they are likely to be given a certain amount of discretion in terms of discounts, credit terms, etc., in order to secure large orders. The range of selling skills required is, therefore, wider than for the rest of the salesforce, who deal with the smaller accounts. Some organizations adopt a three-tier system with senior salespeople negotiating with national accounts, ordinary salespeople selling to medium-sized accounts, and a telephone sales team dealing with small accounts.

New/existing account structure A further method of sales organization is to create two teams of salespeople. The first team services existing accounts, while the second concentrates upon seeking new accounts. This structure recognizes that gaining new customers is a specialized activity, demanding prospecting skills, patience, the ability to accept higher rejection rates than when calling upon existing customers, and the time to cultivate new relationships. Placing this function in the hands of the regular salesforce may result in its neglect, since the salespeople may view it as time which could be better spent with existing customers. Pioneer salespeople were used successfully by trading stamp companies to prospect new customers. Once an account was obtained, it was handed over to a maintenance salesperson who serviced the account.

Training

Training should not be confined to new salespeople. Experienced salespeople require refresher training, which has the benefit of sharpening skills and stimulating thought on new ways of selling. A training programme usually has five components:

1. The company—objectives, policies and organization
2. Its products
3. Its competitors and their products
4. Selling procedure and techniques
5. Work organization and report preparation

The first three components are essentially communicating the required level of knowledge to the salesperson. The first component will probably include a brief history of the company, how it has grown and where it intends to go in the future. Policies relevant to the selling function, for example, how salespeople are evaluated, and the nature of the compensation system will be explained. The way in which the company is organized will be described and the relationship between sales and the marketing function, including advertising and market research, will be described so that the salesperson has an appreciation of the support he or she is receiving from headquarters.

The second component, product knowledge, will include a description of how the products are made and the implications for product quality and reliability, the features of the product and the benefits they confer on the consumer. Salespeople will be encouraged to carry out their own product analysis so that they will be able to identify key features and benefits of new products as they are launched. Competitors will be identified and competitors' products will also be analysed to spotlight differences between them and the company's products.

Some training programmes, particularly within the industrial selling area, stop here, neglecting a major component of a training programme—selling procedures and techniques. This component will include practical sessions where trainees develop skills through role-playing exercises. For experienced salespeople, sales skills will be developed by on-the-job training. They will be accompanied on sales visits by their sales manager who will highlight strengths and weaknesses and provide guidance as to improved performance.

The final component of the programme—work organization and report writing—will endeavour to establish good habits among the trainees in areas which, because of day-to-day pressures, may be neglected. The importance of these activities on a salesperson's performance, and hence earnings, will be stressed.

For new recruits to the salesforce, it is important that they are given a thorough programme of training before operating in the field on their own. It goes without saying that, if successful recruitment has taken place, the salesperson who gets the job will understand the role of selling in the economy in general and the company in particular. The salesperson should also possess communication skills, such as asking appropriate questions, listening and talking in the same 'language' as the customer.

In addition to these areas, formal training will be needed as follows:

- *Preparation*   The salesperson will have to know what aids will be needed prior to meeting the customer.

- *Prospecting*   The importance of new business should be emphasized and the salesperson should be given guidance on how it might be obtained.

- *Opening the sale*   On meeting the customer, it is important that the salesperson conveys the right initial impression.

- *Making sales presentations*   Effective persuasion resulting in a sale is the hallmark of a good salesperson. This will require skill in verbal presentation, handling of visual aids and demonstration of the product. It is suggested by Winkler[11] that this skill is best developed by use of video and video playback techniques.

- *Dealing with objections*   Customers can complain about a variety of issues, e.g. price, delivery. The salesperson should be trained in what to say and how to reply.

- *Closing the sale*   This is the most crucial and highly skilled part of a salesperson's job. Knowing how and when to close a sale is what differentiates a really good salesperson from an average one. The salesperson needs to be trained to recognize, when leading up to a close, both verbal and non-verbal cues from the potential buyer. If the salesperson attempts to close the sale too early, he or she may face an objection that has not been covered and may not have been prepared for. This can create a difficult situation to handle. If, however, the salesperson leaves the close of sale too late, he or she may well go on talking and may tell the buyer something unnecessary, and hence give reasons for a changing of mind. Learning how and when to close a sale is an art. Closing techniques can be taught, but experience has a large part to play also. The good salesperson needs the qualities of a diplomat, a negotiator and a psychologist.

- *Work organization*   The salesperson must be trained in the effective use of time through the use of journey planning and day planning.

After the initial training, field training is then conducted, and it is part of the role of the field sales manager to accompany the salesperson on a normal day's work to observe and offer sales back-up, but not to interfere. The field sales manager should afterwards advise the salesperson of their selling strengths and weaknesses. Once the new salesperson is deemed to be 'competent', there will be no need for the field sales manager to go along on every visit, and as the salesperson becomes still more experienced, so the need to accompany will diminish.

Evaluation and control

The prime reason for evaluation is to attempt to attain company objectives. By measuring actual performance against objectives, shortfalls can be identified and appropriate action taken to improve performance. However, evaluation has other benefits. Evaluation can help improve individual salespeople's motivation and skills. Motivation is affected, since an evaluation programme will identify what is expected of the individual, and what is considered good performance. Second, it provides the opportunity for the recognition of above-average standards of work performance, which improves confidence and motivation. Skills are affected since carefully constructed evaluation allows areas of weakness to be identified, and effort to be directed to the improvement of skills in those areas.

Although sales managers are interested in sales primarily as a percentage of quota or target, in practice a whole range of measures may be used—often for diagnostic purposes. Table 10.1 gives a summary of the more common quantitative measures.

In addition, salespeople may be evaluated on a number of qualitative dimensions. The most usual ones are:

● Sales skills

● Customer relationships

● Self-organization

● Product knowledge

● Cooperation and attitudes

For an evaluation and control system to work efficiently, it is important for the sales team to understand its purpose. To view it simply as a means for management to catch them out and criticize performance is likely to breed resentment. It should be used, and be perceived, as a means for assisting salespeople to improve performance, through

TABLE 10.1   *Quantitative measures of performance*

Sales	Orders
Sales revenue	Number of orders taken
Sales revenue as a percentage of quota	Order per call ratio
Sales revenue per order	Average order value
Sales revenue per call	Average profit contribution per order
Sales revenue from new accounts	
Accounts	*Calls*
Number of new accounts	Number of calls per period
Number of accounts lost	Calls on potential new accounts
Total number of accounts	Calls on existing accounts
Profit	*Expenses*
Gross profit	Sales expenses to sales revenue ratio
Net profit	Average expenses per call
Return on investment	Expenses per square mile of territory
Profit per call ratio	

integration with the company's sales training programme. Indeed, the quantitative output measures themselves can be used as a basis for rewarding performance when targets are met. This chapter has provided a checklist of measurements from which individual sales managers can select the most appropriate one for their particular situation. They are summarized in Table 10.1.

Such improvements in the sales evaluation and control system should result in enhanced effectiveness in the marketplace.

TERRITORY MANAGEMENT

Territories should be designed first of all with one basic principle in mind:

- The most effective form of contact

Perhaps five or six different salespersons from the same firm could be calling upon five or six different customers who are all located in the same area. They might even be calling at the same time. It may seem to be a wasteful use of manpower and expenses, but if the same contact is likely to be more effective by following such a policy, then it could be a profitable one.

The 'sales engineer'

Formulating or designing territories has developed into a highly complicated task. It is rarely sufficient to 'count the heads' and allocate according to population. Even with consumer goods, which may be consumed evenly throughout the country, such a technique is no longer valid. The factors that need to be taken into account are now so complex that some companies employ 'sales engineers'. These executives have nothing to do with engineering in the normally accepted sense of the word. Their task is to build territories and to make adjustments to them as situations change.

It is no accident that specialist organizations have developed which offer a service of designing territories by using sales 'bricks'. The sales brick is a geographical unit in which all the known buyers are listed. The bricks are generally roughly equal in sales potential. For example, one brick may contain 10 buyers of furniture and another brick may have 15. In such an example, the brick would have been calculated on the basis that the 10 buyers are, on average, slightly more important that the 15, but the total purchasing capacities are about the same.

Sales bricks can be constructed for almost every kind of industry. As the bricks are built up, they can be transferred in units from one territory to another. However, to design territories using the brick principle is a long and painstaking task, and not many companies can afford the time or expense to use this method.

Factors that determine territory design

There is an infinite number of factors, some of which are pragmatic and others of which may be personal. A salesperson may be allowed to visit another salesperson's territory and deal with a customer simply because it is known that they get on well together. Individual factors such as these cannot be legislated for but must be dealt with as they arise. Many companies encounter some such problems and try to meet them in the most practical way.

Some of the more practical factors are as follows:

- *Potential business*   An estimate needs to be made of the amount of business that is available in the territory. The estimate should be in two parts. The first should be total business and the second, the share which the company may expect to obtain.

- *Number of active customers*   Assuming the company is already doing business in the area, it should be possible to count the customers or to make an estimate of them. If the company only deals direct, then it will be a simple matter of counting them. If the goods are sold through wholesalers, an estimate or some research may be necessary. As well as the number of customers, it is also necessary to assess or calculate the amount of business they do.

- *Number of potential customers*   There will be potential buyers with whom the company is not yet dealing. The estimate should be realistic and it may be necessary to grade them; sometimes customers are 'registered' agents. If they are registered with competitors, it may not be possible to convert them. If they are 'free' agents, then they are, of course, open to offers. As with the known customers, an estimate should be made of the amount of business they handle.

- *Location of customers*   It is necessary to know not only how many and how important the customers and potential customers are, but also where they are located. The distribution of customers can provide headaches for territory planners.

- *Method of distribution*   Some goods are, by their nature, tied to distribution depots, and territories have to be engineered around these depots.

- *Sales situation*   A run-down area may require a salesperson to build it up; a well-developed area may require splitting because the existing salesperson has too much to do.

- *Frequency of call*   How often should the salesperson call? Much depends upon the buyer, the size of the territory and the ordering frequency. This needs to be associated with the acceptable stock levels that customers are prepared to carry.

- *Mixtures of trade*   When companies sell to several different trades, they may regard it as desirable for each salesperson to have a balanced mixture.

- *Identifiable boundaries*   The characteristics of the territory, whether delineated geographically or by trade classification, must be clearly defined so that each is recognizable by its salesperson and by his or her neighbouring colleagues. Disputes about territory boundaries are unnecessary and can lead to discord.

- *Economics of representation*   The most important factor in delineating territories is whether or not they will be economically viable. It is a common practice for the territory boundaries to be calculated roughly and for an estimate to be made of the likely business that will materialize. The salesperson's expenses are estimated, and the total cost of working the territory is then related to the anticipated turnover. Next, the profitability is calculated. Only then can a realistic assessment be made as to whether or not the new territory is likely to be worth while.

  In making such calculations, attention must be paid to the possible future growth of the territory. Most companies are prepared to tolerate a low level of profitability, or even a loss in the short term, if there is the possibility of long-term profits.

  Because of the high total costs of employing a sales representative, some companies, in the food trade in particular, use brokers to do their selling for them.

DEVELOPMENTS IN SELLING AND SALES MANAGEMENT

We have already suggested that selling is beginning to re-emerge as a central element in overall marketing strategy. This does not mean that selling is becoming more important as such, but a number of trends and developments are changing the nature of selling and sales management. Some of the more important developments include the following:

Key account management

Recent years have witnessed a growth of key account management (KAM) approaches to organizing the selling process. Many factors underpin this growth, but perhaps the key one is the trend towards centralized buying and a resulting shift in the balance of power towards the buyer. This is particularly the case in retail markets, but it is also occurring in industrial markets where industrial concentration is increasing. A good commonsense reason for the growth of KAM, however, is that it simply makes good sense to identify and concentrate on your key accounts. Key account selling means identifying and then focusing on key account customers. Such customers are given higher priority, or if you like special treatment. Key account selling requires the development of special selling and sales management skills. So, for example, key account selling places an increased emphasis on the consultative and ambassadorial roles of the salesperson. In addition, the salesperson must have much more frequent communication with key account customers giving them adequate levels of support to ensure that they remain loyal.

Telesales

Although essentially a form of direct marketing and therefore also part of the channel element of the marketing mix, telesales or to use the full term, 'telephone' selling, has been a major growth area of selling in recent years. Telesales can involve dealing with calls into the company or out to the customer. Like key account management, teleselling requires special skills and training. Some customers do resent unsolicited telesales calls, so effective targeting is important. There are also additional ethical and legal issues involved with this type of selling.

The Internet and new technology

Selling and sales management have not been untouched by developments in technology, and again the Internet is having perhaps the most important impact on this area of marketing. In one sense the Internet removes the need for personal selling. However, it is probably more positive to suggest that the Internet can potentially increase the efficiency of the personal selling process in as much as often the Internet or a website is the first port of call for a customer when considering purchasing a product or brand. This may be followed by a request for further information or even a visit from a salesperson.

In terms of sales management, new technology is facilitating greater control over salesforce activities in the field. The obvious examples are the use of mobile phone networks, e-mails through laptops, etc. Intranet technology, too, is affecting personal selling by allowing speedier and more flexible communication with sales staff. Used properly, Intranet technology can increase salesforce motivation and effectiveness in dealing with customers. Satellite and digital technology are enabling sales conferences to be held through video conferencing which can help considerably where sales staff are scattered globally. Finally, access to powerful and cheap computing power enables very rapid analysis of sales data and sales performance which can be fed through to head office from a modem operated by each salesperson at the end of the sales day.

Relationship marketing

Again, several times, we have mentioned the importance and the growth of relationship marketing and that a more detailed discussion of this development in marketing overall is contained in Chapter 13. In the context of this chapter, however, it is important to acknowledge that one of the most important areas of marketing that the notion of relationship concepts has affected is that of personal selling and sales management. In simple terms, which is sufficient for our purposes here, relationship marketing, remember, looks to develop close long-term relationships with marketing where both customers and suppliers are essentially loyal to each other. This seemingly unimportant shift in emphasis away from more conventional one-off transaction marketing in fact has very major implications for both the philosophy and practice of marketing. Again we would point out that these implications are considered in Chapter 13 where we shall see that very many facets of marketing are being affected by this shift towards relationship marketing, but there is no doubt whatsoever that one of the areas most affected by relationship marketing is that of selling and sales management. Lancaster and Massingham[12] suggest that the following represent some of the shifts in emphasis and approach in the selling process when a company moves towards a relationship marketing approach.

- The sales function is required to take a longer term perspective than that of simply making one-off sales when dealing with customers.
- Effective relationship selling requires much more of a team effort, not only between individual members of the salesforce, but between the salesperson and other functions in the supplying company.
- The salesperson must be proactive with customers, for example, calling or visiting customers at times other than when they think a customer is ready to place an order.
- The salesperson must act as a problem-solver for customers rather than just an order taker or even an order winner.
- The salesperson must act as an exchanger of information at the boundary between his or her own company and the customer.
- The emphasis must be much more on levels of customer service than low prices when attempting to generate sales.

All of this means that the skills and, perhaps more importantly, attitudes, required for successful selling changes with the adoption of a relationship marketing approach.

The relationship salesperson, for example, must be skilled at listening to customers and interpreting their problems. Job satisfaction—and in addition remuneration—must be geared much more to developing customer loyalty and trust rather than immediate sales revenue. The importance and impact of the growth of relationship marketing on selling is such that Kotler[13] suggests that the relationship approach is a major step in the evolution of the salesforce. There is certainly no doubt that relationship marketing is set to continue to change the nature of selling and sales management in organizations.

CHAPTER SUMMARY

This chapter has reviewed the selling and managerial skills necessary for efficient personal selling. The modern marketplace requires sales teams who can not only sell, but also negotiate terms and conditions that result in profitable orders. Sales managers must recognize the full extent of their managerial responsibilities, which include setting objectives and strategy recruitment and selection, motivation, organization, training and control.

The chapter has been written from the viewpoint of a company selling to customers, rather than buyers seeking out sellers. Particularly in industrial markets, the latter is often the case. Chapter 3 was concerned with 'marketing and customers', and buyer behaviour (consumer and organizational) was discussed there in some depth. It can therefore be appreciated that a study of buyer behaviour is an essential prerequisite to good selling, because the seller can then focus appropriate selling points on to the avowed and unavowed needs of buyers.

CHAPTER REVIEW QUESTIONS

1. Discuss the importance of 'needs analysis' within personal selling.
2. Outline the main stages in personal selling and discuss the techniques that can be used to achieve a sale.
3. What are the major functions of sales management? Discuss how the achievement of any *two* functions can be accomplished.
4. How can the links between motivation, training and evaluation lead to better sales performance?
5. It is not possible to motivate, only to demotivate. Discuss.
6. What are some of the key developments in selling and sales management, and what are some of the implications of these for the selling and sales management process?

References

1. J. Saunders, T. Hong-Chung and G. Lancaster, 'Traditional and modern views of personal selling', *Journal of Sales Management* (Monograph), **2** (1), 1985.
2. G. Kennedy, J. Benson and J. MacMillan, *Managing Negotiations*, Business Books, London, 1980.
3. F. Herzberg, B. Mausner and B. Block Snydeman, *The Motivation to Work*, John Wiley, New York, 1959.
4. G. Dessler, *Human Behaviour: Improving Performance at Work*, Prentice-Hall, Englewood Cliffs, NJ, 1979.
5. A. H. Maslow, 'A theory of human motivation', *Psychological Review*, July 1943.
6. V. H. Vroom, *Work and Motivation*, John Wiley, New York, 1964.

7. R. Likert, *New Patterns of Sales Management*, McGraw-Hill, London, 1961.
8. G. Lancaster and D. Jobber, *Selling and Sales Management*, 5th edn, Pitman, London, 2001.
9. M. Wilson, *Managing a Sales Force*, Gower Publishing, Aldershot, 1983.
10. B. Donaldson, *Sales Management: Theory and Practice*, Macmillan, London, 1990, p. 240.
11. J. Winkler, *Winning Sales and Marketing Tactics*, Heinemann, London, 1989, p. 242.
12. G. A. Lancaster and L. Massingham, *Marketing Management*, 3rd edn, McGraw-Hill, Maidenhead, 2001, p. 363.
13. P. Kotler, *Marketing Management: Analysis, Planning, Implementation and Control*, 9th edn, Prentice-Hall, NJ, 1997.

Lepton Mutual CASE STUDY

Lepton Mutual has been trading in the UK since 1932. Its products are principally insurance products encompassing a wide range of insurance services including automobile, life, personal, household and so on. In recent years, Lepton Mutual has concentrated on the personal accident field. Many of its major competitors have de-mutualized, but the company feels that it can offer a better service and return to its customers by not doing so.

Over the past five years, despite intense competition, the company has grown as measured by the revenue from premiums collected over the financial year. New sales in particular have steadily increased. However, over the past two years there has been a disturbing increase in the cancellations of existing policies.

Most policies are sold through the company's own salesforce calling on both business and household customers.

The task of the salesperson in the company is divided into three elements:

First, the salesperson is required to generate a pre-determined and agreed percentage of new business each year.

Second, the salesperson is required to service existing policyholders and in particular to ensure that annual policies are renewed.

Third, and again with regard to existing policyholders, the salesperson is required to attempt to upgrade existing policies, for example by persuading customers to increase their cover.

The company spends little on advertising, but does have some sales promotion. The salesforce rotates its coverage of territories on a six-monthly basis. Obviously then, customers see a representative twice a year where, of course, this can be arranged and agreed by the salesperson.

After relative stability the last two years have seen staff turnover in the salesforce treble to what it was. In fact the average length of employment of a newly appointed salesperson is now between five and six months. Thankfully there still remains, however, a core of long-serving members of the sales team who have long-standing relationships with their customers and who therefore generate most of the sales revenue.

Newly appointed members of the sales team spend two weeks in training to learn the standard sales presentation of the company and, regardless of previous experience, are taken through the stages in the sales process including, for example, how to open a sale, the presentation, dealing with objections, etc.

The company would like to encourage its salesforce to sell to larger businesses and to household customers through bank managers, solicitors and accountants, etc. Most new business is based on cold-calling by salespersons on individual homes and businesses. Salespersons are expected to generate their own leads for new business.

Salesforce remuneration is based on a 50 per cent split of commission and salary. Equal amounts of commission are paid irrespective of the source or nature of the sale, so, for example, equal commission is earned on renewals and upgrades compared to gaining new business. A problem for the sales manager has been in motivating the salesforce to spend as much time and energy in gaining new business as the energy they seem to spend in serving the old.

Questions

1. What factors might explain the high turnover of newly recruited sales staff in this company, and what can Lepton Mutual do to reduce this turnover?

2. How can Lepton Mutual encourage its salesforce to spend more time securing new business, what other marketing activities by the company can help to support this, and what additional training might be required for the salesforce?

Part Three

MARKETING PLANNING AND DECISION-MAKING

M

Chapter Eleven

SALES FORECASTING

LEARNING OBJECTIVES *This chapter will help you to:*

- understand the importance and role of sales forecasting in the marketing planning process;

- appreciate the different time horizons for sales forecasts;

- distinguish between the different techniques of sales forecasting and their uses and limitations.

INTRODUCTION

In this and the following chapter we are going to be looking at the preparation, implementation and control of marketing plans. Sometimes avoided by both marketing practitioner and student alike, the area of sales forecasting is often viewed as being overly technical and/or quantitative. However, an understanding and application of sales forecasting techniques is essential to the preparation, implementation and control processes in effective marketing planning. In fact, the sales forecast, as we shall see, constitutes the first step in the start of the marketing planning process.

FORECASTING AS THE START OF THE PLANNING PROCESS

Individual businesses are becoming more competitive in an increasingly complex and 'internationalized' environment. Competitive circumstances tend to change more quickly nowadays and strategic decisions become increasingly critical and binding.

Companies must be able not only to predict their sales, but also to plan for profits, cash flows, etc. The days are gone when companies could afford to have 'slack' in terms of working capital, labour force, raw materials and finished stocks. Such 'slack' is costly (with higher labour and interest rates), and plant and manpower must nowadays be utilized to its optimum capacity. Inefficient use of such resources is costly, and profit margins are such that a company that does not manage such resources in an efficient manner will be prey to its more efficient competitors.

Forecasting sales must thus be the starting point of the planning process as this is the 'act of giving advance warning for beneficial action to be taken'.[1]

The main problem that exists within many organizations is that forecasting has traditionally been seen as a function of the accountant for purposes of budget preparation for the budget period ahead (normally one year), and this is termed the medium-term forecast. Accountants, naturally, will not tend to over-estimate and they will tend to forecast on the prudent side. Figure 11.1 illustrates a hypothetical situation. In this situation one might be inclined to level the accusation of excessive conservatism against the accountant. However, at the end of the day the cost/management accountant is the one who must attempt to ensure that the organization does not over-spend in reaching its anticipated sales, and, in the absence of an intimate knowledge of what is happening in the marketplace, one can hardly blame the professional for adopting such a prudent approach.

The reality of this situation is that the market will probably grow as anticipated on the extrapolation, but the company cannot meet this growth totally because it is not prepared for it in terms of budget (e.g. there are not enough production facilities available to meet increased sales). The company will thus lose sales because it is not in a position to exploit the market. The irony of this situation is that, inevitably, production can most probably produce more than was budgeted for and sales can sell more than was budgeted for, so over-achieving on sales in this situation means that the exercise is often viewed as being successful on the basis that 'sales and production have done better than expected'! The fact that sales have in truth been lost is not considered.

One can postulate further and state that, if sales proceed better than 'likely sales based on trend', as shown in Fig. 11.1, then the capacity to lose sales will be increased even further. This leads to what McDonald calls a planning gap,[2] where action must be brought about to ensure that sales are not lost because production facilities and marketing resources are not available to meet potential demand.

We have thus established that the sales forecast is the start of the planning process and, for reasons just outlined, if the company is to achieve its maximum or optimum

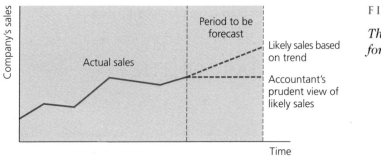

FIGURE 11.1

Theoretical view of a forecasting scenario

share of the market, then marketing must be the department that is responsible for the sales forecast. This fact is often not appreciated by many non-numerate marketing managers, and they are prepared to abrogate what is their direct responsibility to their more numerate colleagues in the finance department.

Once the situation relates to new markets or new products, it is inevitable that marketing must be involved. However, there can be a problem of what Clifton *et al.* refer to as self-protection and inertia.[3] This is where existing suppliers in a market will want to protect their own position and will tend to overstate the degree of competition and understate the market potential, when approached for information, in order to put off potential new entrants. Equally, inertia might rule inside the company, in that individuals within the firm might not want to extend themselves to addressing the problems of exploiting a new product or market. Needless to say, the problems to be overcome in this forecasting scenario rest with marketing analysts and not with cost accountants.

SENSITIVITY ANALYSIS

This is the technique of attempting to evaluate how changing various marketing inputs will affect sales. Forecasting sales for the market and the company can be done by a variety of techniques explained later in this chapter; but clearly, if, say, advertising or personal selling effort is reduced or increased during the period that has been forecasted, then sales will be affected. A forecaster, when forecasting company sales, does so with the advance knowledge that certain marketing mix inputs will take place. Manipulation of these inputs and a consequent assessment of the likely effect upon sales is known as 'sensitivity analysis'.

SHORT-, MEDIUM- AND LONG-TERM FORECASTS

Before we explain each of the above terms, it is perhaps appropriate to state that there are two methods by which forecasting data may be collected:

1. By making a forecast for the industry or total market and then determining what share of this will fall to the company (sometimes called a market forecast).

2. By forecasting sales direct using previous sales data or anticipating sales directly in some other way.

Usually the method used for market and then sales forecasts is termed a 'top-down' approach, in that the ultimate forecast is not obtained from an operational level in the organization. The opposite to this is termed 'bottom-up' forecasting, whereby the data are collected from the marketplace, usually by sales personnel who operate there. These methods are expanded upon in the next chapter.

Battersby produced one of the first UK written texts on forecasting[4] and he differentiated between short-term and long-term forecasts. He introduced medium-term forecasts as being akin to long-term forecasts, but concerned with minor strategic decisions. Since then, the purpose of medium-term forecasting has become far more important, largely because, as has already been elucidated, it is the start of the planning process.

Briefly, each type of forecast may be said to be for the following purposes:

- *Short term* (for up to approximately three months ahead)   Made largely for tactical reasons, e.g. to fulfil seasonal sales demands, for production planning purposes and cash flow requirements.

- *Medium term* (normally for one year ahead)   Made principally for business budgeting. This forecast is the starting-point of the company's planning process. It is also used for predicting manning levels required to achieve these anticipated sales and for plant and machinery requirements.

- *Long term* (5, 10 or 20 years ahead)   These forecasts are for major strategic decisions to be taken by the company. What is 'long term' is largely determined by the type of market in which the company operates. A self-evident example would be computers, where 'long term' is, say, less than five years, and steel production, where 'long term' may be 20 years. Long-term forecasts are used in areas such as management succession, company expansion and long-term financial planning requirements.

Before a company can plan, it must first forecast, as this reduces uncertainty. In this way, plans are based upon more scientific criteria. The problem is that, if the forecast is incorrect, or is based upon spurious premises, then the whole planning exercise will have been fruitless. The importance of accurate forecasts cannot therefore be emphasized enough. Companies can thus prepare for change by planning, in that the forecaster can predict what will happen for a set of decisions in a given set of circumstances. By taking certain actions, the planner can alter the subsequent events relating to a particular situation. A forecast may predict a fall in demand, and in this case management can make plans to counteract this fall in demand, or at least can plan to ensure that it suffers less from the fall in demand than do its competitors.

RELATIONSHIP BETWEEN FORECASTS AND BUDGETS

The forecast determines the budget, and through the sales budget sales are generated. The company sales budget is an amalgam of each individual salesperson's anticipated sales (their individual sales budgets), broken down in detail by product type, by territory and by selling area. Each individual salesperson then receives his or her share of the total sales budget which has to be sold in the period ahead, and this is then termed his or her individual sales quota or sales target.

A budget thus differs from a forecast in that the budget is what is planned to happen, unlike the forecast, which is a prediction of what is expected to happen. The forecast is, therefore, more uncertain as it is affected by external factors, whereas the budget is affected by more controllable internal factors.

One rather obvious, but sometimes ignored, fact is that the sales budget must be coordinated with other budgets within the organization. The sales budget, for instance, should not plan to achieve more sales than production has been budgeted to manufacture.

It must also be borne in mind that budgets should be flexible to allow for changing conditions or unforeseen circumstances. The budget can then be quickly changed to cover such contingencies.

TECHNIQUES OF FORECASTING

This section covers the specific techniques of sales forecasting, although not in sufficient detail to enable the reader to become a forecasting expert or specialist. For a more specialist text that starts from first principles, the reader is directed to *Forecasting for Sales and Materials Management*, by Lancaster and Lomas.[5]

Basically, sales forecasting is divided into qualitative and quantitative techniques. The first set are often called subjective or judgemental methods, as they rely heavily upon opinion in their computation. Quantitative techniques, as the term implies, rely upon mathematics, and such techniques are becoming very popular with the development of computer packages to assist in their application. Quantitative techniques can be split into time-series analysis and causal techniques. In time-series analysis, the variable that the forecaster considers is time and past events are used to predict the future. However, in applying such techniques, it is difficult to predict downturns or upturns, unless the forecaster deliberately manipulates the data. Such techniques are of little use in markets that are unstable or susceptible to sudden irrational changes. Causal techniques assume that there is a relationship between what is to be forecasted and some other measurable independent variable. The value of this independent variable is put into the equation and the forecast is produced from this. Importance must, therefore, be placed upon the choice of a suitable independent variable, and such variables should ideally precede what is to be forecast by a period sufficient to enable production and marketing plans to be implemented in good time. One should not attempt to establish the reasons behind such relationships, and there is often nothing to suppose that such relationships will hold good in the future. The fact is that a relationship has been established in the past, and part of the prediction is that it should probably hold good in the future.

It is logical to look at qualitative techniques first, because these are less scientific in their formulation; in fact, they are sometimes referred to as 'naive' methods. They often precede quantitative methods, and it is these latter that are now being taken increasingly seriously by progressive management, particularly as more sophisticated computational packages become available.

Qualitative techniques

Consumer/user survey method (market research method) This technique basically consists of asking one's customers about their likely purchases for the period it is desired to forecast and then attempting to ascertain what proportion of these anticipated purchases are likely to fall to one's company. It is quite often undertaken by the salesforce in the case of industrial products. Two problems thus arise: the accuracy of the apportionment of likely sales out of anticipated purchases; and the subjective opinion of buyers when giving their estimates to salespeople.

Sometimes it is not possible to ask customers through the salesforce, as is the case for consumer products because they are not usually sold direct to the general public. Here it makes sense to survey a sample of potential consumers through a market research survey (probably as part of an omnibus survey).[6] It is better to assess likely purchasing intentions on a graded answer basis, than on a straightforward dichotomous basis, particularly when the product is not a straightforward purchase. For instance, the decision to purchase a carpet is a complicated matter, and the purchaser goes through a number of different stages of purchasing intention before making the purchase—

unlike, say, the purchase of a can of baked beans, where the decision is far simpler, based upon more immediate needs.

The method is, therefore, quite straightforward, but it is really of most value when there are a small number of purchasers who are likely to signal their intentions to purchase with a reasonable degree of accuracy. Forecasters should also be familiar with competition in the marketplace in order that they can assess more accurately what proportion of likely sales will accrue to their company out of the assessment for the total market. Consequently, its true value tends to be limited to organizational buying situations where purchasers and competitors are few—a rarity for most buying/selling situations!

Panels of executive opinion (jury method) This method is sometimes known as 'panels of expert opinion' because such 'experts' are counselled about the industry with which they are familiar with the object of producing a forecast. Such experts come from both inside and outside the company, including management consultants, professional forecasters and investment analysts. Sometimes the panel or jury can include people from client companies who will be in a position to provide advice from a purchasing standpoint.

The group meets in committee, and the committee produces a composite forecast which might mean having to average the results in the case of disagreement. The basic precept is that each member of the group should have prepared a forecast beforehand and must be able to support this forecast with hard evidence. Such evidence should be presented to the group and discussed, with any inconsistencies being overcome as they arise. As long as agreement is reached after each discussion, a similar set of forecasts should result, because each will represent the majority view; but as was stated earlier, aggregation may be necessary.

'Prudent manager forecasting' is a variation of this approach, when company personnel are asked to assume the position of prospective purchasers and evaluate company sales from a customer's point of view and 'prudently' estimate sales, taking into consideration matters like competitors' products in terms of their design, quality, price, service, etc., together with any other external factors that are considered to be of relevance to evaluating the company's sales.

Much of this type of forecasting is based upon opinion, and can be expensive in terms of the manpower involved in its preparation and discussion. It is a 'top-down' method in that a forecast is produced for the industry and it must then be decided what share of this forecast will accrue to the company. Statistics are not collected from market data (from the 'bottom up'), and there is a problem in deciding what sales will be in terms of individual products and sales territories. Such information is needed for the budgeting procedure, as was explained in the previous chapter. Thus, it has been demonstrated that there are a number of in-built problems associated with this type of forecasting, particularly the fact that it is a 'top-down' method, unlike mathematical forecasting that uses market data.

Salesforce composite This 'bottom-up' method is sometimes referred to as the 'grass-roots' approach, because it entails each salesperson in the company making an individual forecast for his or her particular sales territory. These individual forecasts are agreed with the area manager, who then takes them to the sales manager (or the divisional manager, if this stage exists in the sales hierarchy). A similar exercise is then performed between the area/divisional manager and the sales manager until the figures are agreed.

This method is quite popular, particularly in the area of setting sales quotas or targets. There can be less cause for subsequent complaint, because such figures are based on information stemming initially from the salesforce. A slight variation of this method is called 'detecting differences in figures'. Here, the salesperson prepares the figures suitably broken down by individual customers and by individual products. The area manager then produces a similar set of figures independently, and they then meet and resolve any differences that arise. The process continues in similar vein until it reaches the sales manager, when the final sales forecast is agreed.

This appears to be a good method, and, in so far as non-mathematical methods are concerned, it probably is. It does, however, fall down when the forecast is to be used for future remuneration (as it invariably is, through quotas and targets). There will thus be an inclination on the part of salespeople to produce a pessimistic forecast. This can be overcome in part by linking sales expenses to the forecast. When remuneration is not linked to the sales forecast, there might then be a tendency for the salesforce to produce an optimistic forecast. It is well known that salespeople tend to be optimists, perhaps as a result of optimistic noises made by buyers, all being part of good buyer–seller relationships. The salesforce might not, therefore, be an objective enough starting-point for sales forecasting and might produce an optimistically or pessimistically biased forecast for the reasons stated. In addition, the salesforce is not necessarily aware of the more global economic factors that might affect future sales, and may not take these into consideration when preparing forecasts.

Delphi method   In this method the project leader selects the team and communicates through the post or telephone, but not in committee. He or she sends a questionnaire to members of the team (who may number 20 upwards) and they are asked to respond to questions of a behavioural nature to begin with. Such questions usually concern matters in the nature of a technological breakthrough—e.g. new processes for oil refining, new uses for glass products—that have some bearing on the products that the company makes. The answers are then collected and refined and a summary of the answers is sent out with the next round of questionnaires. This time the questioning can be more pointed, focusing on such matters as: 'If the new processes for oil refining, as predicted from the results of the first round of questionnaires, can be in production by 2005, how can this company benefit?' The rounds of questioning continue, becoming more specific each time, until sufficient useful information is to hand to make marketing and production decisions.

Because the information is not generated in committee, the danger of bandwagon effect of majority opinion is eliminated. However, this method cannot be recommended for the production of a product-by-product and customer-by-customer forecast, because it is more concerned with 'futures', and is really of value only for long-term matters like the viability of the company entering a market, or developing some new form of product or process for the future.

Bayesian decision theory   This method owes its origin to an English cleric of the eighteenth century, but its workings have been refined by statisticians since that date. It is a mixture of subjective and objective material. Its detailed operation cannot be described here, and the reader is directed to more specific texts, like those described at the beginning of this chapter, for a fuller insight into its workings.

A network diagram is used, similar to critical path analysis. Probabilities are estimated by the forecaster for each event in the network. The probabilities thus represent the strength of the decision-maker's feeling regarding the likelihood of the occurrence of the various elements in the network. When making business decisions, one has to decide among alternatives by taking into account the monetary repercussions of actions taken. When one has to select among alternative investments, consideration must be given to the profit and loss situation that might result from each alternative. When applying Bayesian decision theory, this involves selecting an alternative and having a reasonable idea of the economic consequences of choosing that action.

Once the appropriate future events have been identified, and the respective subjective prior probabilities have been assigned, the decision-maker works out the expected payoff for each act and chooses the act with the most attractive payoff.

Generating the probabilities described above is a subjective business, and for this reason many forecasters reject the Bayesian approach. However, it can be useful in solving business problems for which probabilities are often unknown.

Product testing and test marketing   These methods are of most use when little or no previous sales data exist. In such instances it makes sense to anticipate likely demand for the product by testing it on a sample of the potential market beforehand.

The techniques of product testing and test marketing have already been described in Chapter 5. Since product testing involves only a small number of respondents and a summation of their opinions and attitudes towards a new or modified product, test marketing would appear to be the most appropriate medium for producing a sales forecast. Here the product is launched in a limited geographical area and one is thus able to simulate a national launch without committing too many resources in case the product is unsuccessful. Sales are measured during the test and are simply grossed up afterwards to provide a forecast.

The main drawback is that this technique is suitable only for new or substantially modified products of a consumer goods nature. There is also the problem of 'novelty', in that if the unit value is relatively small many people will purchase just to try it out and may never purchase again, which might lead one to produce an optimistic forecast for the national launch. It must also be remembered that it has been known for competitors to attempt deliberately to spoil a test marketing campaign by increasing their promotional activity in the relevant area over the test period.

Quantitative techniques (time series)

Moving averages   This is a very simple technique that smoothes the data in a time series. The longer the moving average, the greater will be the smoothing, and the principle is that one subtracts the earliest sales figure and then adds the latest sales figure. This figure is then divided by the appropriate number of data periods that have been added together to bring it back to an average. The example that follows provides the best explanation, where it can be seen that a longer moving average produces a smoother trend than a shorter moving average. The first moving average is for a three-year period, whereas the second moving average is over a six-year period and it is this one that provides the smoothest pattern of data.

The forecast is produced by extending the trend line, and it is up to the forecaster to decide whether three-year or six-year averaging is better. In the case of a steady trend, it may not be necessary to smooth the data, and in such cases the process is simply called 'trend projection'. As a rule, the more the data fluctuate, the greater will the averaging period have to be. It is, of course, up to the forecaster to decide what averaging period to use: three years and six years have been used in the example in Table 11.1 for reasons of illustration.

In this particular example it can be seen that the three-year moving average would have been enough to provide a trend for purposes of forecasting, and even a two-year moving average would have sufficed. Longer moving-average periods are of more value to the forecaster when the data fluctuate a great deal. The graph in Fig. 11.2 illustrates this point.

Exponential smoothing   A major drawback with the moving-averages technique is that it does not respond immediately to a sudden change in sales, and if the sales trend changes it will take one or more periods before the trend is apparent in the forecast. (The longer the moving average, the longer it will take to reflect the change.) Exponential smoothing helps to overcome this by the apportionment of different weightings to earlier or later parts of the data. The skill lies in how the forecaster judges earlier or later parts of the time series to be more or less typical of the future.

The technique is relatively simple to operate, but it is essentially a technique that needs computer application, particularly if the forecaster is going to 'manipulate' the data to produce a number of different forecasts. The more precise mathematics of the technique cannot be entered into here, and the reader is again pointed to one of the more specialist forecasting or statistical texts mentioned earlier for a more detailed insight.

The technique is best illustrated by reference to the example in Fig. 11.2, annual sales of double-sized duvets for Werman Duvet Company Ltd. The sales are reproduced in Fig. 11.3, and from this it can be seen that weightings have been applied to earlier and later parts of the time series, according to how the forecaster viewed their typicality of how they would reflect the pattern for the future. In this particular example, the

TABLE 11.1   *Practical example of moving averages technique. Werman Duvet Company Ltd: annual unit sales of double-sized duvets, 1987–2002*

Year	Number	Three years		Six years	
		Total	Average	Total	Average
1987	925				
1988	1023	3111	1037		
1989	1163	3886	1295		
1990	1700	4508	1503	8 030	1338
1991	1645	4919	1640	9 101	1517
1992	1574	5215	1738	10 510	1752
1993	1996	6002	2001	11 446	1908
1994	2432	6527	2176	11 924	1987
1995	2099	6709	2236	12 549	2092
1996	2178	6547	2182	13 356	2226
1997	2270	6829	2276	13 605	2268
1998	2381	6896	2299	13 604	2267
1999	2245	7057	2352	14 007	2334
2000	2431	7178	2393	14 156	2359
2001	2502	7260	2420		
2002	2327				

forecaster has a pessimistic view of the future and has apportioned a greater weighting to the downwards parts of the series and less to the upwards parts. Such weightings will produce a downward trend as the forecast, unlike the moving-average example, which produced a flattening yet still increasing trend (see Fig. 11.2).

Time-series analysis   The sales figures over a time period will fluctuate, but beneath this is a trend which the forecaster needs to know in order to apply his forecast. This fluctuation is particularly prevalent when the data contain seasonal figures or cyclical material. Bringing these seasonal or cyclical data down to a trend is called the purgative process. This technique, therefore, is of most use when there is a seasonal pattern that is repeated on a regular basis. The time-series analysis technique analyses these seasonal movements in terms of their deviations from the average trend and then adds them back into the forecast once the trend line has been extrapolated.

Using the Werman Duvet Company's quarterly sales figures over the past five years best describes how the technique works in practice. Sales are given quarterly, and it can be seen that for a product like duvets, the sales fluctuate on a seasonal basis throughout the year, as one would expect. Unit sales are added for the four quarters to produce one year's data. The oldest quarterly period is then subtracted and the newest quarterly period added until the last quarter is reached. The next column adds two years' data, subtracting the oldest and adding the newest. The figure is then divided by 8 to discover the trend (because this contains four quarters over each of two years). Finally, deviations from the trend are calculated by subtracting the trend from the actual sales, or the actual sales from the trend, to produce a positive or negative figure in the form of deviations from the trend.

Table 11.2 gives the quarterly figures for sales of duvets for Werman Duvet Company Ltd and the appropriate calculations to provide the deviations from trend. It can be seen that when the quarterly deviations are totalled there is a positive sum of 21 remaining. The sum should equal zero, otherwise there will be a positive bias in the

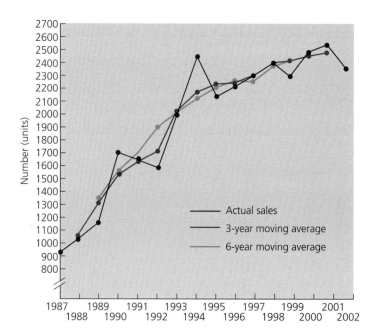

FIGURE 11.2

Werman Duvet Company Ltd: annual sales of double-sized duvets

forecast. The sum comes equally off each quarter's figures (i.e. in this case five from three of the quarters and six from the other quarter, because to fractionalize the amounts exactly would give the forecast a spurious accuracy). In this example we have added four years' data, so the corrected deviations totals will have to be divided by 4 to bring them back to the correct average deviations. The result is as follows:

Quarter	1	2	3	4	
Deviations	−68	−207	−212	+487	= 0

Again, for reasons stated earlier, the sum of the deviations should equal zero.

The graph can now be drawn which will include the actual sales and trend line. From this, the trend line can be extrapolated. Following this, the deviations from trend should be added in as appropriate to produce the seasonal forecast which is then entered into the sales forecast. Figure 11.4 shows this information graphically.

In this particular case, the forecaster has predicted that the downward trend will continue for a short period and then turn upwards. This is where the skill of the forecaster comes in. Information for such a prediction can come from a variety of sources internal and external to the company. In fact, it is possible to apply some of the qualitative techniques described earlier, which are of more value in attempting to ascertain general trend patterns, particularly 'panels of executive opinion' and the 'Delphi' method.

Figure 11.4 shows quarterly sales and the trend line. The trend line has been extended to produce a forecast trend, and the deviations from trend have been entered onto this trend to produce an actual forecast as shown in Table 11.3.

The first two figures for 2002 quarters 3 and 4 have been given as a forecast, but these have passed, so they cannot be entered into the graph. Figure 11.4 actually

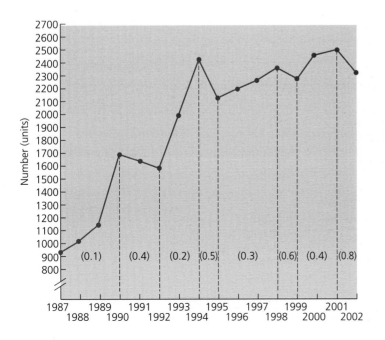

FIGURE 11.3

Werman Duvet Company Ltd: annual sales of double-sized duvets (Note: figures in brackets represent weightings)

produces a forecast for the four quarters of 2003 and it could, of course, have been extended further by extending the trend line and then applying the deviations from the trend.

The technique has much to commend it where there is a seasonality element in previous data. However, there must be an element of subjectivity in the extension of the

TABLE 11.2   *Werman Duvet Company Ltd: quarterly sales of double-sized duvets, 1998 (1)–2002 (4)*

Year	Quarter	Unit sales	Quarterly moving total	Sum of pairs	÷8 to final trend	Deviations from trend
1998	1	542				
	2	368				
	3	334	2381	4789	599	−265
	4	1137	2408	4825	603	+534
1999	1	569	2417	4848	606	−37
	2	377	2431	4676	585	−208
	3	348	2245	4441	555	−207
	4	951	2196	4417	552	+399
2000	1	520	2221	4482	560	−40
	2	402	2261	4692	586	−184
	3	388	2431	4857	607	−219
	4	1121	2426	4818	602	+519
2001	1	515	2392	4874	609	−94
	2	368	2482	4984	623	−255
	3	478	2502	5028	629	−151
	4	1141	2526	5108	638	+503
2002	1	539	2582	5075	634	−95
	2	424	2493	4820	603	−179
	3	389	2327			
	4	975				

Sum of quarterly deviations from trend, 1998–2002

Quarter	1	2	3	4	
Year					
1998			−265	+534	
1999	−37	−208	−207	+399	
2000	−40	−184	−219	+519	
2001	−94	−255	−151	+503	
2002	−95	−179			
Totals	−266	−826	−842	+1955	= +21
Corrected deviations	−271	−831	−847	+1949	= 0

trend line, and it is here that the forecaster must take most care, and apply a soundly thought-out forecast rather than merely extrapolating the general trend.

'Z' charts   'Z' or Zee charts only provide one year's data. For forecasting purposes, the forecaster must prepare a number of these from previous years and then compare them (usually merely by sight) to see whether there are any general patterns of trend that are repeated, so that a prediction can be made for the future. The technique is thus rather subjective, and its true value probably lies in the preparation of sales data, rather than as a serious medium for forecasting.

   Data for two years are needed in order to produce a 'Z' chart and each line of the 'Z' represents previous sales in a different format. The bottom line is the monthly sales, the diagonal line is the cumulative sales and the top line is the moving annual total

TABLE 11.3   *Werman Duvet Company Ltd—Forecast*

Year	Period	Trend	Deviation	Forecast
2002	3	565	−212	353
	4	540	+487	1027
2003	1	600	−68	532
	2	680	−207	473
	3	685	−212	473
	4	690	+487	1177

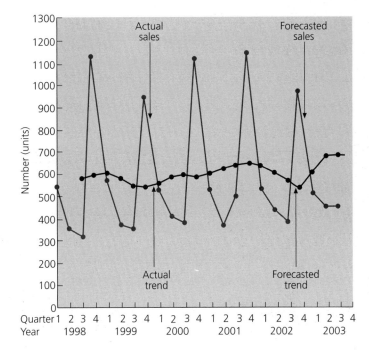

FIGURE 11.4

Werman Duvet Company Ltd: quarterly sales of double-sized duvets

(calculated by taking off the figure 12 months ago and adding on the new month's figure). The technique is best explained by practical example from the monthly sales of Werman Duvet Company for 2001 and 2002, and this is illustrated in Table 11.4 and Fig. 11.5.

Quantitative techniques (causal)

Leading indicator   This method uses the technique of linear regression to establish a relationship between an established measurable observation and what has to be forecasted. Linear regression and its antecedent correlation are described more fully in Rodger's text.[7] Basically, Rodger states that it is possible to infer the existence of correlation (or interrelationship) between two sets of data from the visual inspection of these data on a diagram. One axis measures one set of criteria and the other measures another set. If the measurements come close together in a more or less straight line, the correlation is said to be linear, and there is then a close relationship between the two sets of data. Naturally, for forecasting purposes, if one knows in advance what the data are on one axis, then it is a simple matter to predict what the data will be on the other axis.

However, in real-life forecasting situations matters are not as easy as those just described, and in all probability the relationship between the two sets of data will be only approximately linear. We must, therefore, calculate the 'line of best fit' that runs through the data. This line is called the *line of regression*, and it describes in

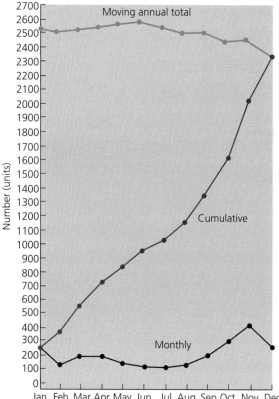

FIGURE 11.5

Werman Duvet Company Ltd: monthly sales of double-sized duvets

quantitative terms the underlying relationship or correlation between the two sets of data.

The technique needs a computer in its application, and there are a number of statistical packages available through which the technique can be used. The following simple illustration describes how the method can be applied:

> The sale of children's clothes will depend upon the size of the child population. Therefore, a clothes manufacturer would use birth statistics as a leading indicator. The number of years that the indicator can precede the forecast, and for which sex of child, depends on the age range and the sex of clothing that the manufacturer caters for.

This is called *leading indicator forecasting* because the indicator precedes the forecast, but it is of course an over-simplification of how the method operates. Forecasting packages are available that combine a number of leading indicators and then provide a permutation of indicators that best fit known previous sales. It may well be that there is no logical reason why the permutation of a number of indicators relates to previous sales statistics. Such a permutation should be constantly under review as time passes the forecasted sales turn into actual sales. The permutation is then modified to take account of the most recent sales.

Simulation   This is a technique that relies heavily upon the computer. It has already been explained that leading indicator forecasting seeks to establish a relationship between something that is measurable and the subject that is to be forecasted. Simulation uses trial and error (or iteration) in arriving at the forecasting relationship.

In a complicated forecasting situation the number of possible outcomes of possibilities is very large. The probabilities of various outcomes can, however, be estimated. This is known as '*Monte Carlo simulation*' (the obvious link being gambling on

T A B L E 11.4   *Werman Duvet Company Ltd: monthly sales of double-sized duvets, 2001–2002*

Month	Unit sales 2001	Unit sales 2002	Cumulative sales, 2002	Moving annual total
Jan.	216	240	240	2526
Feb.	136	122	362	2512
Mar.	163	177	539	2526
Apr.	149	179	718	2556
May	121	135	853	2570
Jun.	98	110	963	2582
Jul.	161	103	1066	2524
Aug.	141	111	1177	2494
Sept.	176	175	1352	2493
Oct.	328	294	1646	2459
Nov.	404	412	2058	2467
Dec.	409	269	2327	2327

estimated probabilities). It depends upon a predetermined chance of a particular event occurring.

The technique is difficult to explain any further without going into complicated discussion and explanations. The reader is again pointed to Rodger's text for a more in-depth explanation than the one provided in this more basic marketing text.[8]

Diffusion models Lancaster and Wright have already provided a forecast of the video market using this technique.[9] In keeping with other causal techniques, the mathematics are complicated, and the reader should seek more specialist help before attempting to apply such methodology. The following explanation attempts to describe the thinking behind the process.

The techniques that have been explained so far have depended upon a series of past sales from the company or the industry to produce the forecast. When totally new products come onto the market there are no past sales to draw upon, and we must then rely on the application of theory called 'the diffusion of innovations'. This theory is discussed more fully in the next chapter, which deals with the product (or service), but it is appropriate to introduce it briefly here in order to describe this technique.

Diffusion theory assumes that new products have four basic elements:

1. The innovation
2. The communication of this innovation among individuals
3. The social system
4. Time

Innovations can be categorized into the following groupings:

- Continuous
- Dynamically continuous
- Discontinuous

These groupings are a hierarchical listing, with the innovations being more widely removed from previous technology as one moves further down the listing. This leads to a lower degree of likely acceptance of the innovation the further down the list the innovation is placed. In the early stages of a product innovation, knowledge must be communicated to as many potential customers as possible, particularly those who are likely to be influential in gaining wider appeal for the innovation. This process of communication is broken down into formal and informal communication. These two elements are fed into the forecasting model. As such, the model can be applied without large amounts of past sales data. The formal communication is controlled by the company and includes such data as advertising expenditure and sales support for the launch. The informal element relates to such matters as family and reference group influences.

After the innovation has been launched onto the market, a measure of the rate of adoption is needed in order to produce a useful forecast. Products are born, they mature and they die. It is important to the forecaster using this technique that the first few points of the launch sales are known in order to be able to determine the rate of adoption. The forecast can then be made using only a small amount of data points covering the early launch period. The assumption is made that the product has a life-cycle curve and that new product acceptance is through a process of imitation in that later purchasers will follow the innovators. The technique also provides a forecast of first-time users and not repeat purchasers.

MISCELLANEOUS

There are a number of further forecasting techniques, such as Box-Jenkins, spectral analysis and X-11, that are very specialized and sophisticated in their application. They are used only in rarefied circumstances, and to attempt an explanation here would perhaps imply that their importance is greater than is really the case. It is sufficient to say that they have been mentioned, and the reader should consider them only if a depth study of sales forecasting is to be undertaken. A more detailed view of these techniques, together with the part that forecasting plays in marketing planning, is provided by Lancaster and Massingham.[10]

CHAPTER SUMMARY

The sales forecast precedes planning, and such plans are needed so that management can organize its activities in an ordered manner. Increasing competition means that businesses have to be more competitive, and this means making a more scientific approach to planning. Such an approach is through better sales forecasting.

Forecasting techniques have been split into qualitative techniques and quantitative techniques, with the latter being divided into time-series analysis and causal techniques.

Qualitative techniques have included: consumer/user survey methods, panels of executive opinion, salesforce composite, Delphi method, Bayesian decision theory and product testing and test marketing. Quantitative techniques (time series) have covered: moving averages, exponential smoothing, time-series analysis and 'Z' charts. Quantitative techniques (causal) have included: leading indicator, simulation and diffusion models.

Now that the market has been researched and forecasted, it is possible to proceed with the preparation of the marketing plan: this is the subject of the next chapter.

CHAPTER REVIEW QUESTIONS

1. As an information flow from the market to the firm, how important is sales forecasting for marketing? Why should such forecasting be the responsibility of marketing as opposed to finance?

2. Distinguish between qualitative and quantitative forecasting methods. State the advantages and drawbacks associated with each.

3. What is the relationship between the sales forecast and the sales budget?

4. How does a market forecast differ from a company forecast? How does a 'top-down' method differ from a 'bottom-up' method?

5. For a company of your choice in an industry of your choice (preferably ones with which you are in some way familiar), justify the forecasting methodology you would undertake in providing:

   a. Medium-term forecasts.
   b. Long-term forecasts.

References

1. G. A. Lancaster and R. A. Lomas, *Forecasting for Sales and Materials Management*, Macmillan, London, 1985, p. 1.
2. M. McDonald, *Marketing Plans: How to Prepare Them*, Heinemann, London, 1990.
3. P. Clifton, H. Nguyer and S. Nutt, *Marketing Analysis and Forecasting*, Heinemann, London, 1985, p. 33.
4. A. Battersby, *Sales Forecasting*, Cassell, London, 1968, p. 7.
5. Lancaster and Lomas, op. cit.
6. This has been covered in Chapter 5, and it is where a company can purchase market research questions on a questionnaire shared with questions purchased by other companies. Costs are thus reduced, because it is unlikely that such questioning will take up more than one or two questions, for which it would not be worth mounting an individual survey.
7. L. W. Rodger, *Statistics for Marketing*, McGraw-Hill, London, 1984, pp. 122–32.
8. Rodger, op. cit., pp. 228–36.
9. G. A. Lancaster and G. Wright, 'Forecasting the future of video using a diffusion model', *European Journal of Marketing*, **17** (2), 1983, pp. 70–9.
10. G. A. Lancaster and L. C. Massingham, *Marketing Management*, 3rd edn, McGraw-Hill, London, 2001, p. 331.

Townends Teeth

CASE STUDY

Townends Teeth is a company supplying local dentists with dental and associated products. For example, they supply materials for fillings and bridges, dentures, crowns, usable materials such as gauze and so on.

The company's customers are dental practices within an approximately 100 mile radius encompassing most dental practices in West Yorkshire where the company is based. The company has several competitors, some of which are multinational operations.

Customers, i.e. dental practices order their products according to demand. In other words, they do not hold stock. In large measure, this is because they are unsure on any weekly basis of just what they will require, but, more importantly, because many of the products have to be made and supplied to specific individual customer orders and requirements as you would expect for products of this kind.

Because of this, one of the problems that Townends Teeth has is in determining what stock to hold of products at any one time. Again, for obvious reasons dentists will not wait weeks and weeks for products to be delivered into Townends warehouses before delivery to their dental practices. Recently Townends has had severe problems with out-of-stock situations because they have been unable to anticipate or forecast demand.

Bob Townend, one of the joint family owners of the company, is responsible for sales and associated activities such as invoicing, delivery, etc. He has decided that the company needs a good sales forecasting system, but is unsure how to proceed in this respect.

Questions

1. What would be the benefits to a company like Townends Teeth of introducing a sales forecasting system?

2. Advise Bob on the range of sales forecasting techniques which the company might use.

Chapter Twelve

MARKETING PLANNING: COMBINING THE MARKETING MIX

LEARNING OBJECTIVES *This chapter will help you to:*

- understand the process and importance of marketing planning

- appreciate the key steps and decisions in the marketing planning process;

- understand some of the key models and techniques used in contemporary marketing planning;

- understand the practical combination of the marketing mix to meet the needs of different target segments including industrial, fast-moving consumer goods, services, small- and medium-sized enterprises and not-for-profit markets.

INTRODUCTION

In this chapter we shall examine the process of marketing planning. In fact, this also includes the organizing, directing and controlling aspects of marketing management activities which all managers, irrespective of the functional specialism in which they spend their working lives, have to perform. We shall start by looking at the nature of the marketing planning process including its link to overall corporate strategic planning. We shall look at the all-important business mission and move through the marketing audit and SWOT analysis to the setting of objectives, strategy identification and selection, and finally the management of the marketing mix. As regards the marketing mix, we shall look at how the marketing setting affects the practical application of the marketing mix including how the marketing mix differs throughout the product life cycle and how the mix is combined and modified to meet the needs of different target segments. We shall also introduce some of the key techniques of strategy appraisal and selection, but the more advanced of these techniques are included as an appendix for the reader who needs more detail on these techniques (see Appendix 1). Controlling and evaluating marketing plans is also an important element of the planning process, we therefore need to consider the main areas of strategic marketing evaluation. Finally, we will consider the people managing aspects of the marketing plan. Marketing managers after all, like other managers, normally rely on getting things done through people. To be effective, the marketing manager must be aware of the importance of managing the human assets under his, or her control. This involves careful selection, training, motivation and leadership of marketing personnel.

As we work through the key steps in the planning process you will note that we shall be re-introducing some of the areas and activities covered in earlier chapters. So, for example, we shall be showing how segmentation targeting (Chapter 4) links in with the marketing plan. Similarly, we shall be considering the analysis of the marketing environment (Chapter 2) in the marketing plan. Even where some of the areas covered in earlier chapters are not explicitly covered again, aspects such as understanding the behaviour of customers (Chapter 3) or the need for effective market research and marketing information (Chapter 5) obviously are key inputs and techniques to the marketing planning process. This is as it should be. After all, the marketing plan incorporates all the techniques and tools of marketing. Hopefully, you will see how the areas you have already studied now come together as a whole.

PLANNING AND MARKETING MANAGEMENT

There is little doubt that the main activity and responsibility of any manager is that of planning. The marketing manager must therefore use all the tools and techniques at his or her disposal to develop effective plans for the marketing activities of the organization. Marketing planning is no different to other areas of management planning in that it involves a series of iterative steps which require marketing management to *set objectives ('Where do we want to go?'), formulate strategies and tactics ('What broad routes do we intend to take to get there and what detailed activities do we need to perform?') and prescribe time scales for the implementation and achievement of these plans ('When do we want to get there?')*. This 'where', 'how' and 'when' content of all plans is encompassed in our definition of the planning role of marketing management which can be summarized as follows:

> The planning role of marketing management comprises the determination of marketing objectives together with the choice of strategies and tactics to achieve these objectives and a time scale for their implementation and achievement.

STEPS IN THE PLANNING PROCESS

There are probably as many different variations or views on the basic marketing planning steps as there are different marketing textbooks. Figure 12.1 represents our view of the key steps in this process. We will take each of these steps in turn.

Corporate objectives/business mission

Irrespective of the type of organization, all of them exist to serve a purpose. This purpose may take a variety of forms and may be classified in a number of ways according to our viewpoint and the particular organization. For example, the business organization aims to create wealth and produce profits. The charitable organization aims to improve the welfare of mankind or help particular selected groups. Corporate objectives may also encompass several areas relating to, for example, growth, innovation, financial performance, corporate reputation, and so on. These overall corporate objectives are, in fact, the start-point of the marketing planning process. Inasmuch as the marketing function, alongside every other function in the business, is there to help identify shape, above all it is there to achieve overall corporate objectives. The marketing plan must therefore reflect, be consistent with and help to achieve overall corporate objectives.

The overall corporate objectives therefore should feed into the start-point of the marketing planning process. The way in which corporate objectives do so can be seen through the business definition stage of the marketing plan. In fact, corporate objectives are best thought of as being a definition of the business, of the order of 'Our business is . . .'. To be useful and relevant, a business definition should ideally fulfil a number of criteria. The following represents the more important of these criteria when thinking about how to define a business which reflects and supports overall corporate objectives:

1. The definition should be neither too broad nor too narrow . . . Definitions such as 'We are in the business of making profits' (too broad) or 'We make lead pencils' (too narrow) are not useful for developing marketing plans.

FIGURE 12.1

The marketing planning process

2. Ideally, the definition should encompass the three dimensions of what Abel[1] refers to as the 'business domain'. These three dimensions are respectively:

   a. Customer groups to be served
   b. Customer needs to be served
   c. Technologies to be utilized

An illustration of how these dimensions might be incorporated into a business mission statement is:

> . . . The business of Acme Trading plc is in the provision of *beauty aids* (customer need) to *female students* (customer group) based on *non-allergic, animal-free products* (technology) with the aim of . . . ; etc

This notion of a business domain is a useful extension to the much vaunted need to avoid 'marketing myopia' advanced by Levitt[2] in the early 1960s. To avoid a narrow non-customer-oriented view of one's business, Levitt argues, it is necessary to define the business in terms of what customer needs a company fulfils rather than in terms of what it provides. For example, the Ford Motor Company would, in Levitt's terms, be said to be in the business of fulfilling the need for transport rather than being in the business of producing vehicles. In fact, you will no doubt have noted that Levitt is actually making the argument for the need to adopt a marketing culture which we discussed in Chapter 1. There is little doubt that Levitt's apparently simple piece of commonsense advice was instrumental in bringing about an increased marketing and customer awareness in organizations throughout the USA and later in Europe.

The additional dimensions added by Abel in his concept of business domain add substantially to the usefulness for marketing planning of the notion of business definition.

3. Finally, the business definition should help to motivate and inspire members of the organization with regard to the future. The business mission should be forward looking and aspirational in nature.

An effective business definition enables the marketer to identify, for example, key customer groups or segments. It also enables the marketer to put 'boundaries' around the organization's market and hence enables the measurement of market size, growth and so on. Business definition also enables competitor identification and analysis. Finally, business definition serves to feed into and shape marketing objectives and strategies which in turn feed into the tactics of the individual elements of the marketing mix.

Marketing audit

The second step in preparing marketing plans involves the marketer in auditing the situation which faces the organization. The audit consists of a detailed appraisal of the organization and its marketing environment. The aim is to build a complete marketing picture of the company and its environment so that a SWOT analysis can be prepared. One side of the marketing audit will therefore encompass the internal activities and performance of the organization. This side feeds into the analysis of strengths and weaknesses (the first two initial letters of our SWOT) whereas the other side of the marketing audit encompasses the external marketing environment and feeds into the identification of opportunities and threats (the second two letters of our SWOT). The marketing audit should be as comprehensive as possible and should be carried out at least once a year. Some companies use outside consultants to conduct the audit because they feel this is more objective. Inside or outside personnel, one of the problems with the marketing audit stage is in trying to ensure that all relevant internal and external factors have been taken into account and that nothing important is missed. Often, therefore, companies use a checklist approach to conducting the marketing audit. The problem here, of course, is that no checklist can ever be totally complete—nor will every item on a checklist always be relevant to every situation.

With these caveats in mind, however, we have provided an example of the sort of checklist that can be used in a marketing audit. This is shown in Table 12.1. (We have given a further example in Chapter 15 where we discuss tackling extended case studies.)

You will see from our checklist for the marketing audit that the external/environmental analysis encompasses the main macro- and micro-environmental forces which we encountered in Chapter 2. The external appraisal of the analysis involves a company in the process of what Argenti[3] has termed 'environmental scanning'. This involves not only keeping abreast of changes in the external environment, but also attempting to forecast or predict these changes. Forecasting the external environment is complicated by the possibility of unanticipated events and the fact that various environmental factors interact with one another. Some of the forecasting techniques discussed in Chapter 11 can be used here.

The internal environment analysis of the audit assesses the effectiveness of marketing activities including the marketing mix elements, marketing systems and procedures etc. and financial aspects.

The audit itself feeds into the next step in the process, which is the SWOT analysis.

Analysing strengths and weaknesses and opportunities and threats (SWOT analysis)

The marketing audit, as the term implies, is really a process of taking stock of the internal and external situation. We need to now analyse the results of the audit and in so doing transform the audit into an assessment of strengths and weaknesses and opportunities and threats, the so-called 'SWOT analysis'.

Remember, strengths and weaknesses are essentially associated with the audit of the internal company environment whereas opportunities and threats stem primarily from the external environmental factors. With regard to these opportunities and threats, as we saw in Chapter 2, it is primarily trends and changes in the external environment which gives rise to these. It is important to recognize that any given environmental change can represent a threat to one company and an opportunity for another. In other words, the SWOT analysis is specific to each individual company.

Similarly, what seem at face value to be, say, apparent strengths in a company, may well turn out to be weaknesses when set against external environmental trends and changes. For example, dominant market share may be a weakness if, as in fact is proposed by the returned Labour government in the UK, new competition and fair trading legislation is planned.

Analysing strengths and weaknesses through the internal audit enables the marketer to move towards achieving a 'strategic fit'. Essentially, this is a matching process between the opportunities and threats presented by trends and changes in the organization's environment and its strengths and weaknesses. The concept of strategic fit and the relationship between the internal and external analysis components of the SWOT analysis is shown in Fig. 12.2.

One might be tempted to think that the internal part of the SWOT analysis, i.e. assessing strengths and weaknesses is easier for the marketer than analysing external opportunities and threats, however, as Lancaster and Massingham[4] suggest, in fact assessing strengths and weaknesses is both conceptually and practically fraught with potential problems and difficulties. It is certainly much more than a simple listing process. An effective strengths and weaknesses assessment involves the following key steps and procedures.

Determining what to include in the strengths and weaknesses assessment

First, the marketing planner must determine what activities and/or resources of the organization should be included in the internal analysis. As we have seen, a checklist can be assembled for this purpose, but again we would reiterate that there are dangers with standard checklists as each company is individual. Care should be taken therefore to establish what are critical strengths and weaknesses for a particular situation. Only strategically significant strengths and weaknesses should be assessed. Examples of attributes that will often form part of an internal appraisal, as can be seen again from our checklist, would often include:

- Marketing strengths and weaknesses
- Financial strengths and weaknesses
- Manufacturing and physical resource strengths and weaknesses
- Personnel strengths and weaknesses
- Research and development strengths and weaknesses

Again we cannot stress enough that these are only examples. Which attributes are vital to assess are company and situation-specific. A further factor to note, and again a problem with simple checklists, is the fact that the attributes in a strengths and weaknesses assessment are interrelated. A combination of seemingly moderate strengths in all of the attributes may result in a company that is in fact extremely strong when it comes to competing in markets or dealing with opportunities and threats from the external environment.

Measuring the degree of strength or weakness

Having identified the key attributes of strengths and weaknesses, the next step is to determine the degree of strength or weakness for each attribute. Are we, for example, very strong with respect to our channels of distribution, or only moderately so? Are we *extremely weak* when it comes to research and product development or simply not very adept in this area? In other words, we should distinguish between where we are particularly strong or weak and where we are moderately so. One approach to this is to use numerical or profiling systems of strengths and weaknesses assessment. So, for example, if we are extremely

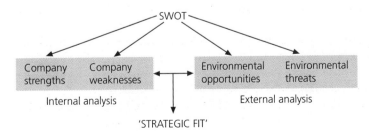

FIGURE 12.2

Achieving a strategic fit: SWOT analysis

TABLE 12.1   *A sample marketing audit checklist*

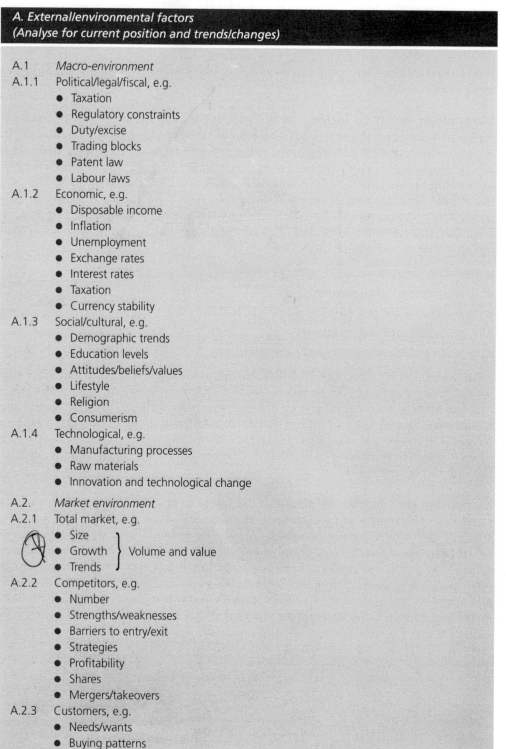

A. External/environmental factors
(Analyse for current position and trends/changes)

A.1   *Macro-environment*
A.1.1   Political/legal/fiscal, e.g.
- Taxation
- Regulatory constraints
- Duty/excise
- Trading blocks
- Patent law
- Labour laws

A.1.2   Economic, e.g.
- Disposable income
- Inflation
- Unemployment
- Exchange rates
- Interest rates
- Taxation
- Currency stability

A.1.3   Social/cultural, e.g.
- Demographic trends
- Education levels
- Attitudes/beliefs/values
- Lifestyle
- Religion
- Consumerism

A.1.4   Technological, e.g.
- Manufacturing processes
- Raw materials
- Innovation and technological change

A.2.   *Market environment*
A.2.1   Total market, e.g.
- Size
- Growth   } Volume and value
- Trends

A.2.2   Competitors, e.g.
- Number
- Strengths/weaknesses
- Barriers to entry/exit
- Strategies
- Profitability
- Shares
- Mergers/takeovers

A.2.3   Customers, e.g.
- Needs/wants
- Buying patterns
- Brand loyalty
- Segments

TABLE 12.1 (*continued*)

A.2.4 Distributors, e.g.
- Principal channels
- Trends in channels
- Purchasing strength/power
- Location
- Terms and conditions of sale, e.g. margins
- Physical distribution/logistics

A.2.5 Suppliers, e.g.
- Number/types
- Bargaining strengths
- Location

B. Internal environment

B.1 *Detailed marketing activity*

B.1.1 Sales/market share, e.g.
- Total sales (volume/value)
- Market share (volume/value)
- Trends in above
- Sales by products, customer, geographical areas

B.1.2 Marketing mix elements, e.g.
- Prices: pricing strategies, discounts, etc.
- Products: range, features, quality, product life cycles, customer service, branding
- Promotion: types, spend, media, salesforce activities, organization, etc.
- Place: channels used, stock levels, warehousing, delivery systems, etc.

B.1.3 Financial aspects:
- Profits and margins
- Cost structures
- Liquidity and cash flow
- Asset structure
- Debt/equity structure
- Capital investment levels

B.2 *Audit of marketing systems, procedures, organization, etc.*

B.2.1 Planning systems, e.g.
- Information gathering/marketing research
- Current company and marketing objectives
- Current strategies and tactics
- Control and budgeting systems
- Planning systems, effectiveness and efficiency

B.2.2 Organization and staffing, e.g.
- Overall company and marketing organization structures
- Coordination and conflict between marketing and other functional areas, e.g. production, finance, R&D, etc.
- Marketing and sales staff: responsibilities, authority, skills and experience

strong in a particular area we could give this a numerical rating of, say, plus 5; on the other hand, extremely weak would be scored as, say, minus 5.

Comparison with competitors   The third step in assessing strengths and weaknesses is to ensure that we compare ourselves to our major existing and potential competitors. It is dangerous to develop plans and strategies based on only own-company strengths when the competitors are even stronger in these areas. The most strategically significant sort of strength is where a company has a strength which is unique. Hamel and Prahalad[5] refer to such distinctive strengths as *'distinctive competences'*.

Assess in relation to opportunities and threats   Once we have refined our analysis of strengths and weaknesses in this way then we can move to assess these in relation to identified opportunities and threats. Remember, a SWOT analysis only makes sense if we consider both internal and external factors together. This is the concept of strategic fit referred to earlier.

Identifying and prioritizing major problems and opportunities: selection of key issues/problem zones   When we begin to look at strengths and weaknesses and opportunities and threats together we can begin to refine our list so as to produce a concise and prioritized list of major problems and major opportunities facing the company. The marketing manager must analyse and distil the SWOT even further so as to identify key issues or, as they are sometimes referred to, *'problem zones'*. We shall be looking at the notion of problem zone identification in more detail in Chapter 15. One way of identifying the key issues or problem zones in a company, however, is to distinguish between what the company would like to achieve and what the company is likely to achieve in the future. Any gaps between these two states represent key issues for the company. The technique of gap analysis discussed later in this chapter when we consider setting objectives, is a similar idea. One may also usefully distinguish between *existing* issues and *anticipated* issues. In the case of anticipated issues, using the SWOT analysis this classification can be further divided into areas for opportunity exploitation and areas to avert the risk of impending threats. Key issues and problem zones need to be prioritized with reference to the scale of the issues and the time-scale for overcoming them.

Having identified key issues from the SWOT we can then analyse these issues in more depth using appropriate qualitative and quantitative techniques and tools on market and financial analysis. This further analysis may lead to a redefinition of the key issues/problem zones. Again, Chapter 15 explores this process in more detail.

Review environmental and resource constraints   In conducting the SWOT analysis the marketing manager must also review the environmental and corporate resource constraints so that plans can be developed within these limitations.

Statement of assumptions   Finally, especially as regards forecasts of changes in the external environment and/or statements regarding corporate resources, the marketing manager must identify and state any assumptions made during the SWOT analysis before proceeding to develop objectives and strategies. These assumptions may encompass many and varied areas. For example, we may have to make assumptions regarding trends and developments in, say, rates of inflation, political developments, legislation and regulations, access to future resources, etc. Clearly the marketing manager should make as few assumptions as possible, but where they are made, he or she should be quite clear what these are, their relevance to marketing strategies and plans, and the consequences of any errors in the assumptions or the forecasts that stem from them.

Business and marketing objectives

Both overall mission statements and SWOT analysis input to this stage of the corporate planning process. The importance of objectives to the planning process cannot be overstated; indeed, many texts on planning cite objective-setting as being the starting-point in the process.

Broadly, setting objectives involves a company in considering the following two questions:

- Where do we wish to go?
- When do we intend to arrive?

Without an answer to these questions, a company can be likened to a ship without a compass; it can move, but it lacks a clear sense of direction. More specifically, among the more important functions that objectives serve in a company are the following:

1. Objectives provide for a *sense of purpose* in a company. Without objectives, companies lack the means to focus and organize their efforts.

2. Objectives help a company to *achieve consistency* between the various levels of decision-making, and between the different functions.

3. Objectives help to *stimulate effort*; they provide a basis for motivating individuals to achieve them.

4. Finally, objectives provide the *basis for control* in a company. Unless we know precisely what is required, it is difficult, if not impossible, to know the extent to which we have achieved it.

In order to fulfil these important functions, objectives must have a number of characteristics. Again, among the most important of these are the following:

- Preferably, objectives should be *quantified*. Quantitative objectives with respect to both levels of performance and time reduce the risk of their being vague or ambiguous.

- Ideally, objectives should be *acceptable* and *agreeable* to those charged with the responsibility of attaining them. It is pointless setting objectives if they are not acted upon—or if the effort to achieve them is given grudgingly.

- A frequent reason for objectives being unacceptable is that they are felt to be too difficult or impossible to achieve. Objectives should be *realistic*, pitched neither too high nor too low.

- Finally, objectives should be *consistent*. As we shall see shortly, often companies have a variety of objectives as opposed to a single one. It is important that these multiple objectives do not conflict one with another in such a way that the achievement of an objective in one area is inconsistent with the achievement of objectives in others. For example, an objective of improved profitability may be inconsistent with an objective of maximum sales.

Having discussed the functions of objectives, and the characteristics that objectives ideally should possess if they are to serve these functions, we can now turn our attention to the variety of corporate objectives that a company might set.

In economic analysis it is often asserted that a firm has one, and only one, objective: namely, 'to maximize its total profits'. Profit-maximizing does not in fact reflect the reality or richness of objective-setting in most companies. Clearly, for many companies profits are enacted for long-run survival, and because of this they will normally formulate objectives in this area. Usually, however, these profit objectives are set in terms of some satisfactory level of profits, often couched in terms of a specified rate of return on the assets employed.

In addition to profit objectives, it is now recognized that companies may have a variety of objectives encompassing a spread of activities. Among some of the most frequently encountered objectives in companies are:

● Profit objectives

● Sales objectives

● Market share objectives

● Growth objectives

● Technical and market standing objectives

● Survival objectives

● Social responsibility objectives

Whatever the mix of objectives, it must be remembered that the objectives themselves relate to some point in the future, hence the importance of specifying a time-scale for their achievement. For an existing business there will also be a past. It is possible, therefore, to measure the past and current performance of the company with respect to those areas in which it has objectives for the future. Management can then compare where it wishes to be (objectives) with where it is likely to be on the basis of a projection from past performance. Any difference constitutes what Ackoff has referred to as a 'planning gap'.[6] This notion of a planning gap is illustrated in Fig. 12.3. The gap stems from the difference between future desired profit objectives and a forecast of projected profit based on past performance.

In the face of such a planning gap, a number of options are available; the intention, however, is to close the gap. For example, the gap could be closed by revising objectives

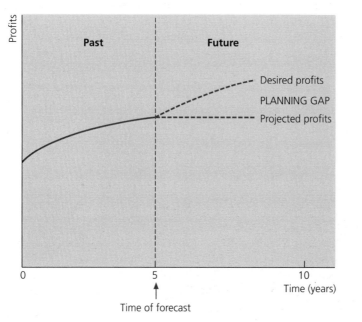

FIGURE 12.3

The planning gap

in a downward direction. Such a step might be taken where the initial objectives are unrealistic. Alternatively, or in addition, the gap could be closed by actions designed to move the company off the projection curve and towards the desired curve. In fact, any movement towards a point at some time in the future requires action decisions—even if the action decision is of the order of 'do nothing', i.e. continue much as we have done in the past. More frequently, these action decisions require the exploration and evaluation of a variety of options, the selection of courses of action from these options, and the commitment of resources. This next step in the process of corporate planning is the formulation of strategies.

Strategy formulation and selection

If objectives relate to the 'where' and 'when' of planning, strategy formulation and selection are concerned with the 'how'.

This idea of strategy is essentially a military one, but it has increasingly been applied in a business context. One of the major difficulties with its application in this context is that the full range of strategic alternatives in marketing is virtually unlimited and is certainly extremely complex.

In an effort to reduce this variety and complexity to manageable proportions, a number of conceptual frameworks have been developed to aid the company in the delineation and choice between strategic options. We shall outline some of the more important of these.

The Ansoff Matrix Ansoff[7] has proposed the idea of 'product/market scope' to aid in the formulation and selection of strategies, particularly for those companies with growth objectives. The basic framework of this approach is shown in Fig. 12.4. The matrix comprises 'markets' on the vertical axis, and on the horizontal axis 'products'. In turn, each axis is subdivided into 'existing' and 'new'. Each cell of the matrix so formed represents a different strategic alternative for achieving growth.

Strategic alternative 1, *market penetration*, is a strategy of expanding sales based on existing products in existing markets. Where the total market is still growing, the strategy may be achieved, for example, through 'natural' market growth. In markets that are static or declining, a market penetration strategy can be achieved only by increasing market share at the expense of competitors.

Strategic alternative 2, *market development*, is a strategy of expansion based on entering new markets, i.e. markets not previously served by the company, with existing products. A good example of this would be a company entering an export market for the first time.

Strategic alternative 3, *product development*, entails developing and launching new products for sale in existing markets.

Product Market	Present	New
Present	1. Market penetration	3. Product development
New	2. Market development	4. Diversification

FIGURE 12.4

Ansoff's product/market scope

Strategic alternative 4, *diversification*, involves a company expanding on the basis of new products *and* new markets. This diversification can take a number of forms. For example, a company might choose to diversify into new product markets by moving through the channel of production and distribution. A car manufacturer taking over a component supplier and both using and marketing the components to other companies would be a good example of this. Alternatively, the diversification may be into an entirely unrelated form of business activity—for example, a tobacco company moving into the production and marketing of children's toys.

Ansoff's product/market matrix is probably one of the best known frameworks for delineating overall marketing strategies.

Boston Consulting Group's (BCG) growth share matrix   In the mid-1960s, the Boston Consulting Group (BCG) was founded to provide advice to strategic marketing planners. BCG developed a simple but useful strategic planning technique based on an analysis of a company's product portfolio. The technique entails assigning each individual product (or strategic business unit) of an organization to one of four possible cells in a simple matrix according to the relative market share and rate of market growth associated with that particular product/business. An example of a completed matrix is shown in Fig. 12.5.

The steps in completing the matrix are as follows:

1. For each product or strategic business unit, determine the annual growth rate in the market. Normally, annual growth rates of 10 per cent or more are considered 'high' and anything less than this, 'low'.

2. Determine the relative market share of each product or strategic business unit by comparing with the share of the largest competitor, and express as a ratio. In order to qualify for the 'high' relative market share category, a ratio of 1.0 or above is required. So, for example, if the market share of the product is 20 per cent and the largest competitor has only 10 per cent, the ratio is 2:1. Clearly, in order to qualify for the 'high' relative market share category, the product or business must be equal to the share leader in the market or above.

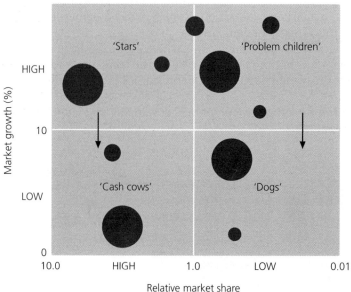

FIGURE 12.5

BCG's growth share index

We now have all the information we need to position products or businesses in the matrix. We can also indicate the relative values of the turnover of each product or business by using a circle, where the area of each circle is proportionate to this turnover.

According to which cell of the matrix the products or businesses are calculated to lie, they are classified as being 'dogs', 'cash cows', 'problem children' or 'stars':

- *'Dogs'* These are products with low market share and slow market growth. Such products are sometimes referred to as 'cash traps', in that they do not generate a significant cash flow to a company and what little is generated is normally required to be reinvested simply to maintain the sales of the product.

- *'Cash cows'* These, on the other hand, are products with high market share and slow market growth. This combination typically means that a product in this category generates large amounts of cash over and above that required to keep the product in this sector.

- *'Problem children'* (sometimes called 'question marks' or 'wildcats') These are products with low market share but in high-growth markets. These products can consume cash resources at alarming rates. The overall net drain on cash with these products is greatest when a company is attempting to increase its market share.

- *'Stars'* These are products in high-growth markets with a relatively high share of the market. Stars can generate a relatively large cash inflow, but this is more often than not matched or exceeded by the outflow of cash necessary to maintain market share. In net terms, therefore, such products provide, at best, modest net cash flows and often are net cash users.

In using and interpreting the product portfolio, a number of factors are important.

1. The portfolio is *dynamic*, i.e. in the absence of any action on the part of a company, products will move their position in the portfolio. Principally because of the product life cycle effect, products have a tendency to move downwards in the portfolio; i.e. 'problem children' become 'dogs', and 'stars' become 'cash cows'. This tendency is indicated by the arrows in Fig. 12.5.

2. The notion is to achieve a certain balance in the portfolio. A balanced portfolio would ideally contain few or no 'dogs', some 'problem children', some 'stars' and some 'cash cows'. The balance between 'problem children', 'stars' and 'cash cows' should be such as to ensure that the company has sufficient net positive cash flow from its 'cash cows' to fund its 'stars' and turn them eventually into 'cash cows'. Funds from 'cash cows' are also used to turn products that are currently 'problem children', because of relatively low market share, into 'stars'. Not all 'problem children' can be moved in this way, and eventually some of them will fall to become 'dogs'. In the long run, all 'dogs' are potential candidates for elimination from the product range.

As a consequence of these two factors, a company must take steps to ensure that the future portfolio mix is as the company wishes it to be. In other words, it must select appropriate strategies in order to achieve in the future a balanced product portfolio. As with most of these techniques, the basic idea of the BCG's product portfolio analysis is to delineate the range of strategies required. The technique, however, is not without its problems and limitations.

Problems and limitations Some of the more frequent criticisms of the problems and limitations of the BCG growth share matrix are:

- Oversimplification
- Problems of classification
- Assumptions
- Application
- Incomplete coverage

Each of these is considered further below.

1. *Oversimplification*   Many critics have argued that the BCG growth share matrix is an oversimplification of product markets and can lead to insufficient management attention to the range of factors that are important in marketing strategy. For example, the matrix is based on only two key factors—market growth and relative market share.

2. *Problems of classification*   There are severe conceptual and practical problems associated with defining what comprises a strategic business unit, a concept essential to the analysis. Similarly, there is some doubt as to precisely where the line should be drawn between what constitutes a high/low relative market share, and what constitutes high/low market growth.

3. *Assumptions*   In common with all the strategic portfolio approaches, the BCG growth share model is derived from a number of key underpinning assumptions. If these assumptions are misplaced or wrong, then the subsequent value of the technique is reduced or removed completely. For example, a central assumption of the matrix is that higher rates of market share are associated with higher profit rates. While there is some considerable evidence to support this assumption, it is by no means invariably the case that higher share equals higher profits.

4. *Application*   The BCG growth share matrix approach implies that managers of different products/strategic business units will cooperate by, for example, not objecting to cash surpluses from their 'cash cows' being used to fund other parts of the business, or by withdrawing certain products in the 'question mark' or 'dog' categories. While it is true that the technique itself makes no claims to address such problems, there is a danger that management may overlook those problems of application.

5. *Incomplete coverage*   The axes used on the BCG growth share matrix mean that this technique effectively ignores new products at the introductory stage of their life cycles and markets that are in the decline stage and hence exhibit negative growth. In Appendix 1 we shall examine a product portfolio matrix that is specifically designed to deal with these problems.

The new BCG matrix   More recently the Boston Consulting Group has developed a model using the two dimensions of, on the one hand, *'the number of possible approaches to achieving a competitive advantage'*: subdivided into *'many'* or *'few'* and as the other dimension, the potential *'size of those advantages'* to a company being subdivided into *'small'* or *'large'* advantages. These dimensions are used to identify four basic types of industries or markets as shown in Figure 12.6.

The characteristics of the four basic types of industries shown in each cell of the matrix are explained below:

1. *Volume*   In this type of industry there are relatively few approaches available for achieving a competitive advantage. For example, a company may achieve a competitive advantage through, say, lower prices, or on the other hand, say, superior service. However, where these relatively few bases of competitive advantage are used effectively by a company, then it achieves an advantage which is often major and long-lasting. Usually, only the largest companies in the industry can achieve and sustain the competitive advantage needed, hence the term 'volume'. Market share

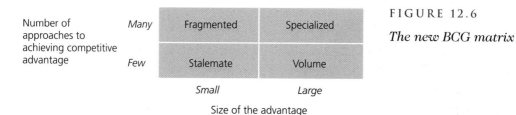

FIGURE 12.6

The new BCG matrix

is essential in this type of industry and the aim must be to be number one and the largest in the industry.

2. *Fragmented*   In these types of industries there are many approaches to achieving differentiation and a competitive advantage. In these types of industries customer needs are varied and often the market is highly segmented. Because of this, we tend to see even small companies differentiating successfully in their own way. However, no one company tends to command a large share of the market and the relative size of the advantage accruing to the individual company is small and often temporary.

3. *Stalemate*   These tend to be mature industries such as shipbuilding, mining, etc., often the products produced are commodity-type products. There are therefore relatively few ways to differentiate and achieve a competitive advantage. Price tends to be the predominant competitive weapon but any advantages accruing from lower prices tend to be relatively short-lived as they are competed away.

4. *Specialized*   In this type of industry there are many approaches available for differentiation and achieving a competitive advantage. Unlike the fragmented industry, however, companies in these sorts of industries can, by becoming specialized, achieve strong competitive advantages which are long lasting in their own particular market niches.

McKinsey/General Electric's multifactor portfolio matrix   Partly because of the limitations and criticisms of the BCG growth share matrix, a number of product/market portfolio techniques now use several factors to analyse strategic business units instead of only the two found in BCG's growth share matrix approach. Working in conjunction with McKinsey & Co., General Electric USA (GE) has developed one of the more popular of these multiple-factor screening methods.

In the GE matrix, strategic business units are evaluated using the two dimensions of *market attractiveness* and *competitive position*. In contrast to the BCG approach, each of these two dimensions is, in turn, further analysed into a number of factors that underpin each dimension. In order to use this technique, the strategic marketing planner must first determine these various factors contributing to market attractiveness and business position.

GE's product/market attractiveness factors   The original GE matrix used the following factors to assess product/market attractiveness.

● Size
● Growth rates
● Competitive diversity and structure
● Historical profit margin
● Technological requirements
● Social impacts
● Environmental impacts
● Legal impacts
● Energy requirements

GE's competitive position factors   For assessing competitive position, the GE matrix uses the following factors:

● Market share
● Share growth rate

- Product quality
- Brand reputation
- Distribution network
- Promotional effectiveness
- Productive capacity
- Productive efficiency
- Unit costs
- R&D performance
- Managerial personnel

GE believe that these are the key factors for their businesses, which, taken together, influence return on investment. (Note that the BCG approach uses cash flow.) However, this list of GE factors can be modified for each company according to its own particular circumstances. Indeed, many of the alternative multiple-factor matrices simply use different checklists of attributes.

Compiling the GE matrix   The five steps in compiling the GE matrix are:

1. Identify strategic business units.
2. Determine factors contributing to market attractiveness.
3. Determine factors contributing to business position.
4. Establish ways of measuring market attractiveness and business position.
5. Rank each strategic business unit according to whether it is high, medium or low on business strength; and high, medium or low on market attractiveness.

The final two factors (measuring and ranking) require that some numerical rating be given to the relative importance of each factor used to assess market attractiveness

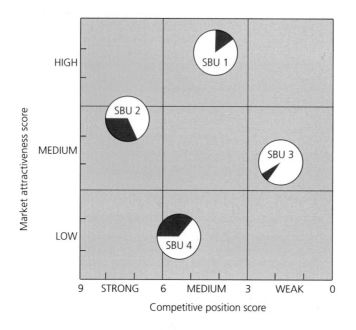

FIGURE 12.7

Illustrative presentation of a GE matrix

(assuming they are not all equally important) and in order to assess competitive position. Multiplying these together and totalling them for each strategic business unit (SBU) then gives an overall composite score which in turn enables the matrix to be compiled. In addition, the total market size for each SBU can be represented by the area of a circle, with the share of the company's SBU in each product market being indicated by a segment in the circle. The approach typically results in a visual portfolio similar to the one shown in Fig. 12.7. As with BCG's matrix, the visual presentation enables a considerable amount of complex information to be presented in an easily digestible form.

Interpreting and using the GE matrix   Having completed the matrix, again as with the BCG approach, the marketing planner can then assess the balances of SBUs in the organization and determine appropriate future strategies for each.

Strategy guidelines   Of itself, the GE matrix does not purport to establish detailed strategies for each SBU. Clearly, this is a task for the management of the company and will require a consideration of many factors. However, according to an SBU's position in the matrix, we can distinguish between three broad strategic guidelines. These are indicated in Fig. 12.8.

Clearly, SBUs that score high or medium on competitive position and market attractiveness are those in which a company should seek at least to maintain investment, and preferably to grow. SBUs that score a combination of low/low or low/medium on competitive position and market attractiveness are candidates for (at the very least) no more investment. Wherever possible, as much cash should be harvested from them as is feasible. SBUs scoring either high/low or medium/medium combinations on competitive position/market attractiveness should be examined to see if some degree of selective investment to maintain or increase earnings would be appropriate.

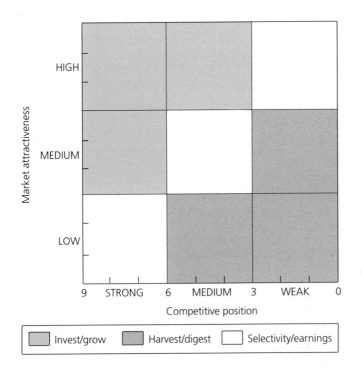

FIGURE 12.8

Strategy guidelines from the GE matrix

A more detailed breakdown of prescriptive strategies for businesses in different cells suggested by Day[8] is shown in Fig. 12.9.

Criticisms and limitations   Because the GE matrix uses several dimensions to assess SBUs instead of only two, and also is based on return on investment rather than simply cash flow, many believe that it offers a substantial improvement over the BCG growth share matrix. However, the approach is not without its limitations and problems:

1. The approach offers only very broad strategy guidelines, with no indication as to precisely what needs to be done to achieve the strategy (e.g. selective growth).

2. There is no precise indication as to how to weight the various elements of market attractiveness, or how to score business strengths against these.

Market attractiveness	STRONG	MEDIUM	WEAK
HIGH	**PROTECT POSITION** – Invest to grow at maximum digestible rate – Concentrate effort on maintaining strength	**INVEST TO BUILD** – Challenge for leadership – Build selectively on strengths – Reinforce vulnerable areas	**BUILD SELECTIVELY** – Specialize around limited strengths – Seek ways to overcome weaknesses – Withdraw if indications of sustainable growth are lacking
MEDIUM	**BUILD SELECTIVELY** – Invest heavily in most attractive segments – Build up ability to counter competition – Emphasize profitability by raising productivity	**SELECTIVITY/ MANAGE FOR EARNINGS** – Protect existing programme – Concentrate investments in segments where profitability is good and risk is relatively low	**LIMITED EXPANSION OR HARVEST** – Look for ways to expand without high risk; otherwise, minimize investment and rationalize investment
LOW	**PROTECT AND REFOCUS** – Manage for current earnings – Concentrate on attractive strengths – Defend strengths	**MANAGE FOR EARNINGS** – Protect position in most profitable segments – Upgrade product line – Minimize investment	**MANAGE FOR EARNINGS** – Sell at a time that will maximize cash value – Cut fixed costs and avoid investment meanwhile

Competitive position

FIGURE 12.9

Prescriptive strategies for cells of a GE matrix

Source: George S. Day, *Analysis for Strategic Market Decisions*, West Publishing Co., St Paul, MN, 1986, p. 204

3. Evaluation and scoring is subjective, as are the points of division of the matrix into high, medium and low segments.

4. The technique is much more complex than the BCG approach, and requires much more extensive data-gathering and processing.

5. The approach does not explicitly take account of possible relationships between various SBUs or product market areas.

6. The GE approach has been criticized on the grounds that it is not supported by empirical evidence or research; what evidence is there, for example, to support the notion that market attractiveness and business position are related to return on investment?

Developments in strategic planning frameworks and tools

There is no doubt that the use of strategic planning frameworks such as the Ansoff, BCG and GE frameworks outlined here is continuing to grow and develop. Used carefully, marketers have found that planning tools such as these can be a major help in the identification and selection of appropriate marketing strategies.

The techniques we have described here represent some of the best known and probably most widely used of the strategic marketing planning tools. However, there are now many other such planning frameworks and tools available, many of them increasingly sophisticated and complex. Some of these more advanced strategic planning tools are included in Appendix 1 of the text specifically for those students who are taking more advanced marketing exams and need to study these. In addition, the interested student is recommended to consult one of the more specialist texts in this area. Those by Greenley[9] and Chisnall[10] are felt to be particularly good.

Segmentation, targeting and positioning strategies

Another key element in marketing strategy is the process of target marketing involving segmentation, targeting and positioning. The importance of this area of marketing strategy is such that you will recall we devoted the whole of Chapter 4 to this area and you might at this stage, therefore, wish to remind yourself of the content of that chapter. To briefly remind you, however, target marketing involves breaking the total market down into sub-sets or segments, each of which have different needs and wants. Having identified and appraised the segments in a market, the marketer must determine which of these segments to target, and on what basis. Targeting strategies remember can be undifferentiated, differentiated or concentrated. Finally, the marketer must position into the targeted segment against competition by combining the marketing mix. This last element of the targeting process illustrates how target marketing strategies feed into the next stage of the marketing planning process, namely marketing tactics and marketing mix decisions.

Marketing tactics/marketing mix decisions

At this stage the marketer is now in a position to plan the more detailed marketing tactics. In essence this involves planning how the different marketing tools will be combined for each target market. The earlier stages of the planning process effectively serve to constrain and delineate these marketing mix decisions.

The term 'marketing mix' is attributed to the American Neil H. Borden[11] and has been touched on several times in earlier chapters. As we have seen, the marketing mix consists of those marketing tools over which the marketer has control and therefore can vary in order to achieve overall marketing objectives and strategies.

The detailed marketing mix strategies and tactics are at the heart of the annual marketing plan and may need to be developed around, say, separate products, different geographical markets, different customer groups, and so on, according to how the company is structured and the range of markets in which it operates. In other words, we would have separate annual marketing plans for, for example, the industrial products and consumer products divisions or for home and export markets.

As a guide to the range of decisions involved in the strategies and tactics for the marketing mix, Lancaster and Massingham[12] suggest some of the factors that the detailed marketing mix plans might consider for what are often referred to as the 'conventional' four Ps as follows:

1. Products
   - Quality
   - Features
   - Options
   - Style
   - Services, installation, warranty
   - Packaging
   - Range, width and depth
   - New product development

2. Price
   - Pricing strategies, e.g. 'skimming vs. penetration'
   - Price changes
   - List prices
   - Discounts
   - Allowances
   - Payment and credit terms

3. Promotion
   - Overall emphasis in promotional mix
   - Objectives, strategies and plans for:
     a. Personal selling
     b. Advertising
     c. Sales promotion
     d. Public relations and publicity
     e. Direct mail

4. Place
   - Channel configuration/coverage/levels
   - Specific types of intermediaries
   - Terms and responsibilities of channel members
   - Order processing systems
   - Warehousing, storage, stocking and delivery policies

As we saw in Chapter 6, with the advent of service markets in particular these four conventional four Ps of the marketing mix have been added to to include a further three Ps, namely

5. People
   - Staff training
   - Staff attitudes
   - Staff appearance

6. Physical evidence
   - Condition of company facilities
   - Corporate image
   - Staff appearance
7. Process
   - Ordering systems
   - Delivery systems
   - Procedures for dealing with imbalances between demand and supply

The range and complexity of marketing mix decisions is added to if we consider that within each individual element of the marketing mix we also need to develop detailed plans for each of the sub-elements. For example, under the promotional element of the mix, we need to develop detailed plans for, say, the advertising element which includes, for example:

- objectives
- copy content/message
- media decisions
- timings/frequency
- measurement of effectiveness/control

With so many decisions in the marketing mix area, it is vitally important that the various marketing mix decisions are combined and coordinated so as to achieve consistency while at the same time fulfilling the strategic objectives of the company, for example with regard to segmentation and positioning. In addition to the large number of decisions in the marketing mix area, numerous factors also affect these decisions such as for example the marketing environment, competitive factors, and, of course, the resources and objectives of the individual company. Because of this you will appreciate that it is inappropriate and indeed dangerous to suggest in specific terms how the marketing mix should be combined for a particular company. This is very much situation and company specific. However, it is appropriate and useful to point in broad terms to the ways in which the combination of marketing mix elements may generally be applied and adapted to different marketing situations, and it is to this area that we now turn our attention.

Combining the marketing mix

So long as we remember that these are only guidelines, we can point to the following marketing situations as having a major effect on how the marketing mix might be combined in different ways and with different emphases.

We would expect it to be combined in different ways according to the following situations.

1. At different stages in the product life cycle
2. In industrial vs. consumer markets
3. In small- and medium-sized enterprises (SMEs)
4. In services marketing
5. In not-for-profit organizations

Taking each of these in turn:

The marketing mix and product life cycle stages   The product life cycle concept was, of course, introduced in Chapter 6. We saw that during the four main stages of the life cycle, namely introduction, growth, maturity and decline, different marketing strategies and therefore a different marketing mix will be required. Indeed, one of the principal uses of the product life cycle concept is the notion that the different stages can help the marketer decide the appropriate combination of marketing mix elements. We will now consider each of the stages of the product life cycle with respect to this combination in more detail:

Introductory stage   Because at this stage the product or service is new to the market, awareness of the new product is likely to be low. Particular emphasis must be given to the promotional and distribution elements of the marketing mix and spending on promotion will be high with lots of sales promotion to try to encourage the trade to stock the new product. Selling efforts will require missionary selling techniques and the product element of the mix is likely to be very basic with few variations. Distribution and logistics will centre on ensuring sufficient stock to ensure effective launch. Price may be set either to skim or penetrate the market depending on the competitive situation.

Growth stage   If the new product is successful we can expect a rapid growth in sales and new competitors can be expected to enter the market. Spending on promotion will still be heavy, and it will still be necessary to use sales promotion to prevent competitors establishing a market position. Product variations may begin to be introduced even at this early stage to meet different customer needs. If during the introductory stage price skimming was used, it is likely that this will shift to emphasizing price competitiveness more as new competitors enter. Distribution strategy is likely to centre on widening the number of channels and intermediaries.

Maturity stage   In the maturity stage, of course, competition is at its peak. Promotion will still be aimed at trying to maintain market share, but also reaching the late adopters and laggards. Further product modifications are likely to take place with further features and even the beginnings of updated products being introduced. Price, although needing to be competitive, still may be less important if sufficient brand loyalty can be established. In this context advertising is likely to take the form of reminder advertising.

Decline stage   Competition will still be intense, but will gradually reduce as companies seek new markets. Sales promotion may be reduced as the market continues to shrink but price competition and price cutting are likely to be intense at this stage. The marketer may seek to extend the product life cycle by introducing style or feature updates including possibly repackaging. Unprofitable products in the range will tend to be phased out at this stage together with unprofitable outlets. Remember, these are only guidelines for how the marketing mix might be combined with different emphases at different stages of the product life cycle. Indeed, some, such as John O'Shaughnessy,[13] advise great care in using the product life cycle stage as a guide to marketing mix decisions.

Industrial versus consumer markets   In Chapter 3, we introduced the notion of two different types of markets or more specifically customers, namely on the one hand industrial or, perhaps more broadly, organizational buyers and on the other consumer buyers. We established that there are many similarities, but also many major differences between these two types of buyers or markets. As a result of the differences in how these different customer groups purchase, why they purchase and the factors which affect their purchasing decisions we often find major differences between how the marketing mix tools are used and combined for these two different types of buyers or markets.

Taking the industrial/organizational buyer first, here the marketing mix is likely to centre on product reliability, distribution systems which afford speed and reliability, an increased emphasis on price, particularly in negotiations, and good after-sales and technical service. In the promotional element of the mix personal selling rather than advertising is likely to predominate. Customers are likely to insist on just-in-time (JIT) supply and therefore logistics is a major part of the marketing mix in such markets. Regarding profit reliability, and related to JIT supply, customers will look for a zero defects policy. As regards the price element, as already mentioned, price is always going to be a key factor and is much more likely to be negotiated. We must be careful, however, not to think that price is always the most important factor and, indeed, increasingly product delivery and reliability are increasingly important. As regards distribution channels, often organizational/industrial buyers are served directly.

In consumer markets, as we would expect, we do find many different combinations of the marketing mix elements. But compared to organizational/industrial markets and particularly for fast-moving consumer goods (fmcgs), the marketing mix often centres around the following key emphases. In terms of the product branding, packaging and logos are often significant elements. The emphasis in the promotional area of the mix will tend to be much more on advertising and sales promotion compared to industrial products. Negotiation is much less the order of the day with regard to pricing in consumer markets, though this, of course, varies between different countries. Particularly for low value, frequently purchased consumer products distribution is likely to be through intermediaries and will require extensive distribution through, say, national retailers.

Small- and medium-sized enterprises (SMEs) An often heard criticism of marketing textbooks is that they tend to assume, at least implicitly, that most marketing is carried out by large and often multi-national organizations and that the marketing problems and requirements of the small- to medium-sized businesses (SMEs) are often neglected. This criticism, of course, is only valid to the extent that the application of marketing concepts and techniques is different in SMEs. In fact, the basic concepts and tools of marketing are essentially the same irrespective of the size and scope of the organization. Having said this, it is often the case that this application does need to reflect the smaller size of such organizations and in particular their access to resources and expertise. This is reflected in many areas of marketing SME organizations, but specifically in the context of the marketing mix the following differences are often found with regard to how the marketing mix elements are combined in SMEs.

First of all the financial and resource limitations of SMEs obviously means that they are not in a position to compete on price in the same way as their larger counterparts. This puts a premium on such companies emphasizing service elements of the marketing mix such as, for example, good after-sales service. Similarly, SMEs cannot hope to spend as much on advertising and promotion as the larger business placing more emphasis in the promotional area of the mix on personal selling. Distribution, too, is likely to be more limited especially as regards geographical spread. Such companies often survive through emphasizing a personal approach to customers and/or offering specialist expertise or skills which their larger counterparts are unwilling or unable to supply. Although strictly not part of the marketing mix, SMEs also find it more problematical to conduct expensive and sophisticated marketing research and therefore will often make more use of secondary, syndicated and shared research such as omnibus surveys in their marketing.

Services marketing   Again remember we introduced some of the issues and differences in service products and marketing in Chapter 6. For example, we saw how the special characteristics of services such as intangibility, non-ownership, inseparability, perishability, and so on, have given rise to the recognition of the need for an extended marketing mix for services to include 'People', 'Physical evidence', and 'Process'. Perhaps services marketing above all explicitly requires a different and special combination of the marketing mix elements. At this stage, it would be useful to reconsider that part of Chapter 6 which considers the implications of marketing service products and especially Table 6.2 which links these implications to the special characteristics of service products. In fact, Chapter 6 covers the most obvious differences in the marketing mix for services in as much as it introduces the extended marketing mix elements listed above. But what about the remaining four conventional/traditional elements of the marketing mix for services? Are there any differences here when we consider marketing service products. Some of the more important considerations of the application of the traditional marketing mix for service products are as follows:

First of all, the product element of the marketing mix places much more emphasis on the quality and attributes of the service and, in particular, on intangibles such as warranties, after-sales facilities and so on. Because of the intangibility of service products, product concepts and benefits are often much more difficult to communicate to customers than it is for their physical product counterparts. New product development and concept testing of new ideas in particular can be problematical, as can the protection and patenting of service products.

With regard to pricing service products, the basic methods of price determination and alternative pricing strategies used for physical products apply just as much but, again as a result of the intangible nature of service products, price does tend to be used much more by customers as a signal of the quality level of the service. In addition, pricing needs to be used much more proactively in services marketing as a tool for matching supply and demand. This may, in turn, require much more flexible pricing methods for services.

The place element of service products, and particularly again the matching of supply to demand, increases the emphasis and importance of effective distribution channels. Admittedly physical distribution as such is not a key problem, but the highly perishable nature of service products outlined in Chapter 6 means that distribution needs to be particularly effective. Where using intermediaries in service products it is very important to remember the inseparability characteristic of services, and great care should be taken in selecting the right distributors that match the positioning of the company and its products and also have the right skills and attitudes towards delivering customer satisfaction.

Finally, with regard to the promotion of services, the marketer of service products needs to place much more emphasis on stressing the benefits rather than the features of the service. Personal selling is particularly important in promoting services, again because of the inseparability element of the service product. Many services rely on the personal qualities and skills of the salesperson in the customer service exchange.

Not-for-profit organizations   As we saw in Chapter 1, marketing is increasingly being used outside the profit making/commercial sectors. A particular growth area for the application of marketing concepts and techniques has been the area of not-for-profit organizations. Before we begin to consider specifically the application of the marketing tools in such organizations it might be useful to consider the background to the application of marketing in these organizations, and indeed whether they really need marketing as such.

Not-for-profit organizations, whether inside or outside the mainstream of the public service, are frequently the subject of criticism for having top-heavy bureaucratic structures, an apathetic attitude to their consumers, and poor and wasteful management which is characterized by a reluctance to innovate. Such criticisms can be summed up as unresponsiveness and lack of communication. These are classic marketing problems, and it is not, therefore, unreasonable to assume that marketing can contribute to their solution. This view can be supported if we examine some of the marketing issues in what constitutes a large proportion of not-for-profit organizations, namely public-sector organizations.

Due to the fact that many public services are (a) virtual monopolies and (b) funded by government, it is not possible to draw significant parallels between such organizations and the commercial sector other than to recognize that both groups have 'marketing' problems. The essential difference is that for many public-sector organizations the principle of consumer sovereignty has a reduced significance. For the most part it has not been possible for consumers to exercise the ultimate sanction—the withdrawal of patronage. This is not to say that all public bodies have failed to respond effectively to their consumers. It is, however, true that where such failure has taken place, had the rules of the commercial sector been applicable, the guilty organizations would probably have been forced to change or go out of existence.

Since the period immediately after the Second World War, the UK has witnessed a dramatic growth in the number of not-for-profit organizations dedicated to the service of the public. At the outset, the level of altruism and the immediate job in hand were probably such that a conscious marketing effort was not thought necessary. Over time, the same changes that have necessitated changes in commercial marketing have also affected the public sector. Changes in life style, levels of affluence and the economy have altered attitudes to institutions which were once considered to be major social benefits. These changes have not been restricted to amenities such as libraries and other public recreational facilities, but have also extended to charities, the police force and the health authorities. It could be argued that the public has little choice but to accept the public services with which they are provided. To accede to such a proposition would, however, be to deny the fundamentals of the marketing concept. While a city library may lose custom because it is not a pleasant place to visit, the only equivalent to such a sanction with respect to more immediately essential services is an unresponsiveness which engenders apathy and eventually hostility. When such a situation occurs, an organization becomes inefficient, not only from an internal viewpoint, but quite clearly from the viewpoint of consumer satisfaction.

The missing element in organizations that have had experiences as described above is 'communication'. Quite simply, the organization has lost touch with its consumers. During the last decade not-for-profit organizations have begun to adopt a 'marketing orientation' which is designed to remedy this, not only in what is physically being offered, but also in terms of image and customer impressions. Like the business sector, there has been a transitional period during which organizations have moved from a 'selling' to a 'marketing' orientation. The providers of public amenities, for example, have recognized that it is not sufficient merely to offer short-term incentives and promotional campaigns; rather they have come to terms with deciding 'what business they are in'! Libraries or public swimming baths are more than what they seem to be if one considers them as satisfying the 'leisure' needs of the community, rather than providing a lending service or a pool of water in which to swim.

That not-for-profit organizations can have marketing problems has not always been recognized. This recognition is the first and principal step of readjustment to the changing needs of society and to better serving those needs that have always existed. The second step is to adopt a marketing approach to management. This can be achieved by viewing the not-for-profit organization as the marketer views the firm and its markets.

The principles of marketing are no different for not-for-profit organizations than they are for any commercial enterprise. The concept of the marketing mix has equal application: just as different companies employ a mix that is appropriate to their markets, the optimum marketing mix for public bodies will depend on the type of organization and the market conditions that prevail.

Applying marketing to not-for-profit organizations is made easier by regarding their marketing structures first as one would regard that of any commercial enterprise. Not-for-profit organizations are made up of the following components:

1. *Production*   This may seem unusual at first sight, but it makes sense if one considers production as an input/output system, whatever the 'product' might be. Input may simply involve the generation of ideas or the acquisition of the means to produce a service. However, this should be subject to the same degree of impetus and control that is applied to any production line of physical goods.

2. *Personnel*   The labour force is an integral part of the total marketing system; the appointment, training and reward structure should be implemented with this 'total' system in mind.

3. *Purchasing*   Just as in business, this should be conducted with cost and finished product in mind.

4. *Marketing*   Marketing is responsible for thinking in terms of the 'product', whether this be a good or a service. Marketing's role should also concern image, the environment and the optimization of the individual components that make up the organization. An actual marketing director is an increasingly evident feature of progressive organizations.

5. *Consumers*   Whatever the degree of choice that consumers have as to their usage of an organization, it should be uppermost in the minds of managers that, although custom may not be lost by inefficiency and poor communication (as in the case of a hospital), these defects imply that the marketing concept is not being successfully implemented. All the factors listed above should, therefore, be focused on the consumers.

6. *Publics*   In addition to the immediate consumer/supplier interface, the list of miscellaneous publics common to any organization should be considered so as to measure and improve goodwill and to afford a monitor on the changing environment.

Although there may need to be some modification to their application, most of the central concepts and techniques of marketing discussed in earlier chapters of this text, such as target marketing, market research and forecasting, analysing consumers, and so on, are equally relevant and useful to the not-for-profit organization. Just as in the profit-oriented organization, the basic aim of not-for-profit organizations is to obtain a desired response from a target market. The desired response may be, for example, a visit to a health centre or increased support for a police force, rather than the exchange of money for products and services, but the principles of marketing remain the same. As regards the application and combination of the marketing mix, in many ways not-for-profit organizations, but more specifically their 'products', are similar in many respects to service products. So, for example, they are often intangible in nature and also share some of the other characteristics of service products such as inseparability, variability, and so on. The additional elements of the marketing mix for services, therefore, come into play together with some of the variations in the application of the conventional four Ps with regard to service products already discussed.

Implementation

Implementation represents that part of the planning process where, what up to now, have simply been planning ideas and often just pieces of paper, plans are turned into action. Implementation involves areas such as budgets, resources, staffing, allocation of detailed responsibilities, timings, and so on. The required organizational structures and systems must also be put in place to ensure that plans can be effectively implemented. This element of the marketing plan introduces the often problematical aspect of managing people. The marketing manager, like any other manager, relies upon people to get things done. Effective marketing planning, and certainly effective implementation of these plans, relies on the effective management of people. In fact, many 'failures' in marketing plans can be traced to the ineffective management of the human asset. The marketing manager must therefore give careful thought to the direction of these assets such that they contribute towards the successful achievement of marketing and company objectives. Effective direction of marketing staff involves recruiting and selecting, training and developing and leading and motivating marketing personnel. The relationship between these elements and effective performance is shown in Fig. 12.10.

Abilities

Every manager will find it difficult to secure maximum performance from the staff if they lack the necessary abilities to function effectively in their duties. Ability, however, is in turn a function of a combination of effective recruitment and selection, plus effective training and development of marketing staff. Normally these aspects of human asset management are seen as being the prerogative of the personnel manager. The marketing manager, however, must not abrogate his or her duties in this area. The personnel department must be kept informed of the essential qualities and skills that must be looked for in job applicants for sales and marketing posts. This, in turn, will require a careful job analysis and the preparation of job descriptions. Marketing managers need to be involved in this process; indeed, there is a greater value to a company in conducting regular job analyses and preparing up-to-date job descriptions. This enhanced value lies in the fact that determining manpower requirements makes it necessary for the marketing manager to think carefully about the tasks the marketing staff is required to perform and the extent to which these tasks are still relevant to the effective performance of the manager's function. Job analyses and descriptions also

FIGURE 12.10

Effective performance and aspects of directing

form the basis for assessing performance and organizing development and training programmes.

Having selected the best available staff for the marketing function, individual potential must be developed and refined; this applies equally to both new entrants and existing staff. The marketing manager should ensure that all members of staff are adequately trained. In the case of new staff this may involve induction training and the development of the basic skills required to do the job. Existing staff, too, may from time to time be required to acquire new skills and patterns of behaviour. The marketing manager should ensure that there is an adequate system of career planning for the human assets in his or her department. Once again, it is recognized that training and development are specialist areas requiring specialist staff, specialist knowledge, and a specialist text.[14] Every marketing manager, however, is directly responsible for ensuring that his or her staff members are given adequate leadership and are motivated.

Effort

Motivation and leadership together constitute the second major element of human asset performance. Surprisingly, the first of these—motivation of marketing staff—is given very little attention in conventional texts on marketing management. 'Surprisingly' because, as we have seen in Chapter 3, an understanding of human motivation is essential for effective marketing decision-making. This understanding should be applied to the motivation of marketing staff. Marketing management should look beyond the simplistic view that what motivates individuals at work is financial inducement: money. In the same way that consumers may be motivated by a variety of complex and often hierarchical factors, so too has research shown that many of the higher-order needs in Maslow's hierarchy[15] can be fulfilled if the work is designed so as to give marketing staff a real feeling of responsibility and achievement.

Finally, in the role of managing the human asset, the marketer must fulfil his or her leadership function. As Handy points out,[16] the 'leadership problem' has attracted countless theories and spawned endless research. The evidence and the theories remain ambiguous and inconclusive. In practice, effective leadership in marketing management requires that the manager achieve a balance between supporting and encouraging members of staff, and ensuring that objectives are successfully met. Above all, the effective leader must constantly strive to win the trust and respect of subordinates.

Monitoring and control

The final stage of the marketing planning process is the establishment and implementation of systems for evaluation and control of the marketing plan. The essentials of any system of evaluation and control are shown in Fig. 12.11. Its essentials are:

- Setting standards for performance
- Evaluating performance against these standards
- Taking action to correct any deviations from standards

As we have already covered the importance of setting specific and preferably quantifiable standards of performance for marketing (as marketing objectives), we shall concentrate here on the evaluative and corrective elements of this process.

Essentially, in evaluating the department's marketing efforts the marketing manager needs to consider the following questions:

● What has happened?
● How does this compare with the standards of performance?
● What explains any differences between standards and actual performance?
● What action needs to be taken and by whom?

In fact, although the control process and the questions that relate to it are common to any control problem, as Kotler[17] points out, four types of marketing control may be distinguished:

● Control of the annual marketing plan
● Control of profitability
● Control of efficiency
● Strategic control

The marketing manager is interested in all four types of control, but the prime concern is with the first and last of these, namely control of the annual plan, and strategic control. We shall examine both the purpose of these two control areas and some of the control techniques or approaches that are associated with each.

Annual plan control

The purpose of annual plan control is to determine the extent to which marketing efforts over the year have been successful. Among the most frequently used control techniques in this evaluation are likely to be sales analysis and analysis of market share.

Sales analysis   Despite exhortations to be marketing- rather than sales-oriented in our approach to customers, overall marketing standards of performance, and therefore techniques of evaluation and control, are often geared to the analysis of sales.

Normally sales analysis will commence with a comparison of budgeted sales revenue against actual sales revenue. Any variations may be due to volume and/or price variances. For example, an unfavourable sales variance may be due to having had to cut prices. The manager must now examine closely the possible reasons for this. Further

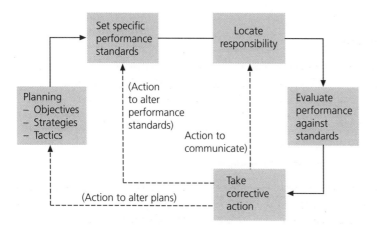

FIGURE 12.11

The control sequence in marketing

detailed analysis may be by individual products, territories, customers, etc., in order to determine more precise information on the nature and extent of price cutting. It should be recognized that these analyses may not lead directly to action. Frequently, data from sales analysis will be used to formulate hypotheses that will form the basis for experimentation. The results of these experiments are actionable. Sevin[18] has referred to the combination of analysis and experiment as *productivity analysis*.

Analysis of market share   Of all the approaches to controlling annual marketing operations, analysis of market share represents one of the most useful and, therefore, widely used techniques. The principal reason for measuring and evaluating market share performance is that it allows a company to assess how well it is doing *vis-à-vis* competitors. For example, a company might find that, while its sales volume has declined over the year, its market share has increased. Clearly, declining sales volume would still represent a cause for concern; nevertheless, an increase in market share would indicate that a company is faring better than competitors in a market that has declined overall. The importance of this conclusion would suggest a very different course of action on the part of marketing management than that suggested by a simple analysis of sales.

A second reason for using market share analysis in marketing control stems from the fact that often overall marketing objectives are couched in terms of market share. Certainly, to some extent market share does indeed represent an overall indication of the efficiency of total marketing efforts compared with competitors. However, as we have seen in Chapter 4 the BCG analysis, perhaps a more pressing reason for stating objectives in terms of market share, is the newly recognized strong link between relative market share and profitability. The general nature of this relationship is shown in Fig. 12.12.

As with sales analysis, measurement of market alone is not sufficient to determine what actions should be taken. The evaluation process requires that marketing management determines the reasons for observed levels of company market share and any significant differences and trends. On the basis of this, the marketing manager must

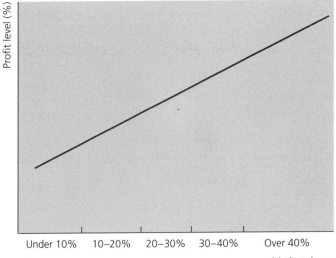

FIGURE 12.2

Generalized relationship between market share and profitability

then determine what actions are required and by whom. Results and conclusions of the evaluation of the annual marketing plan must be discussed with those responsible, and a future plan of action agreed.

Contingency plans   Where there are substantial deviations between desired and achieved performance with regard to the marketing plan, as part of the control process the marketer should have a set of pre-established courses of action to deal with such major deviations. This is especially necessary where the deviations are due to changed circumstances such as, for example, changes in the environmental or to competitive forces and factors such as an unexpected political event or a sudden devaluation. Although part of the control process, in fact contingency plans should be drawn up at the start of the annual planning process. The contingency plans should be linked to any assumptions regarding future developments and trends that have formed part of the analysis and input to the plan. This means that the marketer has plans in reserve ready to cope with circumstances where the assumptions on which the plan is based turn out to be incorrect or ill-founded. For example, the environmental analysis might have suggested an annual inflation rate over the period of the marketing plan of, say, 3 per cent. Where this figure is critical to the marketing plan then contingency plans should be established in advance in case this assumed inflation rate turns out not to be correct.

Strategic control: the marketing audit   More often than not, annual plan control will result in a re-evaluation of objectives, strategies and tactics with a view to preparing next year's plan of action. From time to time, however, a more comprehensive and far-reaching evaluation of marketing objectives, strategies and tactics needs to be undertaken based on a detailed appraisal and evaluation of the total marketing operation, marketing performance and the marketing environment. This type of comprehensive evaluation represents a full marketing audit. You will recognize, of course, that we now have both started and finished the marketing planning process with the marketing audit. This is as it should be, the marketing audit starts the whole process of marketing planning over again. The marketing audit, though, is much more an appraisal of effectiveness rather than of efficiency. The marketing audit both completes and starts the marketing planning process.

CHAPTER SUMMARY

This chapter has considered the overall process and importance of marketing planning detailing each of the steps which the marketer needs to complete in the planning process.

We have looked at the link between the marketing planning process and the overall strategic planning process starting with the all-important business mission and moving through the marketing audit and SWOT analysis to the setting of objectives, strategy identification and selection, and finally the management of the marketing mix. We also introduced some of the key techniques of strategy appraisal and selection including the Ansoff Matrix and some of the more widely used portfolio planning tools. Ultimately, the marketing plan requires the marketer to select target markets and to develop detailed marketing mix strategies in order to position effectively within these target segments. We have looked in some detail therefore at how the marketer can combine the marketing mix in different marketing settings and situations. Finally, we have introduced the notion of the importance of implementing marketing plans and the organizational and human resource aspects of this, together with the process of controlling and evaluating marketing plans.

CHAPTER REVIEW QUESTIONS

1. What do you understand by the term 'business mission' in the context of the marketing planning process, and how does Abel's concept of the 'business domain' help in defining the business mission?
2. Outline the process of conducting a SWOT analysis and discuss the importance of the SWOT analysis for marketing planning purposes.
3. Discuss the use of the Ansoff Matrix in identifying opportunities for growth.
4. Explain how any *one* of the following tools of strategic market planning can be used in helping to identify and select marketing strategies:

   a. Boston Consulting Groups (BCG) growth share matrix.
   b. The new BCG matrix.
   c. McKinsey/General Electrics multifactor portfolio matrix.
5. Briefly outline how the marketing mix might be combined and vary according to the following situations:

   a. At different stages of the product life cycle.
   b. In industrial versus consumer markets.
   c. In services marketing.
   d. In small- and medium-sized enterprises.
   e. In not-for-profit organizations.

References

1. D. Abel, *Defining the Business, The Starting Point of Strategic Planning*, Prentice-Hall, Englewood Cliffs, NJ, 1980.
2. T. Levitt, 'Marketing myopia', *Harvard Business Review*, July/August 1960.
3. J. Argenti, *Systematic Corporate Planning*, John Wiley, Chichester, 1979.
4. G. Lancaster and L. Massingham, *Marketing Management*, 3rd edn, McGraw-Hill, London, 2001, pp. 102–108.
5. G. Hamel and C. K. Prahalad, 'Strategic intent', *Harvard Business Review*, **67** No. 3, 1989, pp. 63–76.
6. R. L. Ackoff, *A Concept of Corporate Planning*, Wiley-Interscience, New York, 1970.
7. I. H. Ansoff, 'Strategies for diversification', *Harvard Business Review*, September/October 1957.
8. G. S. Day, *Analysis for Strategic Marketing Decisions*. West Publishing, St Paul, MN, 1986.
9. G. E. Greenley, *The Strategic and Operational Planning of Marketing*, McGraw-Hill, London, 1986.
10. P. M. Chisnall, *Strategic Industrial Marketing*, Prentice-Hall, Englewood Cliffs, NJ, 1985.
11. N. H. Borden, 'The concept of the marketing mix', in *Science in Marketing*, G. Schwartz (ed.), John Wiley, New York, 1965.
12. G. A. Lancaster and L. Massingham, *Marketing Management*, 3rd edn, McGraw-Hill, London, 2001, pp. 42–44.
13. J. O'Shaughnessy, *Competitive Marketing: A Strategic Approach*, 2nd edn, Unwin Hyman, London, 1988, p. 182.
14. D. S. Markwell and T. J. Roberts, *Organisation of Management Development Programmes*, Gower Press, Aldershot, 1970.
15. A. H. Maslow, 'A theory of human motivation', *Psychological Review*, **50**, 1943, pp. 370–96.
16. C. B. Handy, *Understanding Organizations*, Penguin, Harmondsworth, 1976, pp. 87–104.
17. P. Kotler, *Marketing Management: Analysis, Planning, Implementation and Control*, 8th edn, Prentice-Hall, Englewood Cliffs, NJ, pp. 741–762.
18. C. H. Sevin, *Marketing Productivity Analysis*, McGraw-Hill, New York, 1965.

Icing on the Cake

Jane Asher is probably one of the best known names in the UK when it comes to supplying cakes or materials associated with cake and cake icing/decoration. Jane's company now supplies all the major supermarkets and many other types of outlets with her range of quality products.

In contrast, June, proprietor of Icing on the Cake, is still a relatively small company in this market. June started icing cakes as a hobby, attending evening classes to learn the skills. Initially, icing cakes for friends and relatives on the occasions of birthdays, weddings, etc., June's cake icing and decoration business has gradually expanded to the point where she is now supplying on a commercial basis, albeit locally.

Interviewed by the local newspaper about the success of her business, June stated that she could see that there would be a terrific demand for individually iced and decorated cakes as customers were looking for something more than those that could be bought off the shelf through confectioners and more traditional suppliers.

With an initial capital of £20 000 supplied by her husband who had received damages following a motor bike accident, June rented a small factory, purchased some machinery and began to produce iced cakes to order. Orders come through classified advertising, advertising in local magazines such as, for example, church magazines, but increasingly June is beginning to supply local shops and outlets again to order.

The success of her business is down to her icing skills, but also her individual approach to satisfying customers' requirements. She uses only the best ingredients for her cakes and decorations, and this has been a major factor in her success.

She has recently extended her factory space and now employs six people producing over 200 cakes per week.

Until recently, June's marketing has been confined to the advertising and promotion in the media mentioned above and, of course, careful attention to the product itself. Prices are not the lowest but are competitive.

June is wise enough to realize, however, that the good fortune she has had with her business may not last for ever without a more formal system of marketing planning and control.

You have known June personally for over twenty years and she knows that you lecture in marketing. She has asked you to advise her with regard to the following.

Questions

1. What are the key benefits to be gained by a company like Icing on the Cake from establishing and implementing a more formalized marketing planning system.

2. What are the essential elements of a marketing plan and how would these elements relate to the Icing on the Cake company?

Part Four

MARKETING'S WIDER ISSUES

Chapter Thirteen

CUSTOMER CARE AND RELATIONSHIP MARKETING

LEARNING OBJECTIVES *This chapter will help you to:*

- understand the importance, scope and meaning of customer care and relationship marketing and the links between these two areas of marketing;

- appreciate why customer care and relationship marketing have become important in contemporary marketing;

- understand how to develop policies and programmes to improve standards of customer care in an organization;

- understand how and when to develop policies and programmes of relationship marketing;

- appreciate some of the recent developments in customer care and relationship marketing, and in particular the role of new technology and its impact on these areas.

INTRODUCTION

As you would expect, marketing is an evolving body of thought and practice. We have seen how the original ideas about what marketing is, both as a concept and as a management function, have developed over the years. So, for example, we have seen how the application of the marketing concept and tools has widened from its original primary application in marketing consumer goods in profit-seeking organizations to industrial markets, service markets and not-for-profit organizations. Similarly, we have seen how new technology and technological developments are changing the practice of marketing. In fact, so much is happening with regard to developments in contemporary marketing thinking and practice that it is difficult, and certainly debatable, to select what are the most important and far-reaching of these for the modern marketer. However, most would agree that among the most significant trends and developments in recent years have been the interlinked developments of an increased emphasis on customer care activities, coupled with the growth of relationship marketing. For many, developments in these two areas represent what constitutes an almost seismic shift in marketing thinking and practice. Why this is felt in marketing circles we shall see shortly, together with the implications of this shift. To some extent, however, we have already hinted at the importance of these two areas in the development of marketing inasmuch as we have touched on both customer care and relationship marketing at several points in earlier chapters. In this chapter, we shall concentrate on customer care and relationship marketing examining their implications for the contemporary marketer. We shall start first with customer care and then continue by looking at relationship marketing. It is important to stress, though, that these two areas of contemporary marketing are very much interrelated and in many ways are the two sides of the same coin.

CUSTOMER CARE

Marketers care about customers. We have seen that the marketing concept itself centres on the importance of customers and the absolute necessity of identifying and satisfying their needs and wants. The marketer puts the customer at the centre of the business and the development of organizational strategies. This idea is meat and drink to most marketers and even non-marketers, for example other functions of the business would hesitate to disagree with the notion of the importance and centrality of customers. If this is the case, then why has there been an upsurge in the importance of customer care in marketing programmes in recent years, and how, if at all, does the notion and scope of customer care differ from the traditional marketing concept? Finally, how can a company plan and implement effective customer care programmes in the organization?

The meaning and scope of customer care

There are many views as to the meaning and scope of customer care. The view taken here is that:

> Customer care involves the planning of all the activities involved in the customer/supplier relationship including the pre-, during- and post-transaction stages so as to ensure that customers' expectations with regard to the transaction process are met or exceeded.

This view of customer care stresses the fact that customer care is an all-embracing approach covering every aspect of customer/supplier relationships. It also illustrates that customer care involves planning and activities.

Customer care involves much more than the notion of *customer service*. The notion of customer service focuses more on just the 'order-cycle' related activities in the organization. Certainly customer service is an important facet of overall customer care, but centres more on those activities which involve direct contact with the customer. Customer care is a much more holistic way of looking at customer satisfaction.

Customer care necessitates the involvement of every facet of the company's marketing and customer-related programmes and should affect every stage of the marketing planning and implementation process. But why do we need customer care, and why has it grown in importance in recent years?

The cost of poor customer care

It is increasingly recognized that should the customer's expectations at any point in the supplier/customer relationship not be met, this will result in customer dissatisfaction. Obviously the extent to which the customer feels dissatisfied depends upon the circumstances. So, for example, the customer may be simply mildly dissatisfied or at the other extreme, if you like, 'hopping mad'. Particularly where the latter is the case, however, we know that such customers are unlikely to purchase again from the supplier. Moreover, we know that every dissatisfied customer is likely to talk about this dissatisfaction to other customers or potential customers. Stone and Young[1] suggest that in fact customers with bad experiences are twice as likely to tell others about it as those with good experiences. Quite simply then, poor customer care loses not only the customer involved but perhaps another twenty as well.

The benefits of good customer care

In contrast, satisfied customers are a major business asset. We know that satisfied customers are much more likely to return to buy again, and in fact over time become loyal. This illustrates just one of the links between customer care and relationship marketing. This is particularly important when we look at the costs of acquiring customers compared to keeping them. Kotler[2] has suggested that it can cost as much as ten times more to acquire a new customer than it does to keep an existing one. Certainly, the marketing costs required to persuade a new customer to purchase are much greater than those required to persuade a satisfied customer to purchase again. In this respect, the notion of a 'ladder of loyalty' has been developed. Peck *et al.*[3] show this notion of a ladder of loyalty as involving the steps or rungs shown in Fig. 13.1.

FIGURE 13.1

The relationship marketing ladder of loyalty

Source: H. Peck, A. Payne, M. Christopher, M. Clark, *Relationship Marketing*, Butterworth-Heinemann, 1999, p. 45

The first rung on the ladder 'Prospect' represents an individual or an organization which the marketer could possibly persuade to do business. Once the prospect has been persuaded in this way he, she or it becomes a 'Purchaser', having done business at least once with the organization. The 'Client' is someone who has done business with the marketer's organization on a repeat basis, but is still at best neutral towards the supplier. A supporter, however, is someone who has done business with the marketer on a regular basis, but now begins to like the supplier's organization and will give support if only passively. The penultimate stage on the ladder, the 'Advocate' is a customer who actively recommends the marketer's organization to others, i.e. effectively someone who does your marketing for you. And the highest rung of the ladder is represented by a 'Partner' who is a customer who effectively has the relationship of a partner with the supplying organization.

As we shall see, relationship marketing is aimed at moving customers up the ladder of loyalty until they ultimately become partners. The lifetime value of loyal customers can be huge as measured in sales and profit terms. Given that customer care is a major facet in moving customers up the ladder of loyalty, we can see why marketers have become increasingly interested in the customer care aspects of marketing. This does not explain, however, the growth in importance of customer care.

Customer expectations

Perhaps the major reason for the growth in the importance of customer care is the fact that customers' expectations have changed over the years. Quite simply, customers expect much higher levels of customer care and satisfaction from the marketer. In part, this is as a result of changes in education on the part of many customers. Customers are now much more ready to challenge poor levels of customer care and are much better informed as regards their rights in this respect. Another factor which has contributed to changed customer expectations is the fact that customers now have much better access to information about failings and shortcomings in customer care through much more media exposure in this area. Finally, customers are now much better protected through legislation regarding their rights as customers and what they can realistically and justifiably expect with respect to customer care.

Today's customers therefore will not put up with poor levels of customer care. More and more of them are willing to complain if they feel their expectations have not been met in any way. Moreover, they are increasingly likely to follow up these complaints through some form of formal procedure and even litigation if necessary. It is important to stress, however, that the average customer, even in the USA, where perhaps the highest levels of customer expectation with regard to customer care in the world exist, is still reluctant to complain. So, for example, a report by The White House Office of Consumer Affairs[4] suggested that the average business does not hear from 96 per cent of its unhappy customers, and that for every complaint received there were as many as 30 customers with problems or serious problems. In the UK, where customers are notoriously reluctant to complain, even though, as already suggested, this is changing, these figures are likely to be even higher. One might be tempted therefore to believe that most customers are simply not that concerned about customer care to the extent that they perhaps do not think it is worth complaining. Certainly, many customers probably do not feel it is worth while, but this is probably more a reflection of the fact that they feel that their complaints will go unheeded or fall on deaf ears. Other customers simply may not know how to start to complain in any formal way. This does not mean, of course, that such customers are not concerned about customer care and that the marketer therefore need not be too concerned either. In fact, just the opposite is the case, it is probably the customers who do not complain that are the most important with regard to focusing improved customer care efforts. Such customers represent the majority of those customers who never purchase again and, in addition, represent the main sources of negative information about a company and its products that gets passed on to other potential customers.

Steps in establishing a customer care programme

As already stated, most companies would accept the need for, and benefits of, effective customer care. However, although crucial, mere acceptance of this fact is not sufficient to ensure effective customer care. A series of practical steps must be implemented in establishing effective customer care programmes in an organization. The main steps in this process are as follows:

Identifying customer needs and perceptions
As with all marketing and marketing-related programmes, the start point of effective customer care is the identification of customer needs. Remember, customer care is about ensuring that these needs are met and in particular that the customers' expectations are fulfilled or exceeded. Many companies still do not fully understand what their customers' needs and expectations are with regard to the various facets of the transaction process. Again, remember that customers are often reluctant to complain, and in any event if the customer does complain then it is already too late. The marketer must therefore research customers' needs in order to establish precisely what constitutes customer satisfaction and the customers' expectations with regard to the various facets of the transaction process. The marketer must also at this stage consider the perceptions that customers have with regard to the company and its standards of customer care.

Incorporating customer care standards into company mission statements
Having identified customer needs and perceptions, the next step in establishing a customer care programme is to ensure that customer care is enshrined in the company's overall operating philosophy as evidenced in its overall mission statement. In a way, this is part of the process of establishing a company care philosophy and attitude throughout an organization which we shall return to again shortly.

Establishing customer care standards and specifications
This step in the process involves the company establishing specific levels for customer care and the key activities and processes to be included. These must relate to the customers' expectations and needs established in the first step. So, for example, we need to establish delivery standards, standards for customer responsiveness, courtesy and credibility, product quality and so on. Every facet of the company which may impinge on customer satisfaction needs to be incorporated here and not just marketing activities and personnel. Specific standards for customer care which can be measured and evaluated need to be established at this stage. Although customer care programmes should meet the highest possible level of standards in line with customer expectations, it is important to establish basic minimum level of customer care below which levels of customer care should not drop under any circumstances.

Specifying jobs and activities   Related to required standards and specifications for customer care there needs to be detailed specifications of what this means for people's activities and jobs within the organization. It should include, for example, the designation of tasks and activities, the allocation of responsibilities, the motivation and monitoring and control systems necessary to implement and monitor customer care and the information systems required to facilitate effective customer care programmes.

Ensuring adequate systems for monitoring and evaluating levels of customer care   It is important that effective systems are established for measuring and evaluating standards of customer care including, for example, tracking and monitoring systems, market research and customer evaluation procedures. In addition clear systems and procedures for ensuring effective responses to any problems with customer care levels, including complaints, are necessary.

These, then, are the practical steps in implementing customer care programmes, but over and above these steps, effective customer care as much as anything requires an organization-wide commitment to it. Again, in this respect it is important to stress that this is not just a marketing department responsibility and activity. The importance of customer care and an acceptance of this importance throughout every level and function of the organization is crucial. Customer care must be part of the overall corporate culture. Moreover, it should impinge on every facet of the marketing programme. It is to these two aspects of implementing customer care programmes that we now turn our attention.

Establishing a customer care culture and philosophy

Again, it cannot be stressed enough that effective customer care is not something that can be left solely to the marketing and sales department. Put another way 'customer care' is everyone's business. In much the same way as the adoption of the marketing concept necessitates a culture change within many organizations, so too does the adoption of the customer care concept. However, instilling this philosophy throughout an organization is not easy. Again, as with the marketing concept customers or, to be more specific, customer care is often seen as being someone else's responsibility. Adopting a customer care philosophy starts at the very top of the organization and must have the full support and commitment of the senior management. The importance of customer care must also be 'marketed' throughout the organization. In effect, this is part of the process of 'internal marketing' which we referred to in Chapter 1. Individuals and functions in the organization must be persuaded and shown how their activities relate to overall levels of customer care and the impact they can have on this area. Implementing this philosophy throughout an organization also requires that individuals' tasks, activities, responsibilities and, where appropriate, even promotion and remuneration are linked to customer care. Put another way, customer care responsibilities must be part of everyone's job in the organization.

Needless to say, the marketing function does have a primary role to play in this process, in particular the marketer or marketing function should be responsible for providing up-to-date and reliable information about what it is that customers want with regard to customer care, how various activities in the organization contribute or otherwise to the satisfaction of customer needs and any problems or shortcomings in this respect. The marketer must also ensure that track is kept of competitor levels of customer care and any trends in these levels.

Customer care and the marketing process

Where a commitment to customer care has become part of a company's organizational philosophy we will find that customer care impinges on and informs the whole of the marketing process. This notion can most easily be seen by returning to the typical steps in the marketing planning process which was established in earlier chapters. We can see from this how a company-wide philosophy and commitment to customer care affects the whole marketing process. Each of the steps in the marketing planning process, together with an outline of how customer care relates to each of these steps, is outlined below.

Corporate objectives/business mission   As we have already seen, a commitment to customer care should be reflected and enshrined in the overall corporate objectives and mission statements of the organization. At this stage, mission statements about overall customer care objectives feed into and shape the subsequent stages and strategies of the marketing plan. Mission statements that do not encompass customer care as central to the company's aims are likely to suggest that an organization is not committed to maintaining high levels of caring for customers within the operating framework of the organization.

The marketing audit/SWOT analysis   Remember, the market audit encompasses an appraisal of the internal and external environments of the company. With regard to the external environment analysis, this should help shape required levels of customer care as regards, for example, changing cultural and social values that, in turn, are reflected in customer requirements and expectations for customer care levels. Competitor customer care levels should also be appraised in the external audit. As regards the internal part of the audit, this requires the organization to assess standards of performance regarding customer care and any shortcomings therein. As we have seen, the internal and external audit feed into the SWOT analysis. Part of the SWOT analysis should be an assessment of strengths and weaknesses and opportunities and threats with regard to customer care levels and programmes. So, for example, a company may establish through the audit that it has major weaknesses in certain elements of its customer care activities which need to be remedied. Alternatively, a company may identify possible future opportunities by building on strong levels of customer care compared to competitors.

Marketing objectives and strategies   Marketing objectives and strategies, too, should include customer care elements. Overall, marketing objectives may relate to, for example, growth and market share, but should also include specific objectives with regard to levels of customer care. Again, tools such as gap analysis to correct gaps in required versus achieved levels of customer care may be used here. As regards marketing strategies, clearly different strategies for growth such as diversification will often have customer care implications. If the intention is to pursue new markets, for example, as a strategy for growth, the marketer will need to establish customer needs and expectations regarding customer care levels in these markets.

Marketing tactics/marketing mix decisions   Perhaps one of the most important facets regarding customer care and the marketing mix is to ensure that marketing mix decisions, and in particular specific marketing tactics which can often be short term in nature, do not conflict with or detract from overall planned levels of customer care. So, for example, pricing strategies designed to attract new customers may result in lower levels of customer care than is necessary or required. Virtually every facet of the marketing mix has implications for customer care. Thus delivery and after-sales service stem from distribution and logistics decisions; product decisions, and in particular the augmented product, has a major effect on customer care; promotion should be aimed at building long-term customer relationships; and pricing should reflect overall customer care strategies.

Implementation   We saw earlier that overall objectives for customer care need to be translated into specific action programmes with the allocation of responsibilities, systems and procedures and should include training and motivation of staff. Suitable organizational structures also need to be in place in order to implement effective customer care programmes.

Evaluation and control   It perhaps goes without saying that effective customer care, like all the other areas of marketing, needs to be evaluated and controlled. Systems for monitoring achieved levels of customer care, responses to customer complaints, etc. must be built into the company's overall evaluation and control systems.

As we can see then, customer care affects, and is affected by, every single facet of the marketing planning process. Before we move on to consider the development of relationship marketing, including how this relates to customer care, we need to consider the relationship between customer care and quality, and the distinction between customer care and customer service.

CUSTOMER CARE AND QUALITY

Needless to say there is a very close, but quite complex, relationship between customer care and quality management in the organization. Quality has been a major issue in competitive strategy in recent years, and in particular the pursuit of improved and consistent quality has been a major objective of many companies. This interest in and pursuit of quality has mainly been due to the fact that we know now that quality is a major factor in competitive success. The PIMS programme[5] developed by the Strategic Planning Institute and outlined in Appendix 1 of this text has clearly established the link between good and consistent quality and profitability. Even on an anecdotal level we all know the problems that organizations or even whole countries have experienced in their marketing when they have suffered from quality problems. Obviously, given our definition of customer care, effective standards of customer care are impossible where the quality that the customer experiences or perceives does not match their expectations. Customer care and quality, therefore, are inextricably linked.

One of the major developments in recent years with regard to quality management has been the so-called total quality management (TQM) approach. As the term implies, TQM entails managing every facet of the company's activities with regard to delivering pre-determined standards of quality encompassing every facet of the company's activities. Given that such quality management should revolve around meeting customer requirements and expectations, and that in fact what represents acceptable quality is essentially determined by customers and their requirements, then obviously customer care and TQM are closely related. Quality programmes, however, encompass many other areas than dealing with customers, while customer care programmes are specifically focused on customers and how to improve care. The major influence of TQM on customer care activities is in the notion that with TQM processes all activities including not only those in-company, but, for example, encompassing distributors forward down the chain and suppliers, looking backward down the chain, which can affect quality. Total Quality Management also gives central place to the customer in designing quality systems. In fact customer-driven quality is one of the key distinguishing features of TQM as a philosophy. In many ways then TQM and customer care go hand in hand in the contemporary organization. But what is the relationship between customer care and customer service?

CUSTOMER CARE AND CUSTOMER SERVICE

A degree of confusion exists regarding the relationship and distinction between customer care and customer service. In fact, although the two are closely related there are also some major differences. Some of the key differences are captured by Stone and Young[6] and shown in Table 13.1.

Taking each of these differences in turn, customer service emphasizes the tasks involved in servicing customers rather than customer needs. It is more a supplier's view of the elements of customer requirements as opposed to the customer's perspective. Customer service also focuses primarily on the costs associated with customer requirements, whereas customer care centres on long-term profit and revenue implications. With customer service, much more attention is given to procedures, management processes and hierarchies, and on the technical and administrative requirements associated with customer service. Customer care, on the other hand, emphasizes the importance of procedures which encourage responsiveness to customer needs and ways in which management systems and procedures can support this with a view to achieving commercial as opposed to technical or engineering aims and goals. Having said this, in many companies we still find customer service departments. There is nothing wrong with this as such so long as the elements of customer service and the activities of the customer service department are set and managed in the context of a wider overall company approach and perspective regarding customer care. Put another way, customer service is but a part of the overall customer care activities.

TABLE 13.1 *Differences between customer service and customer care*

Customer service	Customer care
Emphasizes tasks	Emphasizes customers
Focuses on costs	Focuses on profit and revenue
Procedures restrict responsiveness	Procedures enable responsiveness
Hierarchical management	Supportive management
Technical/administrative environment	Commercial environment

Source: M. Stone and L. Young, *Competitive Customer Care: A Guide to Keeping Customers*, Croner, Kingston-upon-Thames, 1992, p. 20

RELATIONSHIP MARKETING

Our second major development in marketing thinking and practice is the growth of relationship marketing. Again we would stress that relationship marketing is very much interlinked with the notion and practice of customer care. We shall therefore highlight these links between the two areas where appropriate as we discuss relationship marketing.

If anything the growth of relationship marketing represents an even more significant shift in marketing thinking and practice than the growth of the philosophy of customer care. So much so that it is often referred to as involving a paradigm shift in the marketing concept itself. Certainly there is no doubt that the development of relationship marketing has had and will continue to have major implications for the marketing manager. Comprehensive accounts of the development, meaning and implications of relationship marketing for the contemporary marketer is given by Lancaster and Massingham.[7] What follows is an overview of these aspects of relationship marketing.

As so often, there are many different views as to the precise nature and hence definition of relationship marketing. So, for example, Gronroos[8] stresses the element of mutual exchange and trust in relationship marketing as follows.

> Relationship marketing is a process including several parties or actors, the objectives of which have to be met. This is done by mutual exchange and fulfilment of promises, a fact that makes trust an important aspect of marketing.

Stone and Woodcock[9] on the other hand put more emphasis on the more traditional tools of sales, communications and customer care techniques. Again, we see the overlap between these two areas.

> Relationship marketing involves the use of a wide range of marketing, sales, communications and customer care techniques and processes to: identify named individual customers, create a relationship between the company and these customers, and manage that relationship to the benefit of both customers and company.

Perhaps one of the simplest and yet most powerful summaries of what relationship marketing is however, is that provided by Buttle.[10]

> At its best, RM (relationship management) is characterized by a genuine concern to meet or exceed the expectations of customers and to provide excellent service in an environment of trust and commitment to the relationship.

Buttle goes on to indicate what is involved in successful relationship marketing and the commitment of the company required to generate this success:

> To be successful relationship marketers, companies must develop a supportive organizational culture, market the RM idea internally, intimately understand customers expectations, create and maintain a detailed customer database, and organize and reward employees in such a way that the objective of RM, customer retention, is achieved.

This illustrates that relationship marketing has major implications for both how we think about marketing and our approach to the practice of marketing. It affects and includes the provision of marketing information, organizational systems and procedures, and the elements of marketing strategy. But what are the characteristics of a relationship marketing approach, and in particular, how does relationship marketing compare and contrast with the more conventional so-called 'transaction marketing approach'. Related to this, why has relationship marketing emerged as a suggested new paradigm for marketing and what are some of the key implications of this new paradigm for the practice of marketing management.

Relation and transaction marketing compared and contrasted

Relationship marketing first became evident in business-to-business marketing, but for reasons we shall see shortly, the relationship marketing approach is now increasingly found in the services sector and in consumer marketing. To understand the nature of relationship marketing it is useful to compare and contrast relationship marketing with the more conventional and traditional transaction marketing approach.

Conventional transaction marketing is based on the seller offering immediate and hopefully attractive combinations of product, price, technical support, etc., in order to generate a sale. The emphasis, although perhaps implicitly, is on completing this individual transaction and in turn this completion is the measure of success of the exchange. The marketer then moves on to finding the next customer and/or with the same customer generating another individual transaction after which the process commences again. The buyer is interested in the best possible value, and the marketer with the revenue from the exchange and there is little emphasis on customer service or long-term relationships by either party. Lancaster[11] argues that this emphasis in traditional transaction marketing on one-off exchange is what distinguishes transaction from relationship marketing. In relationship marketing the emphasis switches to developing a longer term and interactive set of relationships between the marketer and customers. In particular the marketer is concerned to move the customer up the ladder of loyalty discussed earlier to the point where the customer becomes a partner with the supplier. Although transactions and immediate satisfaction are still important to both parties, in relationship marketing the success of the exchange is the extent to which both parties benefit through cooperation and agreement. In the most successful examples of relationship marketing the two parties grow more trusting, more knowledgeable about each others' interests and needs and more interested in helping each other. Transactions cease to be negotiated each and every time and become part of a longer term routine. The outcome of successful relationship marketing is the development of solid, dependable supplier–customer relationships which form the basis of a marketing network and represent a true marketing asset.

In fact, relationship marketing, as opposed to traditional transactional marketing, can be seen as opposite ends of a continuum. The distinctions between transaction marketing and relationship marketing already highlighted, together with additional key areas of difference are well summarized by Kotler[12] and are shown in Table 13.2. We can see from this table that relationship and transaction marketing are indeed at different ends of several spectrums. But why has relationship marketing emerged? What has given rise to this paradigm shift in the concept of marketing?

Reasons for the growth of relationship marketing

The well-established notions of 'exchange' and 'interaction' in marketing provide the theoretical antecedents for the emergence of relationship marketing. To these two acknowledge antecedents, Gummesson[13] adds the notion of 'networks'. Others, however, point out that the growth of relationship marketing may in fact be down to much more hard-nosed pragmatic reasons. These reasons, they assert, are based on the fact that both marketer and customer have increasingly recognized that relationship marketing—and in particular the requirements needed to develop effective relationship marketing such as the building of strong trust and confidence between the two parties, the exchange of information, effective communication and mutual support in a partnership—quite simply makes good business sense.

Perhaps this explains why relationship marketing first began to emerge in business-to-business markets where relationship marketing was much more readily seen to make good commercial sense. For the marketer, building long-term relationships with customers can lead to substantially lower marketing and other costs. For example, lower costs are incurred in advertising and promotion in order to attract and keep customers. Selling costs, too, can be lower, particularly in business-to-business markets where salespeople can spend less time on having to prospect new customers. Both implicitly and explicitly relationship marketing focuses on customer retention. As we saw with customer service, companies have at long last realized the financial value of keeping customers. Cram[14] illustrates that the life time value of loyal customers is potentially huge. Similarly, Kotler[15] suggests that today's companies must pay closer attention to their customer defection rates and take strategic steps to keep these rates to a minimum. In this respect, relationship marketing is one of the key tools in improving customer retention rates in a company. This recognition of the financial pay-off of building long-term, lasting relationships with customers is now being increasingly recognized in consumer goods markets in addition to business-to-business markets.

Needless to say, relationship marketing would not have increased in importance if the other side of the coin were not present, i.e. if there were no benefits for the customer. In fact, relationship marketing can only be of value where it also bestows important and valued benefits to customers. Again, in the case of business-to-business customers these benefits are often readily identified and therefore easier to communicate. These benefits are principally, but not exclusively, financial in nature. For example, for the manufacturing customer, developing effective relationships with suppliers enables more cost-effective systems of production purchasing such as just-in-time (JIT) system. In addition, through relationship marketing more and more companies are able to develop collaborative ventures with their customers or suppliers with regard to developing new products. Clearly both JIT and collaborative new product development require effective long-term relationships between customer and marketer.

TABLE 13.2   *Transaction marketing vs relationship marketing*

Transaction marketing	Relationship marketing
Focus on single sale	Focus on customer retention
Orientation on product features	Orientation on product benefits
Short timescale	Long timescale
Little emphasis on customer service	High customer service emphasis
Limited commitment to customer	High commitment to customer
Moderate customer contact	Extensive customer contact
Quality is primarily concern of production	Quality concern of all functions

Source: Adapted from P. Kotler, *Marketing Management: Analysis, Planning and Control*, 7th edn, Prentice-Hall, Englewood Cliffs, NJ, 1991

Perhaps less obviously a relationship marketing approach also potentially bestows major benefits on the customer in consumer goods markets. For example, if a customer feels they can purchase the same brand every time because they feel they can trust the brand and/or supplier, this can substantially help reduce the time, effort and risk in making a purchase. In addition, many of the relationship marketing campaigns used in consumer markets actually involve some sort of financial inducement for the customer to become involved in a long-term relationship with the marketer. The use of loyalty cards, air miles, and bonus points, etc., are all examples of the sort of inducements designed to encourage the customer up the ladder of loyalty.

Overall, then, as one would expect from any successful relationship, both parties need to feel they can benefit if relationship marketing is to be appropriate and successful. In this respect, Bund-Jackson[16] has suggested that the development of a relationship marketing approach is not always appropriate for all customers. Indeed, she suggests that some customers are in fact better managed through the traditional transaction marketing approach. These customers she refers to as 'always-a-share' customers. These customers include those who have low switching costs in terms of changing suppliers/brands and therefore can change relatively easily. Because of this, they do not value long-term relationships with suppliers and indeed prefer to negotiate individual transactions each time a purchase is made. Other types of customer in this category include customers who are making one-off purchases and hence are obviously not interested in supplier relationships and those customers who are 'brand promiscuous' and want to try out as many different brands as possible in seeking, for example, variety. For this category of customers, any would-be supplier, therefore, is always in a position to gain a share of this type of customer's business. Bund-Jackson points out that relationship marketing with such customers is ineffective and indeed inappropriate.

In contrast, she has termed the customers who are best suited to a relationship marketing approach as 'lost-for-good' customers. The characteristics of such customers are that they have high switching costs in terms of changing suppliers, they tend to have longer time horizons, make a series of purchases over time, and view commitments to particular suppliers or brands as important and preferably relatively permanent. Once a supplier has won this type of account, the customer is likely to remain loyal to the supplier for a long time. If lost, however, the customer often never returns to the supplier, hence Bund-Jackson's term for this particular category of customers. If anything, the incidence of lost-for-good customers, particularly in business-to-business markets, has grown in recent years, again related to developments such as JIT in manufacturing and collaborative ventures between companies. Both JIT and collaboration require close cooperation and high levels of loyalty and trust between supplying and purchasing companies. This can only be achieved by both supplier and buyer taking a long-term relationship marketing approach. Obviously, then, one of the first steps in developing relationship marketing, and indeed in determining whether a relationship marketing approach should be used at all is to identify which customers, if any, merit a relationship approach.

The implications of relationship marketing

There are several far-reaching implications for the marketer associated with the emergence and growth of relationship marketing. Some of the more important of these implications are as follows.

First of all, relationship marketing heightens the need for more effective two-way communication between the marketer and customers. For example, in business-to-business markets electronic data interchange (EDI) systems have facilitated the growth of relationship marketing. In the consumer market direct on-line communication can increasingly help in developing effective customer relationships.

A second major implication of relationship marketing is that everyone in the supplying company and not just the marketing function needs to be concerned with generating customer satisfaction. This is another area where relationship marketing and customer service overlap and interact. To ensure successful relationship marketing there must be effective levels and systems of customer service. Remember, any failings in customer service normally lead to the loss of customers. Like customer service, relationship marketing needs an appropriate supportive organizational culture where everyone in the company is seeking to help build relationships with customers. This again heightens the importance of internal marketing in companies. Recently, some companies have introduced the notion of total relationship marketing (TRM). Zineldin[17] suggests that the main philosophy behind the TRM approach is to facilitate, create, develop, enhance and continuously improve all internal and external relationships with customers, employees and collaborators.

A third implication of relationship marketing is the way in which the customer often leads the whole of the marketing process. Admittedly, this notion is central to the original marketing concept, but with relationship marketing the marketer makes a conscious effort to encourage the customer to tell the marketer what is required and the marketer develops an appropriate marketing programme to respond to this. This process is often referred to as 'reverse marketing'.

Relationship marketing puts a much greater emphasis on systems for enabling constant tracking and assessment of customer satisfaction and needs. Customer databases and other sources of information on customers are central to effective relationship marketing.

Relationship marketing potentially affects every element of the marketing mix. So, for example, as with customer care the elements of the mix should be used carefully so as to encourage customers to become and stay loyal to the company. The use of short-term tactics such as special promotional deals, therefore, while possibly encouraging new customers, may attract the wrong sort of customer who is not ultimately interested in long-term relationships with a supplier or brand. Of all the areas of the marketing mix, however, it is in the area and process of personal selling that we see some of the most far-reaching implications of a relationship as opposed to a transaction approach to marketing. The following represent just some of the shifts in emphasis and perspectives in the selling process when a company moves towards a relationship marketing approach.

- The salesperson must take a longer term perspective than that of simply making a one-off sale when dealing with customers.
- Effective relationship selling requires much more of a team effort not only between individual members of the salesforce, but between the salesperson and other functions in the supplying company.
- The salesperson must be proactive with customers, for example, calling or visiting customers at times other than when they think the customer is ready to place an order.
- The salesperson must act as an exchanger of information between his or her own company and the customer, and vice versa.
- The emphasis must be much more on levels of customer service rather than simply on special deals and attempting to generate sales.

All of the above mean that relationship marketing requires different skills and attitudes for successful selling. The relationship salesperson, for example, must be skilled at listening to customers and interpreting their problems. Moreover, systems for managing and motivating salespersons may need to change. For example, remuneration may need to be geared much more to developing customer loyalty and trust rather than on immediate one-off sales.

Perhaps the most important implication of the growth of relationship marketing is, though, and perhaps obviously, the increased emphasis on the need to approach marketing and develop marketing programmes aimed at building and maintaining customer loyalty. The notion of customer retention therefore is central to the practice of relationship marketing. Kotler[18] discusses three ways in which a company can attempt to build and maintain stronger relationships with existing customers thereby helping to retain them over time.

1. *Adding financial benefits*   Essentially, this involves rewarding customers financially for being loyal. The loyalty schemes mentioned earlier in the chapter, such as reward points or air miles, are examples of these types of benefits. There is some debate about the extent to which such schemes actually do encourage truly loyal customers, or rather simply encourage customers who are looking for the best deal or value.

2. *Adding social benefits*   This involves company personnel increasing their personal and social bonds with customers. So, for example, by learning about customers' individual and specific needs and requirements, and by giving more personal service, 'customers' are turned into 'clients', thereby strengthening the ties and the loyalty which they have to the supplier. Obviously the salesperson can play a key role in this approach to building customer loyalty, but, in addition, the use of more sophisticated databases which can be used to analyse individual customer needs and tailor specific marketing programmes to individual customers is also growing in importance with developments in technology.

3. *Adding structural ties*   There are several ways in which this approach to building customer loyalty and relationships can be implemented. Essentially, it involves providing customer support in the form of expertise and/or equipment which help customers run their business. At the same time, the expertise or equipment provided helps to 'lock' the customer into the supplier. In other words, this approach increases the switching costs, mentioned earlier, for a customer. Examples would include companies providing, say, computer software to a customer which helps the customer run its production schedules, but which is specific to the supplier. Another example would be the supply of electronic data interchange systems for purchasing.

Overall, and together, customer care and relationship marketing are likely to continue to change the way in which marketing is practised.

CHAPTER SUMMARY

In this chapter we have looked at some of the issues associated with the inter-related areas of customer care and relationship marketing. Together, developments in these two areas represent some of the most significant changes in marketing thinking and practice. Both, however, reflect the essential and core concept of marketing inasmuch as they stress the importance of identifying and satisfying customer needs but with the emphasis on building long-term partnerships with customers. Both concepts effectively add further layers to the notion of consumer orientation. Marketers now recognize that building long-term customer loyalty, paying careful attention to retaining customers, and developing effective systems of customer care can provide major long-term benefits to customer and marketer alike.

CHAPTER REVIEW QUESTIONS

1. What do you understand by the term customer care in the context of contemporary marketing, and why has the importance of customer care grown in recent years?
2. Outline the steps in establishing a customer care programme.
3. Explain how customer care relates to the overall marketing planning process.
4. What is relationship marketing and how does it contrast with the more conventional transaction marketing?
5. Outline and discuss the implications of a relationship marketing approach for the practice of marketing.

References

1. S. Stone and L. Young, *Competitive Customer Care: A Guide to Keeping Customers,* Croner Publications, Kingston-upon-Thames, 1992.
2. P. Kotler, *Marketing Management, Analysis, Planning, Implementation and Control,* 9th edn, Prentice-Hall, Englewood Cliffs, NJ, 1997.
3. H. Peck, A. Payne, M. Christopher and M. Clark, *Relationship Marketing: Strategy and Implementation*, Butterworth-Heinemann, Oxford, 1999, p. 45.
4. *Customer Complaints Incidence and Practice.* US Office of Consumer Affairs, The White House, Washington, DC, 1992.
5. R. D. Buzzell and B. T. Gale, *The PIMS Principles: Linking Strategy to Performance*, Free Press, New York, 1984.
6. Stone and Young, op. cit., p. 20.
7. G. A. Lancaster and L. Massingham, *Marketing Management*, 3rd edn, McGraw-Hill, Maidenhead, 2001.

8. C. Gronroos, *Strategic Management and Marketing in the Service Sector*, Marketing Science Institute, Cambridge, MA, 1984.
9. M. Stone and N. Woodcock, *Relationship Marketing*, Kogan Page, London, 1995.
10. F. Buttle, *Relationship Marketing: Theory and Practice*, Paul Chapman, London 1996, p. 13.
11. G. A. Lancaster, 'Marketing and engineering: can there ever be synergy?', *Journal of Marketing Management*, 1993, pp. 141–53.
12. P. Kotler, *Marketing Management: Analysis, Planning and Control*, 7th edn, Prentice-Hall, Englewood Cliffs, NJ, 1991.
13. P. Gummesson, *Total Relationship Marketing*, Butterworth-Heinemann, Oxford, 1999.
14. T. Cram, *The Power of Relationship Marketing—How to Keep Customers for Life*, Pitman, London, 1994.
15. P. Kotler, op. cit., 1997, p. 720.
16. B. Bund-Jackson 'Build customer relationships that last', *Harvard Business Review*, November–December, **63**, 1985, pp. 120–8.
17. N. Zineldin 'Exploring the common ground of total relationship management (TRM) and total quality management (TQM)', *Management Decision*, **37**, 9, pp. 709–18.
18. P. Kotler *Marketing Management: Analysis, Planning, Implementation and Control*, 8th edn, Prentice-Hall, Englewood Cliffs, NJ, 1994, pp. 48–52.

Massingham Electronics have always prided themselves on their level of technical expertise and technical support services. The company, established in 1973, supplies electronic components principally for computers and mobile phones to companies in Singapore and Malaysia.

Looking at the sales figures for the last 18 months, the company chairman and marketing director, Chester Massingham is worried about a substantial dip in sales and market share. As a result, Chester commissioned some market research to explore the possible reasons for this dip in sales.

He is now considering the report based on the results of the research from the market research company he commissioned. To his surprise, the results show that the fall in sales and market share is not due to price or anything to do with product quality, rather the customers in the survey who have turned to competitors reported that they were unhappy with the levels of customer care they had been receiving. Some of the examples of failures in this area which they reported included:

- Incidences of rudeness from some of the sales staff when enquiring at the sales office about progress on orders.

- An assumption that the products were of such good quality that they didn't really need explaining and defending to customers.

- Lack of communication regarding the status of orders so that on occasions customers had experienced stock-outs resulting in loss of production.

Allied to these complaints the report made it clear that competitors were capturing market share because quite simply they seemed more committed to elements of customer care and avoiding the problems referred to above.

Chester simply cannot understand what has happened because he has always had a strong customer service section and all complaints, whenever received, are always followed up by the complaints department in this section.

He is considering looking at ways of improving customer care and is wondering how to proceed in this respect. He is also wondering if he might need to introduce some of the ideas of relationship marketing so as to help improve customer retention rates.

Questions

1. How might Chester approach the problem of improving levels of customer care in the organization?

2. How might Chester develop more of a relationship marketing approach in the organization?

Chapter Fourteen

INTERNATIONAL MARKETING

LEARNING OBJECTIVES   *This chapter will help you to:*

- understand the nature and scope of international marketing;

- appreciate the differences and added complexities which arise when marketing across international boundaries;

- be aware of the key decision areas in planning international marketing strategies;

- understand the issues in managing the marketing mix in international markets;

- understand the product life cycle for international trade;

- be aware of key trends and developments in international marketing.

INTRODUCTION

The aim of this chapter is to give an insight into the complex area of international marketing. There is no suggestion that, having read this, you will have become an expert in marketing overseas or in export procedures, but you should at least be aware of some of the additional implications.

INTERNATIONAL MARKETING DEFINED

Marketers are not agreed that international marketing can be considered a subject separate from marketing on a domestic scale, and this is perhaps one reason why it has been difficult to arrive at a comprehensive yet succinct definition. For the purposes of this chapter, it is proposed to accept the definition put forward by Walsh.[1] International marketing is:

(a) the marketing of goods and services across national frontiers
(b) the marketing operations of an organisation that sells and/or produces within a given country when:
    (i) that organisation is part of, or associated with, an enterprise which also operates in other countries; and
    (ii) there is some degree of influence on or control of that organisation's marketing activities from outside the country in which it sells and/or produces.

In other words, the term 'international marketing' can be applied to the activities of the exporter and of any organization that has some international concern. A small manufacturing company can be an international marketer to a limited degree simply by distributing its products in foreign markets. Companies with overseas sales subsidiaries or overseas manufacturing plant (whether wholly or partly owned, or operating independently and manufacturing under licence) and the multinational corporation are all included in the definition.

From the point of view of the UK, export activity continues to be a significant factor in international marketing activities. As an industrialized nation lacking valuable raw materials, the UK is particularly dependent on international trade. It differs, therefore, from the USA, for example, from whose viewpoint many texts on international marketing have been written, since the latter's domestic market is large enough to absorb its production. Succeeding sections reflect the importance of engaging in international marketing.

MULTINATIONAL CORPORATIONS

The term 'multinational corporation' is widely used and has been variously defined. Once again, Walsh[2] provides a useful working definition. The multinational corporation is a company:

(a) which has a direct investment base in several countries;
(b) which generally derives 20–50 per cent or more of its net profits from foreign operations; and
(c) whose management makes policy decisions based on the alternatives available anywhere in the world.

The key factor is that the company should have a global outlook, making its business decisions with regard to the options available worldwide. It is not, therefore, a domestically based US or Swiss or Dutch company (although many multinational corporations have their origins in single domestic markets), but is a company whose operations span the globe. Manufacturing occurs simultaneously in several different countries and goods are sold worldwide.

The concept of global marketing includes a number of advantages for multinationals:

● *Programme transfers* They can draw upon strategies, products, advertising appeals, sales management practices, promotional ideas and so on that have been tested in actual markets and can apply them in comparable markets.

● *Systems transfers* They can introduce planning, budgeting, new product introduction and other successful systems developed and tested in the company into new markets.

- *People transfers*   They can assign skilled people across national boundaries, thus drawing upon a manpower pool of international rather than merely national dimensions.
- *Scale economies in manufacturing*   Multinational firms, in addition to obtaining traditional single-plant-scale economies, can combine components manufactured in scale-efficient plants in different countries into finished products.
- *Economies of centralization of functional activities*   Instead of duplicating and dispersing its functional staff, multinationals can concentrate activities at single locations and thereby develop greater competence and at the same time reduce costs.
- *Resource utilization*   A major strength of multinational companies is their ability to scan the entire world to identify sources of manpower, money and materials that will enable them most effectively to compete in world markets.
- *Global strategy*   They can scan the world for markets that provide opportunities to apply their skills, match the markets with their resources, and where necessary exploit opportunities, create and shift resources to tap identified opportunities.

Multinational corporations have become increasingly large over time, several having annual sales that equal the GNP of smaller European nations. They are therefore an extremely significant force. For a more detailed discussion, the reader is directed to Chee and Harris's work.[3]

It is useful at this point to distinguish between international marketing and international trade. While trade between nations will inevitably impinge on the activities of international marketing, the terms are not synonymous. World trade used to be until relatively recently, simple exchange of goods. In what was the Eastern bloc, for example, goods are seen as methods of payment rather than as a means of meeting market needs, and hence much trade was by barter.

While some of the activities of marketing may be involved in the exporting process (for example distribution activities), there may well be no marketing management. Terpstra[4] suggests a useful table of comparison (Table 14.1).

TABLE 14.1   *Comparison of international trade and international marketing*

Dimensions	International trade	International marketing
Actors	Nations	Firms
Goods move across frontiers	Yes	Not necessarily
Impetus	Comparative advantage	Company decisions (usually profit motivated)
Information source	Nation's balance of payments	Company records
Marketing activities:		
Buy and sell	Yes	Yes
Physical distribution	Yes	Yes
Pricing	Yes	Yes
Market research	Generally not	Yes
Product development	Generally not	Yes
Promotion	Generally not	Yes
Distribution channel management	No	Yes

Source: V. Terpstra, *International Marketing*, 3rd edn, Dryden Press, Hinsdale, IL, 1983

STAGES OF ECONOMIC DEVELOPMENT OF EXPORT MARKETS

The environment within which marketing operates is continually dynamic and largely uncontrollable. For international marketing this difficulty is magnified; not only are the uncontrollable elements of the environment different from country to country, but the controllable elements of the marketing mix must be adapted to these differing environments. Particularly significant is the diversity that exists between levels of economic activity among nations.

Rostow[5] has provided a description of economies which suggests that all nations are in or are passing through one of the following stages:

- Traditional society
- Preconditions for take-off
- Take-off
- Drive to maturity
- Age of high mass consumption

More common terms are now in use, and while these may change over time (for example, the term 'less developed country' has given way to 'developing country'), they provide a more current classification.

1. *Subsistence economies*   This category consists of those nations dependent on primitive agriculture, with a limited infrastructure and high dependence on foreign aid. Examples include much of Africa (Ethiopia, Burkina Faso) and parts of Asia (Bangladesh).

2. *Developing countries*   There is increasing industrialization and a developing infrastructure in these. Such economies are usually reliant on raw material exports, often based on the extractive industries, including oil (Nigeria, Mexico and parts of the Middle East).

3. *Industrializing countries*   The rapidly industrializing economies of many South American countries (e.g. Brazil) and countries such as Poland and Greece can be considered under this heading.

4. *Industrialized countries*   This includes the major Western industrial countries of Europe, North America and Japan.

An additional sub-grouping, *affluent countries*, usually includes the United States, Sweden and Germany, with their demand for high-quality, sophisticated consumer goods.

Note   While many of the oil-exporting countries of the Middle East have a high GNP *per capita*, in some the development of their infrastructure is still limited and there is a wide disparity between rich and poor. Consequently, they cannot be considered as being truly affluent countries, but perhaps merit a separate category for the purposes of international marketing.

While the above classification is useful, it must be remembered that, as with all environmental factors, it is constantly subject to change. Equally, it may be difficult to place a nation in a particular category.

For the marketer, therefore, the stage in economic development may be a starting-point for researching opportunities overseas, but in itself will provide limited guidance.

IDENTIFYING EXPORT OPPORTUNITIES

Information for marketing decisions was considered in some detail in Part Two of this text. Quantitative and qualitative techniques previously discussed are equally relevant when attempting to identify overseas opportunities. In general, however, the backcloth against which these opportunities are seen is broader.

The number of possible markets is large—over 250 political states are listed in the *United States Statistical Yearbook*; of these over 150 are members of the United Nations. The number of nations that will provide viable market opportunities will, of course, differ from firm to firm and from product to product, and the arguments for concentrating marketing activity within a small group of markets versus spreading to a large number of overseas markets can also be seen to follow this pattern. Be that as it may, a framework for analysing overseas markets is a useful starting-point in a programme of marketing research. The aim of such a programme is to produce a ranked list of overseas markets for future marketing research in depth on the basis of likely potential for the company and its product(s), and to do it in the most cost-effective way. A suggested step-by-step approach is reproduced in Fig. 14.1.

A key factor to consider is market accessibility. This is more than determining how close a country is to the UK or other domestic market. It will include an assessment of both tariff and non-tariff barriers to trade.

A *tariff* can be simply defined as a tax on products crossing a frontier. Tariffs are often imposed by governments to protect local industry from overseas competition. The World Trade Organization (WTO) is an institution established to provide a worldwide forum for discussion in an attempt to reduce the need for tariffs.

Non-tariff barriers include other forms of government action to restrict imports, for example quotas. A *quota* places a specific limit, by volume or value, on the amount of goods exported to a specific market and is usually applied to a specific nation or group of nations. For example, the Multi-Fibre Arrangement (MFA) limited exports of textile products from developing countries to the UK and other European nations. Other non-tariff barriers include discriminatory exchange rate policies, restrictive customs procedures and restrictive administrative and technical regulations. For example, the technical regulations for electrical appliances still differ between the UK and Germany, despite common membership of the European Union (EU). France introduced a regulation whereby all video-cassette recorders imported from Japan were cleared through customs in a limited number of inland towns, effectively reducing the number of imports since only a relatively small number of products could be cleared per day. Non-tariff barriers also include geographic and climatic barriers.

Despite these problems, finding information about accessibility is relatively easy when using government sources such as the Department of Trade and Industry (DTi) Export Initiative. This first stage will reduce the number of potential markets literally from three figures to two, at least as far as direct export is concerned. It may well identify a group of countries for potential joint venture agreements, which are discussed later. Further research can then be considered under the following headings:

1. *Economic*   GNP/GDP; population figures; wage levels and distribution; price levels; inflation; resources.

2. *Market*   Size; stage in product life cycle; market penetration level or average consumption level per annum; competition; market segmentation; availability of media, services, distribution.

3. *Cultural* Material culture (e.g. role of women); social structure and family relationships; social relationships; religion(s); aesthetics; language(s).

4. *Political environment* Incentives for joint venture/wholly owned manufacture (e.g. tax exemptions); protection against competitive imports (tariffs and quotas). *Risks* of appropriation or domestication of foreign owned manufacturing plant.

5. *Legal* There is no true international law, although attempts to reconcile different legal practice have been made. The Madrid Convention, for example, protects trade marks of signatories in all member countries.

Much of the information needed can be obtained from secondary sources, an outline list of which is given in Table 14.2 in addition to the information given in Chapter 5.

As with decisions in domestic marketing, export marketing decisions must be based on up-to-date, accurate information. The reasons for export market research are, therefore, the same as those for domestic marketing, and the basic procedures and techniques encompass those already outlined for any market research activity. The problem must

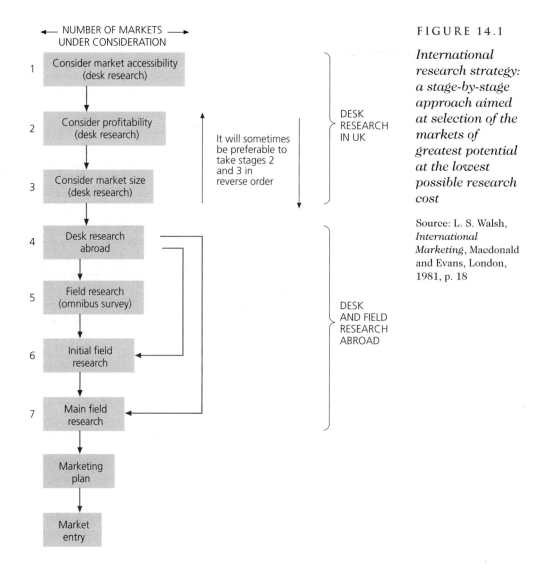

FIGURE 14.1

International research strategy: a stage-by-stage approach aimed at selection of the markets of greatest potential at the lowest possible research cost

Source: L. S. Walsh, *International Marketing*, Macdonald and Evans, London, 1981, p. 18

be identified, objectives must be set for the research, and a careful and systematic research procedure, using first secondary and then primary data, must be established.

The principles, then, are no different. Nevertheless, anyone involved in export marketing research will tell you that there are added complexities in researching across international frontiers. Let us examine some of these problems.

Obtaining secondary data

Differences in the availability and quality of secondary data are important considerations in export market research. Although exporting is recognized as vital to the economic well-being of a country, not all countries—or, more specifically, not all the would-be exporters to them—are equally well served when it comes to published statistical data.

It is a fact that great care should be taken in using any market research information that is derived from secondary sources. In the case of market and statistical information published outside the country of the exporter, great care should be taken in attempting to verify the accuracy of the data.

Differences between countries

Differences between countries are generally much greater than those experienced within a country with respect to social and marketing practices, political and commercial institutions and, of course, language.

TABLE 14.2 *Some sources of secondary data for international market research*

1. Government	Department of Trade and Industry
	Central Office of Information
	HMSO
2. International institutions	Organization for Economic Cooperation and Development
	International Monetary Fund
	World Trade Organization
	European Union
3. Trade associations	
4. Professional bodies	Chartered Institute of Marketing
	Institute of Export
5. Chambers of commerce	
6. Commercial organizations	Market research agencies
	Advertising agencies
7. Consultants	e.g. Economist Intelligence Agency
8. Service industries	Banks
	Airlines
	Freight forwarders
9. European Society for Opinion and Market Research (ESOMAR)	
10. Other published sources, e.g. Axel Springer Publishing Group (Germany)	

In researching export markets, it is important to remember that conditions may vary so much from country to country that each country has to be looked at individually. Above all, it is important not to assume that, because a product or service is a commercial success in one country, it will automatically be so in another. This is true even of countries which, for political or historical reasons, share similar customs, life styles and, indeed, languages.

There are many examples where, because some basic—if apparently small—difference has been overlooked, a great deal of money and effort on the part of the exporter has been wasted. Even within a country, regional variations may be sufficient to require different marketing strategies. These variations add to the complexity of research in export markets and should be considered at a very early stage in research design.

Defining boundaries

Definition of the boundaries of potential export markets adds a further complication to export market research. There is an obvious need to define the boundaries of potential export markets before we begin to research them. But are frontiers the best way of doing this? We can define potential export markets as follows:

- Geographically.
- Administratively—say, according to the location of the international divisions of the company.
- By trading blocs, e.g. EU, EFTA, ASEAN, ANCOM, LAIA.
- Politically.

Clearly, the approach adopted will affect the research procedure and should be defined at the outset.

Cost of research

Managers often flinch at the complexity and cost of export market research, and admittedly, market research, whether in-company or agency-commissioned, can be very expensive. However, if care is taken at the early stages of market assessment, the costs—particularly in relation to the benefits—need not be onerous.

The essence of keeping down market research costs is to approach the assessment of export potential in a step-by-step way.

Preliminary screening of markets   The first step is to conduct a preliminary screening of export markets and to discard those that offer little or no potential. Information provided at this stage may also provide a basis for the decision as to whether or not to export.

Much of the information collected at this stage may be the result of *desk research* using secondary (published) data.

It is difficult and dangerous to list the factors that every company should consider at this preliminary screening stage. Each company must select those criteria for assessment that are relevant to its own particular product markets, objectives and resources. Examples of factors that might be considered are:

- *Accessibility*: distance, freight and similar charges, import duties, quotas, prohibitions, licence requirements, exchange problems—other non-tariff barriers.

- *Market size*: present total size, local production; imports and exports, past trends, future trends.
- *Profitability*: present market price levels in relation to landed costs.

Information sources   Again, it must be stressed that at this stage in market assessment much of the information can be obtained at relatively little cost from published sources. If anything, the potential exporter is rather better served with marketing information than for domestic markets. This again reflects the acknowledgement of the importance of exporting by governments.

Of all the general reference sources available, among the most comprehensive and informative are those produced by government agencies and the commercial banks. For example, in the United Kingdom the government's Department of Trade and Industry (DTi) will provide information on: foreign import regulations and tariffs; agents and business contacts; export market research, etc. Similarly, many of the major banks provide basic market information on developments in the world's major trading nations.

Detailed investigation of export markets

The potential export markets that remain after the screening process should now be subjected to a more detailed analysis based on information obtained from first-hand investigations in the remaining market(s). This information may be collected:

- By visits to the overseas market by company personnel
- By commissioning market research
- By both.

It is important at this stage to remember the following points:

- Field research should be carried out only in markets shown to be promising.
- Market research is unlikely to indicate market entry for all markets; i.e. inevitably there will be some wastage.
- The research terms of reference should be designed right from the start as input to the marketing plan. Details of the plan or brief will, of course, vary according to company, product range and marketing situation.

In order to qualify as a potential export market, it is likely that the following conditions will have to be met:

1. There must be enough potential customers who need the benefits of the product or service.
2. Enough potential customers must recognize these benefits, or it must be possible to persuade them.
3. Potential customers must have the resources to purchase the product/service.
4. It must be possible to reach them via distribution channels efficiently and economically.
5. Total demand at a price must enable the manufacturer to cover costs and make a profit.

Using the press

In many countries there is no national press, regional newspapers being dominant. When trying to assess the value of an advertising campaign, one has to consider at least half a dozen newspapers which have different readerships.

Examination of tastes and customs

On top of all this, there are the varying customs, likes, dislikes and prejudices in each country which have to be examined before any research is undertaken, so that no time is wasted because some basic fact has been overlooked. For instance, if one considers the pet food industry, it must be remembered that in many foreign cities people live in flats where they are precluded by rules from keeping pets. With regard to the do-it-yourself trade in Switzerland, one must take into account the fact that most townspeople again live in flats, where they are often forbidden by the terms of the lease to make any alterations to their apartments, or even, in some cases, to use electric drills or similar tools.

Because of all the above variations, a questionnaire prepared for an English market would be quite meaningless, as many of the questions would not apply, and the factors affecting the customer's decision to buy would be different.

Research overseas must be tailored to the country in question, and in this it is essential not to generalize. Many people are inclined to look upon South America or the Far East as a whole, which is quite wrong; each country is different, and in many cases there is a huge difference between the capital and the rest of the country.

Desk research must be carried out very carefully and very thoroughly. The researchers must endeavour to obtain as much relevant information as they can, and be prepared to have summaries of reports, or even complete reports, translated. When this has been done, it is possible to assess the worth of a visit to the market in question in order to gather more information. In many cases, the best method is to discuss the question in depth with the export department staff dealing with the region in question, as they will be able to fill many of the gaps left by desk research. Once this has been done, the export sales staff will be briefed exactly as to the information that is required, and a selling visit to the overseas country can be coupled with a market research investigation, which will then be relatively inexpensive.

The market research department should by this time have a good idea of the market in question, its distribution channels and its likes and dislikes, and should be in a position to assess roughly the types of product or methods of selling that will be suitable. If the potential appears to be sufficiently large, a market research visit can then be arranged, to go further into the points that have to be settled before the marketing operation starts.

The aim of a marketing research programme is to arrive at a group of markets that offer potential for export and where similarities with the domestic market, rather than differences from it, can be emphasized and exploited.

THE MARKETING MIX APPLIED TO INTERNATIONAL MARKETING

The term 'marketing mix' was introduced in Chapter 1 and its major elements discussed in some detail in Chapter 12 of this text. Again, it must be said that the issues raised are as important to marketing internationally as they are to marketing in the domestic environment. Certain aspects of the mix hold special significance for international marketing.

Distribution

A detailed discussion on channels of distribution has already been provided in Chapter 10, but distribution for international marketing not only includes the structure of channels within a range of overseas markets, but, perhaps more fundamentally, must also address the strategic problem of market entry.

The options available fall into the following broad categories:

- Indirect export
- Direct export
- Manufacture abroad through joint ventures
- Manufacture abroad through independent production

These can be further subdivided as shown in Figs 14.2 and 14.3.

Any or all of these alternatives may be in use in one company, and for a full discussion of all the options listed the reader is directed again to Walsh's work.[6] Certain alternatives have been selected for brief consideration here.

Agency   This may be defined as the legal relationship that exists when one person or company (the agent) is employed by another person or company (the principal) to bring that principal into a contractual relationship with third parties. A sales agent is thus employed to bring about a sales contract between his principal and the third party. The legal title to goods never passes to an agent; it passes, as a result of the agent's efforts, directly from principal to customer, the agent receiving a commission as payment. In marketing practice, however, the expression is loosely used to include distributors.

Distributors   These have been defined as customers who have been granted exclusive or preferential rights to purchase and re-sell a specific range of products in specified

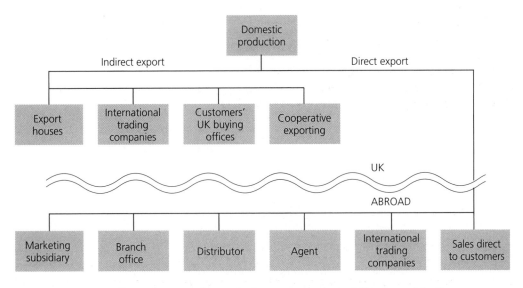

FIGURE 14.2   *Distribution channels between nations (direct and indirect export): principal alternatives*

geographical areas or markets. Distributors are therefore wholesalers, who are 'paid' by the difference between purchase price and resale price (and *not* from any commission from the suppliers). As such, their role is as defined for similar channel intermediaries in domestic operations.

Agents and distributors offer similar advantages to the would-be exporter. They have local experience of market conditions and business practice, valuable to the new exporter, and they involve little or no investment costs. Such advantages should be carefully weighed against the disadvantages. Agents, in particular, are often unable to take a long-term view, which is essential for effective marketing management. Agents have a living to make and are understandably interested in those products that earn commission from the outset. They usually represent various companies and offer a wide range of products. A new product thus might not receive as much attention as a proven successful product.

Agents and distributors are only two options available to exporters, and, while often successful, they should be viewed against the alternatives. A branch office, and company-employed local salesforce, while involving considerable investment, can offer long-term potential for development.

As far as *overseas assembly and manufacture* are concerned, joint ventures require some attention. It would be impossible to consider all the alternatives in a chapter of this length, but the major advantage common to all options is that of market access (where this may be impossible as a result of tariff or quota restrictions). The degree of risk varies—it is relatively low where licensing is concerned and substantial in the case of jointly owned manufacturing facilities, where the possibility of expropriation by the national government adds to the problem of financial outlay.

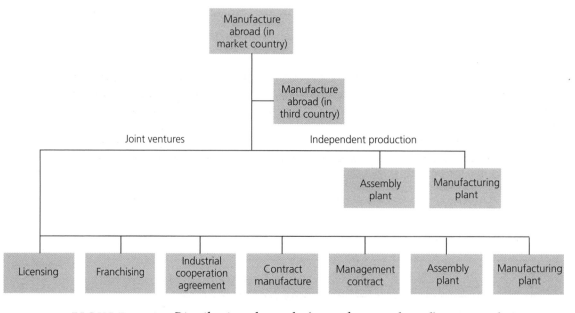

FIGURE 14.3   *Distribution channels (manufacture abroad): principal alternative channels*

Source: L. S. Walsh, *International Marketing*, Macdonald and Evans, London, 1982

For purposes of clarification, some attention is now given to two joint-venture options, licensing and franchising.

Licensing   This is the term used to cover a wide range of agreements relating to the sale or leasing of industrial or commercial expertise. This may include a patent covering a product or process, manufacturing 'know-how', and the use of a trade mark or brand name. In return, the licensee pays a sum, often a minimum amount annually, or an agreed percentage of turnover annually. Licensing can, therefore, be said to involve the sale of intangibles.

Franchising   This is a *form* of licensing and was discussed in some detail in Chapter 8. The franchiser remember provides a standard package of components or ingredients together with management and marketing services and advice. Since franchising involves the transfer of tangibles, it can enable greater control of the operation for the originating manufacturer than licensing. Examples of successful franchising operations include Pepsi Cola, which sells its concentrate to franchises that own bottling plants, employ local staff and control their own promotional budgets; other examples are Benetton, the Italian knitwear manufacturer, whose franchised shops are now a common feature of European high streets, and the Body Shop.

The selection of a channel for market entry is vital to the success of distribution within each overseas market. The shorter the overall channel of distribution, the greater the control. In terms of international marketing, a greater cost is the financial involvement. For smaller firms, some sacrifice of control is thus inevitable in many instances and a balance between these two issues must be achieved.

Finally as in domestic markets, no section on distribution can ignore physical distribution or logistics. The importance of physical distribution for exporting in particular is such that a short section is devoted to this topic at the end of the chapter.

Product

Perhaps the most significant decisions for international marketing are those of product standardization and variety reduction. Examples of the need to meet individual national requirements, in particular where consumer goods are concerned, abound. One particularly descriptive example of the modifications needed to what at that time was the Leyland Mini for successful exporting to Japan is given by Whymant.[7] In addition to overcoming the emission requirements, a wide range of other specifications had to be met:

1. The tyre must not protrude, so on Minis 'eye-brows' have to be fastened on the two front wings.
2. An audible warning device at 110 kph.
3. A red band on the speedometer to show when this speed is reached.
4. A heat shield above the catalyst to stop occupants of the car cooking, and a grass shield underneath so that what grass you do see in Tokyo doesn't catch fire!
5. Special low wattage headlamps.
6. Overheat catalyst warning.
7. Special regulation number plate bracket.

8. Torch for use in breakdown.

9. Modification of emergency parking system for use in breakdown.

10. Side-wing repeater flashers to show when back indicator is on.

11. Reflectors on rear a different size and at a different angle.

While a standard product to meet a global need is attractive to the marketer, not least in terms of economies of scale, it may be impossible in practice. Legal, technical or climatic requirements may make modification mandatory. In addition, local tastes may make it desirable. Certainly, in view of the differing stages of economic development reached by different nations discussed earlier, a similar need may be met by a variety of products. The following section on a product life cycle for international trade highlights this problem.

The eventual result of product modification can lead to an over-full range of products; and, while the review and elimination procedures presented in Chapter 6 remain valid for international marketing, the scale of the problem is often much greater. International product elimination is therefore an area of great importance. In certain circumstances where domestic production costs or small-scale production runs make a product unprofitable, alternative options such as licensing (see above) may enable the marketer to improve profits while retaining market position.

Keegan[8] has identified five possible strategies (Fig. 14.4) for international marketing which encompass the mix elements of product and promotion. These are discussed in brief before considering the promotional element in the next section:

1. *Straight extension*   This is the introduction of the product in the same form and with the same communications in use at home. This is a tempting strategy, as it involves no additional manufacturing or marketing costs. Examples of successful products include Pepsi Cola.

2. *Communications adaptation*   This is where a company modifies its promotional theme but retains an unchanged product. This strategy has a relatively low cost of implementation since major manufacturing costs are not incurred. The example quoted by Keegan is that of bicycles, which are a product designed to meet leisure needs in the USA and other developed countries, but are a basic mode of transport in many developing nations.

3. *Product adaptation*   This involves the modification of a product for reasons discussed earlier, e.g. preferences, while retaining the communications theme. Products that are particularly susceptible to taste, e.g. food and clothing, are such examples.

4. *Dual adaptation*   This involves modifying both product and communications to meet the needs of specific markets. Keegan cites the introduction of instant coffee into the UK, where tastes differed from other European nations in which there is a longer coffee-drinking tradition, and where the initial launch was to a different market segment—the young, who were less traditional and for whom a specific communications message was required.

		Products		
		No change	Adapted	New product
Marketing communications	No change	Straight extension	Product adaptation	
	Adapt	Communication adaptation	Dual adaptation	Product invention

FIGURE 14.4

Keegan's strategies for international marketing

5. *Product inventions*   Where product needs and market conditions are similar to those in the home market, the first four strategies are effective options. In other countries, such as the developing nations, this may not be the case. Product invention, or the development of a new product to meet consumer needs at an affordable price, may be the only alternative. The invention 'backwards' from modern technology of a better manual washing machine for those countries where washing is still done by hand is a good example.

There is no best strategy for a firm—the optimum choice will depend on the specific product–market–company mix.

Promotion

The elements of the communications mix discussed in Chapter 9 are as relevant for international marketing as they are for domestic marketing. For an established company marketing its products overseas, the decisions to be taken hinge on whether a standardized promotional campaign can be contemplated or whether promotion should be adapted to individual national needs.

Complete standardization of all aspects of a campaign is rarely possible—language differences alone ensure this. It is possible, however, for a *common creative idea and message* to be adopted—Coca-Cola is a classic example—using similar media and a common advertising strategy.

The organization of advertising on an international scale is modelled on the US pattern, with branches of many US advertising agencies throughout the world. The environmental differences, discussed above in relation to international marketing research, play a very significant role in international advertising decisions: cultural differences, government attitudes to advertising and, in particular, availability of advertising media are of particular relevance. Even among industrialized nations, commercial television is not always available to the advertiser. Where it is offered, advertising flexibility (by channels in the UK, for example) can be lacking, with lead times of a year being common.

In addition to the national media available within each overseas market, an additional category, international media, can be added to the list of means of promotion for the international marketer. These are publications that aim, as a matter of policy, at coverage in several different countries. They include consumer magazines, such as *Readers' Digest*, *Time*, the various airline publications, trade and technical magazines, international commercial radio and international commercial television which is becoming increasingly significant with the growth of cable and satellite television. Such developments make the prospect of a standardized campaign attractive, particularly in view of cost savings in the production of creative promotional material.

Exhibitions, often considered as an element of below-the-line advertising, are probably of more importance to the international marketer than they are in domestic business. They allow buyer, intermediary and seller to come together, minimizing the costs and time involved for each. Exhibitions range from the giant international trade fairs covering all products and industries, such as Leipzig and Hanover, to the highly specialized international exhibitions specific to a particular product category, for example Pret-à-Porter and the London Boat Show. For a detailed list of international exhibitions, the reader is advised to consult the DTI's *Trade Promotions Guide*.

Agents and distributors have been considered above as intermediaries in the distribution channel. They should also be viewed as an integral part of a company's promotional activities. The representative overseas (and this will include a company employee, whether based locally or in the domestic market) is the first point of contact for the potential buyer. The representative's attitude to the buyer, his or her knowledge of the company and its products, and freedom to negotiate terms have an important (and sometimes adverse) influence. The position of the overseas sales representative is one of isolation from head office, and it is essential to foster two-way communication links.

Pricing

The methods of pricing detailed in Chapter 7 should be used as a basis for any pricing decision in international marketing. However, additional factors must be taken into consideration. Not least of these are the relationship between domestic and overseas pricing and the issue of transfer pricing.

The true marketer will expect to price the product or service according to the needs and requirements of the market. This may or may not be a price similar to that at which goods are sold at home. In practice, various constraints may prevent this, such as inadequate market information (which may not always be the fault of the marketing researcher, but rather a result of the market's stage of development as a whole), a prevailing world price, or the proximity of other markets where the same product is sold. Legal reasons may also be of relevance; the decision of the European Court to ban price differentials for motor cars sold in different member states of the EU was such an example.

The terms of payment under which goods are sold to export markets will add a further dimension to the price. Costs of packing, insurance and freight between buyer and seller all have to be borne and will determine the real selling price of goods. It is beyond the scope of this chapter to consider terms of trade in detail, but your attention is drawn to Terpstra and Sarathy's work[9] which includes a discussion of accepted terms of trade.

Finally, the question of which currency is to be used as a basis for quoting prices overseas is significant. Following the marketing view, the aim of meeting consumers' or industrial buyers' needs would suggest that goods sold in the local currency to intermediaries would be more acceptable. Clearly, such a policy would simplify the buyer's position and would provide a significant competitive advantage in many instances. It must be stated, however, that pricing in the currency of the market may be inappropriate or impossible where developing countries are concerned. Since these currencies may not be freely convertible on the international money market, the decision is then to trade in either the domestic market currency or the currency of a third country (for example US dollars or Swiss francs).

Two final comments will be made before leaving this topic. First, although a price to meet the needs of the market must be desirable to achieve an optimum level of sales, it is undoubtedly simpler to base overseas prices on one of the techniques of cost-based pricing. In some instances, however, this may lose a market for the company, since the initial price may be too high for any significant sales to result; in others, it may cause the company concerned to price a product too low in relation to the established competition, thereby reducing potential profit and perhaps adversely affecting the image of the product in the eyes of the consumer.

Second, there have been allegations of 'dumping' products overseas by a variety of nations. Dumping can be described as the sale of goods in foreign markets at a price lower than the production cost. This appears to contradict the theory of market pricing, but it is true that industrialized countries tend to penalize such imports. To what extent setting a price to meet market demands can, or should, be viewed as dumping is open to debate. It is a question of degree and will, in many instances, depend on the product or industry concerned. In any event, the practice of true dumping, often at marginal prices, can be a high-risk strategy in international marketing. Goods sold at artificially low prices to an overseas buyer can (and often do) return to compete as competitively priced imports in the domestic market.

A second important issue in pricing for international markets is that of transfer pricing. The meaning of, approaches to, and issues involved in transfer pricing are outlined below.

When a company operates in several international markets, with different divisions or units operating as profit centres in each of these markets, it will often find itself transferring components or finished products between the different international divisions. To enable the profit performance of each unit to be evaluated, a price must be established for each inter-unit transaction. This is known as the *transfer price*.

Transfer prices may be established on a number of bases, such as cost, cost plus a standard margin, or arm's-length transfer, i.e. the same price as would be quoted to an independent customer. Central corporate management will usually establish the basis of the transfer price, with the aim of ensuring both a realistic assessment of the contribution of any one unit and the maximization of the profit of the enterprise as a whole.

The transfer price between operating units in different countries can be manipulated to minimize tax or import duty liability or (in effect) to transfer funds. For example:

1. Products may be transferred into high-duty countries at an artificially low transfer price so that, assuming duty is charged *ad valorem*, the duty paid will be low.

2. Products may be transferred into high-tax countries at high transfer prices so that profits in the high-tax country are virtually eliminated and, in effect, are transferred to low-tax countries.

3. Products may be transferred at high prices into a country from which dividend repatriation is restricted or subject to government taxes—in effect, invisible income replaces a formal dividend.

4. Similarly, it is possible to avoid an accumulation of funds in a country with high inflation rates, or where an early devaluation is thought to be a probability, or where expropriation is feared.

For these reasons, national governments are particularly interested in the uses (and abuses) of international transfer pricing. This is a complex area, but essentially we can summarize the attitudes of governments to transfer pricing as follows:

- The government of the *exporting* country has an interest in seeing that the transfer price is not artificially low, and it will endeavour to ensure that appropriate profits are made and taxes paid within its jurisdiction.

- In the *importing* country, the tax authorities are usually on the look-out for unreasonably high transfer prices, which will reduce local profits and, consequently, liability to income tax; while the customs authorities will, in contrast, be watching for low transfer prices designed to minimize duty liability.

As a final comment on this aspect of pricing, we should note that international transfer pricing can also be used as a weapon in the overall marketing strategy: profits can be concentrated, by vertically integrated corporations, at the stage of production where there is least competition. Competitors operating at other stages of production can thus be discouraged by the relatively low profits to be earned.

Pricing is a complex area that, in common with the other elements of the marketing mix, cannot be viewed in isolation. An integrated approach to all four Ps is as essential for international marketing as it is for domestic marketing.

PRODUCT LIFE CYCLE FOR INTERNATIONAL TRADE

The product life cycle theory, as discussed in Chapter 6, has proved useful in identifying future strategies for products and services. By applying it to international trade, Wells[10] has shown the relevance of the theory to importing and exporting a product.

It is contended that exporters would be helped if they had methods of analysing the export potential of their products and had predictors of which products were most likely to be threatened by import competition.

Exporters have traditionally relied upon economic theories which conclude that each country will export those products that use the country's most abundant production factors. However, when such theories are applied to the detailed problems facing business people, they become of limited value.

The trade cycle model has been proposed as an aid to exporters, and this is closely related to the product life cycle concept in marketing. Wells first proposed a theory that combined both, and in order that we might attempt to modify his model, a summary of his proposal is given below.

According to the trade cycle concept, many products follow a pattern that can be divided into four stages:

1. US export strength
2. Start of foreign production
3. Foreign production competitive in export markets
4. Import competition begins

A brief look at the reasoning underlying each of these stages will give some clues that might help the business person to identify the stage at which a particular product may be. The concept can then be of assistance in predicting the future product trade performance, and in understanding what actions the manager can take to modify the pattern for certain products and to profit from different stages of the cycle.

Phase 1   US export strength

The US market is special because it has a large body of very high-income consumers; for this reason, products that satisfy the special demands of such consumers are likely to be introduced in the USA. Moreover, owing to the monopolistic position of the USA as a supplier of new products that satisfy these special demands, they offer the best opportunities for export.

There is no simple relationship between demand and invention, but nevertheless, there can be little doubt that certain products are simply more likely to be developed initially in America. Although labour is cheaper abroad and production costs would be lower, it is more sensible to manufacture in the USA because production is closer to the market and near to specialist supplies. This is because at the early stages of a product's life design is often in a constant state of flux, and demands for design changes must be rapidly translated into more suitable products which require the availability of close communication with specialized suppliers. The existence of a monopoly, or of significant product differentiation at the early stages of the product life cycle, reduces the importance of costs to the manufacturer.

At this point, the American manufacturer has a virtual monopoly for the new product in the world market. US exports start as a trickle and develop into a steady stream as active export programmes are established by the American firms.

Phase 2   Start of foreign production

Product familiarity abroad increases, causing overseas markets to become so large that the product which once appealed primarily to the US consumer comes to have a broad appeal in more prosperous foreign countries. Not only does a potential foreign producer now have a market close at hand, but also, some of his costs will be lower than those of the US producer. Imports from America have to bear duty and overseas freight charges—costs that local products will not carry. Moreover, the potential foreign producer may have to invest less in product development, the US manufacturer having done part of this for him. Some measure of the size of his potential market has been demonstrated by the successful sale of imports. Favourable profit projections based upon a demonstrated market and an ability to underprice imports will eventually induce an entrepreneur in a more prosperous foreign market to commence manufacture.

During this second stage, American exports will still supply most of the world's markets. However, as foreign producers begin to manufacture, US exports to certain markets will decline. The pattern will probably be manifested in a slow-down in the rate of growth of US exports.

Phase 3   Foreign production competitive in export markets

As the early foreign manufacturers become larger and more experienced, their costs should fall. They will begin to reap the advantages of scale economies previously available only to US manufacturers—but, in addition, they will have lower labour costs. Hence their costs may be such that foreign products become competitive with American goods in third markets where goods from both countries have to carry similar freight and duty charges.

During this stage, US producers will be protected from imports in their domestic market where they are not faced with duty and overseas transportation costs. However, foreign goods will gradually take over the markets abroad which were previously held by American exports. The rate of growth of US exports will continue to decline.

Phase 4   Import competition begins

As the foreign manufacturer reaches mass production based on domestic and export markets, the lower labour rates and perhaps new plant may enable it to produce at lower costs than an American manufacturer. The cost savings may be sufficient to pay freight and US duty and still compete with Americans in their own market. This stage will be reached earlier if the foreign producer begins to think in terms of marginal costs for export pricing. If the firm believes that selling can be done above full costs in the home market and excess capacity can be used up by 'dumping' abroad, US producers, who are pricing on full costs, may very quickly be undercut. During this final stage, US exports will be reduced to almost zero, while import competition becomes severe.

Thus the cycle is complete, from the USA as a strong producer and exporter, to the stage where imports may capture a significant share of the American market.

The early foreign producers (usually Western Europeans) will face a cycle similar to that of the US manufacturer. As still lower income markets become large enough, producers in these countries will eventually become competitive, displacing the dominance of the early foreign manufacturers. The manufacture of products moves from country to country in what Hufbauer[11] has called a 'pecking order'.

Clearly, no simple model can explain the behaviour of all products in international trade. However, this model does appear to be useful for understanding trade patterns in manufactured goods. Although no such model should be used by the business person without careful examination of individual products, it does provide some useful hints as to which products might be exportable and which might suffer import competition. The concept can also give clues as to the potential success of various product policies.

To extend the market for a product at home and abroad, the business person may practise a strategy of market segmentation, making design changes in the product to appeal to different types of consumers, but there comes a point where design changes can no longer make a product competitive abroad or safe from imports. Firms may follow two strategies for survival: a continual product roll-over, shifting resources to new products more suited to the unique demands of the market; and/or manufacturing abroad, to take advantage of lower production costs and to save tariffs and transportation charges.

LANCASTER'S MODIFICATION AND EXTENSION TO THE THEORY

According to Wells's theory, as a product moves down the 'pecking order' over time, a series of curves with similar amplitudes will result. However, Lancaster suggests that, the further down the pecking order a product goes, the higher will be its consumption over time.[12] Thus, each product life cycle curve will have a progressively higher amplitude. This is explained diagrammatically in Fig. 14.5.

Curve (1) represents band 1, and we can see that (*a*) represents (band 1) production of a product for the (band 1) market. It is appropriate that the first curve should be the USA, as most new products commence their life there. As this market becomes saturated, the American producers seek export opportunities in developed European markets (band 2), shown in (*b*). The American production of the product continues to supply one market in decline in (c) as European producers begin to market the same product in their home market (*d*). At this stage European production grows as rapidly as American production declines, and eventually European producers are meeting their home market demand by themselves (*e*). In stage (*f*) the developed European producers have reached the pinnacle of production, providing their home market, the American market and next band developing countries (band 3) with the product. However, in section (*g*) sales of the product decline in the European and developing country markets now being supplied, as the developing countries themselves begin to produce the product (*h*). Now developing country production grows as rapidly as European production declines, and eventually developing country producers are meeting their home market demand by themselves (*i*). Now the developing countries have reached the height of their production (*j*), supplying America, Europe, their home market and less developed countries (band 4), and then they move into decline (*k*) as less developed country production increases (*l*). This cycle of trade from one group of countries to another can continue as long as there are countries less developed than the previous ones.

It should be noticed that each curve is higher than the previous one because production increases in relation to the increased demand. This is because the movement of the product from one curve to the next creates active consumers who did not exist before, primarily as a result of product development and experience gained in production, but also because of increased demand as less-developed countries become more affluent.

To give examples of the type of countries involved in the model, 'Europe' denotes Western Europe—those countries that are technically advanced second only to the USA. Such countries would typically be Britain, Germany or France. By developing countries, we mean some European countries and some Far Eastern countries—Portugal, Greece and South Korea would be good examples. Less-developed countries would follow economically and technically after these developing countries, but may be

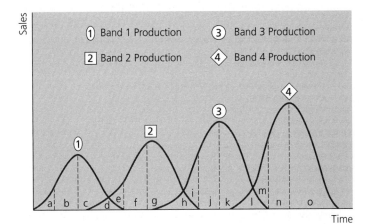

FIGURE 14.5

Lancaster's modification to Wells's theory

Stage	Production	Consumption
a	①	①
b	①	① + ②
c	①	① + ②
d	① + ②	① + ②
e	②	① + ②
f	②	① + ② + ③
g	②	① + ② + ③
h	② + ③	① + ② + ③
i	③	① + ② + ③
j	③	① + ② + ③ + ④
k	③	① + ② + ③ + ④
l	③ + ④	① + ② + ③ + ④
m	④	① + ② + ③ + ④
n	④	① + ② + ③ + ④
o	④	① + ② + ③ + ④

split into various degrees of development. Such countries would typically be The Philippines, Indonesia, Sri Lanka and Nigeria.

Looking at the model cumulatively, we can see a gradual progression in sales of the product. By adding the total consumption levels at each point in time (i.e. by inverting sections *d*, *h* and *l*), we find a straight line of cumulative consumption (see Fig. 14.6). The different stages in each curve can still be identified on this straight line.

In fact, the descriptions given more or less neatly match the definitions given earlier in this chapter, with the USA being an example of an 'affluent country' and so on down the scale to 'subsistence economies'.

LOGISTICS OF EXPORTING

Physical distribution of logistics is an activity often neglected in texts on international marketing. However, as we saw in Chapter 8, it is an extremely important subject, particularly for the export marketer; it is one of the major cost elements in international marketing and has been identified as a crucial factor in non-price competitiveness. Research by Steuer *et al.*[13] showed that in the case of machine tools a rise in waiting time of one month will reduce export orders by approximately 10 per cent.

Logistics includes the three areas of warehousing, inventory control and transport (and, in the case of export marketing, the associated documentation). As far as consumers are concerned, these factors are represented by:

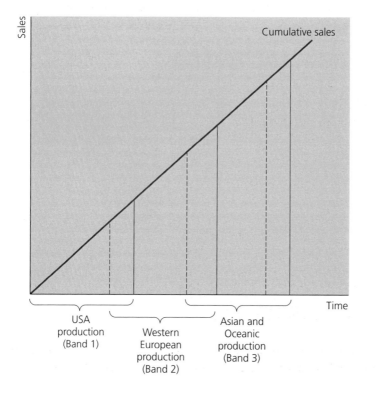

FIGURE 14.6

Cumulative sales, per Lancaster's modification to Wells's theory

- The speed with which orders are filled.
- The ability to meet emergency orders.
- The delivery of goods in acceptable condition.
- The policy on returned goods.
- The options offered on minimum order sizes and transport modes.
- The charges for services (if any).

The concept of total distribution cost has been discussed in Chapter 8. Nowhere is this concept of more importance than in international marketing. The methods of transport potentially available to the export marketer are varied—seafreight, road, rail, canal and airfreight—and it is well known that, on a unit weight or volume rate, the costs of airfreight, for example, are significantly greater than seafreight. This simplistic comparison ignores cost saving in other areas of logistics that can be achieved by airfreight. Greater speed of delivery has a positive effect on cash flow—a company's money is tied up in goods for a shorter period of time; lower safety stock levels reduce the costs of stockholding: cost of insurance, handling and customs clearance can be significantly reduced. This is not to say that airfreight should be the preferred mode of transport—bulk items are clearly excluded—but it serves to indicate that it is unrealistic to consider the freight rate alone in physical distribution decisions. In general terms, however, it can be said that on a regular basis, low-bulk, high-value items are carried by air, while high-bulk, low-value products (e.g. coal) are more effectively moved by sea.

This generalization tends to ignore the other modes of transport already mentioned. Road transport as a means of conveying goods from place of manufacture to place of consumption is highly developed throughout Western Europe, and the use of roll-on/roll-off (ro-ro) ferries is extremely important in trade between the UK and her EU partners. On mainland Europe the canal and river system is commercially viable. The important factor to consider, therefore, is just what is available to reach a specific overseas destination, and how this relates to total distribution costs.

Few export marketers have the knowledge or experience to make all logistics decisions. Traditionally, a freight forwarder has been used to bridge the gap between seller and shipper, whose role has included booking the space on a particular transport mode, documentation and customs procedures and, in many cases, export packaging. Control of logistics was therefore fragmented. Most companies have now replaced at least a part of the international freight forwarder's role by an in-house function. Developments in aligned documentation mean that international documents can be produced as easily as companies' commercial invoices.

The management of international logistics has all the problems of domestic physical distribution, but is complicated by its needs to operate across a wider spectrum of transport modes and accepted practice in differing countries. For a full discussion of this topic you are recommended to consult the text by Phillips *et al.*[14]

TRENDS AND DEVELOPMENTS IN INTERNATIONAL MARKETING

As we might expect, the international marketer is faced with one of the most dynamic and complex of marketing environments. Trade across national frontiers has been one of the fastest growing areas of economic activity over the past twenty years and has witnessed many changes and developments. In fact, the past five years have witnessed some of the most far-reaching trends and developments for international marketers seen during this century. Successful international marketers have been those who have adapted to these trends and developments by seizing the opportunities presented. The next decade, however, is likely to be no different with respect to the speed of change; and to remain successful the international marketer needs to be aware of and respond to these future developments. Four of the most significant of these recent developments affecting international marketing, together with an indication of their implications, are outlined in the following paragraphs.

The single European market: the European Union (EU)

The Single European Act which signalled the ultimate move towards a single market between the member countries of the European Union, together with some of the implications for the marketer was introduced in Chapter 2. We also discussed the move towards a single European currency which, you will recall, the UK has not yet made a decision to join. There is no doubt that the move towards a single market, together with all the implications which this has, such as, for example, eliminating controls on financial and capital movements; harmonizing VAT and other taxation levels; simplifying and often eliminating export documentation and controls, etc., is one of the most significant developments affecting the international and obviously, particularly, the European marketer. The single market will pose increasing opportunities, but also threats to the marketer in the 21st century. Today's marketer needs to be aware of developments in the single European market and plan to take account of the opportunities and threats this will present in the future.

The growth of global marketing

One of the most striking business trends of the past 30 years has been the increase in global marketing; that is, the growing number of firms that view marketing opportunities on a global basis. Of course, companies looking for opportunities in foreign markets is not a new occurrence, after all, nations have traded ever since the start of commerce. However, the 1990s was really the first decade when companies around the world started to think globally. Time and distance have been rapidly shrinking with the advent of new and faster communication, transport and financial flows.

Although many companies such as Nestlé, IBM, Shell, Toshiba and others have been conducting global marketing for many years now, global competition has now intensified to the extent that even purely 'domestic companies' that at one time never even thought about export marketing are beginning to realize that they, too, are affected in their marketing by global competitors.

In addition, the importance of global trade to governments and their economies, has meant that more and more firms are being urged to adopt a global approach, thereby hopefully marketing more of their products abroad and as a consequence adding to a positive balance of payments. This 'urging' has resulted in many governments offering material encouragement to companies to become involved more in global marketing through, for example, grants and loans, offers of expert advice, etc., etc.

Finally, global markets themselves have changed, and are changing with developments such as the single market, already discussed, and other trading blocs. The development of the so-called 'tiger economies' of the Pacific rim, notwithstanding some of the economic problems of the late 1990s, and the collapse of Communism and ensuing growth of more liberal economies in Eastern Europe have given rise to significant new opportunities for those companies willing and able to take advantage of global developments and threats for those who are not.

The newly industrialized countries (NICs)

The pattern of world trade is changing. In recent years we have seen the impact of countries such as South Korea, Singapore, Malaysia and some of the African countries in world markets as they progress to full industrialization.

These countries are likely to present themselves as formidable competitors in world markets in the next decade and beyond. As their economies develop, they will be capable of producing ever more sophisticated goods and services and also will benefit from the relatively low labour costs in these countries. Countries such as South Korea already pose a competitive threat in relatively high-technology products. The whole of the Far East, as well as countries in Africa are now important markets and also formidable competitors. Obviously, marketing strategies of the future—particularly in those companies planning to adopt a global marketing stance—must take the emergence of NICs into account.

Changes in Eastern Europe and the former Soviet Union

Gorbachev's policies of *glasnost* and *perestroika*, which began in the mid-1980s, have resulted in the democratization of the (now former) Soviet Union and an adoption of a more free-market economic philosophy. Other Warsaw Pact countries (for example, both Poland and Hungary) are becoming fully fledged democracies and run their economies more along free-market capitalist lines. Many of the Eastern European countries, including some of those belonging to the former Soviet bloc, are now moving towards membership of the European Union.

These developments present both opportunities and threats to firms in the established Western democracies.[15] It is likely that new markets will open up for existing Western goods and services, particularly high-technology products and financial services. On the other hand, the more marketing-oriented development of these economies will eventually mean greater competition in world markets.

CHAPTER SUMMARY

Any chapter of this length on a topic as wide as international marketing must by its very nature be selective. An attempt has been made to concentrate on those aspects of international marketing that are different from similar areas of activity in domestic marketing by posing additional issues and problems faced by the international marketer.

The chapter has therefore covered the international economic environment, the identification of export opportunities and international physical distribution. A large portion of the chapter has been devoted to the elements of the marketing mix on an international scale, in particular, strategies for entering the overseas market, product and communication alternatives, the concept of the international product life cycle and aspects of pricing as related to overseas marketing.

The principles of marketing are as true for international as for home markets. Customers' needs have to be analysed and understood, objectives must be set and performance must be controlled and measured. Special knowledge is, however, required and special training is necessary, both in the practicalities of export marketing and in the linguistic sense.

Finally, the dynamic nature of international markets means that, more than ever, the international markets must be constantly aware of trends and changes, which give rise to opportunities and threats.

CHAPTER REVIEW QUESTIONS

1. How does the international marketing environment differ from the environment in the domestic market?
2. What are the major difficulties likely to be encountered in carrying out research (both desk and field) for international marketing?
3. What alternative product and communication strategies are open to the international marketer?
4. What are the additional issues to be considered in pricing a product for overseas markets?
5. What are the major alternative market entry strategies, and what benefits and disadvantages do they have?

References

1. L. S. Walsh, *International Marketing*, Macdonald and Evans, London, 1982, p. 4.
2. Walsh, op. cit., pp. 5–6.
3. H. Chee and R. Harris, *Marketing: A Global Perspective*, Pitman Publishing, London, 1993.
4. V. Terpstra, *International Marketing*, 3rd edn, Dryden Press, Hinsdale, IL, 1983.

5. W. W. Rostow, *The Stage of Economic Growth*, Cambridge University Press, Cambridge, 1960.
6. Walsh, op. cit.
7. R. Whymant, 'Why Britain is bamboozled by a bamboo curtain', *Guardian*, 21 October 1980, p. 19.
8. W. J. Keegan, 'Multinational product planning: strategic alternatives', *Journal of Marketing*, **33**, January 1969, pp. 58–62.
9. V. Terpstra and R. Sarathy, *International Marketing*, 5th edn, The Dryden Press, Orlando, FL, 1991, pp. 540–1.
10. L. T. Wells, Jr, 'A product life cycle for international trade', *Journal of Marketing*, **32**, 1968, pp. 1–6.
11. G. C. Hufbauer, *Synthetic Materials and the Theory of International Trade*, Harvard University Press, Cambridge, MA, 1966.
12. G. A. Lancaster and I. Wesenlund, 'A product life cycle theory for international trade: an empirical investigation', *European Journal of Marketing*, **18** (6/7), 1984, pp. 72–89.
13. M. D. Steuer, R. J. Ball and J. R. Eaton, 'The effect of waiting time on foreign orders for machine tools', *Economica*, **33**, pp. 387–403, 1984.
14. C. Phillips, I. Doole and R. Lowe, *International Marketing Strategy*, Routledge, London, 1994, Chapter 10.
15. P. Meller, 'Back to the USSR', *Marketing*, August 1990, pp. 22–3.

Lancaster Designs Ltd　　　　　　　　　　　　　　　　　　　CASE STUDY

Lancaster Designs Ltd is a medium-sized successful firm of interior designers in the UK specializing in the design and completion of interior room designs for hotels and public places. Mike Lancaster combined his design talents with other interior designers, an architect and two furnishing material specialists to form the company some ten years ago. Over the subsequent years they have successfully carried out a number of interior design contracts for hotels around the country. They now offer a complete design service: from the original design or re-design of a room and its furnishings; the acquisition of the materials and furniture, etc; and the completion of the actual installation and decorating work up to the final completion of handing over to the client.

Although sufficient business has been generated over the years to keep all the partners busy, the company see their next step as expansion from the UK into other parts of Europe, particularly with the possible expansion of the European Union and the move towards closer economic and political integration through things such as the single currency.

During a recent partners' business meeting, Mike had raised this prospect with the other partners. Mike travelled extensively throughout Europe, admittedly principally on holiday. He told his partners at the meeting that in his view most of the hotels in which he stayed at could have been considerably improved with regard to their interior designs without much difficulty or great expense. French hotels, in particular, he found abhorrent from an interior design point of view, often with patterns everywhere, pink plastic lampshades and furniture 'out of the ark'. He admitted that perhaps this was simply the French taste, but still felt there was potential for the skills of a business like Lancaster Designs.

He was determined to explore the potential for the services of Lancaster Designs in other parts of Europe further, but he was worried about the extent to which his assessment of the designs in the hotels he had stayed in in Europe was more a reflection of his tastes rather than local tastes. He certainly acknowledged that tastes and cultures were different even in countries as close, both geographically and in many other ways, as France and Germany.

He also understood, that like the UK, many of the international hotels actually had the same 'international' designs for their hotel rooms regardless of where they were in the world. Mike's company had actually designed for some of these companies in the UK such as Holiday Inns for example. He was certain therefore that some of these designs would transfer readily to other countries in Europe.

With the agreement of his partners, he has decided to embark on an initial fact-finding tour encompassing France, Germany, Spain and Italy with a view to assessing the potential for expanding the company's operations into these countries. They have agreed a £10 000 budget to cover this initial fact-finding operation.

The partners all agreed that while continuing with their work within the UK there could be some very good opportunities for their design services abroad in a number of countries. What they needed now was an initial assessment of these opportunities and the extent to which Lancaster Designs' tastes could be transferred to other countries.

Questions

1. Advise Lancaster Designs regarding a research procedure into cultures, tastes and requirements in the countries selected.

2. How might the marketing mix elements for Lancaster Designs differ if they expand into other European countries?

Part Five

CASE STUDIES

Chapter Fifteen

UNDERTAKING EXTENDED CASE STUDIES

LEARNING OBJECTIVES   *This chapter will help you to:*

- understand how to approach and analyse extended case studies;

- distinguish between the techniques for tackling extended as opposed to mini case studies;

- be familiar with our analysis and decision model for undertaking extended case studies.

INTRODUCTION

Although marketing can be studied in its own right as an academic subject, essentially most students of marketing are intending to be, or currently are, practitioners of marketing. This text, although introducing and exploring conceptual and academic frameworks of marketing, is primarily concerned to develop practical application skills in marketing. In this and the following chapter we hope to develop these skills through the use of case studies.

Case studies, of course, are used extensively in the teaching and development of business and management skills. They are particularly widely used in marketing courses and textbooks. In addition to being a vehicle for developing these practical and application skills, they are also widely used to test these skills through examination. So, for example, most undergraduate and postgraduate courses in marketing, including the professional examinations of the Chartered Institute of Marketing in the United Kingdom, use case studies extensively for teaching and examination purposes. Discrete skills can be learned by using case studies, and these include basic analytical skills,

skills of application, creativity, written and oral communication and through awareness of oneself, social skills. In this and the following chapter, therefore, we shall be looking at and encouraging you to tackle marketing case studies. When it comes to case studies, however, we can broadly distinguish between two types of case studies, namely what might be termed 'extended' (maxi case studies) and short situational/scenario type case studies which are often referred to as 'mini cases'.

While these two types of case studies share some similarities with respect to how to approach and undertake them, the simple fact of the difference in the amount of information in each type of case study means that they are often used for different purposes with regard to training and examining, and they certainly require different approaches and techniques of analysis. Many examiners and examining bodies require students to be able to deal with both types of case studies. For example, the Chartered Institute of Marketing uses mini cases throughout its examination schedules in all subjects. However, in what is for many students the final qualifying examination for the CIM, namely the Analysis and Decision paper, an extended maxi case is used.

In this chapter we are going to be looking at how to approach and deal with the maxi-type case study where considerable detail is provided for the student and/or candidate to work on. In the next chapter, however, we are going to be looking at how to approach and deal with the mini type case studies as used, for example, by the Chartered Institute of Marketing.

In both chapters, after providing a framework and guidance of how to approach and analyse each type of case study, we have included two case studies, together with questions, on which to apply the concepts and techniques to which you are introduced. Obviously it is up to you to decide whether or not you want to complete these, but in many ways they represent the culmination of what the text is all about, namely helping you to develop practical and professional skills in the aspects of the fundamentals of marketing. Although the case studies in this and the subsequent chapter are aimed as much at the practising marketing manager as the student preparing for marketing examinations, obviously in the case of the latter it is important to stress examination technique with regard to dealing with case studies. Where appropriate therefore examination technique is also included.

A MODELS APPROACH TO UNDERTAKING EXTENDED CASE STUDIES

As already outlined, the extended case study is usually a detailed and comprehensive set of information covering one or more facets of an organization's marketing problems. As an example of extended case studies, those used by the Chartered Institute of Marketing in their Analysis and Decision syllabus and examination typically run to

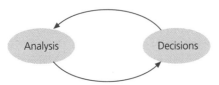

FIGURE 15.1

A simple model of approach to case analysis

thirty or forty pages or more and often include detailed appendices encompassing many facets of the marketing activities of the organization. For the student, or even marketing manager, coming to an extended case study such as this for the first time can be daunting, and in some cases, paralysing. The major problems are often: 'Where do I start; what am I expected to do; how do I deal with all this complexity and information?' In helping to solve these problems a models approach to the analysis of extended case studies is useful.

The most basic question to ask is, What is wrong? Then, What can I do to put it right? Then, Do my suggestions overcome the difficulties I have identified in the case? Figure 15.1 explains in diagrammatic terms.

The dimensions of analysing difficulties in organizations have to be considered in relation to the complexities involved. It is useful, and indeed essential, to attempt to discover and define the boundaries to the difficulties facing the organization, i.e. to view the company in the case study as an 'analysis and decision system' (Fig. 15.2).

As we saw in Chapter 12, two environments need to be examined:

- The internal organizational environment.
- The external organizational environment.

Analysis must be conducted both within the defined boundaries of the organization and beyond, in the external corporate environment.

Analysis conducted both internally and externally will then lead to decision proposals which relate to the internal organizational environment in the context of the wider external company environment.

Therefore, the analysis process must span and bridge the defined boundary to enable the company to be viewed as an 'open system' which interacts with its environment, both taking from and adding to the dynamic status of the 'world' beyond the immediate boundaries of the company.

To jump across the hurdle from analysis to decisions in the context of marketing case studies, a closer look is required at the essential components that comprise the analysis and decision system (see Fig. 15.3).

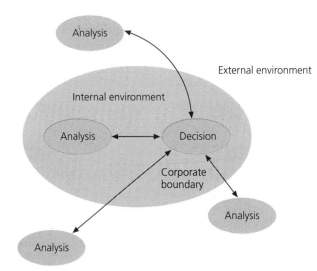

FIGURE 15.2

A sophisticated model of approach to case analysis

The components within this analysis and decision system are interrelated in many ways, the main relationships being demonstrated by arrows in Fig. 15.4. These relationships are the processes that cause the system to function. The relationship diagram in Fig. 15.4 demonstrates the dynamic qualities of the analysis and decision system, showing how the parts relate to the whole system.

To tackle extended marketing case studies, the relationships conveyed may be broken down into a set of systematic processes or procedures, as shown in Fig. 15.5, to (a) prepare a case study, and (b) present the case for examination purposes.

The analysis and decision case study model can now be extended to a set of 20 stages for the preparation and presentation of complex marketing case studies. These stages are:

1. Familiarization.

2. The brief.

3. Initial situation analysis:
   - The information audit.
   - The marketing audit.

4. SWOT analysis.

5. Initial constraint identification.

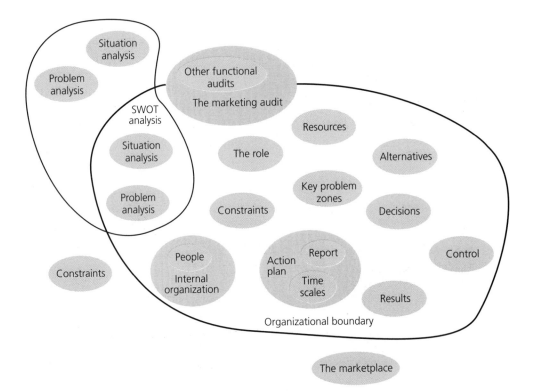

FIGURE 15.3

A marketing case study analysis and decision system

6. Problem identification and analysis:
   - Quantitative analysis.
7. Redefinition of problem zones.
8. Review of environmental and resource constraints.
9. Statement of assumptions.
10. The business mission.
11. Alternative courses of action.
12. Setting time-scales.
13. Setting objectives.
14. Developing strategies.
15. Tactics.
16. Staffing and organizational responsibility.
17. Contingency planning.
18. Results.
19. Control.
20. Report presentation.

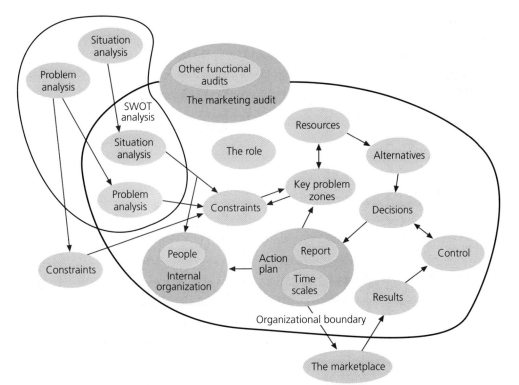

FIGURE 15.4

A marketing case study analysis and decision relationship diagram

USING THE ANALYSIS AND DECISION MODEL

Stage 1   Familiarization

Read through the case study quickly several times to familiarize yourself with the case study scenario.

Read through again, this time more slowly to determine more about the organizational setting, the products/services, and people involved in the environmental context in which the case study scenario is set. Consider the facts presented and the information that can be gleaned from them. Consider how the information presented

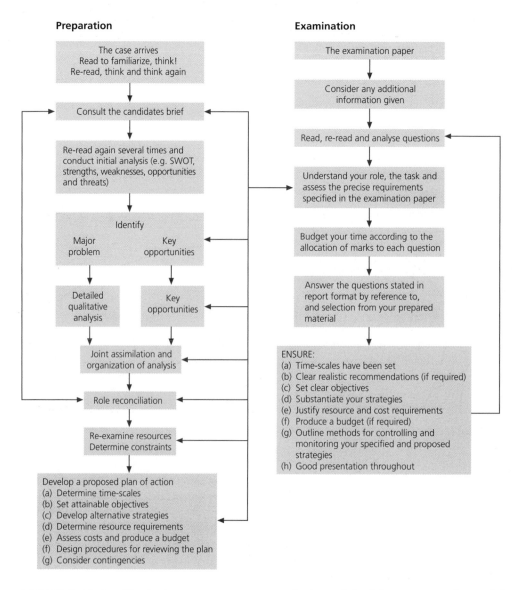

FIGURE 15.5   *Marketing management: analysis and decision case study model*

in the case can best be organized to help you refer back to it for more detailed analysis. At this stage do not discard any of the case material as being invalid.

This is not the time to identify problems or to suggest solutions.

If possible, it is advisable to leave the case for a few hours to help to digest the material to which you have been exposed for the first time.

Above all, remain global in the thoughts you may have marshalled.

At this initial stage avoid all temptation to tackle the detailed aspects with which you have been confronted.

Stage 2   The brief

In certain marketing case studies, as a potential candidate for assessment or examination, you will be given a brief which specifies the role you will be required to take with reference to the case study scenario. Consider your position carefully. In particular:

1. Are you to be a member of the organization? If so:

   a. In what capacity?
   b. Is this a staff or line capacity?
   c. What will be the boundaries of your responsibility?

2. If you are an external consultant to the organization:

   a. What is your position?
   b. What is your brief—actual or anticipated?
   c. Who will be affected by your actions, where, when and how, both within your own consulting organization and in the client company?

Now reconsider the case study material with which you are familiar, in the light of the position in which you are placed.

Stage 3   Initial situation analysis

The information audit   It is time now to transfer your review of the case study into a more detailed description and clearer understanding of the situation and the role you have to perform with respect to the total scenario.

To develop your understanding, it is necessary that you interpret the case facts and data to build up an information bank to establish the actual information you have, assumptions about it and the additional information you may need in the real-life situation.

An assessment, therefore, must be made and the following questions should be posed:

- How reliable are the facts, figures and stated opinions?

- To what extent can the information presented be accepted as precise and valid?

- Are there gaps in the information presented?

- Are these gaps designed purposely by the case study writer for identification and explanation by students?

- Is the information presented likely to be subject to change as a result of the dynamic conditions presented, or to be provided at the examination stage?

- Where are the weak links in the information?

- Are the sources of information given valid?

Students may find it helpful to structure the audit under a series of headings before asking these questions. The structuring will depend upon the case being studied, although functional business areas, issues presented, processes in the organization, time dimensions, personal relationships, and financial and statistical issues are suggested for the beginner.

To complete the information audit, it must be remembered that case studies are rarely written to provide clear facts but rather to encourage the student to use deductive logic to infer or even speculate, to stimulate ideas.

It is necessary, therefore, at the end of the audit to provide a set of assumptions from which to build.

The marketing audit   Having determined the status of the information presented in the case study, it now becomes necessary to conduct a marketing audit on the total case scenario in preparation for a SWOT analysis that will, in turn, lead to the design of a strategic marketing plan.

The marketing audit of the case study must build up an information base to check the validity and reliability of all facts and stated opinions that relate to marketing issues arising in the case study scenario.

Again, as we saw in Chapter 12, a checklist of points needs to be examined. Although no checklist is completely comprehensive and hence foolproof in application, the following major headings distinguish the internal and external audit.

External company environmental factors

1. Macro-economic environment

   a. Political/legal/fiscal
   b. Economic
   c. Social/cultural
   d. Technical

2. The market environment

   a. Market profiles
   b. Customer profiles
   c. Product profiles
   d. Pricing profiles
   e. Communication profile
   f. Channel and physical distribution profile
   g. Industry structural profile
   h. Competitor profiles and profitability

It would be quite impossible to compile a complete list of factors under each heading. Table 12.1 in Chapter 12 gives an example though, of the sort of factors that can be included. The student to complete a 'profile' under each section, should answer the following: Who? What? Where? When? How? Why? and summarize the difficulties arising.

Internal company environmental factors   The internal audit is a complete examination of the situation that currently exists. Remember, we looked at a sample checklist for the internal audit in Chapter 12. Another approach to conducting the internal audit, however, is to examine every element that should be contained in an idealized marketing plan, together with the systems and procedures used to design, develop, implement, control, and review the plan (see Table 15.1).

The marketing audit contributes to the student's SWOT analysis in the following way:

Internal audit → Strengths and weaknesses
External audit → Opportunities and threats

During the process of auditing the case study, where information presented conflicts, as often it does in the real world, candidates must apply common sense, make assessments and state their assumptions before proceeding.

Stage 4   SWOT analysis

The evaluation of the information and marketing audits can now be organized into a SWOT analysis.

Strengths and weaknesses → Historic internal review to date
Opportunities and threats → External current review, forecast
over a future time period

The SWOT analysis provides the basis upon which later stages in the model depend. It should aim to condense the case information in an ordered form for easy subsequent reference.

By committing the SWOT to a written presentation, a better understanding of the total case study emerges. In turn, this assists the student to focus on particular issues to help achieve clear problem definition.

TABLE 15.1   *The marketing audit*

	Current position		
Internal audit elements	Design systems	Implementation systems	Control systems
1. Corporate and market analysis			
2. Constraints			
3. Apparent and stated assumptions			
4. Key problems and potential problem resolution			
5. Resource evaluation			
6. Time dimensions for planning marketing			
7. Objective setting and achievement			
8. Strategic marketing planning			
9. Tactics employed			
10. Organization for marketing			
11. Forecasting			
12. Budgeting systems			
13. Sales analysis			
14. Sales achievement			
15. Market share(s)			
16. Profit performance			
17. Total marketing mix variables			
18. The marketing information system			

The SWOT analysis should be conducted rigorously and is usually best achieved by syndicates working in groups, which often produce creative insights which can be developed to produce distinguished marketing planning proposals.

The content of the SWOT analysis should not appear just as a set of concise, static statements in the pro forma provided in Fig. 15.6, but be *used* to generate *thoughts* for clear problem definition. The real value of a SWOT analysis is to consider the implications that arise from it at corporate and marketing levels. A critical assessment can then be made of the main problem themes facing the company and priorities set for tackling them, and in this way the student can ensure that the key result areas of the business have been appraised.

Stage 5   Constraints

Constraints may impose problems upon an organization. They may also provide the limits within which problems can be both identified and researched.

The audits conducted—i.e. the case information audit, the corporate audit and marketing audit—and analysed in the SWOT analysis will highlight the constraints, both internal and external, which provide limits to organizational performance.

Internal resource constraints and external market constraints provide a framework within which objectives can be set, maximized and achieved.

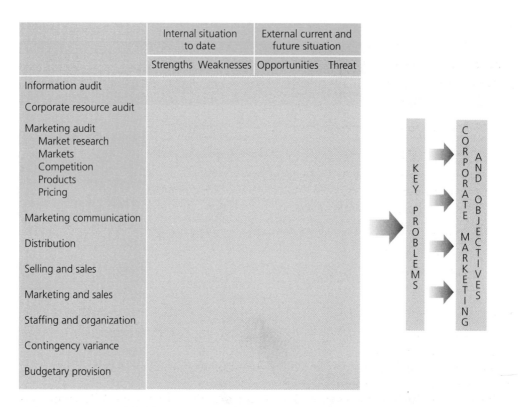

FIGURE 15.6   *SWOT*

Stage 6 *Problem zone identification and problem analysis*

The next extension to the SWOT analysis is to interpret it in terms of key problem areas for attention.

The definition of, and distinction between, problem areas will depend upon the role the student adopts. With a specific role brief, the boundaries of responsibility can be clearly drawn and provide the basis from which an actual perspective can be taken. Where the brief is vague, the case study student must take a variety of perspectives and hence will view the organization from different angles in order to identify a variety of problem areas.

The initial step must be individual or group brainstorming on problem areas to ensure that nothing is discounted at this initial stage.

The definition of problems is quite difficult, because the nature of problems often means that they actually comprise sets of problems, which become problem zones; in turn, there are often related difficulties which are hard to isolate for analysis and action. Complex sets of problems are known as *messes*. The task of the candidate, therefore, is to separate out those problem zones that are containable.

Handling problem zones is a matter of scale. Small-scale problems or difficulties:

- Have an interdefinable boundary.
- Involve a limited number of people.
- Can be treated as a separate matter.
- Have limited applications.
- Are capable of being clearly prioritized.
- Operate over a limited time scale.
- Require information that is known.
- Have a known problem.
- Possess a known solution.

'Messy' problem zones are much larger and poorly defined:

- They have no readily defined boundary.
- They involve more people.
- They cannot be treated individually and disentangled from the context.
- They may have far-reaching implications.
- The time scale is uncertain.
- They are difficult to prioritize.
- Information needed is not specified and is difficult to specify.
- It is not sure what the problem really is.
- No immediate solution is known.

Within marketing case studies simple problems may be posed, but often the problem zone lies between the two extremes above.

One way in which problem zones can be detected is to distinguish between what commonly exists and the desired state for the future.

The tension which exists between the SW area and the OT area in SWOT analysis is a rich source for problem area detection.

Students often consider problems in isolation, where in effect there is usually a causal relationship, which can be quite complex and hence multicausal in origin.

Distinction must be drawn between symptoms and fundamental problems to ensure that the outcomes expected and planned for actually occur.

Students can usefully distinguish between existing problem zones and anticipated problem zones. In the latter area, using the SWOT analysis, this classification can be further divided into problem areas for opportunity exploitation and problem areas to avert the risk of impending threats.

Problem areas defined should be capable of action and hence they need to be prioritized with reference to the scale of the problem area specified and the time scale for overcoming them. Hence the use of a time scale running from the immediate term to the long term over specified years and months is useful.

In many case studies problems may be difficult to define. The student should distinguish between the following problem zones:

- Actual explicit problem zones
- Concealed problem zones
- Potential problem zones

The student should realize that in the first two zones some may be historic or recurrent problems.

The analysis of problem settings in case study scenarios must ultimately be assessed in terms of who and what is affected and to what extent the problem is zone-controllable and by whom.

Problem zones can often be highlighted by the imposition of criteria for organizational assessment. It is against such standards that problems which previously had not been identified become revealed.

Detailed problem analysis—quantitative The identification of problem zones from the SWOT analysis may require, in certain case studies, the application of financial and statistical techniques to assist the depth of analysis required accurately to specify the level of problem(s) facing the company.

Within the space of this text, we cannot provide a comprehensive résumé of such techniques. However, one set of financial assessment techniques often of immediate use is financial ratio analysis.

Financial ratios The subject area of financial analysis is underpinned by ratio analysis. Financial ratios in use are numerous. The marketing student should not need to become a financial analyst to use them but rather should be selective and know the implications of the main categories.

Ratios are not a standard formula for judging the performance of a business. Many ratios are in common use and express standard relationships, but these are only a guide since management cannot be reduced to a formula. What the standard relationships do convey is a logical and important operational sequence of related key control figures. The absolute figures by themselves are of limited value to management.

Ratios are not a substitute for judgement. Management is not provided with answers to its problems by ratios. Judgements must be used not only in the selection of key ratios to suit the business but also in the evaluation of these ratios. Ratios calculated on an industrial basis or for a group of companies operating in a similar type of business, where there is a common basis of calculation, also enable the student to compare company performance with industry performance.

Ratio analysis is a useful financial technique to assist management in the control of the business, provided its limitations are understood.

The marketing student in the analysis of case study profit and loss accounts and balance sheets should be aware of the importance of the following basic ratio types.

1. *Liquidity ratios*

   These are used to assess the company's ability to meet its current financial obligations.

   a. *The current ratio*

Formula:	Current assets divided by current liabilities.
Interpretation:	The number of times current liabilities are covered by current assets. This is a fairly crude measure expressing the company's ability to meet current obligations with a margin of safety, which may arise from the varying quality of the current assets, particularly with reference to stocks and the status of debtors. A more critical measure of the company's solvency is the 'quick ratio', known also as the 'acid test'.

   b. *The acid test*

Formula:	Quick assets divided by current liabilities.
Interpretation:	The number of times current liabilities are covered by quick assets. Quick assets are cash and 'near cash' items, but *not* stock because it may not be quickly convertible to cash. Quick assets are often considered as current assets minus stocks. In most cases this is cash plus debtors, a critical measure which should be in 1:1.

2. *Profitability ratios*

   These are used to assess the company's profit performance with reference to the direct costs and indirect costs of the business and the associated control of both in relation to sales performance.

   a. *Gross profit %*

Formula:	Gross profit divided by sales multiplied by 100.
Interpretation:	As a percentage of sales revenue, gross profit is the margin created from absolute sales for the period minus the direct costs represented by the cost of sales.

   b. *Net profit %*

Formula:	Net profit before tax and depreciation divided by sales multiplied by 100.
Interpretation:	Net profit or loss is the result of charging the indirect costs as revenue expenses of the business against the gross profit margin. To present an objective picture, the net profit figure is taken before depreciation has been charged and corporation tax deducted.

   c. *Return on total assets*

Formula:	Net profit divided by total assets multiplied by 100.
Interpretation:	The ratio measures the rate of profitability achieved on the total assets of the business. Much will depend upon the accuracy of the assets valuation in the company's balance sheet. There is frequent debate over which profit figure to use. The key is to be consistent throughout the analysis. Options include:

   - The figure used in the net profit per cent ratio.
   - Net profit after tax.

   In either case, it is considered appropriate to add back the interest charged on long-term debt to demonstrate objectively the company's capacity to produce profits from total asset utilization.

   d. *Return on capital employed*

Formula:	Net profit before tax and long-term interest divided by total capital employed multiplied by 100.

‌

‌

Interpretation: This is considered to be the primary ratio from which family trees of ratios can be extended to form a pyramid. It expresses the efficiency of management and measures its performance to generate a rate of return on the total capital and reserves of the business.

e. *Return on owner's equity*
   Formula: Pre-tax profits divided by equity capital multiplied by 100.
   Interpretation: This ratio measures the rate of return on the owner's investment in the business. As a percentage, absolute return can also be measured for every £100 invested.

3. *Funds management*
   These ratios are used to assess how efficiently the company uses the available working capital, particularly with reference to inventory holding, debt collection and payment.

   a. *Debtors collection period*
      Formula: Debtors divided by sales multiplied by 365 (days).
      Interpretation: The ratio determines the time taken by the company to collect debts. It provides a clear indication of the efficiency of credit control.

   b. *Average payment period*
      Formula: Creditors divided by purchase multiplied by 365 (days).
      Interpretation: This ratio determines the average time taken for the company to pay its bills. The relationship between 3a and 3b gives an indication of how the company manages cash flow.

   c. *Stock turnover*
      Formula: Sales divided by closing stock.
      Interpretation: This ratio measures the rate at which stock moves through the business. A more critical measure can be made by taking the cost of sales figure. The ratio is expressed as the 'number of times' stock is turned. If this is then divided into 365 days, one can assess the number of days' or months' stock that is tied up on the company shelves. Often less dynamic companies tie up a considerable amount of working capital through poor inventory control.

4. *Ability to borrow*
   These ratios demonstrate the position of the company in relation to the level of indebtedness and the management of the capital structures.

   a. *Debt ratio*
      Formula: Current liabilities divided by total assets multiplied by 100.
      Interpretation: This ratio measures the percentage value of the current liabilities in relation to the total asset value of the business. This demonstrates the amount of current short-term indebtedness which is covered by the company's assets and hence the company's ability to pay off current liabilities from the sale of total assets.

   b. Capital gearing ratio
      Formula: Fixed interest capital divided by shareholders' funds multiplied by 100.
      Interpretation: The ratio reflects the percentage of fixed interest capital and business commitments in relation to the shareholders' funds. It shows the relative position of creditors to the business owner's stake in the company. The fixed interest capital figure is also called net debt and is calculated by adding long-term debt to debentures to overdraft and short-term loans less the cash the company has as a current asset.

Stage 7   Redefinition of problem zones

Owing to the length and associated complexity of some case studies, it is necessary to conduct further financial and statistical analysis to gain a more complete understanding of the material presented.

The results of the quantitative analysis must now be set against the backcloth and market setting of the organization to provide a balanced view. Hence it is the consideration of further quantitative and qualitative analysis that may force the student to redefine the problem zones before proceeding to the next stage of the model.

This provides a natural break, a time to sit back and reflect on the analysis progress to date before adopting a more focused view of the situation. Once the finishing process starts, it is very difficult to revert to take a holistic view again. Therefore, allowing for the time constraints imposed, the longer one can take in problem analysis to provide a global situation summary, the better will be the design of the proposed action plan.

It is at this stage, therefore, before confirming the problem zones for attention, that the candidate should finally reconcile the role(s) in relation to the case study scenario.

Stage 8   Review environmental and resource constraints

Before proceeding to the action plan, students should check that the environmental and corporate resource constraints have been fully appraised and stated so that progress can be planned within these limitations.

In particular, modifications to the design and implementation of resource management can be considered, so that slack or wasted resources can be manipulated to maximize efficient resource utilization.

Stage 9   Statement of assumptions

Based upon the analysis conducted so far, students must state all assumptions before proceeding with the development of objectives and the strategic marketing plan.

Stage 10   The business mission

The corporate plan comprises a statement of the global business mission for the company. This direction is laid out as a set of corporate objectives, corporate strategies with the main tasks for the time period defined, plus corporate financial projections as a set of budgets.

The corporate plan should dictate the changes required for the period. These changes are operated by each strategic business unit in the organization.

The business mission must precede the setting of marketing objectives and the development of marketing strategy, and therefore it provides the foundation for marketing planning.

Simple but demanding questions must be answered:

- What business is the company in now?
- What business is the company *really* in?
- How well is the company doing?
- What assumptions can be made about the future?
- Where should the company be, say, in five years' time, and why?
- What routes can be taken to get there?
- What will be the market reaction?
- What is the level of corporate risk?
- Which direction should the company actually take?

- What resources does the company have, and what will it need?
- How can it be ensured that the company will arrive at the intended destination?
- What action needs to be taken to achieve the business mission, and what will be the total cost?

The answers to these questions should be summarized on a corporate statement which specifies the future business mission for the organization.

Stage 11   Setting objectives

Many marketing case students do not know the questions with which they may be faced in an examination, and hence the most appropriate form of preparation is to draw up a comprehensive marketing plan from which sections can be selected on the day of the examination.

Objectives provide the basis for the plan and should be specified at corporate and marketing levels and then at marketing-scale plan levels so that strategies are designed to relate to the specified objectives at the various levels of the plan.

Marketing objectives should be specified for the prescribed time periods in both quantitative and qualitative terms and should be capable of action, measurement and achievement within the selected periods. They should be both consistent and attainable.

It is vital that objectives are specified clearly so that you can communicate precisely what it is that you wish to do.

The SWOT analysis provides the stimulus from which objectives should be set. Objectives should be designed to overcome the key problems and problem zones that were determined from the SWOT analysis.

A useful technique is to develop an objective tree which starts at global higher-level objectives and obtains a clearer focus for action at the lower marketing-scale plan levels, i.e. a hierarchy of objectives. This hierarchy should specify what is to be achieved at each level.

The setting of marketing objectives should aim to achieve balance within the marketing mix and allow for a degree of flexibility.

Marketing objectives should embrace the company philosophy and encourage the development of revised policy.

Essentially, the following areas cannot be ignored in the design of marketing objectives:

- Market position
- Change
- Output
- Resource utilization
- Staff performance and attitude
- Social responsibility
- Profitability
- Cost control

Stage 12   Setting time-scales

Problem analysis and the selected course or courses of action must be set in the context of time. Realistic time scales must be set for the development of a strategic plan.

Plans are usually devised on a rolling planning basis, and hence a one-year plan can be so rolled over, for example, a three- to five-year period with reviews scheduled at regular intervals.

Students should develop the time horizon for action both within a 12-month period and beyond. Even within the one-year plan there are events that require immediate action—say, within three months. These also should be clearly distinguished.

The complexity of a problem zone may require, for example, a series of sequential actions over a specified time-scale ranging from three months to three years—in which case, students should demonstrate clearly the use of appropriate action phased over the specified time period.

Stage 13   Alternative course of action

Students are now required to take a substantial conceptual leap from problem definition to suggesting alternative solutions.

Creativity is the key! Enjoy the process of generating ideas; have fun; be experimental. So far the process has been quite rigid, yet turgid courses of action are not really required, and rarely do they provide the best solutions for strategic planning.

In some cases, alternatives may be explicit in the case study; the student is merely required to set up criteria by which to weigh the alternatives. Often, though, alternative courses of action are required to embrace, contain and resolve the key problems, prescribed.

Students in these case situations must have an overall appreciation of the global alternatives which are feasible and provide a basis upon which to assess these alternatives to make a firm judgement.

Good solutions are often as good as the ability to define and separate problems for attention.

Problem zones may be too wide to handle in one attempt and hence students must aim to tailor the chosen course of action to lower-level problems.

In all case study work there is no *one* solution, but rather defensible and justifiable courses of action which jointly attempt to resolve the difficulties the organization faces. Owing to the 'soft' nature of many problem settings, solutions may be partial at one end of the continuum and a whole set of problems may be resolved at the other. Rarely will independent courses of action achieve an all-embracing solution to the complexities of a defined problem zone. Rather, it is a set of related and hence integrated combined solutions which serve to make real progress towards overcoming or containing organizational problems.

Courses of action will normally achieve systemic effects both within the organization and beyond, into the environment of the marketplace, and hence alternatives must be assessed objectively to ensure optimization within the previously defined constraints.

Basic cost–benefit analysis of the proposed alterations is suggested. Students should consider the negative outcomes of their proposals as well as the positive effects.

Above all, the selected course of action must be feasible and achievable within the defined limitations of the company scenario posed.

Stage 14   Developing strategies

Marketing objectives specify *what* is to be achieved. Marketing strategies should outline *how* the objectives are to be achieved.

Marketing strategies are determined from objectives, not the other way round; but the student must ensure that the proposed strategy is not over-embracing and does not go beyond the requirements of the specified objective. This is a common fault in student presentations, which in many cases extends to a total reorganization of the company both internally and with reference to its position in the marketplace—albeit to achieve a very modest objective.

Strategy is the route to the achievement of objectives over the specified time intervals for which the objectives have been set.

Balance is a keynote; the internal consistency of the plan must be checked to ensure that the marketing elements for which strategy is designed are integrated and not competitive. When presented, the designed marketing strategy should demonstrate where the emphasis has been placed in order to achieve marketing objectives and the wider business mission.

As a mechanism for marshalling the impact of the developed strategies, financial resource deployment must be specified clearly in the form of a total marketing budget illustrating capital sources, revenues and expenditure.

The strategic marketing plan should demonstrate the utilization of existing resources and those additional resources to be procured to implement the designed strategy.

Stage 15   Marketing action programmes: marketing mix plans

By this stage of the case analysis we should be in a position to develop detailed marketing programmes in order to support broad objectives and strategies. This is best done by detailing tactical plans for each element of the marketing mix and involves specifying the individual activities to be undertaken in each area of the mix with due dates for their achievement.

Stage 16   Staffing and organizational responsibility

People have problems, not organizations; and people design, implement, administer and review plans to overcome problems. Students preparing case studies often demonstrate a total detachment from the human activity system of the organization.

Human resource management is a key factor in the management of the marketing function. Therefore, attention to this critical area is essential in preparing marketing management case studies.

Case material will have varying levels of information about key personnel involved, but where it is provided students must analyse the staff profile, consider the existing position and detect areas where change is required.

Change may mean not simply hiring and firing—even if this is within the remit given in the student brief—but also staff development, training, instruction and progression within the organizational structure.

In particular, the deployment of staff to take responsibility for the implementation of the marketing plan is an essential part of case study preparation.

Staffing should be viewed in a global context to include the appointment and appraisal of external agencies and consultants.

Stage 17   Contingency planning

Strategic planning in the relatively safe internal corporate case environment is one thing. Implementing the plan to achieve the designed strategy is quite another!

The purpose of contingency planning is to enable and even force management to think ahead to answer the question, 'What if our expectations are not realized in the real world?'

Contingency thinking is designed to create answers to the 'What if?' questions so that management will have the answers ready ahead of time if the designed strategy goes wrong. In case study preparation, the vital section on contingencies forces the student to think about a wider range of situations that might occur than when strategies were first designed to meet corporate and marketing objectives.

The student should consider how flexible the designed plan is if conditions should change. Answers to the following questions are needed:

- What is the capability of the organization to adapt to changed conditions?
- How quickly can the organization respond and with what internal and external effects?
- In what way must the organization respond to avert a crisis or the partial achievement of objectives?
- What options are open to the company in the light of anticipated change? How should these options be evaluated and what action should be taken?

At an earlier stage in this case study analysis and decision model the student had to generate ideas and decide between alternative courses of action. Reference back may provide a source for idea generation when designing the contingency plan.

Stage 18   Results

The case study student is often required to produce a strategic and tactical plan in a vacuum where the input is simply the case study material and the output is a well-presented strategic marketing plan. It is assumed that the results of the plan are the achievement of the specified plan objectives. If the objectives have been carefully and clearly communicated in a hierarchy and allocated to responsibility centres for action, monitoring, evaluation and adjustment, the task is usually deemed complete. Often answers to the following questions are overlooked:

- When implemented, what will be the tangible results of the proposed action?
- Can these results be quantified?

Therefore, the projected outcomes should be considered not only in terms of qualitative contribution, but also in financial terms, with reference to anticipated profits and profit contribution.

Stage 19   Control

The management process has been described as planning, organizing, directing, controlling, communicating, coordinating and evaluating organizations and individuals to achieve effective decisions.

The control function needs careful attention in the preparation of a marketing plan.

The control function should monitor feedback and assess performance so that appropriate adjustments can be made to achieve the desired goals and objectives of the organization.

A system of controls should be specified in both qualitative and quantitative terms in accordance with the time dimensions of the designed plan.

By designing a control system to review regularly actual performance against forecasted performance, management should be in a position of *knowing* what may go wrong.

The control system, efficiently administered, should avoid surprise, avert crisis and prevent the plan getting out of control.

To measure progress towards the achievement of goals and objectives, responsibility centres should be designated. No student must consider these without reference to the culture of the organization and the ability to adopt controls.

Despite the stage of organizational development or size of the organization, all managers should be in a position to highlight impending problems that will require immediate attention. This ability produces time in which to diagnose and analyse problem areas, then to design a strategy to resolve the difficulty. Levels of control to be designated should link with the management structure and organizational levels of the company.

To design a control system for the marketing plan, every element in the plan should have a set of specified controls tailored to fit the plan and the organization. Students must be aware that there is not one ubiquitous control model that can be applied to all plans.

The control system should facilitate situational analysis, problem diagnosis and the setting of priorities for feedback, and should specify the form and frequency of controls.

The main aim is for the designed marketing plan to succeed. The control system assists the progression towards success.

In the real world, plans fail frequently owing to a number of often interrelated factors. Typical factors are shown in Fig. 15.7 and should be provided for by the structure in the design of the marketing plan control system.

To assist the control of the marketing plan, the company must have a marketing information system. The complexity of the system will vary considerably depending upon the size of company and style of company management.

The system is a structured, interacting complex of staff, machines and procedures which should be designed to generate an orderly flow of pertinent information. Information is needed from the external and internal organizational environment for use as a basis for decision-making in specified areas of responsibility.

Therefore, the information system lies between the environment and the marketing executive user.

The student must consider what the marketing planning system needs, in what form, and what is economically feasible within the financial resource constraints of the organization.

Budgetary control   The most vital ingredient in business is planning for profit. Without profit, rarely can business survive and grow. An essential activity is profit planning and control, and budgeting is probably the widest-ranging control technique used because it percolates the entire organization.

Budgetary control in the context of the marketing plan is generally designed and adopted to coincide with the financial year of the company.

Correctly applied, the process of budgetary control makes a penetrating, critical and almost uncompromising evaluation of the performance of the marketing plan.

Students must recognize that budgeting and the associated information system provide a major contribution to achieving the objectives of the marketing plan.

The system must be inspired at senior management level and used to set operational standards with accountability for performance. The budgetary control system must be set up to allow for measurement against planned and forecasted performance.

When compiling case study marketing plans, students must realize that budgeting involves more than just forecasting. It provides a framework for evaluating performance.

In the context of case study examinations, students are often required only to list the appropriation of a total budget under relevant cost/profit centres. This is usually the final stage of an exhausting examination. Students must realize that this is only the beginning, and that the budget headings with forecasted income and expenditure have real organizational implications.

Stage 20   Case study report presentation

Written reports must be planned to achieve maximum impact on the reader.

The planning stage starts with the purpose of the report, to whom it is to be presented, what is to be included and how it is to be presented.

The purpose of a written case study report for students of marketing may be for course assessment or formal examinations. The function is to inform the reader of the facts, to explain the proposed course of action and to convince the reader that the recommendations and plans proposed are justifiable in the hope that a favourable reading/assessment is awarded.

A report must be written with a clear understanding of who the readers are and what they know of the situation, so that communication can take place at their knowledge level. For examination case reports, assume that the reader, your examiner, has a low knowledge level; do not overestimate his or her ability. You must be able to *demonstrate*

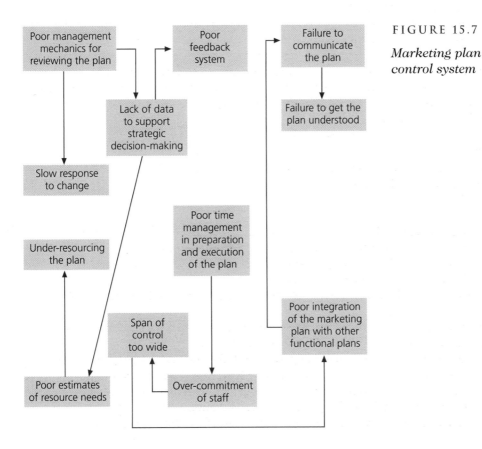

FIGURE 15.7

Marketing plan control system

your knowledge and understanding of the situation. The reader's attitude under conditions of assessment should be objective, but in the real world the writer must be aware of prevailing attitudes so as not to offend the reader.

In both the real world and for course assessment, you must have vision about what the reader wants to receive in terms of content, style and presentation.

Remember that reports are not extended essays but concise statements setting out your thoughts and proposals simply and clearly.

All recommendations should be justified to support your proposed plan of action, but do not bore the reader with in-depth analysis—this is in your working papers for subsequent reference if required.

It is important that the report is so structured that:

- The report is read.
- It is understood.
- It follows a logical sequence leading the reader along a particular path.

Planning the structure of your report before writing is absolutely essential.

For examination candidates, questions posed under examination conditions should be broken down into their component parts and a structure designed to ensure that all component parts have been handled. This structure then forms the headings for your report. Remember to commit to paper the most important points first, just in case your time budget has been exceeded for that particular section of the examination paper. Ensure that conclusions and recommendations are labelled clearly to receive maximum attention by the reader.

The conventions for structuring a report vary considerably. One format used personally is as follows:

1. *Title page*   This contains the report title, to whom it is addressed, the date, author's name and company and the list to whom the report is to be distributed.

2. *Summary*   This is a résumé of the terms of reference of the report with a short statement containing key functions, conclusions and recommendations. (This may also serve as a 'short report' for senior executives not wishing to indulge in the complete work.)

3. *Detailed contents list*   This should show clearly the structure of the report with a numbering system which is used throughout the report. Major headings and sub-headings should be shown and indexed by page number for easy reference.

4. *The main report*   This section contains the detailed facts and plans to support the summary given above. The main report should substantiate the recommendations made to the company in the summary section.

5. *Appendices*   This section should comprise three sub-sections:
   a. Supporting data to back up the main body of the report but which are too detailed for inclusion in the main section and would otherwise disrupt the flow of the report.
   b. Sources of reference, itemizing the bibliography and external sources consulted in the preparation of the report.
   c. Glossary of terms, to assist readers not totally conversant with the more technical aspects of the report.

For examination candidates, this structure may be appropriate only where the one global question has been asked. Where questions are issue-specific, the report must be tailored to the actual examination questions asked. This can be seen clearly in the worked examples included in later chapters of this book.

One alternative structure that may be applied by examination candidates is as follows:

1. *The problem statement* This is an interpretation of the specific examination questions stated in terms of a problem for solution.
2. *The implications of the problem* This section contains a concise résumé of the causes and effects of the problem.
3. *Alternative courses of action* This is a succinct statement of the options that could be taken to solve the problem area.
4. *Conclusions and recommendations* This is a statement of the selected course of action, justifying it and explaining in detail the recommended action to be taken.

Presentation is crucial for a report to be well received. Each page must appear interesting to the reader's eye. The use of white space, headings, indentations and report numbering systems should be applied to create maximum impact.

Remember the reader's attention span may be quite short, so sections and paragraphs should reflect this. In short, write simply, write briefly, write positively, and avoid cluttering the main text with elaborate diagrams, charts and tables.

This, then, completes our comprehensive review of how to approach extended case studies including advice on examination technique, presenting reports and answers etc. We have also included some of the main financial and other ratios that are often needed in the analysis of case studies, and in particular to identify problem zones. A further set of useful concepts and definitions which might be useful in tackling extended case studies, however, is contained in Appendix 2.

Armed with the analysis and decision model we can now introduce you to two case studies on which to practice your skills. These two case studies are in many ways typical of the genre of extended case studies and in particular those found in the Chartered Institute of Marketing's Analysis and Decision case study examination. As already mentioned, whether or not you decide to complete these case studies is of course entirely up to you, but should you decide to do this, our advice would be to attempt them under self imposed examination conditions.

Fisher plc (Hand tools marketing)

Fisher, based in Swansea, Wales, is a public limited company (plc). The 'Fisher Works' in Swansea opened at the turn of the century to provide tools for Welsh industries.

The Welsh steel industry provided many of the raw materials needed in the manufacturing process, and despite the recession in the steel industry, both nationwide and in the Western world, demand for Fisher products today remains active.

Fisher plc (hereafter referred to as Fisher), currently has an estimated 15 per cent share by value of the UK non-power hand tool market. Significant export trade has developed over the past 15 years to secure brand recognition in different countries. Certain Fisher products also are manufactured under licence in Germany and France and are sold throughout Europe. Similar trade has developed in eastern coast states of the USA. Direct exports from the UK to worldwide customers outstrip domestic sales within the UK.

The UK market for Fisher hand tools can be classified as:

- Domestic purchasers
- Professional users (i.e. tradesmen)
- Industrial buyers

Recent research among distribution channels has revealed that approximately 40 per cent by value fall into the first of these categories, with industrial buyers taking 20 per cent.

The Fisher brand has penetrated each of these market segments with considerable success to achieve its overall market position.

A variety of trading agreements on price and volume are used to secure a stable position within the distribution channels. The wholesale trade accounts for 47 per cent of UK turnover; retail trade some 35 per cent; 12 per cent to mail order houses, with the residual sales to direct accounts.

These various channels reach a variety of end users. The company, to quote its marketing manager, has yet to achieve a *complete* picture of 'which type of purchaser and/or end user buys which type of tool from which source of supply—internal estimates rarely agree'.

Market segmentation by end user provides a variety of profiles, ranging from the owner of a screwdriver to the owner and frequent user of a complete range of tools. The end user can be classified on a continuum ranging from the 'non-user' through to the semi-skilled/do-it-yourself enthusiast' to the skilled non-professional' and on to the 'tradesman'.

Among the market classified as 'domestic purchasers' above, 50 per cent are considered 'skilled' users, 40 per cent 'non-skilled' users and the rest 'very occasional users'. The term 'skilled' can be variously defined, but refers to the frequency of use rather than the real ability of the end user.

Market development has been achieved through the trade user to the domestic user over time. This accounts for a wide discrepancy of market shares achieved by type of tool within the defined domestic, professional and industrial markets. To complicate the total market profile further, different types of tools are supplied to each market sector, although many of the tools in the Fisher range are purchased in each sector.

Despite market research findings which have revealed variations in brand quality perception, among end users, of the different types of tools, the Fisher brand is among the leaders in terms of brand recall and brand image when the market is considered as a whole. Furthermore, for specific tools, the Fisher brand has a consistently higher image rating than other market suppliers.

Overall, the company considers itself, and is considered by the markets it serves, to have a good image. Favourable attitudes have been revealed by wholesale and retail distributors as well as tool users. The major attributes cited in recent in-depth research with distributors included 'Products in the range are distinctive'; 'Good reliable tools'; 'Good range of tools'; 'Good variety in different sizes of tools'; 'Effective support and good display materials'; 'The terms of trade are fair—although we never keep pace with demand on certain items.'

Periodic market research is a feature in which the company takes pride. A survey covering the total market for Fisher tools completed in March 2001 revealed the following key findings:

- The major factors influencing all forms of household do-it-yourself (DIY) activity were:
  a. Number of years married.
  b. Age and income of the end user.
  c. Age and type of house.
  d. Period of time residence.
- Readership was confined to the popular national daily press, and DIY magazines.
- All types of consumers recalled a variety of brand names.
- There was an insignificant difference in the 'DIY habit' among the male, 25–55, B, C1, C2, and D socio-economic groups.
- Domestic purchasers appear more brand-loyal than their trade counterparts, who tend to purchase a wide variety of brands and furthermore are more fully aware of suitable substitutes.
- A significant number of domestic purchasers will not accept a substitute for certain Fisher tools.
- Manufacturers' delivery from leading market suppliers appeared to be a general problem associated with this market.
- The need for DIY tools to be sold by specialist retailers is reducing substantially.
- Traditional tool retailers adhere to the manufacturers' recommended prices.
- All retailers offer a cash discount to tradespersons.
- Growth in tool discounting for domestic purchasers in developing at retail 'discount outlets'.
- Many cheap, foreign tools are available on the market.
- A significant number of purchasers of low priced tools are for replacement purposes.
- Quality perception is *the* prime brand purchase motivator among all types of buyers.
- Quality and durability are the key factors considered by the trade users.
- All groups considered the 'effect of advertising as minimal' in influencing the purchase decision.

Within Fisher plc, strategic marketing decisions have depended upon the internal management information system—a fully computerized system totally integrated throughout production, sales and distribution operations.

The board takes pride in the system, which is considered by key users at middle management and executive levels to provide regular up-to-date information at the required level to assist decision-making.

The recently conducted market research now forms part of the marketing information system.

Detailed analysis has revealed the need to review and adjust the marketing plan in the following areas:

1. Pricing

2. Distribution, stock control and ordering procedures

3. New product development

4. Marketing communications

Initial internal discussions have taken place; the preliminary debates have considered:

● The market control that can be secured through a differential pricing policy throughout the various distribution channels and between channel members.

● A revision of minimum order levels to increase order size and thereby reduce the frequency of deliveries.

● More effective product screening and wider use of test marketing prior to the national launch of new products.

● The choice between a generic campaign to promote the Fisher brand across all market segments and product-oriented advertising.

● More effective control of current international business operations and the alternatives for the future.

Each area is considered to be a priority for future marketing operations.

Fisher's London-based advertising agency, Bowland Furness and Lonsdale (BFL), strongly favours a campaign to build the Fisher brand *per se*. Bill Bowland, the accounts director has a clear vision for the next 12-month period. At a recent internal agency meeting, Bill proclaimed:

> We've got to get right through to the end-user—this means promoting Fisher with a big push. The Fisher brand has a good image; we have to build this further to enhance credibility and awareness among non-users to create more sales and yet retain the brand-loyal customers.
>
> The Fisher account is a key plc account; we cannot risk their dissatisfaction—my hunch is that they may ask other agencies to pitch for this campaign if we cannot convince them that the brand image is more important than the product.

Lisa Furness, BFL creative head, claimed:

> The Fisher brand represents a set of consumer-type products, their hand tools are not in any way industrial. Therefore, we are selling to people with competing demands for their cash. We must persuade them that Fisher is best. Above all, the dimensions of the Fisher brand must represent not only quality, durability and good value for money, but also the 'human' dimensions.

Within the London advertising agency circuit Lisa's work was often considered distinctive and above all memorable. BFL accounts were mainly consumer; awards for creativity and poster design are among the accolades achieved. The current range of key accounts covers men's cosmetics, two government accounts, a confectionery manufacturer, a brand of toothpaste, hi-fi equipment, carpets and home computers.

Lisa continued:

> Fisher have a complex understanding, or misunderstanding, of their market. I believe that market segmentation has a place in their marketing strategy, but the bottom line is that tools are tools and people buy brands. The concentration for the campaign must be on media advertising; the integration required is around the Fisher brand so we should capitalize on this—use just one

theme throughout the campaign and create maximum impact. We need a concept now to embody the Fisher brand; the copylines will follow. I will arrange for a brainstorming session—above all, we must be bold, distinctive and simple. We must ensure that Fisher favours Furness—well, BFL—hey?

Within the Fisher marketing department at the quarterly review, sales were down on forecast and some concern was raised about current advertising effectiveness.

Ken Slater, as marketing manager, had recently quarrelled with Lisa Furness over some non-business matters and this may have coloured his comments to the marketing team:

I wonder if BFL really understand our market; we have been with them for three years now and we have only just remained on target. I think that the salesforce need more help to promote our range of products. We must put the product first and our trade relationship cannot be overlooked. Less advertising, more sales promotion and beef up the public relations activities may be the formula for the future. We must be ever mindful of the contribution of market research—we have defined clearly our market segments—each requires special and separate marketing communications activity.

Ken Slater, as a member of the Chartered Institute of Marketing, had attended an open-day event at Moor Hall in April and met a number of advertising personnel. Two individuals left favourable impressions; Lynne Barker and Colin Webb from the Barker Webb agency based in central London. Lynne and Colin had left a large international agency some 18 months previously to form a new outfit with three other young advertising staff from other London-based agencies. With luck, good judgement and the dedication to hard work, the new agency was billing £5.5 million. Good contacts throughout the advertising industry enabled Barker Webb (BW) to offer a full range of services from creative design, market research, sales promotion, display materials, exhibition work, direct mailing apart from the regular business of campaign planning and execution.

Ken Slater, without reference to BFL, had briefed BW. The accounts held by BW covered a broad spectrum of products and services, although its collective experience was wider still. Naturally BW was keen to pitch for the new account. Prior to setting up BW, Colin Webb, in his previous employment, was accounts director for one of Fisher's main competitors.

APPENDICES

Appendix CS1.1 Company Organization Chart and Personnel Profiles

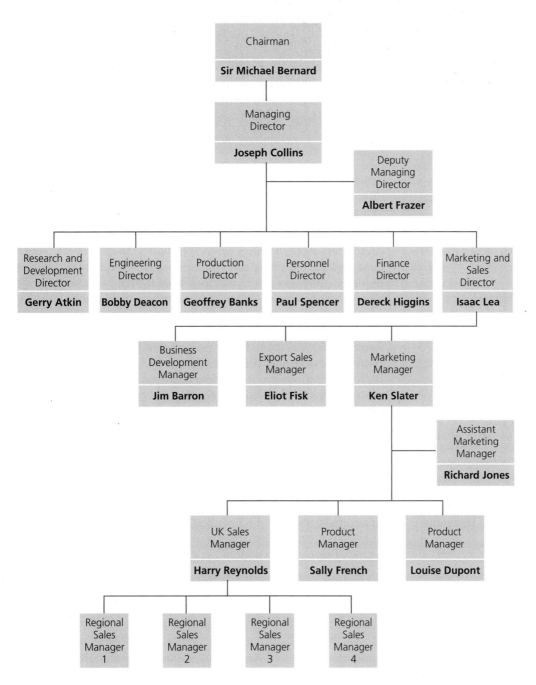

FIGURE APPENDIX CS1.1   *Company organization chart*

Notes to Fisher plc organization chart

Sir Michael Bernard	Appointed 1995. Chairman of three other large manufacturing companies. Serves on a number of government committees. Former Member of Parliament. Aged 70.
Joseph Collins	Appointed 1996. A former finance director. Aged 58, plans to retire at 60 to home in Spain. No other business interests.
Albert Frazer	Appointed 1999 by merchant bankers for a four-year period. Chartered accountant, former business consultant. Aged 46.
Gerry Atkin	Appointed 1981. Former research and development manager. Aged 45. Joined company as a school-leaver. All family links with Wales.
Bobby Deacon	Appointed 1999 on the retirement of former engineering director. American national. Process engineer by training. Previously engineering manager of Kansas Extruder Corporation. Wife born in Wales. Aged 43.
Geoffrey Banks	Appointed 1995. Former group product manager of six years' experience. Five years' sales experience in household furnishing industry. Business graduate from Manchester Business School. Diploma holder from Chartered Institute of Marketing. Aged 38.
Richard Jones	See candidates' brief.
Sally French	Appointed 1999 from Fisher salesforce. Aged 26, single. Currently studying part-time for Chartered Institute of Marketing Diploma. Ambitious to achieve a marketing management position by 30. Recently rejected a job offer by BFL. Handles new products.
Louise Dupont	Appointed 1998. MBA from Manchester Business School. Aged 27, single. Previous experience in market research. French national. Higher education in UK. Father owns an established French tools and tooling equipment company employing 120 people, based in Paris.
Harry Reynolds	Appointed 1983. Aged 55, with 20 years' experience with Fisher in sales positions. Controls 16 representatives across four sales regions through four regional sales managers.
Paul Spencer	Appointed 1993 from Welsh Steel Works. Aged 37, single.
Dereck Higgins	Appointed 1991. Former chief cost accountant, now finance director and company secretary (designate). Works closely with the managing director. Aged 41.
Isaac Lea	Appointed 1991 by Joseph Collins from a major competitor with a brief to achieve marketing integration at board and subordinate levels. Task has yet to be completely achieved—further organizational development is planned. Aged 45.

Jim Barron		Appointed 1983. Previous Fisher UK sales manager. Aged 61. Responsible for international business development. Key role in maintaining links with European and American licensing agreements. Tasks quite separate from Eliot Fisk.
Eliot Fisk		Appointed 1993 from Kansas Extruder Corporation. Aged 39. Role confined to direct export sales from the UK to worldwide customers. May absorb Jim Barron's job in three years' time as export director.
Ken Slater		Appointed 1993 from fast-moving consumer food products manufacturer.

Appendix CS1.2   Report on the UK Market for Hand Tools

To: Ken Slater—Marketing Manager
From: Louise Dupont
Date: 10 May 2001

1. Secondary data
The market for hand tools is poorly documented. The problem, typical of most published statistics, is that figures never conform and estimates vary considerably. Therefore, the figures in this report are to be considered as a guide only because they are very approximate indications. One major reason for this statement is the complex distribution system and the various sources of supply to the end purchaser/user.

2. Market trends
Overall there is a marked decline in the market for traditional hand tools. In volume terms this has amounted to some 35 per cent over the past three years—as a conservative estimate.

Approximately 75 per cent of the UK market is supplied by imported products, which normally are much cheaper at retail selling prices than the British manufactured product.

3. Industry sales (£ million)

	1996	1997	1998	1999	2000
UK manufacturers' sales at ex-factory prices	132	135	112	104	95[E]
Exports	82	81	87	89	n/a
UK manufacturers' sales to home market	49	54	25	22	n/a
Imports	63	82	82	83	n/a
Total UK sales	112	136	107	105	n/a

E = Estimate
Source: Government statistics

Market sizes of selected hand tools 1999	Sales at manufacturer's ex-factory prices
Spanners,* socket sets* and wrenches*	35
Saws and blades	11
Pliers,* pincers* and rippers*	10
Measuring and marking tools	10
Screwdrivers	9
Files and rasps	6
Hammers	4
Wood chisels	2
Planes	2
Carpenters' bits and braces	1
Other hand tools	15

*Products not produced by Fisher
Source: Government statistics

4. Market behaviour

There is a distinct tendency towards the purchase of cheaper tools. The DIY sector appears, during times of recession and high unemployment, to be more price-sensitive and less quality-conscious. The concern appears to be for 'everyday tools', and not 'life-time tools'. It is estimated that the DIY sector accounts for 35 per cent of the market by value at manufacturer's ex-factory prices (i.e. manufacturer's selling prices).

5. Changing pattern of distribution

Large supermarkets, superstores and DIY discount retailers are still increasing in importance.

Specialist tool shops are a very important sector of the retail trade, where the consumer can obtain advice, but they are losing sales to the DIY supermarkets. Manufacturers who had ventured into the retail trade through vertical integration are now reversing this trend.

Builders' merchants, a traditional channel, retain their position, although the majority of sales are to professional users.

The decline in the volume trade to the UK market has led to considerable de-stocking at the retail end, and although this process has now ceased to a great extent, considerable selling effort is required to bring sales back to former levels. As a result, most manufacturers are working at far below production capacity. Increased import penetration means that UK manufacturers must fight harder for domestic market sales.

6. Marketing implications

The implications for Fisher are wide-reaching. A revised marketing plan must be drawn up to select the best strategy for the next three-year period in the hope that the market will be restored to former levels of buoyancy.

Over recent years there has been a marked tendency towards power tools to replace hand tools—further research should be conducted in this area.

Appendix CS1.3 Memorandum—Profit and Sales Performance

To: Ken Slater   Date: 1 May 2001
From: Isaac Lea

I have just received preliminary year-end figures from Dereck Higgins. Our performance for the past four years has not improved in real terms.

The increase in total sales value is between 3 and 4 per cent per year and our ratio of profit before taxation to sales hovers at approximately 2 per cent. It has been made quite clear to me that, for a company of our size and reputation, this is just not good enough—we would be better employed on the money market than in the sale of hand tools. Our shareholders are becoming restless after the recent years of apparent stagnation. We must give active consideration to a revised marketing strategy for the forthcoming year.

Our increased dependence upon overseas trade may necessitate the appointment of an international advertising agency to supplement, or replace, BFL. I would suggest an annual advertisement budget of £400 000 to cover home and export markets.

I would welcome your urgent attention to this matter.

Appendix CS1.4   Sales Analysis—Years Ending 1 April 1995–2000

Home and export sales—year ending 1 April

	1995 H (%)	1995 E (%)	1996 H (%)	1996 E (%)	1997 H (%)	1997 E (%)	1998 H (%)	1998 E (%)	1999 H (%)	1999 E (%)	2000 H (%)	2000 E (%)
Breakdown by product group												
Saws	81	19	55	45	50	50	48	52	45	55	45	55
Measuring tapes	90	10	83	17	82	18	80	20	76	24	75	25
Screwdrivers	78	22	70	30	62	38	61	37	60	40	57	43
Files and rasps	40	60	40	60	41	59	37	63	35	65	30	70
Hammers	41	59	43	57	39	61	34	66	32	68	31	69
Wood chisels	36	64	31	69	30	70	27	73	27	73	22	78
Planes	45	55	39	61	37	63	35	65	31	69	30	70
Carpenters' bits	45	55	38	62	36	64	34	66	31	69	26	74
Vices	40	60	41	59	40	60	36	64	32	68	33	67
Hand drills	45	55	37	63	35	65	34	66	32	68	30	70
Total Fisher products	74	26	53	47	49	51	44	56	40	60	38	62

H = Home
E = Export

Overseas markets for Fisher hand tools*—year ending 1 April

	1992	1995	1997	2000
Western Europe	2	5	8	10
Eastern Europe	2	4	5	7
Asia	3	4	5	7
Middle East	14	15	16	18
Africa	3	12	14	15
South America	2	2	3	1
USA		5	5	4
Total % sales	26	47	56	62

*All export sales are through Fisher appointed agents in the respective markets

Direct home sales analysis—year ending 1 April

	1995 (%)	1996 (%)	1997 (%)	1998 (%)	1999 (%)	2000 (%)
Wholesale	42	23	21	19	17	16
Retail	20	18	17	15	14	13
Mail order	6	6	5	5	4	4
Institutional/industrial	6	6	6	5	5	5
Total % of Fisher sales revenue	74	53	49	44	40	38

Retail sales by type of outlet

	1995 (%)	1996 (%)	1997 (%)	1998 (%)	1999 (%)	2000 (%)
Builders' merchants	1	1	1	1	1	1
Discount stores	1	1	1	2	3	3
Supermarkets	2	2	2	2	2	1
Department/chain stores	2	2	2	2	1	1
Specialist tool shops	4	4	4	3	2	2
Ironmonger/hardware stores	6	4	3	2	2	2
DIY shops	4	4	4	3	3	3
Total sales %	20	18	17	15	14	13

Appendix CS1.5   Selected Abstracts from Market Research Report, April 1998

Hand tool market—competitor profile*
Conducted by Jackson Market Research
Project Leader: Richard Jones
Date of Report: April 2001
Research Commissioned: November 2000

1. Sample composition:

Tradesmen	200
Domestic users	500
Institutional/industrial buyers	15
Mail order	10
Wholesalers	10
Retailers	50

2. Sampling frames:
   Selected without regional bias to provide national representation.

3. Sampling methods and data collection method:

   - *Tradesmen*   Quota sampling—quota controls age and type of trade/profession: personal interviews, on and off the job.
   - *Domestic users*   Random sampling—street interviews: post-survey stratification into levels of skill by usage rate.
   - *Mail order companies*   100 per cent of all registered: telephone interviews—for initial screenings followed by personal interviews at company premises.
   - *Institutional* industrial buyers   A 25 per cent sample of Fisher key accounts: personal interviews.
   - *Wholesalers and retailers*   A 10 per cent sample of Fisher accounts stratified by size of account to provide a representative sample nationally: personal interviews.

Structured interviews were used throughout the survey using recorded questionnaires.

*Abstract from full report

Competitor analysis—year ending April 2001

Company code	UK (%)	Export (%)	UK hand tool market share (%)	Import (%)	UK manufacturer	Hand tool product range code	UK media advertising expenditure (£000)	Size of sales force	Year of market entry
A	65	35	3	nil	✓	Sp, Pl, F, H, C, Wr	10	5	1945
B	42	58	8	10	✓	Sa, H, Wo, Me, C, Y, Spi, O	80	10	1958
C	90	10	2	nil	✓	Sa, Me	5	4	1947
D	45	55	4	nil	✓	Me, H, W, C	—	6	1931
E	20	80	4	5	✓	Wo, V, C, F, Wr, Sc, Pla	10	5	1953
F	38	62	3	5	✓	Sa, Me, Sc, F, H, Wo, Pla, C, O	120	16	1926
G	100	—	20	100	no	Sp, Sa, Pl, Me, Spi, F, H, Wo, Pl, O, Ps	100	12	1979
H	100	—	15	100	no	Sp, Pl, F, H, Wo, O	120	8	1987
I	100	—	29	100	no	Sp, Sa, Pl, V, Me, Spi, F, H, Wo, Pl, O	250	n/a	1973 onwards

NB: Assume UK hand tool market = £100 million at manufacturer's selling prices

Company codes: F = Fisher plc

Other codes = Other importers
= Independent organizations

Product range codes
Sp Spanners
Wr Wrenches
Pl Pliers, pincers, rippers
F Files and rasps
H Hammers
C Carpenters' bits and braces
Sa Saws and blades
Wo Wood chisels
Me Measuring tools
Spi Spirit levels
V Vices
Sc Screwdrivers
Pla Planes
O Others

Competitor rating by tradesmen—Rating scale −5 to +5

	Company codes								
	A	B	C	D	E	F	G	H	I
Value for money	+3	+2	+3	+2	+2	+3	+1	+2	+2
Durability	+4	+2	+5	+2	+5	+3	−2	−1	−2
Appearance	+3	+2	+4	+2	−1	+3	+1	+1	−1
Design	+3	+2	+4	+2	+1	+3	−1	−1	−1
Reliability	+4	+3	+5	+3	+5	+3	−3	−2	−2
Range of products	+3	+3	−4	+2	+2	+4	+4	+4	+5
Advertising	−4	−2	−4	−4	−4	+1	+3	+3	+2
Quality	+4	+3	+5	+3	+4	+3	−1	−1	−1
Guarantees	+3	+1	+4	+2	+3	+3	−1	−1	−1
Packaging	−2	+1	+1	+1	+1	+2	+2	+2	+1
Availability	+1	+4	+1	+4	+3	+4	+3	+3	+5

Competitor rating by institutional/industrial buyers—Rating scale −5 to +5

	Company codes								
	A	B	C	D	E	F	G	H	I
Value for money	+4	+2	+2	+2	+2	+4	−1	−1	−1
Durability	+5	+2	+5	+3	+5	+3	−3	−2	−3
Appearance	+3	+3	+3	+1	−1	+4	−1	−1	−1
Design	+3	+3	+4	+2	+1	+3	+1	+1	+1
Reliability	+5	+3	+4	+4	+5	+3	−2	−2	−2
Range of products	+3	+4	−4	+2	+2	+4	+3	+2	+4
Advertising	−4	+1	−3	−4	−4	+2	+2	+2	+1
Quality	+5	+3	+5	+4	+4	+3	−1	−1	−1
Guarantees	+4	+3	+3	+2	+2	+3	−1	−1	−1
Packaging	−1	+3	+1	−1	−1	+4	+2	+2	+1
Availability	+2	+1	−1	+3	+3	+4	+4	+3	+5

Competitor rating by domestic purchasers—Rating scale −5 to +5

	Company codes								
	A[†]	B	C[‡]	D	E[§]	F	G	H	I
Value for money	+3	+3	+1	+2	+1	+4	+4	+3	+3
Durability	+4	+4	+5	+2	+5	+3	+3	+3	+2
Appearance	+2	+3	+2	+2	−1	+4	+2	+3	+1
Design	+2	+3	+4	+2	−1	+3	+2	+3	+2
Reliability	+4	+4	+5	+2	+5	+4	+3	+3	+2
Range of products	+1	+2	−4	+3	+1	+4	+4	+3	+5
Advertising	−5	+1	−5	−5	−5	+2	+2	+3	+1
Quality	+4	+3	+5	+3	+3	+3	+2	+3	+2
Guarantees	+3	+2	+4	+3	+2	+3	+1	+1	−2
Packaging	−2	+1	+1	+1	+1	+4	+1	+2	−1
Availability	−4	+4	−3	+4	−2	+4	+4	+3	+5

*Small sample response (less than 15%)
[†]Limited brand recognition (35% response)

Competitor rating by wholesale, retail and mail-order channels*—Rating scale −5 to +5

	Company codes								
	A*	B	C*	D	E[†]	F	G	H	I
Value for money	+2	+3	+2	+2	−1	+3	+3	+3	+2
Reliability	+4	+3	+5	+4	+5	+3	−2	+1	+1
Design	+2	+3	+4	+3	−1	+4	+1	+1	+1
Range	+2	+3	−5	+2	+2	+4	+4	+3	+5
Advertising	−5	+2	−5	−5	−4	+2	+2	+2	+1
Guarantees	+2	+2	+2	+2	+3	+3	−2	+1	+1
After-sales service	+2	+2	+1	+2	+3	+3	−2	+1	+2
Customer satisfaction	+4	+3	+5	+3	+2	+3	−1	+1	+1
Trade discount	−1	+1	−2	−3	−3	+1	+4	+4	+5
Delivery service	−1	+1	−3	−1	+1	−1	+3	+4	+5
Packaging	−2	+2	+1	+1	−2	+3	+2	+2	+2
Profit potential	−1	+1	−1	−1	+1	+2	+5	+5	+5

*Results of surveys were very close, hence the mean scores have been applied in this table
[†]Small sample response
[‡]Restricted distribution
[§]Not mail order

APPENDIX CS1.6   Memorandum—BFL Advertising Agency

To: Ken Slater
From: Richard Jones
Date: 10 May 2001

I realize that I am a very new member of the marketing team, but feel that I have a small contribution to make on the above subject, I hope, therefore, that you will treat this memo in the spirit in which it is written. I am not trying to 'teach my grandmother to suck eggs'.

Naturally you are concerned with BFL's performance, and an immediate reaction may be to request another agency to provide a presentation—I would suggest two other agencies. This would keep BFL 'on its toes'. The agency I worked for, Bard, Klein and Mason, would be worth considering; there may have been changes since I left but the man to contact is Colin Webb, my former boss. I can also recommend one of my former market research clients, an advertising agency based here in Swansea, Fortnam and Golde.

Before any decision is taken, it is fair to consider what BFL has achieved; I have a checklist for agency evaluation which you may find helpful.

Should you wish to proceed with other agencies, we should offer BFL the chance to retain the account and notify the company of our intentions. We must not overlook BFL's 10 years' experience as an agency and the billing size of £40 million.

APPENDIX CS1.7   Memorandum—New Product Development

To: Richard Jones
From: Ken Slater
Date: 15 May 2001

I have been aware for some time of the need to diversify beyond hand tools and yet remain within the DIY market.

An opportunity has arisen for Fisher to act as distributors for a Swedish company manufacturing point applicators. The product range comprises paint brushes, paint rollers and a more recent innovation, paint pads. The latter I have no interest in whatsoever.

How do you suggest we proceed?

This is your assignment with the company; please advise me of your progress. I would hope to receive your report by the middle of June.

On the subject of your memo of 10 May, I thank you for your comments and would ask you to supply the checklist you mentioned with your report.

APPENDIX CS1.8   Memorandum—Profitability

To: Dereck Higgins
From: Ken Slater
Date: 16 May 2001

I refer to our conversation of some two weeks ago concerning our profit to sales position.

I have now had time to reflect upon the situation; appropriate attention is being given to the matter but this is under Mr Lea's direct authority. However, at present our information system does not carry financial trend information over the past five years; would you, therefore, provide an outline analysis of the cost impact areas which have a direct influence upon our net profit before tax position? Kindly send a copy also to Mr Lea for information.

My new assistant manager is keen to develop his interest in the financial control area. I am encouraging this and have asked him to talk with you directly.

I understand that Mr Lea approves fully of staff development initiatives.

APPENDIX CS1.9   *Memorandum—Profit to Sales Position*

To: Ken Slater
          c.c. Isaac Lea
From: Dereck Higgins
Date: 17 May 2001

I understand that during Isaac Lea's vacation to the Middle East you have to deal with the running of the department.

The issue of profitability is a number one priority at board level.

I have appended a brief outline of cost trends which contribute to profitability. In marketing you really influence all these areas—including the reduction in numbers of the workforce through poor sales performance.

However, you may feel that additional ratio analysis and financial analysis would be helpful; kindly telephone my secretary to arrange a meeting and bring along your new assistant.

Analysis of Fisher plc profit to sales—year ending 1 April (%)

	1996 M	1996 F	1997 M	1997 F	1998 M	1998 F	1999 M	1999 F	2000 M	2000 F
Pre-tax profits Sales	4.5	2.2	4.5	2.1	4.0	2.2	3.5	2.1	3.5	1.9
Production cost Cost of output	82.1	76.0	81.5	73.3	80.1	72.1	78.3	72.5	78.0	72.5
Distribution cost Cost of output	6.1	9.6	6.3	12.3	6.8	12.9	7.3	12.9	7.5	13.0
Selling cost Cost of output	2.0	4.5	2.5	5.9	3.0	6.3	3.3	6.1	3.5	6.3
Administration cost Cost of output	9.8	7.7	9.7	8.5	10.1	8.7	11.1	8.5	11.0	8.2

M = Median of UK manufacturers A, B, C, D, E
F = Fisher performance

QUESTIONS

As Richard Jones, you are forming a close working relationship with Ken Slater.

Your first report is now due for presentation and should comprise the following sections:

Section 1   Justified recommendations for proceeding with diversification into paint applicators together with a comprehensive specification of the information required at this early stage of new product development.

(20 marks)

Section 2   A checklist for advertising agency evaluation and your judgement of how best to evaluate the alternatives now open to Fisher advertising account.

(20 marks)

Section 3   What you expect from BW at its forthcoming presentation.

(20 marks)

Section 4   An assessment of the current market position of Fisher plc both at home and overseas, with justified options for development to the year 2000.

(40 marks)

A. & C. Watson Ltd (Industrial marketing)

A. & C. Watson Ltd was founded at Coventry in 1954 by two brothers, Alan, an industrial chemist, and Christopher, a mechanical engineer. The brothers were inspired by their father, who held a family tradition in managing Watson Steel Works Ltd. The 'works' has changed operations during its 100-year history from a sheet metal works to a firm specializing in the precision engineering of machine tools which today is managed by Michael Watson, the third and eldest son.

The 'Watson Brothers', as they were known locally, used customized business as their path to growth and business development, and operated successfully by making metal washers and shims* for special applications—albeit largely as a result of trade 'passed on by father'.

Today A. & C. Watson (UK) Ltd (ACW), one of some thirty gasket manufacturers in the UK, is a successful international company owned by an international conglomerate, the Neal Sanders Corporation, whose worldwide consolidated turnover far exceeds £200 million (see CS2.1).

The 1980s saw a major development to the ACW product range; further differentiation of the basic washer and shim types led to considerable product depth by type, size and specification. Fibre washers were introduced made from both asbestos and simple plastic polymers.

Gaskets were developed for a wide range of end-use industries using various materials ranging from mild steel to special metal hardenings, laminated brass and metal–asbestos combinations.

In addition to the development of woven asbestos for insulation end use and special gasketing for 'ring joints', there came the development of the Helitex gasket, which was a completely new concept in industrial sealing (see CS2.2).

This new type of gasket is based upon a series of spirally wound concentric interfacings which combine stainless steel with an asbestos packing. The new gasket withstands much higher stress tolerances and extreme variations in temperature. It also produces a watertight seal and is highly resistant to vibration, corrosion and fire. The uses in the industrial and engineering sectors have consequently appeared almost limitless and are still developing on a worldwide scale.

The late 1980s saw further product development and the first stage of international business development. Export trade to the USA had been growing steadily, and to exploit the market further a new company, A. C. Watson (US), was set up in 1982 to handle East Coast business. Some seven years later, a sister organization was formed in Chicago to supply West Coast industry. Both factories have ensured a firm foothold in the US and Canadian markets and recently have acquired a majority shareholding in the Evans Corporation, which manufactures automobile gaskets.

During the late 1980s and early 1990s two sales subsidiaries were set up by A. C. Watson (US), in Nigeria and Singapore respectively, to supply Africa and the Far East. Currently no plans exist to commence manufacture in these countries, but they will continue to be 'far-off field storage depots'.

*Thin metal packings used to make mechanical parts fit

The latest factory, which operates as an independent manufacturing subsidiary of ACW (UK), was opened in June 1995 in Holland to exploit opportunities within the Dutch petro-chemical refining industries. Over a further three-year period ACW (UK) appointed sales agents in Sweden, Venezuela and Mexico.

A new depot was built in 1985 at Aberdeen to serve the North Sea oil industry.

Diversification into a range of industrial sealants and pneumatic sealing equipment has been achieved and a new sealants salesforce was appointed in 1993 to supplement the existing UK and European sales teams.

Just nine months have passed since the establishment of a special trouble-shooting team which offers technical specialism. Apart from routine maintenance of industrial installations, they have the range of equipment and products to handle most customer requirements in the petrochemical refining industries. This team of seven highly trained engineers has been named 'Force 10'.

Expansion has been at the cost of heavy research and development, re-equipping the manufacturing plant and ensuring the highest standards of precision for Helitex with the installation of micro-computer technology for application to micro-engineering and other production operations. The research and development team, which enjoys the opportunity for speculative research, has a reputation for innovative product designs, many of which are far ahead of the rest of the industry. Extensive tests of existing products, undertaken in the laboratory testing station, are supplemented by yet further research which is in response to technical and scientific leads. Currently, plastics and new polymer compounds are being tested for stress, tolerance, vibration, etc., in the hope that new product ideas will emerge.

Production, although operating at 70 per cent capacity, has not been without setbacks. All production machinery is imported from the USA and delays in delivery times have been a constant source of frustration. The environmentalist lobby on the use of asbestos, and subsequent legislation, has caused an accelerated programme of research and development to produce substitute materials. A close watch is now kept on the market environment to keep the factory alerted to any future threats.

The company enjoys good working relationships at all levels and one worker representative from the trade union attends the monthly board meetings.

ACW enjoys a very low staff turnover, and, despite the recent redundancy of 35 production operatives and early retirement agreed with 15 others at junior administrative levels, employees have remained loyal to the company.

The culture of the ACW organization is one of a high regard for the management hierarchy. The small board of five directors has a separate suite of offices, a separate dining room and kitchen on the first floor and car parking designated by name plates. A high sense of achievement and self-sufficiency is part of the charisma created by the Watson brothers.

Middle management, defined by those with the title 'manager', have a separate dining room adjoining the works canteen. ACW managers share an open-plan office on the ground floor of the main two-storey office building.

Corporate planning is a matter of basic group policy, with the emphasis on setting objectives which match company resources to production requirements.

While lunchtime discussions are dominated invariably by internal influences and priorities, formal board meetings occur monthly with quarterly presentations made to the Neal Sanders board. Budgetary control, sales target achievement and technical considerations receive particular attention, while a positive zest for new innovation permeates every meeting.

Christopher Watson firmly believes that it is the responsibility of his sales and marketing director, Stephen Sutcliffe, merely to sell what ACW produces, an opinion that is also voiced by Mark Sutton, his research and development manager.

A memo sent to Sutcliffe on his appointment gives a clear indication of the MD's convictions (see Appendix CS2.3).

Following Stephen Sutcliffe's appointment, the seals salesforce was reorganized into three regions to increase the accountability of individual representatives. A new 'Midlands' region (Area B) was designated under Bob Pearce, a former ACW representative of some 10 years' standing. Further appointments to the salesforce were made in 2000 when two engineering graduates were taken on to replace David Clarke and Andrew Smith, who had been promoted from the seals salesforce to regional sales management of the newly created sealants salesforce (see Appendix CS2.4).

In all, eight new representatives were appointed and placed on an intensive six-month training programme organized by external sales training consultants. These eight representatives still remain at ACW and two have recently obtained the CIM Diploma by part-time evening study.

Sutcliffe has, on several occasions, consulted the mature salesmen about further training, but the force resents the 'need for re-schooling'. They consider that technical representatives or sales engineers, as they are known, do not require high-pressure selling techniques in this industry, and that the firm's success to date proves this.

All salesmen are paid on a 'salary-only' basis, with a Christmas bonus usually amounting to a further month's money paid at the discretion of Stephen Sutcliffe. This discretionary bonus is on the basis of Sutcliffe's assessment of an individual's performance throughout the year. It is a system that Sutcliffe believes in and one that he considers works best after his 30 years' experience as a technical representative. However, his sales managers do not share the same view. Frank White firmly believes in the need for a commission system, but does not wish to press too hard for this, having been with the company for only two years, and having taken over the job previously handled by Sutcliffe himself!

Advice from Terry Porter has been heeded. 'Frank, don't rock the boat if you want to get on, I say the same to my regional managers and they appear content. Neal Johnson and Max Bennett have been with me for 12 years now and the company looks after them well. Bob Pearce, who has an ambitious wife, is my only potential mutineer.'

André Pascalle, the international member of the sales management team, is a major asset to ACW. Of French and Austrian parents, he speaks French, German, English and Spanish fluently and has local working knowledge of the countries and operational areas of his sales agents, where he spends some 40 per cent of his time. He works closely with Stanley Reed on international contracts, and has four representatives in Germany who return to the UK after a six-week journey cycle. His sphere of influence throughout the company is considerable and he spends more time with the Watson brothers than with his immediate boss. He was offered the board appointment of marketing and sales director before Sutcliffe but turned it down on the basis that it would constrain his movements and stunt his job satisfaction.

Monitoring the movements of the salesforce is achieved by a mandatory 'Friday phone-in'. The German reps are expected to call in each Friday between 10 a.m. and 12 noon to the Coventry office. In the event of André Pascalle's absence, they report direct to Stephen Sutcliffe. The UK sales representatives telephone their regional managers, who, in turn, report in to Terry Porter and Frank White. Sutcliffe expects a report phoned to him at home by 10.30 each Saturday morning.

A monthly UK sales meeting is held at Head Office, and this is supplemented by an annual weekend sales conference held in a London hotel each June after the publication of the annual accounts.

Internal sales office administration and ordering are handled by the customer service department, where complaints and after-sales service enquiries are dealt with swiftly and efficiently. Alan Humphreys, a former sales manager, has spent his entire working life with the company and after an unfortunate road accident decided to stay with paperwork and an office job, rather than be out on the road. As customer service manager, he is a highly valued member of the management team.

The dispatch and onward distribution of products takes place from the main warehouse at Coventry, but the recent downturn in business during the recession in European trade has, despite computerized stock control, produced unusually high stock levels.

ACW has a conscious policy of maintaining high customer service levels and prides itself on providing good delivery times irrespective of cost. Production is often disrupted by urgent orders for Helitex specials, and this is a frequent source of conflict between Len Roberts and Alan Humphreys.

ACW vehicles and sales fleet are maintained to the highest standards and renewed regardless of mileage every two years.

All export orders are air-freighted using the services of a local freight forwarding agency to handle the documentation requirements.

One distinguishing feature at the works is a helicopter pad, itself an attraction and source of newsworthy items. It was built in 1987 to handle the booming business with the oil exploration and refining industries in the North Sea, where a broken pipeline seal or flange can cause a considerable loss in production and delivery times must be kept to a minimum.

In accordance with the board policy 'marketing' activities are kept low-key. No funds are consciously appropriated for media advertising, although trade press coverage is enjoyed from the regular editorial coverage of new applications of Helitex. The majority of the small promotions budget is allocated to sales aids, samples, sales kits and technical data sheets. Being conscious of the firm's corporate image, Christopher Watson commissioned a new 12-page, four-colour brochure and found this to be well received by both actual and potential customers who were largely unaware of the total range of products manufactured by ACW. The success of this brochure has led to further work on the development of a new company logo, new house colours and new letter headings for stationery, etc., to make sure that a new dynamic image is effectively communicated on all company instruments.

Stephen Sutcliffe has read this new move as either a 'change of heart' or as a direct remit from the Neal Sanders Corporation, and, to make sure he is fully aware of market reactions to ACW and the range of products, he has commissioned a small market research survey—of which some desk research is detailed (see Appendix CS2.5).

A lecturer at a local college, a personal friend, has also produced a short statement on the public relations image presented by ACW and its salesforce (see Appendix CS2.6).

Meanwhile, John Mills's team has also been working on a detailed analysis of sales activities and market trends (see Appendix CS2.7).

To complete the 'audit', detailed discussions have been held on pricing policy, pricing strategy and tactics—all previously the realm of Mark Taylor.

Sutcliffe believes that it is now time to take stock of his operations, and make significant changes to meet the challenge of the next five years so that he may be able to hand over the reins of a successful and well-managed operation upon his retirement. He is now giving careful consideration to the final accounts and profit contribution trends (see Appendix CS2.8).

APPENDICES

Appendix CS2.1   The Neal Sanders Corporation

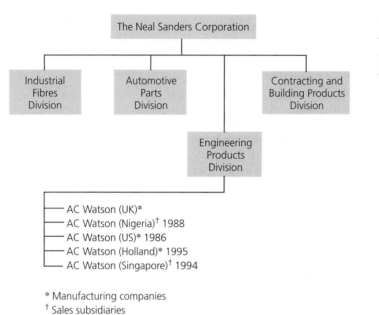

FIGURE
APPENDIX CS2.1

*The Neal Sanders
Company*

* Manufacturing companies
† Sales subsidiaries

Appendix CS2.2   Typical Washers, Shims and Helitex Gaskets

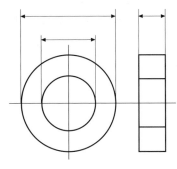

(ALL sizes in millimetres)

BRIGHT WASHERS
Cadmium plated or hardened brass.

Size range

D1	D2	T
1 to 40	2 to 77	0.2 to 6.6

BLACK WASHERS
Cold rolled steel strip-option
zinc plated.

Size range

D1	D2	T
5.5 to 75	9.2 to 120	1 to 11

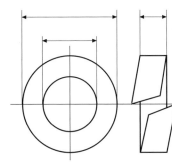

SPRING WASHERS
Carbon steel hardened, tempered
phosphated oil or lanaolin coated.

Size range

D1	D2	T
3.1 to 50	5.5 to 66.5	1 to 8

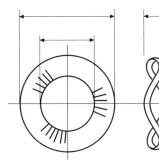

CRINKLE WASHERS

Size range

D1	D2	T
1.7 to 21.2	3.5 to 34.7	0.2 to 2.6

(continued)

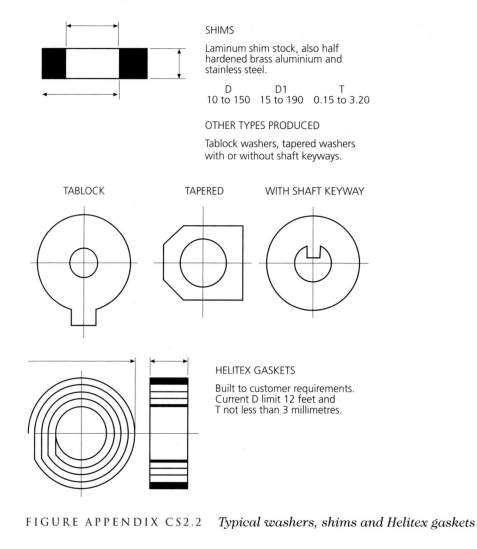

SHIMS

Laminum shim stock, also half hardened brass aluminium and stainless steel.

D	D1	T
10 to 150	15 to 190	0.15 to 3.20

OTHER TYPES PRODUCED

Tablock washers, tapered washers with or without shaft keyways.

TABLOCK   TAPERED   WITH SHAFT KEYWAY

HELITEX GASKETS

Built to customer requirements. Current D limit 12 feet and T not less than 3 millimetres.

FIGURE APPENDIX CS2.2 *Typical washers, shims and Helitex gaskets*

Appendix CS2.3   Memorandum—Appointment of Stephen Sutcliffe

To: Stephen Sutcliffe   Date: 18/9/95
From: C. Watson, Managing Director
Subject: Appointment

Welcome to the board, and to the new job of Marketing and Sales Director. It is a grand title, and 'marketing' is included to be fashionable with the international scene. Frankly, you are my *Sales* Director, I hope you will never forget it!

You have a Marketing Services Manager and a small team—do not let them interfere too much; their job is to generate more sales volume by discovering new potential for our products.

My view is that marketing is a luxury; it costs money, and you can't measure the results of the achievement—all far too woolly. Given a free hand, I would rather have another four reps on the road. Sales are all that matter; they get the orders—or at least it's your job to make sure they do. Our success to date has proven that good sales service is all that is required to run a business effectively and I don't want to be found wrong. I'm fully aware of the problems ahead, but our research and development team are second to none.

Good luck; it is good to have a man of mature years on the board.

Appendix CS2.4(a)   Production and Distribution Organization Structure

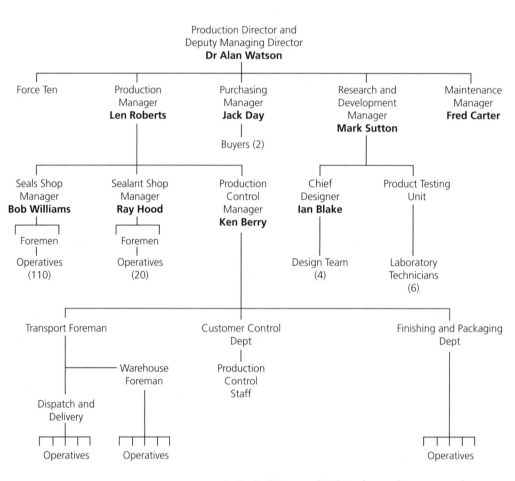

FIGURE APPENDIX CS2.4(A)   *A. & C. Watson (UK) Ltd: production and distribution organizational structure*

Appendix CS2.4(b) *Sales and Marketing Organization Structure*

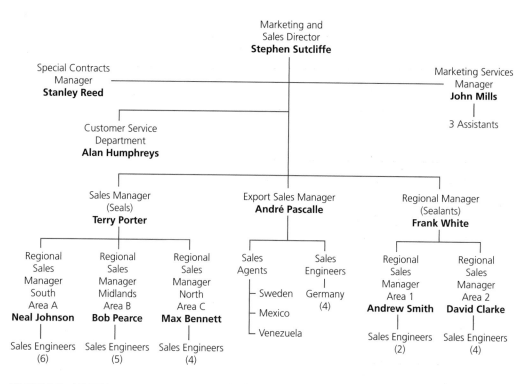

FIGURE APPENDIX CS2.4(B)   *A. & C. Watson (UK) Ltd: sales and marketing organizational structure*

Appendix CS2.4(c)   Sales Areas

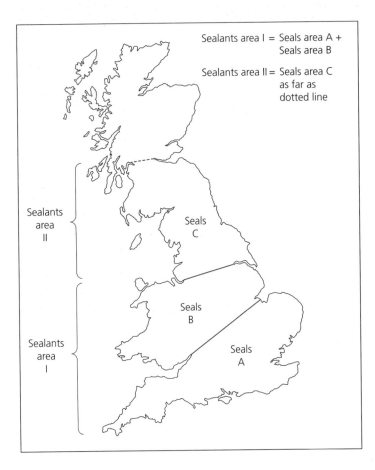

Sealants area I = Seals area A +
Seals area B

Sealants area II = Seals area C
as far as
dotted line

Sealants
area
II

Seals
C

Seals
B

Sealants
area
I

Seals
A

FIGURE
APPENDIX
CS2.4(C)

*A. & C. Watson (UK)
Ltd: sales areas*

Appendix CS2.5(a)   UK Market Trends by Value (Index 1995 = 100)

	1997	1998	1999	2000	2001	2002*
SEALS						
Washers, shims and metal packings	114	114	132	139	143	145
Helitex-type gaskets	129	142	180	201	211	223
Other gaskets for mechanical engineering end use	131	141	174	193	209	237
Fibre washers and jointings	125	146	150	129	141	172
Automotive gaskets	136	147	167	174	179	189
Laminated brass sheeting and foils	112	132	146	169	185	208
SEALANTS						
Mastics	112	123	156	167	189	203
Ring joint sealants	108	117	131	142	153	167
Compound sealant	118	132	147	167	197	213
Waterproof sealant	107	110	133	143	155	160
INDUSTRY						
Natural gas	124	167	208	239	272	301
Natural gas liquids	130	145	179	250	600	700
Crude oil production	150	352	444	903	1396	1514

*Estimate
Source: ACW Marketing Services Department

Appendix CS2.5(b)   Initial Appraisal of Market—2001

Major market segments	Major product groups						
	Washers	Other gaskets	Helitex gaskets	Compound sealants	Ring joint sealants	Fibre washers	Mastics
Oil refineries and petrochemical refining		✓	✓				
Original equipment manufacturing (pumps, compressors and valves)	✓		✓				
Building contractors						✓	✓
Heat exchange and exhaust manufacturing		✓					
The gas industry	✓			✓		✓	
The electrical industry	✓						
Oil exploration companies		✓	✓		✓		
The automotive industry (prime movers)	✓	✓	✓				
Engineering contractors	✓						✓
Specialist end use				✓		✓	
Our competitors			✓			✓	

Appendix CS2.6   Memorandum—Public Relations Perspective

Dear Stephen,

My observations are as follows:

1. On first arriving the company's name was only visible from one direction when approaching the ACW complex.
2. The reception area and visitors' waiting room do not convey a welcoming atmosphere, despite a most efficient receptionist whose telephone manner was commendable.
3. The office staff speak well of the company, are happy in their work and operate with an air of efficiency, and all appear most courteous to visitors.
4. The company has a positive sense of identity, but it is poorly conveyed. The company headed notepaper is old, inappropriate to an international image and does not represent the best possible impression.
5. Little use is made of the Neal Sanders centralized publicity facility in London.
6. The salesforce are motivated by goodwill and a positive sense of corporate identity but receive insufficient information and direction from Head Office. Particular weaknesses appeared to be no guidance for cold calling, no sales targets for product groups, an absence of profit contribution knowledge and infrequent individual assessments by their regional managers.

Yours truly,

Peter

Appendix CS2.7   Sales Analysis—Years Ending 1995–2001

Total ACW sales by product group—years ending April 1995–2001 (£000s)

Product group	1995	1996	1997	1998	1999	2000	2001
SEALS							
Washers and shims/metal packings	572	652	647	866	936	1017	850
Helitex	920	1276	1430	1882	2018	2310	2544
Other gaskets	370	415	497	642	678	688	791
Fibre washers	74	131	230	96	55	72	152
Automotive gaskets	303	474	535	651	704	624	560
Insulation materials	149	193	219	255	94	84	89
Laminated brass sheeting	99	131	153	170	209	123	103
SEALANTS							
Mastics	—	—	—	60	152	332	606
Ring joint sealants	—	—	87	167	180	198	190
Compound sealants	—	—	28	105	195	314	507
Waterproof sealants	—	—	—	11	53	93	132
Total UK sales	2487	3272	3826	4905	5274	5855	6524
Total exports	925	1241	1601	2416	3164	3759	4349
Total sales	3412	4513	5427	7321	8438	9614	10 873

Export sales by product group—years ending April 1997–2001 (percentages)

Exports to	1997				1998				1999				2000				2001			
	A	B	C	D	A	B	C	D	A	B	C	D	A	B	C	D	A	B	C	D
Germany	1.3	7.5	5.6	—	0.9	8.1	4.9	—	0.9	9.2	4.9	—	0.7	9.3	4.5	—	0.5	9.6	3.6	0.3
Sweden	—	1.9	0.8	—	—	2.3	1.3	—	—	3.7	1.5	—	0.3	4.6	2.1	—	0.4	4.8	2.2	0.2
Mexico	—	—	—	—	—	0.3	—	—	0.2	0.6	—	—	0.2	0.9	—	—	0.3	1.7	—	—
Venezuela	—	3.2	5.1	—	—	5.4	6.2	—	0.6	7.3	5.6	—	0.7	9.6	5.0	0.4	0.9	9.9	4.9	0.3
Others*	0.7	2.7	0.7	—	0.4	2.6	0.6	—	0.2	2.4	0.4	—	—	0.8	—	—	—	0.4	—	—
Total export % of ACW sales revenue	29.5%				33.0%				37.5%				39.1%				40%			
Representing (£000s)	£1601				£2416				£3164				£3759				£4349			

A: Washers and shims
B: Helitex
C: Other gaskets for mechanical engineering end use
D: Fibre washers
*Others to: Iran, Libya, United States, Nigeria, Singapore

UK salesforce analysis for year ending April 2001

Salesforce	Call rate No. per week $\bar{X}$	Call rate Coefficient of variation[†] (%)	New prospects Each journey cycle	New prospects Number converted this year	Journey cycle (days)	Value of orders achieved (£)[*]
SEALS						
Area A						
B. Anstey	12	16.7	4	6	20	331 197
A. Majors	10	30.0	5	2	20	380 667
C. Whiffin	14	7.1	3	4	20	403 991
D. Allen	9	22.2	2	1	20	350 123
S. Lawrence	8	12.5	1	2	20	420 871
M. Aldred	13	23.1	3	3	20	397 151
Area B						
E. Lees	15	13.3	7	10	25	156 600
P. Fisher	19	15.8	9	6	25	171 417
C. Smith	20	15.0	6	2	25	233 921
S. Hudson	17	17.6	4	5	25	133 089
W. Tyler	13	15.4	3	3	25	87 089
Area C						
H. Brown	9	22.2	3	2	20	589 416
D. Young	11	18.2	3	2	20	617 032
N. Watson	8	12.5	2	3	20	505 473
K. Fletcher	7	28.6	1	0	20	310 079
SEALANTS						
Area 1						
J. Hood	23	21.7	14	11	30	212 327
K. Neal	25	20.0	16	13	30	246 921
A. Summers	19	10.5	12	9	30	202 427
J. Mason	21	14.3	9	6	30	186 325
Area 2						
T. Old	17	17.6	12	5	30	265 200
L. Raven	15	20.0	10	7	30	321 793

[*]A percentage of orders are placed and the sales accredited to the appropriate territory.

[†]Coefficient of variation $= \dfrac{\text{Standard deviation}}{\text{Mean } \bar{X}} \times 100$

NB: André Pascalle could not offer comparative data

UK sales revenue analysis by region—years ending April 1996–2001 (percentages)

	Seals							Sealants				
	1996	1997	1998	1999	2000	2001		1997	1998	1999	2000	2001
Area A	n/a	40	37	37	35	35	Area 1	2	4	7	10	13
Area B	n/a	23	24	20	18	12						
Area C	n/a	34	32	32	31	31	Area 2	1	3	4	6	9
Totals	100	97	93	89	84	78	Totals	3	7	11	16	22

SEALS			%
Factors	15%	Oil refineries and petrochemical refineries	37
		Engineering contractors	6
		Automotive industry	10
End-user industries	79%	Gas industry	7
		Electrical industries	4
		Oil exploration	9
Competitors	6%	Original equipment manufacturers (pumps and valves and compressors)	6

SEALANTS			%
Factors	28%	Automotive body builders	19
		Building/construction and engineering contracting industries	16
End-user industries	59%	Marine users	7
DIY sector (do-it-yourself)	13%	Specialist end-users including original equipment manufacturers	17

A. & C. Watson (UK) Ltd: home sales breakdown by customer groups

Appendix CS2.8(a) Profit Contribution by Product Group—Years Ending April 1995–2001 (percentages)

Product group	1995 H	1995 E	1996 H	1996 E	1997 H	1997 E	1998 H	1998 E	1999 H	1999 E	2000 H	2000 E	2001 H	2001 E
SEALS														
Washers and shims	16.3	0.8	15.1	1.1	12.2	1.1	12.1	0.7	11.8	1.2	11.1	1.2	10.7	1.3
Helitex	41.1	5.3	37.1	9.4	39.2	10.6	38.0	12.9	37.6	13.0	37.9	17.1	37.8	19.4
Other gaskets	14.1	5.1	12.1	4.9	11.8	4.6	11.1	5.1	10.3	7.1	9.9	7.6	8.4	7.4
Fibre washers	0.3	—	0.6	—	1.1	—	0.2	—	0.1	—	0.2	—	0.7	0.2
Automotive gaskets	12.2	—	14.2	—	13.7	—	12.3	—	11.7	—	8.4	—	6.4	—
Insulation materials	3.2	—	3.7	—	3.7	—	3.9	—	1.8	—	1.0	—	0.7	—
Laminated brass sheeting	1.6	—	1.8	—	1.9	—	1.9	—	2.1	—	1.3	—	0.9	—
	88.8	11.2	84.6	15.4	83.5	16.3	79.5	18.7	75.4	21.3	69.8	25.9	65.6	28.3
SEALANTS														
Mastics	—	—	—	—	—	—	0.2	—	1.2	—	1.9	—	3.3	—
Ring joint sealants	—	—	—	—	0.2	—	1.0	—	0.9	—	0.9	—	0.8	—
Compound sealants	—	—	—	—	*	—	0.6	—	1.0	—	1.1	—	1.5	—
Waterproof sealants	—	—	—	—	—	—	*	—	0.2	—	0.4	—	0.5	—
	—	—	—	—	0.2	—	1.8	—	3.3	—	4.3	—	6.1	—

H: Home trade
E: Export trade
* Insignificant amount

Appendix CS2.8(b)   Profit and Loss Accounts

A. & C. Watson (UK) Ltd* profit and loss accounts, years ending April 1995–2001 (£000s)

	1995	1996	1997	1998	1999	2000	2001
Sales*	3412	4513	5427	7321	8438	9614	10873
Cost of sales	2146	2880	3526	4705	5218	6042	6904
Gross profit	1266	1633	1901	2616	3220	3572	3969
Expenses	921	1173	1315	1767	2309	2870	3230
Profit before tax	345	460	586	849	911	702	739
Tax	170	225	291	420	460	360	381
Net profit	175	235	295	429	451	342	358

*Note final accounts for ACW (UK) only (ACW sales revenue worldwide currently exceeds £25 million).

Appendix CS2.9   Summary Balance Sheets

A. & C. Watson (UK) Ltd summary balance sheets, years ending April 1995–2001

	1995	1996	1997	1998	1999	2000	2001
Fixed assets							
Freehold land and buildings (at cost)	110	250	311	427	530	530	530
Plant, equipment and vehicles (depreciated)	220	320	460	710	779	800	840
Total fixed assets	330	570	771	1137	1309	1330	1370
Current assets							
Stock and WIP	259	315	472	553	687	842	1064
Debtors	287	395	511	732	914	960	1087
Bank	72	89	121	185	472	585	635
Total current assets	618	799	1104	1470	2073	2387	2786
Current liabilities							
Creditors	300	441	597	783	912	1025	1120
Dividends	10	11	12	20	20	35	27
Taxation	170	225	291	420	460	360	381
Total current liabilities	480	677	900	1223	1392	1420	1528
Current assets less current liabilities	138	122	204	247	681	967	1258
Total net assets	468	692	975	1384	1990	2297	2628
Financed by:							
Share capital	175	175	175	175	350	350	350
General reserve—retained profit	293	517	800	1209	1640	1947	2278
	468	692	975	1384	1990	2297	2628

QUESTIONS

Stephen Sutcliffe retired on 1 May 1998 and has emigrated to live with his son and daughter-in-law in Australia.

As Duncan Morris, you have been appointed at the request of the Neal Sanders Corporation to replace Stephen Sutcliffe.

Previously you were a divisional marketing manager at the Evans Corporation, where your track record was regarded highly: much had been achieved during your five years with the company. Now you have returned home to Coventry, where you were employed in sales and sales management positions in the automotive industries.

You have been given a clear brief to review the sales and marketing operations at A. & C. Watson Ltd, where there is now a desire at board level for the company to become more marketing oriented!

You are required to prepare a report for Christopher Watson, your managing director, for subsequent discussion at a special meeting of the Neal Sanders board which you will be required to attend.

Your report should comprise the following sections:

Section 1   Home and export sales and profit forecasts by product group for the next three years, i.e. until April 2001.

(25 marks)

Section 2   A strategy for the achievement of these forecasts to include the following:

a. Internal reorganization of the sales and marketing functions.
b. Management and control of field sales operations.
c. Your marketing mix plans.

(60 marks)

Section 3   An outline budget itemizing expenditure levels for the achievement of Sections 1 and 2 over the specified period.

(15 marks)

Chapter Sixteen

UNDERTAKING MINI CASE STUDIES

LEARNING OBJECTIVES *This chapter will help you to:*

- understand how to approach and analyse mini case studies;

- distinguish between the techniques for tackling mini as opposed to extended case studies;

- develop skills in analysing and preparing answers to exam-type mini case studies

INTRODUCTION

It is tempting to think that undertaking mini case studies, especially in examinations, is much easier and less complex than undertaking extended case studies. However, the fact is that often mini case studies present more difficult problems for the student undertaking them than the more extended case studies which run to pages and pages. Certainly, mini cases require a very different approach and method.

The obvious difference, of course, between mini and extended cases is the amount of material contained in the case study. Again, it is a debatable point as to where mini cases end and extended cases start, but many mini cases contain only a few pages of text and therefore information, and often comprise only one or two sides of information. Because of this, the major difficulty associated with them for many students is a lack of information and ensuing gaps in what is known about the organization and/or the situation in the case. Often mini cases are no more than scenarios used as a framework to allow students to demonstrate their marketing knowledge.

Related to their shorter length, another issue in tackling them under examination conditions is that unlike many extended cases used for examinations, most mini cases are presented unseen to the student, i.e. the first time a candidate gets to look at the case is in the examination itself. Obviously this presents very different issues and problems for the student compared to when the case study, if not the questions, has been issued some time before the examination for candidates to work on.

The use of mini cases for examination purposes is in fact growing, particularly among the professional bodies in marketing. It is now some years, for example, since the Chartered Institute of Marketing introduced mini cases in all their examinations except for the final qualifying Analysis and Decision case which is, of course, an extended case study.

For these reasons, therefore, although you have had the opportunity to attempt mini case studies at the end of each chapter throughout this text, we felt it appropriate and useful to introduce you to a framework for tackling mini cases of the type encountered, for example, in the Chartered Institute of Marketing examination papers. Obviously, although as already mentioned mini cases create their own particular problems compared to their extended case study counterparts, the generally less complex nature of mini cases means that we do not need, and indeed it is not appropriate, to have an extended analysis and decision model for tackling them. The framework and advice for tackling them which follows, therefore, need not be as complex as for the extended type case study.

In line with the advice given at the start of the text regarding the 'route map' for working through the material it contains, many of you may in fact be reading this chapter as a prelude to tackling the mini case studies which appear at the end of each chapter. One of the reasons for including a mini case at the end of each chapter is in fact to give you plenty of practice in tackling them. This is also why, unlike the previous chapter on extended case studies, we have not felt it necessary to include further mini cases in this one. If you have only read through Chapter 1, then, you should now work through this chapter before tackling the first mini case study at the end of Chapter 1. From time to time after this you may wish to return to this chapter to remind yourself of this framework as you work through the rest of the mini cases contained in the text.

A FRAMEWORK FOR UNDERTAKING MINI CASES

We have already mentioned that one of the key differences between the mini cases and the extended case study in examination settings is the fact that the mini case is usually presented unseen to candidates. Associated with this is the certainty that you will, of course, only receive the questions in the examination. The final key difference regarding most mini cases, and certainly, for example, those used in the Chartered Institute of Marketing examinations is that you only have a relatively short time, usually approximately one and a half hours, to tackle the case study and questions.

With these differences in mind a simple framework for undertaking mini cases under examination conditions is shown in Fig. 16.1. Each of the stages within the framework is outlined and discussed below.

Stage 1   Familiarization of case and questions

Although it sounds obvious, not enough students in fact spend enough time familiarizing themselves with the case and question scenario. Because time is felt to be pressing, there is a strong temptation to start writing answers or suggesting detailed solutions to various problems which the candidate has spotted in the case. It is vital, however, to spend at least fifteen minutes reading through the case and questions three or four times to get the feel of what the situation and the company is 'about', and in particular to ensure that you understand the context of the questions and what the examiner is looking for. At this stage, only rough notes should be made about the possible shape of an answer and its content.

Stage 2   Analysis of questions/instructions

Having familiarized yourself with the case you can now turn your attention to the specific questions/instructions which will accompany the mini case. It is most important that you follow these to the letter. It may appear strange to have to stress this obvious point, but in fact examiners regularly report that failure to read and certainly answer the question is always a major point of criticism of candidates by the examiners. So, for example, if the question asks you to advise on a promotional plan do not subsequently advise on a plan for the marketing mix, however much you may feel that the examiner has missed the point.

At this stage you should also note any instructions as to the role you are to assume. For example: Are you to be a member of the organization? If so, in what capacity? Alternatively, for example, you might be asked to assume the role of outside adviser/consultant to the company in the case.

Whatever the role, you should be careful to assume the appropriate stance.

Finally, in analysing the questions/instructions you should carefully note the mark allocation if there is more than one question and/or if the questions are sectionalized. The mark allocation acts as a guide as to the relative importance, and therefore the amount of time, you should devote to each part of your answer.

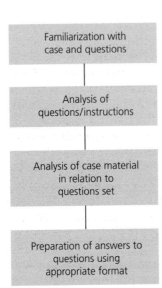

FIGURE 16.1

Tackling mini cases: a framework

Stage 3   Analysis of case material in relation to questions set

Now, and only now, are you in a position to work through the case material in detail. Bearing in mind the tasks set for you by the examiner, you should work through the case noting and writing down your general observations and any salient facts and figures.

Remember, this is your analysis in preparing for your answers, not the answers themselves. You should therefore prepare this outline in rough and cross it out afterwards.

Again, because of the difference in length and therefore the amount of material between mini cases and extended case studies it is unlikely that you will be required, or able, to prepare a detailed SWOT analysis or a full marketing audit. However, so far as it is possible there is nothing wrong with using these and, of course, you must always include them if the examiner asks you to. Overall, your observations of facts and issues should be concise and tailored to the questions themselves.

Stage 4   Preparation of specific answers to questions set

In this final stage of undertaking mini cases under examination conditions you should now be in a position to turn your attention to producing specific answers to the questions set. Clearly, the content of your answers will need to reflect the particular questions on each case, but remember that the mini cases are designed to test your application skills. You will therefore need to select from your acquired knowledge those techniques, concepts and skills which are appropriate to the questions asked. In preparing your answers you should bear these points in mind:

Avoid 'waffle' and extended general introductions   Remember, you have little time to answer the questions set. More importantly, there are no marks for general situation analyses or for observations not directly related to the questions. In particular, do not waste valuable time by writing down the questions again.

Note carefully any constraints and time-scales   One of the most frequent criticisms aimed at mini case answers by the examiners is that the candidate has come up with impractical suggestions. Often, the mini cases deal with the marketing problems of smaller or inexperienced companies. A company with an annual turnover of, say, £½ million is unlikely to be able to afford, for example, a national television advertising campaign or an extensive and expensive programme of international marketing research. The recognition of the limiting effects of such resource constraints—financial, human and organizational—and a reflection of these in a candidate's answers is in fact a test of the candidate's ability to practise marketing. Sometimes the mini case itself or the questions will contain specific information on resources and budgets available, e.g. for promotion. Do not exceed them and wherever possible demonstrate your professional knowledge of current costs and practice. In this context note, too, any indications of time-scales in a mini case. For example, if the case indicates or specifies a plan of action to cover the next twelve months, make sure that your plan covers precisely this period, not the next three months or the next five years. Where a series of actions is required over the requisite period, your answer should demonstrate clearly the timing and sequence of these actions over the specified time-period.

Clearly state any assumptions you have made   Often in case studies you will need to make assumptions. Assumptions play a particularly important role in mini cases due to the fact that you will always lack information for analyses and on which to base your marketing recommendations. So, for example, you may be asked to make recommendations about pricing strategy when the case contains little or no information about important aspects affecting the pricing decision such as detailed cost information, competitor prices and so on. In this situation you will nearly always have to make assumptions. The examiners will be happy to accept any assumption so long as it is reasonable in the context of the case. You should clearly specify any assumptions you have made in arriving at your proposals for courses of action. In fact, so long as your assumptions meet the 'reasonable' criterion, you can use your assumptions to your advantage.

Used wisely and creatively, assumptions can help you to clear away any considerations which, though important, are peripheral to the particular aspects on which the questions centre. They can also be used to support the line of argument in your answers.

Suggest specific courses of action   The need to suggest specific courses of action is in fact common to most types of management and marketing case. Again, taking care to note the examiner's instructions and the specific questions, generally answers should indicate solutions to problems through clearly specified courses of action rather than simply the identification of the problems themselves. In most questions, the action required should be explicit in the questions themselves. Often, alternative courses of action may be open to the company in the case: indeed, you may be asked to identify these. However, wherever possible and appropriate, you should be careful not to use a mere listing of alternatives as a means of avoiding a commitment to a particular alternative. At the very least you should prioritize your alternatives and give supporting reasons for your choice.

Do not over-complicate your answers   Essentially most mini cases are not over-complicated. They are generally testing a candidate's ability to apply key marketing concepts and techniques. Keep your answers brief, to the point and in the format, e.g. memo, report etc., specified.

To summarize, then, here are the key points to remember when preparing answers to mini cases.

- Avoid waffle, extended general introductions, and simply repeating the case material.
- Note constraints and time scales.
- State assumptions.
- Propose relevant action.
- Do not over-complicate.
- Answer the actual questions set.

Finally, remember that, as in most things in life, practice makes perfect. Hopefully the application of the steps and considerations above to the mini cases contained in this text will go some way towards providing this.

APPENDICES

Appendix One

FURTHER STRATEGIC MARKETING PLANNING TOOLS

In Chapter 12 some of the more frequently used strategic marketing planning tools are introduced. However, as pointed out in that chapter, these represent just a few of the strategic marketing planning frameworks available to the contemporary marketer. In this Appendix are outlined some of the newer, and in some ways more complex, strategic marketing planning tools beginning with the so-called 'industry maturity/ market evolution models'.

Further references to each of the models described are provided at the end of the Appendix.

INDUSTRY MATURITY/MARKET EVOLUTION MODELS

A number of strategic marketing planning tools have been developed which are based on the notion that different strategies are required at different stages of the evolution of an industry. Two of the best known examples of these types of strategic planning tools are Porter's model of *Industry/Market Evolution* and Arthur D. Little's *Industry Maturity/Competitive Position Matrix*.

Porter's Model of Industry/Market Evolution

Michael Porter's model[1] is based on the following three main stages in the evolution of an industry/market:

1. Emerging industry
2. Transition to maturity
3. Decline

According to Porter each of these stages has its own particular characteristics, some of the more important of which are listed for each stage.

1. Emerging industry

    a. Uncertainty among buyers over:

        ● Product performance
        ● Potential applications
        ● Likelihood of obsolescence

    b. Uncertainty among sellers over:

        ● Customer needs
        ● Demand levels
        ● Technological developments

2. Transition to maturity

    a. Falling industry profits
    b. Slow-down in growth
    c. Customers knowledgeable about products and competitive offerings
    d. Less product innovation
    e. Competition in non-product aspects

3. Decline

    a. Competition from substitutes
    b. Changing customer needs
    c. Demographic and other macro-environmental forces and factors affecting markets

Porter then uses the characteristics of each stage to suggest the following strategies as being appropriate to each:

1. *Emerging industry* strategies developed to take account of industry competitive structure characteristics, i.e.:

    ● Threat of entry
    ● Rivalry among competitors
    ● Pressure of substitutes
    ● Bargaining power of buyers and suppliers

2. *Transition to maturity*   Strategies focused on:

    ● Developing new market segments
    ● Focusing strategies for specific segments
    ● Developing a more efficient organization

Stage of industry development

Strategic position of organization		Growth	Maturity	Decline
	Leader	– Keep ahead of the field	– Cost leadership – Raise barriers – Deter competitors	– Redefine scope – Direct peripherals – Encourage departures
	Follower	– Imitation at lower cost – Joint ventures	– Differentiation – Focus	– Differentiation – New opportunities

FIGURE A1.1

Industry life cycle and strategic positioning

Source: M. E. Porter, *Competitive Advantage: Creating and Sustaining Superior Performance,* Free Press, NY, p. 192

3. *Decline*
   - Seek pockets of enduring demand
   - Divest

Clearly, this approach is similar to the conventional concept of product life-cycle analysis in identifying the stage, specifying the characteristics of each stage, and suggesting appropriate strategies for each stage. Porter has developed the notion of industry life cycle further by linking it to the 'strategic position' of the individual organization. Strategic position is categorized in terms of whether the individual organization is a leader or a follower. This approach is shown in Fig. A1.1.

Arthur D. Little's industry maturity/competitive position matrix

A similar approach to that developed by Porter is the one used by the business consultants Arthur D. Little.[2] A summary of this approach is shown in Fig. A1.2. As can be seen, the matrix comprises the 'stage of industry maturity' on the horizontal axis and 'competitive position' on the vertical axis.

The stages of industrial maturity are broken down into four categories:

1. Embryonic
2. Growth
3. Maturity
4. Ageing

Which of these four the industry is in is determined by assessing eight key descriptors:

- Rate of market growth
- Industry potential
- Product line
- Number of competitors
- Market share stability
- Purchasing patterns
- Ease of entry
- Technology

Company's competitive position	Stage of industry maturity			
	Embryonic	Growth	Maturity	Ageing
Dominant				
Strong				
Favourable				
Tentative				
Weak				

FIGURE A1.2

The A. D. Little competitive position/industry maturity index

A 'mature' industry, for instance, is characterized by slow or negligible rates of growth; little or no further growth potential; few changes in breadth of product lines; stable or declining numbers of competitors; stable market share positions; established buying patterns; high barriers to entry; and process and materials innovation in technology.

Criticisms and limitations   The major criticisms of this type of model are the lack of empirical evidence to support the underpinning notions, and its simplistic approach to strategy selection. Certainly there is little doubt that industries do pass through different stages and that individual companies in these industries do have different competitive positions. However, these models tend to suggest that analysing just these two factors enables the 'right' strategies to be identified and selected. Needless to say, strategic decisions are much more complex than this implies.

Shell's directional policy matrix   A similar approach to the GE business screen is the Shell directional policy matrix.[3] This approach also has two dimensions—company's competitive capabilities (vertical axis) and prospects for sector profitability (horizontal axis), as shown in Fig. A1.3. The firm's products are plotted into one of the nine cells in the figure and subsequently there is a suggested strategy for each of these cells.

There now follows a brief description of how to complete the matrix and what each of the horizontal and vertical axes in the model means.

The horizontal axis: sector profitability   This includes the criteria of market growth rate, market quality, industry situation and environmental considerations. On each of these factors, a product is given from one to five stars. For instance, the factor of 'market quality' might be judged on the basis of several criteria such as pricing behaviour, or past stability in the profitability of that sector. The qualitative or quantitative evaluation of market quality is then converted into a rating from 0 to 4. The same procedure is followed for each of the other three factors, so that the overall score on sector profitability is the total of the ratings on all four factors.

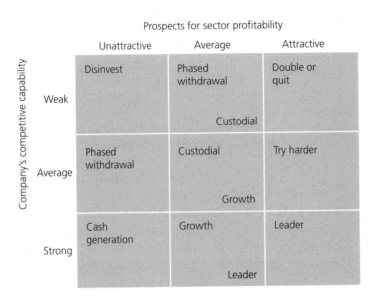

Prospects for sector profitability

FIGURE A1.3

The Shell directional policy matrix

Source: Shell Chemicals UK, *The Directional Policy Matrix, A New Aid to Corporate Planning*, November 1975

The vertical axis: competitive capabilities   The same approach is used here, except that the company's capabilities are assessed on the basis of market position, product research and development, and production capability. These are further divided into sub-factors applicable to any particular industry.

The strategy recommendations contained in the nine cells of the matrix are shown in Fig. A1.3. Shell emphasizes that, whatever strategy is eventually selected, the aim is that it should be 'resilient', i.e. viable in a diverse range of potential futures. Hence, each strategy ideally should be evaluated against all future possible scenarios; the results in all of these should be acceptable, and no potential 'disasters' should result.

Limitations   The directional policy matrix has been criticized on the grounds that, like the BCG approach, it assumes that the same set of factors is universally applicable for assessing the prospects of any product or business. Many critics believe that the relevant factors and their relative importance will vary according to both the firm's products and the individual characteristics of each company. In addition, like the GE technique, the matrix does not provide any guidelines on how to implement the strategies suggested in each cell of the matrix.

Barksdale and Harris's portfolio analysis/product life-cycle matrix

Developed by Barksdale and Harris,[4] the product life-cycle portfolio matrix is specifically designed to deal with the criticisms that the BCG matrix (a) ignores products that are new, and (b) overlooks markets with a negative growth rate, i.e. markets that are in decline. Because of this, the product life cycle portfolio matrix includes a specific focus on the growth and maturity stages of the product life cycle in developing the portfolio technique.

The key underpinning assumptions on which the Barksdale–Harris technique is based are:

1. Products have finite life spans. They enter the market, pass through a period of growth, reach a stage of maturity, subsequently move into a period of decline, and finally disappear.

2. Strategic objectives and marketing strategy should match the market growth rate changes so as to take advantage of the challenges and opportunities as the product goes through the different stages.

3. For most mass-produced products, costs of production are closely linked to experience (volume). Hence for most types of products, the unit cost goes down as volume increases.

4. Expenditures—investment in plant and equipment and marketing expenses—are directly related to rate of growth. Consequently, products in growth markets will use more resources than products in mature markets.

5. Margins and the cash generated are positively related to share of market. Products with a high relative share of their market will be more profitable than products with low shares.

6. When the maturity stage is reached, products with a high market share generate a stream of cash greater than that needed to support them in the market. This cash is available for investment in other products or in research and development to create new products.

Building on these assumptions, Barksdale and Harris also highlight the additional issues that arise out of pioneering new products, which they label *infants*, and products in declining markets, which they label as either *war-horses* (high-share products in declining markets) or *dodos* (low-share products in declining markets). The result is a combined PLC/product portfolio model as shown in Fig. A1.4.

This approach is based on the notions that both the initial and the decline stages of the life cycle are important; more specifically, it recognizes that product innovations as well as products with negative growth rates are important and should not be ignored in strategic analysis. The result is an expanded (2 × 4) portfolio matrix, as shown in Fig. A1.5. The eight-cell matrix is composed of the usual four BCG categories plus the following new categories:

1. *'War-horses'*   When a market begins to exhibit negative growth, 'cash cows' become 'war-horses'. These products still have a high market share and hence can still be substantial cash generators. This transition might require reduced marketing expenditure, or it may take the form of selective withdrawal from market segments or the elimination of certain models.

2. *'Dodos'*   These are products that have low shares of declining markets with little opportunity for growth or cash generation. The appropriate strategy is to remove them from the portfolio, but if competitors have already removed themselves from the market it may still be profitable to remain. Timing is thus critical.

3. *'Infants'*   These are pioneering products that possess a high degree of risk. They do not immediately earn profits, and they consume substantial cash resources. The length of the innovative period can vary from a short time with consumer packaged goods to an extended period with a product that is innovative enough to require a shift in buying habits.

Criticisms and limitations   Barksdale and Harris, the developers of the matrix, claim that it is more comprehensive. Regardless of the level of analysis—corporate, business division or product/market categories—they suggest that the expanded model provides an improved system for classifying and analysing the full range of market situations. Classification of products according to this expanded model is meant to reveal the relative competitive position of products, to indicate the rate of market growth, and to enable the configuration of strategic alternatives in a general sense if not in specific terms.

The key here is that it is only 'general'. Barksdale and Harris admit that the new matrix does not eliminate the problems involved in defining, say, products and markets,

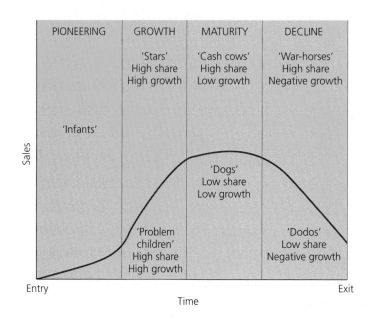

FIGURE A1.4

Combined PLC/product portfolio concepts

Source: H. C. Barksdale and C. E. Harris Jnr, 'Portfolio analysis and the product life cycle', *Journal of Long Range Planning*, **15** (6), 1982

or rates of growth. As with the other strategic planning tools, the benefits a company can achieve are only as good as the inputs upon which they are based.

It is claimed, however, that the matrix does provide an improved framework that identifies the cash flow potential and the investment opportunity for every product offered by an organization. In addition, it helps to conceptualize the strategic alternatives of all product/market categories of an organization.

The strategic position and action evaluation model (SPACE) model

Developed by Rowe *et al.*,[5] this model looks at identifying possible alternative strategies by analysing four key variables, namely:

1. The degree of 'turbulence' in the environment facing the company: ranging from 'stable' to 'unstable'.
2. The financial strength of the company: ranging from 'strong' to 'weak'.
3. The competitive advantage of the company: again, ranging from 'strong' to 'weak'.
4. The attractiveness of the market: ranging from 'high' to 'low'.

Each of these four key variables is evaluated and scored along the appropriate dimensions, and the results profiled as shown in Fig. A1.6 which shows a hypothetical profile for a company.

According to the scores achieved from the analysis of these four key factors and hence the resulting profile, the model suggests four alternative '*strategic thrusts*' which will be best suited to the company. In turn, Rowe *et al.* suggest a number of possible alternative strategies for achieving each strategic thrust. The four basic strategic thrusts identified in the model are as follows, together with the profiles or 'scores' which accompany each of them:

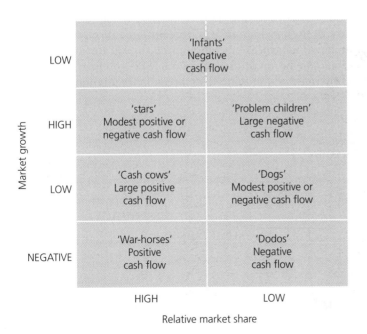

FIGURE A1.5

Product life-cycle portfolio matrix

1. *Strategic thrust: 'aggressive'*   A company which is in a stable environment with a strong competitive and financial position, and where the industry is of high attractiveness, should pursue aggressive strategies. Appropriate strategies under this category would be, for example, growth through acquisition or innovation.

2. *Strategic thrust: 'competitive'*   This strategic thrust is suited to a company operating in an unstable environment with weak financial strengths, where the industry is attractive and the company has a strong competitive advantage. You will note that this profile is that shown for our hypothetical company in Fig. A1.6. Appropriate strategies under this category would be, for example, cost reduction, productivity improvement and mergers with cash-rich companies.

3. *Strategic thrust: 'conservative'*   A company operating in a stable environment, with strong financial strengths, but where the industry is unattractive and the competitive position weak, should pursue a conservative strategic thrust with strategies such as cost reduction and product/service rationalization.

4. *Strategic thrust: 'defensive'*   This strategic thrust favours those companies in unstable markets which are unattractive and where the competitive advantage and financial strengths are both weak. Strategies here include rationalization and divestment.

This model is interesting in as much as it combines both marketing and financial aspects. As with some of the portfolio techniques, however, the 'scoring' to arrive at the different profiles is largely subjective.

Illinitch and Schaltegger's 'green' portfolio planning model

This portfolio analysis model is a good illustration of how these tools of analysis are continuously evolving to meet the needs of the contemporary marketer.[6] Specifically, this portfolio model combines portfolio analysis and the contemporary issue of 'green' marketing. The basic approach in this three-dimensional matrix is based upon trying to quantify the environmental impacts of business activities and comparing them with economic aspects of the business. The model is shown in Fig. A1.7.

The horizontal plane of the matrix consists of the traditional BCG matrix of growth against profitability with the quadrants retaining their respective metaphors. The size of the circle represents the size of the product or firm, in economic or environmental terms. The third, vertical dimension measures environmental impact. Recent developments in accounting mean this can be quantified at plant, SBU, or firm level. The pollution units are calculated by multiplying toxic discharges by regulation standards

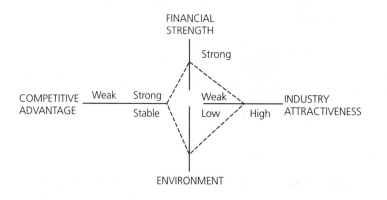

FIGURE A1.6

Strategic position and action evaluation model (SPACE)

Source: A. J. Rowe, R. O. Mason, K. E. Dickel and N. H. Snyder, *Strategic Management: A Methodological Approach*, 3rd edn, Addison-Wesley, London, 1989

weighting co-efficients. Products deemed to be ecologically sound are called '*green*' and their counterparts are called '*dirty*'. Thus we see the notion of the somewhat entertaining '*green cash cow*' and '*dirty dogs*'.

The authors suggest that 'dirty cash cows' are usually old, declining industries that are in the short term very profitable to firms and communities. However, in the long term, the negative publicity and financial penalties make such industries risky. Alternatively, although the 'green dog' is financially unprofitable, the authors argue that the strategic challenge in fact is to make it viable. This, they suggest, can be done by creating a market for the product and/or capturing market share. Creating a market may in turn involve changing customer values and behaviour, whereas capturing market share may involve lowering production costs.

We have included this interesting 'green' portfolio technique not because there is any evidence of it being potentially more valuable to the development of strategic marketing than some of the other recent ideas on portfolio analysis, but rather that it illustrates that portfolio techniques are being constantly improved and have changed substantially since the early days of the original BCG portfolio.

The Strategic Planning Institute's PIMS databank

In the early 1970s the Marketing Science Institute and the Harvard Business School established a joint study to investigate the relationship between management strategies and company profitability.[7] Usually referred to as the PIMS project (Profit Impact of Management Strategies), the study looked at the return on investment (ROI) of a large sample of American and European businesses and compared this with information on the various strategies these businesses were using.

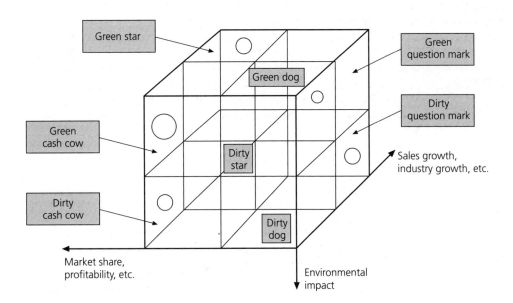

FIGURE A1.7   *The 'green' business portfolio*

Source: A. Y. Illinitch and S. C. Schaltegger, 'Developing a green business portfolio', *Journal of Long Range Planning*, **28** (2), 1995

The essence of PIMS is the use of empirical evidence to establish which strategies are associated with higher levels of profitability in an industry and thereby to advise managers in these industries towards better (more profitable) courses of action.

Some of the basic questions that PIMS seeks to answer include:

- What is the typical profit rate for each type of business?
- Given current strategies in a company, what are future operating results likely to be?
- What strategies are likely to help improve future operating results?

In order to obtain this information for a particular company, the company must subscribe to the PIMS project and provide detailed information, including, for example:

- Competitors and market information
- Balance sheet information
- Assumptions about future sales, costs, strategies, etc.

This information is then compared with the PIMS database and a series of reports prepared for the subscribing company as follows:

1. A 'Par' report—showing the ROI and cash flows that are 'normal' for this type of business given its market, competition, technology and cost structure. Also included is an analysis of strengths and weaknesses that are regarded as explaining high or low par figures compared with other businesses in the database.

2. A 'Strategy Analysis' report, which computes the predicted consequences of each of several alternative strategic actions, judged by information on similar businesses making similar moves, from a similar starting-point and in a similar business environment.

3. A 'Report on Look-Alikes' (ROLA), which examines possible tactics for achieving strategic objectives, such as an increase in market share, by analysing strategically similar businesses more closely.

4. An 'Optimus Strategy' report, which is aimed at predicting the best combination of strategies for that particular company, again based on the experiences of other businesses in 'similar' circumstances.

The advantages of PIMS to the individual businesses are obvious. Not only can the management of that business assess the likely outcome of its proposed strategies, but it can also identify those strategies that would yield the highest return on investment.

If this is the case, then one is bound to ask, why doesn't every company subscribe to PIMS for its strategic planning? There are a number of reasons why not every company can, or will, subscribe. First of all, there is the question of cost. The full range of PIMS services is expensive and not every company can afford them. Second, the amount of data required to be supplied by a company for a PIMS analysis is extensive. Again, this can be not only a costly process but also a time consuming one. Finally, and perhaps most important of all, there are limitations to PIMS itself. For example:

- PIMS data are historical and may be misleading in conditions of rapid change.
- The underlying assumptions of the PIMS model are not clarified and therefore must be taken on trust.
- The statistical basis of PIMS can give rise to problems of interpretation and understanding.

In short, then, PIMS is not a panacea for strategic decision-making in the individual company and is best used as another aid to managerial judgement. In this respect, some of the general findings of PIMS are useful and are much less expensive than an actual subscription.

In general terms, analysis of the PIMS database has shown that some 37 variables together account for almost 80 per cent of the variations in return on investment. These, therefore, are the key factors that most strategic company planners will need to consider in their decision-making. Fortunately, however, the analysis has also shown that, of those 37 variables, some are more significant than others. The key ones appear to be:

- Market share
- Investment intensity
- Market growth
- Life cycle stage
- Marketing expense–sales ratio

For example, PIMS indicates that on average a difference in 10 per cent on market share is accompanied by a difference of about 5 per cent in pre-tax return on investment. Similarly, a low or medium market growth rate combined with low investment intensity gives rise to high positive net cost flow and increased returns on investment.

In conclusion, we can see that the PIMS study offers managers access to one of the most comprehensive empirically based strategic planning tools. The full information, and therefore advantages, of PIMS are available only to a company that subscribes to the PIMS database and is therefore prepared and able to bear the potentially high costs and time commitment involved. However, even for the non-subscribing company, the general and published findings of PIMS regarding key determinants of return on investment have proved to be a useful guide to strategic marketing planning decisions.

Criticisms and limitations   Although PIMS is useful, there is some criticism. The findings are given as conclusions from empirical research, but many of them are self-evident. O'Shaughnessy[8] has suggested that 'the findings cannot distinguish between causal factors and factors in a state of mere co-existence'. He goes on to say: 'Without supporting explanations and appropriate tests, the findings can be misleading in tempting management to deal with symptoms rather than causes.'

Day[9] to some extent agrees with O'Shaughnessy when he states three basic limitations of PIMS:

1. *Interpreting and utilizing PIMS findings*   PIMS has been used to predict profitability; this should not be so because the model does not tell us about causality.
2. *Specification problems*   These concern whether the regression models have omitted any important variables and have been properly structured.
3. *Measurement error*   This happens because of eliminating outliers, standardized inputs, etc.

Abell and Hammond[10] suggest that PIMS does not enable the user to assess the impact of future changes in the market (except for sales, prices and costs) on business strategy. The strategic changes that can be investigated are restricted to modifications of current strategy. PIMS is most useful in assessing the viability of current strategies in the current environment and in suggesting ways to improve it. In this respect, it falls short of some of the other portfolio techniques, such as the GE matrix, which does at least provide the user with a qualitative way to consider the future.

References

1. M. E. Porter, *Competitive Advantage: Creating and Sustaining Superior Performance.* Free Press, New York, 1985.
2. Concepts of market/industry evolution are contained in a series of booklets published by A. D. Little Inc., New York.
3. Shell Chemicals UK, *The Directional Policy Matrix: A New Aid to Corporate Planning*, November 1975.
4. H. C. Barksdale and C. E. Harris Jr, 'Portfolio analysis and the product lifecycle', *Journal of Long Range Planning*, **15** (6), 1982.
5. A. J. Rowe, R. O. Mason, K. E. Dickel and N. H. Snyder, *Strategic Management: A Methodological Approach*, 3rd edn, Addison-Wesley, London, 1989.
6. A. Y. Illinitch and S. C. Schaltegger, 'Developing a green business portfolio', *Journal of Long Range Planning*, **28** (2), 1995, pp. 29–58
7. R. D. Buzzell and B. T. Gale, *The PIMS Principles: Linking Strategy to Performance*, Free Press, 1987, p. 94.
8. J. O'Shaughnessy, *Competitive Marketing: A Strategic Approach*, 2nd edn, Unwin-Hyman, London, 1988, p. 44.
9. G. Day, 'Analytical approaches to strategic market planning', *Review of Marketing*, 1981, pp. 89–95.
10. D. F. Abell and J. S. Hammond, *Strategic Marketing Planning*, Prentice-Hall, Englewood Cliffs, NJ, 1979, pp. 112–113.

Appendix Two

EXTENDED CASE STUDIES: FURTHER USEFUL CONCEPTS AND DEFINITIONS

In Chapter 15 we introduced you to a number of useful financial ratios and definitions for undertaking extended case studies. The following concepts and definitions may also be useful in this respect.

Acknowledgement

The information in this appendix is reproduced from material kindly supplied by Professor E. C. Lea, and Professor B. Kenny, both formerly of the University of Huddersfield.

Accounts payable   Amounts owed by the firm to creditors (US).

Accounts receivable   Amounts owing to the firm by its debtors (US).

Accumulation depreciation   The cumulative amount of depreciation written off a fixed asset.

Acid test   see Quick ratio.

Amortization   The writing off, over a period, of an asset or a liability.

Asset   Any property, tangible or intangible, that can be expressed in monetary terms and that brings benefit to the firm, e.g. plant and equipment, stocks, goodwill.

Asset turnover   Ratio of sales to net tangible assets.

Authorized share capital   The maximum share capital that a company can issue at any given time. The amount, which can be altered by the shareholders in general meeting, is stated in the Memorandum of Association and must be disclosed in the balance sheet. Also called '*Nominal share capital*' or '*Registered share capital*'.

Average collection period   The frequency with which a company collects its debts:

$$\frac{\text{Debtors} \times 365}{\text{Credit sales}} \text{ days}$$

Bonus shares   Shares issued to existing shareholders without further payment on their part. Also referred to as a '*Scrip issue*' or a '*Capitalization issue*'.

Book value   The monetary amount of an asset as stated in the balance sheet. Usually represents acquisition cost less accumulated depreciation.

Business planning   Involves the process of establishing objectives and the development and implementation of strategy, extending down to the development of sales forecasts, establishment of budgets, anticipation of needs for capital and facilities and equipment.

'Cash cows'   Low-growth products that usually generate more cash than is required to maintain market share. Generally regarded as the foundation of the firm.

Convertible loan stock   Loan stock which may be converted at the option of the holder at a future date or dates into ordinary shares at given price ratios.

Cost of capital   The cost to a company's ordinary shareholders of issuing shares or debentures, of retaining profits, or of other sources of funds.

Creditors   Amounts owing by a company resulting from, say, the purchase of materials.

Cumulative preference shares   Preference shares entitled to be paid the arrears of their dividend before any dividend is paid on the ordinary shares. Any arrears must be disclosed as a note to the balance sheet.

Current assets   Those assets that are either already cash or can reasonably be expected to become cash within one year from the date of the balance sheet, e.g. debtors, stock-in-trade. If the directors believe that any of the current assets will not realize their balance sheet values in the ordinary course of business, this fact must be disclosed.

Current liabilities   Liabilities that are expected to have been paid within one year from the date of the balance sheet, e.g. trade creditors, proposed final dividend, current taxation.

Current ratio   Ratio of current assets to current liabilities. A measure of liquidity.

Debentures   Loans that are usually, but not necessarily, secured on the assets of the company. Usually redeemable but may be irredeemable.

Debtors   Amount owing to the company, e.g. from the sale of goods. Usually shown in balance sheets net of provision for debts unlikely to be recovered.

Deferred taxation   Tax that is due beyond one year from the date of the balance sheet.

Depreciation   Expense recording the using up of fixed assets through operations. Usually measured by allocating the historical cost less disposable value of the asset on a straight-line or reducing-balance basis.

Discounted cash flow   The present value of future cash receipts and payment, i.e. their value after taking into account the delay in receiving or paying them.

Diversification A strategy by which the firm's growth objectives are achieved by adding products or services to the existing lines. Concentric diversification takes place when the products added are similar to existing types, from a production, marketing channel, customer or technology point of view. *Conglomerate diversification* refers to growth into areas unrelated to the company's present product/market scope (often associated with acquisitions).

Divestment Refers to retrenchment strategy. The selling off or liquidation of a division or unit of an organization.

Dividend That part of the profits of a company which is distributed to the shareholders. May be interim (paid during the financial year) or final (recommended by the directors for approval by the shareholders at the annual general meeting). Both must be disclosed gross of tax in the profit and loss account. The proposed final dividend is shown gross in the balance sheet as a current liability.

Dividend cover The ratio between earnings per share and the ordinary dividend per share.

Dividend yield The relationship between the ordinary dividend and the market price per ordinary share.

'Dodos' Term for describing low-share, negative-growth products. Used in context of product life cycle/product portfolio analysis.

'Dogs' Products that are at a cost disadvantage and have few opportunities for growth at a reasonable cost. Generally low market share product needing cash to survive and, consequently, not profitable.

Earnings per share Net profit after tax attributable to the ordinary shareholders, divided by the number of ordinary shares.

Earnings yield The relationship between the earnings per ordinary share and the market price per ordinary share. The reciprocal of the price–earning ratio multiplied by 100.

Environment Generally refers to *external* forces affecting the organization. These may be classified under legal, social, political, economic, technological and market forces.

Equity share capital Defined by the Companies Act as any issued share capital that has unlimited rights to participate in either the distribution of dividends or capital. Often more narrowly defined to mean ordinary shares only.

Experience curve A postulate that suggests that, as the firm grows in size and experience, it is able to reduce costs and improve productivity for a given activity.

Financial ratios Relationships among items in financial statements.

Fixed assets Assets held for use in the business rather than for re-sale.

Fixed overheads Those overheads whose amount remains constant over the usual range of activity.

Gearing The relationship between the funds provided to a company by its ordinary shareholders and the long-term sources of funds carrying a fixed interest charge or dividend.

Goodwill   The difference between the 'value' of a company as a whole and the sum of the values of the tangible assets and liabilities taken separately. Usually recorded only when the company is being evaluated for, say, potential purchase.

Historical cost   The usual basis of valuation in published financial statements. Favoured because it is more objective and more easily verifiable by an auditor. Its use is contentious, especially in times of inflation.

Holding company   A company that controls another company, called its '*Subsidiary*'. Balance sheet of holding company must show separately amounts owing to and owed by subsidiaries.

Intangible assets   Assets such as goodwill, patents and trade marks.

Integration   Growth strategy characterized by the extension of the firm's business definition, i.e. vertical (forward and backward) integration. In this case the firm may integrate forwards to assure control of distribution, or backwards to safeguard supplies of raw materials.

Issued expenses   Expenses of making an issue of shares or debentures.

Issued share capital   The amount of the authorized share capital that has been issued; the remainder is the unissued share capital. The amount of the issued capital must be disclosed in the published balance sheet. Not necessarily equal to called-up or paid-up share capital.

Issue price   The price at which a share is issued. Since the issue may be at a premium or a discount, the issue price is not necessarily equal to the par value.

Liabilities   Amounts owing by a company, which must be disclosed in the published balance sheet. For example:

- Aggregate amount of bank loans and overdrafts
- Aggregate amount of other loans
- Amounts owing to subsidiary companies
- Recommended dividend
- Redeemed debentures
- Debtors

Liquid assets   *see* Quick assets.

Loan capital   Funds acquired by non-short-term borrowing from sources other than the shareholders of the company.

Long-term debt   Long-term sources of funds other than equity (share capital and reserves).

MBO (management by objectives)   A technique that establishes a formal approach requiring top, middle and lower management to operate by a system of objectives.

Market price   The price at which a company's securities can be bought or sold on a stock exchange. Not necessarily equal to the par value or the issue price.

Minority interest   That part of a subsidiary company's shareholders' funds that is not held by the holding company. Usually shown as a separate item on the net worth and liabilities side of a consolidated balance sheet.

MIS (management information system)   A formal system of gathering intelligence—information to be used by the strategist. For example, economic data, market reports, technological development, etc., plus data on internal operations.

Net current assets   Another name for working capital.

Net profit ratio   Ratio of net profit to sales.

Net tangible assets   Assets except for intangible assets (goodwill, patents and trade marks), less liabilities.

Net working capital   Another name for working capital.

Net worth   Assets less liabilities. The proprietorship section of a balance sheet, usually referred to in the case of a company as shareholders' funds or share capital and reserves.

Nominal share capital   see Authorized share capital.

Non-voting shares   Shares with no voting rights. Non-voting ordinary shares are usually cheaper to buy than those carrying votes.

Objectives   Desired targets or results which at the basic level may be expressed in financial, product/mission or social–psychological terms; at the fulfilling level, objectives may be defined in more directed fashion, such as relationships with customers or continuous improvement of resources.

Ordinary shares   Shares entitled to share in the profits after payment of debenture interest and preference dividends. Often referred to as the '*Equity capital*'.

Paid-up share capital   The amount of the called-up share capital which has been paid up by the shareholders.

Par value   The face or nominal value of a share or debenture. Not necessarily equal to the issue price or the current market price. Dividend and interest percentages refer to the par value; yields, to the current market price.

PIMS (profit impact of marked strategies)   UK study relating to profitability analysis (see Schoeffler, Buzzell and Heany, 'Impact of Strategic Planning on Profit Performance', *Harvard Business Review*, **52**, March–April 1974, pp. 137–45).

Policies   Broad guidelines to pursuing objectives, and designed to clarify or sharpen up those objectives.

Preference shares   Shares that usually are entitled to a fixed rate of dividend before a dividend is paid on the ordinary shares, and to priority of repayment if the company is wound up. Participating preference shares are also entitled to a further dividend if profits are available. If a preference dividend is not paid, the arrears must be disclosed as a footnote to the balance sheet. Arrears can arise only if the shares are cumulative as distinct from non-cumulative.

Price–earnings ratio   The multiple of the last reported earnings that the market is willing to pay for a company's ordinary shares; the reciprocal of the earnings yield multiplied by 100.

Product portfolio (analysis)   Relates to specific marketing strategies to achieve a balanced mix of products that will produce the maximum long-run effects from scarce cash and management resources.

'Question marks' Sometimes known as *'Problem children'*. High-growth/low-market-share products. Cash generation is low and cash needs high.

Quick assets Current assets less stock-in-trade.

Quick ratio The relationship between quick assets and current liabilities. Also known as *'Liquid ratio'*, or the *'Acid test'*. A measure of liquidity.

Quoted investments Investments for which there is a quotation or permission to deal on a recognized stock exchange or on any reputable stock exchange outside the UK. Must be shown separately in the balance sheet.

Reserves Reserves arise either from the retention of profits or from specific capital transactions such as the issue of shares at a premium or the revaluation of assets. Must not include provisions—unless the directors consider they are excessive—or the taxation equalization account. Not a charge against profits; not necessarily represented by cash on the other side of the balance sheet. Movements in reserves during the financial year must be disclosed.

Reserve fund A reserve that is represented by specially earmarked cash or investments on the other side of the balance sheet.

Retained profits Profits not distributed to shareholders but reinvested in the company. Their cost is less than a new issue of shares, because of the issue costs of the latter.

Return on investments Ratio of profit (usually before interest and tax) to net tangible assets. A measure of profitability.

Revaluation The writing-up of an asset to its current market value.

Revenue reserves Reserves regarded by the directors as being normally available for dividend.

Rights issue An issue of shares in which the existing shareholders have a right to subscribe for the new shares at a stated price. The right can be sold if the shareholder does not wish to subscribe.

Share capital Unless limited by guarantee, a company registered under the Companies Act must have a share capital divided into a fixed amount. The ownership of a share gives the shareholder a proportionate ownership of the company. The share capital is stated in the balance sheet at its part (nominal) value.

Shareholder Member of a company whose part ownership of (share in) the company is evidenced by a share certificate.

Shareholders' funds The proprietorship section of a company balance sheet. Includes the share capital and the reserves (sometimes called *'Net worth'*).

Share premium Results from issuing shares at a price higher than their par value. Must be disclosed in the balance sheet as a reserve. Cannot be used to pay dividends, but can be used to make an issue of bonus shares.

'Stars' Products that are market leaders and also growing at a fast rate. They represent the best opportunity for growth and investment.

Stock-in-trade For a manufacturing company consists of raw materials, work-in-progress and finished goods. Usually valued at the lower of cost or market value.

Stock turnover   Ratio of sales (sometimes, cost of sales) to stock-in-trade.

SBU (strategic business unit)   An operating division of a firm which serves a distinct product-market segment or well-defined set of customers. Generally it has the authority to make its own strategic decisions as long as they meet corporate objectives.

Strategy   As a concept, refers to the total system incorporating the firm's objectives, policies and the planning required to achieve objectives. In the managerial sense, strategy relates to the continuous process of effectively relating the organization's objectives and resources to opportunities in the environment.

Synergy   Exists when the strengths of two companies or units, when put together, more than offset their joint weaknesses:

● Many products resulting in higher utilization of facilities, personnel and overheads (operating synergy).
● Many products using same plant and equipment (investment synergy).
● Management experience in one industry helping to solve problems in another industry (management synergy).

Synergy can thus be gained through application of production, marketing or financial expertise.

Time interest earned   The number of times that a company's interest is covered or earned by its profit before interest and tax.

Turnover   Sales. The profit and loss account must disclose the amount and basis of turnover for the financial year. The directors' report must disclose group turnover and profit (or loss) before the tax is divided among classes of business that differ substantially.

Unquoted investments   Investments for which there is not a quotation or permission to deal on a recognized stock exchange or on any reputable stock exchange outside the UK. If they consist of equity of other companies, directors must give either an estimate of their value or information about income received, profits, etc.

Unsecured loan   Money borrowed by a company without security.

'War horses'   Term used to describe high-share/negative-growth products. Used in context of product life cycle/product portfolio analysis.

Working capital   Current assets less current liabilities.

Work-in-progress   Partly completed manufactured goods.

Yield   The rate of return relating cash invested to cash received (or expected to be received).

INDEX